STUDY GUIDE

STUDY GUIDE

STUDY GUIDE

Richard O. Straub
University of Michigan, Dearborn

to accompany

Exploring
PSYCHOLOGY
IN MODULES

tenth edition

DAVID G. MYERS
HOPE COLLEGE
HOLLAND, MICHIGAN

C. NATHAN DEWALL
UNIVERSITY OF KENTUCKY
LEXINGTON, KENTUCKY

worth publishers
Macmillan Learning
New York

Study Guide
by Richard O. Straub
to accompany
Myers: **Exploring Psychology**, Tenth Edition in Modules

Printed in the United States of America

ISBN 13: 978-1-4641-7776-7
ISBN 10: 1-4641-7776-7

Worth Publishers

One New York Plaza

Suite 4500

New York, New York 10004-1562

www.macmillanhighered.com

Contents

Preface

This Study Guide is designed for use with *Exploring Psychology, Tenth Edition in Modules*, by David G. Myers and C. Nathan DeWall. It is intended to help you learn the material in the textbook, to evaluate your understanding of that material, and then to review any problem areas. You may also want to read "Time Management: How to Be a Great Student and Still Have a Life" in the text, which provides study suggestions based on principles of time management, effective note taking, evaluation of exam performance, and an effective program for improving your comprehension while studying from textbooks.

The tenth edition of this Study Guide offers many useful features. Each module is organized by major text section and one or more learning objectives. Under each objective are fill-in and essay-type questions, as well as art to be labeled. As reminders of important concepts, summary tables—some completed for you—are included for your review. At the end of each module is a Module Review, which contains multiple-choice questions and sometimes essays that cover the entire module, and a list of the key terms in that module, which you should try to define in your own words.

Also included within each module are practical study tips and applications. These tips and applications are designed to help you evaluate your understanding of the text module's broader concepts, and make the text material more meaningful by relating it to your own life. Before You Move On consists of matching, true–false, essay questions, and a crossword puzzle that focus on facts and definitions from the entire unit of modules. For all questions, the correct answers are given; explanations of why the answer is correct are also provided in many cases, as well as why the other choices are incorrect.

General Internet Resources

To obtain general information about psychology-related topics, you might want to consult some of the following websites. Russ Dewey's Psych Web is an effort to compile a great deal of information for psychology students and teachers, including self-quizzes, lists of psychology journals on the web, self-help resources, tip sheets for psychology majors, and psychology departments on the Internet. Psych Web is available at the following site: www.psychwww.com.

Both the American Psychological Association (APA) and the American Psychological Society (APS) have Internet services. These services provide not only information about their organizations but also selected articles from their main journals, information about current research in the discipline, and links to other science-related sites on the Internet. Their locations are as follows:

APA: www.apa.org and APS: www.psychologicalscience.org

Finally, and perhaps most important, is Psychtalk, a list for students interested in discussion topics and controversies related to psychology. Topics that have been discussed over the past few years include child abuse, the nature–nurture issue, homosexuality, and pornography. To subscribe, send a message to:

psychtalk-request@fre.fsu.umd.edu

The message should read "subscribe psychtalk (your name)."

Acknowledgments

I would like to thank all the students and instructors who used this Study Guide in its previous editions and provided such insightful and useful suggestions. Special thanks are also due to Betty Shapiro Probert for her extraordinary editorial contributions and to Don Probert for his skill and efficiency in the composition of this guide. I would also like to thank Edgar Doolan and Stacey Alexander of Worth Publishers for their dedication and energy in skillfully coordinating various aspects of production. Most important, I want to thank Jeremy, Rebecca, Melissa, and Pam for their enduring love and patience.

Richard O. Straub

STUDY GUIDE

STUDY GUIDE

Thinking Critically With Psychological Science

Overview

To counteract our human tendency toward faulty reasoning, psychologists adopt a scientific attitude that is based on curiosity, skepticism, humility, and critical thinking.

Psychology's historical development and current activities lead us to define the field as the science of behavior and mental processes. Module 1 discusses the development of psychology from ancient times until today and the range of behaviors and mental processes being investigated by psychologists in each of the various specialty areas. In addition, it introduces the biopsychosocial approach that integrates the three main levels of analysis followed by psychologists working from the seven major perspectives. Next is an overview of the diverse subfields in which psychologists conduct research and provide professional services.

Module 2 explains the limits of intuition and common sense in reasoning about behavior and mental processes. The module also explains how psychologists, using the scientific method, employ the research strategies of description, correlation, and experimentation in order to objectively describe, predict, and explain behavior. This module also discusses research ethics in psychology, including why animal research is relevant, whether laboratory experiments are ethical, and whether psychology's principles don't have the potential for misuse

The final section of Module 2 provides an explanation of how to get your study of psychology off on the right foot by learning (and pledging to follow!) the SQ3R study method. This study method is also discussed in the essay at the beginning of the text.

Module 2 introduces a number of concepts and issues that will play an important role in later modules. Pay particular attention to the strengths and weaknesses of descriptive and correlational research. In addition, make sure that you understand the method of experimentation, especially the importance of control conditions and the difference between independent and dependent variables.

NOTE: Answer guidelines for all Modules 1 and 2 questions begin on page 20.

Outline

Instructions

First, skim each section, noting headings and boldface items. After you have read the section, review each objective by answering the fill-in and essay-type questions that follow it. In some cases, Study Tips explain how best to learn a difficult concept, while Applications and Module Reviews help you to know how well you understand the material. As you proceed, evaluate your performance by consulting the answers on page 20. Do not continue until you understand each answer. If you need to, review or reread a troublesome section in the textbook before continuing.

Before You Move On includes activities that test you on material from the entire unit.

The History and Scope of Psychology

The Scientific Attitude: Curious, Skeptical, and Humble and Critical Thinking

Objective 1-1: Explain how the three main components of the scientific attitude relate to critical thinking.

1. The scientific approach is characterized by the attitudes of _____ , _____ , and _____ .

2. Scientific inquiry thus encourages reasoning that examines assumptions, appraises the sources, discerns hidden values, evaluates evidence, and assesses conclusions, which is called _____ _____ .

STUDY TIP: Try applying a scientific attitude toward how you evaluate your knowledge of psychology in preparation for an upcoming quiz or exam. As is true of researchers, many students develop a false sense of overconfidence in their mastery of course material. Be skeptical! Remain humble! You'll likely do better.

APPLICATIONS:

3. The scientific attitude in psychology refers to the fact that
   a. psychologists study only observable behaviors.
   b. psychologists study thoughts and actions with an attitude of skepticism and derive their conclusions from direct observations.
   c. psychological research should be free of value judgments.
   d. all of these statements are true.

4. The scientific attitude of humility is based on the idea that
   a. researchers must evaluate new ideas and theories objectively rather than accept them blindly.
   b. scientists should approach a research question with some idea of the eventual answer.
   c. simple explanations of behavior are more reliable than complex explanations.
   d. researchers must be prepared to reject their own ideas in the face of conflicting evidence.

Psychology's Roots

Objective 1-2: Describe some important milestones in psychology's early development.

5. The Greek naturalist and philosopher _____ developed early theories about _____ , _____ , _____ , _____ , _____ , and _____ .

6. The first psychological laboratory was founded in 1879 by Wilhelm _____ . Another psychologist, _____ , introduced the school of _____ , which explored the basic elements of mind using the method of _____ . This method proved _____ (reliable/unreliable).

7. Under the influence of evolutionary theorist Charles Darwin, philosopher-psychologist _____ assumed that thinking developed because it was _____ . As a _____ , he focused on how mental and behavioral processes enable the organism to adapt and survive. In 1890, he published an important psychology textbook.

8. The first female president of the American Psychological Association was a distinguished memory researcher, _____ , who was mentored by _____ . The first woman to receive a Ph.D. in psychology was _____ , who was the second female APA president and author of *The Animal Mind*.

Objective 1-3: Describe how psychology continued to develop from the 1920s through today.

9. In its earliest years, psychology was defined as the science of _____ life. After the 1920s into the 1960s, psychology in America was redefined by _____ and _____ as the science of _____ behavior.

10. The other major force was Freudian psychology, which emphasized the ways our _____ thought processes and our _____ responses to childhood experiences affect our behavior.

11. As a response to Freudian psychology and
_____ , which they considered
too limiting, pioneers _____
and _____ forged
_____ psychology. This new perspective emphasized people's _____
potential.

12. The text author defines *psychology* as the scientific
study of _____ and
_____ processes. In this defini-
tion, "behavior" refers to any action that we can
_____ and _____ ,
and "mental processes" refers to the internal,
_____ _____ we
_____ from behavior.

13. As a science, psychology is less a set of findings
than a way of _____
_____ .

APPLICATIONS:

14. *Psychology* is defined as the "science of behavior
and mental processes." Wilhelm Wundt would
have omitted which of the following words from
this definition?
   a. science
   b. behavior and
   c. and mental processes
   d. Wundt would have agreed with the definition
   as stated.

15. Matthew believes that psychologists should go
back to using introspection as a research tool.
This technique is based on
   a. the scientific attitude.
   b. evolutionary principles.
   c. self-examination of mental processes.
   d. the study of observable behavior.

16. Dharma's term paper on the history of American
psychology notes that
   a. psychology began as the science of mental
   life.
   b. from the 1920s into the 1960s, psychology was
   defined as the scientific study of observable
   behavior.
   c. contemporary psychologists study both overt
   behavior and covert thoughts.
   d. all of these statements are true.

17. During his presentation on the history of psychology, Sanjay notes that Darwin's theory led most
directly to the development of the school of
   a. structuralism.   c. functionalism.
   b. behaviorism.   d. humanism.

18. The psychological views of William James are to
those of Edward Titchener as _____ is to
_____ .
   a. motivation; emotion
   b. emotion; motivation
   c. structuralism; functionalism
   d. functionalism; structuralism

Contemporary Psychology

Objective 1-4: Discuss how our understanding of
biology and experience, culture and gender, and
human flourishing has shaped contemporary
psychology.

19. The historical roots of psychology include the
fields of _____ and
_____ .

20. Some early psychologists included Ivan Pavlov,
who pioneered the study of _____ ;
the personality theorist _____ ; and
Jean Piaget, who studied _____ .

21. Worldwide, the number of psychologists is
_____ (increasing/decreasing).
Thanks to international publications and meetings, psychological science is also
_____ .

22. During the 1960s, psychology underwent a
_____ revolution as it began to
recapture interest in how our _____
perceives, processes, and retains information. The
study of brain activity linked with mental activity
is called _____
_____ .

23. The nature–nurture issue is the controversy over
the relative contributions of _____
and _____ .

24. The Greek philosopher who assumed that character and intelligence are inherited is
_____ . The Greek philosopher
who argued that all knowledge comes from sensory experience is _____ .

25. In 1859, naturalist _____
explained species variation by proposing the
process of _____ , which works
through the principle of _____
_____ .

26. Today's psychologists explore the relative contributions of biology and experience. How we humans are alike because of our common biology and history is the focus of _____ _____ . How we differ because of our differing genes and environments is the focus of _____ .

27. Although the debate continues, we will see that _____ works on what _____ endows and that every _____ event is simultaneously a _____ event.

━━━━━━━━━━━━━━━━━━━━━━━━━━━━━

STUDY TIP: The nature–nurture issue is psychology's biggest and most persistent debate. Psychologists explore the issue by asking, for example, how differences in intelligence, personality, and psychological disorders are influenced by heredity and by environment. Today, contemporary science recognizes that *nurture works on what nature endows.* Our species is biologically endowed with an enormous capacity to learn and to adapt. Moreover, every *psychological event is simultaneously a biological event.*

━━━━━━━━━━━━━━━━━━━━━━━━━━━━━

28. The enduring behaviors, ideas, attitudes, values, and traditions of a group of people and transmitted from one generation to the next defines the group's _____ .

29. Although specific attitudes and behaviors vary across cultures, the underlying _____ are the same. For instance, throughout the world people diagnosed with _____ _____ _____ exhibit the same _____ malfunction. Likewise, similarities between the _____ and _____ far outweigh differences.

30. _____ scientifically explores human strengths and human flourishing.

31. A friend majoring in anthropology is critical of psychological research because it often ignores the influence of culture on thoughts and actions. You point out that
    a. there is very little evidence that cultural diversity has a significant effect on specific behaviors and attitudes.
    b. most psychologists assign participants to research conditions in such a way as to fairly represent the cultural diversity of the people under study.
    c. it is impossible for psychologists to control for every possible factor that might influence research participants.
    d. even when specific thoughts and actions vary across cultures, as they often do, the underlying processes are much the same.

Objective 1-5: Describe psychology's three main levels of analysis and related perspectives.

32. Each person is a complex _____ that is part of a larger _____ _____ and at the same time composed of smaller systems. For this reason, psychologists work from three main _____ of _____ — biological , _____ , and _____-_____ — which together form an integrated _____ approach to the study of behavior and mental processes.

33. Psychologists who study how the body and brain enable emotions, memories, and sensory experiences are working from the _____ perspective.

34. Psychologists who study how natural selection influences behavior tendencies are working from the _____ perspective, whereas those concerned with the relative influences of genes and environment on individual differences are working from the _____ _____ perspective.

35. Psychologists who believe that behavior springs from unconscious drives and conflicts are working from the _____ perspective.

36. Psychologists who study the mechanisms by which observable responses are acquired and

changed are working from the
_____ perspective.

37. The _____ perspective explores how we encode, process, store, and retrieve information.

38. Psychologists who study how thinking and behavior vary in different situations are working from the _____-_____ perspective.

39. The different perspectives on the big issues _____ (contradict/complement) one another.

STUDY TIP: This section describes a number of perspectives in psychology. Keep in mind that each perspective is nothing more than how certain psychologists feel behavior and mental processes should be investigated. For example, a clinical psychologist could approach the study of abnormal behavior from any of the perspectives discussed. Typically, however, psychologists work from a combination of perspectives rather than exclusively from only one. To deepen your understanding of the various perspectives, review the following chart. In the first column are listed psychology's contemporary perspectives. In the second column are listed historical roots and the pioneers who contributed to each modern-day perspective and the subfield that derives from it. As you work through the modules, you might want to annotate this chart to include what you know about these psychologists.

Perspective	Historical Roots and Pioneers
Neuroscience	Aristotle (perception, emotion), Wundt
Evolutionary	Darwin, Freud
Behavior Genetics	Darwin
Psychodynamic	Aristotle (personality), Freud
Behavioral	Aristotle (learning), Pavlov, Watson, Skinner
Cognitive	Aristotle (memory), Wundt (quantifying mental processes), Piaget
Social-Cultural	Piaget, Rogers, Maslow

APPLICATIONS:

40. The philosophical views of Aristotle are to those of Plato as _____ is to _____ .
   a. nature; nurture
   b. nurture; nature
   c. rationality; irrationality
   d. irrationality; rationality

41. Professor Gutierrez, who believes that human emotions are best understood as being jointly determined by heredity, learning, and the individual's social and cultural contexts, is evidently a proponent of the
   a. psychodynamic perspective.
   b. biopsychosocial approach.
   c. evolutionary perspective.
   d. neuroscience perspective.

42. In concluding her report on the "nature–nurture issue in contemporary psychology," Karen notes that
   a. most psychologists believe that nature is a more important influence on the development of most human traits.
   b. most psychologists believe that nurture is more influential.
   c. the issue is more heatedly debated than ever before.
   d. nurture works on what nature endows.

43. Dr. Waung investigates how a person's interpretation of a situation affects his or her reaction. Evidently, Dr. Waung is working from the _____ perspective.
   a. neuroscience   c. cognitive
   b. behavioral   d. social-cultural

44. The psychological perspective that places the MOST emphasis on how observable responses are learned is the _____ perspective.

    a. behavioral   **c.** behavior genetics

    b. cognitive   **d.** evolutionary

45. During a dinner conversation, a friend says that the cognitive and behavioral perspectives are quite similar. You disagree and point out that the cognitive perspective emphasizes _____, whereas the behavioral perspective emphasizes _____.

    a. conscious processes; observable responses

    b. unconscious processes; conscious processes

    c. overt behaviors; covert behaviors

    d. introspection; experimentation

46. Concerning the major psychological perspectives on behavior, the text author suggests that

    a. researchers should work within the framework of only one of the perspectives.

    b. only those perspectives that emphasize objective measurement of behavior are useful.

    c. the different perspectives often complement one another; together, they provide a fuller understanding of behavior than provided by any single perspective.

    d. psychologists should avoid all of these traditional perspectives.

Objective 1-6: Identify psychology's main subfields.

47. Psychologists may be involved in conducting

_____,

which builds psychology's knowledge base, or

_____,

which seeks solutions to practical problems.

48. Psychologists who help people cope with problems in living are called _____ psychologists. Psychologists who study, assess, and treat troubled people are called _____ psychologists.

49. Medical doctors who provide psychotherapy and treat physical causes of psychological disorders are called _____.

50. Psychologists who work to create healthy social and physical environments are called

_____.

51. Terrence wants to talk to a professional to help him cope with some academic challenges he's facing. You recommend that he contact a(n)

    a. industrial-organizational psychologist.

    b. developmental psychologist.

    c. counseling psychologist.

    d. psychiatrist.

52. Dr. Aswad is studying people's enduring inner traits. Dr. Aswad is most likely a(n)

    a. clinical psychologist.

    b. psychiatrist.

    c. personality psychologist.

    d. industrial-organizational psychologist.

MODULE REVIEW:

53. The scientific attitude of skepticism is based on the belief that

    a. people are rarely candid in revealing their thoughts.

    b. mental processes can't be studied objectively.

    c. the scientist's intuition about behavior is usually correct.

    d. ideas need to be tested against observable evidence.

54. In its earliest days, psychology was defined as the

    a. science of mental life.

    b. study of conscious and unconscious activity.

    c. science of observable behavior.

    d. science of behavior and mental processes.

55. Who introduced the early school of structuralism?

    a. Edward Titchener

    b. Wilhelm Wundt

    c. William James

    d. Mary Whiton Calkins

56. The first psychology laboratory was established by _____ in the year _____.

    a. Wundt; 1879   **c.** Freud; 1900

    b. James; 1890   **d.** Watson; 1913

57. Who would be most likely to agree with the statement, "Psychology is the science of mental life"?

    a. Wilhelm Wundt

    b. John Watson

    c. Ivan Pavlov

    d. virtually any American psychologist during the 1960s

58. Who would be most likely to agree with the statement, "Psychology should investigate only behaviors that can be observed"?

    a. Wilhelm Wundt

    b. Sigmund Freud

    c. John B. Watson

    d. William James

59. Who wrote an important 1890 psycology text-book?
    a. Wilhelm Wundt
    b. Ivan Pavlov
    c. Jean Piaget
    d. William James

60. In psychology, *behavior* is best defined as
    a. anything a person says, does, or feels.
    b. any action we can observe and record.
    c. any action, whether observable or not.
    d. anything we can infer from a person's actions.

61. Carl Rogers and Abraham Maslow are most closely associated with
    a. cognitive psychology.
    b. behaviorism.
    c. psychodynamic theory.
    d. humanistic psychology.

62. Today, *psychology* is defined as the
    a. science of mental phenomena.
    b. science of conscious and unconscious activity.
    c. science of behavior.
    d. science of behavior and mental processes.

63. Which of the following exemplifies the issue of the relative importance of nature and nurture on our behavior?
    a. the issue of the relative influence of biology and experience on behavior
    b. the issue of the relative influence of rewards and punishments on behavior
    c. the debate as to the relative importance of heredity and instinct in determining behavior
    d. the debate as to whether mental processes are a legitimate area of scientific study

64. Psychologists who study the degree to which genes influence our personality are working from the _____ perspective.
    a. behavioral
    b. evolutionary
    c. behavior genetics
    d. neuroscience

65. Which psychological perspective emphasizes the interaction of the brain and body in behavior?
    a. neuroscience
    b. cognitive
    c. behavioral
    d. behavior genetics

66. A psychologist who explores how Asian and North American definitions of attractiveness differ is working from the _____ perspective.
    a. behavioral
    b. evolutionary
    c. cognitive
    d. social-cultural

67. A psychologist who conducts experiments solely intended to build psychology's knowledge base is engaged in
    a. basic research.
    b. applied research.
    c. industrial-organizational research.
    d. clinical research.

68. Psychologists who study, assess, and treat troubled people are called
    a. basic researchers.
    b. applied psychologists.
    c. clinical psychologists.
    d. psychiatrists.

69. Today, psychology is a discipline that
    a. connects with a diversity of other fields.
    b. is largely independent of other disciplines.
    c. is focused primarily on basic research.
    d. is focused primarily on applied research.

70. Psychologists who study how brain activity is linked to memory, perception, and other thought processes are called
    a. humanistic psychologists.
    b. psychiatrists.
    c. clinical psychologists.
    d. cognitive neuroscientists.

71. In defining *psychology*, the text notes that psychology is most accurately described as a
    a. way of asking and answering questions.
    b. field engaged in solving applied problems.
    c. set of findings related to behavior and mental processes.
    d. nonscientific approach to the study of mental disorders.

72. Two historical roots of psychology are the disciplines of
    a. philosophy and chemistry.
    b. physiology and chemistry.
    c. philosophy and biology.
    d. philosophy and physics.

73. The way we encode, process, store, and retrieve information is the primary concern of the _____ perspective.
    a. neuroscience
    b. evolutionary
    c. social-cultural
    d. cognitive

74. Which of the following individuals is also a physician?
    a. clinical psychologist
    b. experimental psychologist
    c. psychiatrist
    d. biological psychologist

75. Dr. Jones' research centers on the relationship between changes in our thinking over the life span and changes in moral reasoning. Dr. Jones is most likely a
    a. clinical psychologist.
    b. personality psychologist.
    c. psychiatrist.
    d. developmental psychologist.

76. Which subfield is most directly concerned with studying human behavior in the workplace?
    a. clinical psychology
    b. personality psychology
    c. industrial-organizational psychology
    d. psychiatry

77. Dr. Ernst explains behavior in terms of different situations. Dr. Ernst is working from the _____ perspective.
    a. behavioral   c. social-cultural
    b. evolutionary   d. cognitive

78. Which perspective emphasizes the learning of observable responses?
    a. behavioral   c. neuroscience
    b. social-cultural d. cognitive

79. A psychologist who studies how worker productivity might be increased by changing office layout is engaged in _____ research.
    a. applied   c. clinical
    b. basic   d. developmental

80. The biopsychosocial approach emphasizes the importance of
    a. different levels of analysis in exploring behavior and mental processes.
    b. basic research over pure research.
    c. pure research over basic research.
    d. having a single academic perspective to guide research.

TERMS AND CONCEPTS TO REMEMBER:

81. critical thinking
82. structuralism
83. functionalism
84. behaviorism
85. humanistic psychology
86. psychology
87. cognitive neuroscience
88. nature–nurture issue
89. natural selection
90. evolutionary psychology
91. behavior genetics
92. culture
93. positive psychology
94. levels of analysis
95. biopsychosocial approach
96. basic research
97. applied research
98. counseling psychology
99. clinical psychology
100. psychiatry
101. community psychology

ESSAY QUESTION

Explain how researchers working from each of psychology's major perspectives might investigate an emotion such as love. (Use the space below to list the points you want to make, and organize them. Then write the essay on a separate piece of paper.)

Research Strategies: How Psychologists Ask and Answer Questions

The Need for Psychological Science

Objective 2-1: Explain how our everyday thinking sometimes leads us to a wrong conclusion.

1. An effortless, immediate, automatic feeling or thought is called _____.

2. The tendency to perceive an outcome that has occurred as being obvious and predictable is called the _____ _____. This phenomenon is _____ (rare/common) in _____ (children/adults/both children and adults).

3. Our everyday thinking is also limited by _____ in what we think we know. Most people are _____ (better/worse/equally wrong) in predicting their social behavior.

4. Another common tendency is to perceive order in _____ _____.

5. Patterns and streaks in random sequences occur _____ (more/less) often than people expect, and they _____ (do/do not) appear random.

The Scientific Method

Objective 2-2: Describe how theories advance psychological science.

6. Psychological science uses the _____ _____ to evaluate ideas. They make careful _____ and form _____, which are _____ based on new _____.

7. An explanation using an integrated set of principles that organizes observations and implies testable predictions is a _____. The testable predictions that allow a scientist to evaluate a theory are called _____. These predictions specify what results will _____ _____.

8. To prevent theoretical biases from influencing scientific observations, research must be reported precisely—using clear _____ _____ of all concepts—so that

others can _____ _____ the findings.

9. The test of a useful theory is the extent to which it effectively _____ a range of self-reports and observations and implies clear _____.

10. Psychologists conduct research using _____, _____, and _____ methods.

Objective 2-3: Describe how psychologists use case studies, naturalistic observations, and surveys to observe and describe behavior, and explain why random sampling is important.

11. The research strategy in which one individual or group is studied in depth in order to reveal universal principles of behavior is the _____ _____.

12. Although case studies can suggest fruitful ideas, a potential problem with this method is that any given individual may be _____.

13. The research method in which people or animals are directly observed in their natural environments is called _____ _____.

14. Using naturalistic observation, researchers have found that people are more likely to laugh in _____ situations than in _____ situations. Also, using observations of walking speed and the speed of postal clerks, researchers have concluded that the pace of life _____ (varies/ does not vary) from one culture to another.

15. The method in which a group of people is questioned about their attitudes or behavior is the _____. An important factor in the validity of survey research is the _____ of questions.

16. We are more likely to overgeneralize from samples we observe, especially _____ ones.

17. Surveys try to obtain a _____ sample, one that will be representative of the _____ being studied. In such a sample, every person _____ (does/does not) have a chance of being included.

18. Large, representative samples _____ (are/are not) better than small ones.

19. Case studies, surveys, and naturalistic observation do not explain behavior; they simply _____ it.

Objective 2-4: Describe positive and negative correlations, and discuss why correlations enable prediction but not cause-effect explanation.

20. When changes in one factor are accompanied by changes in another, the two factors are said to be _____ , and one is thus able to _____ the other. The statistical expression of this relationship is called a _____ _____ .

21. If two factors increase or decrease together, they are _____ _____ . If, however, one decreases as the other increases, they are _____ _____ . Another way to state the latter is that the two variables relate _____ .

22. A negative correlation between two variables does not indicate the _____ of the relationship.

If your level of test anxiety goes down as your time spent studying for the exam goes up, would you say these events are positively or negatively correlated? Explain your reasoning.

23. A correlation between two events or behaviors means only that one event can be _____ from the other.

24. Because two events may both be caused by some other _____ , a correlation does not mean that one _____ the other. For this reason, correlation thus does not enable _____ .

Objective 2-5: Describe the characteristics of experimentation that make it possible to isolate cause and effect.

25. To isolate _____ and _____ , researchers control for other _____ .

26. Research studies have found that breast-fed infants _____ (do/do not) grow up with higher intelligence scores than those of infants who are bottle-fed. To study cause-effect relationships, psychologists conduct _____ . Using this method and _____ assigning participants to groups, a researcher _____ the factor of interest while _____ _____ (controlling) other factors.

27. If a _____ changes when an _____ factor is varied, the researcher knows the factor is having an _____ .

28. An experiment must involve at least two conditions: the _____ condition, in which the experimental treatment is present, and the _____ condition, in which it is absent.

29. To ensure that the two groups are identical, experimenters rely on the _____ _____ of individuals to the experimental conditions.

30. The factor that is being manipulated in an experiment is called the _____ variable. The measurable factor that may change as a result of these manipulations is called the _____ variable. Other factors that can potentially influence the results of an experiment are called _____ _____ .

STUDY TIP: Students often confuse independent variables and dependent variables. Remember that independent variables are manipulated (controlled) directly by the researcher to determine how they affect dependent variables. Dependent variables are the behaviors and mental processes that psychologists are trying to understand. In a sense, dependent variables *depend* on the actions of independent variables. When you are struggling to distinguish two variables, ask yourself, "Which of these two variables can affect the other?" Consider, for example, a researcher investigating caffeine and reaction time. After randomly assigning different students to groups that drink a highly caffeinated drink and a weakly caffeinated drink, she measures each student's speed in pushing a button in response to a signal light. Which variable is the independent variable, and which is the dependent variable? If the answer is not obvious, try the test question, "Which variable can affect the other?" Clearly, reaction time cannot affect caffeine. So, in this example, the dose of caffeine is the independent variable and reaction time is the dependent variable.

---

28. When neither the participants nor the person collecting the data knows which condition a participant is in, the researcher is making use of the _____-_____ procedure.

29. Researchers sometimes give certain participants a pseudotreatment, called a _____ , and compare their behavior with that of participants who receive the actual treatment. When merely thinking that one is receiving a treatment produces results, a _____ _____ is said to occur.

30. The aim of an experiment is to _____ a(n) _____ variable, measure the _____ variable, and _____ all other variables.

Explain at least one advantage of the experiment as a research method.

Objective 2-6: Discuss whether laboratory conditions can illuminate everyday life.

31. In laboratory experiments, psychologists' concern is not with specific behaviors but with the underlying theoretical _____ .

32. Psychologists conduct experiments on simplified behaviors in a laboratory environment to gain _____ over the many variables present in the "real world." In doing so, they are able to test _____ _____ of behavior that also operate in the real world.

STUDY TIP/APPLICATIONS: The concepts of control and operational definition are important in experimental research. In an experiment, researchers strive to hold constant (control) the possible effects of all variables on the dependent variable, except the one that is being manipulated (independent variable). Operational definitions, which were explained earlier, are like recipes for measuring a variable so that other researchers can replicate your results. They are much more precise than dictionary definitions. For example, the dictionary might define *intelligence* as "the capacity to reason." Because this definition is too vague for research purposes, a psychologist might create the operational definition of *intelligence* as "a person's answers to a specific set of IQ test questions." Test your understanding of these important concepts by completing the following exercises.

33. You decide to test your belief that men drink more soft drinks than women by finding out whether more soft drinks are consumed per day in the men's dorm than in the women's dorm. Your belief is a(n) _____, and your research prediction is a(n) _____.
  a. hypothesis; theory
  b. theory; hypothesis
  c. independent variable; dependent variable
  d. dependent variable; independent variable

34. The concept of control is important in psychological research because
    a. without control over independent and dependent variables, researchers cannot describe, predict, or explain behavior.
    b. experimental control allows researchers to study the influence of one or two independent variables on a dependent variable while holding other potential influences constant.
    c. without experimental control, results cannot be generalized from a sample to a population.
    d. of all of these reasons.

35. Martina believes that high doses of caffeine slow a person's reaction time. To test this belief, she has five friends each drink three 8-ounce cups of coffee and then measures their reaction time on a learning task. What is wrong with Martina's research strategy?
    a. No independent variable is specified.
    b. No dependent variable is specified.
    c. There is no control condition.
    d. There is no provision for replication of the findings.

36. Rashad, who is participating in a psychology experiment on the effects of alcohol on perception, is truthfully told by the experimenter that he has been assigned to the "high-dose condition." What is wrong with this experiment?
    a. There is no control condition.
    b. Rashad's expectations concerning the effects of "high doses" of alcohol on perception may influence his performance.
    c. Rashad was given a placebo, so the results may be tainted.
    d. All of these statements are correct.

37. Which of the following procedures is an example of the use of a placebo?
    a. In a test of the effects of a drug on memory, a participant is led to believe that a harmless pill actually contains an active drug.
    b. A participant in an experiment is led to believe that a pill, which actually contains an active drug, is harmless.
    c. Participants in an experiment are not told which treatment condition is in effect.
    d. Neither the participants nor the experimenter knows which treatment condition is in effect.

APPLICATIONS:

38. Your roommate is conducting a survey to learn how many hours the typical student studies each day. She plans to pass out her questionnaire to the members of her sorority. You point out that her findings will be flawed because
    a. she has not specified an independent variable.
    b. she has not specified a dependent variable.

c. the sample will probably not be representative of the population of interest.
d. of all of these reasons.

39. A professor constructs a questionnaire to determine how students at the university feel about nuclear disarmament. Which of the following techniques should be used to survey a random sample of the student body?
    a. Every student should be sent the questionnaire.
    b. Only students majoring in psychology should be asked to complete the questionnaire.
    c. Only students living on campus should be asked to complete the questionnaire.
    d. From an alphabetical listing of all students, every tenth (or fifteenth, e.g.) student should be asked to complete the questionnaire.

40. A researcher was interested in determining whether her students' test performance could be predicted from their proximity to the front of the classroom. So she matched her students' scores on a math test with their seating position. This study is an example of
    a. experimentation.
    b. correlational research.
    c. a survey.
    d. naturalistic observation.

41. If eating saturated fat and the likelihood of contracting cancer are positively correlated, which of the following is true?
    a. Saturated fat causes cancer.
    b. People who are prone to develop cancer prefer foods containing saturated fat.
    c. A separate factor links the consumption of saturated fat to cancer.
    d. None of these statements is necessarily true.

42. If height and body weight are positively correlated, which of the following is true?
    a. There is a cause-effect relationship between height and weight.
    b. As height increases, weight decreases.
    c. Knowing a person's height, one can predict his or her weight.
    d. All of these statements are true.

43. Your best friend criticizes psychological research for being artificial and having no relevance to behavior in real life. In defense of psychology's use of laboratory experiments you point out that
    a. psychologists make every attempt to avoid artificiality by setting up experiments that closely simulate real-world environments.
    b. psychologists who conduct basic research are not concerned with the applicability of their findings to the real world.

c. most psychological research is not conducted in a laboratory environment.

d. psychologists intentionally study behavior in simplified environments in order to gain greater control over variables and to test general principles that help to explain many behaviors.

Psychology's Research Ethics

Objective 2-7: Explain why psychologists study animals, and describe the ethical guidelines that safeguard human and animal research participants. Discuss how human values influence psychology.

44. Many psychologists study animals because they are fascinating. More important, they study animals because of the _____ (similarities/differences) between humans and other animals. These studies have led to treatments for human _____ and to a better understanding of human functioning.

45. Some people question whether experiments with animals are _____ . They wonder whether it is right to place the _____ of humans over those of animals.

46. Opposition to animal experimentation also raises the question of what _____ should protect the well-being of animals.

47. The ethics code of the _____ _____ _____ and Britain's BPS urge researchers to obtain partici-

pants' _____ _____ and fully _____ people after the research.

Describe two other ethical guidelines for psychological research.

48. Psychologists' values _____ (do/do not) influence what they study, how they study it, and how they interpret results.

49. Although psychology _____ (can/cannot) be used to manipulate people, its purpose is to _____ .

SUMMARY STUDY TIP: As we will note through this Study Guide, preparing a table to summarize what you have learned about a topic is a good way to promote understanding. Table 1.2 in the text compares the three research methods. Without looking at the text, try to complete the table below on your own. We've partially filled in a couple of column entries for you.

COMPARING RESEARCH METHODS

Research Method	Basic Purpose	How Conducted	What Is Manipulated	Weaknesses
Descriptive		Do case studies, surveys, or naturalistic observations	Nothing	
Correlational	To detect naturally			
Experimental	To explore			

Improve Your Retention—and Your Grades

Objective 2-8: Explain how psychological principles can help you learn and remember.

50. Repeated _____ and _____ of material improves retention of information. This phenomenon is called the _____ _____ .

51. To master any subject, you must _____ process it.

52. The _____ study method incorporates five steps: **a.** _____ ,
    b. _____ , **c.** _____ ,
    d. _____ , and
    e. _____ .

List four additional study tips identified in the text.

a. _____

b. _____

c. _____

d. _____

APPLICATIONS:

53. Your roommate announces that her schedule permits her to devote three hours to studying for an upcoming quiz. You advise her to
    a. spend most of her time reading and rereading the text material.
    b. focus primarily on her lecture notes.
    c. space study time over several short sessions.
    d. cram for three hours just before the quiz.

54. A fraternity brother rationalizes the fact that he spends very little time studying by saying that he "doesn't want to peak too soon and have the test material become stale." You tell him that
    a. he is probably overestimating his knowledge of the material.
    b. if he devotes extra time to studying, his retention of the material will be improved.
    c. the more often students test themselves on the material, the better their exam scores.
    d. all of these statements are true.

55. Brad, who prepares for exams simply by reading the textbook assignment several times, evidently has not heard about
    a. functionalism.
    b. positive psychology.

    c. the testing effect.
    d. the nature–nurture issue.

MODULE REVIEW:

56. Juwan eagerly opened an online trading account, believing that his market savvy would allow him to pick stocks that would make him a rich day trader. This belief best illustrates
    a. the I-knew-it-all-along phenomenon.
    b. the scientific attitude.
    c. hindsight bias.
    d. overconfidence.

57. Which of the following BEST describes the hindsight bias?
    a. Events seem more predictable before they have occurred.
    b. Events seem more predictable after they have occurred.
    c. A person's intuition is usually correct.
    d. A person's intuition is usually not correct.

58. After detailed study of a gunshot wound victim, a psychologist concludes that the brain region destroyed is likely to be important for memory functions. Which type of research did the psychologist use to deduce this?
    a. the case study   **c.** correlation
    b. a survey   **d.** experimentation

59. In an experiment to determine the effects of exercise on motivation, exercise is the
    a. control condition.
    b. confounding variable.
    c. independent variable.
    d. dependent variable.

60. To determine the effects of a new drug on memory, one group of people is given a pill that contains the drug. A second group is given a sugar pill that does not contain the drug. This second group constitutes the
    a. random sample.   **c.** control group.
    b. experimental group.   **d.** test group.

61. *Theories* are defined as
    a. testable propositions.
    b. factors that may change in response to manipulation.
    c. statistical indexes.
    d. principles that help to organize observations and predict behaviors or events.

62. A psychologist studies the play behavior of young children by watching groups during recess at school. Which type of research is being used?
    a. correlation
    b. case study
    c. experimentation
    d. naturalistic observation

63. To ensure that other researchers can repeat their work, psychologists use
    a. control groups.
    b. random assignment.
    c. double-blind procedures.
    d. operational definitions.

64. Which of the following is NOT a basic research technique used by psychologists?
    a. description
    b. replication
    c. experimentation
    d. correlation

65. Psychologists' personal values
    a. have little influence on how their experiments are conducted.
    b. do not influence the interpretation of experimental results because of the use of statistical techniques that guard against subjective bias.
    c. can bias both scientific observation and interpretation of data.
    d. have little influence on investigative methods but a significant effect on interpretation.

66. If shoe size and IQ are negatively correlated, which of the following is true?
    a. People with large feet tend to have high IQs.
    b. People with small feet tend to have high IQs.
    c. People with small feet tend to have low IQs.
    d. IQ is unpredictable based on a person's shoe size.

67. Which of the following would be best for determining whether alcohol impairs memory?
    a. case study   c. survey
    b. naturalistic observation d. experiment

68. Well-done surveys measure attitudes in a representative subset, or _____ , of an entire group, or _____ .
    a. population; random sample
    b. control group; experimental group
    c. experimental group; control group
    d. random sample; population

69. Which of the following research methods does NOT belong with the others?
    a. case study   c. naturalistic observation
    b. survey   d. experiment

70. To prevent the possibility that a placebo effect or researchers' expectations will influence a study's results, scientists employ
    a. control groups.
    b. experimental groups.
    c. random assignment.
    d. the double-blind procedure.

71. Which statement about the ethics of experimentation with people and animals is FALSE?
    a. The same processes by which humans learn are present in rats, monkeys, and other animals.
    b. Views on whether it is right to place the well-being of humans above that of animals are the same in every culture.
    c. The American Psychological Association and the British Psychological Society have set strict guidelines for the care and treatment of human and animal subjects.
    d. Most psychological studies are free of such stress as the delivery of electric shock.

72. In an experiment to determine the effects of attention on memory, memory is the
    a. control condition.
    b. confounding variable.
    c. independent variable.
    d. dependent variable.

73. The procedure designed to ensure that the experimental and control groups do not differ in any way that might affect the experiment's results is called
    a. variable controlling.
    b. random assignment.
    c. representative sampling.
    d. stratification.

74. Debriefing refers to
    a. the perception that two negatively correlated variables are positively correlated.
    b. explaining the purpose of a research study after its conclusion.
    c. an insignificant correlation.
    d. a correlation that equals –1.0.

75. The strength of the relationship between two vivid events will most likely be
    a. significant.   c. negative.
    b. positive.   d. overestimated.

76. Which of the following is true, according to the text?
    a. Because laboratory experiments are artificial, any principles discovered cannot be applied to everyday behaviors.
    b. Psychological science demonstrates why we cannot rely on intuition and common sense.
    c. Psychology's theories reflect common sense.
    d. Psychology has few ties to other disciplines.

77. Which type of research would allow you to determine whether students' grades accurately predict later income?
    a. case study   c. experimentation
    b. naturalistic observation d. correlation

78. In a test of the effects of air pollution, groups of students performed a reaction-time task in a polluted or an unpolluted room. To what condition were students in the unpolluted room exposed?
    a. experimental   c. randomly assigned
    b. control   d. dependent

79. To study the effects of lighting on mood, Dr. Cooper had students fill out questionnaires in brightly lit or dimly lit rooms. In this study, the independent variable consisted of
    a. the number of students assigned to each group.
    b. the students' responses to the questionnaire.
    c. the room lighting.
    d. the subject matter of the questions asked.

80. A major principle underlying the SQ3R study method is that
    a. people learn and remember material best when they actively process it.
    b. many students overestimate their mastery of text and lecture material.
    c. study time should be spaced over time rather than crammed into one session.
    d. overlearning disrupts efficient retention.

81. In order, the sequence of steps in the SQ3R method is
    a. survey, review, retrieve, question, read.
    b. review, question, survey, read, retrieve.
    c. question, review, survey, read, retrieve.
    d. survey, question, read, retrieve, review.

TERMS AND CONCEPTS TO REMEMBER:

82. intuition
83. hindsight bias
84. theory
85. hypothesis
86. operational definition
87. replication
88. case study
89. naturalistic observation
90. survey
91. population
92. random sample
93. correlation
94. correlation coefficient
95. experiment
96. experimental group
97. control group
98. random assignment
99. double-blind procedure
100. placebo effect
101. independent variable
102. confounding variable
103. dependent variable
104. informed consent
105. debriefing
106. testing effect
107. SQ3R

ESSAY QUESTION

Elio has a theory that regular exercise for 1 month can improve thinking. Help him design an experiment evaluating this theory. (Use the space below to list the points you want to make, and organize them. Then write the essay on a separate piece of paper.)

Before You Move On

Matching Items 1

Match each psychological perspective, school, and subfield with its definition or description.

Terms

_____ 1. neuroscience perspective
_____ 2. social-cultural perspective
_____ 3. psychiatry
_____ 4. clinical psychology
_____ 5. behavior genetics perspective
_____ 6. behavioral perspective
_____ 7. industrial-organizational psychology
_____ 8. cognitive perspective
_____ 9. basic research
_____ 10. applied research
_____ 11. evolutionary perspective
_____ 12. psychodynamic perspective
_____ 13. positive psychology
_____ 14. community psychology
_____ 15. behaviorism
_____ 16. cognitive neuroscience

Definitions or Descriptions

a. behavior in the workplace

b. how people differ as products of different environments

c. the study of practical problems

d. the scientific study of the strengths and virtues of human functioning

e. the mechanisms by which observable responses are acquired and changed

f. how the body and brain create emotions, memories, and sensations

g. how we encode, process, store, and retrieve information

h. the view that psychology should be an objective science that avoids reference to mental processes

i. how natural selection favors traits that promote the perpetuation of one's genes

j. the study, assessment, and treatment of troubled people

k. brain activity linked with perception, thinking, memory, and language

l. the disguised effects of unfulfilled wishes and childhood traumas

m. adds to psychology's knowledge base

n. how people interact with their social environment and how social institutions affect individuals and groups

o. how much genes and environment contribute to individual differences

p. the medical treatment of psychological disorders

Matching Items 2

Match each psychological perspective, school, and subfield with its definition or description.

Terms

_____ 1. culture
_____ 2. placebo effect
_____ 3. hindsight bias
_____ 4. critical thinking
_____ 5. insight

Definitions or Descriptions

a. I-knew-it-all-along phenomenon

b. reasoning that does not blindly accept arguments

c. an effortless, immediate, automatic feeling or thought

d. shared ideas and behaviors passed from one generation to the next

e. experimental results caused by expectations alone

Matching Items 3

Match each term with its definition or description.

Terms

_____ 1. hypothesis
_____ 2. theory
_____ 3. independent variable
_____ 4. dependent variable
_____ 5. experimental group
_____ 6. control group
_____ 7. case study
_____ 8. survey
_____ 9. replication
_____ 10. random assignment
_____ 11. experiment
_____ 12. double-blind
_____ 13. debriefing
_____ 14. informed consent

Definitions or Descriptions

a. an in-depth observational study of one person
b. the variable being manipulated in an experiment
c. the variable being measured in an experiment
d. giving research participants information that enables them to choose whether to participate
e. testable proposition
f. repeating an experiment to see whether the same results are obtained
g. the process in which research participants are selected by chance for different groups in an experiment
h. an explanation using an integrated set of principles that organizes observations and predicts behaviors or events
i. the research strategy in which the effects of one or more variables on behavior are tested
j. the "treatment-present" group in an experiment
k. the research strategy in which a representative sample of individuals is questioned
l. experimental procedure in which neither the research participant nor the experimenter knows which condition the participant is in
m. the "treatment-absent" group in an experiment
n. explaining the purpose of a research study after its conclusion

True–False Items

Place a *T* or an *F* in the blank next to each statement.

_____ 1. Psychology's three main levels of analysis often contradict each other.
_____ 2. The primary research tool of the first psychologists was the experiment.
_____ 3. The subject matter of psychology has changed over the history of the field.
_____ 4. Every psychological event is simultaneously a biological event.
_____ 5. Today, most psychologists work within the behavioral perspective.

_____ 6. The major perspectives in psychology contradict one another.
_____ 7. Repeated self-testing and rehearsal promotes better retention than rereading.
_____ 8. Overlearning hinders retention.
_____ 9. A major goal of psychology is to teach us how to ask important questions and to think critically as we evaluate competing ideas.
_____ 10. The school of structuralism fell from favor in part because the method of introspection was unreliable.

Cross Check

As you learned in Module 2, reviewing and overlearning of material are important to the learning process. After you have written the definitions of the key terms in these modules, you should complete the crossword puzzle to ensure that you can reverse the process—recognize the term, given the definition.

ACROSS

4. Condition in which research participants are exposed to the independent variable being studied.
7. Sample in which every member of the population has an equal chance of being included.
8. Careful reasoning that examines assumptions, discerns hidden values, evaluates evidence, and assesses conclusions.
9. When a research participant's expectations produce the results of an experiment, it is called a _____ effect.
10. In the longstanding controversy over the relative contributions that genes and experience make to the development of psychological traits and behaviors, experience is referred to as _____ .
12. Control procedure in which neither the experimenter nor the research participants are aware of which condition is in effect.
13. Descriptive research strategy in which one person is studied in great depth.
14. Measure that indicates the extent to which one factor predicts another factor.
16. Testable prediction, often implied by a theory.
17. The interdisciplinary study of the brain activity linked with cognition (including perception, thinking, memory, and language) is cognitive _____ .

DOWN

1. The view that psychology should be an objective science that studies behavior without reference to mental processes.
2. Early school of thought promoted by James and influenced by Darwin; explored how mental and behavioral processes function—how they enable the organism to adapt, survive, and flourish.
3. A precise definition of the procedures used to identify a variable.
5. In an experiment, the variable being manipulated and tested by the investigator.
6. Research method in which behavior is observed and recorded in naturally occurring situations without any manipulation or control.
11. The bias in which we believe, after learning an outcome, that we could have foreseen it.
14. The enduring behaviors, ideas, attitudes, values, and traditions shared by a group of people and transmitted from one generation to the next.
15. Experimental condition in which the treatment of interest is withheld.

Answers

The History and Scope of Psychology

The Scientific Attitude: Curious, Skeptical, and Humble and *Critical Thinking*

1. curiosity; skepticism; humility

2. critical thinking

3. **b.** is the answer. Psychologists approach their studies of behavior and mental processes with attitudes of curiosity, skepticism, and humility.
a. Psychologists study both overt (observable) behaviors and covert thoughts and feelings.
c. Psychologists' values definitely do influence their research.

4. **d.** is the answer.
a. This follows from the attitude of skepticism, rather than humility.
b. Scientists should be open-minded about the outcome of their research.
c. Neither type of explanation is more reliable than the other.

Psychology's Roots

5. Aristotle; learning; memory; motivation; emotion; perception; personality

6. Wundt; Edward Titchener; structuralism; introspection; unreliable

7. William James; adaptive; functionalist

8. Mary Calkins; William James; Margaret Floy Washburn

9. mental; John B. Watson; B. F. Skinner; observable

10. unconscious; emotional

11. behaviorism; Carl Rogers; Abraham Maslow; humanistic; growth

12. behavior; mental; observe; record; subjective experiences; infer

13. asking and answering questions

14. **b.** is the answer.
a. As the founder of the first psychology laboratory, Wundt's research certainly would be scientific.
c. The earliest psychologists, including Wilhelm Wundt, were concerned with the self-examination of covert thoughts, feelings, and other mental processes.

15. **c.** is the answer.

16. **d.** is the answer.

17. **c.** is the answer. Like Darwin, James assumed that thinking, like smelling, developed because it was adaptive.

18. **d.** is the answer. James emphasized the adaptive value of our thoughts and behaviors (functionalism). Titchener used the method of introspection to examine the basic contents of the mind (structuralism).

Contemporary Psychology

19. biology; philosophy

20. learning; Sigmund Freud; children

21. increasing; globalizing

22. cognitive; mind; cognitive neuroscience

23. biology; experience

24. Plato; Aristotle

25. Charles Darwin; evolution; natural selection

26. evolutionary psychology; behavior genetics

27. nurture; nature; psychological; biological

28. culture

29. processes; specific learning disorder; brain; genders

30. Positive psychology

31. **d.** is the answer.

32. system; social system; levels; analysis; psychological; social-cultural; biopsychosocial

33. neuroscience

34. evolutionary; behavior genetics

35. psychodynamic

36. behavioral

37. cognitive

38. social-cultural

39. complement

40. **b.** is the answer. Aristotle believed that all knowledge comes from experience (nurture). Plato believed that some ideas are innate (nature).

    c. & d. The text does not discuss the views of these philosophers regarding this issue.

41. **b.** is the answer.
a., c., & d. Each of these perspectives is too narrow to apply to Professor Gutierrez's belief. Moreover, the psychodynamic perspective (a.) emphasizes unconscious processes, in which Professor Gutierrez has not expressed a belief.

42. **d.** is the answer. Because both nature and nurture influence most traits and behaviors, the tension surrounding this issue has dissolved.

43. **c.** is the answer.
a. This perspective emphasizes the influences of physiology on behavior.
b. This perspective emphasizes environmental influences on observable behavior.
d. This perspective emphasizes how behavior and thinking vary across situations and cultures.

44. **a.** is the answer.

45. **a.** is the answer.
b. Neither perspective places any special emphasis on unconscious processes.
c. Neither perspective emphasizes covert behaviors.
d. Introspection was a research method used by the earliest psychologists, not those working from the cognitive perspective.

46. **c.** is the answer.
a. The text suggests just the opposite: By studying behavior from several perspectives, psychologists gain a fuller understanding.
b. & d. Each perspective is useful in that it calls researchers' attention to different aspects of behavior. This is equally true of those perspectives that do not emphasize objective measurement.

47. basic research; applied research

48. counseling; clinical

49. psychiatrists

50. community psychologists

51. **c.** is the answer.
a. Industrial-organizational psychologists study and advise on behavior in the workplace.
b. Developmental psychologists investigate behavior and mental processes over the life span.
d. Psychiatrists are medical doctors who treat medical disorders. There is no indication that Terrence is suffering from a medical disorder.

52. **c.** is the answer.
a. Clinical psychology is concerned with the study and treatment of psychological disorders.
b. Psychiatry is the branch of medicine concerned with the physical diagnosis and treatment of psychological disorders.
d. Industrial-organizational psychologists study behavior in the workplace.

Module Review:

53. **d.** is the answer.

54. **a.** is the answer.
b. Psychology has never been defined in terms of conscious and unconscious activity.

c. From the 1920s into the 1960s, psychology was defined as the scientific study of observable behavior.
d. Psychology today is defined as the scientific study of behavior and mental processes. In its earliest days, however, psychology focused exclusively on mental phenomena.

55. **a.** is the answer.

56. **a.** is the answer.

57. **a.** is the answer.
b. & d. John Watson, like many American psychologists during this time, believed that psychology should focus on the study of observable behavior.
c. Because he pioneered the study of learning, Pavlov focused on observable behavior and would certainly have *disagreed* with this statement.

58. **c.** is the answer.
a. Wilhelm Wundt, the founder of the first psychology laboratory, was seeking to measure the simplest mental processes.
b. Sigmund Freud developed an influential theory of personality that focused on unconscious processes.
d. William James, author of the early textbook *Principles of Psychology*, was a philosopher and was more interested in mental phenomena than observable behavior.

59. **d.** is the answer
a. Wilhelm Wundt founded the first psychology laboratory.
b. Ivan Pavlov pioneered the study of learning.
c. Jean Piaget was the twentieth century's most influential observer of children.

60. **b.** is the answer.

61. **d.** is the answer.

62. **d.** is the answer.
a. In its earliest days psychology was defined as the science of mental phenomena.
b. Psychology has never been defined in terms of conscious and unconscious activity.
c. From the 1920s into the 1960s, psychology was defined as the scientific study of behavior.

63. **a.** is the answer. Biology and experience are internal and external influences, respectively.
b. Rewards and punishments are both external influences on behavior.
c. Heredity and instinct are both internal influences on behavior.
d. The legitimacy of the study of mental processes does not relate to the internal/external issue.

64. **c.** is the answer.

65. **a.** is the answer.
    b. The cognitive perspective is concerned with how we encode, process, store, and retrieve information.
    c. The behavioral perspective studies the mechanisms by which observable responses are acquired and changed.
    d. The behavior genetics perspective focuses on the relative contributions of genes and environment to individual differences.

66. **d.** is the answer.
    a. Behavioral psychologists investigate how learned behaviors are acquired. They generally do not focus on subjective opinions, such as attractiveness.
    b. The evolutionary perspective studies how natural selection favors traits that promote the perpetuation of one's genes.
    c. Cognitive psychologists study the mechanisms of thinking and memory, and generally do not investigate attitudes. Also, because the question specifies that the psychologist is interested in comparing two cultures, d. is the best answer.

67. **a.** is the answer.
    b. & c. Applied and industrial-organizational psychologists tackle practical problems.
    d. Clinical psychologists (and researchers) focus on treating troubled people.

68. **c.** is the answer.
    d. Psychiatrists are medical doctors rather than psychologists.

69. **a.** is the answer.
    c. & d. Psychologists are widely involved in *both* basic and applied research.

70. **d.** is the answer.

71. **a.** is the answer.
    b. Psychology is equally involved in basic research.
    c. Psychology's knowledge base is constantly expanding.
    d. Psychology is the *scientific study* of behavior and mental processes.

72. **c.** is the answer.

73. **d.** is the answer.
    a. The neuroscience perspective studies the biological bases for a range of psychological phenomena.
    b. The evolutionary perspective studies how natural selection favors traits that promote the perpetuation of one's genes.
    c. The social-cultural perspective is concerned with variations in behavior across situations and cultures.

74. **c.** is the answer. After earning their M.D. degrees, psychiatrists specialize in the diagnosis and treatment of mental health disorders.
    a., b., & d. These psychologists generally earn a Ph.D. rather than an M.D.

75. **d.** is the answer. The emphasis on change during the life span indicates that Dr. Jones is most likely a developmental psychologist.
    a. Clinical psychologists study, assess, and treat people who are psychologically troubled.
    b. Personality psychologists study our inner traits.
    c. Psychiatrists are medical doctors.

76. **c.** is the answer.
    a. Clinical psychologists study, assess, and treat people with psychological disorders.
    b. & d. Personality psychologists and psychiatrists do not usually study people in work situations.

77. **c.** is the answer.
    a. Psychologists who follow the behavioral perspective emphasize observable, external influences on behavior.
    b. The evolutionary perspective focuses on how natural selection favors traits that promote the perpetuation of one's genes.
    d. The cognitive perspective places emphasis on conscious, rather than unconscious, processes.

78. **a.** is the answer.

79. **a.** is the answer. The research is addressing a practical issue.
    b. Basic research is aimed at contributing to the base of knowledge in a given field, not at resolving particular practical problems.
    c. & d. Clinical and developmental research would focus on issues relating to psychological disorders and life-span changes, respectively.

80. **a.** is the answer.
    b. & c. The biopsychosocial approach has nothing to do with the relative importance of basic research and applied research and is equally applicable to both.
    d. On the contrary, the biopsychosocial approach is based on the idea that single academic perspectives are often limited.

Terms and Concepts to Remember:

81. **Critical thinking** is careful reasoning that examines assumptions, appraises the source, discerns hidden values, evaluates evidence, and assesses conclusions.

82. **Structuralism** was an early school of thought promoted by Wundt and Titchener; used introspection to re-veal the structure of the human mind.

83. **Functionalism** was an early school of thought promoted by James and influenced by Darwin; explored how mental and behavioral processes function—how they enable the organism to adapt, survive, and flourish.

84. **Behaviorism** is the view that psychology should focus only on the scientific study of observable behaviors without reference to mental processes.

85. **Humanistic psychology** is a historically significant perspective that emphasized the growth potential of healthy people.

86. **Psychology** is the scientific study of behavior and mental processes.

87. **Cognitive neuroscience** is the interdisciplinary study of how brain activity is linked with cognition (including thinking, language, memory, and perception).

88. The **nature–nurture issue** is the controversy over the relative contributions that genes (nature) and experience (nurture) make to the development of psychological traits and behaviors.

89. **Natural selection** is the principle that those traits of a species that contribute to reproduction and survival are most likely to be passed on to succeeding generations.

90. **Evolutionary psychology** is the study of the evolution of behavior and the mind, using princples of natural selection.

91. **Behavior genetics** is the study of the relative power and limits of genetic and environmental influences on behavior.

92. **Culture** refers to the enduring behaviors, ideas, attitudes, values, and traditions shared by a group of people and passed from one generation to the next.

93. **Positive psychology** is the scientific study of the strengths and virtues of human functioning that help people and communities thrive.

94. Psychologists analyze behavior and mental processes from differing complementary views, or **levels of analysis,** from biological to psychological to social-cultural.

95. The **biopsychosocial approach** is an integrated perspective that focuses on biological, psychological, and social-cultural levels of analysis for a given behavior or mental process.

96. **Basic research** is pure science that aims to increase psychology's scientific knowledge base rather than to solve practical problems.

97. **Applied research** is scientific study that aims to solve practical problems.

98. **Counseling psychology** is the branch of psychology that helps people with challenges in their daily lives and in achieving greater well-being.

99. **Clinical psychology** is the branch of psychology concerned with the study, assessment, and treatment of people with psychological disorders.

100. **Psychiatry** is the branch of medicine concerned with the physical diagnosis and treatment of psychological disorders.

101. **Community psychology** is the branch of psychology concerned with how people interact with their social environments and how social institutions affect individuals and groups.

Essay Question

A psychologist working from the neuroscience perspective might study the brain circuits and body chemistry that trigger attraction and sexual arousal. A psychologist working from the evolutionary perspective might analyze how love has facilitated the survival of our species. A psychologist working from the behavior genetics perspective might attempt to compare the extent to which the emotion is attributable to our genes and the extent to which it is attributable to our environment. A psychologist working from the psychodynamic perspective might search for evidence that a person's particular emotional feelings are disguised effects of unfulfilled wishes. A psychologist working from the behavioral perspective might study the external stimuli, such as body language, that elicit and reward approach behaviors toward another person. A psychologist working from the cognitive perspective might study how our thought processes, attitudes, and beliefs foster attachment to loved ones, and a psychologist working from the social-cultural perspective might explore situational influences on attraction and how the development and expression of love vary across cultural groups.

MODULE
2

Research Strategies: How Psychologists Ask and Answer Questions

The Need for Psychological Science

1. insight

2. hindsight bias; common; both children and adults

3. overconfidence; equally wrong

4. random events

5. more; do not

The Scientific Method

6. scientific method; observations; theories; revised; observations

7. theory; hypotheses; confirm our theory or lead us to revise or reject it

8. operational definitions; replicate

9. organizes; predictions

10. descriptive; correlational; experimental

11. case study

12. atypical

13. naturalistic observation

14. social; solitary; varies

15. survey; wording

16. vivid

17. random; population; does

18. are

19. describe

20. correlated; predict; correlation coefficient

21. positively correlated; negatively correlated; inversely

22. strength

This is an example of a negative correlation. As one factor (time spent studying) increases, the other factor (anxiety level) decreases.

23. predicted

24. event; caused; explanation

25. cause; effect; factors

26. do; experiments; randomly; manipulates; holding constant

27. behavior; experimental; effect

28. experimental; control

29. random assignment

30. independent; dependent; confounding variables

28. double-blind

29. placebo; placebo effect

30. manipulate; independent; dependent; control

Experimentation has the advantage of increasing the investigator's control of both relevant and irrelevant variables that might influence behavior. Experiments also permit the investigator to go beyond observation and description to uncover cause-effect relationships in behavior.

31. principles

32. control; general principles

33. **b.** is the answer. A general belief such as this one is a theory; it helps organize, explain, and generate testable predictions (called hypotheses) such as "men drink more soft drinks than women."
c. & d. Independent and dependent variables are experimental treatments and behaviors, respectively. Beliefs and predictions may involve such variables, but are not themselves those variables.

34. **b.** is the answer.
a. Although the descriptive methods of case studies, surveys, naturalistic observation, and correlational research do not involve control of variables, they nevertheless enable researchers to describe and predict behavior.
c. Whether a sample is representative of a population, rather than control over variables, determines whether results can be generalized from a sample to a population.

35. **c.** is the answer. To determine the effects of caffeine on reaction time, Martina needs to measure reaction time in a control, or comparison, group that does not receive caffeine.
a. Caffeine is the independent variable.
b. Reaction time is the dependent variable.
d. Whether Martina's experiment can be replicated is determined by the precision with which she reports her procedures, which is not an aspect of research strategy.

36. **b.** is the answer.
a. The low-dose comparison group is the control group.
c. Rashad was not given a placebo.

37. **a.** is the answer.
b. Use of a placebo tests whether the behavior of a research participant, who mistakenly believes that a treatment (such as a drug) is in effect, is the same as it would be if the treatment were actually present.
c. & d. These are examples of *blind* and *double-blind* control procedures.

38. **c.** is the answer. The members of one sorority are likely to share more interests, traits, and attitudes than will the members of a random sample of college students.
a. & b. Unlike experiments, surveys do not specify or directly manipulate independent and dependent variables. In a sense, survey questions are independent variables, and the answers, dependent variables.

39. **d.** is the answer. Selecting every tenth (or fifteenth) person would probably result in a representative sample of the entire population of students at the university.
a. It would be difficult, if not impossible, to survey every student on campus.

b. Psychology students are not representative of the entire student population.

c. This answer is incorrect for the same reason as b. This would constitute a biased sample.

40. **b.** is the answer.

a. This is not an experiment because the researcher is not manipulating the independent variable (seating position); she is merely measuring whether variation in this factor predicts test performance.

c. If the study were based entirely on students' self-reported responses, this would be a survey.

d. This study goes beyond naturalistic observation, which merely describes behavior as it occurs, to determine if test scores can be predicted from students' seating position.

41. **d.** is the answer.

a. Correlation does not imply causality.

b. Again, a positive correlation simply means that two factors tend to increase or decrease together; further relationships are not implied.

c. A separate factor may or may not be involved. That the two factors are correlated does not imply a separate factor. There may, for example, be a direct causal relationship between the two factors themselves.

42. **c.** is the answer. If height and weight are positively correlated, increased height is associated with increased weight. Thus, one can predict a person's weight from his or her height.

a. Correlation does not imply causality.

b. This situation depicts a negative correlation between height and weight.

43. **d.** is the answer.

Psychology's Research Ethics

44. similarities; diseases

45. ethical; well-being

46. safeguards

47. American Psychological Association; informed consent; debrief

Ethical guidelines require investigators to protect research participants from harm and discomfort and treat information obtained from participants confidentially.

48. do

49. can; enlighten

SUMMARY STUDY TIP: COMPARING RESEARCH METHODS (For your convenience the text table is repeated here.)

Research Method	Basic Purpose	How Conducted	What Is Manipulated	Weaknesses
Descriptive	To observe and record behavior	Do case studies, surveys, or naturalistic observations	Nothing	No control of variables; single cases may be misleading
Correlational	To detect naturally occurring relationships; to assess how one variable predicts another	Collect data on two or more variables; no manipulation	Nothing	Does not specify cause and effect
Experimental	To explore cause and effect	Manipulate one or more factors; use random assignment	The independent variable(s)	Sometimes not feasible; results may not generalize to other contexts; not ethical to manipulate certain variables

Improve Your Retention—and Your Grades

50. self-testing; rehearsal; testing effect

51. actively

52. SQ3R; a. survey; b. question; c. read; d. retrieve; e. review
   a. Distribute study time.
   b. Process class information actively.
   c. Overlearn material.
   d. Learn to think critically.

53. **c.** is the answer.

a. To be effective, study must be active rather than passive in nature.

b. Most exams are based on lecture and textbook material.

d. Cramming hinders retention.

54. **d.** is the answer.

55. **c.** is the answer.

Module Review:

56. d. is the answer.
a. & c. Both of these refer to the tendency to believe, after learning an outcome, that one could have foreseen it.
b. The scientific attitude involves curiosity, skepticism, and humility, none of which is present in Juwan's thinking.

57. b. is the answer.
a. The phenomenon is related to hindsight rather than foresight.
c. & d. The phenomenon doesn't involve whether the intuitions are correct but rather people's attitude that they had the correct intuition.

58. a. is the answer. In a case study, one person is studied in depth.
b. In survey research, a group of people is interviewed.
c. Correlations identify whether two factors are related.
d. In an experiment, an investigator manipulates one variable to observe its effect on another.

59. c. is the answer. Exercise is the variable being manipulated in the experiment.
a. A control condition for this experiment would be a group of people not permitted to exercise.
b. A confounding variable is a variable other than those being manipulated that may influence behavior.
d. The dependent variable is the behavior measured by the experimenter—in this case, the effects of exercise.

60. c. is the answer. The control condition is that for which the experimental treatment (the new drug) is absent.
a. A random sample is a subset of a population in which every person has an equal chance of being selected.
b. The experimental condition is the group for which the experimental treatment (the new drug) is present.
d. "Test group" is an ambiguous term; both the experimental and control group are tested.

61. d. is the answer.
a. Hypotheses are testable propositions.
b. Dependent variables are factors that may change in response to manipulated independent variables.
c. Statistical indexes may be used to test specific hypotheses (and therefore as indirect tests of theories), but they are merely mathematical tools, not general principles, as are theories.

62. d. is the answer. In this case, the children are being observed in their normal environment rather than in a laboratory.
a. Correlational research measures relationships between two factors. The psychologist may later want to determine whether there are correlations between the variables studied under natural conditions.
b. In a case study, one subject is studied in depth.
c. This is not an experiment because the psychologist is not directly controlling the variables being studied.

63. d. is the answer.

64. b. is the answer. Replication is the repetition of an experiment to determine whether its findings are reliable. It is not a research method.

65. c. is the answer.
a., b., & d. Psychologists' personal values can influence all of these.

66. b. is the answer.
a. & c. These answers would have been correct had the question stated that there is a *positive* correlation between shoe size and IQ. Actually, there is probably no correlation at all!

67. d. is the answer. In an experiment, it would be possible to manipulate alcohol consumption and observe the effects, if any, on memory.
a., b., & c. These answers are incorrect because only by directly controlling the variables of interest can a researcher uncover cause-effect relationships.

68. d. is the answer.
a. A sample is a subset of a population.
b. & c. Control and experimental groups are used in experimentation, not in survey research.

69. d. is the answer. Only experiments can reveal cause-effect relationships; the other methods can only *describe* relationships.

70. d. is the answer.
a. & b. The double-blind procedure is one way to create experimental and control groups.
c. Research participants are randomly assigned to either an experimental or a control group.

71. b. is the answer. Just the opposite is true. Cultures differ in their views about valuing human well-being over animal well-being.

72. d. is the answer.
a. The control condition is the comparison group, in which the experimental treatment (the treatment of interest) is absent.
b. Memory is a directly observed and measured dependent variable in this experiment. A confounding variable is a variable other than those being manipulated that may influence behavior.

c. Attention is the independent variable, which is being manipulated.

73. **b.** is the answer. If enough participants are used in an experiment and they are randomly assigned to the two groups, any differences that emerge between the groups should stem from the experiment itself.
a., c., & d. None of these terms describes precautions taken in setting up groups for experiments.

74. **b.** is the answer.

75. **d.** is the answer. Because we are sensitive to dramatic or unusual events, we are especially likely to perceive a relationship between them.
a., b., & c. The relationship between vivid events is no more likely to be significant, positive, or negative than that between less dramatic events.

76. **b.** is the answer.
a. In fact, the artificiality of experiments is part of an intentional attempt to create a controlled environment in which to test theoretical principles that are applicable to all behaviors.
c. Some psychological theories go against what we consider common sense; furthermore, on many issues that psychology addresses, it's far from clear what the "common sense" position is.
d. Psychology has always had ties to other disciplines, and in recent times, these ties have been increasing.

77. **d.** is the answer. Correlations show how well one factor can be predicted from another.
a. Because a case study focuses in great detail on the behavior of an individual, it's probably not useful in showing whether predictions are possible.
b. Naturalistic observation is a method of describing, rather than predicting, behavior.
c. In experimental research the effects of manipulated independent variables on dependent variables are measured. It is not clear how an experiment could help determine whether IQ tests predict academic success.

78. **b.** is the answer. The control condition is the one in which the treatment—in this case, pollution—is absent.
a. Students in the polluted room would be in the experimental condition.
c. Presumably, all students in both conditions were randomly assigned to their groups. Random assignment is a method for establishing groups, rather than a condition.
d. The word *dependent* refers to a kind of variable in experiments; conditions are either experimental or control.

79. **c.** is the answer. The lighting is the factor being manipulated.
a. & d. These answers are incorrect because they involve aspects of the experiment other than the variables.
b. This answer is the dependent, not the independent, variable.

80. **a.** is the answer.
b. & c. Although each of these is true, SQ3R is based on the more *general* principle of active learning.
d. In fact, just the opposite is true.

81. **d.** is the answer.

Terms and Concepts to Remember:

82. **Intuition** refers to automatic feelings and thoughts, as contrasted with those that come with conscious reasoning.

83. **Hindsight bias** refers to the tendency to believe, after learning an outcome, that one would have foreseen it; also called the *I-knew-it-all-along phenomenon.*

84. A **theory** is an explanation using an integrated set of principles that organizes observations and predicts behaviors or events.

85. A **hypothesis** is a testable prediction, often implied by a theory. Testing the hypothesis helps scientists to test the theory.

86. An **operational definition** is a carefully worded statement of the exact procedures (operations) used in a research study.

87. **Replication** is the process of repeating the essence of a research study, often with different participants and in different situations, to see whether the basic finding extends to other people and circumstances.

88. The **case study** is a descriptive technique in which one person or group is studied in great depth in the hope of revealing universal principles.

89. **Naturalistic observation** is a descriptive technique in which behavior is observed and recorded in naturally occurring situations without trying to manipulate and control the situation.

90. The **survey** is a descriptive technique for ascertaining the self-reported attitudes or behaviors of a representative, random sample of people.

91. A **population** consists of all the members of a group being studied, from which samples may be drawn.

92. A **random sample** is one that is representative because every member of the population has an equal chance of being included.

93. **Correlation** is a measure of the extent to which two factors vary together, and thus of how well either factor predicts the other.

94. The **correlation coefficient** is a statistical measure of the relationship between two things. It can be positive or negative (from –1 to +1).

    Example: If there is a positive correlation between air temperature and ice cream sales, the warmer (higher) it is, the more ice cream is sold. If there is a negative correlation between air temperature and sales of cocoa, the cooler (lower) it is, the more cocoa is sold.

95. An **experiment** is a research method in which a researcher directly manipulates one or more factors (independent variables) to observe the effect on some behavior or mental process (the dependent variable); experiments therefore make it possible to establish cause-effect relationships.

96. The **experimental group** in an experiment is one in which participants are exposed to the independent variable being studied.

    Example: In the study of the effects of a new drug on reaction time, participants in the **experimental group** would actually receive the drug being tested.

97. The **control group** in an experiment is one in which the treatment of interest, or independent variable, is withheld so that comparison to the experimental condition can be made.

    Example: The **control group** in an experiment testing the effects of a new drug on reaction time would be a group of participants given a placebo (inactive drug or sugar pill) instead of the drug being tested.

98. **Random assignment** is the procedure of assigning participants to the experimental and control conditions by chance, thus minimizing preexisting differences between those assigned to the different groups.

99. A **double-blind procedure** is an experimental procedure in which both the experimenter and the research participants are ignorant (blind) about whether the research participants have received the treatment or a placebo. It is used to prevent experimenters' and participants' expectations from influencing the results of an experiment.

100. The **placebo effect** occurs when the results of an experiment are caused by expectations alone.

101. The **independent variable** of an experiment is the factor being manipulated and tested by the investigator.

    Example: In the study of the effects of a new drug on reaction time, the drug is the **independent variable**.

102. In an experiment, a **confounding variable** is a factor other than the independent variable that might influence the results.

103. The **dependent variable** of an experiment is the factor being measured by the investigator, that is, the factor that may change in response to manipulations of the independent variable.

    Example: In the study of the effects of a new drug on reaction time, the participants' reaction time is the **dependent variable.**

104. **Informed consent** is the ethical practice of giving research participants enough information to enable them to choose whether they wish to take part in a study.

105. **Debriefing** is the ethical practice of explaining a study, including its purpose and any deceptions, to participants after they have finished.

106. The **testing effect** (also called the *retrieval practice effect* or *test-enhanced learning*) refers to the beneficial effects on memory of actively retrieving, rather than simply reading, information.

107. **SQ3R** is a study method consisting of five steps: *s*urvey, *q*uestion, *r*ead, *r*etrieve, and *r*eview.

Essay Question

Elio's hypothesis is that daily aerobic exercise for one month will improve memory. Exercise is the independent variable. The dependent variable is memory. Exercise could be manipulated by having people in an experimental group jog for 30 minutes each day. Memory could be measured by comparing the number of words they recall from a test list studied before the exercise experiment begins, and again afterward. A control group that does not exercise *is* needed so that any improvement in the experimental group's memory can be attributed to exercise, and not to some other factor, such as the passage of one month's time or familiarity with the memory test. The control group should engage in some nonexercise activity for the same amount of time each day that the experimental group exercises. The participants should be randomly selected from the population at large, and then randomly assigned to the experimental and control groups.

Before You Move On

Matching Items 1

1. f	7. a	13. d
2. b	8. g	14. n
3. p	9. m	15. h
4. j	10. c	16. k
5. o	11. i	
6. e	12. l	

Matching Items 2

1. d	4. b
2. e	5. c
3. a	

Matching Items 3

1. e	5. j	9. f	13. n
2. h	6. m	10. g	14. d
3. b	7. a	11. i	
4. c	8. k	12. l	

True–False Items

1. F	5. F	9. T
2. F	6. F	10. T
3. T	7. T	
4. T	8. F	

Cross-Check

ACROSS	DOWN
4. experimental	1. behaviorism
7. random	2. functionalism
8. critical thinking	3. operational
9. placebo	5. independent
10. nurture	6. naturalistic
12. double-blind	11. hindsight
13. case study	14. culture
14. correlation	15. control
16. hypothesis	
17. neuroscience	

The Biology of Behavior

Overview

Modules 3–6 are concerned with the functions of the brain and its component neural systems, as well as the role of heredity and environment in organizing and "wiring" the brain. Under the direction of the brain, the nervous and endocrine systems coordinate a variety of voluntary and involuntary behaviors and serve as the body's mechanisms for communication with the external environment.

Knowledge of the workings of the brain has increased with advances in neuroscientific methods. The brain's increasing complexity arises from new brain systems built on top of old. Within the brainstem are the oldest regions, the medulla and the reticular formation. The thalamus sits atop the brainstem and the cerebellum extends from the rear. The limbic system includes the amygdala, the hippocampus, and the hypothalamus. The cerebral cortex, representing the highest level of brain development, is responsible for our most complex functions.

Each hemisphere of the cerebral cortex has four geographical areas: the frontal, parietal, occipital, and temporal lobes. Although small, well-defined regions within these lobes control muscle movement and receive information from the body senses, most of the cortex—its association areas—are free to process other information. Studies of split-brain patients have also given researchers a great deal of information about the specialized functions of the brain's right and left hemispheres. Studies of people with intact brains indicate that each hemisphere makes unique contributions to the integrated functions of the brain.

The field of behavior genetics studies twins and adopted children to weigh genetic and environmental influences on behaviors. The next section discusses psychology's use of evolutionary principles to answer universal questions about human behavior.

NOTE: Answer guidelines for all Modules 3–6 questions begin on page 50.

Outline

Instructions

First, skim each section, noting headings and boldface items. After you have read the section, review each objective by answering the fill-in, essay-type, and multiple-choice questions for that section. In some cases, Study Tips explain how best to learn a difficult concept and Applications and Module Reviews help you to know how well you understand the material. Finally, try to define the important terms and concepts using your own words. As you proceed, evaluate your performance by consulting the answers on page 50. Do not continue until you understand each answer. If you need to, review or reread a troublesome section in the textbook before continuing.

Before You Move On includes activities that test you on material from the entire unit.

STUDY TIP: Many students find the technical material in these modules difficult to master. Not only are there many terms for you to remember, but you must also know the organization and function of the various divisions of the nervous system. Learning this material will require a great deal of active processing, testing yourself frequently to be sure you know and understand the many structures and their functions. Answer the fill-in and essay questions several times, drawing and labeling brain diagrams, making flash cards, and mentally defining the terms are all useful techniques for learning this type of material.

 Neural and Hormonal Systems

Introduction

Objective 3-1: Explain why psychologists are concerned with human biology.

1. In the most basic sense, every idea, mood, memory, and behavior that an individual has ever experienced is a _____ happening.

2. Researchers who study the links between biology and behavior are referred to as

_____ .

APPLICATIONS:

3. A biological psychologist would be more likely to study
   a. how you learn to express emotions.
   b. how to help people overcome emotional disorders.
   c. life-span changes in the expression of emotion.
   d. the chemical changes that accompany emotions.

4. Cite some possible areas a biological psychologist would be likely to study.

Neural Communication

Objective 3-2: Describe neurons, and explain how they transmit information.

5. Our body's neural system is built from billions of nerve cells, or _____ .

6. The extensions of a neuron that receive messages from other neurons are the _____ .
The extension of a neuron that transmits information to other neurons is the _____ .
Some of these extensions are insulated by a fatty tissue called the _____

_____ , which helps speed the neuron's impulses.

7. Identify the major parts of the neuron diagrammed below.

   a. _____   c. _____
   b. _____   d. _____

8. The cells that support, protect, and nourish cortical neurons are called _____
_____ . These cells may also play a role in _____ and _____ .

9. The neural impulse, or _____
_____ , is a brief electrical charge that travels down a(n) _____ .

10. The fluid interior of a resting axon carries mostly _____ (positively/negatively) charged ions, while the fluid outside has mostly _____ (positively/negatively) charged ions. This polarization, called the _____
_____ , occurs because the cell membrane is _____
_____ .

11. An action potential occurs when the first part of the axon opens its gates and _____ (positively/negatively) charged ions rush in, causing that part of the neuron to become _____ . Neurons need tiny breaks between action potentials. During a resting pause

called the _____ _____
action potentials do not occur until the axon
returns to its _____

_____. Then the neuron can fire
again.

12. To trigger a neural impulse, _____
signals minus _____ signals must
exceed a certain intensity, called the

_____. Increasing a stimulus above
this level _____ (will/will not)
increase the neural impulse's intensity. This phenomenon is called an _____-

_____-_____
response.

13. The strength of a stimulus _____
(does/does not) affect the intensity of a neural
impulse. A strong stimulus _____
(can/cannot) trigger more neurons to fire and to
fire more often.

Objective 3-3: Describe how nerve cells communicate
with other nerve cells.

14. The junction between two neurons is called a
_____, and the gap is called the
_____. This
discovery was made by _____.

15. The chemical messengers that convey information across the gaps between neurons are called
_____. These chemicals bind to
receptor sites and unlock tiny channels, allowing
electrically charged _____ to enter
the neuron.

16. Neurotransmitters influence neurons either by
_____ or _____ their
readiness to fire. Excess neurotransmitters drift
away, are broken down by enzymes, or are reab-
sorbed by the sending neuron in a process
called _____.

Outline the sequence of reactions that occur when a
neural impulse is generated and transmitted from one
neuron to another.

Objective 3-4: Describe how neurotransmitters influence behavior, and explain how drugs and other
chemicals affect neurotransmission.

17. A neurotransmitter that is important in muscle
contraction is _____; it is also
important in learning and _____.

18. Naturally occurring opiate-like neurotransmitters
that are present in the brain are called
_____. When the brain is flooded
with drugs such as _____ or
_____, it may stop producing these
neurotransmitters.

19. Drugs that increase a neurotransmitter's action
are called _____. Drugs that
decrease a neurotransmitter's action by
_____ or _____ their
action are called _____. While certain _____ drugs create a tempo-
rary "high" by mimicking the endorphins, the
poison _____ produces paralysis by
blocking ACh release.

STUDY TIP: To understand the relationships among
excitatory and inhibitory synapses, threshold, and
the all-or-none response, you should think of the
neuron as a simple switch that is always either "on"
or "off." This "all-or-none" response is in contrast
to the graded, "partially on" response of the more
complex dimmer switch. Whether the all-or-none
response occurs depends on whether the input to
the neuron is sufficient to allow it to reach its threshold—much as a simple light switch requires a certain
amount of force to operate. In the neuron's case, the
"force" refers to the combination of excitatory inputs

(which promote a response) and inhibitory inputs (which promote the neuron's remaining in its resting state).

APPLICATIONS:

20. Several shy neurons send an inhibitory message to neighboring neuron Joni. At the same time, a larger group of party-going neurons sends Joni excitatory messages. What will Joni do?
    a. fire, assuming that her threshold has been reached
    b. not fire, even if her threshold has been reached
    c. enter a refractory period
    d. become hyperpolarized

21. I am a relatively fast-acting chemical messenger that influences muscle action, learning, and memory. What am I?
    a. dopamine   c. acetylcholine
    b. a hormone   d. glutamate

22. Since Malcolm has been taking a drug prescribed by his doctor, he has been depressed. His doctor explains that this is because the drug
    a. triggers release of dopamine.
    b. inhibits release of dopamine.
    c. triggers release of ACh.
    d. inhibits release of ACh.

23. Lolita is feeling depressed for no particular reason. It is possible that she has an undersupply of _____ .

24. Punjab had lunch at the local Chinese restaurant. Afterward, he suffered a migraine, most likely caused by an _____ of _____ .

The Nervous System

Objective 3-5: Describe the functions of the nervous system's main divisions, and identify the three main types of neurons.

25. Taken altogether, the neurons of the body form the _____ _____ .

26. The brain and spinal cord form the _____ nervous system.

27. The neurons that link the brain and spinal cord to the rest of the body form the _____ nervous system.

28. Axons are bundled into electrical cables called _____ , which link the CNS with muscles, glands, and sensory receptors.

29. Information arriving in the brain and spinal cord from the body's tissues and sensory receptors travels in _____ neurons. Instructions from the brain and spinal cord are sent to the body's tissues via _____ neurons. The neurons that enable internal communication within the brain and spinal cord are called _____ .

30. The division of the peripheral nervous system that enables voluntary control of the skeletal muscles is the _____ nervous system.

31. Responses of the glands and muscles of internal organs are controlled by the _____ nervous system.

32. The body is made ready for action by the _____ division of the autonomic nervous system.

33. The _____ division of the autonomic nervous system produces relaxation. These systems work together to keep us in a steady internal state called _____ .

Describe and explain the sequence of physical reactions that occur in the body as an emergency is confronted and then passes.

34. The brain's neurons cluster into work groups called _____ _____ .

35. Automatic responses to stimuli, called _____ , illustrate the work of the _____ _____ . Simple pathways such as these are involved in the _____-_____ response and in the _____ reflex.

Beginning with the sensory receptors in the skin, trace the course of a spinal reflex as a person reflexively jerks his or her hand away from an unexpectedly hot burner on a stove.

STUDY TIP: To keep the various functions of the peripheral nervous system (PNS) straight, remember that the PNS consists of two main divisions: somatic and autonomic. The somatic ("S") division primarily regulates "S functions," the *skeletal* muscles. The autonomic ("A") division regulates *automatic* ("A") physical systems that do not require conscious attention. These include breathing, heart rate, and digestion, to name a few.

APPLICATIONS:

36. You are sitting at your desk at home, studying for an exam. No one else is home, but you hear creaking floorboards. You sneak downstairs, only to discover your parents have returned home early. Describe and explain the sequence of physical reactions that occurred in your body as you felt fear and then relief.

37. You are able to pull your hand quickly away from hot water before pain is felt because
   a. movement of the hand is a reflex that involves intervention of the spinal cord only.
   b. movement of the hand does not require intervention by the central nervous system.
   c. the brain reacts quickly to prevent severe injury.
   d. the autonomic division of the peripheral nervous system intervenes to speed contraction of the muscles of the hand.

38. Following Jayshree's near-fatal car accident, her physician noticed that the pupillary reflex of her eyes was abnormal. This MAY indicate that Jayshree's _____ _____ _____ was damaged in the accident.

39. Your brother has been taking prescription medicine and experiencing a number of unpleasant side effects, including unusually rapid heartbeat and excessive perspiration. It is likely that the medicine is exaggerating activity in the
   a. central nervous system.
   b. sympathetic nervous system.
   c. parasympathetic nervous system.
   d. somatic nervous system.

The Endocrine System

Objective 3-6: Describe how the endocrine system transmits information and interacts with the nervous system.

40. The body's chemical communication network is called the _____ _____ . This system transmits information through chemical messengers called _____ at a much _____ (faster/slower) rate than the nervous system, and its effects last _____ (a longer time/a shorter time).

41. In a moment of danger, the autonomic nervous system orders the _____ glands to release _____ and _____ . These hormones increase _____ , _____ , and _____ , providing a surge of energy.

42. The most influential gland is the _____ , which, under the control of an adjacent brain area called the _____ , helps regulate _____ and the release of hormones by other endocrine glands. The hormone _____ enables contractions associated with birthing, milk flow during nursing, and orgasm. It also promotes _____ _____ .

Write a paragraph describing the feedback system that links the nervous and endocrine systems.

APPLICATIONS:

43. I am a relatively slow-acting (but long-lasting) chemical messenger carried throughout the body by the bloodstream. What am I?

  a. a hormone   **c.** acetylcholine
  b. a neurotransmitter **d.** dopamine

44. A bodybuilder friend suddenly seems to have grown several inches in height. You suspect that your friend's growth spurt has occurred because he has been using drugs that affect the

  a. pituitary gland.   **c.** adrenal glands.
  b. pancreas.   **d.** parathyroids.

MODULE REVIEW:

45. The axons of certain neurons are covered by a layer of fatty tissue that helps speed neural transmission. This tissue is

  a. dopamine.   **c.** acetylcholine.
  b. the myelin sheath.   **d.** an endorphin.

46. Heartbeat, digestion, and other self-regulating bodily functions are governed by the

  a. voluntary nervous system.
  b. autonomic nervous system.
  c. sympathetic division of the autonomic nervous system.
  d. somatic nervous system.

47. A strong stimulus can increase the

  a. speed of the impulse the neuron fires.
  b. intensity of the impulse the neuron fires.
  c. number of times the neuron fires.
  d. threshold that must be reached before the neuron fires.

48. The pain of heroin withdrawal may be attributable to the fact that

  a. under the influence of heroin the brain ceases production of endorphins.
  b. under the influence of heroin the brain ceases production of all neurotransmitters.
  c. during heroin withdrawal the brain's production of all neurotransmitters is greatly increased.
  d. heroin destroys endorphin receptors in the brain.

49. The effect of a drug that is an antagonist is to

  a. cause the brain to stop producing certain neurotransmitters.
  b. mimic a particular neurotransmitter.
  c. block a particular neurotransmitter.
  d. disrupt a neuron's all-or-none firing pattern.

50. Which is the correct sequence in the transmission of a simple reflex?

  a. sensory neuron, interneuron, sensory neuron
  b. interneuron, motor neuron, sensory neuron
  c. sensory neuron, interneuron, motor neuron
  d. interneuron, sensory neuron, motor neuron

51. In a resting state, the axon is

  a. depolarized, with mostly negatively charged ions outside and positively charged ions inside.
  b. depolarized, with mostly positively charged ions outside and negatively charged ions inside.
  c. polarized, with mostly negatively charged ions outside and positively charged ions inside.
  d. polarized, with mostly positively charged ions outside and negatively charged ions inside.

52. Dr. Hernandez is studying neurotransmitter abnormalities in depressed patients. She would most likely be working as a _____ psychologist.

  a. personality   **c.** psychoanalytic
  b. phrenology   **d.** biological

53. Voluntary movements, such as writing with a pencil, are directed by the

  a. sympathetic nervous system.
  b. somatic nervous system.
  c. parasympathetic nervous system.
  d. autonomic nervous system.

54. A neuron will generate action potentials when it

  a. remains below its threshold.
  b. receives an excitatory input.
  c. receives more excitatory than inhibitory inputs.
  d. is stimulated by a neurotransmitter.

55. Which is the correct sequence in the transmission of a neural impulse?

  a. axon, dendrite, cell body, synapse
  b. dendrite, axon, cell body, synapse
  c. synapse, axon, dendrite, cell body
  d. dendrite, cell body, axon, synapse

56. Chemical messengers produced by endocrine glands are called

  a. agonists.   **c.** hormones.
  b. neurotransmitters. **d.** enzymes.

57. Which of the following is true of a refractory period?
    a. A neurotransmitter's action is increased because it remains in the synaptic gap.
    b. Action potentials cannot occur.
    c. The inhibitory signals exceed the excitatory signals.
    d. A neurotransmitter's action is decreased by blocking its production or release.

58. When Sandy scalded her toe in a tub of hot water, the pain message was carried to her spinal cord by the _____ nervous system.
    a. somatic
    b. sympathetic
    c. parasympathetic
    d. central

59. Which of the following are governed by the simplest neural pathways?
    a. emotions
    b. physiological drives, such as hunger
    c. reflexes
    d. movements, such as walking

60. Melissa has just completed running a marathon. She is so elated that she feels little fatigue or discomfort. Her lack of pain is probably the result of the release of
    a. ACh.
    b. endorphins.
    c. dopamine.
    d. norepinephrine.

61. The myelin sheath that is on some neurons
    a. increases the speed of neural transmission.
    b. slows neural transmission.
    c. regulates the release of neurotransmitters.
    d. prevents positive ions from passing through the membrane.

62. I am a relatively fast-acting chemical messenger that affects mood, hunger, sleep, and arousal. What am I?
    a. acetylcholine
    b. dopamine
    c. norepinephrine
    d. serotonin

63. The neurotransmitter acetylcholine (ACh) is most likely to be found
    a. at the junction between sensory neurons and muscle fibers.
    b. at the junction between motor neurons and muscle fibers.
    c. at junctions between interneurons.
    d. in all of these locations.

64. The gland that regulates body growth is the
    a. adrenal.
    b. thyroid.
    c. hypothalamus.
    d. pituitary.

65. Epinephrine and norepinephrine are _____ that are released by the _____ gland.
    a. neurotransmitters; pituitary
    b. hormones; pituitary
    c. neurotransmitters; thyroid
    d. hormones; adrenal

66. The effect of a drug that is an agonist is to
    a. cause the brain to stop producing certain neurotransmitters.
    b. mimic a particular neurotransmitter.
    c. block a particular neurotransmitter.
    d. disrupt a neuron's all-or-none firing pattern.

TERMS AND CONCEPTS TO REMEMBER:

Using your own words, on a piece of paper write a brief definition or explanation of each of the following terms.

67. biological psychology
68. neuron
69. dendrites
70. axon
71. myelin sheath
72. glial cells (glia)
73. action potential
74. threshold
75. refractory period
76. all-or-none response
77. synapse
78. neurotransmitters
79. reuptake
80. endorphins
81. agonist
82. antagonist
83. nervous system
84. central nervous system (CNS)
85. peripheral nervous system (PNS)
86. nerves
87. sensory (afferent) neurons
88. motor (efferent) neurons
89. interneurons
90. somatic nervous system
91. autonomic nervous system
92. sympathetic nervous system

93. parasympathetic nervous system
94. reflex
95. endocrine system
96. hormones
97. adrenal glands
98. pituitary gland

ESSAY QUESTION

Discuss how the endocrine and nervous systems become involved when a student feels stress—such as that associated with an upcoming final exam. (Use the space below to list the points you want to make, and organize them. Then write the essay on a separate sheet of paper.)

MODULE 4 Tools of Discovery and Older Brain Structures

The Tools of Discovery: Having Our Head Examined

Objective 4-1: Describe how neuroscientists study the brain's connections to behavior and mind.

1. Researchers sometimes study brain function by producing _____ or by selectively destroying brain cells. The oldest technique for studying the brain involves _____ _____ of patients with brain injuries or diseases.

2. The _____ is an amplified recording of the waves of electrical activity that sweep across the brain's surface.

3. The technique depicting the level of activity of brain areas by measuring the brain's consumption of glucose is called the _____.

Briefly explain the purpose of the PET scan.

4. A technique that produces clearer images of the brain (and other body parts) by using magnetic fields and radio waves is known as _____ .

5. By comparing scans taken less than a second apart, the _____ detects oxygen-laden bloodflow to the part of the brain thought to control the bodily activity being studied. Using this technique, researchers found that bloodflow to the back of the brain _____ (increases/decreases) when people view a scene because that is where _____ information is processed. When the brain is unoccupied, blood continues to flow via a web of brain regions called the _____ _____ .

STUDY TIP/APPLICATIONS: To help keep the various research methods for studying the brain straight, think of the methods as falling into two categories: (1) those that measure ongoing electrical or metabolic brain activity in real time (EEG, PET scan, fMRI) and (2) those that merely provide a momentary picture of the brain's anatomical structure (MRI).

6. **a.** Which method would be most useful to a neurologist attempting to locate a tumor in a patient's brain?

_____

   b. Which method would be most useful to a researcher attempting to pinpoint the area of the brain that is most critical to speaking aloud?

_____

   c. What are some other instances in which a researcher would be best advised to use methods that give a picture of the brain's structure?

d. What are some other instances in which a researcher would be best advised to use methods that measure brain activity?

Older Brain Structures

Objective 4-2: Identify the structures that make up the brainstem, and summarize the functions of the brainstem, thalamus, reticular formation, and cerebellum.

7. The oldest and innermost region of the brain is the _____ .

8. At the base of the brainstem, where the spinal cord enters the skull, lies the _____ , which controls _____ and _____ . Just above this part is the _____ , which helps coordinate movements and control sleep.

9. Nerves from each side of the brain cross over to connect with the body's opposite side in the _____ .

10. At the top of the brainstem sits the _____ , which serves as the brain's sensory control center, receiving information from all the senses except _____ and routing it to the regions dealing with those senses. These egg-shaped structures also receive replies from the higher regions, which they direct to the _____ and to the _____ .

11. A network of neurons, the _____ _____ , extends from the spinal cord right up through brainstem and into the thalamus and plays an important role in controlling _____ . Electrically stimulating this area will produce an _____ animal. Lesioning this area will cause an animal to lapse into a _____ .

12. At the rear of the brainstem lies the _____ , which enables _____ _____ and skill memory. It also helps us judge time, modu-

late our _____ , and discriminate sounds and textures; and (with help from the pons) it coordinates voluntary _____ .

13. The lower brain functions occur without _____ effort, indicating that our brains process most information _____ (inside/outside) of our awareness.

Objective 4-3: Describe the structures and functions of the limbic system.

14. Between the brainstem and cerebral hemispheres is the _____ system. Aggression or fear will result from stimulation of different regions of the lima-bean-sized neural clusters, the _____ (a).

15. We must remember, however, that the brain _____ (is/is not) neatly organized into structures that correspond to our categories of behavior. For example, aggressive behavior _____ (does/does not) involve neural activity in many brain levels.

16. Below the thalamus is the _____ (b), which regulates bodily maintenance behaviors such as _____ , _____ , _____ _____ , and _____ behavior, thus helping to maintain a steady (_____) internal state. This area also regulates behavior by secreting _____ that enable it to control the _____ gland. Olds and Milner discovered that this region also contains _____ centers, which animals will work hard to have stimulated. Later research has revealed other reward centers, such as the _____ _____ in front of the hypothalamus.

17. Some researchers believe that substance use disorders, binge eating, and other _____ disorders may stem from a genetic _____

_____ _____ in the natural brain systems for pleasure and well-being.

18. The part of the limbic system that processes conscious, explicit memories is the _____ (c), which _____ (increases/decreases) in size and function as we age.

MODULE REVIEW:

19. The brain research technique that involves monitoring the brain's usage of glucose is called (in abbreviated form) the
    a. PET scan.   **c.** EEG.
    b. fMRI.   **d.** MRI.

20. Though there is no single "control center" for emotions, their regulation is primarily attributed to the brain region known as the
    a. limbic system.   **c.** brainstem.
    b. reticular formation. **d.** cerebellum.

21. Following a head injury, a person has ongoing difficulties staying awake. Most likely, the damage occurred to the
    a. thalamus.   **c.** reticular formation.
    b. corpus callosum.   **d.** cerebellum.

22. The technique that uses magnetic fields and radio waves to produce computer images of structures within the brain is called
    a. the EEG.   **c.** a PET scan.
    b. a lesion.   **d.** MRI.

23. Jessica experienced difficulty keeping her balance after receiving a blow to the back of her head. It is likely that she injured her
    a. medulla.   **c.** hypothalamus.
    b. thalamus.   **d.** cerebellum.

24. Moruzzi and Magoun caused a cat to lapse into a coma by severing neural connections between the cortex and the
    a. reticular formation. **c.** thalamus.
    b. hypothalamus.   **d.** cerebellum.

TERMS AND CONCEPTS TO REMEMBER:

25. lesion
26. electroencephalogram (EEG)
27. PET (positron emission tomography) scan
28. MRI (magnetic resonance imaging)
29. fMRI (functional MRI)
30. brainstem
31. medulla
32. thalamus
33. reticular formation
34. cerebellum
35. limbic system
37. amygdala
38. hypothalamus
36. hippocampus

⟫ The Cerebral Cortex and Our Divided Brain

The Cerebral Cortex

Objective 5-1: Describe the functions of the various cerebral cortex regions.

1. The most complex functions of human behavior are linked to the most developed part of the brain, the _____ _____. This thin layer of interconnected neural cells is the body's ultimate control and _____-_____ center.

2. Compared with the cortexes of lower mammals, the human cortex has a _____ (smoother/more wrinkled) surface. This _____ (increases/decreases) the overall surface area of our brains.

3. Each hemisphere's cortex is subdivided into four lobes, separated by prominent _____, or folds. List the four lobes of the brain.
    a. _____   c. _____
    b. _____   d. _____

4. Electrical stimulation of one side of the _____ cortex, an arch-shaped region at the back of the _____ lobe, will produce movement on the opposite side of the body. The more precise the control needed, the _____ (smaller/greater) amount of cortical space occupied.

5. Research with _____-_____ computers is underway to determine whether they will help people who have suffered paralysis

or amputation. For example, recording electrodes implanted in the _____ _____ of a 25-year-old man's brain have enabled him to mentally control a TV, draw shapes on a screen, and play video games.

6. At the front of the parietal lobes lies the _____ cortex, which, when stimulated, elicits a sensation of _____ . The more sensitive a body region, the greater the area of _____ _____ devoted to it.

7. Visual information is received in the _____ lobes, whereas auditory information is received in the _____ lobes.

APPLICATION:

10. In the diagrams to the right, the numbers refer to brain locations that have been damaged. Match each location with its probable effect on behavior.

Location		Behavioral Effect
_____	1.	a. vision disorder
_____	2.	b. insensitivity to touch
_____	3.	c. motor paralysis
_____	4.	d. hearing problem
_____	5.	e. lack of coordination
_____	6.	f. abnormal hunger
_____	7.	g. split brain
_____	8.	h. sleep/arousal
_____	9.	disorder
		i. altered personality

8. Areas of the brain that don't receive sensory information or direct movement but, rather, integrate, interpret, and act on information received by other regions are known as _____ _____ . Approximately _____ of the human cortex is of this type. Such areas in the _____ lobe are involved in judging, planning, and processing of new memories and in some aspects of personality. In the _____ lobe, these areas enable mathematical and spatial reasoning, and an area of the _____ lobe enables us to recognize faces.

9. Although the mind's subsystems are localized in particular brain regions, the brain _____ (does/does not) act as a unified whole.

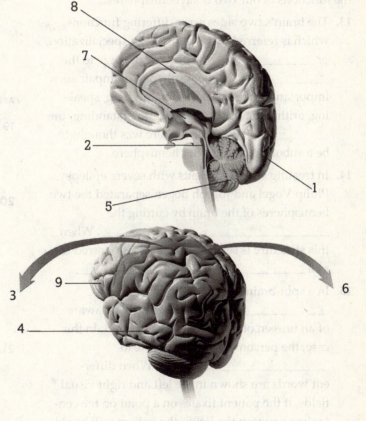

Objective 5-2: Discuss the extent to which a damaged brain can reorganize itself, and define *neurogenesis*.

11. The quality of the brain that makes it possible for undamaged brain areas to take over the functions of damaged regions is known as _____ . This quality is especially apparent in the brains of _____ (young children/adolescents/adults).

12. Although severed neurons usually _____ (will/will not) regenerate, some neural tissue can _____ in response to damage. Research has found that adult mice, birds, monkeys, and humans _____ (can/cannot) generate new brain cells through a process called _____ . Research also reveals the existence of master _____ cells in the human embryo that can develop into any type of brain cell.

Our Divided Brain

Objective 5-3: Describe what split brains reveal about the functions of our two brain hemispheres.

13. The brain's two sides serve differing functions, which is referred to as hemispheric specialization, or _____ . Because damage to the _____ hemisphere will impair such important functions as reading, writing, speaking, arithmetic reasoning, and understanding, the _____ hemisphere was thought to be a subordinate or minor hemisphere.

14. In treating several patients with severe epilepsy, Philip Vogel and Joseph Bogen separated the two hemispheres of the brain by cutting the _____ _____ . When this structure is severed, the result is referred to as a _____ _____ .

15. In a split-brain patient, only the _____ hemisphere will be aware of an unseen object held in the left hand. In this case, the person would not be able to _____ the object. When different words are shown in the left and right visual fields, if the patient fixates on a point on the center line between the fields, the patient will be able to say only the word shown on the _____ .

Explain why a split-brain patient would be able to read aloud the word *pencil* flashed to his or her right visual field, but would be unable to identify a *pencil* by touch using only the left hand.

16. When the "two minds" of a split brain are at odds, the _____ hemisphere tries to rationalize what it doesn't understand. The _____ hemisphere excels at making inferences. The brain often acts on autopilot; it acts first and then explains itself. This phenomenon demonstrates that the _____ mind _____ (can/cannot) control our behavior.

17. Deaf people use the _____ hemisphere to process sign language.

18. Although the _____ hemisphere is better at making literal interpretations of language, the _____ hemisphere excels in modulating our _____ and orchestrating our _____ .

APPLICATIONS:

19. The part of the human brain that is most like that of a fish is the
    a. cortex.
    b. amygdala.
    c. brainstem.
    d. right hemisphere.

20. To pinpoint the location of a tumor, a neurosurgeon electrically stimulated parts of the patient's somatosensory cortex. If the patient was conscious during the procedure, which of the following was probably experienced?
    a. "hearing" faint sounds
    b. "seeing" random visual patterns
    c. movement of the arms or legs
    d. a sense of having the skin touched

21. If Dr. Rogers wishes to conduct an experiment on the effects of stimulating the reward centers of a rat's brain, he should insert an electrode into the
    a. thalamus.
    b. somatosensory cortex.
    c. hypothalamus.
    d. corpus callosum.

22. A split-brain patient has a picture of a knife flashed to her left hemisphere and that of a fork to her right hemisphere. She will be able to
    a. identify the fork using her left hand.
    b. identify a knife using her left hand.
    c. identify a knife using either hand.
    d. identify a fork using either hand.

23. Anton is applying for a technician's job with a neurosurgeon. In trying to impress his potential employer with his knowledge of the brain, he says, "After my father's stroke I knew immediately that the blood clot had affected his left cerebral hemisphere because he no longer recognized a picture of his friend." Should Anton be hired?
    a. Yes. Anton obviously understands brain structure and function.
    b. No. The right hemisphere, not the left, specializes in picture recognition.
    c. Yes. Although blood clots never form in the left hemisphere, Anton should be rewarded for recognizing the left hemisphere's role in picture recognition.
    d. No. Blood clots never form in the left hemisphere, and the right hemisphere is more involved than the left in recognizing pictures.

24. Dr. Johnson briefly flashed a picture of a key in the right visual field of a split-brain patient. The patient could probably
    a. verbally report that a key was seen.
    b. write the word key using the left hand.
    c. draw a picture of a key using the left hand.
    d. do none of these things.

25. In primitive vertebrate animals, the brain primarily regulates _____ ; in lower mammals, the brain enables _____ .
    a. emotion; memory
    b. memory; emotion
    c. survival functions; emotion
    d. reproduction; emotion

26. A scientist from another planet wishes to study the simplest brain mechanisms underlying emotion and memory. You recommend that the scientist study the
    a. brainstem of a frog.
    b. limbic system of a dog.
    c. cortex of a monkey.
    d. cortex of a human.

27. Raccoons have much more precise control of their paws than dogs. You would expect that raccoons have more cortical space dedicated to "paw control" in the _____ of their brains.
    a. frontal lobes   c. temporal lobes
    b. parietal lobes   d. occipital lobes

MODULE REVIEW:

28. Which of the following is typically controlled by the right hemisphere?
    a. language
    b. learned voluntary movements
    c. arithmetic reasoning
    d. perceptual tasks

29. An experimenter flashes the word FLYTRAP onto a screen facing a split-brain patient so that FLY projects to her right hemisphere and TRAP to her left hemisphere. When asked what she saw, the patient will
    a. say she saw FLY.
    b. say she saw TRAP.
    c. point to FLY using her right hand.
    d. point to TRAP using her left hand.

30. Cortical areas that are not primarily concerned with sensory, motor, or language functions are
    a. called projection areas.
    b. called association areas.
    c. located mostly in the parietal lobe.
    d. located mostly in the temporal lobe.

31. The visual cortex is located in the
    a. occipital lobe.   c. frontal lobe.
    b. temporal lobe.   d. parietal lobe.

32. Which of the following is typically controlled by the left hemisphere?
    a. modulating speech
    b. word recognition
    c. the left side of the body
    d. perceptual skills

33. Research has found that the amount of representation in the motor cortex reflects the
    a. size of the body parts.
    b. degree of precise control required by each of the parts.
    c. sensitivity of the body region.
    d. area of the occipital lobe being stimulated by the environment.

34. The nerve fibers that enable communication between the right and left cerebral hemispheres and that have been severed in split-brain patients form a structure called the
    a. reticular formation.   c. corpus callosum.
    b. association areas.   d. parietal lobes.

35. Beginning at the front of the brain and moving toward the back of the head, then down the skull and back around to the front, which of the following is the correct order of the cortical regions?

   a. occipital lobe; temporal lobe; parietal lobe; frontal lobe
   b. temporal lobe; frontal lobe; parietal lobe; occipital lobe
   c. frontal lobe; occipital lobe; temporal lobe; parietal lobe
   d. frontal lobe; parietal lobe; occipital lobe; temporal lobe

36. Following a nail gun wound to his head, Jack became more uninhibited, irritable, dishonest, and profane. It is likely that his personality change was the result of injury to his

   a. parietal lobe.   c. occipital lobe.
   b. temporal lobe.   d. frontal lobe.

37. Three-year-old Marco suffered damage to the speech area of the brain's left hemisphere when he fell from a swing. Research suggests that

   a. he may never speak again.
   b. his motor abilities may improve so that he can easily use sign language.
   c. his right hemisphere may take over much of the language function.
   d. his earlier experience with speech may enable him to continue speaking.

TERMS AND CONCEPTS TO REMEMBER:

38. cerebral cortex
39. frontal lobes
40. parietal lobes
41. occipital lobes
42. temporal lobes
43. motor cortex
44. somatosensory cortex
45. association areas
46. plasticity
47. neurogenesis
48. corpus callosum
49. split brain

MODULE 6 Genetics, Evolutionary Psychology, and Behavior

Behavior Genetics: Predicting Individual Differences

Objective 6-1: Define *chromosomes*, *DNA*, *genes*, and the human *genome*, and describe how behavior geneticists explain our individual differences.

1. Our similarities as human beings include our common _____ _____ , our shared _____ architecture, and our _____ behaviors.

2. Our differences as humans include our _____ , _____ , and _____ and _____ backgrounds.

3. A fundamental question in psychology deals with the extent to which we are shaped by our genes, or our _____ , and by external influences, called our _____ .

4. Researchers who study the relative powers of genetic and environmental influences are called _____ _____ .

5. The master plans for development are stored in the _____ . In number, each person inherits _____ of these structures, _____ from each parent. Each is composed of a coiled chain of the molecule _____ .

6. If chromosomes are the chapters of heredity, the words that make each of us a distinctive human being are called _____ .

7. Genes can either be _____ (active) or inactive. Genes are "turned on" by _____ _____ . When turned on, genes provide the code for creating _____ _____ , our body's building blocks.

8. The complete instructions for making an organism are referred to as the human _____ .

9. Most of our traits are influenced by _____ (single/multiple) genes.

STUDY TIP: To keep the relationship among genes, DNA, and chromosomes straight, try thinking about them visually. Chromosomes are the largest of the units. They are made of up genes, which are in turn made up of DNA. Test your understanding by identifying the elements of heredity in the drawing below. Note that (c) is the unit that contains the code for proteins, and (d) is the spiraling, complex molecule.

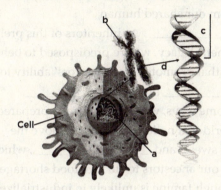

10. a. _____   c. _____
    b. _____   d. _____

Objective 6-2: Discuss how twin and adoption studies help us understand the effects and interactions of nature and nurture.

11. To study the power and limits of genetic influences on behavior, researchers use _____ and _____ studies.

12. Twins who developed from a single (monozygotic) egg are genetically _____ . Twins who developed from different (dizygotic) fertilized eggs are no more genetically alike than siblings and are called _____ twins.

13. In terms of the personality traits of extraversion and neuroticism, identical twins are _____ (more/no more) alike than are fraternal twins.

14. Twin pairs reported _____ (being treated alike/being treated differently). However, their similarities _____ (could/could not) be attributed to how they were treated.

15. Through research on identical twins raised apart, psychologists are able to study the influence of the _____ .

16. Studies tend to show that the personality traits such as extraversion and agreeableness of adopted children _____ (do/do not) closely resemble those of their adoptive parents. However, adoption studies show that parenting _____ (does/does not) matter. For example, many adopted children score _____ (higher/lower) than their biological parents on intelligence tests. Furthermore, parents influence their children's _____ , _____ , manners, politics, and _____ .

APPLICATION:

17. My sibling and I developed from a single fertilized egg. Who are we?
    a. opposite-sex identical twins
    b. same-sex identical twins
    c. opposite-sex fraternal twins
    d. same-sex fraternal twins

Objective 6-3: Describe how heredity and environment work together.

18. The difference between any two people is an effect of environment. But it is also the product a biological mechanism: _____ .

19. Genes are self-_____ ; rather than acting as _____ that always lead to the same result, they _____ to the environmental context. Therefore, genes and environment—nature and nurture— _____ .

20. The field of _____ studies the _____ mechanism by which _____ _____ trigger or block _____ expression.

21. Our experiences also lay down _____ , which may "turn off" a specific gene.

22. Environmental factors such as _____ , _____ , and stress can affect the _____ molecules that regulate gene expression.

APPLICATIONS:

23. Which of the following is an example of an interaction?
    a. Swimmers swim fastest during competition against other swimmers.
    b. Swimmers with certain personality traits swim fastest during competition, while those with other personality traits swim fastest during solo time trials.
    c. As the average daily temperature increases, sales of ice cream decrease.
    d. As the average daily temperature increases, sales of lemonade increase.

24. Despite growing up in the same home environment, Karen and her brother John have personalities as different from each other as two people selected randomly from the population.
    a. Personality is inherited. Because Karen and John are not identical twins, it is not surprising they have very different personalities.
    b. Gender is the most important factor in personality. If Karen had a sister, the two of them would probably be much more alike.
    c. The interaction of their individual genes and nonshared experiences accounts for the common finding that children in the same family are usually very different.
    d. Their case is unusual; children in the same family usually have similar personalities.

25. Dr. Gonzalez is conducting research on whether people who do well in school can thank their genes or their environment for their success. To distinguish how much genetic and environmental factors affect school success, Dr. Gonzalez should compare children with _____ (the same/different) genes and _____ (the same/different) environments.

Evolutionary Psychology: Understanding Human Nature

Objective 6-4: Describe evolutionary psychologists' use of natural selection to explain behavior tendencies.

26. Researchers who study natural selection and the adaptive nature of human behavior are called _____ .

27. Researchers in this field focus mostly on what makes people so _____ (much alike/different from one another).

28. According to the principle of _____ _____ , traits that lead to increased reproduction and survival will most likely be passed on to succeeding generations.

29. Genetic _____ are random errors in genetic replication that lead to _____ .

30. Our behavioral and biological similarities arise from our shared human _____ . As inheritors of this prehistoric genetic legacy, we are predisposed to behave in ways that promoted our ancestors' ability to _____ and _____ . But in some ways, we are biologically prepared for a world that no longer exists. We love the tastes of sweets and _____ , which enabled our ancestors to survive food shortages , even though famine is unlikely in industrialized societies.

MODULE REVIEW:

31. If a fraternal twin develops schizophrenia, the likelihood of the other twin developing serious mental illness is much lower than with identical twins. This suggests that
    a. schizophrenia is caused by genes.
    b. schizophrenia is influenced by genes.
    c. environment is unimportant in the development of schizophrenia.
    d. identical twins are especially vulnerable to mental disorders.

32. Of the following, the best way to separate the effects of genes and environment in research is to study
    a. fraternal twins.
    b. identical twins.
    c. adopted children and their adoptive parents.
    d. identical twins raised in different environments.

33. Unlike _____ twins, who develop from a single fertilized egg, _____ twins develop from separate fertilized eggs.
    a. fraternal; identical
    b. identical; fraternal
    c. placental; nonplacental
    d. nonplacental; placental

34. Each cell of the human body has a total of
    a. 23 chromosomes.   c. 46 chromosomes.
    b. 23 genes.   d. 46 genes.

35. Genes direct our physical development by synthesizing
   a. hormones.
   b. proteins.
   c. DNA.
   d. chromosomes.

36. The term *genome* refers to
   a. a complex molecule containing genetic information that makes up the chromosomes.
   b. a segment of DNA.
   c. the complete instructions for making an organism.
   d. the code for synthesizing protein.

37. Most human traits are
   a. learned.
   b. determined by a single gene.
   c. influenced by many genes acting together.
   d. unpredictable.

38. Several studies of long-separated identical twins have found that these twins
   a. have little in common because of the different environments in which they were raised.
   b. have many similarities, in everything from medical histories to personalities.
   c. have similar personalities, but very different likes, dislikes, and lifestyles.
   d. are no more similar than are fraternal twins reared apart.

39. Adoption studies show that the personalities of adopted children
   a. closely match those of their adoptive parents.
   b. bear more similarities to their biological parents than to their adoptive parents.
   c. closely match those of the biological children of their adoptive parents.
   d. closely match those of other children raised in the same home, whether or not they are biologically related.

40. Chromosomes are composed of a coiled chain of
   a. DNA molecules that contain genes.
   b. DNA molecules that contain neurotransmitters.
   c. DNA molecules that contain endorphins.
   d. DNA molecules that contain enzymes.

41. When the effect of one factor (such as environment) depends on another (such as heredity), we say there is a(n) _____ between the two factors.
   a. genome
   b. positive correlation
   c. negative correlation
   d. interaction

42. Through natural selection, the traits that are most likely to be passed on to succeeding generations are those that contribute to
   a. extraversion.
   b. survival.
   c. aggressiveness.
   d. social power.

43. When evolutionary psychologists use the word *fitness,* they are specifically referring to
   a. an animal's ability to adapt to changing environments.
   b. the diversity of a species' gene pool.
   c. the total number of members of the species currently alive.
   d. our ability to survive and reproduce.

44. Mutations are random errors in _____ replication.
   a. gene
   b. chromosome
   c. DNA
   d. protein

45. An evolutionary psychologist would be most interested in studying
   a. why most parents are so passionately devoted to their children.
   b. hereditary influences on skin color.
   c. why certain diseases are more common among certain age groups.
   d. genetic differences in personality.

TERMS AND CONCEPTS TO REMEMBER:

46. environment

47. heredity

48. behavior genetics

49. chromosomes

50. DNA (deoxyribonucleic acid)

51. genes

52. genome

53. identical (monoygotic) twins

54. fraternal (dizygotic) twins

55. interaction

56. epigenetics

57. evolutionary psychology

58. natural selection

59. mutation

Before You Move On

Complete the following exercises after you thoroughly understand the material in all the modules.

Matching Items 1

Match each structure or technique with its corresponding function or description.

Structures or Techniques

_____ 1. hypothalamus
_____ 2. lesion
_____ 3. EEG
_____ 4. fMRI
_____ 5. reticular formation
_____ 6. MRI
_____ 7. thalamus
_____ 8. corpus callosum
_____ 9. cerebellum
_____ 10. amygdala
_____ 11. medulla
_____ 12. behavior genetics
_____ 13. heredity
_____ 14. genes

Functions or Descriptions

a. amplified recording of brain waves
b. technique that uses radio waves and magnetic fields to image brain anatomy
c. serves as sensory control center
d. contains reward centers
e. tissue destruction
f. technique that uses radio waves and magnetic fields to show brain function
g. helps control arousal
h. links the cerebral hemispheres
i. influences rage and fear
j. regulates breathing and heartbeat
k. enables coordinated movement
l. the genetic transfer of characteristics
m. the study of genetic and environmental influences
n. the biochemical units of heredity

Matching Items 2

Match each structure or term with its corresponding function or description.

Structures or Terms

_____ 1. right hemisphere
_____ 2. brainstem
_____ 3. temporal lobes
_____ 4. occipital lobes
_____ 5. plasticity
_____ 6. neurogenesis
_____ 7. reuptake
_____ 8. limbic system
_____ 9. association areas
_____ 10. left hemisphere
_____ 11. glial cells
_____ 12. chromosomes
_____ 13. environment

Functions or Descriptions

a. the formation of new neurons
b. specializes in rationalizing reactions
c. support cells of the nervous system
d. specializes in spatial relations
e. brain areas containing the auditory cortex
f. brain areas containing the visual cortex
g. oldest part of the brain
h. regulates emotion
i. the brain's capacity for modification
j. absorption of excess neurotransmitters
k. brain areas involved in higher mental functions
l. nongenetic influences
m. threadlike structures made of DNA

Cross-Check

As you learned in Module 2, reviewing and overlearning of material are important to the learning process. After you have written the definitions of the key terms in these modules, you should complete the crossword puzzle to ensure that you can reverse the process—recognize the term, given the definition.

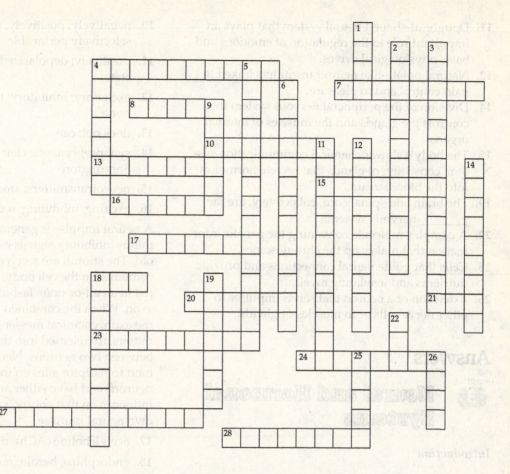

ACROSS

4. The division of the nervous system that connects the brain and spinal cord to the body's sense receptors, muscles, and glands.
7. Located on the sides of the brain, these lobes contain the auditory areas, which receive information from the ears.
8. Located at the back of the frontal lobe, the part of the cortex that controls voluntary movement.
10. Located just behind the forehead, these lobes are involved in speaking and muscle movements and in making plans and judgments.
13. Glands that produce the hormones epinephrine and norepinephrine.
15. Located in the brainstem, this structure controls breathing and heartbeat.
16. The thin outer covering of the cerebral hemispheres.
17. Junction between the axon tip of the sending neuron and the dendrite or cell body of the receiving neuron.
18. Amplified recording of the waves of electrical activity of the brain.
20. Destruction of tissue.
21. Technique that uses magnetic fields and radio waves to produce computer-generated images of brain structures.
23. Located at the back and base of the brain, these lobes contain the visual cortex, which receives

information from the eyes.
24. The part of the limbic system involved in regulation of the emotions of fear and rage.
27. The study of environmental influences on gene expression.
28. Situated between the frontal and occipital lobes, these lobes contain the sensory cortex.

DOWN

1. The biochemical units of heredity that make up the chromosomes.
2. Limbic system structure that regulates hunger, thirst, and body temperature and contains the so-called reward centers of the brain.
3. Large band of neural fibers that links the right and left hemispheres.
4. Technique that measures the levels of activity of different areas of the brain by tracing their consumption of a radioactive form of glucose.
5. Neural impulse generated by the movement of positively charged atoms in and out of channels in the axon's membrane.
6. Neurotransmitter that triggers muscle contractions.
9. Simple, automatic, inborn response to a sensory stimulus.

11. Doughnut-shaped neural system that plays an important role in the regulation of emotions and basic physiological drives.

12. Natural opiate-like neurotransmitters linked to pain control and to pleasure.

14. Division of the peripheral nervous system that controls the glands and the muscles of internal organs.

18. The body's slower chemical communication system, consisting of glands that secrete hormones into the bloodstream.

19. The brain and spinal cord, collectively, are the _____ nervous system.

22. A complex molecule containing the genetic information that makes up the chromosomes.

25. Cells that guide neural connections and provide nutrients and insulating myelin.

26. Extension of a neuron that sends impulses to other nerve cells or to muscles or glands.

Answers

 MODULE 3

Neural and Hormonal Systems

Introduction

1. biological

2. biological psychologists

3. **d.** is the answer. A biological psychologist studies the links between biology (chemical changes in this example) and behavior (emotions in this example).
   a., b., & c. Experimental, clinical, and developmental psychologists would be more concerned with the learning of emotional expressions, the treatment of emotional disorders, and life-span changes in emotions, respectively.

4. A biological psychologist might study chemical changes that accompany emotions, how muscle tension varies with facial expression, how heart rate changes as people become angry, and so on.

Neural Communication

5. neurons

6. dendrites; axon; myelin sheath

7. **a.** dendrites
   b. cell body
   c. axon
   d. myelin sheath

8. glial cells; learning; thinking

9. action potential; axon

10. negatively; positively; resting potential; selectively permeable

11. positively; depolarized; refractory period; resting state

12. excitatory; inhibitory; threshold; will not; all-or-none

13. does not; can

14. synapse; synaptic cleft (gap); Sir Charles Sherrington

15. neurotransmitters; atoms

16. exciting; inhibiting; reuptake

A neural impulse is generated by excitatory signals minus inhibitory signals exceeding a certain threshold. The stimuli are received through the dendrites, combined in the cell body, and electrically transmitted in an all-or-none fashion down the length of the axon. When the combined signal reaches the end of the axon, chemical messengers called neurotransmitters are released into the synaptic cleft, or gap, between two neurons. Neurotransmitter molecules bind to receptor sites on the dendrites of neighboring neurons and have either an excitatory or inhibitory influence on that neuron's tendency to generate its own neural impulse.

17. acetylcholine (ACh); memory

18. endorphins; heroin; morphine

19. agonists; inhibiting; blocking; antagonists; opiate; curare

20. **a.** is the answer.
    b. Because she has reached her threshold, she will probably fire.
    c. The refractory period is a resting period. Because Joni has received a large number of excitatory messages, she will not be at rest.
    d. *Hyperpolarization* is not a term.

21. **c.** is the answer.

22. **b.** is the answer.
    a. By triggering release of dopamine, such a drug would probably enhance Malcolm's enjoyment of the pleasures of life.
    c. & d. ACh is the neurotransmitter at synapses between motor neurons and muscle fibers.

23. norepinephrine. An undersupply can cause depression.

24. oversupply; glutamate. Glutamate is in MSG, which is sometimes used in Chinese cooking. Glutamate can cause migraines because an oversupply can overstimulate the brain.

The Nervous System

25. nervous system

26. central

27. peripheral

28. nerves

29. sensory; motor; interneurons

30. somatic

31. autonomic

32. sympathetic

33. parasympathetic; homeostasis

The sympathetic division of the autonomic nervous system becomes aroused in response to an emergency. The physiological changes that occur include accelerated heartbeat, elevated blood sugar, slowing of digestion, and increased perspiration to cool the body. When the emergency is over, the parasympathetic nervous system produces the opposite physical reactions.

34. neural networks

35. reflexes; spinal cord; knee-jerk; pain

From sensory receptors in the skin the message travels via sensory neurons to an interneuron in the spinal cord, which in turn activates a motor neuron. This motor neuron causes the muscles in the hand to contract, and the person jerks his or her hand away from the heat.

36. When you hear the creaking, you become afraid. The sympathetic division of your autonomic nervous system becomes aroused, causing these physiological changes: accelerated heartbeat, elevated blood sugar, increase in blood pressure, slowing of digestion, and increased perspiration to cool the body. When you realize it's only your parents, your parasympathetic nervous system produces the opposite physical reactions, calming your body.

37. **a.** is the answer. Because this reflex is an automatic response and involves only the spinal cord, the hand is jerked away before the brain has even received the information that causes the sensation of pain.
    b. The spinal cord, which organizes simple reflexes such as this one, is part of the central nervous system.
    c. The brain is not involved in directing spinal reflexes.
    d. The autonomic nervous system controls the glands and the muscles of the internal organs; it does not influence the skeletal muscles controlling the hand.

38. autonomic nervous system

39. **b.** is the answer. Sympathetic arousal produces several effects, including accelerated heartbeat and excessive perspiration.

a. & d. Activation of the central nervous system and the somatic nervous system does not have these effects.
c. Arousal of the parasympathetic nervous system would have effects opposite to those stated.

The Endocrine System

40. endocrine system; hormones; slower; a longer time

41. adrenal; epinephrine; norepinephrine; heart rate; blood pressure; blood sugar

42. pituitary; hypothalamus; growth; oxytocin; pair bonding, group cohesion, and social trust

The hypothalamus in the brain influences secretions by the pituitary. The pituitary regulates other endocrine glands, which release hormones that influence the brain, which directs behavior.

43. **a.** is the answer.
    b., c., & d. Acetylcholine and dopamine are fast-acting neurotransmitters released at synapses, not in the bloodstream.

44. **a.** is the answer. Hormones of the pituitary gland regulate body growth.
    b. The pancreas regulates the level of sugar in the blood.
    c. The adrenal glands produce hormones that provide energy during emergencies; they are not involved in regulating body growth.
    d. The parathyroids help regulate the level of calcium in the blood.

Module Review:

45. **b.** is the answer.
    a. Dopamine is a neurotransmitter that influences movement, learning, attention, and emotion.
    c. Acetylcholine is a neurotransmitter that triggers muscle contraction.
    d. Endorphins are opiatelike neurotransmitters linked to pain control and to pleasure.

46. **b.** is the answer. The autonomic nervous system controls internal functioning, including heartbeat, digestion, and glandular activity.
    a. The functions mentioned are all automatic, not voluntary, so this answer cannot be correct.
    c. This answer is incorrect because most organs are affected by both divisions of the autonomic nervous system.
    d. The somatic nervous system transmits sensory input to the central nervous system and enables voluntary control of skeletal muscles.

47. **c.** is the answer. Stimulus strength can affect only the number of times a neuron fires or the number of neurons that fire.

a., b., & d. These answers are incorrect because firing is an all-or-none response, so intensity remains the same regardless of stimulus strength. Nor can stimulus strength change the neuronal threshold or the impulse speed.

48. **a.** is the answer. Endorphins are neurotransmitters that function as natural painkillers. When the body has a supply of artificial painkillers such as heroin, endorphin production stops.
    b. The production of neurotransmitters other than endorphins does not cease.
    c. Neurotransmitter production does not increase during withdrawal.
    d. Heroin makes use of the same receptor sites as endorphins.

49. **c.** is the answer.

50. **c.** is the answer. In a simple reflex, a sensory neuron carries the message that a sensory receptor has been stimulated to an interneuron in the spinal cord. The interneuron responds by activating motor neurons that will enable the appropriate response.

51. **d.** is the answer.

52. **d.** is the answer. Biological psychologists study the links between biology (in this case, neurotransmitters) and psychology (depression, in this example).

53. **b.** is the answer.
    a., c., & d. The autonomic nervous system, which is divided into the sympathetic and parasympathetic divisions, is concerned with regulating basic bodily maintenance functions.

54. **c.** is the answer.
    a. An action potential will occur only when the neuron's threshold is *exceeded*.
    b. An excitatory input that does not reach the neuron's threshold will not trigger an action potential.
    d. This answer is incorrect because some neurotransmitters inhibit a neuron's readiness to fire.

55. **d.** is the answer. A neuron receives incoming stimuli on its dendrites and cell body. These electrochemical signals are combined in the cell body, generating an impulse that travels down the axon, causing the release of neurotransmitter substances into the synaptic cleft or gap.

56. **c.** is the answer.
    a. Agonists are drugs that excite neural firing by mimicking a particular neurotransmitter.
    b. Neurotransmitters are the chemicals involved in synaptic transmission in the nervous system.
    d. Enzymes are chemicals that facilitate various chemical reactions throughout the body but are

not involved in communication within the endocrine system.

57. **b.** is the answer.
    a. This describes an absolute refractory period.
    c. This is the opposite of what occurs when the threshold is reached and a neuron is able to fire.
    d. This describes the action of an antagonist.

58. **a.** is the answer. Sensory neurons in the somatic nervous system relay such messages.
    b. & c. These divisions of the autonomic nervous system are concerned with the regulation of bodily maintenance functions such as heartbeat, digestion, and glandular activity.
    d. The spinal cord itself is part of the central nervous system, but the message is carried to the spinal cord by the somatic division of the peripheral nervous system.

59. **c.** is the answer. As automatic responses to stimuli, reflexes are the simplest complete units of behavior and require only simple neural pathways.
    a., b., & d. Emotions, drives, and voluntary movements are all behaviors that are much more complex than reflexes and therefore involve much more complicated neural pathways.

60. **b.** is the answer. Endorphins are neurotransmitters that function as natural painkillers and are evidently involved in the "runner's high" and other situations in which discomfort or fatigue is expected but not experienced.
    a. ACh is a neurotransmitter involved in muscular control.
    c. Dopamine is a neurotransmitter involved in, among other things, movement.
    d. Norepinephrine is an adrenal hormone released to help us respond in moments of danger.

61. **a.** is the answer.
    c. & d. Myelin sheaths are not involved in regulating the release of neurotransmitters.

62. **d.** is the answer.

63. **b.** is the answer. ACh is a neurotransmitter that causes the contraction of muscle fibers when stimulated by motor neurons. This function explains its location.
    a. & c. Sensory neurons and interneurons do not directly stimulate muscle fibers.

64. **d.** is the answer. The pituitary regulates body growth, and some of its secretions regulate the release of hormones from other glands.
    a. The adrenal glands are stimulated by the autonomic nervous system to release epinephrine and norepinephrine.

b. The thyroid gland affects metabolism, among other things.
c. The hypothalamus, which is not a gland, regulates the pituitary but does not itself directly regulate growth.

65. **d.** is the answer. Also known as adrenaline and noradrenaline, epinephrine and norepinephrine are hormones released by the adrenal glands.

66. **b.** is the answer.
a. Abuse of certain drugs, such as heroin, may have this effect.
c. This describes the effect of an antagonist.
d. Drugs do not have this effect on neurons.

Terms and Concepts to Remember:

67. A **biological psychologist** is concerned with the links between biology and behavior.

68. The **neuron**, or nerve cell, is the basic building block of the nervous system.

69. The **dendrites** of a neuron are the bushy, branching extensions that receive messages from other nerve cells and conduct impulses toward the cell body.

70. The **axon** of a neuron is the extension that sends impulses to other nerve cells or to muscles or glands.

71. The **myelin sheath** is a layer of fatty tissue that segmentally covers many axons and helps speed neural impulses.

72. More numerous than cortical neurons, the **glial cells** of the brain guide neural connections, provide nutrients and insulating myelin, and help remove excess ions and neurotransmitters.

73. An **action potential** is a neural impulse generated by the movement of positively charged atoms in and out of channels in the axon's membrane.

74. A neuron's **threshold** is the level of stimulation required to trigger a neural impulse.

75. The **refractory period** is a brief resting period after a neuron has fired; subsequent action potentials cannot occur until the axon returns to its resting state.

76. Neurons have an **all-or-none response,** that is, they either fire or do not fire.

77. A **synapse** is the junction between the axon tip of the sending neuron and the dendrite or cell body of the receiving neuron. The tiny gap at this junction is called the *synaptic gap* or *cleft*.

78. **Neurotransmitters** are chemicals that are released into synaptic gaps and so transmit neural messages from neuron to neuron.

79. **Reuptake** is the absorption of excess neurotransmitters by a sending neuron.

80. **Endorphins** are natural, opiate-like neurotransmitters linked to pain control and to pleasure.
Memory aid: Endorphins *end* pain.

81. An **agonist** is a molecule that mimics a neurotransmitter and stimulates a response.

82. An **antagonist** is a molecule that binds to receptors and inhibits a response.

83. The **nervous system** is the speedy, electrochemical communication system, consisting of all the nerve cells in the peripheral and central nervous systems.

84. The **central nervous system (CNS)** consists of the brain and spinal cord; it is located at the *center*, or internal core, of the body.

85. The **peripheral nervous system (PNS)** includes the sensory and motor neurons that connect the central nervous system to the body's sense receptors, muscles, and glands; it is at the *periphery* of the body relative to the brain and spinal cord.

86. **Nerves** are bundles of neural axons, which are part of the PNS, that connect the central nervous system with muscles, glands, and sense organs.

87. **Sensory (afferent) neurons** carry incoming information from the sensory receptors to the brain and spinal cord.

88. **Motor (efferent) neurons** carry outgoing information from the brain and spinal cord to muscles and glands.

89. **Interneurons** are the neurons of the central nervous system that link the sensory and motor neurons in the transmission of sensory inputs and motor outputs.

90. The **somatic nervous system** is the division of the peripheral nervous system that enables voluntary control of the skeletal muscles; also called the *skeletal nervous system.*

91. The **autonomic nervous system** is the division of the peripheral nervous system that controls the glands and the muscles of internal organs and thereby controls internal functioning; it regulates the *automatic* behaviors necessary for survival.

92. The **sympathetic nervous system** is the division of the autonomic nervous system that arouses the body, mobilizing its energy.

93. The **parasympathetic nervous system** is the division of the autonomic nervous system that calms the body, conserving its energy.

94. A **reflex** is a simple, automatic response to a sensory stimulus; it is governed by a very simple neural pathway.

95. The **endocrine system**, the body's "slower" chemical communication system, consists of glands that secrete hormones into the bloodstream.

96. **Hormones** are chemical messengers, mostly manufactured by the endocrine glands, that are produced in one tissue and circulate through the bloodstream to their target tissues, on which they have specific effects.

97. The **adrenal glands** are a pair of endocrine glands that produce epinephrine and norepinephrine, hormones that help arouse the body in times of stress.

98. The **pituitary gland**, under the influence of the hypothalamus, regulates growth and controls other endocrine glands; it is the endocrine system's most influential gland.

Essay Question

The body's response to stress is regulated by the nervous system. As the date of the exam approaches, the stressed student's cerebral cortex activates the hypothalamus, triggering the release of hormones that in turn activate the sympathetic branch of the autonomic nervous system and the endocrine system. The autonomic nervous system controls involuntary bodily responses such as breathing, heartbeat, and digestion. The endocrine system contains glands that secrete hormones into the bloodstream that regulate the functions of body organs.

In response to activation by the hypothalamus, the student's pituitary gland would secrete a hormone which in turn triggers the release of epinephrine, norepinephrine, and other stress hormones from the adrenal glands. These hormones would help the student's body manage stress by making nutrients available to meet the increased demands for energy stores the body often faces in coping with stress. These hormones activate the sympathetic division of the autonomic system, causing increased heart rate, breathing, and blood pressure and the suppression of digestion. After the exam date has passed, the student's body would attempt to restore its normal, pre-stress state. The parasympathetic branch of the autonomic system would slow the student's heartbeat and breathing and digestive processes would no longer be suppressed, perhaps causing the student to feel hungry.

MODULE 4

Tools of Discovery and Older Brain Structures

Tools of Discovery: Having Our Head Examined

1. lesions; clinical observation

2. electroencephalogram (EEG)

3. PET (positron emission tomography) scan

By depicting the brain's consumption of temporarily radioactive glucose, the PET scan allows researchers to see which brain areas are most active as a person performs various tasks by tracking the gamma rays released. This provides additional information on the specialized functions of various regions of the brain.

4. MRI (magnetic resonance imaging)

5. functional MRI; increases; visual; default network

6. a. MRI
   b. PET scan
   c. to study developmental changes in brain structure, to compare brain anatomy in women and men
   d. to learn which areas of the brain become active during strong emotions, to determine whether brain activity is abnormal in people suffering from neurocognitive disorder (memory and language problems)

Older Brain Structures

7. brainstem

8. medulla; breathing; heartbeat; pons

9. brainstem

10. thalamus; smell; medulla; cerebellum

11. reticular formation; arousal; alert (awake); coma

12. cerebellum; nonverbal learning; emotions; movement

13. conscious; outside

14. limbic; amygdala

15. is not; does

16. hypothalamus; hunger; thirst; body temperature; sexual; homeostatic; hormones; pituitary; reward; nucleus accumbens

17. addictive; reward deficiency syndrome

18. hippocampus; decreases

Module Review:

19. **a.** is the answer. The PET scan measures glucose consumption in different areas of the brain to determine their levels of activity.

b. The fMRI compares MRI scans taken less than a second apart to reveal brain structure and function.

c. The EEG is a measure of electrical activity in the brain.

d. MRI uses magnetic fields and radio waves to produce computer-generated images of soft tissues of the body.

20. **a.** is the answer.

b. The reticular formation is linked to arousal.

c. The brainstem governs the mechanisms of basic survival—heartbeat and breathing, for example— and has many other roles.

d. The cerebellum coordinates movement output and balance.

21. **c.** is the answer. The reticular formation plays an important role in arousal.

a. The thalamus relays sensory input.

b. The corpus callosum links the two cerebral hemispheres.

d. The cerebellum is involved in coordination of movement output and balance.

22. **d.** is the answer.

a. The EEG is an amplified recording of the brain's electrical activity.

b. A lesion is destruction of tissue.

c. The PET scan is a visual display of brain activity that detects the movement of a radioactive form of glucose as the brain performs a task.

23. **d.** is the answer. The cerebellum is involved in the coordination of voluntary muscular movements.

a. The medulla regulates breathing and heartbeat.

b. The thalamus relays sensory inputs to the appropriate higher centers of the brain.

c. The hypothalamus is concerned with the regulation of basic drives and emotions.

24. **a.** is the answer. The reticular formation controls arousal via its connections to the cortex. Thus, separating the two produces a coma.

b., c., & d. None of these structures controls arousal. The hypothalamus regulates hunger, thirst, sexual behavior, and other basic drives; the thalamus is a sensory relay station; and the cerebellum is involved in the coordination of voluntary movement.

Terms and Concepts to Remember:

25. A **lesion** is destruction of tissue; studying the consequences of lesions in different regions of the brain—both surgically produced in animals and naturally occurring—helps researchers to determine the normal functions of these regions.

26. An **electroencephalogram (EEG)** is an amplified recording of the waves of electrical activity of the brain. *Encephalo* comes from a Greek word meaning "related to the brain."

27. The **PET (positron emission tomography) scan** measures the levels of activity of different areas of the brain by tracing their consumption of a radioactive form of glucose, the brain's fuel.

28. **MRI (magnetic resonance imaging)** uses magnetic fields and radio waves to produce computer-generated images that show brain structures more clearly.

29. In an **fMRI (functional magnetic resonance imaging),** MRI scans taken less than a second apart are compared to reveal bloodflow and, therefore, brain function.

30. The **brainstem**, the oldest and innermost region of the brain, is an extension of the spinal cord and is the central core of the brain; its structures direct automatic survival functions.

31. Located in the brainstem, the **medulla** controls breathing and heartbeat.

32. Located atop the brainstem, the **thalamus** routes incoming messages to the appropriate cortical centers and transmits replies to the medulla and cerebellum.

33. The **reticular formation** is a nerve network that travels through the brainstem into the thalamus. It plays an important role in controlling arousal.

34. The **cerebellum** processes sensory input and coordinates movement output and balance.

35. The **limbic system** is a neural system associated with emotions such as fear and aggression and basic physiological drives.

Memory aid: Its name comes from the Latin word *limbus*, meaning "border"; the **limbic system** is at the border of the brainstem and cerebral hemispheres.

37. The **amygdala** is part of the limbic system and influences the emotions of fear and aggression.

38. Also part of the limbic system, the **hypothalamus** regulates hunger, thirst, body temperature, and sexual behavior; helps govern the endocrine system via the pituitary gland; and contains the so-called reward centers of the brain.

36. The **hippocampus** is a neural center in the limbic system that processes explicit memories.

MODULE

5

The Cerebral Cortex and Our Divided Brain

The Cerebral Cortex

1. cerebral cortex; information-processing

2. more wrinkled; increases

3. fissures
   a. frontal lobe
   b. parietal lobe
   c. occipital lobe
   d. temporal lobe
4. motor; frontal; greater
5. brain-controlled; motor cortex
6. somatosensory; touch; somatosensory cortex
7. occipital; temporal
8. association areas; three-fourths; prefrontal; parietal; temporal
9. does
10. Brain Damage Diagram

1. a	4. d	7. f
2. h	5. e	8. g
3. c	6. b	9. i

11. plasticity; young children
12. will not; reorganize; can; neurogenesis; stem

Our Divided Brain

13. lateralization; left; right
14. corpus callosum; split brain
15. right; name; right

The word *pencil* when flashed to a split-brain patient's right visual field would project only to the opposite, or left, hemisphere of the patient's brain. Because the left hemisphere contains the language control centers of the brain, the patient would be able to read the word aloud. The left hand is controlled by the right hemisphere of the brain. Because the right hemisphere would not be aware of the word, it would not be able to guide the left hand in identifying a pencil by touch.

16. left; right; unconscious; can
17. left
18. left; right; speech; self-awareness
19. c. is the answer. The brainstem is the oldest and most primitive region of the brain. It is found in lower vertebrates, such as fish, as well as in humans and other mammals. The structures mentioned in the other choices are associated with stages of brain evolution beyond that seen in the fish.
20. d. is the answer. Stimulation of the somatosensory cortex elicits a sense of touch, as the experiments of Penfield demonstrated.
   a., b., & c. Hearing, seeing, or movement might be expected if the temporal, occipital, and motor regions of the cortex, respectively, were stimulated.
21. c. is the answer. As Olds and Milner discovered,

electrical stimulation of the hypothalamus is a highly reinforcing event because it is the location of the animal's reward centers. The other brain regions mentioned are not associated with reward centers.
22. a. is the answer. The left hand, controlled by the right hemisphere, would be able to identify the fork, the picture of which is flashed to the right hemisphere.
23. b. is the answer.
   a., c., & d. The left hemisphere does not specialize in picture recognition. And blood clots can form anywhere in the brain.
24. a. is the answer. The right visual field projects directly to the verbal left hemisphere.
   b. & c. The left hand is controlled by the right hemisphere, which, in this situation, would be unaware of the word since the picture has been flashed to the left hemisphere.
25. c. is the answer.
   d. Reproduction is only one of the basic survival functions the brain regulates.
26. b. is the answer. The hippocampus of the limbic system is involved in processing memory. The amygdala of the limbic system influences fear and anger.
   a. The brainstem controls vital functions such as breathing and heartbeat; it is not directly involved in either emotion or memory.
   c. & d. These answers are incorrect because the limbic system is an older brain structure than the cortex. Its involvement in emotions and memory is therefore more basic than that of the cortex.
27. a. is the answer. The motor cortex, which determines the precision with which various parts of the body can be moved, is located in the frontal lobes.
   b. The parietal lobes contain the somatosensory cortex, which controls sensitivity to touch.
   c. The temporal lobes contain the primary projection areas for hearing and, on the left side, are also involved in language use.
   d. The occipital lobes contain the primary projection areas for vision.

Module Review:

28. d. is the answer.
   a. In most persons, language is primarily a left hemisphere function.
   b. Learned movements are unrelated to hemispheric specialization.
   c. Arithmetic reasoning is generally a left hemisphere function.
29. b. is the answer.

30. **b.** is the answer. Association areas interpret, integrate, and act on information from other areas of the cortex.

31. **a.** is the answer. The visual cortex is located at the very back of the brain.

32. **b.** is the answer.
a., c., & d. modulating speech, perceptual skills, and the left side of the body are primarily influenced by the right hemisphere.

33. **b.** is the answer.
c. & d. These refer to the somatosensory cortex.

34. **c.** is the answer. The corpus callosum is a large band of neural fibers linking the right and left cerebral hemispheres. To sever the corpus callosum is in effect to split the brain.

35. **d.** is the answer. The frontal lobe is in the front of the brain. Just behind is the parietal lobe. The occipital lobe is located at the very back of the head and just below the parietal lobe. Next to the occipital lobe and toward the front of the head is the temporal lobe.

36. **d.** is the answer. As demonstrated in the case of Phineas Gage, injury to the frontal lobe may produce such changes in personality.
a. Damage to the parietal lobe might disrupt functions involving the somatosensory cortex.
b. Damage to the temporal lobe might impair hearing.
c. Occipital damage might impair vision.

37. **c.** is the answer.

Terms and Concepts to Remember:

38. The **cerebral cortex** is a thin intricate covering of interconnected neural cells atop the cerebral hemispheres. The seat of information processing, the cortex is responsible for those complex functions that make us distinctively human.
Memory aid: Cortex in Latin means "bark." As bark covers a tree, the **cerebral cortex** is the "bark of the brain."

39. Located at the front of the brain, just behind the forehead, the **frontal lobes** are involved in speaking and muscle movements and in making plans and judgments.

40. Situated between the frontal and occipital lobes, the **parietal lobes** contain the somatosensory cortex, which receives sensory input for touch and body position.

41. Located at the back and base of the brain, the **occipital lobes** contain the visual cortex, which receives information from the eyes.

42. Located on the sides of the brain, the **temporal lobes** contain the auditory cortex, which receive information from the ears.
Memory aid: The **temporal lobes** are located near the *temples.*

43. Located at the back of the frontal lobe, the **motor cortex** controls voluntary movement.

44. The **somatosensory cortex** is located at the front of the parietal lobes, just behind the motor cortex. It registers and processes body touch and movement sensations.

45. Located throughout the cortex, **association areas** of the brain are involved in higher mental functions, such as learning, remembering, and abstract thinking.
Memory aid: Among their other functions, **association areas** of the cortex are involved in integrating, or *associating*, information from different areas of the brain.

46. **Plasticity** is the brain's capacity for modification, as evidenced by brain reorganization following damage (especially in children).

47. **Neurogenesis** is the formation of new neurons.

48. The **corpus callosum** is the large band of neural fibers that links the right and left cerebral hemispheres. Without this band of nerve fibers, the two hemispheres could not interact.

49. **Split brain** is a condition in which the major connections between the two cerebral hemispheres (the corpus callosum) are severed, literally resulting in a split brain.

MODULE 6 Genetics, Evolutionary Psychology, and Behavior

Behavior Genetics: Predicting Individual Differences

1. biological heritage; brain; social
2. personalities; interests; cultural; family
3. heredity; environment
4. behavior geneticists
5. chromosomes; 46; 23; DNA
6. genes
7. expressed; environmental events; protein molecules
8. genome
9. multiple
10. **a.** cell nucleus   **b.** chromosome
    c. gene   **d.** DNA

11. twin; adoption

12. identical; fraternal

13. more

14. being treated alike; could not

15. environment

16. do not; does; higher; attitudes; values; faith

17. **b.** is the answer.
    a. Because they are genetically the same, identical twins are always of the same sex.
    c. & d. Fraternal twins develop from two fertilized eggs.

18. adaptation

19. regulating; blueprints; react; interact

20. epigenetics; molecular; environmental events; genetic

21. epigenetic marks

22. diet; drugs; epigenetic

23. **b.** is the answer.
    a. An interaction requires at least two variables; in this example there is only one (competition).
    c. This is an example of a negative correlation.
    d. This is an example of a positive correlation.

24. **c.** is the answer.
    a. Although heredity does influence certain traits, such as outgoingness and emotional instability, it is the interaction of heredity and experience that ultimately molds personality
    b. There is no single "most important factor" in personality. Moreover, for the same reason two sisters or brothers often have dissimilar personalities, a sister and brother may be very much alike.
    d. Karen and John's case is not at all unusual.

25. the same; different

Evolutionary Psychology: Understanding Human Nature

26. evolutionary psychologists

27. much alike

28. natural selection

29. mutations; change

30. genome; survive; reproduce; fats

Module Review:

31. **b.** is the answer.
    a. & c. Although an identical twin is at increased risk, the relationship is far from perfect. Mental disorders, like all psychological traits, are influenced by *both* nature and nurture.
    d. This is not at all implied by the evidence from twin studies.

32. **d.** is the answer.
    a., b., & c. To pinpoint the influence of one of the two factors (genes and environment), it is necessary to hold one of the factors constant.

33. **b.** is the answer.
    c. & d. There are no such things as "placental" or "nonplacental" twins. All twins have a placenta during prenatal development.

34. **c.** is the answer.
    b. & d. Each cell of the human body contains hundreds of genes.

35. **b.** is the answer.
    a. Hormones are chemical messengers produced by the endocrine glands.
    c. & d. Genes are segments of DNA, which are the makeup of chromosomes.

36. **c.** is the answer.
    a. This defines DNA.
    b. This defines a gene.
    d. The genes provide the code for synthesizing proteins.

37. **c.** is the answer.

38. **b.** is the answer.
    a., c., & d. Despite being raised in different environments, long-separated identical twins often have much in common, including likes, dislikes, and lifestyles. This indicates the significant heritability of many traits.

39. **b.** is the answer.
    a., c., & d. The personalities of adopted children do not much resemble those of their adoptive parents (therefore, not a.) or other children reared in the same home (therefore, not c. or d.).

40. **a.** is the answer.

41. **d.** is the answer.
    a. A genome is the complete instructions for making an organism.
    b. & c. When two factors are correlated, it means either that increases in one factor are accompanied by increases in the other (positive correlation) or that increases in one factor are accompanied by decreases in the other (negative correlation).

42. **b.** is the answer.

43. **d.** is the answer.
    a. Survival ability is only one aspect of fitness.
    b. & c. Neither of these is related to fitness.

44. **a.** is the answer.

45. **a.** is the answer. This is an example of a trait that contributes to survival of the human species and the perpetuation of one's genes.
    b., c., & d. These traits and issues would likely be of greater interest to a behavior geneticist because

they concern the influence of specific genes on behavior.

Terms and Concepts to Remember:

46. In behavior genetics, **environment** refers to every nongenetic, or external, influence on our traits and behaviors.

47. **Heredity** is the genetic transfer of characteristics from parents to offspring.

48. **Behavior genetics** is the study of the relative power and limits of genetic and environmental influences on behavior.

49. **Chromosomes** are threadlike structures made of DNA molecules that contain the genes. In conception, the 23 chromosomes in the egg are paired with the 23 chromosomes in the sperm.

50. **DNA (deoxyribonucleic acid)** is a complex molecule containing the genetic information that makes up the chromosomes.

51. **Genes** are the biochemical units of heredity that make up the chromosomes; they are segments of the DNA molecules capable of synthesizing a protein.

52. A **genome** is the complete genetic instructions for making an organism.

53. **Identical (monozygotic) twins** develop from a single fertilized egg that splits in two and therefore are genetically identical.

54. **Fraternal (dizygotic) twins** develop from two separate eggs fertilized by different sperm and therefore are no more genetically similar than ordinary siblings.

55. **Epigenetics** is the study of influences on gene expression that occur without a change in DNA.

56. **Interaction** refers to the interplay that occurs when the effect of one factor (such as environment) depends on another factor (such as heredity).

57. **Evolutionary psychology** is the study of the evolution of behavior and the mind, using principles of natural selection.

58. **Natural selection** is the evolutionary principle that traits that lead to increased reproduction and survival are the most likely to be passed on to succeeding generations.

59. **Mutations** are random errors in gene replication that lead to change.

Before You Move On

Matching Items 1

1. d	5. g	9. k	13. l
2. e	6. b	10. i	14. n
3. a	7. c	11. j	
4. f	8. h	12. m	

Matching Items 2

1. d	5. i	9. k	13. l
2. g	6. a	10. b	
3. e	7. j	11. c	
4. f	8. h	12. m	

Cross-Check

ACROSS	DOWN
4. peripheral	1. gene
7. temporal	2. hypothalamus
8. motor	3. corpus callosum
10. frontal	4. PET scan
13. adrenal	5. action potential
15. medulla	6. acetylcholine
16. cortex	9. reflex
17. synapse	11. limbic system
18. EEG	12. endorphins
20. lesion	14. autonomic
21. MRI	18. endocrine
23. occipital	19. central
24. amygdala	22. DNA
27. epigenetics	25. glial
28. parietal	26. axon

Consciousness and the Two-Track Mind

Overview

Consciousness—our awareness of ourselves and our environment—can be experienced in various states. Module 7 examines normal consciousness, Module 7 explores sleep and dreaming, and Module 9 covers drug-altered states. Cognitive neuroscientists study the links between brain activity and mental processes. Our awareness focuses on a limited aspect of all that we experience. Research indicates that we have a two-track mind. Conscious information processing enables us to exercise control and to communicate our mental states to others. Beneath the surface, unconscious processing occurs simultaneously on many parallel tracks.

Our daily schedule of waking and sleeping is governed by a biological clock known as circadian rhythm. Our sleep also follows a repeating cycle. Awakening people during REM sleep yields predictable dreamlike reports that are mostly of ordinary events. Freud's view that dreams can be traced back to erotic wishes is giving way to newer theories, for example, that dreams help us process information and fix it in memory or that dreams erupt from neural activity.

Psychoactive drugs also alter consciousness. Depressants act by depressing neural functioning. Although their effects are pleasurable, they impair memory and self-awareness and may have other physical consequences. Stimulants act at the synapses by influencing the brain's neurotransmitters. Hallucinogens can distort judgment of time and can alter sensations and perceptions. A number of those who survive a brush with death later recall visionary experiences. Drug effects depend on dosage and the user's personality and expectations.

NOTE: Answer guidelines for all Module 7–9 questions begin on page 77.

Outline

Instructions

First, skim each section, noting headings and boldface items. After you have read the section, review each objective by answering the fill-in, essay-type, and multiple-choice questions for that section. In some cases, Study Tips explain how best to learn a difficult concept and Applications and Module Reviews help you to know how well you understand the material. Finally, try to define the important terms and concepts using your own words. As you proceed, evaluate your performance by consulting the answers on page 77. Do not continue until you understand each answer. If you need to, review or reread a troublesome section before continuing.

Before You Move On includes activities that test you on material from the entire unit.

MODULE 7 Consciousness: Some Basic Concepts

Defining and Studying Consciousness

Objective 7-1: Describe the place of consciousness in psychology's history.

1. The study of _____ was central in the early years of psychology and in recent decades, but for quite some time it was displaced by the study of observable _____ .

2. Advances in neuroscience made it possible to relate _____ _____ to various mental states; as a result, psychologists once again affirmed the importance of _____ .

Define *consciousness* in a sentence.

3. The interdisciplinary study of how brain activity is linked with mental processes is called _____ _____ .

Selective Attention

Objective 7-2: Discuss how selective attention directs our perceptions.

4. When we focus our conscious awareness on a particular stimulus, we are using _____ .

5. Your ability to attend to only one voice among many is called the _____ _____ .

6. When researchers distracted participants with a counting task, the participants failed to notice a gorilla-suited assistant who passed through, thus displaying _____ . One form of this phenomenon is _____ _____ .

7. Some stimuli are so powerful they demand our attention, causing us to experience _____ .

APPLICATION:

8. When we become absorbed in reading a book, we do not hear the people talking around us. This *selective attention* is most accurately defined as
   a. the focusing of conscious awareness on a particular stimulus.
   b. our awareness of ourselves and our environment.
   c. failing to see visible objects when our attention is directed elsewhere.
   d. separating our conscious awareness to focus on two tasks at the same time.

Dual Processing: The Two-Track Mind

Objective 7-3: Describe the *dual processing* being revealed by today's cognitive neuroscience.

9. Much of our everyday thinking, feeling, and acting operate outside of our _____ awareness.

10. Unconscious information processing occurs _____ on _____ (sequential/parallel) tracks.

11. Solving new problems _____ (requires/does not require) conscious attention and is usually best served by _____ (parallel/sequential) processing. For routine business, we typically make use of _____ (parallel/sequential) processing.

12. The principle that information is often processed on a deliberate, _____ "high road" and an automatic, _____ "low road" is called _____ . The high road is _____ , and the low road is _____ .

13. The condition in which a person responds to a visual stimulus without consciously experiencing it is called _____ .

14. Our vision is actually a _____-_____ system with a visual _____ track enabling us to recognize things and plan future actions and a visual _____ track guiding our moment-to-moment movements.

APPLICATION:

15. Concluding his presentation on levels of information processing, Miguel states that:
    a. humans process both conscious and unconscious information in parallel.
    b. conscious processing occurs in parallel, while unconscious processing is sequential.
    c. conscious processing is sequential, while unconscious processing is parallel.
    d. all information processing is sequential in nature.

MODULE REVIEW:

16. As defined by the text, *consciousness* includes which of the following?
    a. focused attention
    b. sleeping
    c. hypnosis
    d. all of these conditions

17. Which of the following best illustrates dual processing?
    a. Jack is watching a scary movie and doesn't notice the person in a Dracula costume walk in front of the screen.
    b. Despite the loud conversations around her, Karen is able to concentrate on what her friend is saying.
    c. At the soccer game, Gavin misses seeing a goal kick when his cell phone rings.
    d. While listening to the symphony, Marisol concentrates on what the pianist plays while automatically responding to the tempo and theme of the overall performance.

18. At its beginning, psychology focused on the study of
    a. observable behavior.
    b. consciousness.
    c. abnormal behavior.
    d. all of these behaviors.

19. *Consciousness* is defined in the text as
    a. mental life.
    b. selective attention to ongoing perceptions, thoughts, and feelings.
    c. information processing.
    d. our awareness of ourselves and our environment.

TERMS AND CONCEPTS TO REMEMBER:

20. consciousness

21. cognitive neuroscience

25. selective attention

26. inattentional blindness

27. change blindness

22. dual processing

23. blindsight

24. parallel processing

MODULE 8 Sleep and Dreams

Objective 8-1: Define *sleep*.

Define *sleep* in a sentence.

Biological Rhythms and Sleep

Objective 8-2: Describe how our biological rhythms influence our daily functioning

1. Our bodies' internal "clocks" control several _____ _____ .

2. The sleep-waking cycle follows a 24-hour clock called the _____ _____ .

3. Body temperature _____ (rises/falls) as morning approaches and begins to _____ (rise/fall) again before we go to sleep.

4. When people are at their daily peak in circadian arousal, _____ is sharpest and _____ is most accurate.

5. Our circadian rhythm is altered by _____ and _____ . Most 20-year-olds are _____-energized "owls"; most older adults are _____-loving "larks."

Objective 8-3: Describe the biological rhythm of our sleeping and dreaming stages.

6. The sleep cycle consists of _____ distinct stages.

7. The rhythm of sleep cycles was discovered when Aserinsky noticed that, at periodic intervals during the night, the _____ of a sleeping child moved rapidly. This stage of sleep, during which _____ occur, is called _____ _____ .

8. The relatively slow brain waves of the awake but relaxed state are known as _____ waves. As you grow tired, you slip into _____ .

9. During non-REM stage 1 (NREM-1) sleep, people often experience _____ sensations similar to _____ . These sensations may later be incorporated into _____ .

10. The bursts of brain-wave activity that occur during NREM-2 sleep are called _____ _____ .

11. Large, slow brain waves are called _____ waves. They occur in non-REM stage _____ , which is therefore called _____-_____ sleep. A person in this stage

APPLICATIONS:

14. Match the sleep stage with a description of that stage or an activity that occurs then.

Sleep Stage

_____ 1. NREM-1 sleep
_____ 2. NREM-2 sleep
_____ 3. NREM-3 sleep
_____ 4. REM sleep

15. Given that REM is referred to as *paradoxical sleep*, which of the following is true about what happens when Nicholas dreams that he is running around the school track?
   a. Studies of people deprived of REM sleep indicate that REM sleep is unnecessary.
   b. The body's muscles remain relaxed while other body systems are active.

of sleep generally will be _____ (easy/difficult) to awaken. It is during this stage that children may _____ .

Describe the bodily changes that accompany REM sleep.

12. During REM sleep, the motor cortex is _____ (active/relaxed), while the muscles are _____ (active/relaxed), so much so that you are essentially _____ . For this reason, REM is often referred to as _____ sleep.

13. The sleep cycle repeats itself about every _____ minutes. As the night progresses, deep NREM-3 sleep becomes _____ (longer/briefer) and REM and NREM-2 periods become _____ (longer/briefer). Approximately _____ percent of a night's sleep is spent in REM sleep.

Description or Example
   a. Bonita dreams that she's dancing with Hugh Jackman at a grand ball.
   b. Manfred feels like he's floating above the bed.
   c. Rapid, rhythmic brain-wave activity indicates you are clearly asleep.
   d. You are in slow-wave sleep and you do not awaken easily.

   c. It is very easy to awaken a person from REM sleep.
   d. The body's muscles are very tense while the brain is in a nearly meditative state.

16. Although her eyes are closed, Adele's brain is generating bursts of electrical activity. It is likely that Adele is
    a. is in deep sleep.
    b. is at the peak of her circadian rhythm.
    c. in REM sleep.
    d. has been deprived of sleep for 24 hours.

Objective 8-4: Explain how biology and environment interact in our sleep patterns.

17. Newborns spend nearly _____ (how much?) of their day asleep, while adults spend no more than _____ .

18. In studying sleep patterns researchers are discovering the _____ that regulate sleep in humans and animals . Sleep is also influenced by _____ , as indicated by the fact that people now sleep _____ (more/less) than they did a century ago.

19. Our biological clock is reset each day by exposure to _____ _____ , which triggers proteins in the _____ of the eyes to signal the brain's _____ _____ (a), which causes the brain's (b) gland to increase or decrease its production of _____ , a sleep-inducing hormone.

Why Do We Sleep?

Objective 8-5: Describe sleep's functions.

20. Two possible reasons for sleep are to _____ us and to help us _____ by restoring the _____ _____ and repairing _____ tissue. Animals with high waking _____ produce an abundance of chemical _____ _____ that are toxic to _____ . Sleep also facilitates our _____ of the day's experiences and stimulates _____ thinking.

21. During deep sleep, a growth hormone that is necessary for _____ development is released by the _____ gland. Adults spend _____ (more/less) time in deep sleep than children and so release _____ (more/less) growth hormone.

22. A full night's sleep _____ (improves/disrupts) athletic performance.

APPLICATIONS:

23. Concluding her presentation on contemporary theories of why sleep is necessary, Marilynn makes all of the following points, EXCEPT that
    a. sleep may have evolved because it kept our ancestors safe during potentially dangerous periods.
    b. sleep gives the brain time to heal, as it restores and repairs damaged neurons.
    c. sleep encourages growth through a hormone secreted during deep sleep.
    d. slow-wave sleep provides a "psychic safety valve" for stressful waking experiences.

24. Arsenio is participating in a sleep experiment. While he sleeps, a PET scan of his brain reveals increased activity in the amygdala of the limbic system. This most likely indicates that Arsenio is in _____ sleep.

Sleep Deprivation and Sleep Disorders

Objective 8-6: Describe how sleep loss affects us, and identify the major sleep disorders.

25. Allowed to sleep unhindered, most people will sleep _____ (how many?) hours a night.

26. For students, less sleep predicts more _____ in friendships and romantic relationships. Also, students who sleep _____ (how many?) or fewer hours each night have a higher risk of _____ than those who sleep _____ hours or more.

27. Another effect of sleep deprivation is to promote weight gain by increasing the hormone _____ and decreasing the hormone _____ , by decreasing _____ rate, increasing the stress hormone _____ , and

enhancing _____ brain responses to the sight of food.

28. Sleep deprivation may also suppress the functioning of the body's _____ system and slow our _____ _____ on visual attention tasks.

29. Another indication of the hazards of this state is that the rate of _____ tends to increase immediately after the spring time change in Canada and the United States.

30. A persistent difficulty in falling or staying asleep is characteristic of _____ . Sleeping pills and alcohol may make the problem worse since they tend to _____ (increase/reduce) REM sleep. Such aids can also lead to _____ , a state in which increasing doses are needed to produce an effect.

State several tips for those suffering from insomnia.

31. The sleep disorder in which a person experiences uncontrollable sleep attacks is _____ . People with severe cases of this disorder may collapse directly into _____ sleep and experience a loss of _____ _____ .

32. Individuals suffering from _____ _____ stop breathing while sleeping. This disorder is associated with _____ .

33. The sleep disorder characterized by extreme fright and doubled heart and breathing rates is called _____ _____ . Unlike nightmares, these episodes usually happen early in the night, during the first few hours of NREM-_____ sleep. The same is true of episodes of _____ and _____ , problems that _____ (run/do not run) in families. These sleep episodes

are most likely to be experienced by _____ (young children/adolescents/older adults), in whom this stage tends to be the _____ and _____ .

34. Norbert's wife complains that she has to stay up all night to be sure he starts breathing again each time he stops breathing for a minute or so. Norbert consults his doctor and learns that he is suffering from
   a. sleep apnea.   c. night terrors.
   b. narcolepsy.   d. insomnia.

35. A person who falls asleep in the midst of a heated argument probably suffers from
   a. sleep apnea.   c. night terrors.
   b. narcolepsy.   d. insomnia.

Dreams

Objective 8-7: Describe our dreams.

36. Dreams experienced during _____ sleep are vivid, emotional, and often bizarre.

37. On average, people spend _____ (how many?) years of life in dreams.

38. For both men and women, 8 in 10 dreams are marked by _____ (positive/negative) event or emotion, such as fears of _____ _____ .

39. Most dreams _____ (incorporate/do not incorporate) traces of previous days' experiences.

40. While we sleep, our mind _____ (monitors/does not monitor) stimuli in the environment. While sleeping, we _____ (can/cannot) learn to associate a sound with a mild electric shock; we _____ (do/do not) remember recorded information played while we are asleep.

Objective 8-8: Describe the functions of dreams proposed by theorists.

41. Freud referred to the actual content of a dream as its _____ content. Freud believed that this is a censored, symbolic version of the

true meaning, or _____ content, of the dream.

42. According to Freud, most of the dreams of adults reflect _____ wishes and are the key to understanding inner _____ . To Freud, dreams serve as a psychic _____ _____ that discharges otherwise unacceptable feelings.

43. Researchers who believe that dreams serve an _____-processing function receive support from the fact that REM sleep facilitates _____ .

44. Brain scans confirm the link between _____ sleep and _____ .

45. Other theories propose that dreaming serves some _____ function, for example, that REM sleep provides the brain with needed _____ . Such an explanation is supported by the fact that _____ (infants/adults) spend the most time in REM sleep.

46. Still other theories propose that dreams are elicited by random bursts of _____ activity originating in lower regions of the brain, such as the _____ . According to the _____-_____ theory, dreams are the brain's attempt to _____ random neural activity. The bursts have been shown by PET scans to be given their emotional tone by the brain's _____ system, especially the _____ . Other theorists see dreams as a natural part of brain _____ and _____ development. These theorists emphasize our mind's _____-_____ control of our dream content.

47. Researchers agree that we _____ (need/do not need) REM sleep. After being deprived of REM sleep, a person spends more time in REM sleep; this is the _____ _____ effect.

48. REM sleep _____ (does/does not) occur in other mammals. Animals such as fish, whose behavior is less influenced by learning,

_____ (do/do not) dream. This finding supports the _____-_____ theory of dreaming.

APPLICATIONS:

49. Barry has participated in a sleep study for the last four nights. He was awakened each time he entered REM sleep. Now that the experiment is over, Barry will most likely show a(n) _____ (increase/ decrease) in REM sleep, a phenomenon known as _____ _____ .

50. Bahara dreams that she trips and falls as she walks up the steps to the stage to receive her college diploma. Her psychoanalyst suggests that the dream might symbolize her fear of moving on to the next stage of her life—a career. The analyst is evidently attempting to interpret the _____ content of Bahara's dream.

51. Six-month-old Piper spend two-thirds of the day sleeping and most of that time in REM sleep. Her 25-year-old mother sleeps only 8 hours with fewer hours in REM sleep than her daughter. According to a physiological theory of dreaming, this makes sense because the brain activity associated with REM sleep
    a. fixes the day's activities in memory.
    b. gives meaning to random neural activity.
    c. provides the brain with periodic stimulation.
    d. keeps the infant in deep sleep.

MODULE REVIEW:

52. The cluster of brain cells that control the circadian rhythm is the
    a. amygdala.
    b. suprachiasmatic nucleus.
    c. visual cortex.
    d. pineal.

53. Sleep spindles predominate during which stage of sleep?
    a. NREM-1   c. NREM-2
    b. NREM-3   d. REM sleep

54. During which stage of sleep does the body experience increased heart rate, rapid breathing, and genital arousal?
    a. NREM-2   c. NREM-1
    b. NREM-3   d. REM sleep

55. The sleep cycle is approximately _____ minutes.
    a. 30   c. 75
    b. 50   d. 90

56. The effects of chronic sleep deprivation include
    a. suppression of the immune system.
    b. diminished productivity.
    c. depression.
    d. all of these effects.

57. One effect of sleeping pills is to
    a. decrease REM sleep.
    b. increase REM sleep.
    c. decrease NREM-2 sleep.
    d. increase NREM-2 sleep.

58. People who heard unusual phrases prior to sleep were awakened each time they began REM sleep. The fact that they remembered less the next morning provides support for the _____ theory of dreaming.
    a. manifest content
    b. physiological
    c. information-processing
    d. cognitive development

59. According to Freud, dreams are
    a. a symbolic fulfillment of erotic wishes.
    b. the result of random neural activity in the brainstem.
    c. the brain's mechanism for self-stimulation.
    d. the transparent expressions of inner conflicts.

60. Which of the following is NOT a theory of dreaming mentioned in the text?
    a. Dreams facilitate information processing.
    b. Dreaming stimulates the developing brain.
    c. Dreams result from random neural activity originating in the brainstem.
    d. Dreaming is an attempt to escape from social stimulation.

61. The sleep-waking cycles of young people who stay up too late typically are _____ hours in duration.
    a. 23   c. 25
    b. 24   d. 26

62. Which of the following statements regarding REM sleep is true?
    a. Adults spend more time than infants in REM sleep.
    b. REM sleep deprivation results in a REM rebound.
    c. People deprived of REM sleep adapt easily.
    d. Sleeping medications tend to increase REM sleep.

63. A person whose EEG shows a high proportion of alpha waves is most likely
    a. dreaming.   c. in NREM-3 sleep.
    b. in NREM-2 sleep.   d. awake and relaxed.

64. Circadian rhythms are the
    a. brain waves that occur during deep sleep.
    b. neural pathways of NREM-1 sleep.
    c. regular body cycles that occur on a 24-hour schedule.
    d. brain waves that are indicative of NREM-2 sleep.

65. Which of the following is NOT an example of a biological rhythm?
    a. the circadian rhythm
    b. the 90-minute sleep cycle
    c. the four sleep stages
    d. sudden sleep attacks during the day

66. Which of the following is characteristic of REM sleep?
    a. genital arousal
    b. increased muscular tension
    c. night terrors
    d. alpha waves

67. According to one physiological theory, dreaming represents
    a. the brain's efforts to integrate unrelated bursts of activity in visual brain areas with the emotional tone provided by limbic system activity.
    b. a mechanism for coping with the stresses of daily life.
    c. a symbolic depiction of a person's unfulfilled wishes.
    d. an information-processing mechanism for converting the day's experiences into long-term memory.

TERMS AND CONCEPTS TO REMEMBER:

68. sleep

69. circadian rhythm

70. REM sleep

71. alpha waves

72. hallucinations

73. delta waves

74. suprachiasmatic nucleus (SCN)

75. insomnia

76. narcolepsy

77. sleep apnea

78. night terrors

79. dream

80. manifest content

81. latent content

82. REM rebound

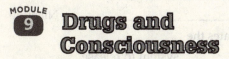

MODULE 9 — Drugs and Consciousness

Tolerance and Addiction

Objective 9-1: Explain what substance use disorders are, and describe the roles played by tolerance, withdrawal, and addiction in these disorders.

1. Drugs that alter moods and perceptions are called _____ drugs. Continued craving and use of a drug despite significant life disruption indicates a _____ _____ _____ .

2. A drug's effect depends not only on its biological effects but also on the user's _____ , which vary with _____ and _____ contexts.

3. Drug users who require increasing doses to experience a drug's effects have developed _____ for the drug. With continued use of alcohol and some other drugs, the user's brain chemistry adapts to offset the drug effect; thus, the user experiences _____ .

4. If a person abruptly stops taking a drug, he or she may experience the undesirable side effects of _____ . A person who has a compulsive craving for drugs or certain behaviors despite adverse consequences is _____ to that substance.

Objective 9-2. Discuss how the concept of addiction has changed.

(Thinking Critically) Briefly state three reasons addictions may not be as irresistible as commonly believed.

APPLICATION:

5. Dan has recently begun using an addictive, euphoria-producing drug. Which of the following will probably occur if he repeatedly uses this drug?
   a. As tolerance to the drug develops, Dan will experience increasingly pleasurable "highs."
   b. The dosage needed to produce the desired effect will increase.
   c. After each use, he will become more and more elated.
   d. Addiction will become less of a problem.

Types of Psychoactive Drugs

6. The three broad categories of drugs discussed in the text include _____ , which tend to slow bodily functions; _____ , which speed bodily functions; and _____ , which alter perception. These drugs all work by mimicking, stimulating, or inhibiting the activity of the brain's _____ .

Objective 9-3: Identify the depressants, and describe their effects.

7. Depressants _____ neural activity and _____ body function. Low doses of alcohol, which is classified as a _____ , slow the activity of the _____ nervous system.

8. Alcohol is a _____ ; it may make a person more _____ or more _____ aggressive. Alcohol can disrupt memory formation and can have long-term effects on the brain and _____ because binge drinking contributes to _____ _____ death and reduces the birth of new _____ _____ . It also impairs the growth of _____ connections. Also, blackouts after drinking result from alcohol's suppression of _____ _____ .

9. A drive to continue problematic use of alcohol indicates _____ _____ , which can _____ the brain. _____ (Women/Men), who have less of a stomach enzyme that digests alcohol, are more vulnerable. Alcohol also reduces _____ and focuses one's

attention on an _____ situation and away from _____ _____ and _____ consequences.

Describe how a person's expectations can influence the behavioral effects of alcohol.

10. Tranquilizers, which are also known as _____, have effects similar to those of alcohol. Sometimes prescribed to induce sleep or reduce _____, in larger doses, they can impair _____ and judgment.

11. Opium, morphine, and heroin all _____ (excite/depress) neural functioning. Together, these drugs are called the _____. When they are present, the brain eventually stops producing _____.

Objective 9-4: Identify the stimulants, and describe their effects.

12. The most widely used stimulants are _____, _____, the _____, _____, _____, and _____. Stimulants _____ (can be/cannot be) addictive.

13. Eliminating _____ would increase life expectancy more than any other preventive measure. The highly addictive drug in tobacco is _____. Smokers _____ (do/do not) develop tolerance to the drug. Quitting causes _____ symptoms

that include _____ _____.

14. Nicotine quickly triggers the release of _____ and _____, two neurotransmitters that diminish _____ and boost _____ and _____ _____. Nicotine also stimulates the _____ _____ system to release _____ and _____, neurotransmitters that calm _____ and reduce sensitivity to _____.

15. Cocaine and crack deplete the brain's supply of the neurotransmitters _____, _____, and _____ and result in depression as the drugs' effects wear off. They do this by blocking the _____ of the neurotransmitters, which remain in the nerve cells' _____.

16. Cocaine's psychological effects depend not only on dosage and form but also on the user's _____ and _____ and the _____.

17. Methamphetamine triggers the release of the neurotransmitter _____, which stimulates brain cells that enhance _____ and _____. Its aftereffects may include _____ _____.

18. The drug _____, or MDMA, is both a _____ and a _____ _____. This drug triggers the release of the neurotransmitters _____ and _____ and blocks the reabsorption of _____. Within a half-hour, users experience high _____, emotional elevation, and, in a social context, _____. Among the adverse effects of this drug are disruption of the body's _____ clock, suppression of the _____ _____, impaired _____, and slow _____.

Objective 9-4: Identify the hallucinogens, and describe their effects.

19. Hallucinogens, which are also referred to as _____, distort _____ and evoke _____ _____ in the absence of sensory input. Two common synthetic hallucinogens are _____ and _____ .

20. The reports of people who have had _____-_____ _____ are very similar to the _____ reported by drug users. These experiences may be the result of a deficient supply of _____ or other insults to the brain.

21. Discovered by Albert Hoffman in 1943, _____ produces effects that vary from euphoria to detachment to _____ , depending on the user's current _____ and _____ .

22. The active ingredient in marijuana is abbreviated _____ . In some cases, legal _____ marijuana use has been granted to relieve the pain and nausea associated with diseases such as AIDS and _____ .
Describe some of the physical and psychological effects of marijuana.

23. All psychoactive drugs trigger _____ _____ , which helps explain both _____ and _____ .

APPLICATIONS:

24. Roberto is moderately intoxicated by alcohol. Which of the following changes in his behavior is likely to occur?
    a. If angered, he is more likely to become aggressive than when he is sober.
    b. He will be less self-conscious about his behavior.

c. If sexually aroused, he will be less inhibited about engaging in sexual activity.
    d. All of these changes are likely.

25. Which of the following statements concerning marijuana is true?
    a. The by-products of marijuana are cleared from the body more slowly than are the by-products of alcohol.
    b. Regular users may need a larger dose of the drug to achieve a high than occasional users would need to get the same effect.
    c. Marijuana is as addictive as nicotine or cocaine.
    d. Even small doses of marijuana hasten the loss of brain cells.

26. I am a synthetic stimulant and mild hallucinogen that produces euphoria and social intimacy by triggering the release of dopamine and serotonin. What am I? _____

27. Lyndall was in a car accident that required critical surgery to repair her damaged internal organs. During surgery, she had a sense of being outside her body, floating above the operating room. These _____-_____ experiences are similar to sensations of an LSD "trip."

28. Which of the following statements concerning near-death experiences is true?
    a. Fewer than 1 percent of patients who come close to dying report having them.
    b. They typically consist of fantastic, mystical imagery.
    c. They are more commonly experienced by women than by men.
    d. They are more commonly experienced by men than by women.

Influences on Drug Use

Objective 9-5: Explain why some people become regular users of consciousness-altering drugs.

29. Drug use by North American youth _____ (increased/declined) during the 1970s, then declined until the early 1990s because of increased _____ _____ and efforts by the media to deglamorize drug use.

30. Adopted individuals are more susceptible to alcohol use disorder if they had a(n) _____ (adoptive/biological) parent with a history of alcohol use disorder. Boys who at age 6 are _____ (more/less) excitable are more likely as teens to smoke, drink, and use other drugs. Genes that are more common among people predisposed to alcohol use disorder may cause deficiencies in the brain's _____ _____ system.

Identify some of the psychological and social-cultural roots of drug use.

31. Among teenagers, drug use _____ (varies/is about the same) across _____ and _____ groups.

32. Smoking usually begins during _____ _____ . Because these people are _____ and often think the world is watching their every move, they are more vulnerable to smoking's allure.

33. Studies reveal that African-American teens have _____ (higher/lower) rates of drinking, smoking, and cocaine use. Alcohol and other drug addiction have also been low among actively _____ people. A major social influence on drug use is the _____ culture.

34. State three possible channels of influence for drug prevention and treatment programs.

    a. _____

    b. _____

    c. _____

APPLICATIONS:

35. Which of the following statements concerning alcohol use disorder is NOT true?
    a. Adopted individuals are more susceptible to alcohol use disorder if they had an adoptive parent with alcohol use disorder.
    b. Having an identical twin with alcohol use disorder puts a person at increased risk for alcohol problems.
    c. Geneticists have identified genes that are more common among people predisposed to alcohol use disorder.
    d. Researchers have bred rats that prefer alcohol to water.

36. Which of the following was NOT suggested by the text as an important aspect of drug prevention and treatment programs?
    a. education about the long-term costs of a drug's temporary pleasures
    b. efforts to boost people's self-esteem and purpose in life
    c. attempts to modify peer associations
    d. "scare tactics" that frighten prepubescent children into avoiding drug experimentation

37. Which of the following statements concerning the roots of drug use is true?
    a. Heavy users of alcohol, marijuana, and cocaine often are always on a high.
    b. If an adolescent's friends use drugs, odds are that he or she will, too.
    c. Teenagers who are academically average students seldom use drugs.
    d. It is nearly impossible to predict whether a particular adolescent will experiment with drugs.

STUDY TIP: This module discusses three major categories of psychoactive drugs, drugs that when abused may lead to clinically significant impairment or distress. Information about their psychological effects and their actions on the nervous system is best organized in the form of a chart. To help you review this material, complete the missing information in the chart on the next page. To get you started, the first drug category has already been filled in. In combination with text Table 9.2, you should have a useful summary of substance use and addictive disorders.

38. Psychoactive Drug Category	Specific Drugs in This Category	Psychological Effects of These Drugs	How These Drugs Affect the Nervous System
Depressants	alcohol, barbiturates, opiates	disrupt judgment and inhibition, induce sleep, reduce anxiety	decrease neural activity, slow body functions
Stimulants			
Hallucinogens			

MODULE REVIEW:

39. Cocaine and crack produce a euphoric rush by
   a. blocking the actions of serotonin.
   b. depressing neural activity in the brain.
   c. blocking the reuptake of dopamine in brain cells.
   d. stimulating the brain's production of endorphins.

40. Which of the following is classified as a depressant?
   a. methamphetamine
   b. LSD
   c. marijuana
   d. alcohol

41. Which of the following preventive measures would have the greatest impact on average life expectancy?
   a. eliminating obesity
   b. eliminating smoking
   c. eliminating use of crack
   d. eliminating binge drinking

42. Psychoactive drugs affect behavior and perception through
   a. the power of suggestion.
   b. the placebo effect.
   c. alteration of neural activity in the brain.
   d. psychological, not physiological, influences.

43. All of the following are common misconceptions about addiction, EXCEPT the statement that
   a. to overcome an addiction a person almost always needs professional therapy.
   b. psychoactive and medicinal drugs very quickly lead to addiction.
   c. biological factors place some individuals at increased risk for addiction.

   d. many other repetitive, pleasure-seeking behaviors fit the drug-addiction-as-disease-needing-treatment model.

44. The lowest rates of drug use among high school seniors is reported by
   a. Asian-Americans.
   b. Hispanic-Americans.
   c. African-Americans.
   d. Native Americans.

45. Which of the following is NOT true of alcohol?
   a. It slows sympathetic nervous system activity.
   b. It signals the central nervous system to release epinephrine.
   c. It reduces self-awareness.
   d. It suppresses REM sleep.

46. A person who requires increasing amounts of a drug in order to feel its effect is said to have developed
   a. tolerance.
   b. an addiction.
   c. withdrawal symptoms.
   d. resistance.

47. Which of the following is NOT a stimulant?
   a. amphetamines
   b. caffeine
   c. nicotine
   d. alcohol

48. Which of the following was NOT cited in the text as evidence that heredity influences alcohol use?

   a. Children whose parents abuse alcohol have a lower tolerance for multiple alcoholic drinks taken over a short period of time.

   b. Boys who are impulsive and fearless at age 6 are more likely to drink as teenagers.

   c. Laboratory mice have been selectively bred to prefer alcohol to water.

   d. Adopted children are more susceptible if one or both of their biological parents have a history of alcohol use disorder.

49. Which of the following is usually the most powerful determinant of whether teenagers begin using drugs?

   a. family strength   **c.** school adjustment

   b. religion   **d.** peer influence

50. THC is the major active ingredient in

   a. nicotine.   **c.** marijuana.

   b. MDMA.   **d.** cocaine.

51. I am a synthetic stimulant and mild hallucinogen that produces euphoria and social intimacy by triggering the release of dopamine and serotonin. What am I?

   a. LSD   **c.** THC

   b. MDMA   **d.** cocaine

52. How a particular psychoactive drug affects a person depends on

   a. the dosage and form in which the drug is taken.

   b. the user's expectations and personality.

   c. the situation in which the drug is taken.

   d. all of these conditions.

TERMS AND CONCEPTS TO REMEMBER:

53. psychoactive drugs

54. substance use disorder

55. tolerance

56. addiction

57. withdrawal

58. depressants

59. alcohol use disorder

60. barbiturates

61. opiates

62. stimulants

63. amphetamines

64. nicotine

65. cocaine

66. methamphetamine

67. Ecstasy (MDMA)

68. hallucinogens

69. near-death experience

70. LSD

71. THC

ESSAY QUESTION

You have just been assigned the task of writing an article tentatively titled "Alcohol and Alcohol Use Disorder: Roots, Effects, and Prevention." What information should you include in your article? (Use the space provided to list the points you want to make, and organize them. Then write the essay on a separate piece of paper.)

Before You Move On

Matching Items 1

Match each term with its appropriate definition or description.

Definitions or Descriptions

_____ 1. surface meaning of dreams

_____ 2. deeper meaning of dreams

_____ 3. stage of sleep associated with delta waves

_____ 4. stage of sleep associated with muscular relaxation

_____ 5. sleep disorder in which breathing stops

_____ 6. sleep disorder occurring in NREM-3 sleep

_____ 7. depressant

_____ 8. hallucinogen

_____ 9. stimulant

_____ 10. simultaneous unconscious and conscious tracks

_____ 11. disorder in which sleep attacks occur

_____ 12. study of how brain activity is linked to mental activity

_____ 13. twilight stage of sleep associated with imagery resembling hallucinations

Terms

a. marijuana

b. alcohol

c. NREM-1 sleep

d. cognitive neuroscience

e. manifest content

f. cocaine

g. narcolepsy

h. sleep apnea

i. NREM-3 sleep

j. REM sleep

k. latent content

l. night terrors

m. dual processing

Matching Items 2

Match each term with its appropriate definition or description.

Definitions or Descriptions

_____ 1. drug that is both a stimulant and mild hallucinogen

_____ 2. drugs that increase energy and stimulate neural activity

_____ 3. brain wave of awake, relaxed person

_____ 4. unconscious response to a visual stimulus

_____ 5. sleep stage associated with dreaming

_____ 6. drugs that reduce anxiety and depress central nervous system activity

_____ 7. natural painkillers produced by the brain

_____ 8. focusing conscious awareness on a particular stimulus

_____ 9. our awareness of ourselves and our environment

_____ 10. theory that dreaming reflects our erotic drives

_____ 11. neurotransmitter that LSD resembles

_____ 12. brain-wave activity during NREM-2 sleep

Terms

a. Freud's theory

b. serotonin

c. Ecstasy

d. alpha

e. amphetamines

f. consciousness

g. sleep spindle

h. endorphins

i. REM

j. barbiturates

k. selective attention

l. blindsight

Cross-Check

As you learned in Module 2, reviewing and overlearning of material are important to the learning process. After you have written the definitions of the key terms in this unit, you should complete the crossword puzzle to ensure that you can reverse the process—recognize the term, given the definition.

ACROSS

2. Term for REM sleep reflecting that the body is aroused but the muscles are relaxed.
8. Widely used stimulant that is inhaled.
9. Brain wave that is predominant in NREM-3 sleep.
10. Powerful hallucinogen first used by Albert Hofmann.
11. Type of brain wave that occurs during NREM-2 sleep.
12. NREM-1 dream sensation similar to a hallucination.
13. Also known as tranquilizers.
15. Drug category that includes alcohol.

DOWN

1. Relatively slow brain waves of a relaxed, awake state.
3. Drugs that "speed up" neural activity.
4. Drugs that depress neural activity, temporarily lessening pain.
5. Theory suggesting that dreams help fix daily experiences in our memories.
6. Drug that disrupts the processing of recent experiences into long-term memories.
7. Neurotransmitter whose reuptake is blocked by cocaine.
12. Divided consciousness (as during hypnosis).
13. Depressant that causes a rush of euphoria.
14. Active ingredient in marijuana.

Answers

 Consciousness: Some Basic Concepts

Defining and Studying Consciousness

1. consciousness; behavior

2. brain activity; cognition

Consciousness is our awareness of ourselves and our environment.

3. cognitive neuroscience

Selective Attention

4. selective attention

5. cocktail party effect

6. inattentional blindness; change blindness

7. popout

8. **a.** is the answer.
   b. This is the definition of consciousness.
   c. This defines inattentional blindness.
   d. In selective attention, awareness is focused on one stimulus.

Dual Processing: The Two-Track Mind

9. conscious

10. simultaneously; parallel

11. requires; sequential; parallel

12. conscious; unconscious; dual processing; reflective; intuitive

13. blindsight

14. dual-processing; perception; action

15. **c.** is the answer.

Module Review:

16. **d.** is the answer.

17. **d.** is the answer.
   a. Jack is exhibiting inattentional blindness.
   b. Karen is demonstrating selective attention.
   c. Gavin's experience is an example of inattentional blindness.

18. **b.** is the answer.
   a. The behaviorists' emphasis on observable behavior occurred much later in the history of psychology.
   c. Psychology has never been primarily concerned with abnormal behavior.

19. **d.** is the answer.

Terms and Concepts to Remember:

20. For most psychologists, **consciousness** is our awareness of ourselves and our environment.

21. **Cognitive neuroscience** is the interdisciplinary study of the links between brain activity and cognition (including perception, thinking, memory, and language).

25. **Selective attention** is the focusing of conscious awareness on a particular stimulus.

26. **Inattentional blindness** is a perceptual error in which we fail to see visible objects when our attention is directed elsewhere.

27. **Change blindness** occurs when we fail to notice changes in the environment.

22. **Dual processing** is the principle that information is often simultaneously processed on separate conscious and unconscious tracks.

23. **Blindsight** is a condition in which a person responds to a visual experience without consciously experiencing it.

24. **Parallel processing** is the processing of many aspects of a problem simultaneously; the brain's natural mode of information processing for many functions.

 Sleep and Dreams

Sleep is a periodic, natural loss of consciousness—as distinct from unconsciousness resulting from a coma, general anesthesia, or hibernation.

Biological Rhythms and Sleep

1. biological rhythms

2. circadian rhythm

3. rises; fall

4. thinking; memory

5. age; experience; evening; morning

6. four

7. eyes; dreams; REM sleep

8. alpha; sleep

9. hypnagogic; hallucinations; memories

10. sleep spindles

11. delta; 3; slow-wave; difficult; wet the bed

During REM sleep, brain waves become as rapid and saw-toothed as those of NREM-1 sleep, heart rate rises and breathing becomes rapid and irregular, and genital arousal and rapid eye movements occur.

12. active; relaxed; paralyzed; paradoxical

13. 90; briefer; longer; 20 to 25

14. 1. b   3. d

    2. c   4. a

15. **b.** is the answer. Although the body is aroused internally, the messages of the activated motor cortex do not reach the muscles.

    a. Studies of REM-deprived people indicate just the opposite.

    c. It is difficult to awaken a person from REM sleep.

    d. Just the opposite occurs in REM sleep: the muscles are relaxed, yet the brain is aroused.

16. **c.** is the answer. The rapid eye movements of REM sleep coincide with bursts of activity in brain areas that process visual images.

17. two-thirds; one-third

18. genes; culture; less

19. bright light; retinas; suprachiasmatic nucleus; pineal; melatonin

Why Do We Sleep?

20. protect; recuperate; immune system; brain; metabolism; free radicals; neurons; memory; creative

21. muscle; pituitary; less; less

22. improves

23. **d.** is the answer. Freud's theory proposed that dreams, which occur during fast-wave, REM sleep, serve as a psychic safety valve.

24. REM. The amygdala is involved in emotion, and dreams during REM sleep often tend to be emotional.

Sleep Deprivation and Sleep Disorders

25. 9

26. conflicts; 5; depression; 8

27. ghrelin; leptin; metabolic; cortisol; limbic

28. immune; reaction time

29. accidents

30. insomnia; reduce; tolerance

Tips for promoting healthy sleep include exercising regularly during the day; avoiding caffeine after early afternoon and food and drink before bedtime; sleeping on a regular schedule; relaxing before bedtime; hiding the time so you aren't tempted to check repeatedly; reassuring yourself that temporary sleep loss causes no great harm; focusing your mind on nonarousing, engaging thoughts, such as song lyrics, TV programs, or vacation travel; and, if all else fails, settle for less sleep, either going to bed later or getting up earlier.

31. narcolepsy; REM; muscular tension

32. sleep apnea; obesity

33. night terrors; 3; sleepwalking; sleeptalking; run; young children; lengthiest; deepest

34. **a.** is the answer. With sleep apnea, the person stops breathing for a minute or so, then is awakened by decreased blood oxygen and snorts in the air. This happens hundreds of times each night.

35. **b.** is the answer. Narcolepsy is characterized by uncontrollable sleep attacks.

    a. Sleep apnea is characterized by the temporary cessation of breathing while asleep.

    c. Night terrors are characterized by high arousal and terrified behavior, occurring during NREM-3 sleep.

    d. Insomnia refers to chronic difficulty in falling or staying asleep.

Dreams

36. REM

37. six

38. negative; repeatedly failing in an attempt to do something; being attacked, pursued, or rejected; or experiencing misfortune

39. incorporate

40. monitors; can; do not

41. manifest; latent

42. erotic; conflicts; safety valve

43. information; memory

44. REM; memory

45. physiological; stimulation; infants

46. neural; brainstem; activation-synthesis; synthesize; limbic; amygdala; maturation; cognitive; top-down

47. need; REM rebound

48. does; do not; information-processing

49. increase; REM rebound

50. latent. The analyst is evidently trying to go beyond the events in the dream and understand the dream's hidden meaning, or the dream's latent content.

51. **c.** is the answer.

Module Review:

52. **b.** is the answer.

    a. The amygdala is an emotion center in the limbic system.

    c. The visual cortex is the part of the brain that receives raw input from the eyes.

    d. The pineal is a gland that produces the sleep-inducing hormone melatonin.

53. **c.** is the answer.

a. NREM-1 sleep is characterized by slowed breathing and irregular brain waves.
b. Delta waves predominate during NREM-3.
d. Faster, nearly waking brain waves occur during REM sleep.

54. **d.** is the answer.
a., b., & c. During non-REM stages 1–3 heart rate and breathing are slow and regular and the genitals are not aroused.

55. **d.** is the answer.

56. **d.** is the answer.

57. **a.** is the answer. Like alcohol, sleeping pills carry the undesirable consequence of reducing REM sleep and may make insomnia worse in the long run.
b., c., & d. Sleeping pills do not produce these effects.

58. **c.** is the answer. They remembered less than if they were awakened during other stages.

59. **a.** is the answer. Freud saw dreams as psychic safety valves that discharge unacceptable feelings that are often related to erotic wishes.
b. & c. These physiological theories of dreaming are not associated with Freud.
d. According to Freud, dreams represent the individual's conflicts and wishes but in disguised, rather than transparent, form.

60. **d.** is the answer.
a., b., & c. Each of these describes a valid theory of dreaming that was mentioned in the text.

61. **c.** is the answer. We can reset our biological clocks by adjusting our sleep schedules. Thus, young adults adopt something closer to a 25-hour day by staying up too late to get 8 hours of sleep.

62. **b.** is the answer. Following REM deprivation, people temporarily increase their amount of REM sleep, in a phenomenon known as REM rebound.
a. Just the opposite is true: the amount of REM sleep is greatest in infancy.
c. Deprived of REM sleep by repeated awakenings, people return more and more quickly to the REM stages after falling back to sleep. They by no means adapt easily to the deprivations.
d. Just the opposite occurs: they tend to suppress REM sleep.

63. **d.** is the answer.
a. The brain waves of REM sleep (dream sleep) are more like those of NREM-1 sleepers.
b. NREM-2 is characterized by sleep spindles.
c. NREM-3 characterized by slow delta waves.

64. **c.** is the answer.

65. **d.** is the answer.

66. **a.** is the answer.
b. During REM sleep, muscular tension is low.
c. Night terrors are associated with NREM-3 sleep.
d. Alpha waves are characteristic of the relaxed, awake state.

67. **a.** is the answer.
b. & c. These essentially Freudian explanations of the purpose of dreaming are based on the idea that a dream is a psychic safety valve that harmlessly discharges otherwise inexpressible feelings.
d. This explanation of the function of dreaming is associated with the information-processing viewpoint.

Terms and Concepts to Remember:

68. **Sleep** is the natural loss of consciousness, on which the body and mind depend for healthy functioning; as distinct from unconsciousness resulting from a coma, general anesthesia, or hibernation.

69. A **circadian rhythm** is any regular bodily rhythm, such as body temperature and sleep-wakefulness, that follows a 24-hour cycle.
Memory aid: In Latin, *circa* means "about" and *dies* means "day." A **circadian rhythm** is one that is about a day, or 24 hours, in duration.

70. **REM sleep** (rapid eye movement sleep) is the recurring sleep stage in which the muscles are relaxed but other body systems are active, and vivid dreaming occurs; also known as *paradoxical sleep.*
Memory aid: **REM** is an acronym for rapid eye movement, the distinguishing feature of this sleep stage that led to its discovery.

71. **Alpha waves** are the relatively slow brain waves characteristic of an awake, relaxed state.

72. **Hallucinations** are false sensory experiences that occur without any sensory stimulus.

73. **Delta waves** are the large, slow brain waves associated with deep sleep.

74. **The suprachiasmatic nucleus (SCN)** is a pair of cell clusters in the hypothalamus that controls circadian rhythm. In response to light, the SCN causes the pineal gland to adjust melatonin production, thus modifying our feelings of sleepiness.

75. **Insomnia** is a sleep disorder in which the person regularly has difficulty in falling or staying asleep.

76. **Narcolepsy** is a sleep disorder in which the victim suffers sudden, uncontrollable sleep attacks, often characterized by entry directly into REM.

77. **Sleep apnea** is a sleep disorder in which the person ceases breathing while asleep, briefly arouses to gasp for air, falls back asleep, and repeats this cycle throughout the night.

    Example: One theory of the sudden infant death syndrome is that it is caused by **sleep apnea**.

78. A person suffering from **night terrors** experiences episodes of high arousal with apparent terror. Night terrors usually occur during NREM-3 sleep and are seldom remembered.

79. **Dreams** are sequences of images, emotions, and thoughts passing through a sleeping person's mind, the most vivid of which occur during REM sleep.

80. In Freud's theory of dreaming, the **manifest content** is the remembered story line.

81. In Freud's theory of dreaming, the **latent content** is the underlying but censored meaning of a dream.

    Memory aids for 80 and 81: *Manifest* means "clearly apparent, obvious"; *latent* means "hidden, concealed." A dream's **manifest content** is that which is obvious; its **latent content** remains hidden until its symbolism is interpreted.

82. **REM rebound** is the tendency for REM sleep to increase following REM sleep deprivation.

⟩⟩ Drugs and Consciousness

Tolerance and Addiction

1. psychoactive; substance use disorder

2. expectations; social; cultural

3. tolerance; neuroadaptation

4. withdrawal; addicted

Addiction may not be as irresistible as commonly believed. For example, the following are not true.

  a. Taking a psychoactive drug automatically leads to addiction.

  b. A person cannot overcome an addiction without professional help.

  c. The addiction-as-disease-needing-treatment model is applicable to a broad spectrum of pleasure-seeking behaviors.

5. **b.** is the answer. Continued use of a drug produces a tolerance; to experience the same "high," Dan will have to use larger and larger doses.

Types of Psychoactive Drugs

6. depressants; stimulants; hallucinogens; neurotransmitters

7. calm; slow; depressant; sympathetic

8. disinhibitor; helpful; sexually; cognition; nerve cell; nerve cells; synaptic; REM sleep

9. alcohol use disorder; shrink; Women; self-awareness; arousing; normal inhibitions; future

Studies have found that if people believe that alcohol affects social behavior in certain ways, then, when they drink alcohol (or even mistakenly think that they have been drinking alcohol), they will behave according to their expectations, which vary by culture. For example, if people believe alcohol promotes sexual feeling, on drinking they are likely to behave in a sexually aroused way.

10. barbiturates; anxiety; memory

11. depress; opiates; endorphins

12. caffeine; nicotine; amphetamines; cocaine; Ecstasy; methamphetamine; can be

13. smoking; nicotine; do; withdrawal; craving, insomnia, anxiety, irritability, and distractibility

14. epinephrine; norepinephrine; appetite; alertness; mental efficiency; central nervous; dopamine; opioids; anxiety; pain

15. dopamine; serotonin; norepinephrine; reuptake (reabsorption); synapses

16. expectations; personality; situation

17. dopamine; energy; mood; irritability, insomnia, hypertension, seizures, social isolation, depression, and occasional violent outbursts

18. Ecstasy; stimulant; mild hallucinogen; dopamine; serotonin; serotonin; energy; connectedness; circadian; immune system; memory; thinking

19. psychedelics; perceptions; sensory images; Ecstasy (MDMA); LSD

20. Near-death experiences; hallucinations; oxygen

21. LSD; panic; mood; expectations

22. THC; medical; cancer

Like alcohol, marijuana relaxes, disinhibits, and may produce a euphoric feeling. Also like alcohol, marijuana impairs perceptual and motor skills. Marijuana is a mild hallucinogen; it can amplify sensitivity to colors, sounds, tastes, and smells. Marijuana also interrupts memory formation. Unlike alcohol, THC remains in the body for a week or more. Also, the users' experience can vary with the situation.

23. negative aftereffects; tolerance; withdrawal

24. **d.** is the answer. Alcohol loosens inhibitions and reduces self-consciousness, making people more likely to act on their feelings of anger or sexual arousal.

25. a. is the answer. THC, the active ingredient in marijuana, and its by-products linger in the body for a week or more.

26. Ecstasy (MDMA)

27. near-death

28. b. is the answer.
a. Approximately 12 to 40 percent of people who have come close to death report some sort of near-death experience.
c. & d. There is no gender difference in the prevalence of near-death experiences.

Influences on Drug Use

29. increased; drug education

30. biological; more; dopamine reward

A psychological factor in drug use is the feeling that one's life is meaningless and lacks direction. Regular users of psychoactive drugs often have experienced stress or failure and are depressed. Drug use often begins as a temporary way to relieve depression, anger, anxiety, or insomnia. A powerful social factor in drug use, especially among adolescents, is peer influence. Peers shape attitudes about drugs, provide drugs, and establish the social context for their use.

31. varies; cultural; ethnic

32. early adolescence; self-conscious

33. lower; religious; peer

34. a. education about the long-term costs of a drug's temporary pleasures
b. efforts to boost people's self-esteem and purpose in life
c. attempts to "inoculate" youths against peer pressures

35. a. is the answer. Adopted individuals are more susceptible to alcohol use disorder if they had a *biological* parent with alcohol use disorder.
b., c., & d. Each of these is true, which indicates that susceptibility to alcohol use disorder is at least partially determined by heredity.

36. d. is the answer.

37. b. is the answer.

38. Stimulants include caffeine, nicotine, amphetamines, cocaine, Ecstasy, and methamphetamine. They enhance energy and mood and can be addictive. They excite neural activity and speed up body functions.
Hallucinogens include Ecstasy, LSD, and marijuana. They distort perceptions and evoke sensory images in the absence of sensory input. They produce their effects by interfering with the serotonin neurotransmitter system.

Module Review:

39. c. is the answer. They also block the reuptake of serotonin and norepinephrine.
a. This answer describes the effect of LSD.
b. Depressants such as alcohol have this effect. Cocaine and crack are classified as stimulants.
d. None of the psychoactive drugs has this effect. Opiates, however, *suppress* the brain's production of endorphins.

40. d. is the answer. Alcohol, which slows body functions and neural activity, is a depressant.
a. Methamphetamine is a stimulant.
b. & c. LSD and marijuana are hallucinogens.

41. b. is the answer.

42. c. is the answer. Such drugs work primarily at synapses, altering neural transmission.
a. What people believe will happen after taking a drug will likely have some effect on their individual reactions, but psychoactive drugs actually work by altering neural transmission.
b. Because a placebo is a substance without active properties, this answer is incorrect.
d. This answer is incorrect because the effects of psychoactive drugs on behavior, perception, and so forth have a physiological basis.

43. c. is the answer. This is true. Heredity, for example, influences tendencies toward alcohol use disorder.

44. c. is the answer.

45. b. is the answer. This is true of nicotine.

46. a. is the answer.
b. Addiction is compulsive craving of drugs or certain behaviors despite known adverse consequences.
c. Withdrawal refers to the discomfort and distress that follow discontinuing an addictive drug or behavior.
d. There is no such thing as drug "resistance."

47. d. is the answer. Alcohol is a depressant.

48. a. is the answer. Compared with other children, children whose biological parents abuse alcohol are more susceptible to alcohol use disorder, which means that they have a *higher* tolerance for multiple drinks, making it more likely that they will, in fact, consume more alcohol.

49. d. is the answer. If adolescents' friends use drugs, the odds are that they will, too.
a., b., & c. These are also predictors of drug use but seem to operate mainly through their effects on peer association.

50. c. is the answer.

51. b. is the answer.

a. & c. Unlike stimulants, LSD and THC do not speed up body functions.
d. Unlike hallucinogens, cocaine is a stimulant and does not generally distort perceptions.

52. **d.** is the answer.

Terms and Concepts to Remember:

53. **Psychoactive drugs**—which include stimulants, depressants, and hallucinogens—are chemical substances that alter moods and perceptions. They work by stimulating, inhibiting, or mimicking the activity of neurotransmitters.

54. **Substance use disorder** involves continued substance craving and use despite significant life disruption and/or physical risk.

55. **Tolerance** is the diminishing of a psychoactive drug's effect that occurs with repeated use, requiring progressively larger doses to produce the same effect.

56. An **addiction** is a compulsive craving of drugs or certain behaviors despite known adverse consequences.

57. **Withdrawal** refers to the discomfort and distress that follow discontinuing an addictive drug or behavior.

58. **Depressants** are psychoactive drugs, such as alcohol, opiates, and barbiturates, that reduce neural activity and slow body functions.

59. **Alcohol use disorder** (popularly known as *alcoholism*) is alcohol use that is marked by tolerance, withdrawal, and a drive to continue problematic use.

60. **Barbiturates** are depressants, sometimes used to induce sleep or reduce anxiety, that impair memory and judgment.

61. **Opiates** are depressants derived from the opium poppy, such as opium, morphine, and heroin; they reduce neural activity and temporarily lessen pain and anxiety.

62. **Stimulants** are psychoactive drugs, such as caffeine, nicotine, amphetamines, Ecstasy, methamphetamine, and cocaine, that excite neural activity and speed up body functions.

63. **Amphetamines** are a type of stimulant and, as such, speed up body functions and neural activity.

64. **Nicotine** is the stimulating and highly addictive psychoactive drug found in tobacco.

65. **Cocaine** is a powerful and addictive stimulant derived from the cocoa plant; produces temporarily increased alertness and euphoria.

66. **Methamphetamine** is a powerfully addictive stimulant that stimulates the central nervous systems, speeds up body functions, and is associated with energy and mood changes.

67. Classified as both a synthetic stimulant and a mild hallucinogen, **Ecstasy (MDMA)** produces short-term euphoria by increasing serotonin levels in the brain. Repeated use may permanently damage serotonin neurons, suppress immunity, and impair memory and other cognitive functions.

68. **Hallucinogens** are psychedelic drugs, such as LSD and marijuana, that distort perceptions and evoke sensory images in the absence of sensory input.

69. The **near-death experience** is an altered state of consciousness that has been reported by some people who have had a close brush with death.

70. **LSD** (lysergic acid diethylamide) is a powerful hallucinogen capable of producing vivid false perceptions and disorganization of thought processes.

71. The major active ingredient in marijuana, **THC** is classified as a mild hallucinogen.

Essay Question

As a depressant, alcohol slows neural activity and body functions. Although low doses of alcohol may produce relaxation, with larger doses reactions slow, speech slurs, skilled performance deteriorates, and memory formation is disrupted. Alcohol also reduces self-awareness and may facilitate sexual and aggressive urges the individual might otherwise resist.

Some people may be biologically vulnerable to alcohol use disorder. This is indicated by the fact that individuals who have a biological parent with alcohol use disorder, or people who have an identical twin with alcohol use disorder, are more susceptible to alcohol use disorder.

Stress, depression, and the feeling that life is meaningless and without direction are common feelings among heavy users of alcohol and may create a psychological vulnerability to alcohol use disorder.

Especially for teenagers, peer group influence is strong. If an adolescent's friends use alcohol, odds are that he or she will, too.

Research suggests three important channels of influence for drug prevention and treatment programs: (1) education about the long-term consequences of alcohol use; (2) efforts to boost people's self-esteem and purpose in life; and (3) attempts to counteract peer pressure that leads to experimentation with drugs.

Before You Move On

Matching Items 1

1. e	6. l	11. g
2. k	7. b	12. d
3. i	8. a	13. c
4. j	9. f	
5. h	10. m	

Matching Items 2

1. c	5. i	9. f
2. e	6. j	10. a
3. d	7. h	11. b
4. l	8. k	12. g

Cross-Check

ACROSS	DOWN
2. paradoxical	1. alpha
8. nicotine	3. amphetamines
9. delta	4. opiates
10. LSD	5. information processing
11. spindle	6. alcohol
12. hypnagogic	7. dopamine
13. barbiturates	12. heroin
15. depressant	15. THC

Developing Through the Life Span

Overview

Developmental psychologists study the life cycle, from conception to death. Modules 10–13 cover physical, cognitive, and social development over the life span and introduces three major issues in developmental psychology: (1) the relative impact of genes and experience on behavior (2) whether development is best described as gradual and continuous or as a discontinuous sequence of stages and (3) whether the individual's personality remains stable or changes over the life span.

Although there are not too many terms to learn in these modules, there are a number of important research findings to remember. Pay particular attention to the stage theories of Piaget, Kohlberg, and Erikson, as well as to the discussion regarding intellectual stability during adulthood.

NOTE: Answer guidelines for all Modules 10–13 questions begin on page 102.

Outline

Instructions

First, skim each section, noting headings and boldface items. After you have read the section, review each objective by answering the fill-in, essay-type, and multiple-choice questions for that section. In some cases, Study Tips explain how best to learn a difficult concept and Applications and Module Reviews help you to know how well you understand the material. Finally, try to define the important terms and concepts using your own words. As you proceed, evaluate your performance by consulting the answers on page 102. Do not continue until you understand each answer. If you need to, review or reread a troublesome section before continuing.

Before You Move On includes activities that test you on material from the entire unit

Developmental Issues, Prenatal Development, and the Newborn

Developmental Psychology's Major Issues

Objective 10-1: Identify three issues that have engaged developmental psychologists.

1. Scientists who study physical, cognitive, and social changes throughout the life cycle are called _____ _____ .

2. One of the major issues in developmental psychology concerns the relative importance of genetic inheritance and experience in determining behavior; this is called the issue of _____ and _____ .

3. A second developmental issue concerns whether developmental changes are gradual or abrupt; this is called the issue of _____ and _____ . Researchers who see development as a slow, continuous shaping process emphasize _____ and _____ .

4. Stage theories that have been considered include the theory of cognitive development proposed by _____ , the theory of moral development proposed by _____ , and the theory of psychosocial development proposed by _____ .

5. Although research casts doubt on the idea that life proceeds through age-linked _____ , there are spurts of _____ growth during childhood and puberty that correspond roughly to the stages proposed by _____ .

6. A third controversial issue concerns the consistency of personality and whether development is characterized more by _____ over time or by change. Research on the consistency of personality shows that some traits, such as those related to _____ , are more stable than others, such as social attitudes.

Prenatal Development and the Newborn

Objective 10-2: Describe the course of prenatal development, and explain how teratogens affect that development.

7. Conception begins when a woman's _____ releases a mature _____ .

8. The few _____ from the man that reach the egg release digestive _____ that eat away the egg's protective covering. As soon as one sperm penetrates the egg, the egg's surface _____ all other sperm.

9. The egg and sperm _____ fuse and become one.

10. Fertilized human eggs are called _____ . During the first week, the cells in this cluster begin to specialize in structure and function, that is, they begin to _____ . About 10 days after conception, the fertilized egg attaches to the mother's _____ wall.

11. From about 2 until 8 weeks of age the developing human, formed from the inner cells of the fertilized egg, is called a(n) _____ . Many of the outer cells become the _____ , which transfers _____ and _____ from mother to fetus. Along with nutrients, a range of harmful substances known as _____ can pass through the placenta.

12. During the final stage of prenatal development, the developing human is called a(n) _____ .

13. Moderate consumption of alcohol during pregnancy _____ (usually does not affect/can affect) the fetal brain. If a mother drinks heavily, her baby is at risk for the birth defects and lower intelligence that accompany _____ _____ _____ . The fetal damage may occur because alcohol has a(n) _____ effect.

APPLICATION:

14. Marisa has just learned that she is two months pregnant. She is concerned about her baby's health because in the last few months she has been drinking heavily. Marisa is afraid that her unborn child may be at risk for birth defects and for future behavior problems, _____ , and lower _____ .

Objective 10-3: Describe some newborn abilities, noting how researchers explore infants' mental abilities.

15. When an infant's cheek is touched, it will vigorously _____ for a nipple. Other infant reflexes include _____ , _____ , _____ , and _____ .

16. American psychologist _____ believed that the newborn experiences a "blooming, buzzing confusion." This belief is _____ (correct/incorrect).

Give some evidence supporting the claim that a newborn's sensory equipment is biologically prewired to facilitate social responsiveness.

17. To study infants' thinking, developmental researchers have used _____ , which involves a _____ in responding with repeated stimulation. Researchers have found that infants prefer sights, such as faces, and sounds that facilitate _____ responsiveness.

APPLICATION:

18. Leonardo is only 6 months old so he can't tell his Mom what he likes. However, by looking away from a mobile that now seems to bore him, he is

saying that he sees and remembers the mobile. His behavior indicates that he has _____ to the mobile.

MODULE REVIEW:

19. Dr. Joan Goodman is studying how memory changes as people get older. She is most likely a(n) _____ psychologist.
    a. social
    b. cognitive
    c. developmental
    d. experimental

20. Newborns vigorously root for a nipple when
    a. their foot is tickled.
    b. their cheek is touched.
    c. they hear a loud noise.
    d. they make eye contact with their caregiver.

21. A child can be born a drug addict because
    a. drugs used by the mother will pass into the child's bloodstream.
    b. addiction is an inherited personality trait.
    c. drugs used by the mother create genetic defects in her chromosomes.
    d. the fetus' blood has not yet developed a resistance to drugs.

22. A child whose mother drank heavily when she was pregnant is at heightened risk of
    a. being emotionally excitable during childhood.
    b. becoming insecurely attached.
    c. being born with the physical and cognitive abnormalities of fetal alcohol syndrome.
    d. addiction to a range of drugs throughout life.

23. Which is the correct order of stages of prenatal development?
    a. zygote, fetus, embryo
    b. zygote, embryo, fetus
    c. embryo, zygote, fetus
    d. embryo, fetus, zygote

24. Teratogens are
    a. physical abnormalities in the developing fetus.
    b. cognitive abnormalities in the developing fetus.
    c. chemicals and viruses that cross the placenta and may harm the developing fetus.
    d. fertilized eggs.

TERMS AND CONCEPTS TO REMEMBER:

25. developmental psychology

26. zygote

27. embryo

28. fetus

29. teratogens

30. fetal alcohol syndrome (FAS)

31. habituation

MODULE 11   Infancy and Childhood

Physical Development

Objective 11-1: Describe how the brain and motor skills develop during infancy and childhood.

1. Biological growth processes that enable orderly changes in behavior, relatively uninfluenced by experience, are called _____ .

2. The developing brain _____ (overproduces/underproduces) neurons. At birth, the human nervous system _____ (is/is not) fully mature.

3. Between 3 and 6 years of age, the brain is developing most rapidly in the _____ lobes, which enable _____ _____ . The last cortical areas to develop are the _____ _____ linked with _____ , _____ , and _____ .

4. Fiber pathways supporting _____ , _____ , and _____ proliferate into puberty. After puberty, a process of _____ or _____ shuts down some neural connections and strengthens others.

5. Your _____ dictate your overall brain architecture, but _____ fills in the details. Rosenzweig, Krech, and their colleagues discovered that rats raised from a young age in enriched environments had _____ (thicker/thinner) brain cortexes than animals raised in solitary confinement.

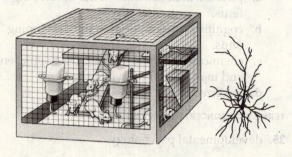

Describe the effects of sensory stimulation on neural development.

6. During early childhood, youngsters can most easily master such skills as the _____ and accent of another language. We seem to have a _____ _____ for some skills.

7. Infants pass the milestones of _____ development at different rates, but the basic _____ of stages is fixed. Infants roll over before they _____ and walk before they _____ .

8. Genes play a _____ (major/minor) role in motor development. Until the necessary muscular and neural maturation is complete, including the rapid development of the brain's _____ , experience has a _____ (large/small) effect on learning to walk, for example.

9. Our earliest memories generally do not occur before age _____ . This phenomenon has been called _____ _____ .

10. Research has shown that babies _____ (are/are not) capable of learning.

APPLICATION:

11. Calvin, who is trying to impress his psychology professor with his knowledge of infant motor development, asks why some infants learn to roll over before they lift their heads from a prone position, while others develop these skills in the opposite order. What should Calvin's professor conclude from this question?

    a. Calvin clearly understands that the sequence of motor development is not the same for all infants.

b. Calvin doesn't know what he's talking about. Although some infants reach these developmental milestones ahead of others, the order is the same for all infants.

c. Calvin needs to be reminded that rolling over is an inherited reflex, not a learned skill.

d. Calvin understands an important principle: Motor development is unpredictable.

Cognitive Development

Objective 11-2: Describe how a child's mind develops from the perspectives of Piaget, Vygotsky, and today's researchers.

12. *Cognition* refers to all the mental activities associated with _____ , _____ , _____ , and _____ .

13. The first researcher to show that the thought processes of adults and children are very different was _____ .

14. To organize and interpret his or her experiences, the developing child constructs cognitive concepts called _____ . The interpretation of new experiences in terms of existing ideas is called _____ . The adaptation of existing ideas to fit new experiences is called _____ .

15. In Piaget's first stage of development, the _____ stage, children experience the world through their motor and sensory interactions with objects. This stage occurs between birth and nearly age _____ .

16. The awareness that things continue to exist even when they are removed from view is called _____ . This awareness begins to develop at about _____ months of age.

17. Developmental researchers have found that Piaget and his followers _____ (overestimated/underestimated) young children's competence. For instance, babies have an intuitive grasp of simple laws of _____ , as seen in their reaction to a ball stopping in midair, and an understanding of _____ , as Karen Wynn demonstrated.

18. According to Piaget, during the preschool years and up to age _____ , children are in the _____ stage.

19. The principle that the quantity of a substance remains the same even when the shape of its container changes is called _____ . Piaget believed that preschoolers _____ (have/have not) developed this concept.

20. A child who can perform mental operations can think in _____ and enjoy _____ _____ . Researchers have found that that this ability appears at an earlier age than Piaget supposed.

21. Preschoolers have difficulty perceiving things from another person's point of view. This inability is called _____ . Even adults may overestimate the extent to which others share their opinions and perspectives, a trait known as the _____ _____ _____ .

22. The child's growing ability to take another's perspective is evidence that the child is acquiring a _____ _____ _____ . Between the ages of about 3½ and 4½, children come to realize that others may hold _____ _____ .

23. Piaget believed that children acquire the mental abilities needed to comprehend mathematical transformations and conservation by about _____ years of age. At this time, they enter the _____ _____ stage.

24. In Piaget's final stage, the _____ _____ stage, reasoning expands from the purely concrete to encompass _____ thinking. Piaget believed most children begin to enter this stage by age _____ .

25. Russian psychologist _____ noted that by age _____ children stop thinking aloud and instead rely on _____ _____ . Talking to themselves helps children control their _____ and _____ and master new skills.

26. Complementing Piaget's emphasis on interaction with the _____ environment is Vygotsky's emphasis on interaction with the

_____ environment. To Vygotsky, children were young _____ mentored by parents and others who give them new words. Thus they provide a _____ the child uses to build higher-level thinking.

STUDY TIP: Jean Piaget was the first major theorist to realize that each stage of life has its own characteristic way of thinking. To deepen your understanding of Jean Piaget's stages of cognitive development, fill in the blanks in the chart below. Do as much as you can without reviewing the text. To get you started, the first stage has been completed.

27. Typical Age Range	Stage	New Developments	Test to Determine If Someone Is in This Stage
Birth to nearly 2 years	Sensorimotor	Stranger anxiety Object permanence	Have the child's mother leave the room Hide a toy under a blanket
2 to _____	_____		
_____	Concrete		
About 12 through _____	_____		

APPLICATIONS:

28. Compared with when he was younger, 4-year-old Antonio is better able to empathize with his friend's feelings. This growing ability to take another's perspective indicates that Antonio is acquiring a _____ _____ .

29. As 8-year-old Gabriella observes, liquid is transferred from a tall, thin tube into a short, wide jar. She is asked if there is now less liquid in order to determine if she has mastered the concept of _____ .

30. Caleb is 14 months old and he behaves as though "out of sight is out of existence." He is in Piaget's _____ stage of cognitive development.

Explain briefly how contemporary researchers view Piaget's theory.

31. Makayla is 3 years old, can use language, and has trouble taking another person's perspective. She is in Piaget's _____ stage of cognitive development.

32. Four-year-old Jamail has a younger sister. When asked if he has a sister, he is likely to answer _____ (yes/no); when asked if his sister has a brother, Jamail is likely to answer _____ (yes/no).

33. In Piaget's theory, conservation is to egocentrism as the _____ stage is to the _____ stage.
    a. sensorimotor; formal operational
    b. formal operational; sensorimotor
    c. preoperational; sensorimotor
    d. concrete operational; preoperational

Objective 11-3: Describe autism spectrum disorder.

34. The disorder characterized by significant deficiencies in _____ and _____ interaction and an impaired _____ _____, as well as rigidly fixated interests and _____ behaviors, is referred to as _____ _____ _____ .

35. This disorder is related to poor communication among brain areas that normally work together to enable taking another's _____ .

ASD has differing levels of severity. Describe the characteristics of those who generally function at a high level (those formerly diagnosed with Asperger's syndrome).

36. Biological factors, including _____ _____ and _____ _____ _____, contribute to ASD. Research on the brain's structure have revealed _____ (fewer than normal fiber tracts connecting the front of the brain to the back).

37. Baron-Cohen's theory proposes that autism spectrum disorder represents an "extreme _____ brain." According to this theory, girls tend to be _____, who are better than boys at reading facial expressions and gestures. Boys tend to be _____, who understand things in terms of rules or laws.

Social Development

Objective 11-4: Describe how parent-infant attachment bonds form.

38. Soon after _____ _____ emerges and children become mobile, a new fear, called _____ _____, emerges. This fear emerges at about age _____ .

39. The development of a strong emotional bond between infant and parent is called _____ .

40. The Harlows' studies of monkeys have shown that mother-infant attachment does not depend on the mother providing nourishment as much as it does on her providing the comfort of _____ _____ . Another key to attachment is _____ .

41. Human attachment involves one person providing another with a _____ _____ when distressed and a _____ _____ from which to explore.

42. In some animals, attachment will occur only during a restricted time called a _____ _____ . Konrad Lorenz discovered that ducklings would follow almost any object if it were the first moving thing they observed. This phenomenon is called _____ .

43. Human infants _____ (do/do not) have a precise critical period for becoming attached. However, because of _____ _____, they attach to what they know.

APPLICATION:

44. In a 1998 movie, a young girl finds that a flock of geese follows her wherever she goes because she was the first "object" they saw after they were born. This is an example of

   a. conservation.   c. egocentrism.

   b. imprinting.   d. basic trust.

Objective 11-5: Describe how psychologists have studied attachment differences, and discuss what they have learned.

45. Placed in a research setting called the _____ _____, children show one of two patterns of attachment: _____ attachment or _____ attachment, marked either by _____ or avoidance.

Contrast the responses of securely and insecurely attached infants to strange situations.

Discuss the impact of responsive parenting on infant attachment.

46. A father's love and acceptance for his children are _____ (comparable to/less important than) a mother's love in predicting their children's health and well-being.

47. Separation anxiety peaks in infants around _____ months, then _____ (gradually declines/remains constant for about a year). This is true of children _____ (in North America/throughout the world).

48. According to Erikson, securely attached infants approach life with a sense of _____ _____ .

49. Most researchers now believe that early attachments _____ (do/do not) form the basis of adult attachments.

Describe the relationship between early attachments and adult attachments.

APPLICATION:

50. Layla and Christian Bishop have a 13-month-old boy. According to Erikson, the Bishops' sensitive, loving care of their child contributes to the child's _____ _____ .

Objective 11-6: Describe how childhood neglect or abuse affects children's attachment.

51. The Harlows found that when monkeys reared in social isolation were placed with other monkeys, they reacted with either fear or _____ .

52. Although most children who grow up under adversity are _____ and become normal adults, early abuse and excessive exposure to _____ _____ may alter the development of the brain chemical _____ .

53. Most abused children _____ (do/do not) later become abusive parents.

Objective 11-7: Describe three parenting styles, and explain how children's traits relate to them.

54. Parents who are coercive, who impose rules and expect obedience are exhibiting a(n) _____ style of parenting.

55. Parents who are unrestraining, who make few demands of their children and tend to submit to their children's desires are identified as _____ parents.

56. Setting and enforcing standards after discussion with their children is the approach taken by confrontive, _____ parents. Studies have shown that these parents tend to have children with the highest _____ , _____ , and social competence.

Explain why the correlation between authoritative parenting and social competence does not necessarily reveal cause and effect.

57. Whereas most Western parents place more emphasis on _____ (emotional closeness/independence) in their children, many Asian and African parents focus on cultivating

_____ (emotional closeness/independence). These cultures encourage a strong sense of _____ _____ , a sense that what shames or honors the person also shames or honors the family.

MODULE REVIEW:

58. In Piaget's stage of concrete operational intelligence, the child acquires an understanding of the principle of
    a. conservation.
    b. deduction.
    c. attachment.
    d. object permanence.

59. Piaget held that egocentrism is characteristic of the
    a. sensorimotor stage.
    b. preoperational stage.
    c. concrete operational stage.
    d. formal operational stage.

60. During which stage of cognitive development do children acquire object permanence?
    a. sensorimotor
    b. preoperational
    c. concrete operational
    d. formal operational

61. The Harlows' studies of attachment in monkeys showed that
    a. provision of nourishment was the single most important factor motivating attachment.
    b. a cloth mother produced the greatest attachment response.
    c. whether a cloth or wire mother was present mattered less than the presence or absence of other infants.
    d. attachment in monkeys is based on imprinting.

62. When psychologists discuss maturation, they are referring to stages of growth that are NOT influenced by
    a. conservation.
    b. nature.
    c. nurture.
    d. continuity.

63. The developmental theorist who suggested that securely attached children develop an attitude of basic trust is
    a. Piaget.
    b. Harlow.
    c. Vygotsky.
    d. Erikson.

64. Research findings on infant motor development are consistent with the idea that
    a. cognitive development lags significantly behind motor skills development.
    b. maturation of physical skills is relatively unaffected by experience.
    c. in the absence of relevant earlier learning experiences, the emergence of motor skills will be slowed.
    d. in humans, the process of maturation may be significantly altered by cultural factors.

65. According to Piaget, the ability to think logically about abstract propositions is indicative of the stage of
    a. preoperational thought.
    b. concrete operations.
    c. formal operations.
    d. postconventional thought.

66. Stranger anxiety develops soon after
    a. the concept of conservation.
    b. egocentrism.
    c. a theory of mind.
    d. the concept of object permanence.

67. Before Piaget, people were more likely to believe that
    a. the child's mind is a miniature model of the adult's.
    b. children think about the world in radically different ways from adults.
    c. the child's mind develops through a series of stages.
    d. children interpret their experiences in terms of their current understandings.

68. Which is the correct sequence of stages in Piaget's theory of cognitive development?
    a. sensorimotor, preoperational, concrete operational, formal operational
    b. sensorimotor, preoperational, formal operational, concrete operational
    c. preoperational, sensorimotor, concrete operational, formal operational
    d. preoperational, sensorimotor, formal operational, concrete operational

69. The term *critical period* refers to
    a. prenatal development.
    b. the initial 2 hours after a child's birth.
    c. the preoperational stage.
    d. an optimal period for normal development of some skills.

70. Which of the following was NOT found by the Harlows in socially deprived monkeys?
    a. They had difficulty mating.
    b. They showed extreme fear or aggression when first seeing other monkeys.
    c. They showed abnormal physical development.
    d. The females were abusive mothers.

71. Most people's earliest memories do not predate _____ of age.
    a. 6 months   c. 2 years
    b. 1 year   d. 3 years

72. Insecurely attached infants who are left by their mothers in an unfamiliar setting often will
    a. hold fast to their mothers on their return.
    b. explore the new surroundings confidently.
    c. be indifferent toward their mothers on their return.
    d. display little emotion at any time.

73. Compared with Westerners, children in Asian and African cultures
    a. have a stronger sense of family self.
    b. are encouraged to be independent.
    c. think first about your personal needs.
    d. tend to follow their conscience.

TERMS AND CONCEPTS TO REMEMBER:

74. maturation
75. critical period
76. cognition
77. schema
78. assimilation
79. accommodation
80. sensorimotor stage
81. object permanence
82. preoperational stage
83. conservation
84. egocentrism
85. theory of mind
86. concrete operational stage
87. autism spectrum disorder
88. formal operational stage
89. stranger anxiety
90. attachment
91. imprinting
92. temperament
93. basic trust

MODULE
12 Adolescence

Physical Development

Objective 12-1: Define *adolescence*, and explain how physical changes affect developing teens.

1. *Adolescence* is defined as the transition period between _____ and _____ .

2. The "storm and stress" view of adolescence is credited to _____ , one of the first American psychologists to describe adolescence.

3. Adolescence begins with the time of developing sexual maturity known as _____ .

4. The _____ (timing/sequence) of pubertal changes is more predictable than their _____ (timing/sequence).

5. The first menstrual period, called _____ , has a _____ (more/less) predictable sequence than timing.

6. Boys who mature _____ (early/late) tend to be more popular, self-assured, and independent; they also are at increased risk for _____ .
   For girls, _____ (early/late) maturation can be a challenge, especially when their bodies are out of sync with their _____ .

7. The adolescent brain undergoes a selective _____ of unused neurons and connections. Also, teens' occasional impulsiveness, risky behaviors, and emotional storms may be due, in part, to the fact that development in the brain's _____ _____ lags behind that of the _____ _____ . The growth of the fatty tissue that forms around axons and speeds neurotransmission (_____) enables better communication with other brain regions, which bring improved judgment, impulse control, and _____-_____ .

APPLICATION:

8. Based on the text discussion of maturation and popularity, who among the following is probably the most popular sixth grader?
   a. Jessica, the most physically mature girl in the class
   b. Roger, the most intellectually mature boy in the class
   c. Rob, the tallest, most physically mature boy in the class
   d. Cindy, who is average in physical development and is on the school debating team

Cognitive Development

Objective 12-2: Describe adolescent cognitive and moral development, according to Piaget, Kohlberg, and later researchers.

9. During the early teen years, reasoning is often _____, as adolescents often feel their experiences are unique.

10. Adolescents' developing cognitive ability enables them to think about what is _____ possible and _____ that with imperfect reality.

11. Piaget's final stage of cognitive development is the stage of _____ _____. Adolescents in this stage are capable of reasoning _____ and _____ consequences. This enables them to detect _____ in others' reasoning and to spot hypocrisy.

12. The theorist who proposed that moral thought progresses through stages is _____. These stages are divided into three basic levels: _____, _____, and _____.

13. In the preconventional stages of morality, characteristic of children, the emphasis is on obeying rules to avoid _____ or gain concrete _____.

14. Conventional morality usually emerges by early _____. The emphasis is on gaining social _____ or maintaining the social _____.

15. Individuals who base moral judgments on their own perceptions of basic ethical principles are said by Kohlberg to employ _____ morality.

Explain why critics fault Kohlberg's theory of moral development.

16. The idea that moral feelings precede moral reasoning is expressed in the moral _____ view of morality. Research studies using _____ _____ support the idea that moral judgment involves more than merely thinking; it is also gut-level feeling.

17. Morality involves doing the right thing, and what we do depends on _____ influences. Today's _____ _____ _____ focus on moral issues and doing the right thing.

18. Our capacity to delay _____ is basic to our future _____, _____, and _____ success. Children with this capacity are rated by teachers and parents as more _____.

APPLICATIONS:

19. Thirteen-year-old Irene has no trouble defeating her 11-year-old brother at a detective game that requires following clues in order to deduce the perpetrator of a crime. How might Piaget explain Irene's superiority at the game?
   a. Being older, Irene has had more years of schooling.
   b. Girls develop intellectually at a faster rate than boys.
   c. Being an adolescent, Irene is beginning to develop abstract reasoning skills.
   d. Girls typically have more experience than boys at playing games.

20. Jake, a junior in high school, regularly attends church because his family and friends think he should. Jake is in Kohlberg's _____ stage of moral reasoning.

21. In Jada's country, people believe in family togetherness above all else. Because her culture does not give priority to _____, Kohlberg would say that she is not at his highest level of moral reasoning, the _____ level.

Social Development

Objective 12-3: Describe the social tasks and challenges of adolescence.

Complete the missing information in the following table of Erikson's stages of psychosocial development.

Group Age	Psychosocial Stage
Infancy	_____
_____	Autonomy vs. shame and doubt
Preschool	_____
_____	Competence vs. inferiority
Adolescence	_____
_____	Intimacy vs. isolation
Middle adulthood	_____
_____	Integrity vs. despair

22. To refine their sense of identity, adolescents in individualist cultures experiment with different "_____" in different situations. The result may be role _____, which is resolved by forming a self-definition, or _____ . The aspect of people's self-concept that forms around their group membership is their _____ _____ .

23. Some adolescents forge their identity early, simply by _____ their parents' values and expectations. Others may adopt the identity of a particular _____ _____ .

24. During the early to mid-teen years, self-esteem generally _____ (rises/falls/remains stable). During the late teens and twenties, self-esteem generally _____ (rises/falls/remains stable) and agreeableness and emotional stability scores _____ (increase/decrease).

25. Erikson saw the formation of identity as a prerequisite for the development of _____ in young adulthood.

Objective 12-4: Discuss how parents and peers influence adolescents.

26. Adolescence is typically a time of increasing influence from one's _____ and decreasing influence from _____ .

27. Most adolescents report that they _____ (do/do not) get along with their parents. They see their parents as having the most influence in shaping their _____ _____ , for example.

28. Research on social relationships between parents and their adolescent children shows that high school girls who have the most _____ relationships with their mothers tend to enjoy the most _____ friendships with girlfriends.

29. When excluded adolescents withdraw, they are vulnerable to _____ , low _____ , and _____ .

APPLICATION:

30. Fourteen-year-old Cassandra feels freer and more open with her friends than with her family. Knowing this is the case, Cassandra's parents should
    a. be concerned, because deteriorating parent-teen relationships, such as this one, are often followed by a range of problem behaviors.
    b. encourage Cassandra to find new friends.
    c. seek family counseling.
    d. not worry, since adolescence is typically a time of growing peer influence and diminishing parental influence.

Emerging Adulthood

Objective 12-5: Define *emerging adulthood*.

31. Together, later _____ and earlier _____ _____ have widened the once-brief interlude between biological maturity and social independence.

32. Because the time from 18 to the mid-twenties is increasingly a not-yet-settled phase of life, some

psychologists refer to this period as a time of

_____ _____ .

MODULE REVIEW:

33. According to Erikson, the central psychological challenges pertaining to adolescence, young adulthood, and middle age, respectively, are
    a. identity formation; intimacy; generativity.
    b. intimacy; identity formation; generativity.
    c. generativity; intimacy; identity formation.
    d. intimacy; generativity; identity formation.

34. In preconventional morality, the person
    a. obeys out of a sense of social duty.
    b. conforms to gain social approval.
    c. obeys to avoid punishment or to gain concrete rewards.
    d. follows the dictates of his or her conscience.

35. Which of the following is correct?
    a. Early maturation places both boys and girls at a distinct social advantage.
    b. Early maturing girls are more popular and self-assured than girls who mature late.
    c. Early maturation places both boys and girls at a distinct social disadvantage.
    d. Early maturing boys are more popular and self-assured than boys who mature late.

36. After puberty, the self-concept usually becomes
    a. more positive in boys.
    b. more positive in girls.
    c. more positive in both boys and girls.
    d. more negative in both boys and girls.

37. Adolescence is marked by the onset of
    a. an identity crisis.
    b. parent-child conflict.
    c. the concrete operational stage.
    d. puberty.

38. Whose stage theory of moral development was based on how people reasoned about ethical dilemmas?
    a. Erikson   c. Harlow
    b. Piaget   d. Kohlberg

39. To which of Kohlberg's levels would moral reasoning based on the existence of fundamental human rights pertain?
    a. preconventional morality
    b. conventional morality
    c. postconventional morality
    d. generative morality

40. The idea that morality is rooted in moral intuitions rather than moral reasoning is the basis for
    a. Lawrence Kohlberg's theory.
    b. Jean Piaget's theory.
    c. Jonathan Haidt's theory.
    d. Erik Erikson's theory.

41. In Erikson's theory, individuals generally focus on developing _____ during adolescence and then _____ during young adulthood.
    a. identity; intimacy
    b. intimacy; identity
    c. basic trust; identity
    d. identity; basic trust

TERMS AND CONCEPTS TO REMEMBER:

42. adolescence

43. puberty

44. identity

45. social identity

46. intimacy

47. emerging adulthood

Essay Question

Sheryl is a 12-year-old living in the United States. She is in the sixth grade. Describe the developmental changes she is likely to be experiencing according to Piaget, Kohlberg, and Erikson. (Use the space below to list the points you want to make, and organize them. Then write the essay on a separate sheet of paper.)

 MODULE 13 Adulthood

Physical Development

Objective 13-1: Identify the physical changes that occur during middle and late adulthood.

1. During adulthood, age _____
   (is/is not) a very good predictor of people's traits.

2. In our mid-twenties, _____,
_____, _____,
_____, _____,
_____, and _____
_____ begin a slight decline.
Because they mature earlier, _____
(women/men) also peak earlier.

3. During early and middle adulthood, physical
vigor has less to do with _____
than with a person's _____
and _____ habits.

4. With age, men experience a more gradual decline
in _____ count, level of the hormone
_____, and speed of erection and
ejaculation during later life.

5. Women experience the cessation of the menstrual
cycle, known as _____, which
occurs within a few years of _____.
A woman's emotional experience during this time
depends largely on her _____ and
_____.

6. With age, the eye's pupil _____
(shrinks/enlarges) and its lens becomes
_____ (more/less) transparent. As a
result, the amount of light that reaches the retina
is _____ (increased/reduced).

7. Other senses, such as _____ and
_____ diminish with age.

8. Although older adults are _____
(more/less) susceptible to life-threatening ailments, they suffer from short-term ailments such
as flu _____ (more/less) often than
younger adults.

9. Aging _____ (slows/speeds/has no
effect on) neural processing and causes a gradual
loss of _____ _____.

10. The good news is that the aging brain is
_____, and partly compensates for
what it loses by recruiting and reorganizing
_____.

11. Physical exercise stimulates _____
_____ development and
_____ connections, thanks perhaps
to increased _____ and nutrient
flow.

12. With age, the tips of our chromosomes, called
_____, wear down. This wear and
tear is accelerated by _____,
_____, and stress. However, these
tips are maintained by _____.

Cognitive Development

Objective 13-2: Describe how memory changes with
age.

13. Looking back in later life, adults asked to recall
the one or two most important events over the
last half-century tend to name events from their
teens or twenties, a phenomenon referred to as a
"_____ _____."

14. Studies of developmental changes in learning
and memory show that during adulthood there is
a decline in the ability to _____
(recall/recognize) new information but not in the
ability to _____ (recall/recognize)
such information. One factor that influences
memory in older people is the
_____ of material.

15. Cognitive abilities among 70-year-olds are
_____ (less/more) varied than
among 20-year-olds.

16. A research study in which people of various ages
are compared with one another is called a
_____-_____ study.

17. A research study in which the same people are
retested over a period of years is called a
_____ study.

18. Age is less a predictor of memory and intelligence
than is _____.
Especially in the last three or four years of
life, cognitive decline typically accelerates.
Researchers call this near-death drop
_____ _____.

19. Which statement illustrates cognitive development during the course of adult life?
a. Forty-three-year-old Sophia has better recognition memory than 72-year-old Kylie.
b. Both Sophia and Kylie have strong recall and
recognition memory.
c. Kylie's recognition memory decreased sharply
at age 50.

d. Forty-three-year-old Sophia has better recall memory than 72-year-old Kylie.

Social Development

Objective 13-3: Discuss the themes and influences that mark our social journey from early adulthood to death.

20. Contrary to popular opinion, job and marital dissatisfaction do not surge during the forties, thus suggesting that the midlife transition is not a _____ .

21. The term used to refer to the culturally preferred timing for leaving home, getting a job, marrying, and so on is the _____ _____ . Today, the timing of such life events is becoming _____ (more/less) predictable. Even _____ _____ can have lasting significance.

22. According to Erikson, the two basic tasks of adulthood are achieving _____ and _____ .

23. According to Freud, the healthy adult is one who can _____ and _____ .

24. Human societies have nearly always included a relatively _____ bond. Straight and gay romantic relationships sealed with _____ more often endure.

25. Such bonds are usually lasting when couples marry after age _____ and are _____ _____ .

26. Compared with the period between 1960 and 1980, the divorce rate today has _____ (increased/decreased/leveled off).

27. Couples who live together before marrying have a _____ (higher/lower) divorce rate than those who do not.

28. Marriage is a predictor of _____ , _____ _____ , _____ , and physical and mental _____ . Lesbian couples report _____ (greater/less) well-being than those who are alone.

29. As children begin to absorb time and energy, satisfaction with the marriage itself may _____ (increase/decrease). This is particularly true among _____ women, who shoulder most of the burden.

30. For most couples, the children's leaving home produces a(n) _____ (increase/decrease) in marital satisfaction.

31. During the first two years of college or university, most students _____ (can/cannot) predict their later careers.

32. After a series of unfulfilling relationships, 30-year-old Carlos tells a friend that he doesn't want to marry because he is afraid of losing his freedom and independence. Erikson would say that Carlos is having difficulty with the psychosocial task of
    a. trust versus mistrust.
    b. autonomy versus doubt.
    c. intimacy versus isolation.
    d. identity versus role confusion.

Objective 13-4: Discuss how our well-being changes across the life span.

33. From early adulthood to midlife, people typically experience a strengthening sense of _____ , _____ , and _____ .

34. During the over-65 years, _____ feelings tend to grow, and _____ feelings subside. Compared with teens and young adults, older adults tend to have a _____ (smaller/larger) social network, with _____ (fewer/more) friendships.

35. As we age, the brain area called the _____ shows _____ (increased/decreased) activity in response to negative events.

36. More and more people flourish into later life, thanks to _____ influences.

APPLICATION:

37. The text discusses well-being across the life span. Which of the following people is likely to report the greatest life satisfaction?
    a. Billy, a 7-year-old second-grader
    b. Kathy, a 17-year-old high-school senior
    c. Mildred, a 70-year-old retired teacher
    d. too little information to tell

Objective 13-5: Describe the range of reactions to the death of a loved one.

38. Grief over a loved one's death is especially severe when it comes _____

    _____.

39. Reactions to a loved one's death _____ (do/do not) vary according to cultural norms. Those who express the strongest grief immediately _____ (do/do not) purge their grief more quickly.

40. Terminally ill and bereaved people _____ (do/do not) go through predictable stages.

41. According to Erikson, the final task of adulthood is to achieve a sense of

    _____ .

MODULE REVIEW:

42. An older person who can look back on life with satisfaction and reminisce with a sense of completion has attained Erikson's stage of
    a. generativity.   c. isolation.
    b. intimacy.   d. integrity.

43. The cognitive ability that has been shown to decline during adulthood is the ability to
    a. recall new information.
    b. recognize new information.
    c. learn meaningful new material.
    d. use judgment in dealing with daily life problems.

44. Which of the following statements concerning the effects of aging is true?
    a. Aging almost inevitably leads to total memory failure if the individual lives long enough.
    b. Aging increases susceptibility to short-term ailments such as the flu.
    c. Significant increases in life satisfaction are associated with aging.
    d. The aging process can be significantly affected by the individual's activity patterns.

45. Longitudinal research
    a. compares people of different ages.
    b. studies the same people at different times.
    c. usually involves a larger sample than does cross-sectional research.
    d. usually involves a smaller sample than does cross-sectional research.

46. Cross-sectional research
    a. compares people of different ages with one another.
    b. studies the same group of people at different times.
    c. is used for studying cognitive development during infancy.
    d. is used for studying social development during infancy.

47. The *social clock* refers to
    a. an individual or society's distribution of work and leisure time.
    b. adulthood responsibilities.
    c. typical ages for starting a career, marrying, and so on.
    d. age-related changes in one's circle of friends.

48. After their grown children have left home, most couples experience
    a. the distress of the empty nest syndrome.
    b. increased strain in their marital relationship.
    c. the need to have their children visit often.
    d. greater happiness and enjoyment in their relationship.

49. In terms of incidence, susceptibility to short-term illnesses _____ with age and susceptibility to long-term ailments _____ with age.
    a. decreases; increases
    b. increases; decreases
    c. increases; increases
    d. decreases; decreases

50. Research on the American family indicates that
    a. 23 percent of unmarried adults, but 40 percent of married adults, report being "very happy" with life.
    b. the divorce rate is now one-half the marriage rate.
    c. children born to cohabiting parents are five times more likely to experience their parents' separation.
    d. all of these statements are true.

51. The popular idea that terminally ill and bereaved people go through predictable stages, such as denial, anger, and so forth
    a. is widely supported by research.
    b. more accurately describes grieving in some cultures than others.
    c. is true of women but not men.
    d. is not supported by research studies.

TERMS AND CONCEPTS TO REMEMBER:

52. menopause
53. cross-sectional study
54. longitudinal study
55. social clock

Before You Move On

True–False Items

Indicate whether each statement is true or false by placing *T* or *F* in the blank next to the item.

_____ 1. Most abused children later become abusive parents.
_____ 2. At birth, the brain and nervous system of a healthy child are fully developed.

Cross-Check

As you learned in Module 2, reviewing and overlearning of material are important to the learning process. After you have written the definitions of the key terms in this unit, you should complete the crossword puzzle to ensure that you can reverse the process—recognize the term, given the definition.

ACROSS

3. The developing human organism from 9 weeks after conception until birth.
4. In Piaget's theory, changing an existing schema to incorporate new information.
6. Process by which certain animals form attachments during a critical period.
9. The developing human organism from 2 weeks through 2 months after conception.
11. Mental concepts or frameworks that organize information.

_____ 3. The sequence in which children develop motor skills varies from one culture to another.
_____ 4. Current research shows that young children are more capable and development is more continuous than Piaget believed.
_____ 5. The process of grieving is much the same throughout the world.
_____ 6. The most self-confident children are raised by authoritarian parents.
_____ 7. During adulthood, age only moderately correlates with people's traits.
_____ 8. By the age of 50, most adults have experienced a "midlife crisis."
_____ 9. Compared with those who are younger, older people are more susceptible to short-term ailments such as flu and cold viruses.
_____ 10. The symptoms of Alzheimer's disease are simply an intensified version of normal aging.

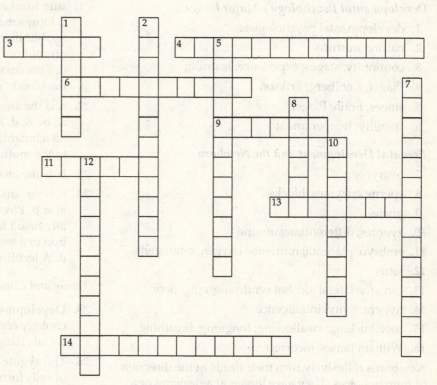

13. The first menstrual period.
14. A study in which the same people are retested over a period of years.

DOWN

1. A childhood disorder marked by deficiencies in communication and social interaction is _____ spectrum disorder.
2. In Piaget's theory, interpreting a new experience in terms of an existing schema.
5. Principle that properties such as number or volume remain constant despite changes in appearance.
7. A study in which people of different ages are compared with one another.
8. Fertilized human egg.
10. Any drug, virus, or other toxic substance that crosses the mother's placenta.
12. Decreasing responsiveness to a stimulus that is repeatedly presented.

Answers

 Developmental Issues, Prenatal Development, and the Newborn

Developmental Psychology's Major Issues

1. developmental psychologists
2. nature; nurture
3. continuity; stages; experience; learning
4. Piaget; Kohlberg; Erikson
5. stages; brain; Piaget
6. stability; temperament

Prenatal Development and the Newborn

7. ovary; egg
8. sperm; enzymes; blocks
9. nuclei
10. zygotes; differentiate; uterine
11. embryo; placenta; nutrients; oxygen; teratogens
12. fetus
13. can affect; fetal alcohol syndrome; epigenetic
14. hyperactivity; intelligence
15. root; sucking; swallowing; tonguing; breathing
16. William James; incorrect

Newborns reflexively turn their heads in the direction of human voices. They gaze longer at a drawing of a face-like image. They focus best on objects about 8 to 12 inches away, which is about the distance between a nursing infant's eyes and the mother's. Within days, they recognize their mother's smell.

17. habituation; decrease; social

18. habituated

Module Review:

19. **c.** is the answer. Developmental psychologists study physical, cognitive (memory, in this example), and social change throughout the life span.
a. Social psychologists study how people influence and are influenced by others.
b. Cognitive psychologists *do* study memory; because Dr. Goodman is interested in life-span *changes* in memory, she is more likely a developmental psychologist.
d. Experimental psychologists study physiology, sensation, perception, learning, and other aspects of behavior. Only developmental psychologists focus on developmental changes in behavior and mental processes.

20. **b.** is the answer. The infant turns its head and begins sucking when its cheek is stroked.
a., c., & d. These stimuli produce other reflexes in the newborn.

21. **a.** is the answer. Any drug taken by the mother passes through the placenta and enters the child's bloodstream.
b. Addiction cannot be inherited; it requires exposure to an addictive drug.
c. Drugs may disrupt the mechanisms of heredity, but there is no evidence that such changes promote addiction.
d. This answer is incorrect because at no age does the blood "resist" drugs.

22. **c.** is the answer.
a., b., & d. A child's emotional temperament, attachment, and addiction have not been linked to the mother's drinking while pregnant.

23. **b.** is the answer.

24. **c.** is the answer.
a. & b. Physical and cognitive abnormalities usually result from teratogens, but that's not a definition of a teratogen.
d. A fertilized egg is a zygote.

Terms and Concepts to Remember:

25. **Developmental psychology** is the branch of psychology concerned with physical, cognitive, and social change throughout the life span.

26. The **zygote** is the fertilized egg, that is, the cluster of cells formed during conception by the union of sperm and egg.

27. The **embryo** is the developing prenatal organism from about 2 weeks through 2 months after conception; formed from the inner cells of the zygote.

28. The **fetus** is the developing prenatal human from 9 weeks after conception to birth.

29. **Teratogens** (literally, "monster makers") are agents, such as chemicals and viruses, that cross the mother's placenta and can harm the developing embryo or fetus.

30. **Fetal alcohol syndrome (FAS)** refers to the physical and cognitive abnormalities that heavy drinking by a pregnant woman may cause in the developing child.

31. **Habituation** is decreasing responsiveness to a stimulus that is repeatedly presented. It is used by researchers to find out what infants see, hear, smell, and think.

MODULE 11   Infancy and Childhood

Physical Development

1. maturation

2. over; is not

3. frontal; rational planning; association areas; thinking; memory; language

4. agility; language; self-control; pruning

5. genes; experience; thicker

Research has shown that human and animal infants given extra sensory stimulation develop faster neurologically. Throughout life, sensory stimulation activates and strengthens particular neural connections, while other connections weaken with disuse. In this way, our experiences shape the very structure of the neural pathways that process those experiences.

6. grammar; critical period

7. motor; sequence; sit; run

8. major; cerebellum; small

9. 3; infantile amnesia

10. are

11. **b.** is the answer.
    a. & d. Although the rate of motor development varies from child to child, the basic sequence is universal and, therefore, predictable.
    c. Rolling over and head lifting are both learned.

Cognitive Development

12. thinking; knowing; remembering; communicating

13. Jean Piaget

14. schemas; assimilation; accommodation

15. sensorimotor; 2

16. object permanence; 8

17. underestimated; physics; numbers

18. 6 or 7; preoperational

19. conservation; have not

20. symbols; pretend play

21. egocentrism; curse of knowledge

22. theory of mind; false beliefs

23. 6 or 7; concrete operational

24. formal operational; abstract; 12

25. Lev Vygotsky; 7; inner speech; behavior; emotions

26. physical; social; apprentices; scaffold

Contemporary researchers see development as more continuous than did Piaget. By detecting the beginnings of each type of thinking at earlier ages, they have revealed conceptual abilities Piaget missed. They also see formal logic as a smaller part of cognition than Piaget did. Despite these revisions to Piaget's theory, studies support the basic idea that cognitive development unfolds in the sequence Piaget described.

27. Piaget's stages are summarized below.

Typical Age Range	Stage	New Developments	Test to Determine If Someone Is in This Stage
Birth to nearly 2 years	Sensorimotor	Stranger anxiety Object permanence	Have the child's mother leave the room Hide a toy under a blanket
2 to 6 or 7 years	Preoperational	Egocentrism Not yet logical	Ask questions to determine child's ability to take another's perspective
6 or 7 to 11 years	Concrete operational	Conservation Simple math	Transfer liquid from a tall, thin glass into a short, wide glass
About 12 through adulthood	Formal operational	Abstract logic	Give child a hypothetical reasoning problem

28. theory of mind

29. conservation. This test is designed to determine if the child understands that the quantity of liquid is conserved, despite the shift to a container that is different in shape.

30. sensorimotor. The sensorimotor period is Piaget's first stage. Object permanence develops some time during this period.

31. preoperational. This child's age, ability to use language, and egocentrism clearly place her within Piaget's preoperational stage.

32. yes; no. Being 4 years old, Jamail would be in Piaget's preoperational stage. Preoperational thinking is egocentric, which means Jamail would find it difficult to "put himself in his sister's shoes" and perceive that she has a brother.

33. d. is the answer. Conservation is a hallmark of the concrete operational stage; egocentrism is a hallmark of the preoperational stage.

34. communication; social; theory of mind; repetitive; autism spectrum disorder

35. viewpoint (perspective)

They have normal intelligence, often accompanied by exceptional skill or talent in a specific area, but deficient social and communication skills and a tendency to become distracted by irrelevant stimuli.

36. genetic influences; abnormal brain development; underconnectivity

37. male; empathizers; systemizers

Social Development

38. object permanence; stranger anxiety; 8 months

39. attachment

40. body contact; familiarity

41. safe haven; secure base

42. critical period; imprinting

43. do not; mere exposure

44. b. is the answer.
    a. Conservation is the ability to realize that the amount of an object does not change even if its shape changes.
    c. Egocentrism is having difficulty perceiving things from another's perspective.
    d. According to Erikson, basic trust is feeling that the world is safe as a result of sensitive, loving caregivers.

45. strange situation; secure; insecure; anxiety

Placed in a strange situation, securely attached infants play comfortably, happily exploring their new environment. In contrast, insecurely attached infants are less likely to explore their surroundings and may even

cling to their mothers. When separated from their mothers, insecurely attached infants are much more distressed than securely attached infants. When reunited with their mothers, insecurely attached infants may be indifferent.

Research studies conducted by Mary Ainsworth have revealed that sensitive, responsive mothers tend to have securely attached infants, whereas insensitive, unresponsive mothers often have insecurely attached infants. Other studies have found that temperamentally difficult infants whose mothers receive training in responsive parenting are more likely to become securely attached than are control infants. This points to the importance of considering the infant's temperament in studying attachment.

46. comparable to

47. 13; gradually declines; throughout the world

48. basic trust

49. do

People who report secure relationships with their parents tend to enjoy secure friendships. When leaving home, they tend to adjust well. Feeling insecurely attached to others may take either of two main forms. With one, insecure-anxious attachment, people constantly crave acceptance but remain alert to signs of rejection. With insecure-avoidant attachment, people experience discomfort getting close to others and use avoidant strategies to maintain distance from others.

50. basic trust. Although loving parents will also produce securely attached children, Erikson's theory deals with trust or mistrust.

51. aggression

52. resilient; stress hormones; serotonin

53. do not

54. authoritarian

55. permissive

56. authoritative; self-esteem; self-reliance

There are at least three possible explanations for the correlation between authoritative parenting and social competence in children. (1) Parenting may foster children's competence. (2) Children's competence may promote authoritative parenting. (3) A third factor, such as heredity, may foster both authoritative parenting and child competence.

57. independence; emotional closeness; family self

Module Review:

58. a. is the answer.
    b. Deduction, or deductive reasoning, is a formal operational ability.
    c. Piaget's theory is not concerned with attachment.

d. Attaining object permanence is the hallmark of sensorimotor thought.

59. **b.** is the answer. The preoperational child sees the world from his or her own vantage point.
a. As immature as egocentrism is, it represents a significant cognitive advance over the sensorimotor child, who knows the world only through senses and actions. Even simple self-awareness takes a while to develop.
c. & d. As children attain the operational stages, they become more able to see the world through the eyes of others.

60. **a.** is the answer. Before object permanence is attained, "out of sight" is truly "out of mind."
b., c., & d. Developments during the preoperational, concrete operational, and formal operational stages include the use of language, conservation, and abstract reasoning, respectively.

61. **b.** is the answer.
a. When given the choice between a wire mother with a bottle and a cloth mother without, the monkeys preferred the cloth mother.
c. The presence of other infants made no difference.
d. Imprinting plays no role in the attachment of higher primates.

62. **c.** is the answer. Through maturation—an orderly sequence of biological growth processes that are relatively unaffected by experience—all humans develop.
a. Conservation is the cognitive awareness that objects do not change with changes in shape.
b. The forces of nature *are* those that direct maturation.
d. The issue of continuity and stages has to do with whether development is a gradual and continuous process or a discontinuous, stagelike process. Those who emphasize maturation see development as occurring in stages, not continuously.

63. **d.** is the answer. Erikson proposed that development occurs in a series of stages, in the first of which the child develops an attitude of either basic trust or mistrust.
a. Piaget's theory is concerned with cognitive development.
b. Harlow conducted research on attachment and deprivation.
c. Vygotsky focused on the influence of social factors on cognitive development.

64. **b.** is the answer.

65. **c.** is the answer. Once formal operational thought has been attained, thinking is no longer limited to concrete propositions.

a. & b. Preoperational thought and concrete operational thought emerge before, and do not include, the ability to think logically about abstract propositions.
d. Postconventional thought is Kohlberg's final stage of moral development.

66. **d.** is the answer. With object permanence, a child develops schemas for familiar objects, including faces, and may become upset by a stranger who does not fit any of these schemas.
a. The concept of conservation develops during the concrete operational stage, whereas stranger anxiety develops during the sensorimotor stage.
b. & c. Egocentrism and a theory of mind both develop during the preoperational stage. This follows the sensorimotor stage, during which stranger anxiety develops.

67. **a.** is the answer.
b., c., & d. Each of these is an understanding developed by Piaget.

68. **a.** is the answer.

69. **d.** is the answer. A critical period is an optimal time during which an organism must be exposed to certain influences or experiences for particular skills to develop.
a. Critical periods refer to developmental periods after birth.
b. Critical periods vary from behavior to behavior, but they are not confined to the hours following birth.
c. Critical periods are not specifically associated with the preoperational period.

70. **c.** is the answer. Deprived monkeys were impaired in their social behaviors but not in their physical development.
a., b., & d. Each of these was found in socially deprived monkeys.

71. **d.** is the answer. This is because of a lack of neural connections before that age.

72. **c.** is the answer.
a. Insecurely attached infants often cling to their mothers when placed in a new situation; yet, when the mother returns after an absence, the infant's reaction tends to be one of indifference.
b. These behaviors are characteristic of securely attached infants.
d. Insecurely attached infants in unfamiliar surroundings will often exhibit a range of emotional behaviors.

73. **a.** is the answer. All the other characteristics are more true of Western children.

Terms and Concepts to Remember:

74. **Maturation** refers to the biological growth processes that enable orderly changes in behavior, relatively uninfluenced by experience.

    Example: The ability to walk depends on a certain level of neural and muscular **maturation**. For this reason, until the toddler's body is physically ready to walk, practice "walking" has little effect.

75. A **critical period** is an optimal period shortly after birth during which an organism must be exposed to certain stimuli or experiences if it is to develop properly.

76. **Cognition** refers to all the mental processes associated with thinking, knowing, remembering, and communicating.

77. In Piaget's theory of cognitive development, **schemas** are mental concepts or frameworks that organize and interpret information.

78. In Piaget's theory, **assimilation** refers to interpreting a new experience in terms of an existing schema.

79. In Piaget's theory, **accommodation** refers to changing an existing schema to incorporate new information that cannot be assimilated.

80. In Piaget's theory of cognitive stages, the **sensorimotor stage** lasts from birth to nearly age 2. During this stage, infants gain knowledge of the world through their senses and their actions.

81. **Object permanence,** which develops during the sensorimotor stage, is the awareness that things do not cease to exist when not perceived.

82. In Piaget's theory, the **preoperational stage** lasts from about 2 to 6 or 7 years of age. During this stage, language development is rapid, but the child is unable to understand the mental operations of concrete logic.

83. **Conservation** is the principle that properties such as number, volume, and mass remain constant despite changes in the forms of objects; it is acquired during the concrete operational stage.

84. In Piaget's theory, **egocentrism** refers to the difficulty that preoperational children have in considering another's viewpoint. *Ego* means "self," and *centrism* indicates "in the center"; the preoperational child is "self-centered."

85. Our ideas about our own and others' thoughts, feelings, and perceptions and the behaviors these might predict constitute our **theory of mind**.

86. During the **concrete operational stage,** lasting from about ages 7 to 11, children can think logically about concrete events and objects.

87. **Autism spectrum disorder** is a disorder that appears in childhood and is marked by deficient communication, social interaction, and understanding of others' states of mind. Interests are rigidly fixated and behaviors are repetitive.

88. In Piaget's theory, the **formal operational stage** normally begins about age 12. During this stage people begin to think logically about abstract concepts.

    Memory aid: To help differentiate Piaget's stages remember that "operations" are mental transformations. *Pre*operational children, who lack the ability to perform transformations, are "before" this developmental milestone. Concrete operational children can operate on real, or concrete, objects. Formal operational children can perform logical transformations on abstract concepts.

89. **Stranger anxiety** is the fear of strangers that infants begin to display by about 8 months of age.

90. **Attachment** is an emotional tie with another person, shown in young children by their seeking closeness to a caregiver and showing distress on separation.

91. **Imprinting** is the process by which certain animals form strong attachments during early life.

92. **Temperament** is a person's characteristic emotional reactivity and intensity.

93. According to Erikson, **basic trust** is a sense that the world is predictable and trustworthy, a concept that infants form if their needs are met by responsive caregiving.

MODULE
 12   Adolescence

Physical Development

1. childhood; adulthood

2. G. Stanley Hall

3. puberty

4. sequence; timing

5. menarche; more

6. early; alcohol use, delinquency, and premature sexual activity; early; emotional maturity

7. pruning; frontal lobe; limbic system; myelin; long-term planning

8. **c.** is the answer. Early maturing boys tend to be more popular.

    a. Early maturing girls may temporarily suffer embarrassment and be the objects of teasing.

    b. & d. The social benefits of early or late maturation are based on physical development, not on cognitive skills.

Cognitive Development

9. self-focused

10. ideally; compare

11. formal operations; hypothetically; deducing; inconsistencies

12. Lawrence Kohlberg; preconventional; conventional; postconventional

13. punishment; rewards

14. adolescence; approval; order

15. postconventional

Kohlberg's critics note that his postconventional stage is culturally limited, appearing mostly among people who prize individualism.

16. intuitionist; moral paradoxes

17. social; character education programs

18. gratification; academic; vocational; social; self-controlled

19. c. is the answer.
    a., b., & d. Piaget did not link cognitive ability to amount of schooling, gender, or differences in how boys and girls are socialized.

20. conventional. Conventional morality is based in part on a desire to gain others' approval.

21. individualism; postconventional

Social Development

Erikson's stages of psychosocial development

Group Age	Psychosocial Stage
Infancy	Trust vs. mistrust
Toddlerhood	Autonomy vs. shame and doubt
Preschool	Initiative vs. guilt
Elementary school	Competence vs. inferiority
Adolescence	Identity vs. role confusion
Young adulthood	Intimacy vs. isolation
Middle adulthood	Generativity vs. stagnation
Late adulthood	Integrity vs. despair

22. selves; confusion; identity; social identity

23. adopting; peer group

24. falls; rises; increase

25. intimacy

26. peers; parents

27. do; religious faith

28. affectionate; intimate

29. loneliness; self-esteem; depression

30. d. is the answer.
    a. This description of Cassandra's feelings does not suggest that her relationship with her parents is deteriorating. Cassandra's social development, like that of most adolescents, is coming under increasing peer influence and diminishing parental influence.
    b. & c. Because Cassandra's feelings are normal, there is no reason for her to change her circle of friends or for her parents to seek counseling.

Emerging Adulthood

31. independence; sexual maturity

32. emerging adulthood

Module Review:

33. a. is the answer.

34. c. is the answer. At the preconventional level, moral reasoning centers on self-interest, whether this means obtaining rewards or avoiding punishment.
    a. & b. Moral reasoning based on a sense of social duty or a desire to gain social approval is associated with the conventional level of moral development.
    d. Reasoning based on ethical principles is characteristic of the postconventional level of moral development.

35. d. is the answer. Boys who show early physical maturation are generally stronger and more athletic than boys who mature late; these qualities may lead to greater popularity and self-assurance.
    a. & c. Early maturation tends to be socially advantageous for boys but not for girls.
    b. Early maturing girls often suffer embarrassment and are objects of teasing.

36. c. is the answer. Because the late teen years provide many new opportunities for trying out possible roles, adolescents' identities typically incorporate an increasingly positive self-concept.

37. d. is the answer. The physical changes of puberty mark the onset of adolescence.
    a. & b. An identity crisis or parent-child conflict may or may not occur during adolescence; neither of these formally marks its onset.
    c. Formal operational thought, rather than concrete reasoning, typically develops in adolescence.

38. d. is the answer.
    a. Erikson is known for his theory of psychosocial development.
    b. Piaget is known for his theory of cognitive development.

c. Harlow is known for his studies of attachment in infant monkeys.

39. **c.** is the answer.
    a. Preconventional morality is based on avoiding punishment and obtaining rewards.
    b. Conventional morality is based on gaining the approval of others and/or on following the law and social convention.
    d. There is no such thing as generative morality.

40. **c.** is the answer.
    a. Kohlberg focused on moral reasoning.
    b. Piaget studied cognitive development in children.
    d. Erikson proposed eight stages of social development throughout the life span.

41. **a.** is the answer.
    b. According to Erikson, identity develops before intimacy.
    c. & d. The formation of basic trust is the task of infancy.

Terms and Concepts to Remember:

42. **Adolescence** refers to the life stage from puberty to independent adulthood, denoted physically by sexual maturity, cognitively by the onset of formal operational thought, and socially by the formation of identity.

43. **Puberty** is the early adolescent period of sexual maturation, during which a person becomes capable of reproducing.

44. In Erikson's theory, establishing an **identity**, or one's sense of self, is the primary task of adolescence.

45. **Social identity** refers to person's self-concept as defined by the groups to which he or she belongs.

46. In Erikson's theory, **intimacy**, or the ability to establish close, loving relationships, is the primary task of late adolescence and early adulthood.

47. For some people in modern cultures, **emerging adulthood** is the period from the late teens to mid-twenties, bridging the gap between adolescent dependence and full independence and responsible adulthood.

Essay Question

Sheryl's age would place her at the threshold of Piaget's stage of formal operations. Although her thinking is probably still somewhat self-focused, Sheryl is becoming capable of abstract, logical thought. This will increasingly allow her to reason hypothetically and deductively. Because her logical thinking also enables her to detect inconsistencies in others' reasoning and between their ideals and actions, Sheryl and her parents may be having some heated debates about now.

According to Kohlberg, Sheryl is probably at the threshold of postconventional morality. When she was younger, Sheryl probably abided by rules in order to gain social approval, or simply because "rules are rules" (conventional morality). Now that she is older, Sheryl's moral reasoning will increasingly be based on her own personal code of ethics and an affirmation of people's agreed-upon rights.

According to Erikson, psychosocial development occurs in eight stages, each of which focuses on a particular task. As an adolescent, Sheryl's psychosocial task is to develop a sense of self by testing roles, then integrating them to form a single identity. Erikson called this stage *identity versus role confusion*.

MODULE
13   Adulthood

Physical Development

1. is not
2. muscular strength; reaction time; sensory keenness; cardiac output; women
3. age; health; exercise
4. sperm; testosterone
5. menopause; 50; expectations; attitude
6. shrinks; less; reduced
7. smell; hearing
8. more; less
9. slows; brain cells
10. plastic; neural networks
11. brain cell; neural; oxygen
12. telomeres; smoking; obesity; exercise

Cognitive Development

13. reminiscence bump
14. recall; recognize; meaningfulness
15. more
16. cross-sectional
17. longitudinal
18. proximity to death; terminal decline
19. **d.** is the answer.
    a. & c. In tests of recognition memory, the performance of older persons shows little decline.
    b. The ability to recall material, especially meaningless material, declines with age.

Social Development

20. crisis
21. social clock; less; chance events
22. intimacy; generativity
23. love; work

24. monogamous; commitment

25. 20; well educated

26. leveled off

27. higher

28. happiness; sexual satisfaction; income; health; greater

29. decrease; employed

30. increase

31. cannot

32. **c.** is the answer. Carlos' age and struggle to form a close relationship place him squarely in this stage.
   a. Trust versus mistrust is the psychosocial task of infancy.
   b. Autonomy versus doubt is the psychosocial task of toddlerhood.
   d. Identity versus role confusion is the psychosocial task of adolescence.

33. identity; confidence; self-esteem

34. positive; negative; smaller; fewer

35. amygdala; decreased

36. biopsychosocial

37. **d.** is the answer. Research has not uncovered a tendency for people of any particular age group to report greater feelings of satisfaction or well-being.

38. suddenly and before its expected time on the social clock

39. do; do not

40. do not

41. integrity

Module Review:

42. **d.** is the answer.
   a. Generativity is associated with middle adulthood.
   b. & c. Intimacy and isolation are associated with young adulthood.

43. **a.** is the answer.
   b., c., & d. These cognitive abilities remain essentially unchanged as the person ages.

44. **d.** is the answer. "Use it or lose it" seems to be the rule: Often, changes in activity patterns contribute significantly to problems regarded as being part of usual aging.
   a. Most older people suffer some memory loss but remember some events very well.
   b. Although older people are more subject to long-term ailments than younger adults, they actually suffer fewer short-term ailments.
   c. People of all ages report equal happiness or satisfaction with life.

45. **b.** is the answer.

46. **a.** is the answer.
   b. This answer describes the longitudinal research method.
   c. Cross-sectional studies compare people of different ages throughout the life span, generally beginning after the person is able to verbalize.
   d. Cross-sectional studies do not deal with social development.

47. **c.** is the answer. Different societies and eras have somewhat different ideas about the age at which major life events should ideally occur.

48. **d.** is the answer.
   a., b., & c. Most couples do not feel a loss of purpose or marital strain following the departure of grown children.

49. **a.** is the answer.

50. **d.** is the answer.

51. **d.** is the answer.

Terms and Concepts to Remember:

52. **Menopause** is the cessation of menstruation and typically occurs within a few years of age 50. It also refers to the biological changes experienced during a woman's years of declining ability to reproduce.

53. In a **cross-sectional study,** people of different ages are compared with one another.

54. In a **longitudinal study,** the same people are tested and retested over a period of years.

55. The **social clock** refers to the culturally preferred timing of social events, such as leaving home, marrying, having children, and retiring.

Before You Move On

True–False Items

1. F	5. F	9. F
2. F	6. F	10. F
3. F	7. T	
4. T	8. F	

Cross-Check

ACROSS	DOWN
3. fetus	1. autism
4. accommodation	2. assimilation
6. imprinting	5. conservation
9. embryo	7. cross-sectional
11. schema	8. zygote
13. menarche	10. teratogen
14. longitudinal	12. habituation

Sex, Gender, and Sexuality

Overview

Module 14 explores how genes and environment interact to shape both the biological and social aspects of our gender. In the end, the message is clear: Our genes and our experience together form who we are.

Module 15 discusses human sexuality, including the sexual response cycle, how hormones influence sexual motivation, and the impact of external and imagined stimuli on sexual arousal. Sexually transmitted infections and adolescents' use of contraceptives are also explored. Sexual motivation in men and women is triggered less by physiological factors and more by external incentives. Even so, research studies demonstrate that sexual orientation is neither willfully chosen nor easily changed. An evolutionary explanation of gender differences and mating preferences points out that male and female traits are selected because they contribute to survival and reproduction.

Module 15 concludes with reflections on nature–nurture interactions in sex, gender, and sexuality.

NOTE: Answer guidelines for all Module 14 and 15 questions begin on page 122.

Outline

Instructions

First, skim each section, noting headings and boldface items. After you have read the section, review each objective by answering the fill-in, essay-type, and multiple-choice questions for that section. In some cases, Study Tips explain how best to learn a difficult concept and Applications and Module Reviews help you to know how well you understand the material. Finally, try to define the important terms and concepts using your own words. As you proceed, evaluate your performance by consulting the answers on page 122. Do not continue until you understand each answer. If you need to, review or reread a troublesome section before continuing.

Before You Move On includes activities that test you on material from the entire unit.

MODULE 14 Gender Development

Objective 14-1: Explain how the meaning of *gender* differs from the meaning of *sex*.

1. The biologically influenced characteristics by which people define *males* and *females* constitute _____ , which is defined by their _____ and _____ .

2. The learned and socially influenced characteristics by which people define *men* and *women* constitute _____ . These characteristics are the product of the interplay among our _____ _____ , our _____ _____ , and our current situations.

How Are We Alike? How Do We Differ?

Objective 14-2: Describe some ways in which males and females tend to be alike and to differ.

3. Among your _____ (how many?) chromosomes, _____ (how many?) are unisex.

4. Compared with the average man, the average woman enters puberty 2 years _____ (earlier/later) than the average man and lives 5 years _____ (more/less). She also expresses _____ more freely and can detect fainter _____ , for example. Women are more likely than men to suffer from _____ , _____ , and _____ .

5. Compared with women, men are more likely to commit _____ and to suffer _____ _____ . They are also more likely to be diagnosed with _____ _____ _____ , _____ - _____ , _____ , _____ - _____ / _____ , and _____ , and _____ _____ .

6. *Aggression* is defined as _____ or _____ behavior that is _____ to hurt someone physically or emotionally.

7. Although men are more likely to commit more extreme _____ violence, women are slightly more likely to commit _____ aggression.

8. Throughout the world, men are more likely than women to engage in _____ , _____ , _____ , and _____ _____ .

9. Compared with women, in most societies men place more importance on _____ and _____ and are socially _____ . As leaders, they tend to be more _____ , while women are more _____ .

10. When interacting, men have been more likely to offer _____ , the _____ , women to express _____ .

11. In everyday behavior, men talk assertively, _____ , initiating _____ , and _____ . And they smile and _____ less.

12. The difference in social connectedness is noticeable in how children _____ , and it continues throughout the teen and adult years. Girls play in groups that are _____ and less _____ than boys' groups. In late adolescence, they spend more time on _____ - _____ websites. In other words, males tend to be _____ , and females tend to be _____ .

13. Brain scans suggest that women's brains are better wired to improve _____ _____ , and men's brains to connect _____ _____ _____ .

14. Both men and women have reported their friendships with women as more _____ , enjoyable, and _____ .

15. Women tend and befriend—for example, they turn to others for _____ , especially when coping with _____ .

16. Gender differences in power, connectedness, and other traits peak in late _____ and early _____ . By age 50, most parent-related gender differences have _____ (decreased/increased).

APPLICATION:

17. Mackenzie and Zachary live next door to Ella and Michael. They've become good friends, and every Sunday they get together for dinner. Zachary and Michael discuss the best way to clean their roofs, demonstrating the male tendency to _____ _____ . Mackenzie and Ella talk about how to make their new neighbors feel welcome, demonstrating the female tendency to _____ _____ .

The Nature of Gender: Our Biological Sex

Objective 14-3: Explain how sex hormones influence prenatal and adolescent sexual development, and describe a *disorder of sexual development*.

18. The twenty-third pair of chromosomes determines the developing person's _____ . The mother always contributes a(n) _____ chromosome. When the father contributes a(n) _____ chromosome, the testes begin producing the hormone _____ . In about the _____ (what week?), this hormone initiates the development of male sex organs. Females _____ (do/do not) have this hormone.

19. Sex chromosomes control _____ that influence the brain's wiring.

20. Adolescence begins with the time of developing sexual maturity known as _____ . A two-year period of rapid physical development begins in girls at about the age of _____ and in boys at about the age of _____ . This growth spurt is marked by the development of the reproductive organs and external genitalia, or _____ _____ characteristics, as well as by the development of traits such as pubic hair and enlarged breasts in females and facial hair in males. These nonreproductive traits are known as _____ _____ characteristics.

21. The first menstrual period is called _____ . Genes play a major role in age of onset. Environment also matters. Early onset is more likely following stresses related to _____ _____ , sexual _____ , insecure _____ , or a history of a mother's smoking during pregnancy.

22. In boys, the first ejaculation is called _____ , which usually occurs during sleep by about age _____ .

23. The inherited condition involving the unusual development of sex chromosomes and anatomy results in a _____ _____ _____ . In the past, medical professionals often recommended _____-_____ for some children with this condition.

The Nurture of Gender: Our Culture and Experiences

Objective 14-4: Describe how gender roles and gender identity differ.

24. The social expectations about the way men and women behave define our culture's _____ .

25. Gender roles _____ (are/are not) rigidly fixed by evolution, as evidenced by the fact that they vary across _____ and over _____ . For instance, in _____ societies there tends to be minimal division of labor by sex; by contrast, in _____ societies, women remain close to home while men roam freely, herding cattle or sheep.

26. Our personal sense of being male, female, or, occasionally, some combination of the two is called our _____ . The degree to which we exhibit traditionally male or female traits and interests is called _____ .

27. According to _____ _____ theory, children learn gender-linked behaviors by observing and imitating others and being rewarded or punished for acting in certain ways. Even when their families discourage traditional gender behavior, some children _____ (do/do not) organize themselves into "boy worlds" and "girl worlds." Others seem to prefer a blend of male and female roles, or _____ . These people tend to be more _____ . They tend to be more resilient and _____ , and they experience less _____ .

28. Children also learn from their _____ _____ what it means to be male or female and adjust their behavior accordingly, thereby demonstrating that _____ is important in the formation of gender identity.

29. People who are _____ have a sense of being male or female that differs from their birth sex. Some of these people are also _____ : They prefer to live as members of the other birth sex.

APPLICATIONS:

30. Rod has always felt pressure to be the driver when traveling in a car with Sue because he learned that this was expected of men. Rod's feelings illustrate the influence of
    a. chromosomes.
    b. gender roles.
    c. puberty.
    d. androgyny.

31. Pat and Alex have been married for about 10 years. During that time, Alex is the one most likely to spend less time at work, more time with household chores, and more time caring for the very young and the very old. Alex is most likely _____ (male/female).

32. When his son cries because another child has taken his favorite toy, Brandon admonishes him by saying, "Big boys don't cry." Evidently, Brandon is an advocate of _____ _____ in accounting for the development of gender-linked behaviors.

33. Three-year-old Caleb shares a toy chest with his 18-month-old sister Elena. Caleb has put all cars, trucks, and superheros to his side of the chest and all the dolls, stuffed animals, and miniature furniture to Elena's side. Caleb has clearly formed a _____ _____ about gender-linked behaviors.

34. Four-year-old Sarah, who has very specific ideas about what it means to be female and frequently adjusts her behavior accordingly, is demonstrating the importance of _____ in the formation of gender identity.
    a. gender schemas
    b. androgyny
    c. genes
    d. menarche

MODULE REVIEW:

35. *Gender* refers to
    a. the socially influenced characteristics by which people define *men* and *women*.
    b. the biologically influenced characteristics by which people define *male* and *female*.
    c. one's sense of being male or female.
    d. the extent to which one exhibits traditionally male or female traits.

36. The fertilized egg will develop into a boy if, at conception,
    a. the sperm contributes an X chromosome.
    b. the sperm contributes a Y chromosome.
    c. the egg contributes an X chromosome.
    d. the egg contributes a Y chromosome.

37. The hormone testosterone
    a. is found only in females.
    b. determines the sex of the developing person.
    c. stimulates growth of the female sex organs.
    d. stimulates growth of the male sex organs.

38. Androgynous children tend to
    a. be more resilient and self-accepting.
    b. be traditionally masculine or feminine.
    c. exhibit less flexible gender roles.
    d. suffer from depression.

39. Some children who are raised by parents who discourage traditional gender typing
    a. are less likely to display gender-typed behaviors themselves.
    b. often become confused and develop an ambiguous gender identity.

c. nevertheless organize themselves into "girl worlds" and "boy worlds."

d. display excessively masculine and feminine traits as adults.

40. Genetically male children who underwent sex-reassignment surgery and were raised as girls later

a. all described themselves as female.

b. all described themselves as male.

c. all had an unclear sexual identity.

d. described themselves either as female or male, or had an unclear sexual identity.

TERMS AND CONCEPTS TO REMEMBER:

41. sex

42. gender

43. aggression

44. relational aggression

45. X chromosome

46. Y chromosome

47. testosterone

48. puberty

49. primary sex characteristics

50. secondary sex characteristics

51. spermarche

52. menarche

53. disorder of sexual development

54. role

55. gender role

56. gender identity

57. social learning theory

58. gender typing

59. androgyny

60. transgender

MODULE
15   Human Sexuality

The Physiology of Sex

Objective 15-1: Describe how hormones influence human sexual motivation.

1. In most mammals, females are sexually receptive only during ovulation, when the hormones,

called _____ (such as _____), have peaked.

2. The importance of the hormone _____ to male sexual arousal is confirmed by the fact that sexual interest declines in animals if their _____ are removed. In women, low levels of the hormone _____ may cause a waning of sexual interest.

3. Hormones affect human sexual behavior _____ (as much as/more than/less than) they do other mammals. Among women with mates, sexual desire rises slightly at _____, when there is a surge of _____ and a smaller surge of _____.

4. Hormone levels surge or decline at two predictable times in the life span: the _____ surge triggers the development of sex _____ and sexual interest, and in _____ (middle adulthood/ late adulthood), _____ levels fall, and women experience _____. A third hormone shift may occur as a result of _____ or _____.

Objective 15-2: Describe the human sexual response cycle, and explain how sexual dysfunctions and paraphilias differ.

5. The two researchers who identified a four-stage sexual response cycle are _____ and _____. In order, the stages of the cycle are the _____ phase, the _____ phase, _____, and the _____ phase. During resolution, males experience a _____ _____, during which they are incapable of another orgasm.

6. Problems that consistently impair sexual arousal or functioning are called _____ _____. Examples of such problems include _____ _____ , _____ _____, and _____ _____.

7. When a person's sexual arousal is from fantasies, behaviors, or urges involving nonhuman objects, the suffering of self or others, and/or nonconsenting persons, it is called a _____ . Examples include _____ , _____ , and _____ .

Objective 15-3: Explain how sexually transmitted infections can be prevented.

8. Every day, more than 1 million people worldwide acquire a _____ _____ _____ . Teenage girls, because of their not yet fully mature biological development and lower levels of protective _____ , may be especially vulnerable to STIs.

9. Condoms are about _____ percent effective in preventing transmission of _____ —the virus that causes _____ .

10. Rates of AIDS are increasing fastest in _____ (women/men).

11. Oral sex _____ (has/has not) been linked to the transmission of STIs, such as the _____ _____ .

12. One factor that increases the risk of STI transmission from oral sex is the _____ _____ .

The Psychology of Sex

Objective 15-4: Describe how external and imagined stimuli contribute to sexual arousal.

13. Although both men and women are aroused by erotic stimuli, _____ (men's/women's) feelings of sexual arousal have much more closely mirrored their genital response than have _____ (men's/women's).

14. With repeated exposure, the emotional response to an erotic stimulus often _____ .

Explain some of the possible harmful consequences of sexually explicit material.

15. Most women and men _____ (have/do not have) sexual fantasies. Compared with women's fantasies, men's sexual fantasies are more _____ _____ . Sexual fantasies _____ (do/do not) indicate sexual problems or dissatisfaction.

Objective 15-5: Discuss the factors that influence teenagers' sexual behaviors and use of contraceptives.

16. Compared with European teens, American teens have _____ (higher/lower) rates of teen pregnancy and _____ (higher/lower) rates of STIs.

17. Teens attend to other teens, who, in turn, are influenced by popular media. Media help write the _____ _____ that affect their perceptions and actions.

State four factors that influence teen sexual behaviors.

18. (caption) Most characters in top-selling video games are _____ (males/females). The _____ (male/female) characters in video games are likely to be _____ , which means that they are _____ _____ . Such depictions contribute to the early _____ of girls, which leads to _____ _____ about sexuality.

State several predictors of sexual restraint (reduced teen sexuality and pregnancy).

19. Which of the following was NOT identified as an influence on teenagers' sexual behavior?

    a. alcohol use
    b. thrill-seeking
    c. mass media sexual norms
    d. guilt

20. Which of the following teens is most likely to delay the initiation of sex?

    a. Jack, who has below-average intelligence
    b. Jason, who is not religiously active
    c. Ron, who regularly volunteers his time in community service
    d. It is impossible to predict.

Sexual Orientation

Objective 15-6: Summarize what research has taught us about sexual orientation.

21. A person's sexual attraction toward members of a particular sex is referred to as _____ _____ .

    Attraction to members of our own sex is a _____ orientation, to the opposite sex is a _____ orientation, and to both sexes is a _____ orientation.

22. Studies in Europe and the United States indicate that approximately _____ percent of men and _____ percent of women are exclusively homosexual. This finding suggests that popular estimates of the rate of homosexuality are _____ (high/low/accurate).

23. Some homosexuals struggle with their sexual orientation. Without social support, the result may be lower _____ and higher _____ and depression, as well as an increased risk of contemplating _____ .

24. A person's sexual orientation _____ (does/does not) appear to be voluntarily chosen. Several research studies reveal that sexual orientation among _____ (women/men) tends to be less strongly felt and potentially more changeable than among the other sex. This phenomenon has been called a difference in _____ _____ .

25. Childhood events and family relationships _____ (are/are not) important factors in determining a person's sexual orientation. Also, homosexuality _____ (does/does not) involve a fear of the other sex that leads people to direct their sexual desires toward members of their own sex.

26. Sex hormone levels _____ (do/do not) predict sexual orientation.

27. As children, most homosexuals _____ (were/were not) sexually victimized.

28. Same-sex attraction _____ (does/does not) occur in other species.

29. Researcher Simon LeVay discovered a cluster of cells in the _____ that is larger in _____ men than in all others.

30. Gays and lesbians differ from their straight counterparts in their preference for sex-related _____ .

31. Studies of twins suggest that genes probably _____ (do/do not) play a role in homosexuality. Research has confirmed that homosexual men have more homosexual relatives on their _____ (mother's/father's) side than on their _____ (mother's/father's) side, which is called the _____ _____ . However, because sexual orientation differs in some _____ _____ , other factors might also be at work.

32. Sexual orientation has been altered by abnormal _____ conditions during prenatal development. In humans, prenatal exposure to hormone levels typical of _____ , particularly between the _____ _____ , may predispose an attraction to males.

33. Men who have older brothers are somewhat _____ (more/less) likely to be gay. This phenomenon, which has been called the _____ _____-_____ _____ , may represent a defensive maternal _____ response to substances produced by _____ (male/female) fetuses.

34. Gays and lesbians may have certain physical traits that fall midway between straight males and females, including their scores on tests of _____ _____ .

35. The consistency of brain, genetic, and prenatal findings suggests that _____ plays the larger role in predisposing sexual orientation, which explains why sexual orientation is _____ (difficult/relatively easy) to change.

APPLICATION:

36. Summarizing his presentation on the origins of homosexuality, Dennis explains that the fraternal birth-order effect refers to the fact that
   a. men who have younger brothers are somewhat more likely to be gay.
   b. men who have older brothers are somewhat more likely to be gay.
   c. women with older sisters are somewhat more likely to be gay.
   d. women with younger sisters are somewhat more likely to be gay.

An Evolutionary Explanation of Human Sexuality

Objective 15-7: Discuss how an evolutionary psychologist might explain male-female differences in sexuality and mating preferences.

37. Compared with women, men think _____ (equally/more/less) about sex, and they are _____ (equally/more/less) likely to initiate sexual activity.

38. The _____ explanation of male-female differences in attitudes toward sex is based on differences in the optimal strategy by which women and men pass on their _____ . According to this view, men and women _____ (are/are not) selected for different patterns of sexuality.

39. Research reveals that men judge women as more attractive if they have a _____ appearance, which conveys _____ and _____ ; whereas women judge men who appear _____ , _____ , _____ , and _____ as more attractive.

Objective 15-8: List the key criticisms of evolutionary explanations of human sexuality, and describe how evolutionary psychologists respond.

40. Critics of the evolutionary explanation of the gender sexuality difference argue that it often works _____ (forward/backward) to explain what happened.

41. Other critics invoke _____ _____ theory to explain human sexuality, suggesting that people learn _____ _____ for how they should act in certain situations.

42. A third criticism points to the potential social _____ of accepting an evolutionary explanation, such as excusing men's sexual aggression.

43. Evolutionary psychologists counter the criticisms by noting that the sexes, having faced similar adaptive problems, are more _____ (alike/different) than they are _____ (alike/different). They also note that evolutionary principles offer testable _____ .

Social Influences on Human Sexuality

Objective 15-9: Describe the role that social factors play in our sexuality, and discuss how nature, nurture, and our own choices influence gender roles and sexuality.

44. The study of sexual behavior and what motivates it _____ (can/cannot) be free of values. How we label a behavior depends on our _____ toward that behavior. Labels describe, but they also _____ .

45. Those whose relationship first developed to a deep commitment, such as marriage, not only reported greater _____ _____ and stability but also better _____ .

Reflections on the Nature and Nurture of Sex, Gender, and Sexuality

46. As brute strength becomes _____ (more/less) relevant to power and status, gender roles are _____ (converging/diverging).

47. We are the product of both _____ and _____ , but we are also a system that is _____ . We know this because a _____ approach to development shows that no single factor is all-powerful.

MODULE REVIEW:

48. Some scientific evidence makes a preliminary link between homosexuality and
    a. late sexual maturation.
    b. the age of an individual's first erotic experience.
    c. atypical prenatal hormones.
    d. early problems in relationships with parents.

49. The correct order of the stages of Masters and Johnson's sexual response cycle is
    a. plateau; excitement; orgasm; resolution.
    b. excitement; plateau; orgasm; resolution.
    c. excitement; orgasm; resolution; refractory.
    d. plateau; excitement; orgasm; refractory.

50. Which of the following is NOT true regarding sexual orientation?
    a. Sexual orientation is neither willfully chosen nor willfully changed.
    b. Some homosexuals struggle with their sexual orientation.
    c. Men's sexual orientation is potentially more fluid and changeable than women's.
    d. Women, regardless of sexual orientation, respond to both female and male erotic stimuli.

51. Castration of male rats results in
    a. reduced testosterone and sexual interest.
    b. reduced testosterone, but no change in sexual interest.
    c. reduced estradiol and sexual interest.
    d. reduced estradiol, but no change in sexual interest.

52. Exposure of a fetus to the hormones typical of females during the _____ may predispose the developing human to become attracted to males.
    a. first trimester
    b. second trimester
    c. third trimester
    d. entire pregnancy

53. Which of the following statements concerning homosexuality is true?
    a. Homosexuals have abnormal hormone levels.
    b. As children, most homosexuals were molested by an adult homosexual.
    c. Homosexuals had a domineering opposite-sex parent.
    d. Research indicates that sexual orientation may be at least partly physiological.

54. According to Masters and Johnson, the sexual response of males is most likely to differ from that of females during
    a. the excitement phase.
    b. the plateau phase.
    c. orgasm.
    d. the resolution phase.

55. Through natural selection, the traits that are most likely to be passed on to succeeding generations are those that contribute to
    a. temperament.   c. aggressiveness.
    b. survival.   d. social scripts.

56. Which of the following is NOT true regarding the sexuality of men and women?
    a. Men more often than women attribute a woman's friendliness to sexual interest.
    b. Women are more likely than men to cite affection as a reason for first intercourse.
    c. Men are more likely than women to initiate sexual activity.
    d. Male-female differences in sexuality are noticeably absent among gay men and lesbian women.

57. Evolutionary psychologists attribute male-female differences in sexuality to the fact that women have
    a. greater reproductive potential than do men.
    b. lower reproductive potential than do men.
    c. weaker sex drives than men.
    d. stronger sex drives than men.

58. According to evolutionary psychology, men are drawn sexually to women who seem _____ , while women are attracted to men who seem _____ .
    a. nurturing; youthful
    b. youthful and fertile; mature and affluent
    c. slender; muscular
    d. exciting; dominant

59. Evolutionary explanations of male-female differences in sexuality have been criticized because
    a. they offer "after-the-fact" explanations.
    b. standards of attractiveness vary with time and place.
    c. they underestimate cultural influences on sexuality.
    d. of all of these reasons.

60. An evolutionary psychologist would be most interested in studying
   a. why most parents are so passionately devoted to their children.
   b. hereditary influences on skin color.
   c. why certain diseases are more common among certain age groups.
   d. genetic differences in personality.

Essay Question

Lakia's new boyfriend has been pressuring her to become more sexually intimate than she wants to be at this early stage in their relationship. Strongly "macho" in attitude, Jerome is becoming increasingly frustrated with Lakia's hesitation, while Lakia is starting to wonder if a long-term relationship with this type of man is what she really wants. In light of your understanding of the evolutionary explanation of gender differences in sexuality, explain why the tension between Lakia and Jerome would be considered understandable.

TERMS AND CONCEPTS TO REMEMBER:

61. asexual

62. estrogens

63. sexual response cycle

64. refractory period

65. sexual dysfunction

66. erectile disorder

67. female orgasmic disorder

68. paraphilias

69. AIDS (acquired immune deficiency syndrome)

70. social script

71. sexual orientation

Before You Move On

Matching Items

Match each term with its corresponding definition or description.

Terms

_____ 1. X chromosome
_____ 2. Y chromosome
_____ 3. gender role
_____ 4. gender identity
_____ 5. gender typing
_____ 6. transgender
_____ 7. primary sex characteristics
_____ 8. secondary sex characteristics

Functions or Descriptions

a. one's personal sense of being female, male, or some combination of the two
b. nonreproductive sexual traits
c. a term used to describe people whose gender identity or expression doesn't match their birth sex
d. the acquisition of a traditional gender role
e. the sex chromosome found only in men
f. body structures that make sexual reproduction possible
g. a set of expected behaviors for males and females
h. the sex chromosome found in both women and men

True–False Items

Indicate whether each statement is true or false by placing *T* or *F* in the blank next to the item.

_____ 1. Gender differences in mate preferences vary widely from one culture to another.
_____ 2. Nature selects behavioral tendencies that aid survival and reproduction.
_____ 3. According to Masters and Johnson, only males experience a plateau period in the cycle of sexual arousal.
_____ 4. Testosterone affects the sexual arousal of the male only.
_____ 5. Unlike men, women tend not to be aroused by sexually explicit material.
_____ 6. One's sexual orientation is not voluntarily chosen.
_____ 7. Eighty percent of people in the United States think homosexuality is never justified.

Cross-Check
As you learned in Module 2, reviewing and overlearning of material are important to the learning process. After you have written the definitions of the key terms in this unit, you should complete the crossword puzzle to ensure that you can reverse the process—recognize the term, given the definition.

ACROSS

2. Hormones secreted in greater amounts by females than by males.
4. The body structures that enable reproduction are the _____ characteristics.
8. The sex chromosome found in both men and women.
10. A resting period after orgasm, during which a male cannot be aroused to another orgasm.
11. A life-threatening sexually transmitted infection caused by HIV.
12. People whose gender identity does not match their birth sex.

DOWN

1. The most important male sex hormone.
3. The socially constructed roles and characteristics by which a culture defines *male* or *female*.
4. The early adolescent period of sexual maturation.
5. The first period.
6. Masters and Johnson's four stages of sexual responding are referred to as the _____ cycle.
7. A cluster of prescribed behaviors expected of those who occupy a particular social position.
9. The acquisition of a traditional feminine or masculine is referred to as gender _____ .
13. One sense of being male or female is one's gender _____ .

Answers

1. sex; chromosomes; anatomy
2. gender; biological dispositions; developmental experiences

How Are We Alike? How Are We Different?

3. 46; 45
4. earlier; more; emotions; odors; depression; anxiety; eating disorders

5. suicide; alcohol use disorder; autism spectrum disorder; color-deficient vision; attention-deficit/hyperactivity disorder; antisocial personality disorder

6. physical; verbal; intended

7. physical; relational

8. hunting; fighting; warring; supporting war

9. power; achievement; dominant; directive; democratic

10. opinions; support

11. interrupting; touches; staring; apologize

12. play; smaller; competitive; social-network; independent; interdependent

13. social relationships; perception with action

14. intimate; nurturing

15. support; stress

16. adolescence; adulthood; decreased

17. communicate solutions; explore relationships

The Nature of Gender: Our Biological Sex

18. sex; X; Y; testosterone; seventh; do

19. hormones

20. puberty; 11; 12; primary sex; secondary sex

21. menarche; father absence; abuse; attachment

22. spermarche; 14

23. disorder of sexual development; sex-reassignment surgery

The Nurture of Gender: Our Culture and Experiences

24. gender roles

25. are not; time; place; nomadic; agricultural

26. gender identity; gender typing

27. social learning; do; androgyny; adaptable; self-accepting; depression

28. gender schemas; thinking

29. transgender; transsexual

30. **b.** is the answer.

31. female

32. gender typing

33. gender schema

34. **a.** is the answer.
    b. *Androgyny* refers to a blend of male and female roles.
    c. Genes apply to inherited characteristics. Here, we are talking about learned behavior.
    d. Menarche is the female's first menstrual period.

Module Review:

35. **a.** is the answer.
    b. This defines a person's sex.
    c. This defines gender identity.
    d. This defines gender typing.

36. **b.** is the answer.
    a. In this case, a female would develop.
    c. & d. The egg can contribute only an X chromosome. Thus, the sex of the child is determined by which chromosome the sperm contributes.

37. **d.** is the answer.
    a. Although testosterone is the principal male hormone, it is present in both females and males.
    b. This is determined by the sex chromosomes.
    c. In the absence of testosterone, female sex organs will develop.

38. **a.** is the answer.

39. **c.** is the answer.
    b. & d. There is no evidence that being raised in a "gender neutral" home confuses children or fosters a backlash of excessive gender typing.

40. **d.** is the answer. Some later described themselves as female, and some as male.

Terms and Concepts to Remember:

41. In psychology, **sex** refers to the biologically influenced characteristics by which people define *male* and *female*.

42. In psychology, **gender** refers to the socially influenced characteristics by which people define *men* and *women*.

43. **Aggression** is physical or verbal behavior intended to hurt someone physically or emotionally.

44. **Relational aggression** is physical or verbal behavior intended to harm a person's relationship or social standing.

45. The **X chromosome** is the sex chromosome found in both men and women. Females inherit an X chromosome from each parent.

46. The **Y chromosome** is the sex chromosome found only in men. Males inherit an X chromosome from their mothers and a Y chromosome from their fathers.

47. **Testosterone** is the most important male sex hormone. During prenatal development, testosterone stimulates the development of the male sex organs. During puberty, it stimulates the development of the male sex characteristics.

48. **Puberty** is the early adolescent period of sexual maturation, during which a person becomes capable of reproducing.

49. The **primary sex characteristics** are the body structures (ovaries, testes, and external genitalia) that enable reproduction.

50. The **secondary sex characteristics** are the non-reproductive sexual characteristics, for example, female breasts, male voice quality, and body hair.

51. **Spermarche** is the first ejaculation.

52. **Menarche** is the first menstrual period.

53. A **disorder of sexual development** is an inherited condition involving unusual development of sex chromosomes and anatomy.

54. A **role** is a cluster of prescribed behaviors expected of those who occupy a particular social position.

55. A **gender role** is a set of expected behaviors for males or for females.

56. **Gender identity** is one's sense of being male, female, or some combination of the two.

57. According to **social learning theory,** people learn social behavior (such as gender roles) by observing and imitating and by being rewarded or punished for acting a certain way.

58. **Gender typing** is the acquisition of a traditional feminine or masculine role.

59. **Androgyny** is displaying both traditional feminine and masculine characteristics.

60. **Transgender** refers to people whose gender identity or expression differs from that associated with their birth sex.

MODULE 15   Human Sexuality

The Physiology of Sex

1. estrogens; estradiol

2. testosterone; testes; testosterone

3. less than; ovulation; estrogens; testosterone

4. pubertal; characteristics; late adulthood, estrogen; menopause; surgery; drugs

5. William Masters; Virginia Johnson; excitement; plateau; orgasm; resolution; refractory period

6. sexual dysfunctions; premature ejaculation; erectile disorder; female orgasmic disorder

7. paraphilia; exhibitionism; necrophilia; pedophilia

8. sexually transmitted infection (STI); antibodies

9. 80; HIV; AIDS

10. women

11. has; human papillomavirus (HPV)

12. number of sexual partners a person has

The Psychology of Sex

13. men's; women's

14. habituates

Erotic material may increase the viewer's acceptance of the false idea that women enjoy rape, may increase men's willingness to hurt women, may lead people to devalue their partners and relationships, and may diminish people's satisfaction with their own sexual partners.

15. have; often, physical, and less romantic; do not

16. higher; lower

Among the factors that influence teen sexual behaviors are (1) minimal communication about birth control, (2) guilt related to sexual activity, (3) alcohol use that influences judgment, and (4) mass media norms of unprotected promiscuity.

18. males; female; hypersexualized; partially nude or revealingly clothed, with large breasts and tiny waists; sexualization; unrealistic expectations

Teens with high intelligence test scores, those who are actively religious, those whose father is present, and those who participate in service learning programs more often delay sex.

19. b. is the answer.

20. c. is the answer.
    a., b., & d. Teens with high rather than average intelligence (therefore, not a.), and those who are religiously active (therefore, not b.) are most likely to delay sex.

Sexual Orientation

21. sexual orientation; homosexual; heterosexual; bisexual

22. 3 or 4; 2; high

23. self-esteem; anxiety; suicide

24. does not; women; erotic plasticity

25. are not; does not

26. do not

27. were not

28. does

29. hypothalamus; heterosexual

30. odors

31. do; mother's; father's; fertile female theory; twin pairs

32. hormone; females; second trimester

33. more; fraternal birth-order effect (or older brother effect); immune; male

34. spatial abilities

35. biology; difficult

36. b. is the answer.

An Evolutionary Explanation of Human Sexuality

37. more; more

38. evolutionary; genes; are

39. youthful; health; fertility; mature; dominant; bold; affluent

40. backward

41. social learning; social scripts

42. consequences

43. alike; different; predictions

Social Influences on Human Sexuality

44. cannot; attitude; evaluate

45. relationship satisfaction; sex

Reflections on the Nature and Nurture of Sex, Gender, and Sexuality

46. less; converging

47. nature; nurture; open; biopsychosocial

Module Review:

48. c. is the answer.
a., b., & d. None of these is linked to homosexuality.

49. b. is the answer.

50. c. is the answer. Research studies suggest that women's sexual orientation is potentially more fluid and changeable than men's.

51. a. is the answer.
c. & d. Castration of the testes, which produce testosterone, does not alter estrogen levels.

52. b. is the answer. The second trimester may be a critical period for the brain's neurohormonal control system. Exposure to abnormal hormonal conditions at other times has no effect on sexual orientation.

53. d. is the answer. Although the basis for sexual orientation remains unknown, recent evidence points more to a physiological basis.

54. d. is the answer. During the resolution phase males experience a refractory period.
a., b., & c. The male and female responses are very similar in each of these phases.

55. b. is the answer.

56. d. is the answer. Such differences characterize both heterosexual and homosexual people.

57. b. is the answer. Women must conceive and protect a fetus inside her body for at least nine months.

c. & d. The text does not suggest that there is a difference in the strength of the sex drive in men and women.

58. b. is the answer.
a. According to this perspective, women prefer mates with the potential for long-term nurturing investment in their joint offspring.
c. While men are drawn to women whose waists are roughly a third narrower than their hips, the text does not suggest that women equate muscularity with fertility.
d. Excitement was not mentioned as a criterion for mating.

59. d. is the answer.

60. a. is the answer. This is an example of a trait that contributes to survival of the human species and the perpetuation of one's genes.
b., c., & d. These traits and issues would likely be of greater interest to a behavior geneticist because they concern the influence of specific genes on behavior.

Essay Question

Evolutionary psychologists would not be surprised by the tension between Lakia and Jerome. Because eggs are expensive, compared with sperm, women prefer mates with the potential for long-term investment in their joint offspring. According to this perspective, this may be why Lakia is not in a hurry to become sexually intimate with Jerome. Men, on the other hand, are selected for "pairing widely" but not necessarily wisely in order to maximize the spreading of their genes. This is especially true of men like Jerome, who have traditional masculine attitudes.

Terms and Concepts to Remember:

61. A person who is **asexual** has no sexual attraction to others.

62. **Estrogens** are sex hormones, such as estradiol, secreted in greater amounts by females than by males and contributing to female sex characteristics. In mammals other than humans, estrogen levels peak during ovulation and trigger sexual receptivity.

63. The **sexual response cycle** described by Masters and Johnson consists of four stages of bodily reaction: excitement, plateau, orgasm, and resolution.

64. The **refractory period** is a resting period after orgasm, during which a male cannot be aroused to another orgasm.

65. A **sexual dysfunction** is a problem—such as erectile disorder, premature ejaculation, and female orgasmic disorder—that consistently impairs sexual arousal or functioning.

53. **Erectile disorder** is a sexual dysfunction in which a man is unable to have or maintain an erection due to insufficient bloodflow to the penis.

54. **Female orgasmic disorder** is a sexual dysfunction in which a woman feels distress over infrequently or never experiencing orgasm.

55. **Paraphilias** involve experiencing sexual arousal from fantasies, behaviors, or urges involving nonhuman objects, the suffering of self or others, and/or nonconsenting persons.

56. **AIDS** (acquired immune deficiency syndrome) is a sexually transmitted infection caused by the *human immunodeficiency virus* (HIV) that depletes the immune system, leaving a person vulnerable to life-threatening infections.

26. A **social script** is a culturally modeled guide for how to act in various situations.

57. **Sexual orientation** refers to a person's enduring attraction to members of either the same sex, the opposite sex, or both sexes.

Before You Move On

Matching Items

1. h		**5.** d	
2. e		**6.** c	
3. g		**7.** f	
4. a		**8.** b	

True–False Items

1. F		**5.** F	
2. T		**6.** T	
3. F		**7.** F	
4. F			

Cross-Check

ACROSS

2. estrogens
4. primary sex
8. X chromosome
10. refractory
11. AIDS
12. transgender

DOWN

1. testosterone
3. gender
4. puberty
5. menarche
6. sexual response
7. role
9. typing
13. identity

Sensation and Perception

Overview

Module 16 explores the processes by which our sense receptors and nervous system represent our external environment (sensation), as well as how we mentally organize and interpret this information (perception). The senses of vision, hearing, taste, touch, smell, and body position and movement are described in Modules 17 and 18. In discussing vision, the text describes the ways in which we organize stimuli in the environment to perceive form; depth; and constant shape, size, and brightness. To enhance your understanding of these processes, Module 17 also discusses research findings from studies of perceptual set, subliminal stimulation, sensory restriction, recovery from blindness, adaptation to distorted environments, and extrasensory perception.

In these modules there are many terms to learn and several theories you must understand. Many of the terms are related to the structure of the eye, ear, and other sensory receptors. Answering the fill-in, multiple-choice, and essay-type questions several times, labeling the diagrams, and rehearsing the material frequently will help you to memorize these structures and their functions. The theories discussed include the Young-Helmholtz three-color and opponent-process theories of color vision, the Gestalt theory of form perception. the place and frequency theories of hearing, and the gate-control theory of pain. As you study these theories, concentrate on understanding the strengths and weaknesses (if any) of each.

NOTE: Answer guidelines for all Modules 16–18 questions begin on page 148.

Outline

Instructions

First, skim each section, noting headings and boldface items. After you have read the section, review each objective by answering the fill-in, essay-type, and multiple-choice questions for that section. In some cases, Study Tips explain how best to learn a difficult concept and Applications and Module Reviews help you to know how well you understand the material. Finally, try to define the important terms and concepts using your own words. As you proceed, evaluate your performance by consulting the answers on page 148. Do not continue until you understand each answer. If you need to, review or reread a troublesome section before continuing.

Before You Move On includes activities that test you on material from the entire unit

Basic Concepts of Sensation and Perception

Processing Sensation and Perception

Objective 16-1: Define *sensation* and *perception*, and explain what we mean by *bottom-up processing* and *top-down processing*.

1. The perceptual disorder in which a person has lost the ability to recognize familiar faces is
_____ .

2. The process by which we receive stimulus energies from the environment and encode them as neural signals is _____ . The process by which sensations are organized and interpreted is _____ .

3. Sensory analysis, which starts at the entry level and works up, is called _____-
_____ _____ .

   Perceptual analysis, which works from our experience and expectations, is called
_____-_____
_____ .

STUDY TIP: An excellent way to study all the technical material in these modules is to organize it into a chart. For each sense you need to know several facts, including the nature of the stimulus input, the type of receptor that transmits the stimulus energy, and how the information is processed in the brain. To help you review your understanding of sensation and perception, refer often to the summary chart on page 144.

APPLICATIONS:

4. Sensation is to _____ as perception is to _____ .
   a. recognizing a stimulus; interpreting a stimulus
   b. detecting a stimulus; recognizing a stimulus
   c. interpreting a stimulus; detecting a stimulus
   d. seeing; hearing

5. Superman's eyes used _____ , while his brain used _____ .
   a. perception; sensation
   b. top-down processing; bottom-up processing
   c. bottom-up processing; top-down processing

6. Concluding her presentation on sensation and perception, Kelly notes that
   a. perception is bottom-up processing.
   b. sensation is top-down processing.
   c. without sensation there is no perception.
   d. sensation and perception blend into one continuous process.

Transduction

Objective 16-2: Identify the three steps that are basic to all our sensory systems.

7. All our senses perform three basic steps; they _____ sensory information, _____ that stimulation into neural impulses that our brain can use, and _____ that neural information to our brain.

8. The process of converting one form of energy into another that our brain can use is called _____ .

Thresholds

Objective 16-3: Distinguish between absolute thresholds and difference thresholds, and discuss what effect, if any, stimuli below the absolute threshold have on us.

9. Gustav _____ referred to the minimum stimulation necessary for a stimulus to be detected _____ percent of the time as the _____ _____ .

10. According to _____ _____ theory, a person's experience, expectations, motivation, and alertness all influence the detection of a stimulus.

11. Stimuli you cannot detect 50 percent of the time are _____ . However, under certain conditions, an invisible image or word can _____ a person's response to a later question. This illustrates that much of our information processing occurs _____ .

12. The minimum difference required to distinguish two stimuli 50 percent of the time is called the _____ _____ . Another term for this value is the _____ _____ .

13. The principle that the difference threshold is not a constant amount, but a constant proportion, is known as _____ _____ . The proportion depends on the _____ .

STUDY TIP: The concept of threshold can be confusing. Since you can count on at least one exam question on this topic, be sure you understand the concept: "Below threshold" means the stimulus is undetectable; "above threshold" means the stimulus is strong enough to be detected.

APPLICATION:

14. In shopping for a new stereo, you discover that you cannot differentiate between the sounds of models X and Y. The difference between X and Y is below your
    a. absolute threshold.
    b. subliminal threshold.
    c. receptor threshold.
    d. difference threshold.

Objective 16-4: Discuss whether subliminal sensation enables subliminal persuasion.

15. (Thinking Critically) Some entrepreneurs claim that exposure to "below threshold," or _____ , stimuli can be persuasive, but their claims are probably unwarranted. Some weak stimuli may trigger in our sensory receptors a response that is processed by the brain, even though the response doesn't cross the threshold into _____ awareness.

Sensory Adaptation

Objective 16-5: Explain the function of sensory adaptation.

16. After constant exposure to an unchanging stimulus, the receptor cells of our senses begin to fire less vigorously; this phenomenon is called
    _____ _____ .

17. This phenomenon illustrates that sensation is designed to focus on _____ changes in the environment.

18. If we stare at an object without flinching, it does not vanish because _____
    _____ .

APPLICATION:

19. Calvin usually runs his fingertips over a cloth's surface when trying to decide whether the texture is right for what he wants. By moving his fingers over the cloth, he prevents the occurrence of _____ _____ to the feel.

Perceptual Set, Context Effects, and Motivation and Emotion

Objective 16-6: Explain how our expectations, contexts, motivation, and emotions influence our perceptions.

20. Through experience we form concepts, or _____ , that organize and interpret unfamiliar information. This produces a mental predisposition that influences perception, which is called a _____
    _____ .

21. How a stimulus is perceived depends on our perceptual _____ and the _____ in which it is experienced.

22. The context of a stimulus creates a _____ (top-down/bottom-up) expectation that influences our perception as we match our _____ (top-down/bottom-up) signal against it.

23. In everyday life, our perceptions are also influenced by _____ about gender and the _____ context of our experiences.

24. Our perceptions are also directed by our _____ , as when a water bottle appears closer if we are thirsty.

APPLICATION:

25. Although carpenter Smith perceived a briefly viewed object as a screwdriver, police officer Wesson perceived the same object as a knife. This illustrates that perception is guided by
    a. bottom-up processing.
    b. sensory adaptation.
    c. transduction.
    d. perceptual set.

MODULE REVIEW:

26. Which of the following is true?
    a. The absolute threshold for any stimulus is a constant.
    b. The absolute threshold for any stimulus varies somewhat.
    c. The absolute threshold is defined as the minimum amount of stimulation necessary for a stimulus to be detected 75 percent of the time.
    d. The absolute threshold is the minimum amount of stimulation necessary for a stimulus to be detected 60 percent of the time.

27. If you can just notice the difference between 10- and 11-pound weights, which of the following weights could you differentiate from a 100-pound weight?
    a. 101-pound weight
    b. 105-pound weight
    c. 110-pound weight
    d. There is no basis for prediction.

28. A decrease in sensory responsiveness accompanying an unchanging stimulus is called
    a. sensory fatigue.
    b. bottom-up processing.
    c. sensory adaptation.
    d. transduction.

29. Which of the following is an example of sensory adaptation?
    a. finding the cold water of a swimming pool warmer after you have been in it for a while
    b. developing an increased sensitivity to salt the more you use it in foods
    c. becoming very irritated at the continuing sound of a dripping faucet
    d. All of these are examples.

30. _____ processing refers to how the physical characteristics of stimuli influence their interpretation.
    a. Top-down   c. Signal detection
    b. Bottom-up   d. Absolute threshold

31. The study of perception is primarily concerned with how we
    a. detect sights, sounds, and other stimuli.
    b. sense environmental stimuli.
    c. develop sensitivity to illusions.
    d. interpret sensory stimuli.

32. Which of the following influences perception?
    a. biological maturation
    b. the context in which stimuli are perceived
    c. expectations
    d. all of these factors

33. The process by which sensory information is converted into neural energy is
    a. sensory adaptation.   c. the threshold.
    b. signal detection.   d. transduction.

34. Weber's law states that
    a. the absolute threshold for any stimulus is a constant.
    b. the jnd for any stimulus is a constant.
    c. the absolute threshold for any stimulus is a constant proportion.

    d. the jnd for any stimulus is a constant proportion.

35. Concerning the evidence for subliminal stimulation, which of the following is the best answer?
    a. The brain processes some information without our awareness.
    b. Stimuli too weak to cross our thresholds for awareness may trigger a response in our sense receptors.
    c. Because the absolute threshold is a statistical average, we are able to detect weaker stimuli some of the time.
    d. All of these statements are true.

36. The phenomenon that refers to the ways in which an individual's expectations influence perception is called
    a. perceptual set.
    b. signal detection.
    c. bottom-up processing.
    d. sensory adaptation.

37. _____ processing refers to how our knowledge and expectations influence perception.
    a. Top-down   c. Signal detection
    b. Bottom-up   d. Sensory adaptive

38. Given normal sensory ability, a person standing atop a mountain on a dark, clear night can see a candle flame atop a mountain 30 miles away. This is a description of vision's
    a. difference threshold.   c. absolute threshold.
    b. jnd.   d. feature detection.

TERMS AND CONCEPTS TO REMEMBER:

39. sensation

40. perception

41. bottom-up processing

42. top-down processing

43. transduction

44. absolute threshold

45. signal detection theory

46. subliminal

47. priming

48. difference threshold

49. Weber's law

50. sensory adaptation

51. perceptual set

MODULE 17 Vision: Sensory and Perceptual Processing

Light Energy and Eye Structures

Objective 17-1: Describe the characteristics of the energy that we see as visible light, and identify the structures in the eye that help focus that energy.

1. The visible spectrum of light is a small portion of the larger spectrum of _____ energy.

2. The distance from one light wave peak to the next is called _____ . This value determines the wave's color, or _____ .

3. The amount of energy in light waves, or _____ , determined by a wave's _____ , or height, influences the _____ of a light.

STUDY TIP: The stimulus energy for vision can be described as a traveling wave that varies in wavelength and amplitude. The wavelength of a visual stimulus is measured as the distance from the peak of one wave to the next—the shorter the distance, the greater the frequency of the waves. Short, high frequency waves produce "cool" or bluish colors for visual stimuli. Long, low frequency waves produce "warm" or reddish colors.

The wave's amplitude is measured as the distance from the top of its peak to the bottom. High amplitude waves produce bright colors, while low amplitude waves produce dull colors.

To test your understanding, take a look at these two waves.

4. Assuming that these two waves were light energy, would they differ in appearance? How so?

---

5. Light enters the eye through the _____ , then passes through a small opening called the _____ ; the size of this opening is controlled by the colored muscle, the _____ . This muscle also respond to our _____ and emotional states.

6. By changing its curvature, the _____ can focus the image of an object onto the _____ , the light-sensitive inner surface of the eye. The process by which the lens changes shape to focus images is called _____ .

7. The retina receives an inverted mirror image in the form of particles of _____ _____ , which its receptor cells convert into _____ _____ that they send to the brain, where a complete image is assembled. Along the way, visual information percolates through progressively more _____ levels.

Information Processing in the Eye and Brain

Objective 17-2: Describe how rods and cones process information, as well as the path information travels from the eye to the brain.

8. The retina's receptor cells are the _____ and _____ .

9. The light energy in the rods and cones triggers _____ changes that would spark _____ signals, activating nearby _____ cells, which then activate a network of _____ cells.

10. The axons of ganglion cells converge to form the _____ _____ , which carries the visual information to the _____ . In the brain, the information first goes to the _____ , which distributes it to travels to the _____ _____ .

11. Where this nerve leaves the eye, there are no receptors; thus, the area is called the _____ .

12. Most cones are clustered around the retina's point of central focus, called the _____ , whereas the rods are concentrated in more _____ regions of the retina. Many cones have their own _____ cells to communicate with the visual cortex. Rods _____ (do/do not) have direct links.

13. It is the _____ (rods/cones) of the eye that permit the perception of color, whereas _____ (rods/cones) enable black-and-white vision. Rods are also sensitive to _____ .

14. Unlike cones, in dim light the rods are _____ (sensitive/insensitive). Adapting to a darkened room will take the retina approximately _____ minutes.

APPLICATIONS:

15. To maximize your sensitivity to fine visual detail you should
    a. stare off to one side of the object you are attempting to see.
    b. close one eye.
    c. decrease the intensity of the light falling upon the object.
    d. stare directly at the object.

16. Which of the following is true of cones?
    a. Cones enable color vision.
    b. Cones are highly concentrated in the foveal region of the retina.
    c. Cones have a higher absolute threshold for brightness than rods.
    d. All of these statements are true.

17. Assuming that the visual systems of humans and other mammals function similarly, you would expect that the retina of a nocturnal mammal (one active only at night) would contain
    a. mostly cones.
    b. mostly rods.
    c. an equal number of rods and cones.
    d. more bipolar cells than an animal active only during the day.

18. As the football game continued into the night, LeVar noticed that he was having difficulty distinguishing the colors of the players' uniforms. This is because the _____ , which enable color vision, have a _____ absolute threshold for brightness than the available light intensity.
    a. rods; higher   c. rods; lower
    b. cones; higher   d. cones; lower

Objective 17-3: Describe how we perceive color in the world around us.

19. An object appears to be red in color because it _____ the long wavelengths of red and because of our mental _____ of the color.

20. One out of every 50 people is color deficient; this is usually a male because the defect is genetically _____ .

21. According to the _____- _____ _____ theory, the eyes have three types of color receptors: one reacts most strongly to _____ , one to _____ , and one to _____ .

22. After staring at a green square for a while, you will see the color red, its _____ color, as an _____ .

23. Hering's theory of color vision is called the _____-_____ theory. According to this theory, color vision is enabled by three sets of opponent retinal processes: _____ versus _____ , _____ versus _____ , and _____ versus _____ .
Summarize the two stages of color processing.

APPLICATIONS:

24. I am a cell in the thalamus that is excited by red and inhibited by green. I am a(n)
    a. rod.
    b. cone.
    c. bipolar cell.
    d. opponent-process cell.

25. After staring at a very intense red stimulus for a few minutes, Carrie shifted her gaze to a beige wall and "saw" the color _____ . Carrie's experience provides support for the _____ theory.
    a. green; trichromatic
    b. blue; opponent-process
    c. green; opponent-process
    d. blue; trichromatic

Objective 17-4: Describe the location and function of the feature detectors.

26. As noted earlier, visual information is routed by the _____ to higher-level brain areas. Hubel and Wiesel discovered that certain neurons in the _____ _____ of the brain's _____ _____ respond only to specific features of what is viewed. They called these neurons _____ _____ .

27. Feature detectors pass their information to other cortical areas, where teams of cells (_____ _____) respond to complex patterns. Research has shown that in monkey brains feaure detectors specialize in responding to a specific _____ , _____ , _____ , or _____ _____ .

Objective 17-5: Explain how the brain uses parallel processing to construct visual perceptions.

28. The brain achieves its remarkable speed in visual perception by processing several subdivisions (_____ , _____ , _____ , and color) of a stimulus _____ (simultaneously/sequentially). This procedure, called _____ _____ , may explain why people who have suffered a stroke may lose just one aspect of vision.

29. Other brain-damaged people may demonstrate _____ by responding to a stimulus that is not consciously perceived.

Perceptual Organization

Objective 17-6: Describe how Gestalt psychologists understood perceptual organization, and explain how figure-ground and grouping principles contribute to our perceptions.

30. According to the _____ school of psychology, we tend to organize a cluster of sensations into a _____ , or form.

31. When we view a scene, we see the central object, or _____ , as distinct from surrounding stimuli, or the _____ .

32. Proximity, continuity, and closure are examples of Gestalt rules of _____ .

33. The principle that we organize stimuli into smooth, continuous patterns is called _____ . The principle that we fill in gaps to create a complete, whole object is _____ . The grouping of items that are close to each other is the principle of _____ .

APPLICATION:

34. Studying the road map before her trip, Colleen had no trouble following the route of the highway she planned to travel. Colleen's ability illustrates the principle of
    a. closure.
    b. figure-ground.
    c. continuity.
    d. proximity.

Objective 17-7: Explain how we use binocular and monocular cues to perceive the world in three dimensions.

35. The ability to see objects in three dimensions despite their two-dimensional representations on our retinas is called _____ . It enables us to estimate _____ .

36. Gibson and Walk developed the _____ _____ to test depth perception in infants. They found that each species, by the time it is _____ , has the perceptual abilities it needs.

Summarize the results of Gibson and Walk's studies of depth perception.

For questions 37–45, identify the depth perception cue that is defined.

37. Any cue that requires both eyes:

_____.

38. The greater the difference between the images received by the two eyes, the nearer the object:
_____ _____. 3-D movies simulate this cue by photographing each scene with two cameras.

39. Any cue that requires either eye alone:

_____.

40. If two objects are presumed to be the same size, the one that casts a smaller retinal image is perceived as farther away:
_____ _____.

41. An object partially covered by another is seen as farther away: _____.

42. Objects lower in the visual field are seen as nearer: _____ _____.

43. As we move, objects at different distances appear to move at different rates:
_____ _____.

44. Parallel lines appear to converge in the distance:
_____ _____.

45. The dimmer of two objects seems farther away:
_____ _____
_____.

STUDY TIP: Monocular depth cues are used by either eye alone to determine the distance of objects. They include relative height and size, interposition, linear perspective, and light and shadow.

46. Test your understanding of these cues by drawing a picture (in the box in the next column) of a person on a bus or train, a fence, a house, and trees. Use each cue at least once, and in your

drawing place the objects in the following order (closest to most distant): person, fence, house, and trees.

APPLICATIONS:

47. When two familiar objects of equal size cast unequal retinal images, the object that casts the smaller retinal image will be perceived as being
   a. closer than the other object.
   b. more distant than the other object.
   c. larger than the other object.
   d. smaller than the other object.

48. As her friend Milo walks toward her, Noriko perceives his size as remaining constant because his perceived distance _____ at the same time that her retinal image of him _____ .
   a. increases; decreases
   b. increases; increases
   c. decreases; decreases
   d. decreases; increases

49. How do we perceive a pole that partially covers a wall?
   a. as farther away
   b. as nearer
   c. as larger
   d. There is not enough information to determine the object's size or distance.

50. An artist paints a tree orchard so that the parallel rows of trees converge at the top of the canvas. Which cue has the artist used to convey distance?
   a. interposition
   b. retinal disparity
   c. linear perspective
   d. figure-ground

51. Objects higher in our field of vision are perceived as _____ due to the principle of _____ .
   a. nearer; relative height
   b. nearer; linear perspective
   c. farther away; relative height
   d. farther away; linear perspective

Objective 17-8: Explain how perceptual constancies help us construct meaningful patterns.

52. Our tendency to see objects as unchanging while the stimuli from them change in size, shape, color, and brightness is called _____ _____ .

53. The brain computes an object's brightness _____ (relative to/independent of) surrounding objects.

54. The perception of brightness constancy depends on the amount of light an object reflects relative to its surroundings, called _____ _____ .

55. The experience of color depends on the surrounding _____ in which an object is seen. In an unvarying context, a familiar object will be perceived as having consistent color, even as the light changes. This phenomenon is called _____ _____ .

56. We see color as a result of our brains' computations of the light _____ by any object relative to its _____ .

57. Due to shape and size constancy, familiar objects _____ (do/do not) appear to change shape or size despite changes in our _____ images of them.

58. Several illusions, including the _____ illusion, are explained by the interplay between perceived _____ and perceived _____ . When distance cues are removed, these illusions are _____ (diminished/strengthened).

APPLICATIONS:

59. The fact that a white object under dim illumination appears lighter than a gray object under bright illumination is called
 a. relative luminance.
 b. perceptual adaptation.
 c. color contrast.
 d. brightness constancy.

60. In the absence of perceptual constancy
 a. objects would appear to change size as their distance from us changed.
 b. depth perception would be based exclusively on monocular cues.
 c. depth perception would be based exclusively on binocular cues.
 d. depth perception would be impossible.

61. Your friend tosses you a Frisbee. You know that it is getting closer instead of larger because of
 a. shape constancy.
 b. relative motion.
 c. size constancy.
 d. all of these factors.

Perceptual Interpretation

Objective 17-9: Describe what research on restored vision, sensory restriction, and perceptual adaptation reveals about the effects of experience on perception.

62. The idea that knowledge comes from inborn ways of organizing sensory experiences was proposed by the philosopher _____ .

63. On the other side were philosophers who maintained that we learn to perceive the world by experiencing it. One philosopher of this school was _____ .

64. Studies of cases in which vision has been restored to a person who was blind from birth show that, upon seeing tactilely familiar objects for the first time, the person _____ (can/cannot) recognize them. They _____ (can/cannot) distinguish figure from ground and they _____ (can/cannot) sense color.

65. Studies of sensory restriction demonstrate that visual experiences during _____ are crucial for perceptual development. Such experiences suggest that there is a _____ _____ for normal sensory and perceptual development.

66. Humans given glasses that shift or invert the visual field _____ (will/will not) adapt to the distorted perception. This is an example of _____ _____ . Animals such as chicks _____ (adapt/do not adapt) to distorting lenses.

MODULE REVIEW:

67. The size of the pupil is controlled by the
 a. lens.   c. cornea.
 b. retina.   d. iris.

68. The process by which the lens changes its curvature is
    a. accommodation.
    b. parallel processing.
    c. feature detection.
    d. transduction.

69. The receptor of the eye that functions best in dim light is the
    a. fovea.
    b. cone.
    c. bipolar cell.
    d. rod.

70. The Young-Helmholtz theory proposes that
    a. there are three different types of color-sensitive cones.
    b. retinal cells are excited by one color and inhibited by its complementary color.
    c. there are four different types of cones.
    d. rod, not cone, vision accounts for our ability to detect fine visual detail.

71. The transduction of light energy into nerve impulses takes place in the
    a. iris.
    b. retina.
    c. lens.
    d. optic nerve.

72. The brain breaks vision into separate dimensions such as motion, form, depth, and color, and works on each aspect simultaneously. This is called
    a. feature detection.
    b. parallel processing.
    c. accommodation.
    d. opponent processing.

73. One light may appear reddish and another greenish if they differ in
    a. wavelength.
    b. amplitude.
    c. opponent processes.
    d. brightness.

74. Which of the following explains why a rose appears equally red in bright and dim light?
    a. the Young-Helmholtz theory
    b. the opponent-process theory
    c. feature detection
    d. color constancy

75. Most color-deficient people will probably
    a. lack functioning red- or green-sensitive cones.
    b. see the world in only black and white.
    c. also suffer from poor vision.
    d. have above-average vision to compensate for the deficit.

76. The historical movement associated with the statement "The whole may exceed the sum of its parts" is
    a. philosophy.
    b. behavioral psychology.
    c. functional psychology.
    d. Gestalt psychology.

77. Figures tend to be perceived as whole, complete objects, even if spaces or gaps exist in the representation, thus demonstrating the principle of
    a. interposition.
    b. linear perspective.
    c. continuity.
    d. closure.

78. The figure-ground relationship has demonstrated that
    a. perception is largely innate.
    b. perception is simply a point-for-point representation of sensation.
    c. the same stimulus can trigger more than one perception.
    d. different people see different things when viewing a scene.

79. When we stare at an object, each eye receives a slightly different image, providing a depth cue known as
    a. interposition.
    b. linear perspective.
    c. relative motion.
    d. retinal disparity.

80. As we move, viewed objects cast changing shapes on our retinas, although we do not perceive the objects as changing. This is part of the phenomenon of
    a. perceptual constancy.
    b. relative motion.
    c. linear perspective.
    d. continuity.

81. Kittens and monkeys raised seeing only diffuse, unpatterned light
    a. later had difficulty distinguishing color and brightness.
    b. later had difficulty perceiving color and brightness, but eventually regained normal sensitivity.
    c. later had difficulty perceiving the shape of objects.
    d. showed no impairment in perception, indicating that neural feature detectors develop even in the absence of normal sensory experiences.

82. Adults who are born blind but later have their vision restored
    a. are almost immediately able to recognize familiar objects.
    b. typically fail to recognize familiar objects.
    c. are unable to follow moving objects with their eyes.
    d. have excellent eye-hand coordination.

83. Which of the following is NOT a monocular depth cue?
    a. light and shadow
    b. relative height
    c. retinal disparity
    d. interposition

84. The Moon illusion occurs in part because distance cues at the horizon make the Moon seem
    a. farther away and therefore larger.
    b. closer and therefore larger.
    c. farther away and therefore smaller.
    d. closer and therefore smaller.

85. Figure is to ground as _____ is to _____ .
    a. night; day
    b. top; bottom
    c. cloud; sky
    d. sensation; perception

86. According to the opponent-process theory
    a. there are three types of color-sensitive cones.
    b. the process of color vision begins in the cortex.
    c. neurons involved in color vision are stimulated by one color's wavelength and inhibited by another's.
    d. all of these statements are true.

87. Hubel and Wiesel discovered feature detectors in the visual
    a. fovea.
    b. optic nerve.
    c. iris.
    d. cortex.

88. Which of the following is the correct order of the structures through which light passes after entering the eye?
    a. lens, pupil, cornea, retina
    b. pupil, cornea, lens, retina
    c. pupil, lens, cornea, retina
    d. cornea, pupil, lens, retina

89. In the opponent-process theory, the three pairs of processes are
    a. red-green, blue-yellow, black-white.
    b. red-blue, green-yellow, black-white.
    c. red-yellow, blue-green, black-white.
    d. dependent upon the individual's experience.

90. Wavelength is to _____ as _____ is to brightness.
    a. hue; intensity
    b. intensity; hue
    c. frequency; amplitude
    d. brightness; hue

91. Which of the following is the most accurate description of how we process color?
    a. Throughout the visual system, color processing is divided into separate red, green, and blue systems.
    b. Red-green, blue-yellow, and black-white opponent processes operate throughout the visual system.
    c. Color processing occurs in two stages: (1) a three-color system in the retina and (2) opponent-process cells en route to the visual cortex.
    d. Color processing occurs in two stages: (1) an opponent-process system in the retina and (2) a three-color system en route to the visual cortex.

92. One reason that your ability to detect fine visual details is greatest when scenes are focused on the fovea of your retina is that
    a. there are more feature detectors in the fovea than in the peripheral regions of the retina.
    b. cones in the fovea are nearer to the optic nerve than those in peripheral regions of the retina.
    c. many rods, which are clustered in the fovea, have individual bipolar cells to relay their information to the cortex.
    d. many cones, which are clustered in the fovea, have individual bipolar cells to relay their information to the cortex.

93. The tendency to organize stimuli into smooth, uninterrupted patterns is called
    a. closure.
    b. continuity.
    c. interposition.
    d. proximity.

94. Which of the following statements is consistent with the Gestalt theory of perception?
    a. Perception develops largely through learning.
    b. Perception is the product of heredity.
    c. The mind organizes sensations into meaningful perceptions.
    d. Perception results directly from sensation.

95. Experiments with distorted visual environments demonstrate that
    a. adaptation rarely takes place.
    b. animals adapt readily, but humans do not.
    c. humans adapt readily, while lower animals typically do not.
    d. adaptation is possible during a critical period in infancy but not thereafter.

96. According to the philosopher _____, we learn to perceive the world.
    a. Locke   c. Gibson
    b. Kant   d. Walk

97. The phenomenon of size constancy is based on the close connection between an object's perceived _____ and its perceived _____.
    a. size; shape   c. size; brightness
    b. size; distance   d. shape; distance

98. Which of the following statements best describes the effects of sensory restriction?
    a. It produces functional blindness when experienced for any length of time at any age.
    b. It has greater effects on humans than on animals.
    c. It has more damaging effects when experienced during infancy.
    d. It has greater effects on adults than on children.

99. The depth cue that occurs when we watch stable objects at different distances as we are moving is
    a. linear perspective.   c. relative height.
    b. interposition.   d. relative motion.

100. Each time you see your car, it projects a different image on the retinas of your eyes, yet you do not perceive it as changing. This is because of
    a. perceptual adaptation.
    b. retinal disparity.
    c. perceptual constancy.
    d. figure-ground.

101. The term *gestalt* means
    a. grouping.   c. perception.
    b. sensation.   d. whole.

102. Studies of the visual cliff have provided evidence that much of depth perception is
    a. innate.
    b. learned.
    c. innate in lower animals, learned in humans.
    d. innate in humans, learned in lower animals.

103. All of the following are laws of perceptual organization, EXCEPT
    a. proximity.   c. continuity.
    b. closure.   d. retinal disparity.

104. You probably perceive the diagram above as three separate objects due to the principle of
    a. proximity.   c. closure.
    b. continuity.   d. linear perspective.

TERMS AND CONCEPTS TO REMEMBER:

105. wavelength and hue
106. intensity
107. retina
108. accommodation
109. rods and cones
110. optic nerve
111. blind spot
112. fovea
113. Young-Helmholtz trichromatic (three-color) theory
114. opponent-process theory
115. feature detectors
116. parallel processing
117. gestalt
118. figure-ground
119. grouping
120. depth perception
121. visual cliff
122. binocular cue
123. retinal disparity
124. monocular cue
125. perceptual constancy
126. color constancy
127. perceptual adaptation

ESSAY QUESTION:

In many movies from the 1930s, dancers performed seemingly meaningless movements which, when viewed from above, were transformed into intricate patterns and designs. Similarly, the formations of marching bands often create pictures and spell words. Identify and describe at least four Gestalt principles of grouping that explain the audience's perception of the images created by these types of formations. (Use the space below to list the points you want to make, and organize them. Then write the essay on a separate piece of paper.)

SUMMING UP:

Use the diagram at the top of the next column to identify the parts of the eye, then describe how each contributes to vision. Also, briefly explain the role of each structure.

The Eye

1. _____

   _____

2. _____

   _____

3. _____

   _____

4. _____

   _____

5. _____

   _____

6. _____

   _____

7. _____

   _____

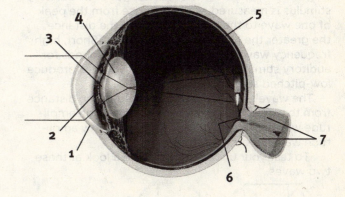

MODULE
18

The Nonvisual Senses

Hearing

Objective 18-1: Describe the characteristics of air pressure waves that we hear as sound.

1. The stimulus for hearing, or _____ , is sound waves, created by the compression and expansion of
_____ _____ .

2. The amplitude of a sound wave determines the sound's _____ .

3. The frequency of a sound wave determines the _____ we perceive.

4. Sound energy is measured in units called _____ . The absolute threshold for hearing is arbitrarily defined as _____ such units.
Every 10 decibels correspond to a _____ increase in sound intensity.

STUDY TIP: The stimulus energy for hearing can be described as a traveling wave that varies in wavelength and amplitude. The wavelength of an auditory stimulus is measured as the distance from the peak of one wave to the next—the shorter the distance, the greater the frequency of the waves. Short, high frequency waves produce high-pitched sounds for auditory stimuli. Long, low frequency waves produce low-pitched sounds.

The wave's amplitude is measured as the distance from the top of its peak to the bottom. High amplitude waves produce loud sounds, while low amplitude waves produce soft sounds.

To test your understanding, take a look at these two waves.

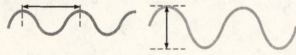

5. Assuming that these two waves were sound energy, would they sound the same? How would they differ?

Objective 18-2: Explain how the ear transforms sound energy into neural messages.

6. The ear is divided into three main parts: the _____ ear, the _____ ear, and the _____ ear.

7. The outer ear channels sound waves through the _____ _____ to the _____ , a tight membrane that then vibrates.

8. The middle ear transmits the vibrations through a piston made of three small bones: the _____ , _____ , and _____ .

9. In the inner ear, a coiled, bony, fluid-filled tube called the _____ contains the receptor cells for hearing. The incoming vibrations cause the _____ _____ to vibrate the fluid that fills the tube, which causes ripples in the _____ , bending the _____ _____ that line its surface. This movement triggers impulses in the adjacent nerve cells. Axons of those cells converge to form the auditory canal, which carries the neural messages (via the _____) to the _____ lobe's auditory cortex.

10. Damage to the cochlea's hair cell receptors or their associated auditory nerves can cause _____ hearing loss. It may be caused by disease, but more often it results from the biological changes linked with heredity, _____ , and prolonged exposure to ear-splitting noise or music.

11. Problems in the mechanical system that conducts sound waves to the cochlea may cause _____ _____ _____ .

12. An electronic device that restores hearing among nerve-deafened people is a _____ _____ .

APPLICATIONS:

13. Which of the following correctly lists the order of structures through which sound travels after entering the ear?
    a. auditory canal, eardrum, middle ear, cochlea
    b. eardrum, auditory canal, middle ear, cochlea
    c. eardrum, middle ear, cochlea, auditory canal
    d. cochlea, eardrum, middle ear, auditory canal

14. Dr. Frankenstein has forgotten to give his monster an important part; as a result, the monster cannot transform sound into neural messages. Dr. Frankenstein omitted the
    a. eardrum.
    b. middle ear.
    c. semicircular canals.
    d. basilar membrane.

Objective 18-3: Explain how we detect loudness, discriminate pitch, and locate sounds.

15. The brain interprets loudness from the
    _____ of hair cells a sound activates.

16. One theory of pitch perception proposes that different pitches activate different places on the cochlea's basilar membrane; this is the
    _____ theory. This theory has difficulty accounting for how we hear
    _____-pitched sounds, which do not have such localized effects.

17. A second theory proposes that the frequency of neural impulses, sent to the brain at the same frequency as sound waves, allows the perception of different pitches. This is the _____ (or temporal) theory. This theory fails to account for the perception of _____-pitched sounds because individual neurons cannot fire faster than _____ times per second.

18. For the higher pitches, cells may alternate their firing to match the sound's frequency, according to the _____ principle. Pitches in the intermediate range are handled by
    _____ .

19. We locate a sound by sensing differences in the
    _____ and _____
    with which it reaches our ears.

20. A sound that comes from directly ahead will be
    _____ (easier/harder) to locate than a sound that comes from off to one side.

The Other Senses

Objective 18-4: Describe how we sense touch.

21. The sense of touch is a mixture of at least four senses: _____ ,
    _____ , _____ , and
    _____ . Other skin sensations, such as tickle, itch, hot, and wetness, are
    _____ of the basic ones.

22. The _____-_____
    influence on touch is illustrated by the fact that a self-produced tickle produces less activation in the _____ _____
    than someone else's tickle.

Objective 18-5: Describe the biological, psychological, and social-cultural influences that affect our experience of pain, and discuss how placebos, distraction, and hypnosis help control pain.

23. People born without the ability to feel pain may be unaware of experiencing severe
    _____ . More numerous are those who live with _____ pain in the form of persistent headaches and backaches, for example.

24. Pain sensitivity varies, depending on
    _____ , _____ ,
    _____ , _____ , and
    our surrounding _____ .

25. The pain system _____ (is/is not) triggered by one specific type of physical energy. The body has specialized _____ , sensory receptors located in our skin,
    _____ , and organs that detect harmful stimuli.

26. Melzack and Wall have proposed a theory of pain called the _____-
    _____ theory, which proposes that there is a neurological _____ in the _____ _____
    that blocks pain signals or lets them through. It may be opened by activation of
    _____ (small/large) nerve fibers

and closed by activation of _____ (small/large) fibers or by information from the

_____ .

27. Pain-producing brain activity may be triggered with or without _____

_____ . A sensation of pain in an amputated leg is referred to as a _____

_____ sensation. Another example is _____ , experienced by people who have a ringing-in-the-ears sensation.

28. Because our experience of pain is also influenced by psychological factors as well as our social situation and our _____

traditions, we can say our perception of pain is a

_____ phenomenon.

List some pain control techniques used in health care situations.

29. (Thinking Critically) Hypnosis _____ (can/cannot) relieve pain. Two theories have proposed explanations of how it works. The

_____ _____ proposes that hypnosis is a by-product of normal social and mental processes. Another theory views hypnosis as a special dual-processing state of

_____ , a split between different levels of consciousness. This theory explains why people may carry out _____

_____ after they are not longer hypnotized.

APPLICATIONS:

30. The phantom limb sensation indicates that
   a. pain is a purely sensory phenomenon.
   b. the central nervous system plays only a minor role in the experience of pain.
   c. pain involves the brain's interpretation of neural activity.
   d. all of these are true.

31. While competing in the Olympic trials, marathoner Kirsten O'Brien suffered a stress fracture in her left leg. That she did not experience significant pain until the race was over is probably attributable to the fact that during the race
   a. the pain gate in her spinal cord was closed by information coming from her brain.
   b. her body's production of endorphins decreased.
   c. an increase in the activity of small pain fibers closed the pain gate.
   d. a decrease in the activity of large pain fibers closed the pain gate.

32. How does pain differ from other senses?
   a. It has no special receptors.
   b. It has no single stimulus.
   c. It is influenced by both physical and psychological phenomena.
   d. All of these statements are true.

Objective 18-6: Explain how our sense of taste and smell are similar, and how they differ.

33. The basic taste sensations are _____ ,

_____ , _____ ,

_____ , and a meaty taste called

_____ .

34. Taste, which is a _____ sense, is enabled by the 200 or more _____

_____ on the top and sides of the tongue. Each contains a _____ that catches food chemicals. Inside each are 50 to 100 taste _____ _____ that project antenna-like hairs that sense food molecules.

35. Taste receptors reproduce themselves every _____ . As we age, the number of taste buds _____ (increases/decreases/remains unchanged) and our taste sensitivity _____ (increases/decreases/remains unchanged), which is accelerated by _____ and by _____ use.

36. Like taste, smell (or _____) is a

_____ sense. There _____

(is/is not) a distinct receptor for each detectable odor. The olfactory receptor cells are located at the top of each _____

_____ .

37. For humans, the attractiveness of smells depends on _____ associations.

38. Odors are able to evoke memories and feelings because there is a direct link between the brain area that gets information from the nose and the ancient _____ centers associated with memory and emotion.

APPLICATIONS:

39. Seventy-year-old Mrs. Martinez finds that she must spice her food heavily or she cannot taste it. Unfortunately, her son often finds her cooking inedible because it is so spicy. What is the likely explanation for their taste differences?
    a. Women have higher taste thresholds than men.
    b. Men have higher taste thresholds than women.
    c. Being 70 years old, Mrs. Martinez probably has fewer taste buds than her son.
    d. All of these are likely explanations.

40. Tamiko hates the bitter taste of her cough syrup. Which of the following would she find most helpful in minimizing the syrup's bad taste?
    a. tasting something very sweet before taking the cough syrup
    b. keeping the syrup in her mouth for several seconds before swallowing it
    c. holding her nose while taking the cough syrup
    d. gulping the cough syrup so that it misses her tongue

Objective 18-7: Explain how we sense our body's position and movement.

41. The system for sensing the position and movement of body parts is called _____ . The receptors for this sense are located in the _____ , _____ , and _____ .

42. The sense that monitors the position and movement of the head (and thus the body) is the _____ _____ . The receptors for this sense are located in the _____ _____ and _____ _____ of the inner ear.

Sensory Interaction

Objective 18-8: Describe how sensory interaction influences our perceptions, and define *embodied cognition*.

43. When the sense of smell is blocked, as when we have a cold, foods do not taste the same; this illustrates the principle of _____ _____ . The _____ effect occurs when we _____ a speaker saying one syllable while _____ another.

44. The influence of bodily sensations, gestures, and other states on our cognitive preferences and judgments is called _____ _____ .

45. In a few people, one sort of sensation involuntarily produces another, a phenomenon called _____ .

Refer often to the following chart summarizing our sensory systems.

Sense	Stimulus Input	Receptors	Notes
Vision	Visible electromagnetic energy	Rods and cones	Wavelength = hue; intensity = brightness; rods = black and white; cones = color
Hearing	Sound waves of moving air molecules	Hair cells in the cochlea	wavelength = pitch; amplitude = loudness
Touch	Pressure, warmth, cold, pain	Specialized nerve endings	Cold + pressure = wetness; side-by-side pressure = tickle
Pain	No one type of stimulus	No special receptors	Natural endorphins relieve pain; hypnosis used for treating pain
Taste	Chemical molecules corresponding to sweet, salty, sour, bitter, and umami	Hair cells in the taste pores	Sensory interaction: smell influences; taste; smell + texture = taste = flavor
Smell	Airborne chemical molecules	Olfactory receptor cells in the nasal cavity	The brain's circuitry for smell connects with areas involved in memory storage
Body position and movement	Changes in body's position (kinesthesia) Changes in head position (vestibular sense)	Sensors in muscles, tendons, and joints Hairlike receptors in the ear's semicircular canals and vestibular sacs of the inner ear	Millions of position and motion sensors Messages sent to the brain's cerebellum

46. The river of perception is fed by streams of sensation, _____ , and
_____ .

APPLICATION:

47. Which of the following is an example of sensory interaction?

   a. finding that despite its delicious aroma, a weird-looking meal tastes awful
   b. finding that food tastes bland when you have a bad cold
   c. finding it difficult to maintain your balance when you have an ear infection
   d. All of these are examples.

(Thinking Critically) ESP—Perception Without Sensation?

Objective 18-9: List the claims of ESP, and discuss the conclusions of most research psychologists after putting these claims to the test.

48. Perception outside the range of normal sensation is called _____
_____ .

49. Psychologists who study ESP are called
_____ .

50. The form of ESP in which people claim to be capable of reading others' minds is called
_____ . A person who "senses"
that a friend is in danger might claim to have the ESP ability of _____ .
An ability to "see" into the future is called
_____ . A person who claims to be able to levitate and move objects is claiming the power of _____ .

51. Analyses of psychic visions and premonitions reveal _____ (high/meager) accuracy. Nevertheless, some people continue to believe in their accuracy because vague predictions often are later _____ to match events that have already occurred. In addition, people are more likely to recall or _____ dreams that seem to have come true.

52. Critics point out that a major difficulty for parapsychology is that ESP phenomena are not consistently _____ .

53. Daryl Bem, who has been skeptical of stage psychics, conducted research in which Cornell University participants _____ (did/did not) accurately guess the position of an erotic scene.

APPLICATIONS:

54. Regina claims that she can bend spoons, levitate furniture, and perform many other "mind over matter" feats. Regina apparently believes she has the power of

a. telepathy.
b. clairvoyance.
c. precognition.
d. psychokinesis.

55. Which of the following is true of the predictions of leading psychics?

a. They are often ambiguous prophecies later interpreted to match actual events.
b. They are no more accurate than guesses made by others.
c. They are nearly always inaccurate.
d. All of these statements are true.

MODULE REVIEW:

56. Frequency is to pitch as _____ is to_____.

a. wavelength; loudness
b. amplitude; loudness
c. wavelength; intensity
d. amplitude; intensity

57. Our experience of pain when we are injured depends on

a. our biological makeup and the type of injury we have sustained.
b. how well medical personnel deal with our injury.
c. our physiology, experiences and attention, and surrounding culture.
d. what our culture allows us to express in terms of feelings of pain.

58. According to the gate-control theory, a way to alleviate chronic pain would be to stimulate the _____ nerve fibers that _____ the spinal gate.

a. small; open
b. small; close
c. large; open
d. large; close

59. Kinesthesia involves

a. the bones of the middle ear.
b. information from the tendons, joints, and muscles.
c. membranes within the cochlea.
d. the body's sense of balance.

60. A person claiming to be able to read another's mind is claiming to have the ESP ability of

a. psychokinesis.
b. precognition.
c. clairvoyance.
d. telepathy.

61. Jack claims that he often has dreams that predict future events. He claims to have the power of

a. telepathy.
b. clairvoyance.
c. precognition.
d. psychokinesis.

62. Which of the following is true regarding scientific investigations of precognition?

a. A growing body of research demonstrates that some people are truly "psychic."
b. Studies that seem to provide evidence of precognitive ability have been criticized for being badly flawed.
c. The search for a valid test of ESP has resulted in only a handful of studies.
d. All of these statements are true.

63. The frequency theory of hearing is better than place theory at explaining our sensation of

a. the lowest pitches.
b. pitches of intermediate range.
c. the highest pitches.
d. all of these pitches.

64. Which of the following is NOT one of the basic tastes?

a. sweet
b. salty
c. umami
d. bland

65. The receptors for taste are located in the

a. taste buds.
b. cochlea.
c. vestibular sacs.
d. cortex.

66. The inner ear contains receptors for

a. audition and kinesthesia.
b. kinesthesia and the vestibular sense.
c. audition and the vestibular sense.
d. audition, kinesthesia, and the vestibular sense.

67. What enables you to feel yourself wiggling your toes even with your eyes closed?

a. vestibular sense
b. kinesthesia
c. the skin senses
d. sensory interaction

68. The principle that one sense may influence another is

a. place theory.
b. gate-control theory.
c. kinesthesia.
d. sensory interaction.

69. Psychologists who study ESP are called

a. clairvoyants.
b. telepaths.
c. parapsychologists.
d. levitators.

70. Which of the following statements concerning ESP is true?
    a. Most ESP researchers are quacks.
    b. There have been a large number of reliable demonstrations of ESP.
    c. Most research psychologists are skeptical of the claims of defenders of ESP.
    d. There have been reliable laboratory demonstrations of ESP, but the results are no different from those that would occur by chance.

71. The place theory of pitch perception cannot account for how we hear
    a. low-pitched sounds.
    b. middle-pitched sounds.
    c. high-pitched sounds.
    d. chords (three or more pitches simultaneously).

72. Sensorineural hearing loss is caused by
    a. wax buildup in the outer ear.
    b. damage to the eardrum.
    c. blockage in the middle ear because of infection.
    d. damage to the cochlea.

TERMS AND CONCEPTS TO REMEMBER:

73. audition
74. frequency and pitch
75. middle ear
76. cochlea
77. inner ear
78. sensorineural hearing loss
79. conduction hearing loss
80. cochlear implant
81. place theory
82. frequency theory
83. gate-control theory
84. hypnosis
85. dissociation
86. postyhypnotic suggestion
87. kinesthesia
88. vestibular sense
89. sensory interaction
90. embodied cognition
91. extrasensory perception (ESP)
92. parapsychology

SUMMING UP:

Use the diagram to identify the parts of the ear, then describe how each contributes to hearing. Also, briefly explain the role of each structure.

The Ear

1. _____
   _____
2. _____
   _____
3. _____
   _____
4. _____
   _____
5. _____
   _____
6. _____
   _____

7. _____
   _____
8. _____
   _____

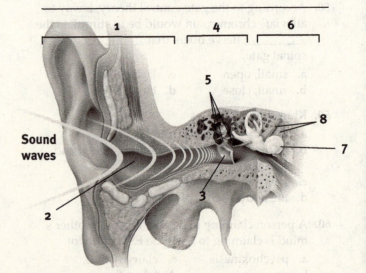

Sound waves

Before You Move On

Complete the following exercises after you thoroughly understand the material in all the modules.

Matching Items

Match each of the structures with its function or description.

Structures or Conditions

_____ 1. lens
_____ 2. iris
_____ 3. pupil
_____ 4. rods
_____ 5. cones
_____ 6. middle ear
_____ 7. inner ear
_____ 8. large nerve fiber
_____ 9. small nerve fiber
_____ 10. semicircular canals
_____ 11. sensors in joints

Functions or Descriptions

a. amplifies sounds
b. closes pain gate
c. vestibular sense
d. controls pupil
e. accommodation
f. opens pain gate
g. admits light
h. vision in dim light
i. transduction of sound
j. kinesthesia
k. color vision

True–False Items

Indicate whether each statement is true or false by placing _T_ or _F_ in the blank next to the item.

_____ 1. Once we perceive an item as a figure, it is impossible to see it as ground.

_____ 2. Laboratory experiments have laid to rest all criticisms of ESP.

_____ 3. Six-month-old infants will cross a visual cliff if their mother calls.

_____ 4. Unlike other animals, humans have no critical period for visual stimulation.

_____ 5. Immanuel Kant argued that experience determined how we perceive the world.

_____ 6. It is just as easy to touch two pencil tips together with only one eye open as it is with both eyes open.

_____ 7. After some time, humans are able to adjust to living in a world made upside down by distorting goggles.

_____ 8. As our distance from an object changes, the object's size seems to change.

_____ 9. Perception is influenced by psychological factors such as set and expectation as well as by physiological events.

_____ 10. John Locke argued that perception is inborn.

Essay Question

A dancer in a chorus line uses many sensory cues when performing. Discuss three senses that dancers rely on, and explain why each is important. (Use the space below to list the points you want to make, and organize them. Then write the essay on a separate sheet of paper.)

Cross-Check

As you learned in Module 2, reviewing and overlearning of material are important to the learning process. After you have written the definitions of the key terms in this unit, you should complete the crossword puzzle to ensure that you can reverse the process—recognize the term, given the definition.

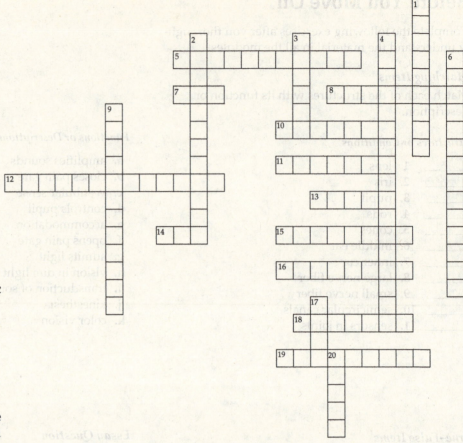

ACROSS

5. The sense of the position and movement of the parts of the body.
7. Psychological characteristic of light that is determined by wavelength.
8. Part of the ear in which sounds are converted to nerve impulses.
10. The ear's membrane that is lined with hair cells.
11. Grouping principle that we fill in gaps in visual stimuli to create a complete, whole image.
12. Monocular depth cue in which we perceive an object that partially blocks our view of another object as closer.
13. Receptors that enable color vision.
14. Another term for the difference threshold (abbreviation).
15. Information processing in which several aspects of a problem are processed simultaneously.
16. Minimum stimulation needed to detect a stimulus 50 percent of the time is the _____ threshold.
18. Snail-like structure of the inner ear that contains the receptors for hearing.
19. A binocular cue for perceiving depth.

DOWN

1. Number of complete wavelengths that pass a given point in a given time.
2. The organization of the visual field into two parts is referred to as the _____ relationship.
3. Part of the eye that contains the rods and cones.
4. Monocular cue for perceiving distance that involves the convergence of parallel lines.
6. The study of ESP.
9. Divided consciousness (as during hypnosis).

17. Visual receptors that are concentrated in the periphery of the retina.
20. Psychological characteristic of a sound that is determined by its frequency.

Answers

MODULE
16

Basic Concepts of Sensation and Perception

Processing Sensation and Perception

1. prosopagnosia
2. sensation; perception
3. bottom-up processing; top-down processing
4. **b.** is the answer.
   a. Both recognition and interpretation are examples of perception.
   c. This answer would have been correct if the question had read, "Perception is to sensation as _____ is to _____."
   d. Sensation and perception are important processes in both hearing and seeing.
5. **c.** is the answer.
6. **d.** is the answer.

Transduction

7. receive; transform; deliver
8. transduction

Thresholds

9. Fechner; 50; absolute threshold
10. signal detection
11. subliminal; prime; automatically
12. difference threshold; just noticeable difference (jnd)
13. Weber's law; stimulus
14. **d. is the answer.**
   a. The absolute threshold refers to whether a single stimulus can be detected, not to whether two stimuli can be differentiated.
   b. Subliminal refers to stimuli below the absolute threshold.
   c. A receptor threshold is a minimum amount of energy that will elicit a neural impulse in a receptor cell.
15. subliminal; conscious

Sensory Adaptation

16. sensory adaptation
17. informative
18. our eyes are constantly moving
19. sensory adaptation. This occurs when we remain fixed on a stimulus. Moving his fingers prevents his sense of touch from adapting.

Perceptual Set, Context Effects, and Motivation and Emotion

20. schemas; perceptual set
21. set; context
22. top-down; bottom-up
23. stereotypes; emotional
24. motives
25. **d. is the answer.** The two people interpreted a briefly perceived object in terms of their perceptual sets, or mental predispositions, in this case conditioned by their work experiences.
   a. Their different interpretations reflect top-down processing.
   b. Sensory adaptation refers to the decreased sensitivity that occurs with continued exposure to an unchanging stimulus.
   c. Transduction is the transformation of one form of energy into another.

Module Review:

26. **b.** is the answer. Psychological factors can affect the absolute threshold for a stimulus.

a. The absolute threshold for detecting a stimulus depends not only on the strength of the stimulus but also on psychological factors such as experience, expectations, motivation, and fatigue. Thus, the threshold cannot be a constant.
c. & d. The absolute threshold is the minimum stimulus that is detected 50 percent of the time.

27. **c. is the answer.** According to Weber's law, the difference threshold is a constant proportion of the stimulus. There is a 10 percent difference between 10 and 11 pounds; since the difference threshold is a constant proportion, the weight closest to 100 pounds that can nonetheless be differentiated from it is 110 pounds (or 100 pounds plus 10 percent).

28. **c. is the answer.**
   a. "Sensory fatigue" is not a term in psychology.
   b. Bottom-up processing is analysis that begins with the sensory receptors and works up to the brain's integration of sensory information.
   d. Transduction refers to the conversion of one form of energy into another.

29. **a. is the answer.** Sensory adaptation means a diminishing sensitivity to an unchanging stimulus. Only the adjustment to cold water involves a decrease in sensitivity; the other examples involve an increase.

30. **b. is the answer.**
   a. Top-down processing refers to how our knowledge and expectations influence perception.
   c. Signal detection explains precisely how and when we detect the presence of a faint stimulus (*signal*) amid background stimulation (*noise*).
   d. The absolute threshold is the minimum stimulation necessary to detect a particular stimulus 50 percent of the time.

31. **d. is the answer.**
   a. & b. The study of sensation is concerned with these processes.
   c. Although studying illusions has helped psychologists understand ordinary perceptual mechanisms, it is not the primary focus of the field of perception.

32. **d. is the answer.**

33. **d. is the answer.**
   a. Sensory adaptation refers to the diminished sensitivity that occurs with unchanging stimulation.
   b. Signal detection explains precisely how and when we detect the presence of a faint stimulus (*signal*) amid background stimulation (*noise*).
   c. Threshold refers to the amount of stimulation necessary either to detect a stimulus or to determine the difference between two stimuli.

34. **d.** is the answer. Weber's law concerns difference thresholds (jnd's), not absolute thresholds, and states that these are constant proportions of the stimuli, not that they remain constant.

35. **d.** is the answer.

36. **a.** is the answer.
    b. Signal detection theory explains how and when we detect the presence of a faint stimulus.
    c. Bottom-up processing is analysis that begins with the sensory receptors and works up to the brain's integration of sensory information.
    d. Sensory adaptation refers to the decreased sensitivity that occurs with continued exposure to an unchanging stimulus.

37. **a.** is the answer.
    b. Bottom-up processing refers to the physical characteristics of stimuli rather than their perceptual interpretation.
    c. Signal detection explains precisely how and when we detect the presence of a faint stimulus (*signal*) amid background stimulation (*noise*).
    d. Sensory adaptation refers to the decreased sensitivity that occurs with continued exposure to an unchanging stimulus.

38. **c.** is the answer. The absolute threshold is the minimum stimulation needed to detect a stimulus.
    a. & b. The difference threshold, which is also known as the jnd, is the minimum difference between two stimuli that a person can detect. In this example, there is only one stimulus—the sight of the flame.
    d. Feature detection refers to nerve cells in the brain responding to specific features of a stimulus.

Terms and Concepts to Remember:

39. **Sensation** is the process by which our sensory receptors and nervous system receive and represent stimulus energies from our environment.

40. **Perception** is the process by which we organize and interpret sensory information, enabling us to recognize meaningful objects and events.

41. **Bottom-up processing** is analysis that begins with the sensory receptors and works up to the brain's integration of sensory information.

42. **Top-down processing** is information processing guided by higher-level mental processes.

43. **Transduction** refers to the conversion of one form of energy into another. In sensation, it is the process by which receptor cells in the eyes, ears, skin, and nose convert stimulus energies into neural impulses our brain can interpret.

44. The **absolute threshold** is the minimum stimulus energy needed to detect a stimulus 50 percent of the time.

45. **Signal detection theory** explains precisely how and when we detect the presence of a faint stimulus (*signal*) amid background stimulation (*noise*). Detection depends partly on experience, expectations, motivation, and alertness.

46. A stimulus that is **subliminal** is one that is below the absolute threshold for conscious awareness.
    Memory aid: Limen is the Latin word for "threshold." A stimulus that is subliminal is one that is sub- ("below") the limen, or threshold.

47. **Priming** is the activation, often unconsciously, of certain associations, the effect of which is to predispose a perception, memory, or response.

48. The **difference threshold** (also called the *just noticeable difference,* or *jnd*), is the minimum difference between two stimuli required for detection 50 percent of the time.

49. **Weber's law** is the principle that, to be perceived as different, the just noticeable difference between two stimuli must differ by a constant minimum percentage (rather a constant amount).
    Example: If a difference of 10 percent in weight is noticeable, Weber's law predicts that a person could discriminate 10- and 11-pound weights or 50- and 55-pound weights.

50. **Sensory adaptation** refers to the decreased sensitivity that occurs with continued exposure to an unchanging stimulus.

51. **Perceptual set** is a mental predisposition to perceive one thing and not another.

MODULE 17 — Vision: Sensory and Perceptual Processing

Light Energy and Eye Structures

1. electromagnetic
2. wavelength; hue
3. intensity; amplitude; brightness
4. yes. The left-hand wave has lower amplitude and the colors would be duller. The right-hand wave has similar frequency (and therefore hue) but a higher amplitude, making it brighter.
5. cornea; pupil; iris; cognitive
6. lens; retina; accommodation
7. light energy; neural impulses; abstract

Information Processing in the Eye and Brain

8. rods; cones
9. chemical; neural; bipolar; ganglion

10. optic nerve; brain; thalamus; visual cortex

11. blind spot

12. fovea; peripheral; bipolar; do not

13. cones; rods; movement

14. sensitive; 20

15. **d.** is the answer. Greater sensitivity to fine visual detail is associated with the cones, which have their own bipolar cells to relay information to the cortex. The cones are concentrated in the fovea, the retina's point of central focus. For this reason, staring directly at an object maximizes sensitivity to fine detail.
    a. If you stare off to one side, the image falls onto peripheral regions of the retina, where rods are concentrated and sensitivity to fine visual detail is poor.
    b. Sensitivity to detail is not directly influenced by whether one or both eyes are stimulated.
    c. Decreasing the intensity of light would only impair the functioning of the cones, which are sensitive to visual detail but have a high threshold for light intensity.

16. **d.** is the answer.

17. **b.** is the answer. Rods and cones enable vision in dim and bright light, respectively. If an animal is active only at night, it is likely to have more rods than cones in its retinas.
    d. Bipolar cells link both cones and rods to ganglion cells. There is no reason to expect that a nocturnal mammal would have more bipolar cells than a mammal active during the day and at night. If anything, because several rods share a single bipolar cell, whereas many cones have their own, a nocturnal animal (with a visual system consisting mostly of rods) might be expected to have fewer bipolar cells than an animal active during the day (with a visual system consisting mostly of cones).

18. **b.** is the answer.
    a. & c. It is the cones, rather than the rods, that enable color vision.
    d. If the cones' threshold were lower than the available light intensity, they would be able to function and therefore detect the colors of the players' uniforms.

19. reflects (rejects); construction

20. sex linked

21. Young-Helmholtz trichromatic; red; green; blue

22. opponent; afterimage

23. opponent-process; red; green; yellow; blue; black; white

In the first stage of color processing, the retina's red, green, and blue cones respond in varying degrees to different color stimuli, as suggested by the three-color theory. The resulting signals are then processed in the retina and the thalamus by red-green, blue-yellow, and black-white opponent-process cells, which are turned "on" by one wavelength and turned "off" by its opponent.

24. **d.** is the answer.
    a., b., & c. Rods, cones, and bipolar cells are located in the retina. Moreover, neither are excited by some colors and inhibited by others.

25. **c.** is the answer.
    a. The trichromatic theory cannot account for the experience of afterimages.
    b. & d. Afterimages are experienced as the complementary color of a stimulus. Green, not blue, is red's complement.

26. thalamus; visual cortex; occipital lobe; feature detectors

27. supercell clusters; gaze; head angle; posture; body movement

28. motion; form; depth; simultaneously; parallel processing

29. blindsight

Perceptual Organization

30. Gestalt; whole

31. figure; ground

32. grouping

33. continuity; closure; proximity

34. **c.** is the answer. She perceives the line for the road as continuous, even though it is interrupted by lines indicating other roads.
    a. Closure refers to the perceptual filling in of gaps in a stimulus to create a complete, whole object.
    b. Figure-ground refers to the organization of the visual field into two parts: the figure and its background.
    d. Proximity is the tendency to group objects near to one another as a single unit.

35. depth perception; distance

36. visual cliff; mobile

Research on the visual cliff suggests that in many species the ability to perceive depth is present at, or very shortly after, birth. Learning seems to be involved because crawling seems to increase infants' fear of heights.

37. binocular

38. retinal disparity

39. monocular
40. relative size
41. interposition
42. relative height
43. relative motion
44. linear perspective
45. light and shadow
46.

47. **b.** is the answer. The phenomenon described is the basis for the monocular cue of relative size.

   a. The object casting the *larger* retinal image would be perceived as closer.

   c. & d. Because of size constancy, the perceived size of familiar objects remains constant, despite changes in their retinal image size.

48. **d.** is the answer.

49. **b.** is the answer. This is an example of the principle of interposition in depth perception.

   a. The partially obscured object is perceived as farther away.

   c. The perceived size of an object is not altered when that object overlaps another.

50. **c.** is the answer.

   a. Interposition is a monocular depth cue in which an object that partially covers another is perceived as closer.

   b. Retinal disparity refers to the difference between the two images received by our eyes that allows us to perceive depth. It has nothing to do with the way the artist placed the trees.

   d. Figure-ground refers to the organization of the field into objects that stand out from their surroundings.

51. **c.** is the answer.

   b. & d. Linear perspective is the apparent convergence of parallel lines as a cue to distance.

52. perceptual constancy
53. relative to
54. relative luminance
55. context; color constancy
56. reflected; surrounding objects

57. do not; retinal
58. Moon; size; distance; diminished
59. **d.** is the answer. Although the amount of light reflected from a white object is less in dim light than in bright light—and may be less than the amount of light reflected from a brightly lit gray object—the brightness of the white object is perceived as remaining constant. Because a white object reflects a higher percentage of the light falling on it than does a gray object, and the brightness of objects is perceived as constant despite variations in illumination, white is perceived as brighter than gray even under dim illumination.

   a. Relative luminance refers to the relative intensity of light falling on surfaces that are in proximity. Brightness constancy is perceived despite variations in illumination.

   b. Perceptual adaptation refers to the ability to adjust to an artificially modified perceptual environment, such as an inverted visual field.

   c. Color contrast is not discussed in this text.

60. **a.** is the answer. Because we perceive the size of a familiar object as constant even as its retinal image grows smaller, we perceive the object as being farther away.

   b. & c. Perceptual constancy is a cognitive, rather than sensory, phenomenon. Therefore, the absence of perceptual constancy would not alter sensitivity to monocular or binocular cues.

   d. Although the absence of perceptual constancy would impair depth perception based on the size-distance relationship, other cues to depth, such as linear perspective, could still be used.

61. **a.** is the answer.

Perceptual Interpretation

62. Immanuel Kant
63. John Locke
64. cannot; can; can
65. infancy; critical period
66. will; perceptual adaptation; do not adapt

Module Review:

67. **d.** is the answer.
   a. The lens lies behind the pupil and focuses light on the retina.
   b. The retina is the inner surface of the eyeball and contains the rods and cones.
   c. The cornea lies in front of the pupil and is the first structure that light passes through as it enters the eye.

68. **a.** is the answer.

b. Parallel processing is information processing in which several aspects of a stimulus are processed simultaneously.

c. Feature detection is the process by which neural cells in the brain respond to specific visual features.

d. Transduction refers to the conversion of an environmental stimulus, such as light, into a neural impulse by a receptor—a rod or a cone.

69. **d.** is the answer.
a. The fovea is not a receptor; it is a region of the retina that contains only cones.
b. Cones have a higher threshold for brightness than rods and therefore do not function as well in dim light.
c. Bipolar cells are not receptors; they are neurons in the retina that link rods and cones with ganglion cells, which make up the optic nerve.

70. **a.** is the answer. The Young-Helmholtz theory proposes that there are red-, green-, and blue-sensitive cones.
b. This answer describes Hering's opponent-process theory.
c. The Young-Helmholtz theory proposes that there are three types of cones, not four.
d. The Young-Helmholtz theory concerns only color vision, not the detection of visual detail.

71. **b.** is the answer.
a. The iris controls the diameter of the pupil.
c. The lens accommodates its shape to focus images on the retina.
d. The optic nerve carries nerve impulses from the retina to the visual cortex.

72. **b.** is the answer.
a. Feature detection is the process by which nerve cells in the brain respond to specific visual features of a stimulus, such as movement or shape.
c. Accommodation is the process by which the lens changes its curvature to focus images on the retina.
d. The opponent-process theory suggests that color vision depends on the response of brain cells to red-green, yellow-blue, and black-white opposing colors.

73. **a.** is the answer. Wavelength determines hue.
b. & d. The amplitude of light determines its brightness.
c. Opponent processes are neural systems involved in color vision, not properties of light.

74. **d.** is the answer. Color constancy is the perception that a familiar object has consistent color, even if changing illumination alters the wavelengths reflected by that object.

a. & b. These theories explain how the visual system detects color; they do not explain why colors do not seem to change when lighting does.
c. Feature detection explains how the brain recognizes visual images by analyzing their distinctive features of shape, movement, and angle.

75. **a.** is the answer. Thus, they have difficulty discriminating these two colors.
b. Those who are color deficient are usually not "color blind" in a literal sense. Instead, they are unable to distinguish certain hues, such as red from green.
c. Failure to distinguish red and green is separate from, and does not usually affect, general visual ability.
d. Color deficiency does not enhance vision. A deficit in one sense often is compensated for by overdevelopment of another sense—for example, hearing in blind people.

76. **d.** is the answer. Gestalt psychology, which developed in Germany early in the twentieth century, was interested in how clusters of sensations are organized into "whole" perceptions.
a. Philosophers Immanuel Kant and John Locke argued over whether our perceptual abilities should be attributed to our nature or to our nurture.
b. & c. Behavioral and functional psychology developed later in the United States.

77. **d.** is the answer.
a. Interposition is the tendency to perceive objects that partially block our view of another object as closer.
b. Linear perspective is when parallel lines appear to meet in the distance.
c. Continuity refers to the tendency to group stimuli into smooth, continuous patterns.

78. **c.** is the answer. Although we always differentiate a stimulus into figure and ground, those elements of the stimulus we perceive as figure and those as ground may change. In this way, the same stimulus can trigger more than one perception.
a. The idea of a figure-ground relationship has no bearing on the issue of whether perception is innate.
b. Perception cannot be simply a point-for-point representation of sensation, since in figure-ground relationships a single stimulus can trigger more than one perception.
d. Figure-ground relationships demonstrate the existence of general, rather than individual, principles of perceptual organization. Significantly, even the same person can see different figure-ground relationships when viewing a scene.

79. d. is the answer. The greater the retinal disparity, or difference between the images, the less the distance.

a. Interposition is the monocular distance cue in which an object that partially blocks another object is seen as closer.

b. Linear perspective is the monocular distance cue in which parallel lines appear to converge in the distance.

c. Relative motion is the monocular distance cue in which objects at different distances change their relative positions in our visual image, with those closest moving most.

80. a. is the answer. Perception of constant shape, like perception of constant size, is part of the phenomenon of perceptual constancy.

b. Relative motion is a monocular distance cue in which objects at different distances appear to move at different rates.

c. Linear perspective is a monocular distance cue in which lines we know to be parallel converge in the distance, thus indicating depth.

d. Continuity is the perceptual tendency to group items into continuous patterns.

81. c. is the answer.

a. & b. The kittens had difficulty only with lines they had never experienced, and never regained normal sensitivity.

d. Both perceptual and feature-detector impairment resulted from visual restriction.

82. b. is the answer. Because they have not had early visual experiences, these adults typically have difficulty learning to perceive objects.

a. Such patients typically could not visually recognize objects with which they were familiar by touch, and in some cases this inability persisted.

c. Being able to perceive figure-ground relationships, patients are able to follow moving objects with their eyes.

d. This answer is incorrect because eye-hand coordination is an acquired skill and requires much practice.

83. c. is the answer. Retinal disparity is a binocular cue; all the other cues mentioned are monocular.

84. a. is the answer. The Moon appears larger at the horizon than overhead in the sky because objects at the horizon provide distance cues that make the Moon seem farther away and therefore larger. In the open sky, of course, there are no such cues.

85. c. is the answer. We see a cloud as a figure against the background of sky.

a., b., & d. The figure-ground relationship refers to the organization of the visual field into objects (figures) that stand out from their surroundings (ground).

86. c. is the answer. After leaving the receptor cells, visual information is analyzed in terms of pairs of opponent colors; neurons stimulated by one member of a pair are inhibited by the other.

a. The idea that there are three types of color-sensitive cones is the basis of the Young-Helmholtz three-color theory.

b. According to the opponent-process theory, and all other theories of color vision, the process of color vision begins in the retina.

87. d. is the answer. Feature detectors are cortical neurons and hence are located in the visual cortex.

a. The fovea contains cones.

b. The optic nerve contains neurons that relay nerve impulses from the retina to higher centers in the visual system.

c. The iris is simply a ring of muscle tissue, which controls the diameter of the pupil.

88. d. is the answer.

89. a. is the answer.

90. a. is the answer. Wavelength determines hue, and intensity determines brightness.

91. c. is the answer.

a. This answer is incorrect because separate red, green, and blue systems operate only in the retina.

b. This answer is incorrect because opponent-process systems operate en route to the brain, after visual processing in the receptors is completed.

d. This answer is incorrect because it reverses the correct order of the two stages of processing.

92. d. is the answer.

a. Feature detectors are nerve cells located in the visual cortex, not in the fovea of the retina.

b. The proximity of rods and cones to the optic nerve does not influence their ability to resolve fine details.

c. Rods are concentrated in the peripheral regions of the retina, not in the fovea; moreover, several rods share a single bipolar cell.

93. b. is the answer.

a. Closure refers to the tendency to perceptually fill in gaps in recognizable objects in the visual field.

c. Interposition is the tendency to perceive objects that partially block our view of another object as closer.

d. Proximity refers to the tendency to group items that are near one another.

94. c. is the answer.

a. & b. The Gestalt psychologists did not deal with the origins of perception; they were more concerned with its form.

d. In fact, they argued just the opposite: Perception is more than mere sensory experience.

95. **c.** is the answer. Humans are able to adjust to upside-down worlds and other visual distortions, figuring out the relationship between the perceived and the actual reality; lower animals, such as chicks, are typically unable to adapt.

a. Humans are able to adapt quite well to distorted visual environments (and then to readapt).

b. This answer is incorrect because humans are the most adaptable of creatures.

d. Humans are able to adapt at any age to distorted visual environments.

96. **a.** is the answer.

b. Kant claimed that knowledge is inborn.

c. & d. Gibson and Walk make no claims about the origins of perception.

97. **b.** is the answer.

98. **c.** is the answer. There appears to be a critical period for perceptual development, in that sensory restriction has severe, even permanent, disruptive effects when it occurs in infancy but not when it occurs later in life.

a. & d. Sensory restriction does not have the same effects at all ages, and it is more damaging to children than to adults. This is because there is a critical period for perceptual development; whether functional blindness will result depends in part on the nature of the sensory restriction.

b. Research studies have not indicated that sensory restriction is more damaging to humans than to animals.

99. **d.** is the answer. When we move, stable objects we see also appear to move, and the distance and speed of the apparent motion cue us to the objects' relative distances.

a., b., & c. These depth cues are unrelated to movement and thus work even when we are stationary.

100. **c.** is the answer. Because of perceptual constancy, we see the car's shape and size as always the same.

a. Perceptual adaptation refers to our ability to adjust to an artificially displaced or even inverted visual field.

b. Retinal disparity means that our right and left eyes each receive slightly different images.

d. Figure-ground refers to the organization of the visual field into two parts.

101. **d.** is the answer. *Gestalt* means a "form" or "whole."

102. **a.** is the answer. Most infants refused to crawl out over the "cliff" even when coaxed, suggesting that much of depth perception is innate. Studies with the young of "lower" animals show the same thing.

103. **d.** is the answer.

104. **a.** is the answer. Proximity is the tendency to group objects near to one another. The diagram is perceived as three distinct units.

b. Continuity is the tendency to group stimuli into smooth, uninterrupted patterns. There is no such continuity in the diagram.

c. Closure is the perceptual tendency to fill in gaps in a form. In the diagram, three disconnected units are perceived rather than a single whole.

d. Linear perspective is when parallel lines appear to meet in the distance.

Terms and Concepts to Remember:

105. **Wavelength**, which refers to the distance from the peak of one light or sound wave to the next, gives rise to the perceptual experiences of **hue**, or color, in vision.

106. The **intensity** of light and sound is determined by the amplitude of the waves and is experienced as brightness and loudness, respectively.

107. The **retina** is the light-sensitive, multilayered inner surface of the eye that contains the rods and cones as well as neurons that form the beginning of the optic nerve.

108. **Accommodation** is the process by which the lens of the eye changes shape to focus near objects on the retina.

109. The **rods** and **cones** are visual receptors that convert light energy into neural impulses. The rods are concentrated in the periphery of the retina, the cones in the fovea. The rods have poor sensitivity; detect black, white, and gray; function well in dim light; and are needed for peripheral vision. The cones have excellent sensitivity, enable color vision, and function best in daylight or bright light.

110. Composed of the axons of retinal ganglion cells, the **optic nerve** carries neural impulses from the eye to the brain.

111. The **blind spot** is the region of the retina where the optic nerve leaves the eye. Because there are no rods or cones in this area, there is no vision here.

112. The **fovea** is the retina's point of central focus. It contains only cones; therefore, images focused on the fovea are the clearest.

113. The **Young-Helmholtz trichromatic (three-color) theory** maintains that the retina contains red-, green-, and blue-sensitive color receptors that in combination can produce the perception of any color. This theory explains the first stage of color processing.

114. The **opponent-process theory** maintains that color vision depends on pairs of opposing retinal processes (red-green, yellow-blue, and white-black). This theory explains the second stage of color processing.

115. **Feature detectors**, located in the visual cortex of the brain, are nerve cells that selectively respond to specific visual features, such as movement, shape, or angle. Feature detectors are evidently the basis of visual information processing.

116. **Parallel processing** is information processing in which several aspects of a stimulus are processed simultaneously.

117. **Gestalt** means "whole" or "form." The Gestalt psychologists emphasized our tendency to integrate pieces of information into meaningful wholes.

118. **Figure-ground** refers to the organization of the visual field into two parts: the figure, which stands out from its surroundings, and the surroundings, or background.

119. **Grouping** is the perceptual tendency to organize stimuli into coherent groups. Gestalt psychologists identified various principles of grouping.

120. **Depth perception** is the ability to see objects in three dimensions although the images that strike the retina are two-dimensional; it allows us to judge distance.

121. The **visual cliff** is a laboratory device for testing depth perception, especially in infants and young animals. In their experiments with the visual cliff, Gibson and Walk found strong evidence that depth perception is at least in part innate.

122. **Binocular cues** are depth cues that depend on information from both eyes.

    Memory aid: Bi- indicates "two"; *ocular* means something pertaining to the eye. **Binocular cues** are cues for the "two eyes."

123. **Retinal disparity** refers to the differences between the images received by the left eye and the right eye as a result of viewing the world from slightly different angles. It is a binocular depth cue, since the greater the difference between the two images, the nearer the object.

124. **Monocular cues** are depth cues that depend on information from either eye alone.

    Memory aid: Mono- means one; a monocle is an eyeglass for one eye. A **monocular cue** is one that is available to either the left or the right eye.

125. **Perceptual constancy** is the perception that objects have consistent lightness, color, shape, and size, even as illumination and retinal images change.

126. **Color constancy** is the perception that familiar objects have consistent color despite changes in illumination that shift the wavelengths they reflect.

127. **Perceptual adaptation** refers to our ability to adjust to changed sensory input, including an artificially displaced or even inverted visual field. Given distorting lenses, we perceive things accordingly but soon adjust by learning the relationship between our distorted perceptions and the reality.

Essay Question

1. *Proximity.* We tend to perceive items that are near each other as belonging together. Thus, a small section of dancers or members of a marching band may separate themselves from the larger group in order to form part of a particular image.

2. *Similarity.* Because we perceive similar figures as belonging together, choreographers and band directors often create distinct visual groupings within the larger band or dance troupe by having the members of each group wear a distinctive costume or uniform.

3. *Continuity.* Because we perceive smooth, continuous patterns rather than discontinuous ones, dancers or marching musicians moving together (as in a column, for example) are perceived as a separate unit.

4. *Closure.* If a figure has gaps, we complete it, filling in the gaps to create a whole image. Thus, we perceptually fill in the relatively wide spacing between dancers or marching musicians in order to perceive the complete words or forms they are creating.

Summing Up

The Eye

1. Cornea. Light enters the eye through this transparent membrane, which protects the inner structures from the environment.

2. Iris. The colored part of the eye, the iris controls the size of the pupil to optimize the amount of light that enters the eye.

3. Pupil. The adjustable opening in the iris, the pupil allows light to enter.

4. Lens. This transparent structure behind the pupil changes shape to focus images on the retina.

5. Retina. The light-sensitive inner surface of the eye, the retina contains the rods and cones, which transduce light energy into neural impulses.

6. Blind spot. The region of the retina where the optic nerve leaves the eye, the blind spot contains no rods or cones and so there is no vision here.

7. Optic nerve. This bundle of nerve fibers carries neural impulses from the retina to the brain.

 MODULE 18 **The Nonvisual Senses**

Hearing

1. audition; air molecules

2. loudness

3. pitch

4. decibels; zero; tenfold

5. yes. The sounds have similar frequency (and therefore pitch), but the right-hand sound has higher amplitude and would therefore be louder.

6. outer; middle; inner

7. auditory canal; eardrum

8. hammer; anvil; stirrup

9. cochlea; oval window; basilar membrane; hair cells; thalamus; temporal

10. sensorineural; aging

11. conduction hearing loss

12. cochlear implant

13. a. is the answer.

14. d. is the answer. The hair cells, which transform sound energy into neural messages, are located on the basilar membrane.
a. & b. The eardrum and bones of the middle ear merely conduct sound waves to the inner ear, where they are transformed.
c. The semicircular canals are involved in the vestibular sense, not hearing.

15. number

16. place; low

17. frequency; high; 1000

18. volley; some combination of place and frequency theories

19. speed (timing); intensity

20. harder

The Other Senses

21. pressure; warmth; cold; pain; variations

22. top-down; somatosensory cortex

23. injury; chronic

24. genes; physiology; experience; attention; culture

25. is not; nociceptors; muscles

26. gate-control; gate; spinal cord; small; large; brain

27. sensory input; phantom limb; tinnitus

28. cultural; biopsychosocial

Pain control techniques include drugs, surgery, acupuncture, thought distraction, exercise, hypnosis, relaxation training, electrical stimulation, and massage. Even an inert placebo can help. Similarly, for burn victims, distraction during painful wound care can be created by immersion in a computer-generated 3-D world.

29. can; social influence; dissociation; posthypnotic suggestions

30. c. is the answer. Since pain is felt in the limb that does not exist, the pain is simply the brain's (mis)interpretation of neural activity.
a. If pain were a purely sensory phenomenon, phantom limb pain would not occur, since the receptors are no longer present.
b. That pain is experienced when a limb is missing indicates that the central nervous system, especially the brain, is where pain is sensed.

31. a. is the answer.
b. Since endorphins relieve pain, a decrease in their production would have made Kirsten more likely to experience pain. Moreover, because endorphins are released in response to pain, their production probably would have increased.
c. Neural activity in small fibers tends to open the pain gate.
d. An increase in large-fiber activity would tend to close the pain gate.

32. d. is the answer.

33. sweet; sour; salty; bitter; umami

34. chemical; taste buds; pore; receptor cells

35. week or two; decreases; decreases; smoking; alcohol

36. olfaction; chemical; is not; nasal cavity

37. learned

38. limbic

39. **c.** is the answer. As people age they lose taste buds and their taste thresholds increase. For this reason, Mrs. Martinez needs more concentrated tastes than her son to find food palatable.

    a. & b. There is no evidence that women and men differ in their absolute thresholds for taste.

40. **c.** is the answer. Because of the powerful sensory interaction between taste and smell, eliminating the odor of the cough syrup should make its taste more pleasant.

    a. If anything, the contrasting tastes might make the bitter syrup even less palatable.

    b. If Tamiko keeps the syrup in her mouth for several seconds, it will ensure that her taste pores fully "catch" the stimulus, thus intensifying the bitter taste.

    d. It's probably impossible to miss the tongue completely.

41. kinesthesia; tendons; joints; muscles

42. vestibular sense; semicircular canals; vestibular sacs

Sensory Interaction

43. sensory interaction; McGurk; see; hearing

44. embodied cognition

45. synesthesia

46. cognition; emotion

47. **d.** is the answer. Each of these is an example of the interaction of two senses—vision and taste in the case of (a.), taste and smell in the case of (b.), and hearing and the vestibular sense in the case of (c.).

(Thinking Critically) ESP: Perception Without Sensation?

48. extrasensory perception

49. parapsychologists

50. telepathy; clairvoyance; precognition; psychokinesis

51. meager; interpreted (retrofitted); reconstruct

52. reproducible (replicable)

53. did

54. **d.** is the answer.

    a. Telepathy is the claimed ability to "read" minds.

    b. Clairvoyance refers to the claimed ability to perceive remote events.

    c. Precognition refers to the claimed ability to perceive future events.

55. **d.** is the answer.

Module Review:

56. **b.** is the answer. Just as wave frequency deter-

mines pitch, so wave amplitude determines loudness.

    a. Amplitude is the physical basis of loudness; wavelength determines frequency and thereby pitch.

    c. & d. Wavelength, amplitude, and intensity are physical aspects of light and sound. Because the question is based on a relationship between a physical property (frequency) of a stimulus and its psychological attribute (pitch), these answers are incorrect.

57. **c.** is the answer. The biopsychosocial approach tells us that our experience of pain depends on biological, psychological, and social-cultural factors.

58. **d.** is the answer. The small fibers conduct most pain signals; the large fibers conduct most other sensory signals from the skin. The gate either allows pain signals to pass on to the brain or blocks them from passing. When the large fibers are stimulated, the pain gate is closed and other sensations are felt in place of pain.

59. **b.** is the answer. Kinesthesia, or the sense of the position and movement of body parts, is based on information from the tendons, joints, and muscles.

    a. & c. The ear plays no role in kinesthesia.

    d. Equilibrium, or the vestibular sense, is not involved in kinesthesia but is, rather, a companion sense.

60. **d.** is the answer.

    a. Psychokinesis refers to the claimed ability to perform acts of "mind over matter."

    b. Precognition refers to the claimed ability to perceive future events.

    c. Clairvoyance refers to the claimed ability to perceive remote events.

61. **c.** is the answer.

    a. This answer would be correct had Jack claimed to be able to read someone else's mind.

    b. This answer would be correct had Jack claimed to be able to sense remote events, such as a friend in distress.

    d. This answer would be correct had Jack claimed to be able to levitate objects or bend spoons without applying any physical force.

62. **b.** is the answer.

63. **a.** is the answer. Frequency theory best explains the lowest pitches. Place theory best explains the highest pitches, and some combination of the two theories probably accounts for our sensation of intermediate-range pitches.

64. **d.** is the answer.

65. **a.** is the answer.
    b. The cochlea contains receptors for hearing.
    c. The vestibular sacs are involved in the body's position and movement.
    d. The cortex is the outer layer of the brain, where information detected by the receptors is processed.

66. **c.** is the answer. The inner ear contains the receptors for audition (hearing) and the vestibular sense; those for kinesthesia are located in the tendons, joints, and muscles.

67. **b.** is the answer. Kinesthesia, the sense of movement of body parts, would enable you to feel your toes wiggling.
    a. The vestibular sense is concerned with movement and position, or balance, of the whole body, not of its parts.
    c. The skin, or tactile, senses are pressure, pain, warmth, and cold; they have nothing to do with movement of body parts.
    d. Sensory interaction, the principle that the senses influence each other, does not play a role in this example, which involves only the sense of kinesthesia.

68. **d.** is the answer.
    a. Place theory is the theory that the pitch we hear depends on the place on the basilar membrane that is stimulated.
    b. Gate-control theory maintains that a "gate" in the spinal cord determines whether pain signals are permitted to reach the brain.
    c. Kinesthesia is the sense of the position and movement of the parts of the body.

69. **c.** is the answer.
    a., b., & d. These psychics claim to exhibit the phenomena studied by parapsychologists.

70. **c.** is the answer.
    a. Many ESP researchers are sincere, reputable researchers.
    b. & d. There have been no reliable demonstrations of ESP.

71. **a.** is the answer.
    b. & c. Although the localization of low-pitched sounds along the basilar membrane is poor, that for sounds of middle and, especially, high pitch is good. Therefore, place theory accounts well for high-pitched sounds and, together with frequency theory, can account for middle-pitched sounds.
    d. As long as the notes of a chord are within the range of responsiveness of the basilar membrane, place theory can account for chord perception.

72. **d.** is the answer. Sensorineural hearing loss is caused by destruction of neural tissue as a result of problems with the cochlea's receptors or the auditory nerve.
    a. & c. Wax buildup and blockage because of infection are temporary states; sensorineural hearing loss is permanent. Moreover, sensorineural hearing loss involves the inner ear rather than the outer or middle ear.
    b. Damage to the eardrum impairs the mechanical system that conducts sound waves; it could therefore cause conduction hearing loss, not sensorineural hearing loss.

Terms and Concepts to Remember:

73. **Audition** refers to the sense of hearing.

74. **Frequency** is directly related to wavelength: longer waves produce lower pitch; shorter waves produce higher pitch. The **pitch** of a sound is determined by its frequency, that is, the number of complete wavelengths that can pass a point in a given time.

75. The **middle ear** is the chamber between the eardrum and cochlea containing the three bones (hammer, anvil, and stirrup) that concentrate the eardrum's vibrations on the cochlea's oval window.

76. The **cochlea** is the coiled, bony, fluid-filled tube of the inner ear through which sound waves trigger neural impulses.

77. The **inner ear** contains the semicircular canals and the cochlea, which includes the receptors that transform sound energy into neural impulses. Because it also contains the vestibular sacs, the inner ear plays an important role in balance, as well as in audition.

78. **Sensorineural hearing loss** (nerve deafness) is hearing loss caused by damage to the auditory receptors of the cochlea or to the auditory nerve due to disease, aging, or prolonged exposure to ear-splitting noise.

79. **Conduction hearing loss** refers to the hearing loss that results from damage in the mechanical system of the outer or middle ear, which impairs the conduction of sound waves to the cochlea.

80. A **cochlear implant** is an electronic device that converts sounds into electrical signals that stimulate the auditory nerve.

81. The **place theory** of hearing states that we hear different pitches because sound waves of various frequencies trigger activity at different places on the cochlea's basilar membrane.
    Memory aid: **Place theory** maintains that the *place* of maximum vibration along the cochlea's membrane is the basis of pitch discrimination.

82. The **frequency theory** of hearing presumes that the rate, or frequency, of nerve impulses in the auditory nerve matches the frequency of a tone, thus enabling us to sense its pitch.

83. Melzack and Wall's **gate-control theory** maintains that a "gate" in the spinal cord determines whether pain signals are permitted to reach the brain. Neural activity in small nerve fibers opens the gates; activity in large fibers or information from the brain closes the gate.

    Example: The **gate-control theory** gained support with the discovery of endorphins. Production of these opiate-like chemicals may be the brain's mechanism for closing the spinal gate.

84. **Hypnosis** is a social interaction in which the hypnotist suggests to the subject that certain perceptions, feelings, or behaviors will occur.

85. **Dissociation** is a split in consciousness, which allows some thoughts and behaviors to occur simultaneously with others.

86. A **posthypnotic suggestion** is a suggestion, made during hypnosis, to be carried out after the subject is no longer hypnotized.

87. **Kinesthesia** is the sense of the position and movement of the parts of the body.

88. The sense of body movement and position, including the sense of balance, is called the **vestibular sense**.

89. **Sensory interaction** is the principle that one sense may influence another.

90. **Embodied cognition** refers to the influence of bodily sensations, gestures, and other states on cognitive preferences and judgments.

91. **Extrasensory perception (ESP)** refers to the controversial claim that perception can occur without sensory input. Supposed ESP powers include telepathy, clairvoyance, and precognition.

    Memory aid: Extra- means "beyond" or "in addition to"; **extrasensory perception** is perception outside or beyond the normal senses.

92. **Parapsychology** is the study of ESP, psychokinesis, and other paranormal forms of interaction between the individual and the environment.

    Memory aid: Para-, like *extra*-, indicates "beyond"; thus, paranormal is beyond the normal and **parapsychology** is the study of phenomena beyond the realm of psychology and known natural laws.

Summing Up

The Ear

1. Outer ear. Hearing begins as sound waves enter the auditory canal of the outer ear.

2. Auditory canal. Sound waves passing through the auditory canal are brought to a point of focus at the eardrum.

3. Eardrum. Lying between the outer and middle ear, this membrane vibrates in response to sound waves.

4. Middle ear. Lying between the outer and inner ear, this air-filled chamber contains the hammer, anvil, and stirrup.

5. Hammer, anvil, and stirrup. These tiny bones of the middle ear concentrate the eardrum's vibrations on the cochlea's oval window.

6. Inner ear. This region of the ear contains the cochlea and the semicircular canals, which play an important role in balance.

7. Cochlea. This fluid-filled multichambered structure contains the hair cell receptors that transduce sound waves into neural impulses.

8. Auditory nerve. This bundle of fibers carries nerve impulses from the inner ear to the brain.

Before You Move On

Matching Items

1. e	6. a	11. j
2. d	7. i	
3. g	8. b	
4. h	9. f	
5. k	10. c	

True–False Items

1. F	5. F	9. T
2. F	6. F	10. F
3. F	7. T	
4. F	8. F	

Essay Question

The senses that are most important to dancers are vision, hearing, kinesthesia, and the vestibular sense. Your answer should refer to any three of these senses and include, at minimum, the following information.

Dancers rely on vision to gauge their body position relative to other dancers as they perform specific choreographed movements. Vision also helps dancers assess the audience's reaction to their performance. Whenever dance is set to music, hearing is necessary so that the dancers can detect musical cues for certain parts of their routines. Hearing also helps the dancers keep their movements in time with the music. Kinesthetic receptors in dancers' tendons, joints, and muscles provide their brains with information about the position and movement of body parts to determine if they are in the proper positions. Receptors for the vestibular sense located in the dancers' inner ears send messages to their brains that help them maintain their balance and determine the correctness of the position and movement of their bodies.

Cross-Check

ACROSS

5. kinesthesia
7. hue
8. inner ear
9. basilar
10. closure
11. interposition
12. cones
13. jnd
14. parallel
15. absolute
17. cochlea
18. disparity

DOWN

1. frequency
2. figure-ground
3. retina
4. linear perspective
6. parapsychology
9. dissociation
16. rods
20. pitch

Learning

Overview

"No topic is closer to the heart of psychology than learning," a relatively permanent change in an organism's behavior due to experience.

Modules 19–21 cover the basic principles of three forms of learning: classical, or respondent, conditioning, in which we learn associations between events; operant conditioning, in which we learn to engage in behaviors that are rewarded and to avoid behaviors that are punished; and observational learning, in which we learn by observing and imitating others.

Module 21 also covers several important issues, including the generality of principles of learning, the role of cognitive processes in learning, and the ways in which learning is constrained by the biological predispositions of different species.

NOTE: Answer guidelines for all Modules 19–21 questions begin on page 179.

Outline

Instructions

First, skim each section, noting headings and boldface items. After you have read the section, review each objective by answering the fill-in, essay-type, and multiple-choice questions for that section. In some cases, Study Tips explain how best to learn a difficult concept and Applications and Module Reviews help you to know how well you understand the material. Finally, try to define the important terms and concepts using your own words. As you proceed, evaluate your performance by consulting the answers on page 179. Do not continue until you understand each answer. If you need to, review or reread a troublesome section before continuing.

Before You Move On includes activities that test you on material from the entire unit

Basic Learning Concepts and Classical Conditioning

How Do We Learn?

Objective 19-1: Define *learning*, and identify some basic forms of learning.

1. The process of acquiring through experience new and relatively enduring information or behaviors is called _____ .

2. One way we learn is by _____ events that occur in sequence. Even simple animals, such as the sea slug *Aplysia*, can learn simple_____ between stimuli. This type of learning is called _____ _____ .

3. The type of learning in which the organism learns to associate two stimuli and thus to anticipate events is _____ conditioning. A situation or event that evokes a response is a _____ . Behavior that occurs as an automatic response to a stimulus is called _____ behavior.

4. The tendency of organisms to associate a response and its consequence forms the basis of _____ conditioning. Behavior that operates on the environment, producing consequences, is called _____ behavior.

5. We acquire mental information that guides our behavior through _____ _____ . Complex animals often learn behaviors merely by _____ others perform them. This is called _____ _____ .

Classical Conditioning

Objective 19-2: Describe behaviorism's view of learning.

6. Classical conditioning was first explored by the Russian physiologist _____ . Early in the twentieth century, psychologist _____ urged psychologists to discard references to inner thoughts, feelings, and motives in favor of studying observable behavior. This view, called _____ , influenced American psychology during the first half of that century.

Objective 19-3: Describe who Pavlov was, and identify the basic components of classical conditioning.

7. Pavlov, who had a _____ degree, earned a Nobel Prize for his work studying the _____ system.

8. In Pavlov's classic experiment, a tone, or _____ , is sounded just before food, the _____ _____ , is placed in the animal's mouth. An animal will salivate when food is placed in its mouth. This salivation is called the _____ _____ .

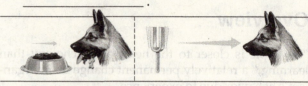

9. Eventually, the dogs in Pavlov's experiment would salivate on hearing the tone, now called the _____ _____ . This salivation is called the _____ .

STUDY TIP: Students often confuse *stimulus* with *response* and *conditioned* with *unconditioned*. The stimulus is the event that causes something else, the response, to happen. Unconditioned means "unlearned"; conditioned means "learned." Thus, an unconditioned response (UR) is an event that occurs naturally in response to some stimulus. An unconditioned stimulus (US) is something that naturally and automatically triggers the unlearned response. A conditioned stimulus (CS) is an originally neutral stimulus (NS) that, through learning, comes to be associated with some unlearned response. A conditioned response (CR) is the learned response to the originally neutral but now conditioned stimulus.

Stimulus (event or other trigger) → Response
Unconditioned = unlearned
Conditioned = learned
So, unconditioned stimulus   +   conditioned stimulus
↓   ↓
unconditioned response   conditioned response

APPLICATIONS:

Classical conditioning is all around us. It is especially common in the realm of emotional behavior. Test your understanding of the basic elements of classical conditioning in the following example. Then, consider whether there are emotions of your own that might have developed as the product of classical conditioning.

As a child, you were playing in the yard one day when a neighbor's cat wandered over. Your mother (who has a terrible fear of animals) screamed and snatched you into her arms. Her behavior caused you to cry. You now have a fear of cats.

10. The NS, then CS is _____

11. The US is _____

12. The CR is _____

13. The UR is _____

14. You always rattle the box of dog biscuits before giving your dog a treat. As you do so, your dog salivates. At first, rattling the box is a _____ , which eventually becomes a _____ . Your dog's salivation to the rattling is a _____ .

    a. NS; CS; CR   **c.** NS; US; CR
    b. CS; NS; UR   **d.** US; NS; UR

Objective 19-4: Summarize the processes of *acquisition, extinction, spontaneous recovery, generalization,* and *discrimination* in classical conditioning.

Use the following graph as a reference for the answers to 15(a), 19(b), and 20(c).

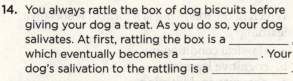

15. The initial learning of a conditioned response is called (a) _____ . For many conditioning situations, the optimal interval between a neutral stimulus and the US is

_____ _____ .

16. When the US is presented prior to a neutral stimulus, conditioning _____ (does/does not) occur.

17. Sexual conditioning studies with quail demonstrate that classical conditioning is highly adaptive because it helps animals _____ and _____ .

18. If a CS is repeatedly presented without the US, (b) _____ soon occurs; that is, the CR diminishes.

19. Following a pause, however, the CR reappears in response to the CS; this phenomenon is called (c) _____ _____ .

20. Subjects often respond to a similar stimulus as they would to the original CS. This phenomenon is called _____ .

21. Humans and other animals can also be trained not to respond to _____ stimuli. This learned ability is called _____ .

22. Being able to recognize differences among stimuli has _____ value because it lets us limit our learned responses to appropriate stimuli.

STUDY TIP: Some students find the terms *discrimination* and *generalization* confusing because of their negative social connotations. In the context of classical conditioning, discrimination is a healthy sign that the subject of conditioning has learned the difference between two stimuli, much as a "discriminating coffee lover" can taste subtle variations between two coffee blends. Generalization is apparent when discrimination does not occur.

APPLICATION:

Bill had an American-made car that was in the shop more than it was out. Since then he will not even consider owning an American-made car.

23. Bill's attitude is an example of _____ . Bill's friend Andy also had an American-made car with similar problems. Deciding that it was just that brand, Andy decided to try another brand. Rather than bunch all American-made cars together, he was a _____ buyer of cars.

Objective 19-5: Explain why Pavlov's work remains so important.

24. Classical conditioning is one way that virtually all organisms learn to _____ to their environment.

25. Another aspect of Pavlov's legacy is that he showed how a process such as learning could be studied _____.

Explain why the study of classical conditioning is important.

Objective 19-6: Identify some applications of Pavlov's work to human health and well-being, and describe how Watson applied Pavlov's principles to learned fears.

26. Through classical conditioning, former drug users often feel a _____ when they are in the _____ associated with previous highs.

27. Research studies demonstrate that the body's immune system _____ (can/cannot) be classically conditioned.

28. Pavlov's work also provided a basis for Watson's idea that human _____ and behaviors, though _____ influenced, are mainly a bundle of conditioned responses.

Describe the Watson and Rayner experiment.

MODULE REVIEW:

29. *Learning* is best defined as
  a. any behavior produced by an organism without being provoked.
  b. a change in the behavior of an organism.
  c. a relatively permanent change in the behavior of an organism due to experience.
  d. behavior based on operant rather than respondent conditioning.

30. In Pavlov's original experiment with dogs, the meat served as a
  a. CS.   c. US.
  b. CR.   d. UR.

31. In Pavlov's original experiment with dogs, the tone was initially a(n) _____ stimulus; after it was paired with meat, it became a(n) _____ stimulus.
  a. conditioned; neutral
  b. neutral; conditioned
  c. conditioned; unconditioned
  d. unconditioned; conditioned

32. When a conditioned stimulus is presented without an accompanying unconditioned stimulus, _____ will soon take place.
  a. generalization   c. extinction
  b. discrimination   d. aversion

33. In Pavlov's original experiment with dogs, salivation to meat was the
  a. CS.   c. US.
  b. CR.   d. UR.

34. Which of the following is a form of associative learning?
  a. classical conditioning
  b. cognitive learning
  c. observational learning
  d. all of these types of learning

35. For the most rapid conditioning, a CS should be presented
  a. about 1 second after the US.
  b. about one-half second before the US.
  c. about 15 seconds before the US.
  d. at the same time as the US.

36. During extinction, the _____ is omitted; as a result, the _____ seems to disappear.
  a. US; UR   c. US; CR
  b. CS; CR   d. CS; UR

37. In Watson and Rayner's experiment, the loud noise was the _____ and the white rat was the _____ .
  a. CS; CR   c. CS; US
  b. US; CS   d. US; CR

38. In which of the following may classical conditioning play a role?
  a. emotional problems
  b. the body's immune response
  c. helping drug addicts
  d. in all of these cases

39. In Pavlov's studies of classical conditioning of a dog's salivary responses, spontaneous recovery occurred
  a. during acquisition, when the CS was first paired with the US.

b. during extinction, when the CS was first presented by itself.

c. when the CS was reintroduced following extinction of the CR and a rest period.

d. during discrimination training, when several conditioned stimuli were introduced.

TERMS AND CONCEPTS TO REMEMBER:

40. learning
41. associative learning
42. stimulus
43. respondent behavior
44. operant behavior
45. cognitive learning
46. classical conditioning
47. behaviorism
48. neutral stimulus (NS)
49. unconditioned response (UR)
50. unconditioned stimulus (US)
51. conditioned response (CR)
52. conditioned stimulus (CS)
53. acquisition
54. extinction
55. spontaneous recovery
56. generalization
57. discrimination

MODULE 20 **Operant Conditioning**

Objective 20-1: Define *operant conditioning*.

1. In operant conditioning, organisms associate their own actions with _____ . Actions followed by _____ increase; actions followed by _____ decrease. Thus, the behavior _____ on the environment. This differs from classical conditioning, which involves automatic _____ behavior.

Skinner's Experiments

Objective 20-2: Describe who Skinner was, and explain how operant behavior is reinforced and shaped.

2. B. F. Skinner was an _____ major who studied psychology in graduate school. He became modern _____'s most influential and controversial figure.

3. Skinner used Thorndike's _____ _____ as a starting point in developing a behavioral technology that revealed principles of _____ _____ . Thorndike's principle states that _____ behavior is likely to _____ .

4. Skinner designed an apparatus, called the _____ , to investigate learning in animals. This design creates a stage on which organisms act out Skinner's concept of _____ , any event that increases the frequency of a preceding response.

5. The procedure in which a person teaches an animal to perform an intricate behavior by building up to it in small steps is called _____ . This method involves reinforcing successive _____ of the desired behavior.

6. In experiments to determine what an animal can perceive, researchers have found that animals are capable of forming _____ and _____ between stimuli. Similar experiments have been conducted with babies, who also can't verbalize their responses.

7. A situation, event, or signal that a certain response will be reinforced is a _____ _____ .

APPLICATION:

8. Which of the following is an example of shaping?
   a. A dog learns to salivate at the sight of a box of dog biscuits.
   b. A new driver learns to stop at an intersection when the light changes to red.
   c. A parrot is rewarded first for making any sound, then for making a sound similar to "Laura," and then for "speaking" its owner's name.

Objective 20-3: Discuss the differences between positive and negative reinforcement, and identify the basic types of reinforcers.

9. A stimulus that strengthens a response by presenting a typically pleasurable stimulus after a response is a _____

_____ .

10. A stimulus that strengthens a response by reducing or removing an aversive (unpleasant) stimulus is a _____ _____ .

11. Reinforcers, such as food and shock, that are related to basic needs and therefore do not rely on learning are called _____

_____ .

12. Reinforcers that must be conditioned and therefore derive their power through association are called _____ _____ .

13. Children who are able to delay gratification tend to become _____ (more/less) socially competent and high-achieving adults.

14. Immediate consequences _____ (are/are not) sometimes more alluring than their alternative, _____ reinforcement. This explains in part the tendency of some teens to engage in risky, _____

_____ .

STUDY TIP: Some students have a problem differentiating positive and negative reinforcers because they naturally think "positive" indicates a "good," or desirable, outcome, while "negative" connotes a "bad," or undesirable, outcome. Remember that from the organism's point of view, reinforcement is always a desirable outcome. You may find it useful to think of a photography analogy. A "negative" is a reverse image in which the "positive" photographic image is not present. So too, negative reinforcement involves taking away an event—in this case, one that is undesirable.

Objective 20-4: Explain how the different reinforcement schedules affect behavior.

15. A _____ is a pattern specifying how often a _____

_____ is reinforced.

16. The procedure involving reinforcement of each and every response is called

_____ _____ .

Under these conditions, learning is _____ (rapid/slow). When this type of reinforcement is discontinued, extinction is _____ (rapid/slow).

17. The procedure in which responses are reinforced only part of the time is called _____ reinforcement. Under these conditions, learning is generally _____ (faster/slower) than it is with continuous reinforcement. Behavior reinforced in this manner is _____ (very/not very) resistant to extinction.

18. When behavior is reinforced after a set number of responses, a _____-_____ schedule is in effect. An example of this schedule is _____

_____ .

19. Three-year-old Yusef knows that if he cries when he wants a treat, his mother will sometimes give in. When, as in this case, reinforcement occurs after an unpredictable number of responses, a _____-_____

schedule is being used.

20. Reinforcement of the first response after a set interval of time defines the

_____-_____

schedule. An example of this schedule is

_____ .

21. When the first response after varying amounts of time is reinforced, a _____-_____ schedule is in effect. An example of this schedule is _____

_____ .

Describe the typical patterns of response under fixed-interval, fixed-ratio, variable-interval, and variable-ratio schedules of reinforcement.

APPLICATIONS:

22. You are expecting an important letter in the mail. As the regular delivery time approaches you glance more and more frequently out the window, searching for the letter carrier. Your behavior in this situation typifies that associated with which schedule of reinforcement?

    a. fixed-ratio
    b. variable-ratio
    c. fixed-interval
    d. variable-interval

23. From a casino owner's viewpoint, which of the following jackpot-payout schedules would be the most desirable for reinforcing customer use of a slot machine?

    a. variable-ratio
    b. fixed-ratio
    c. variable-interval
    d. fixed-interval

24. Lars, a shoe salesman, is paid every two weeks, whereas Tom receives a commission for each pair of shoes he sells. Evidently, Lars is paid on a _____ schedule of reinforcement, and Tom on a _____ schedule of reinforcement.

    a. fixed-ratio; fixed-interval
    b. continuous; intermittent
    c. fixed-interval; fixed-ratio
    d. variable-interval; variable-ratio

25. Jack finally takes out the garbage in order to get his father to stop pestering him. Jack's behavior is being influenced by _____ _____ .

26. Your instructor invites you to her home as part of a select group of students to discuss possible careers in psychology. The invitation is an example of a _____ _____ .

Objective 20-5: Discuss how punishment and negative reinforcement differ, and explain how punishment affects behavior.

27. Negative reinforcement _____ (increases/decreases) a response by _____ an aversive stimulus after that response. Punishment _____ (increases/decreases) a response by _____ an aversive stimulus after that response.

28. An aversive consequence that decreases the likelihood of the behavior that preceded it is called _____ . If an aversive stimulus is administered, it is called _____ . If a desirable stimulus is withdrawn, it is called _____ _____ .

29. Because punished behavior is merely _____ , it may reappear. Also, punishment teaches _____ , that behavior that is unacceptable in one context may be acceptable in another. Punishment can also teach the person to associate _____ not only with the undesirable behavior but also with _____ and _____ .

30. Punishment also often increases _____ and does not guide the individual toward more desirable behavior.

STUDY TIP/APPLICATION: To avoid the natural tendency to confuse punishment and negative reinforcement, remember that positive reinforcement and negative reinforcement both lead to an *increase* in behavior, while punishment *decreases* behavior. In punishment, something bad occurs following an undesirable behavior; in negative reinforcement, something bad is removed. Complete the chart on the next page of examples of punishment and negative reinforcement. The first example has been filled in for you.

31.

Behavior	Consequence	Which Is Taken Away, Something Good or Bad?	Is This Punishment or Negative Reinforcement?
Driving while intoxicated	Lose driver's license	Good	Punishment
a. Forgetting to give your roommate a phone message			
b. Putting on your coat so that you are no longer cold			
c. Getting a drink when you are thirsty			
d. Using your laptop until the battery dies			
e. Your brother nagging you until you help him with his homework			

Skinner's Legacy

Objective 20-6: Discuss why Skinner's ideas provoked controversy, and identify how his operant conditioning principles might be applied at school, in sports, at work, and at home.

32. Skinner's views were controversial because he insisted that _____ influences, rather than _____ _____ and _____ , shape behavior.

33. Skinner also advocated the use of _____ principles to influence people in ways that promote more desirable _____ .

34. Skinner's critics argued that he _____ people by neglecting their personal _____ and by seeking to _____ their actions.

35. The use of teaching machines and programmed textbooks was an early application of the operant conditioning procedure of _____ to education. Online _____ , software that is _____ , and _____ -based learning are newer examples of this application of operant principles. Reinforcement principles can also be used to enhance _____ abilities by shaping successive approximations of new skills.

36. In boosting productivity in the workplace, positive reinforcement is _____ (more/less) effective when applied to specific behaviors than when given to reward general merit and when the desired performance is well defined and _____ . For such behaviors, immediate reinforcement is _____ (more/no more) effective than delayed reinforcement.

37. In using operant conditioning to change your own behavior, you would follow these five steps
a. _____
b. _____
c. _____
d. _____
e. _____

APPLICATIONS:

38. The manager of a manufacturing plant wishes to use positive reinforcement to increase the productivity of workers. Which of the following procedures would probably be the most effective?
a. Deserving employees are given a general merit bonus at the end of each fiscal year.
b. A productivity goal that seems attainable, yet is unrealistic, is set for each employee.
c. Employees are given immediate bonuses for specific behaviors related to productivity.
d. Employees who fail to meet standards of productivity receive pay cuts.

39. Reggie's mother tells him that he can go on Facebook after he cleans his room. Evidently, Reggie's mother is attempting to use _____ to increase room cleaning.

a. operant conditioning
b. secondary reinforcement
c. positive reinforcement
d. all of these procedures

Contrasting Classical and Operant Conditioning

Objective 20-7: Describe how operant conditioning differs from classical conditioning.

40. Classical conditioning and operant conditioning are both forms of _____ _____ .

41. Both types of conditioning involve similar processes of _____ , _____ , _____ _____ , _____ , and _____ .

42. Classical conditioning associates _____ stimuli with stimuli that

trigger responses that are _____ . Thus, in this form of conditioning, the organism _____ (does/does not) control the responses.

43. The reflexive responses of classical conditioning involve _____ behavior.

44. In contrast, behavior that is more spontaneous and that is influenced by its consequences is called _____ behavior.

45. Classical and operant conditioning are both subject to the influences of _____ processes and _____ predispositions.

___

STUDY TIP/APPLICATION: If you still find yourself confusing classical conditioning and operant conditioning, try the following. Ask yourself two questions: (1) Is the behavior voluntary (operant conditioning) or involuntary (classical conditioning)? (2) Does the learning involve an association between two stimuli (classical conditioning) or between a response and an outcome (operant conditioning)? Test your understanding with the following examples.

46.

Behavior	Is the Behavior Voluntary or Involuntary?	Type of Conditioning
a. After receiving a mild shock from the "invisible fence" surrounding his yard, a dog no longer crosses the boundary.		
b. You flinch when someone yells, "Duck!"		
c. You ask more questions in class after the professor praises you for a good question.		
d. The pupil of your eye dilates (opens wider) after you enter a darkened theater.		

MODULE REVIEW:

47. The type of learning associated with Skinner is

a. classical conditioning.
b. operant conditioning.
c. respondent conditioning.
d. associative learning.

48. Which of the following statements concerning reinforcement is correct?

a. Learning is most rapid with intermittent reinforcement, but continuous reinforcement produces the greatest resistance to extinction.

b. Learning is most rapid with continuous reinforcement, but intermittent reinforcement produces the greatest resistance to extinction.

c. Learning is fastest and resistance to extinction is greatest after continuous reinforcement.

d. Learning is fastest and resistance to extinction is greatest following intermittent reinforcement.

49. The highest and most consistent rate of response is produced by a _____ schedule.

a. fixed-ratio   c. fixed-interval
b. variable-ratio   d. variable-interval

50. A response that leads to the removal of an unpleasant stimulus is one being
    a. positively reinforced.
    b. negatively reinforced.
    c. punished.
    d. extinguished.

51. One difference between classical and operant conditioning is that
    a. in classical conditioning, the responses operate on the environment to produce rewarding or punishing stimuli.
    b. in operant conditioning, the responses are triggered by preceding stimuli.
    c. in classical conditioning, the responses are automatically triggered by stimuli.
    d. in operant conditioning, the responses are reflexive.

52. Punishment is a controversial way of controlling behavior because
    a. behavior is not forgotten and may return.
    b. punishing stimuli often create fear.
    c. punishment often increases aggressiveness.
    d. of all of these reasons.

53. Which of the following is an example of reinforcement?
    a. presenting a positive stimulus after a response
    b. removing an unpleasant stimulus after a response
    c. being told that you have done a good job
    d. All of these are examples.

54. Shaping is a(n) _____ technique for _____ a behavior.
    a. operant; establishing
    b. operant; suppressing
    c. respondent; establishing
    d. respondent; suppressing

55. For operant conditioning to be most effective, when should the reinforcers be presented in relation to the desired response?
    a. immediately before
    b. immediately after
    c. at the same time as
    d. at least a half hour before

56. In distinguishing between negative reinforcers and punishment, we note that
    a. punishment, but not negative reinforcement, involves use of an aversive stimulus.
    b. in contrast to punishment, negative reinforcement decreases the likelihood of a response by the presentation of an aversive stimulus.

    c. in contrast to punishment, negative reinforcement increases the likelihood of a response by the presentation of an aversive stimulus.
    d. in contrast to punishment, negative reinforcement increases the likelihood of a response by the termination of an aversive stimulus.

57. The "piecework," or commission, method of payment is an example of which reinforcement schedule?
    a. fixed-interval   c. fixed-ratio
    b. variable-interval   d. variable-ratio

58. Putting on your coat when it is cold outside is a behavior that is maintained by
    a. discrimination learning.
    b. punishment.
    c. negative reinforcement.
    d. classical conditioning.

59. On an intermittent reinforcement schedule, reinforcement is given
    a. in very small amounts.
    b. randomly.
    c. for successive approximations of a desired behavior.
    d. only some of the time.

60. You teach your dog to fetch the paper by giving him a doggie treat each time he does so. This is an example of
    a. operant conditioning.
    b. classical conditioning.
    c. conditioned reinforcement.
    d. partial reinforcement.

61. Leon's psychology instructor has scheduled an exam every third week of the term. Leon will probably study the most just before an exam and the least just after an exam. This is because the schedule of exams is reinforcing studying according to which schedule?
    a. fixed-ratio   c. fixed-interval
    b. variable-ratio   d. variable-interval

62. Online testing systems and interactive software are applications of the operant conditioning principles of
    a. shaping and immediate reinforcement.
    b. immediate reinforcement and punishment.
    c. shaping and primary reinforcement.
    d. continuous reinforcement and punishment.

63. Which of the following is the best example of a conditioned reinforcer?
    a. putting on a coat on a cold day

b. relief from pain after the dentist stops drilling your teeth

c. receiving a cool drink after washing your mother's car on a hot day

d. receiving an approving nod from the boss for a job well done

64. To obtain a reward, a monkey learns to press a lever when a 1000-Hz tone is on but not when a 1200-Hz tone is on. What kind of training is this?

a. extinction
b. generalization
c. classical conditioning
d. discrimination

TERMS AND CONCEPTS TO REMEMBER:

65. operant conditioning
66. law of effect
67. operant chamber
68. reinforcement
69. shaping
70. positive reinforcement
71. negative reinforcement
72. primary reinforcer
73. conditioned reinforcer
74. reinforcement schedule
75. continuous reinforcement
76. partial (intermittent) reinforcement
77. fixed-ratio schedule
78. variable-ratio schedule
79. fixed-interval schedule
80. variable-interval schedule
81. punishment

Essay Question

Describe the best way for a pet owner to condition her dog to roll over. (Use the space below to list the points you want to make, and organize them. Then write the essay on a separate piece of paper.)

MODULE

21

Biology, Cognition, and Learning

1. Today's learning theorists recognize that learning is the product of the interaction of

_____ , _____ , and

_____-_____

influences.

Biological Constraints on Conditioning

Objective 21-1: Explain how biological constraints affect classical and operant conditioning.

2. Some psychologists once believed that any natural _____ could be conditioned to any neutral _____ . More than the early behaviorists realized, as Gregory Kimble acknowledged, an animal's capacity for conditioning is limited by

_____ _____

3. John Garcia discovered that rats would associate _____ with taste but not with sights or sounds. Garcia found that taste-aversion conditioning _____ (would/would not) occur when the delay between the CS and the US was as late as several hours. Conditioning is speedier, stronger, and more durable when the CS is _____ relevant.

4. Results such as these support Darwin's principle that _____ _____ favors traits that aid survival. They demonstrate that the principles of learning are constrained by the _____ predispositions of each animal species and that they help each species _____ to its environment.

5. Operant conditioning _____ (is/is not) constrained by an animal's biological predispositions.

6. For instance, with animals it is difficult to use food as a _____ to _____ behaviors that are not naturally associated with _____ .

7. Biological constraints predispose organisms to learn associations that are naturally _____. When animals revert to their biologically predisposed patterns, they are exhibiting what is called _____.

APPLICATIONS:

8. A pigeon can easily be taught to flap its wings to avoid shock but not for food reinforcement. According to the text, this is most likely so because
   a. pigeons are biologically predisposed to flap their wings to escape aversive events and to use their beaks to obtain food.
   b. shock is a more motivating stimulus for birds than food is.
   c. hungry animals have difficulty delaying their eating long enough to learn any new skill.
   d. of all of these reasons.

9. Last evening May-Ling ate her first cheeseburger and french fries at an American fast-food restaurant. A few hours later she became ill. It can be expected that May-Ling will
   a. develop an aversion to the sight of a cheeseburger and french fries.
   b. develop an aversion to the taste of a cheeseburger and french fries.
   c. not associate her illness with the food she ate.
   d. associate her sickness with something she experienced immediately before she became ill.

Cognition's Influence on Conditioning

Objective 21-2: Explain how cognitive processes affect classical and operant conditioning.

10. The early behaviorists believed that to understand behavior in various organisms, any presumption of _____ was unnecessary.

11. Experiments by Robert Rescorla and Allan Wagner demonstrate that a CS must reliably _____ the US for an association to develop and, more generally, that _____ processes play a role in conditioning. It is as if the animal learns to _____ that the US will occur.

12. The importance of cognitive processes in human conditioning is demonstrated by the failure of classical conditioning as a treatment for _____ _____.

13. B. F. Skinner and other behaviorists resisted the growing belief that expectations, perceptions, and other _____ processes have a valid place in the science of psychology.

14. When a well-learned route in a maze is blocked, rats sometimes choose an alternative route, acting as if they were consulting a _____ _____.

15. Animals may learn from experience even when reinforcement is not available. When learning is not apparent until reinforcement has been provided, _____ _____ is said to have occurred.

16. Excessive rewards may undermine _____ _____, which is the desire to perform a behavior for its own sake. The motivation to seek external rewards and avoid punishment is called _____ _____.

APPLICATIONS:

17. After discovering that her usual route home was closed due to road repairs, Sharetta used her knowledge of the city and sense of direction to find an alternative route. This is an example of
    a. latent learning.
    b. classical conditioning.
    c. a biopsychosocial influence.
    d. using a cognitive map.

18. Two rats are independently placed in a maze. One rat is rewarded with food in the goal box. The other receives no food reward. On a later trial, food is placed in the goal box for the "unrewarded" rat. What can you say about the rat's behavior on that trial?
    a. The "unrewarded" rat will run to the goal box just as quickly as the rewarded rat.
    b. The rat will wander around the maze and never find the food reward.
    c. The rat will find the food reward, but it will take much longer than the rewarded rat.
    d. The rat will not even try to find the food reward.

19. Nancy decided to take introductory psychology because she has always been interested in human behavior. Jack enrolled in the same course because he thought it would be easy. Nancy's behavior was motivated by _____ , Jack's by _____ .
    a. extrinsic motivation; intrinsic motivation
    b. intrinsic motivation; extrinsic motivation
    c. drives; incentives
    d. incentives; drives

Learning by Observation

Objective 21-3: Discuss how observational learning differs from associative learning, and explain how observational learning may be enabled by neural mirroring.

20. Learning by observing and imitating others is called _____ , or _____ _____ . This form of learning _____ (occurs/ does not occur) in species other than our own.

21. The psychologist best known for research on observational learning is _____ .

22. In one experiment, the child who viewed an adult punch an inflatable doll played _____ (more/less) aggressively than the child who had not observed the adult.

23. Bandura believes people imitate a model because of _____ _____ and _____ _____ , those received by the model as well as by imitators.

24. Models are most effective when they are perceived as _____ , _____ , or _____ .

25. Neuroscientists have found _____ neurons in the brain's _____ lobe that may provide a neural basis for everyday imitation and _____ learning. These neurons have been observed to fire when monkeys perform a simple task and when they _____ .

26. By age _____ , infants will imitate various novel gestures. By age _____ , they will imitate acts modeled on television. So

strong is the human predisposition to learn from watching adults that 2- to 5-year-olds will _____ . Children's brains enable their _____ and their _____ _____ .

27. After watching coverage of the Olympics on television recently, Lynn and Susan have been staging their own "summer games." Which of the following best accounts for their behavior?
    a. classical conditioning
    b. observational learning
    c. latent learning
    d. prosocial learning

Objective 21-4: Discuss the impact of prosocial modeling and of antisocial modeling.

28. People will model positive, or _____ , behaviors. Models are also most effective when their words and actions are _____ .

29. People will also model negative, or _____ , behaviors. This may help explain why _____ parents might have _____ children. However, _____ factors may also be involved.

30. During their first 18 years, children in developed countries spend more time _____ _____ than they spend in school.

31. Compared with the real world, television depicts a much higher percentage of crimes as being _____ in nature.

32. (Thinking Critically) Correlational studies _____ (link/do not link) watching television and video violence, and playing violent video games with violent behavior.

33. (Thinking Critically) Correlation does not prove _____ . Most researchers believe that watching violence to some extent _____ (does/does not) lead to aggressive behavior, especially when an attractive person commits seemingly _____ , realistic violence that goes _____ and causes no visible pain or harm.

34. (Thinking Critically) The violence-viewing effect stems from several factors, including _____ of observed aggression and the tendency of prolonged exposure to violence to _____ viewers.

APPLICATIONS: Children—and, of course, adults—learn a great deal by watching other people. Depending on the models, the behavior they learn may be good or bad.

35. During holiday breaks Lionel watches wrestling, which _____ his aggressive tendencies. His brother Michael won't watch the wrestling because he feels the pain of the choke hold, for example, as reflected in his brain's

_____ _____ .

Instead, Michael spends time with Grandma, who cooks for the poor during the holiday season, helping Michael to learn _____ behavior.

36. Mrs. Ramirez often tells her children that it is important to buckle their seat belts while riding in the car, but she rarely does so herself. Her children will probably learn to

  a. use their seat belts and tell others it is important to do so.

  b. use their seat belts but not tell others it is important to do so.

  c. tell others it is important to use seat belts but rarely use them themselves.

  d. neither tell others that seat belts are important nor use them.

MODULE REVIEW:

37. Cognitive processes are

  a. unimportant in classical and operant conditioning.

  b. important in both classical and operant conditioning.

  c. more important in classical than in operant conditioning.

  d. more important in operant than in classical conditioning.

38. In Garcia and Koelling's studies of taste-aversion learning, rats learned to associate

  a. taste with electric shock.

  b. sights and sounds with sickness.

  c. taste with sickness.

  d. taste and sounds with electric shock.

39. Learning by imitating others' behaviors is called _____ learning. The researcher best known for studying this type of learning is _____ .

  a. operant; Skinner

  b. observational; Bandura

  c. classical; Pavlov

  d. observational; Watson

40. Classical conditioning experiments by Rescorla and Wagner demonstrate that an important factor in conditioning is

  a. the research participant's age.

  b. the strength of the stimuli.

  c. the predictability of an association.

  d. the similarity of stimuli.

41. Mirror neurons are found in the brain's _____ and are believed by some scientists to be the neural basis for _____ .

  a. frontal lobe; observational learning

  b. frontal lobe; classical conditioning

  c. temporal lobe; operant conditioning

  d. temporal lobe; observational learning

42. In promoting observational learning, the most effective models are those that we perceive as

  a. similar to ourselves.

  b. respected and admired.

  c. successful.

  d. having any of these characteristics.

43. A cognitive map is a

  a. mental representation of one's environment.

  b. sequence of thought processes leading from one idea to another.

  c. set of instructions detailing the most effective means of teaching a particular concept.

  d. biological predisposition to learn a particular skill.

44. After exploring a complicated maze for several days, a rat subsequently ran the maze with very few errors when food was placed in the goal box for the first time. This performance illustrates

  a. classical conditioning.

  b. discrimination learning.

  c. observational learning.

  d. latent learning.

45. Experiments on taste-aversion learning demonstrate that

  a. for the conditioning of certain stimuli, the US need not immediately follow the CS.

  b. any perceivable stimulus can become a CS.

  c. all animals are biologically primed to associate illness with the taste of a tainted food.

  d. all of these statements are true.

46. Regarding the impact of watching television or video violence on children, most researchers believe that
    a. aggressive children simply prefer violent programs.
    b. these media simply reflect, rather than contribute to, violent social trends.
    c. watching violence on television or a video leads to aggressive behavior.
    d. there is only a weak correlation between exposure to violence and aggressive behavior.

TERMS AND CONCEPTS TO REMEMBER:

47. cognitive map
48. latent learning
49. intrinsic motivation
50. extrinsic motivation
51. observational learning
52. modeling
53. mirror neurons
54. prosocial behavior

Before You Move On

Matching Items

Match each definition or description with the appropriate term.

Definitions or Descriptions

_____ 1. presentation of a desired stimulus
_____ 2. tendency for similar stimuli to evoke a CR
_____ 3. removal of an aversive stimulus
_____ 4. an innately reinforcing stimulus
_____ 5. an acquired reinforcer
_____ 6. responses are reinforced after an unpredictable amount of time
_____ 7. the motivation to perform a behavior for its own sake
_____ 8. reinforcing closer and closer approximations of a behavior
_____ 9. the reappearance of a weakened CR
_____ 10. presentation of an aversive stimulus
_____ 11. learning that becomes apparent only after reinforcement is provided
_____ 12. each and every response is reinforced
_____ 13. a desire to perform a behavior because of promised rewards
_____ 14. the process of observing and imitating a specific behavior
_____ 15. learning by observing others

Terms

a. shaping
b. punishment
c. spontaneous recovery
d. latent learning
e. observational learning
f. positive reinforcement
g. negative reinforcement
h. primary reinforcer
i. generalization
j. intrinsic motivation
k. conditioned reinforcer
l. continuous reinforcement
m. variable-interval schedule
n. extrinsic motivation
o. modeling

True–False Items

Indicate whether each statement is true or false by placing *T* or *F* in the blank next to the item.

_____ 1. Operant conditioning involves behavior that is primarily reflexive.

_____ 2. The optimal interval between CS and US is about 15 seconds.

_____ 3. Negative reinforcement decreases the likelihood that a response will recur.

_____ 4. The learning of a new behavior proceeds most rapidly with continuous reinforcement.

_____ 5. As a rule, variable schedules of reinforcement produce more consistent rates of responding than fixed schedules.

_____ 6. Cognitive processes are of relatively little importance in learning.

_____ 7. Although punishment may be effective in suppressing behavior, it can have several undesirable side effects.

_____ 8. All animals, including rats and birds, are biologically predisposed to associate taste cues with sickness.

_____ 9. Whether the CS or US is presented first seems not to matter in terms of the ease of classical conditioning.

_____ 10. Spontaneous recovery refers to the tendency of extinguished behaviors to reappear suddenly.

_____ 11. Elementary schoolchildren with heavy exposure to media violence also tend to get into more fights.

Cross-Check

As you learned in Module 2, reviewing and overlearning of material are important to the learning process. After you have written the definitions of the key terms in this unit, you should complete the crossword puzzle to ensure that you can reverse the process—recognize the term, given the definition.

ACROSS

1. Behavior that occurs as an automatic response to a stimulus.
4. Relatively permanent change in behavior due to experience.
6. Reinforcer that, when removed after a response, strengthens the response.
9. Type of stimulus that naturally triggers an unconditioned response.
12. Unlearned, involuntary response.
14. Type of behavior that is positive and helpful.
17. Behavior that produces reinforcing or punishing stimuli.
20. Procedure that involves reinforcing successive approximations of a behavior.

21. Learned response to a previously neutral stimulus.

22. Learning that occurs in the absence of reinforcement but only becomes apparent when an incentive is introduced.

23. Initial stage of conditioning, in which a new response is established.

DOWN

2. Type of reinforcement in which responding is intermittently reinforced.

3. Schedule in which the first response following a set period of time is reinforced.

5. Tendency for stimuli similar to the original CS to evoke a CR.

7. This occurs when a response is no longer reinforced.

8. Mental picture of the environment

10. Responding differently to stimuli that signal whether a behavior will be reinforced.

11. Learning that involves watching and imitating others.

13. Stimulus that automatically triggers an unconditioned response.

14. The presentation of an aversive stimulus, which decreases the behavior it follows.

15. Type of learning also called Pavlovian conditioning.

16. The process of watching and then imitating a behavior.

18. Motivation to perform a behavior in order to obtain a reward or avoid a punishment.

19. Originally neutral stimulus that comes to trigger a conditioned response.

Answers

Basic Learning Concepts and Classical Conditioning

How Do We Learn?

1. learning

2. associating; associations; associative learning

3. classical; stimulus; respondent

4. operant; operant

5. cognitive learning; observing; observational learning

Classical Conditioning

6. Ivan Pavlov; John Watson; behaviorism

7. medical; digestive

8. neutral stimulus; unconditioned stimulus; unconditioned response

9. conditioned stimulus; conditioned response

10. the cat

11. your mother's behavior

12. your fear today

13. your crying

14. **a.** is the answer. Your dog had to learn to associate the rattling sound with the food. Rattling is therefore a conditioned, or learned, stimulus, and salivation in response to this rattling is a learned, or conditioned, response.

15. acquisition; one-half second

16. does not

17. survive; reproduce

18. extinction

19. spontaneous recovery

20. generalization

21. similar; discrimination

22. adaptive

23. generalization; discriminating

24. adapt

25. objectively

Classical conditioning is one way that virtually all organisms learn to adapt to their environment. Classical conditioning also provided an example to the young field of psychology of how complex processes could be studied with objective laboratory procedures. In addition, classical conditioning has proven to have many helpful applications to human health and well-being.

26. craving; context

27. can

28. emotions; biologically

In Watson and Rayner's experiment, classical conditioning was used to condition fear of a rat in Albert, an 11-month-old infant. When Albert touched the white rat (neutral stimulus), a loud noise (unconditioned stimulus) was sounded. After several pairings of the rat with the noise, Albert began crying at the mere sight of the rat. The rat had become a conditioned stimulus, triggering a conditioned response of fear. This led many psychologists to wonder whether each us might be a walking warehouse of conditioned responses. The experiment, however, would be unacceptable by today's ethical standards.

Module Review:

29. **c.** is the answer.

a. This answer is incorrect because it simply describes any behavior that is automatic rather than being triggered by a specific stimulus.

b. This answer is too general, since behaviors can change for reasons other than learning.

d. Respondently conditioned behavior also satisfies the criteria of our definition of learning.

30. **c.** is the answer. Meat automatically triggers the response of salivation and is therefore an unconditioned stimulus.

    a. A conditioned stimulus acquires its response-triggering powers through learning. A dog does not learn to salivate to meat.

    b. & d. Responses are behaviors triggered in the organism, in this case the dog's salivation. The meat is a stimulus.

31. **b.** is the answer. Prior to its pairing with meat (the US), the tone did not trigger salivation and was therefore a neutral stimulus (NS). Afterward, the tone triggered salivation (the CR) and was therefore a conditioned stimulus (CS).

    c. & d. Unconditioned stimuli, such as meat, innately trigger responding. Pavlov's dogs had to learn to associate the tone with the food.

32. **c.** is the answer. In this situation, the CR will decline, a phenomenon known as extinction.

    a. Generalization occurs when the subject makes a CR to stimuli similar to the original CS.

    b. Discrimination is when the subject does not make a CR to stimuli other than the original CS.

    d. An aversion is a CR to a CS that has been associated with an unpleasant US, such as shock or a nausea-producing drug.

33. **d.** is the answer. A dog does not have to learn to salivate to food; therefore, this response is unconditioned.

    a. & c. Salivation is a response, not a stimulus.

34. **a.** is the answer.

35. **b.** is the answer.

    a. Backward conditioning, in which the US precedes the CS, is ineffective.

    c. This interval is longer than is optimum for the most rapid acquisition of a CS-US association.

    d. Simultaneous presentation of CS and US is ineffective because it does not permit the subject to anticipate the US.

36. **c.** is the answer.

37. **b.** is the answer. The loud noise automatically triggered Albert's fear and therefore functioned as a US. After being associated with the US, the white rat acquired the power to trigger fear and thus became a CS.

38. **d.** is the answer.

39. **c.** is the answer.

    a., b., & d. Spontaneous recovery occurs after a CR has been extinguished, and in the absence of the US. The situations described here all involve the continued presentation of the US and, therefore, the further strengthening of the CR.

Terms and Concepts to Remember:

40. **Learning** is the process of acquiring new and relatively enduring information or behaviors through experience.

41. In **associative learning**, organisms learn that certain events occur together. The events may be two stimuli (as in classical conditioning) or a response and its consequences (as in operant conditioning).

42. A **stimulus** is any situation or event that evokes a response.

43. **Respondent behavior** is behavior that occurs as an automatic response to some stimulus.

    Example: In classical conditioning, conditioned and unconditioned responses are examples of **respondent behavior** in that they are automatic responses triggered by specific stimuli.

44. **Operant behavior** is behavior that operates on the environment, producing consequences.

45. **Cognitive learning** is the acquisition of mental information that guides our behavior, whether by observing events, by watching others, or through language.

46. **Classical conditioning** is a type of learning in which one learns to link two or more stimuli and anticipate events; specifically, a neutral stimulus becomes capable of triggering a conditioned response after having become associated with an unconditioned stimulus.

47. **Behaviorism** is the view that psychology (1) should be an objective science that (2) studies only observable behaviors without reference to mental processes. Most research psychologists today agree with (1) but not with (2).

    Example: Because he was an early advocate of the study of observable behavior, John Watson is often called the father of **behaviorism.**

48. In classical conditioning, a **neutral stimulus (NS)** is one that elicits no response before conditioning.

49. In classical conditioning, the **unconditioned response (UR)** is an unlearned, naturally occurring response to an unconditioned stimulus.

50. In classical conditioning, the **unconditioned stimulus (US)** is a stimulus that naturally and automatically triggers a reflexive unconditioned response.

51. In classical conditioning, the **conditioned response (CR)** is a learned response to a previously neutral (but now conditioned) stimulus, which results from the acquired association between the CS and US.

52. In classical conditioning, the **conditioned stimulus (CS)** is an originally neutral stimulus that comes to trigger a CR after association with an unconditioned stimulus.

53. In a learning experiment, **acquisition** refers to the initial stage of conditioning in which the new response is established and gradually strengthened. In operant conditioning, it is the strengthening of a reinforced response.

54. **Extinction** refers to the diminishing of a CR when the CS is no longer followed by the US; in operant conditioning, extinction occurs when a response is no longer reinforced.

55. **Spontaneous recovery** is the reappearance of an extinguished CR after a pause.

56. **Generalization** refers to the tendency, once a response has been conditioned, for stimuli similar to the original CS to elicit similar responses.

57. **Discrimination** in classical conditioning refers to the ability to distinguish the CS from similar stimuli that do not signal a US.

MODULE 20 Operant Conditioning

1. consequences; reinforcers; punishers; operates; respondent

Skinner's Experiments

2. English; behaviorism

3. law of effect; behavior control; rewarded; recur

4. Skinner box (operant chamber); reinforcement

5. shaping; approximations

6. concepts; discriminating

7. discriminative stimulus

8. **c.** is the answer. The parrot is reinforced for making successive approximations of a goal behavior. This defines shaping.
   a. Shaping is an operant conditioning procedure; salivation at the sight of dog biscuits is a classically conditioned response.
   b. Shaping involves the systematic reinforcement of successive approximations of a more complex behavior. In this example there is no indication that the response of stopping at the intersection involved the gradual acquisition of simpler behaviors.

9. positive reinforcer

10. negative reinforcer

11. primary reinforcers

12. conditioned (secondary) reinforcers

13. more

14. are; delayed; unprotected sex

15. reinforcement schedule; desired response

16. continuous reinforcement; rapid; rapid

17. partial (intermittent); slower; very

18. fixed-ratio; getting a free cup of coffee after purchasing 10 cups

19. variable-ratio

20. fixed-interval; checking the mail as delivery time approaches

21. variable-interval; waiting for a tweet response

Following reinforcement on a fixed-interval schedule, there is a pause in responding and then an increasing rate of response as time for the next reinforcement draws near. On a fixed-ratio schedule there also is a postreinforcement pause, followed, however, by a return to a consistent, high rate of response. Both kinds of variable schedules produce steadier rates of response, without the pauses associated with fixed schedules. In general, schedules linked to responses produce higher response rates and variable schedules produce more consistent responding than the related fixed schedules.

22. **c.** is the answer. Reinforcement (the letter) comes after a fixed interval, and as the likely end of the interval approaches, your behavior (glancing out the window) becomes more frequent.
   a. & b. These answers are incorrect because with ratio schedules, reinforcement is contingent upon the number of responses rather than on the passage of time.
   d. Assuming that the mail is delivered at about the same time each day, the interval is fixed rather than variable. Your behavior reflects this, since you glance out the window more often as the delivery time approaches.

23. **a.** is the answer. Ratio schedules maintain higher rates of responding—gambling in this example—than do interval schedules. Furthermore, variable schedules are not associated with the pause in responding following reinforcement that is typical of fixed schedules. The slot machine would therefore be used more often, and more consistently, if jackpots were scheduled according to a variable-ratio schedule.

24. **c.** is the answer. Whereas Lars is paid (reinforced) after a fixed period of time (fixed-interval), Tom is reinforced for each sale (fixed-ratio) he makes.

25. negative reinforcement. By taking out the garbage, Jack terminates a negative stimulus—his father's nagging.

26. conditioned reinforcer. Being invited to your instructor's home as part of a select group is a conditioned reinforcer in that it doesn't satisfy an innate need but has become linked with desirable consequences.

27. increases; removing; decreases; presenting

28. punishment; positive punishment; negative punishment

29. suppressed; discrimination; fear; the person who administered it

30. aggressiveness

31. **a.** Punishment. You lose something good—conversation with your roommate.
    b. Negative reinforcement. You are no longer cold, which means something bad has been removed.
    c. Negative reinforcement. You are no longer thirsty, so something bad has been removed.
    d. Punishment. You can't use your laptop; certainly, something good has been taken away.
    e. Negative reinforcement. Your brother stops nagging you, so something bad has been removed.

Skinner's Legacy

32. external; internal thoughts; feelings

33. operant; behavior

34. dehumanized; freedom; control

35. shaping; testing; interactive; web; athletic

36. more; achievable; more

37. **a.** State your goal in measurable terms.
    b. Decide how, when, and where you will work toward your goal.
    c. Monitor how often you engage in your desired behavior.
    d. Reinforce the desired behavior.
    e. Reduce the rewards gradually.

38. **c.** is the answer.
    a. Positive reinforcement is most effective in boosting productivity in the workplace when specific behavior, rather than vaguely defined general merit, is rewarded. Also, immediate reinforcement is much more effective than the delayed reinforcement described in a.
    b. Positive reinforcement is most effective in boosting productivity when performance goals are achievable, rather than unrealistic.
    d. The text does not specifically discuss the use of punishment in the workplace. However, it makes

the general point that although punishment may temporarily suppress unwanted behavior, it does not guide one toward more desirable behavior. Therefore, workers who receive pay cuts for poor performance may learn nothing about how to improve their productivity.

39. **d.** is the answer. By making a more preferred activity (going on Facebook) contingent on a less preferred activity (room cleaning), Reggie's mother is employing the operant conditioning technique of positive reinforcement.

Contrasting Classical and Operant Conditioning

40. associative learning

41. acquisition; extinction; spontaneous recovery; generalization; discrimination

42. neutral; automatic; does not

43. respondent

44. operant

45. cognitive; biological

46. **a.** voluntary; operant conditioning
    b. involuntary; classical conditioning
    c. voluntary; operant conditioning
    d. involuntary; classical conditioning

Module Review:

47. **b.** is the answer.
    a. & c. Classical conditioning is associated with Pavlov; respondent conditioning is another name for classical conditioning.
    d. Associative learning is the broad term that would apply to both Pavlov and Skinner.

48. **b.** is the answer. A continuous association will naturally be easier to learn than one that occurs on only some occasions, so learning is most rapid with continuous reinforcement. Yet, once the continuous association is no longer there, as in extinction training, extinction will occur more rapidly than it would have had the organism not always experienced reinforcement.

49. **b.** is the answer.
    a. With fixed-ratio schedules, there is a pause following each reinforcement.
    c. & d. Because reinforcement is not contingent on the rate of response, interval schedules, especially fixed-interval schedules, produce lower response rates than ratio schedules.

50. **b.** is the answer.
    a. Positive reinforcement involves presenting a favorable stimulus following a response.
    c. Punishment involves presenting an unpleasant stimulus following a response.

d. In extinction, a previously reinforced response is no longer followed by reinforcement. In this situation, a response causes a stimulus to be terminated or removed.

51. c. is the answer.
a. In *operant* conditioning the responses operate on the environment.
b. In *classical* conditioning responses are triggered by preceding stimuli.
d. In *classical* conditioning responses are reflexive.

52. d. is the answer.

53. d. is the answer. a. is an example of positive reinforcement, b. is an example of negative reinforcement, and c. is an example of conditioned reinforcement.

54. a. is the answer. Shaping works on operant behaviors by reinforcing successive approximations to a desired goal.

55. b. is the answer.
a., c., & d. Reinforcement that is delayed, presented before a response, or at the same time as a response does not always increase the response's frequency of occurrence.

56. d. is the answer.
a. Both involve an aversive stimulus.
b. All reinforcers, including negative reinforcers, increase the likelihood of a response.
c. In negative reinforcement, an aversive stimulus is withdrawn following a desirable response.

57. c. is the answer. Payment is given after a fixed number of pieces have been completed.
a. & b. Interval schedules reinforce according to the passage of time, not the amount of work accomplished.
d. Fortunately for those working on commission, the work ratio is fixed and therefore predictable.

58. c. is the answer. By learning to put on your coat before going outside, you have learned to reduce the aversive stimulus of the cold.
a. Discrimination learning involves learning to make a response in the presence of the appropriate stimulus and not other stimuli.
b. Punishment is the suppression of an undesirable response by the presentation of an aversive stimulus.
d. Putting on a coat is a response that operates on the environment. Therefore, this is an example of operant, not classical, conditioning.

59. d. is the answer.
a. Intermittent reinforcement refers to the ratio of responses to reinforcers, not the overall quantity of reinforcement delivered.
b. Unlike intermittent reinforcement, in which

the delivery of reinforcement is contingent on responding, random reinforcement is delivered independently of the subject's behavior.
c. This defines the technique of shaping, not intermittent reinforcement.

60. a. is the answer. You are teaching your dog by rewarding him when he produces the desired behavior.
b. This is not classical conditioning because the treat is a primary reinforcer presented after the operant behavior of the dog fetching the paper.
c. Food is a primary reinforcer; it satisfies an innate need.
d. Rewarding your dog each time he fetches the paper is continuous reinforcement.

61. c. is the answer. Because reinforcement (earning a good grade on the exam) is available according to the passage of time, studying is reinforced on an interval schedule. Because the interval between exams is constant, this is an example of a fixed-interval schedule.

62. a. is the answer. Online testing applies operant principles such as reinforcement, immediate feedback, and shaping to the teaching of new skills.
b. & d. Online testing provides immediate, and continuous, reinforcement for correct responses, but does not use aversive control procedures such as punishment.
c. Online testing is based on feedback for correct responses; this feedback constitutes conditioned, rather than primary, reinforcement.

63. d. is the answer. An approving nod from the boss is a conditioned reinforcer in that it doesn't satisfy an innate need but has become linked with desirable consequences. Cessation of cold, cessation of pain, and a drink are all primary reinforcers, which meet innate needs.

64. d. is the answer. In learning to distinguish between the conditioned stimulus and another, similar stimulus, the monkey has received training in discrimination.
a. In extinction training, a stimulus and/or response is allowed to go unreinforced.
b. Generalization training involves responding to stimuli similar to the conditioned stimulus; here the monkey is being trained not to respond to a similar stimulus.
c. This cannot be classical conditioning since the monkey is acting in order to obtain a reward. Thus, this is an example of operant conditioning.

Terms and Concepts to Remember:

65. Operant conditioning is a type of learning in which behavior is strengthened if followed by a reinforcer or diminished if followed by a punisher.

Example: Unlike classical conditioning, which works on automatic behaviors, **operant conditioning** works on behaviors that operate on the environment.

66. E. L. Thorndike proposed the **law of effect**, which states that behaviors followed by favorable consequences are likely to recur, and that behaviors followed by unfavorable consequences become less likely.

67. An **operant chamber** *(Skinner box)* is an experimental chamber for the operant conditioning of an animal such as a pigeon or rat. The controlled environment enables the investigator to present visual or auditory stimuli, deliver reinforcement or punishment, and precisely measure simple responses such as bar presses or key pecking.

68. In operant conditioning, **reinforcement** is any event that strengthens the behavior it follows.

69. **Shaping** is the operant conditioning procedure for establishing a new response by reinforcing successive approximations of the desired behavior.

70. In operant conditioning, **positive reinforcement** strengthens a response by *presenting* a typically pleasurable stimulus after that response.

71. In operant conditioning, **negative reinforcement** strengthens a response by *removing* an aversive stimulus after that response.

72. The powers of **primary reinforcers** are inborn and do not depend on learning.

73. **Conditioned reinforcers** are stimuli that acquire their reinforcing power through their association with primary reinforcers; also called *secondary reinforcers*.

74. In operant conditioning, a **reinforcement schedule** is a pattern that defines how often a desired response will be reinforced.

75. **Continuous reinforcement** is the operant procedure of reinforcing the desired response every time it occurs. In promoting the acquisition of a new response it is best to use continuous reinforcement.

76. **Partial (intermittent) reinforcement** is the operant procedure of reinforcing a response intermittently. A response that has been partially reinforced is much more resistant to extinction than one that has been continuously reinforced.

77. In operant conditioning, a **fixed-ratio schedule** is one in which reinforcement is presented after a set number of responses.

Example: Continuous reinforcement is a special kind of **fixed-ratio schedule**: Reinforcement is presented after *each* response, so the ratio of reinforcements to responses is one to one.

78. In operant conditioning, a **variable-ratio schedule** is one in which reinforcement is presented after a varying number of responses.

79. In operant conditioning, a **fixed-interval schedule** is one in which a response is reinforced after a specified time has elapsed.

80. In operant conditioning, a **variable-interval schedule** is one in which responses are reinforced after varying intervals of time.

81. In operant conditioning, **punishment** is the presentation of an aversive stimulus, such as shock, which decreases the behavior it follows.

Memory aid: People often confuse negative reinforcement and **punishment**. The former strengthens behavior, while the latter weakens it.

Essay Question

The first step in shaping an operant response, such as rolling over, is to find an effective reinforcer. Some sort of biscuit or dog treat is favored by animal trainers. This primary reinforcement should be accompanied by effusive praise (secondary reinforcement) whenever the dog makes a successful response.

Rolling over (the goal response) should be divided into a series of simple approximations, the first of which is a response, such as lying down on command, that is already in the dog's repertoire. This response should be reinforced several times. The next step is to issue a command, such as "Roll over," and withhold reinforcement until the dog (usually out of frustration) makes a closer approximation (such as rotating slightly in one direction). Following this example, the trainer should gradually require closer and closer approximations until the goal response is attained. When the new response has been established, the trainer should switch from continuous to partial reinforcement, in order to strengthen the skill.

MODULE 21 Biology, Cognition, and Learning

1. biological; psychological; social-cultural

Biological Constraints on Conditioning

2. response; stimulus; biological constraints

3. sickness; would; ecologically

4. natural selection; biological; adapt

5. is

6. reinforcer; shape; food

7. adaptive; instinctive drift

8. **a.** is the answer. As in this example, conditioning must be consistent with the particular organism's biological predispositions.

   b. Some behaviors, but certainly not all, are acquired more rapidly than others when shock is used as negative reinforcement.

   c. Pigeons are able to acquire many new behaviors when food is used as reinforcement.

9. **b.** is the answer.

   a., c., & d. Taste-aversion research demonstrates that humans and some other animals, such as rats, are biologically primed to associate illness with the taste of tainted food, rather than with other cues, such as the food's appearance. Moreover, taste aversions can be acquired even when the interval between the CS and the illness is several hours.

Cognition's Influence on Conditioning

10. cognition

11. predict; cognitive; expect

12. alcohol use disorder

13. cognitive

14. cognitive map

15. latent learning

16. intrinsic motivation; extrinsic motivation

17. **d.** is the answer. Sharetta is guided by her mental representation of the city, or cognitive map.

    a. Latent learning, or learning in the absence of reinforcement that is demonstrated when reinforcement becomes available, has no direct relevance to the example.

    b. Classical conditioning refers to automatic responses to stimuli.

    c. Biopsychosocial refers to the influences of biological, psychological, and social-cultural factors.

18. **a.** is the answer. The unrewarded rat is demonstrating latent learning. It has developed a cognitive map of the maze.

19. **b.** is the answer. Wanting to do something for its own sake is intrinsic motivation; wanting to do something for a reward (in this case, presumably, a high grade) is extrinsic motivation.

    a. The opposite is true. Nancy was motivated to take the course for its own sake, whereas Jack was evidently motivated by the likelihood of a reward in the form of a good grade.

    c. & d. A good grade, such as the one Jack is expecting, is an incentive. Drives, however, are aroused states that result from physical deprivation; they are not involved in this example.

Learning by Observation

20. modeling; observational learning; occurs

21. Albert Bandura

22. more

23. vicarious rewards; vicarious punishments

24. similar; successful; admirable

25. mirror; frontal; observational; observe other monkeys performing the same task

26. 8 to 16 months; 14 months; overimitate; empathy; theory of mind

27. **b.** is the answer. The girls are imitating behavior they have observed and admired.

    a. Because these behaviors are clearly willful rather than involuntary, classical conditioning plays no role.

    c. Latent learning plays no role in this example.

    d. Prosocial learning involves the learning of positive, helpful behavior. Their behavior is neither prosocial nor antisocial.

28. prosocial; consistent

29. antisocial; abusive; aggressive; genetic

30. watching television

31. violent

32. link

33. causation; does; justified; unpunished

34. imitation; desensitize

35. increases; mirror neurons; prosocial

36. **c.** is the answer. Studies indicate that when a model says one thing but does another, subjects do the same and learn not to practice what they preach.

Module Review:

37. **b.** is the answer.

    c. & d. The text does not present evidence regarding the relative importance of cognitive processes in classical and operant conditioning.

38. **c.** is the answer.

    a. & d. These studies also indicated that rats are biologically predisposed to associate visual and auditory stimuli, but not taste, with shock.

    b. Rats are biologically predisposed to associate taste with sickness.

39. **b.** is the answer.

    a. Skinner' studies of *operant* learning did not involve imitating another person's behavior.

    c. Pavlov's classical conditioning also did not involve imitating another's behavior.

    d. Watson is best known as an early proponent of behaviorism.

40. c. is the answer.

a., b., & d. Rescorla and Wagner's research did not address the importance of these factors in classical conditioning.

41. a. is the answer.

42. d. is the answer.

43. a. is the answer.

44. d. is the answer. The rat had learned the maze but did not display this learning until reinforcement became available.

a. Negotiating a maze is clearly operant behavior.

b. This example does not involve learning to distinguish between stimuli.

c. This is not observational learning because the rat has no one to observe!

45. a. is the answer. Taste-aversion experiments demonstrate conditioning even with CS-US intervals as long as several hours.

b. Despite being perceivable, a visual or auditory stimulus cannot become a CS for illness in some animals, such as rats.

c. Some animals, such as birds, are biologically primed to associate the *appearance* of food with illness.

46. c. is the answer.

Terms and Concepts to Remember:

47. A **cognitive map** is a mental representation of the layout of one's environment.

48. Latent learning is learning that occurs in the absence of reinforcement but only becomes apparent when there is an incentive to demonstrate it.

49. Intrinsic motivation is the desire to perform a behavior effectively for its own sake, rather than for some external reason.

Memory aid: Intrinsic means "internal": A person who is **intrinsically motivated** is motivated from within.

50. Extrinsic motivation is the desire to perform a behavior to receive promised rewards or avoid threatened punishment.

Memory aid: Extrinsic means "external": A person who is **extrinsically motivated** is motivated by some outside factor.

51. Observational learning is learning by watching and imitating the behavior of others.

52. Modeling is the process of watching and then imitating a specific behavior and is thus an important means through which observational learning occurs.

53. Found in the brain's frontal lobe, **mirror neurons** may be the neural basis for observational learning. These neurons generate impulses that some scientists believe fire when certain actions are performed or when another individual who performs those actions is observed.

54. The opposite of antisocial behavior, **prosocial behavior** is positive, helpful, and constructive and is subject to the same principles of observational learning as is undesirable behavior, such as aggression.

Before You Move On

Matching Items

1. f	**6.** m	**11.** d
2. i	**7.** j	**12.** l
3. g	**8.** a	**13.** n
4. h	**9.** c	**14.** o
5. k	**10.** b	**15.** e

True–False Items

1. F	**5.** T	**9.** F
2. F	**6.** F	**10.** T
3. F	**7.** T	**11.** T
4. T	**8.** F	

Cross-Check

ACROSS
1. respondent
4. learning
6. negative
9. unconditioned
12. UR
14. prosocial
17. operant
20. shaping
21. CR
22. latent
23. acquisition

DOWN
2. partial
3. fixed-interval
5. generalization
7. extinction
8. cognitive map
10. discrimination
11. observational
13. US
14. punishment
15. classical
16. modeling
18. extrinsic
19. CS

Memory

Overview

Module 22 explores human memory as a system that processes information in three steps, beginning with encoding, whereby information is put into the memory system. The module also discusses the important role of meaning, distributed practice, and organization in encoding new memories.

Module 23 continues the discussion by examining memory storage, which is the mechanism by which information is maintained in memory, and retrieval, is the process by which information is accessed from memory through recall or recognition.

Module 24 explains how memory is represented physically in the brain, and how forgetting may result from failure to encode or store information or to find appropriate retrieval cues. This module also discusses the issue of memory construction. How "true" are our memories of events? A particularly controversial issue in this area involves suspicious claims of long-repressed memories of sexual abuse and other traumas that are "recovered" with the aid of hypnosis and other techniques. As you study these modules, try applying some of the memory and studying tips discussed in the text.

NOTE: Answer guidelines for all Module 22–24 questions begin on page 201.

Outline

Instructions

First, skim each section, noting headings and boldface items. After you have read the section, review each objective by answering the fill-in, essay-type, and multiple-choice questions for that section. In some cases, Study Tips explain how best to learn a difficult concept and Applications and Module Reviews (help you to know how well you understand the material. Finally, try to define the important terms and concepts using your own words. As you proceed, evaluate your performance by consulting the answers on page 201. Do not continue until you understand each answer. If you need to, review or reread a troublesome \ before continuing.

Before You Move On includes activities that test you on material from the entire unit.

187

MODULE 22 Studying and Encoding Memories

Studying Memory

Objective 22-1: Define *memory*, and explain how it is measured.

1. Learning that persists over time indicates the existence of _____ for that learning.

2. The ability to retrieve information not in conscious awareness but that was learned at an earlier time is called _____ . The ability to identify previously learned items is called _____ .

3. Researchers found that 25 years after graduation, people were not able to _____ (recall/recognize) the names of their classmates but were able to _____ (recall/recognize) 90 percent of their names and their yearbook pictures.

4. If you have learned something and then forgotten it, you will probably be able to _____ it _____ (more/less) quickly than you did originally. This idea was first tested by pioneering memory researcher _____ , who used _____ _____ to test his memory.

5. Additional rehearsal of learned material, called _____ , _____ (increases/does not increase) retention.

APPLICATION:

6. Complete this analogy: Fill-in-the-blank test questions are to multiple-choice questions as

   a. encoding is to storage.
   b. storage is to encoding.
   c. recognition is to recall.
   d. recall is to recognition.

Objective 22-2: Explain how psychologists describe the human memory system.

7. Both human memory and computer memory can be viewed as _____-
   _____ systems that perform three tasks: _____ , _____ ,

and _____ . Unlike the computer, which processes _____ (sequentially/simultaneously), our brain processes many things _____ (sequentially/simultaneously). This is called _____ _____ . The model called _____ views memory as emerging from interconnected _____ _____ .

8. The classic model of memory has been Atkinson and Shiffrin's _____-
   _____ _____ model. According to this model, we first record information as a fleeting _____ _____ , from which it is processed into _____-_____ memory, where the information is _____ through rehearsal into _____-_____ memory for later retrieval.

9. _____ and other psychologists have clarified the phenomenon of short-term memory with the concept of _____ memory, which focuses more on the _____ processing of briefly stored information. In this model, a _____ _____ handles this focused processing.

STUDY TIP: To remember the material in these three modules, you might find it helpful to use the concept of a three-part model as a retrieval cue. In Module 22, the modified three-stage information-processing model proposes that external events are processed through separate stages of sensory memory, short-term/working memory, and long-term memory. In this module and the next two, the three processes of (1) getting information into the memory system (encoding), (2) retaining information over time (storage), and (3) getting information out of memory storage (retrieval) are described. Each process (encoding, storage, and retrieval) can occur at each memory stage (sensory memory, short-term memory, long-term memory). The chart on the next page applies what can happen at each stage to the example of getting the written words of a memorable poem in and out of memory. To bolster your understanding of these important concepts, you might try using this type of chart as the basis for an example you create.

Sensory Memory	Working/Short-Term Memory	Long-Term Memory
Encoding: light reflecting from printed words in the poem automatically triggers a response in the eye's receptor cells	*Encoding:* automatic processing of location of words on the page; effortful processing of meaning	*Encoding:* Memorable passage triggers deep processing of material from STM to LTM
Storage: image of each word persists in the visual system for about 1/2 sec.	*Storage:* limited capacity and duration of storing words on the page	*Storage:* relatively permanent and limitless; meaningful passage stays with you
Retrieval: visual image is attended to as it passes into STM/Working memory	*Retrieval:* conscious working allows reader to process the meaning of the poem's words	*Retrieval:* recall, recognition, or relearning of memorized passage from the poem

Encoding Memories

Objective 22-3: Distinguish between explicit and implicit memories.

10. Facts and experiences that we can consciously declare make up _____ memory, which is also called _____ memory. Such memories are processed through conscious, _____ processing. Processing that happens without our awareness, called

_____ _____ , produces _____ memories, which are also called _____

_____ .

APPLICATION:

11. Elderly Mr. Flanagan, a retired electrician, can easily remember how to wire a light switch, but he cannot remember the name of the president of the United States. Evidently, Mr. Flanagan's _____ memory is better than his _____ memory.
    a. implicit; explicit
    b. explicit; implicit
    c. declarative; nondeclarative
    d. explicit; declarative

Objective 22-4: Identify the information we process automatically.

12. Implicit memories include _____ memory for skills and associations among stimuli formed by _____ _____ . Mental feats such as vision, thinking, and memory are not single abilities. Rather, we split information into different components for _____ and _____ processing.

Give examples of material that is typically encoded with little or no effort.

APPLICATION:

13. The first thing Karen did when she discovered that she had misplaced her keys was to re-create in her mind the day's events. That she had little difficulty in doing so illustrates _____ processing.

Objective 22-5: Explain how sensory memory works.

14. Stimuli from the environment are first recorded in _____ memory.

15. George Sperling found that when people were briefly shown three rows of letters, they could recall _____ (virtually all/about half) of them. When Sperling sounded a low, high, or medium tone to indicate which letters were to be recalled, the participants were much _____ (more/less) accurate. This suggests that people have a brief photographic, or _____ , memory lasting about a few tenths of a second.

16. Sensory memory for sounds is called _____ memory. This memory fades _____ (more/less) rapidly than photographic memory, lasting for as long as _____ .

Objective 22-6: Describe the capacity of our short-term memory.

17. Our short-term memory capacity is about _____ chunks of information. This capacity was discovered by _____ .

18. Peterson and Peterson found that when _____ was prevented by asking people to count backward, memory for letters was gone after 12 seconds. Without _____ processing, short-term memories have a limited life.

19. Working-memory capacity varies, depending on _____ and other factors. Those with a large working-memory capacity tend also to _____

_____ .

APPLICATION:

20. Brenda has trouble remembering her new five-digit ZIP plus four-digit address code. What is the most likely explanation for the difficulty Brenda is having?
    a. Nine digits are at or above the upper limit of most people's short-term memory capacity.
    b. Nine digits are at or above the upper limit of most people's iconic memory capacity.
    c. The extra four digits cannot be organized into easily remembered chunks.
    d. Brenda evidently has an impaired implicit memory.

Objective 22-7: Describe the effortful processing strategies that help us remember new information.

21. Memory may be aided by grouping information into meaningful units called _____ .

22. Memory aids are known as _____ devices. Using a jingle, such as the one that begins "one is a bun," is an example of the _____-_____ system.

23. Another memory aid involves forming words from the first letters of to-be-remembered words; the resulting word is called an

_____ .

24. When people develop expertise in an area, they process information into _____ .

25. The early memory researcher _____ found that distributed rehearsal is more effective for retention; this is called the _____ . Other researchers have found that the _____ (shorter/longer) the space between practice sessions, the better the retention.

26. Repeated self-testing is a good way to _____ practice. Henry Roediger and Jeffrey Karpicke called this the

_____ .

Objective 22-8: Describe the levels of processing, and explain how they affect encoding.

27. Encoding material on a basic level based on _____ or the _____ of words is called _____ _____ . Encoding material _____ , based on the meaning of words, is called _____

_____ . _____

(Shallow/Deep) processing tends to yield the best retention.

28. Material that is not _____ is difficult to process. We have especially good recall for information we can meaningfully relate to ourselves, called the _____ effect.

29. Thus, the amount remembered depends both on

_____

_____

MODULE REVIEW:

30. The process of getting information out of memory storage is called
    a. encoding.   c. rehearsal.
    b. retrieval.   d. storage.

31. Visual sensory memory is referred to as
    a. iconic memory.   c. photomemory.
    b. echoic memory.   d. semantic memory.

32. Echoic memories fade after approximately
    a. 1 hour.   c. 1 second.
    b. 1 minute.   d. 3 to 4 seconds.

33. Which of the following is NOT a measure of retention?
    a. recall   c. relearning
    b. recognition   d. retrieval

34. Our short-term memory span is approximately _____ items.
    a. 2   c. 7
    b. 5   d. 10

35. Memory techniques such as acronyms and the peg-word system are called
    a. consolidation devices.
    b. imagery techniques.
    c. encoding strategies.
    d. mnemonic devices.

36. One way to increase the amount of information in memory is to group it into larger, familiar units. This process is referred to as
    a. consolidating.   c. encoding.
    b. organization.   d. chunking.

37. The spacing effect means that
    a. distributed study yields better retention than cramming.
    b. retention is improved when encoding and retrieval are separated by no more than 1 hour.
    c. learning causes a reduction in the size of the synaptic gap between certain neurons.
    d. delaying retrieval until memory has consolidated improves recall.

38. In Sperling's memory experiment, research participants were shown three rows of three letters, followed immediately by a low, medium, or high tone. The participants were able to report
    a. all three rows with perfect accuracy.
    b. only the top row of letters.
    c. only the middle row of letters.
    d. any one of the three rows of letters.

39. Memory for skills is called
    a. explicit memory.   c. prime memory.
    b. declarative memory.   d. implicit memory.

40. When Gordon Bower presented words grouped by category or in random order, recall was
    a. the same for all words.
    b. better for the categorized words.
    c. better for the random words.
    d. improved when participants developed their own mnemonic devices.

41. The three-stage processing model of memory was proposed by
    a. Atkinson and Shiffrin.
    b. Hermann Ebbinghaus.
    c. Henry Roediger.
    d. George Sperling.

42. Which of the following measures of retention is the least sensitive in triggering retrieval?
    a. recall   c. relearning
    b. recognition   d. They are equally sensitive.

43. Which type of word processing results in the greatest retention?
    a. shallow   c. visual
    b. deep   d. auditory

44. Information is maintained in short-term memory only briefly unless it is
    a. encoded.   c. iconic or echoic.
    b. rehearsed.   d. retrieved.

45. Textbook chapters are often organized into ____ to facilitate information processing.
    a. mnemonic devices   c. hierarchies
    b. chunks   d. recognizable units

46. Semantic encoding is a type of
    a. mnemonic.
    b. shallow processing.
    c. deep processing.
    d. echoic memory.

TERMS AND CONCEPTS TO REMEMBER:

47. memory

48. recall

49. recognition

50. relearning

51. encoding

52. storage

53. retrieval

54. parallel processing

55. sensory memory

56. short-term memory

57. long-term memory

58. working memory

59. explicit memory

60. effortful processing

61. automatic processing

62. implicit memory

63. iconic memory

64. echoic memory

65. chunking

66. mnemonics

67. spacing effect

68. testing effect

69. shallow processing

70. deep processing

MODULE
23   **Storing and Retrieving Memories**

Memory Storage

Objective 23-1: Describe the capacity of long-term memory, and discuss whether our long-term memories are processed and stored in specific locations.

1. In contrast to short-term memory—and contrary to popular belief—the capacity of permanent memory is essentially_____ .

2. Psychologist _____ attempted to locate memory by cutting out pieces of rats' _____ after they had learned a maze. He found that no matter where he cut, the rats _____ (did/did not) retain a partial memory of how to navigate the maze.

Objective 23-2: Describe the roles of the frontal lobes and hippocampus in memory processing.

3. Explicit, conscious memories are either _____ (facts and general knowledge) or _____ (experienced events).

4. Many brain regions send input to your _____ lobes for working memory processing. The neural center of the limbic system that is particularly important in memory is the _____ . This brain structure is important in the processing and storage of _____ memories. Damage on the

left side of this structure impairs _____ memory; damage on the right side impairs memory for _____ designs and locations. The rear part of this structure processes _____ memory.

5. The hippocampus seems to function as a zone where the brain _____ (temporarily/permanently) stores the elements of a memory. This process is called _____ _____ . However, memories _____ (do/do not) migrate for storage elsewhere. The hippocampus is active during _____ sleep, as memories are processed and filed for later retrieval. _____ lobe areas surrounding the hippocampus support the processing and storing of explicit memories.

APPLICATIONS:

6. Brad, who suffered accidental damage to the left side of his hippocampus, has trouble remembering
   a. visual designs.
   b. locations.
   c. all nonverbal information.
   d. verbal information.

7. After suffering damage to the hippocampus, a person would probably
   a. lose memory for skills such as bicycle riding.
   b. be incapable of being classically conditioned.
   c. lose the ability to store new facts.
   d. experience all of these changes.

Objective 23-3: Describe the roles played by the cerebellum and basal ganglia in memory processing.

8. The cerebellum is important in the processing of _____ memories. People with a damaged cerebellum are incapable of simple _____ conditioning.

9. Deep brain structures called the _____ _____ , which are also involved in _____ movement, facilitate formation of _____ memories for skills.

10. The dual explicit-implicit memory system helps explain _____ amnesia. We do not have explicit memories of our first three years for two reasons: explicit memory requires the use of words that nonspeaking children

_____ (have/have not) learned and the _____ is one of the last brain structures to mature.

Objective 23-4: Discuss how emotions affect our memory processing.

11. Emotions trigger _____ hormones that _____ (influence/do not influence) memory formation by making more _____ available to fuel brain activity.

12. Stress hormones provoke the _____ to initiate a _____ _____ that boosts activity in the brain's memory-forming areas.

13. Memories for surprising, significant moments that are especially clear are called _____ memories. Like other memories, these memories _____ (can/cannot) err.

APPLICATION:

14. Which of the following is the best example of a flashbulb memory?
   a. suddenly remembering to buy bread while standing in the checkout line at the grocery store
   b. recalling the name of someone from high school while looking at his or her yearbook snapshot
   c. remembering to make an important phone call
   d. remembering what you were doing on September 11, 2001, when terrorists crashed planes into the World Trade Center towers

Objective 23-5: Explain how changes at the synapse level affect our memory processing.

15. Eric Kandel and James Schwartz have found that when learning occurs in the sea slug, *Aplysia*, the neurotransmitter _____ is released in greater amounts, making synapses more efficient.

16. After learning has occurred, a sending neuron needs _____ (more/less) prompting to release its neurotransmitter, and the number of connections between neurons _____ (increases/decreases). This phenomenon, called _____-

_____ _____, may be the neural basis for learning and remembering associations.

17. Blocking this process with a specific _____ , or by genetic engineering that causes the absence of an _____ , interferes with learning. Rats given a drug that enhanced _____ learned a maze _____ (faster/more slowly).

18. After LTP has occurred, an electric current passed through the brain _____ (will/will not) disrupt old memories and _____ (will/will not) wipe out recent experiences.

Memory Retrieval

Objective 23-6: Describe how external cues, internal emotions, and order of appearance influence memory retrieval.

19. The best retrieval cues come from the associations formed at the time we _____ a memory.

20. The process by which associations can lead to retrieval is called _____ . This process is often _____ . It may affect _____ as well as memory.

21. Studies have shown that retention is best when learning and testing are done in _____ (the same/different) contexts.

22. What we learn in one condition is best remembered in that condition, called _____-_____ memory. For example, we tend to recall experiences that are consistent with our current emotional state, which is called _____-_____ memory.

Describe the effects of mood on memory.

23. People who are currently depressed may recall their parents as _____ _____ . People who have recovered from depression typically recall their parents about the same as do people who _____ _____ .

24. The tendency to remember the first and last items in a list best is called the _____ _____ .

25. People briefly recall the last items in a list quickly and well, called the_____ effect. Following a delay, first items are remembered _____ (better/less well) than last items, called the _____ effect.

APPLICATIONS:

26. The above figure depicts the recall of a list of words under two conditions. Which of the following best describes the difference between the conditions?
   a. In A, the words were studied and retrieved in the same context; in B, the contexts were different.
   b. In B, the words were studied and retrieved in the same context; in A, the contexts were different.
   c. The delay between presentation of the last word and the test of recall was longer for A than for B.
   d. The delay between presentation of the last word and the test of recall was longer for B than for A.

27. Being in a bad mood after a hard day of work, Susan could think of nothing positive in her life. This is best explained as an example of
   a. priming.
   b. flashbulb memory.
   c. mood-congruent memory.
   d. working memory.

28. In an effort to remember the name of the classmate who sat behind her in fifth grade, Martina mentally recited the names of other classmates who sat near her. Martina's effort to refresh her memory by activating related associations is an example of
   a. priming.
   b. two-track processing.
   c. encoding.
   d. the serial position effect.

29. Walking through the halls of his high school 10 years after graduation, Tom experienced a flood of old memories. Tom's experience showed the role of
   a. state-dependent memory.
   b. context effects.
   c. implicit memory.
   d. explicit memory.

MODULE REVIEW:

30. Semantic memory is to _____ as episodic memory is to _____ .
   a. priming; encoding
   b. encoding; priming
   c. knowledge; personal events
   d. personal events; knowledge

31. Kandel and Schwartz have found that when learning occurs, more of the neurotransmitter _____ is released into synapses.
   a. ACh   c. serotonin
   b. dopamine   d. noradrenaline

32. In a study on context cues, people learned words while on land or when they were underwater. In a later test of recall, those with the best retention had
   a. learned the words on land, that is, in the more familiar context.
   b. learned the words underwater, that is, in the more exotic context.
   c. learned the words and been tested on them in different contexts.
   d. learned the words and been tested on them in the same context.

33. Studies demonstrate that learning causes permanent neural changes in the _____ of animals' neurons.
   a. myelin   c. synapses
   b. cell bodies   d. all of these parts

34. The basal ganglia of the brain play a critical role in the formation of
    a. working memory.
    b. emotional memory.
    c. procedural memory.
    d. explicit memory.

35. Which area of the brain is most important in the processing of implicit memories?
    a. hippocampus   c. hypothalamus
    b. cerebellum   d. amygdala

36. According to the serial position effect, when recalling a list of words you should have the greatest difficulty with those
    a. at the beginning of the list.
    b. at the end of the list.
    c. at the end and in the middle of the list.
    d. in the middle of the list.

37. Experimenters gave people a list of words to be recalled. When the participants were tested after a delay, the items that were best recalled were those
    a. at the beginning of the list.
    b. in the middle of the list.
    c. at the end of the list.
    d. at the beginning and the end of the list.

38. Lashley's studies, in which rats learned a maze and then had various parts of their brains surgically removed, showed that the memory
    a. was lost when surgery took place within 1 hour of learning.
    b. was lost when surgery took place within 24 hours of learning.
    c. was lost when any region of the brain was removed.
    d. remained no matter which area of the brain was tampered with.

39. Long-term potentiation refers to
    a. the disruptive influence of old memories on the formation of new memories.
    b. the disruptive influence of recent memories on the retrieval of old memories.
    c. our tendency to recall experiences that are consistent with our current mood.
    d. the increased efficiency of synaptic transmission between certain neurons following learning.

TERMS AND CONCEPTS TO REMEMBER:

40. semantic memory
41. episodic memory
42. hippocampus
43. memory consolidation
44. flashbulb memory
45. long-term potentiation (LTP)
46. priming
47. mood-congruent memory
48. serial position effect

MODULE
24

Forgetting, Memory Construction, and Improving Memory

Forgetting

Objective 24-1: Explain why we forget.

1. Without the ability to _____ , we would constantly be overwhelmed by information.

2. The disorder involving an inability to form new memories is called _____ _____ . The disorder involving an inability to retrieve old memories is called _____ _____ .

3. People who cannot form new memories can learn _____ _____ and can be _____ _____ . However, they have no _____ memory of having learned these things.

4. Forgetting may have various causes. One reason for forgetting is _____ failure. This type of forgetting occurs because some of the information that we sense never actually _____ .

5. One reason for age-related memory decline is that the brain areas responsible for _____ new information are _____ (more/less) responsive in older adults.

6. Studies by Hermann Ebbinghaus and by Harry Bahrick indicate that most forgetting occurs _____ (soon/a long time) after the material is learned.

7. This type of forgetting is known as _____ _____ , which may be caused by a gradual fading of the physical _____ _____ .

8. When information that is stored in memory temporarily cannot be found, _____ failure has occurred.

9. Research suggests that memories are also lost as a result of _____ , which is especially possible if we simultaneously learn similar, new material.

10. The disruptive effect of previous learning on current learning is called _____ _____ . The disruptive effect of learning new material on efforts to recall material previously learned is called _____ _____ .

11. John Jenkins and Karl Dallenbach found that if people went to sleep after learning, their memory for a list of nonsense syllables was _____ (better/worse) than it was if they stayed awake.

12. In some cases, old information facilitates our learning of new information. This is called _____ _____ .

13. Freud proposed that motivated forgetting, or _____ , may protect a person from painful or unacceptable memories.

14. Increasing numbers of memory researchers think that motivated forgetting _____ (often/sometimes/rarely) occurs.

When Do We Forget?

Sensory memory
The senses momentarily register amazing detail.

Working (short-term) memory
A few items are both noticed and encoded.

Long-term storage
Some items are altered or lost.

Retrieval from long-term memory
Depending on interference, retrieval cues, moods, and motives, some things get retrieved, some don't.

Information bits

APPLICATIONS:

15. At your high school reunion you cannot remember the last name of your homeroom teacher. Your failure to remember is most likely the result of _____ failure.

16. Which of the following sequences would be best to follow if you wanted to minimize interference-induced forgetting in order to improve your recall on the psychology midterm?
    a. study, eat, test
    b. study, sleep, test
    c. study, listen to music, test
    d. study, exercise, test

17. When Carlos was promoted, he moved into a new office with a new phone extension. Every time he is asked for his phone number, Carlos first thinks of his old extension, illustrating the effects of
    a. proactive interference.
    b. retroactive interference.
    c. encoding failure.
    d. storage failure.

18. Lewis cannot remember the details of the torture he experienced as a prisoner of war. According to Freud, Lewis' failure to remember these painful memories is an example of
    a. repression.
    b. retrieval failure.
    c. encoding failure.
    d. proactive interference.

19. After finding her old combination lock, Janice can't remember its combination because she keeps confusing it with the combination of her new lock. She is experiencing
    a. proactive interference.
    b. retroactive interference.
    c. encoding failure.
    d. storage failure.

Memory Construction Errors

Objective 24-2: Explain how misinformation, imagination, and source amnesia influence our memory construction, and describe how we decide whether a memory is real or false.

20. As memories are replayed, they are often modified. This process is called _____ .

21. When witnesses to an event receive misleading information about it, they may experience a _____ _____ and misremember the event. A number of

experiments have demon-strated that false memories _____ (can/cannot) be created when people are induced to imagine nonexistent events; that is, these people later experience _____ _____ . This occurs in part because visualizing something and actually perceiving it _____ _____ .

Describe what Loftus' studies have shown about the effects of misleading postevent information.

22. At the heart of many false memories is _____ _____ , which occurs when we _____ an event to the wrong source. This phenomenon helps explain _____ _____ , which is the sense that a current situation has already been experienced. This feeling of famil-iarity with a stimulus without a clear idea of where we encountered it before occurs when our _____ _____ processing is out of sync with our _____ and _____ _____ processing.

23. Because memory is reconstruction as well as reproduction, we _____ (can/can-not) be sure whether a memory is real by how real it feels.

24. Memory construction explains why memories "refreshed" under _____ are often inaccurate.

APPLICATION:

25. Which of the following illustrates the construc-tive nature of memory?

   a. Janice keeps calling her new boyfriend by her old boyfriend's name.

b. After studying all afternoon and then getting drunk in the evening, Don can't remember the material he studied.

c. After studying Latin, Malcolm was better able to learn his French vocabulary.

d. Although Mrs. Harvey, who has Alzheimer's disease, has many gaps in her memory, she invents sensible accounts of her activities so that her family will not worry.

Objective 24-3: Discuss the reliability of young chil-dren's eyewitness descriptions.

26. Whether a child produces an accurate eyewitness memory depends heavily on how he or she is _____ . Children are most accurate when it is a first interview with a _____ person who asks _____ questions.

Objective 24-4: Explain why reports of repressed and recovered memories are so hotly debated.

27. (Thinking Critically) Researchers increasingly agree that memories obtained under the influence of hypnosis or using other "memory work" tech-niques _____ (are/are not) reliable.

28. (Thinking Critically) Memories of events that happened before age _____ are unreliable. As noted earlier, this phenomenon is called _____ _____ .

Improving Memory

Objective 24-5: Describe how you can use memory research findings to do better in this and other courses.

29. The SQ3R study technique identifies five strate-gies for boosting memory: _____ , _____ , _____ , _____ , and _____ .

Discuss several specific strategies for improving memory.

MODULE REVIEW:

30. Research on memory construction reveals that memories
   a. are stored as exact copies of experience.
   b. reflect a person's biases and assumptions.
   c. may be chemically transferred from one organism to another.
   d. even if long term, usually decay within about five years.

31. The eerie feeling of having been somewhere before is an example of
   a. repression.   **c.** reconsolidation.
   b. encoding failure.   **d.** déjà vu.

32. "Hypnotically refreshed" memories may prove inaccurate—especially if the hypnotist asks leading questions—because of
   a. encoding failure.
   b. déjà vu.
   c. proactive interference.
   d. memory construction.

33. Which of the following best describes the typical forgetting curve?
   a. a steady, slow decline in retention over time
   b. a steady, rapid decline in retention over time
   c. a rapid initial decline in retention becoming stable thereafter
   d. a slow initial decline in retention becoming rapid thereafter

34. Jenkins and Dallenbach found that memory was better in people who were
   a. awake during the retention interval, presumably because decay was reduced.
   b. asleep during the retention interval, presumably because decay was reduced.
   c. awake during the retention interval, presumably because interference was reduced.
   d. asleep during the retention interval, presumably because interference was reduced.

35. Amnesia victims typically have experienced damage to the _____ of the brain.
   a. frontal lobes   **c.** thalamus
   b. cerebellum   **d.** hippocampus

36. Anterograde amnesia is the inability to
   a. retrieve old memories.
   b. remember where information came from.
   c. form new memories.
   d. hold more than 7 items in working memory.

37. Repression is an example of
   a. encoding failure.   **c.** motivated forgetting.
   b. memory decay.   **d.** all of these things.

38. Studies by Loftus and Palmer, in which people were quizzed about a film of an accident, indicate that
   a. when quizzed immediately, people can recall very little because of the stress of witnessing an accident.
   b. when questioned as little as one day later, their memory was very inaccurate.
   c. most people had very accurate memories as much as 6 months later.
   d. people's recall may easily be affected by misleading information.

39. Which of the following was NOT recommended as a strategy for improving memory?
   a. use of mnemonic devices
   b. activation of retrieval cues
   c. speed reading
   d. encoding meaningful associations

40. Amnesia patients typically experience disruption of
   a. implicit memories.
   b. explicit memories.
   c. motor skills.
   d. classically conditioned behaviors.

41. Memory researchers are suspicious of long-repressed memories of traumatic events that are "recovered" with the aid of drugs or hypnosis because
   a. such experiences usually are vividly remembered.
   b. such memories are unreliable and easily influenced by misinformation.
   c. memories of events happening before about age 3 are especially unreliable.
   d. of all of these reasons.

42. The misinformation effect provides evidence that memory
   a. is constructed during encoding.
   b. is unchanging once established.
   c. may be reconstructed during recall according to how questions are framed.
   d. is highly resistant to misleading information.

TERMS AND CONCEPTS TO REMEMBER:

43. anterograde amnesia

44. retrograde amnesia

45. proactive interference

46. retroactive interference
47. repression
48. reconsolidation
49. misinformation effect
50. source amnesia
51. déjà vu

Essay Question

Discuss the points of agreement among experts regarding the validity of recovered memories of child abuse. (Use the space below to list the points you want to make, and organize them. Then write the essay on a separate piece of paper.)

Before You Move On

Matching Items

Match each definition or description with the appropriate term.

Definitions or Descriptions

_____ 1. sensory memory that decays more slowly than visual sensory memory
_____ 2. the process by which information gets into the memory system
_____ 3. the blocking of painful memories
_____ 4. the phenomenon in which one's mood can influence retrieval
_____ 5. memory for a list of words is affected by word order
_____ 6. "one is a bun, two is a shoe" mnemonic device
_____ 7. word that chunks to-be-remembered information into a more familiar form
_____ 8. new learning interferes with previous knowledge
_____ 9. a measure of memory
_____ 10. old knowledge interferes with new learning
_____ 11. misattributing the origin of an event
_____ 12. changing retrieved memories before they are stored again
_____ 13. encoding the meaning of words
_____ 14. inability to form new memories
_____ 15. inability to retrieve old memories

Terms

a. repression
b. relearning
c. serial position effect
d. anterograde amnesia
e. peg-word system
f. acronym
g. proactive interference
h. deep processing
i. retroactive interference
j. source amnesia
k. retrograde amnesia
l. mood-congruent memory
m. echoic memory
n. encoding
o. reconsolidation

True–False Items

Indicate whether each statement is true or false by placing *T* or *F* in the blank next to the item.

_____ 1. Studying that is distributed over time produces better retention than cramming.
_____ 2. Preschool children can be induced to report false events through the use of suggestive interview techniques.
_____ 3. Most people do not have memories of events that occurred before the age of 3.
_____ 4. Studies by Ebbinghaus show that most forgetting takes place soon after learning.
_____ 5. The persistence of a memory is a good clue as to whether it derives from an actual experience.

_____ 6. Recall of newly acquired knowledge is no better after sleeping than after being awake for the same period of time.

_____ 7. Time spent in developing imagery, chunking, and associating material with what you already know is more effective than time spent repeating information again and again.

_____ 8. Although repression has not been confirmed experimentally, most psychologists believe it happens.

_____ 9. Overlearning material by continuing to restudy it beyond mastery often disrupts recall.

Cross-Check

As you learned in Module 2, reviewing and overlearning of material are important to the learning process. After you have written the definitions of the key terms in this unit, you should complete the crossword puzzle to ensure that you can reverse the process—recognize the term, given the definition.

ACROSS

1. Example of motivated forgetting.
4. Sensory memories of auditory stimuli.
6. Encoding of information according to its meaning. Also, a type of explicit memory.
7. Activating associations in order to retrieve a specific memory.
10. Mental pictures.
13. Believed to be the neural basis for learning and memory.
14. Visual sensory memory.
18. Organizing material into familiar, meaningful units.
19. Unusually vivid memory of an emotionally important moment.
20. Loss of memory.
21. Effortful repetition of information.

DOWN

1. A measure of retention that requires identifying previously learned material.
2. The immediate, initial recording of information in memory.
3. An effect in which eyewitnesses to an event incorporate misleading information into their memories.
4. Type of processing that requires attention and some degree of work.

5. Brain area that processes explicit memories for storage.

8. Type of memory of skills, preferences, and dispositions.

9. Memory aids.

11. Unconscious encoding of incidental information into memory.

12. Type of interference in which old knowledge interferes with new learning.

15. Relatively permanent memory that is unlimited in capacity.

16. Baddeley's model of working memory includes _____ input and auditory rehearsal of new information.

17. The false sense of having already experienced a situation.

22. Explicit memory for personal events.

Answers

MODULE
22 Studying and Encoding Memories

Studying Memory

1. memory

2. recall; recognition

3. recall; recognize

4. relearn; more; Hermann Ebbinghaus; nonsense syllables

5. overlearning; increases

6. **d.** is the answer.
a. & b. To correctly answer either type of question, the knowledge must have been encoded and stored.
c. With fill-in-the-blank questions, the answer must be recalled with no retrieval cues other than the question. With multiple-choice questions, the correct answer merely has to be recognized from among several alternatives.

7. information-processing; encoding; storage; retrieval; sequentially; simultaneously; parallel processing; connectionism; neural networks

8. three-stage processing; sensory memory; short-term; encoded; long-term

9. Alan Baddeley; working; active; central executive

Encoding Memories

10. explicit; declarative; effortful; automatic processing; implicit; nondeclarative memories

11. **a.** is the answer.

b., c., & d. Explicit memory, also called declarative memory, is the memory of facts that one can consciously "declare." Nondeclarative memory is what Mr. Flanagan has retained.

12. procedural; classical conditioning; separate; simultaneous

Automatic processing includes the encoding of information about space, time, and frequency.

13. automatic

14. sensory

15. about half; more; iconic

16. echoic; less; 3 or 4 seconds

17. 7; George Miller

18. rehearsal; active

19. age; retain more information and be creative problem solvers

20. **a.** is the answer. Short-term memory capacity is approximately seven digits.
b. Because iconic memory lasts no more than a few tenths of a second, regardless of how much material is experienced, this cannot be the explanation for Brenda's difficulty.
c. The final four digits should be no more difficult to organize into chunks than the first five digits of the address code.
d. Memory for digits is an example of explicit, rather than implicit, memory.

21. chunks

22. mnemonic; peg-word

23. acronym

24. hierarchies

25. Hermann Ebbinghaus; spacing effect; longer

26. distribute; testing effect

27. letters; sound; shallow processing; semantically; deep processing; Deep

28. meaningful; self-reference

29. the time spent learning and on your making it meaningful for deep processing

Module Review:

30. **b.** is the answer.
a. Encoding is the process of getting information *into* memory.
c. Rehearsal is the conscious repetition of information in order to maintain it in memory.

d. Storage is the maintenance of encoded material over time.

31. **a.** is the answer. Iconic memory is our fleeting memory of visual stimuli.
    b. Echoic memory is auditory sensory memory.
    c. There is no such thing as photomemory.
    d. Semantic memory is memory for meaning, not a form of sensory memory.

32. **d.** is the answer. Echoic memories last 3 to 4 seconds.

33. **d.** is the answer. Retrieval refers to the *process* of remembering.

34. **c.** is the answer.

35. **d.** is the answer.
    a. There is no such term as "consolidation techniques."
    b. & c. Imagery and encoding strategies are important in storing new memories, but mnemonic device is the general designation of techniques that facilitate memory, such as acronyms and the peg-word system.

36. **d.** is the answer.
    a. There is no such process of "consolidating."
    b. Organization *does* enhance memory, but it does so through hierarchies, not grouping.
    c. Encoding refers to the processing of information into the memory system.

37. **a.** is the answer.
    b. & d. The text does not suggest that there is an optimal interval between encoding and retrieval.
    c. Learning increases the efficiency of synaptic transmission in certain neurons, but not by altering the size of the synapse.

38. **d.** is the answer. When asked to recall all the letters, participants could recall only about half; however, if immediately after the presentation they were signaled to recall a particular row, their recall was near perfect. This showed that they had a brief photographic memory—so brief that it faded in less time than it would have taken to say all nine letters.

39. **d.** is the answer.
    a. & b. Explicit memory (also called declarative memory) is memory of facts and experiences that one can consciously know and declare.
    c. There is no such thing as prime memory.

40. **b.** is the answer. When the words were organized into categories, recall was two to three times better, indicating the benefits of hierarchical organization in memory.
    d. This study did not examine the use of mnemonic devices.

41. **a.** is the answer.

b. Hermann Ebbinghaus conducted pioneering studies of verbal learning and memory.
c. Henry Roediger demonstrated that distributed practice leads to better long-term retention.
d. George Sperling is known for his research studies of iconic memory.

42. **a.** is the answer. A test of recall presents the fewest retrieval cues and usually produces the most limited retrieval.

43. **b.** is the answer.
    a., c., & d. Visual and auditory processing, both of which are examples of shallow processing, are not as effective in enhancing memory formation as deep processing.

44. **b.** is the answer.
    a. Information in short-term memory has *already* been encoded.
    c. Iconic and echoic are types of *sensory* memory.
    d. Retrieval is the process of getting material out of storage and into conscious, short-term memory. Thus, all material in short-term memory has either already been retrieved or is about to be placed in storage.

45. **c.** is the answer. By breaking concepts down into subconcepts and yet smaller divisions and showing the relationships among these, hierarchies facilitate information processing. Use of main heads and subheads is an example of the organization of textbook chapters into hierarchies.
    a. Mnemonic devices are the method of loci, acronyms, and other memory *techniques* that facilitate retention.
    b. Chunks are organizations of knowledge into familiar, manageable units.
    d. Recognition is a measure of retention.

46. **c.** is the answer.
    a. Mnemonics are memory aids such as acronyms and peg-words.
    b. Shallow processing is encoding words on a basic level based on their appearance or some other superficial characteristic.
    d. Echoic memory is the momentary sensory memory of auditory stimuli.

Terms and Concepts to Remember:

47. **Memory** is the persistence of learning over time through the storage and retrieval of information.

48. **Recall** is a measure of memory in which the person must retrieve information that is not currently in conscious awareness but that was learned earlier.

49. **Recognition** is a measure of memory in which one need only identify, rather than recall, previously learned information.

50. **Relearning** is a measure of memory that assesses the amount of time saved when learning material again.

51. **Encoding** is the first step in memory; information is translated into some form that enables it to enter our memory system.

52. **Storage** is the process by which encoded information is maintained over time.

53. **Retrieval** is the process of getting information out of memory storage.

54. **Parallel processing** is the processing of many aspects of a problem simultaneously.

55. **Sensory memory** is the immediate, very brief recording of sensory information in the memory system.

56. **Short-term memory** is activated memory, which can hold about seven items for a short time.

57. **Long-term memory** is the relatively permanent and limitless capacity memory system into which information from short-term memory may pass. It includes knowledge, skills, and experiences.

58. **Working memory** is the newer way of conceptualizing short-term memory as a work site for the active processing of incoming auditory and visual-spatial information, and of information retrieved from long-term memory.

59. **Explicit memories** are memories of facts, including names, images, and events. They are also called *declarative memories*.

60. **Effortful processing** is encoding that requires attention and conscious effort.

61. **Automatic processing** refers to our unconscious encoding of incidental information such as space, time, and frequency and of well-learned information.

62. **Implicit memories** are procedural memories for automatic skills and classically conditioned associations among stimuli. They are also called *nondeclarative memories*.

63. **Iconic memory** is the visual sensory memory consisting of a perfect photographic memory, which lasts no more than a few tenths of a second.
Memory aid: *Icon* means "image" or "representation." **Iconic memory** consists of brief visual images.

64. **Echoic memory** is the momentary sensory memory of auditory stimuli, lasting about 3 or 4 seconds.

65. **Chunking** is the memory technique of organizing material into familiar, manageable units.

66. **Mnemonics** are memory aids (acronyms, pegwords, and so on), which often use vivid imagery and organizational devices.

67. The **spacing effect** is the tendency for distributed study or practice to yield better long-term retention than massed study or practice.

68. The **testing effect** is the phenomenon in which memory is enhanced more by retrieval of the information than simply rereading it. Also sometimes referred to as a *retrieval practice effect* or *test enhanced learning*.

69. **Shallow processing** is encoding words on a basic level based on the letters in the word or some other superficial characteristic.

70. **Deep processing** is encoding words based on their meaning (semantic encoding).

MODULE 23

Storing and Retrieving Memories

Memory Storage

1. unlimited (limitless)

2. Karl Lashley; cortexes; did

3. semantic; episodic

4. frontal; hippocampus; explicit; verbal; visual; spatial

5. temporarily; memory consolidation; do; deep; Temporal

6. **d.** is the answer.
   a., b., & c. Damage to the right side, not the left side, of the hippocampus would cause these types of memory deficits.

7. **c.** is the answer. The hippocampus is involved in processing new facts for storage.
   a., b., & d. Classical conditioning and skill memory are controlled by other regions of the brain.

8. implicit; eyeblink

9. basal ganglia; motor; procedural

10. infantile; have not; hippocampus

11. stress; influence; glucose

12. amygdala; memory trace

13. flashbulb; can

14. **d.** is the answer. Flashbulb memories are unusually clear memories of emotionally significant moments in life.

15. serotonin

16. less; increases; long-term potentiation

17. drug; enzyme; LTP; faster

18. will not; will

Memory Retrieval

19. encode

20. priming; unconscious; behavior

21. the same

22. state-dependent; mood-congruent

When happy, for example, we perceive things in a positive light and recall happy events; these perceptions and memories, in turn, prolong our good mood.

23. rejecting, punitive, and guilt-promoting; have never suffered depression

24. serial position effect

25. recency; better; primacy

26. **d.** is the answer.
   a. & b. A serial position effect would presumably occur whether the study and retrieval contexts were the same or different.
   c. As researchers found, when recall is delayed, only the first items in a list are recalled more accurately than the others. With immediate recall, both the first and last items are recalled more accurately.

27. **c.** is the answer. Susan's memories are affected by her bad mood.
   a. Priming refers to the conscious or unconscious activation of particular associations in memory.
   b. A flashbulb memory is a vivid memory of a traumatic event.
   d. Working memory is the part of memory involved in the conscious, active processing of incoming auditory and visual-spatial information.

28. **a.** is the answer. Priming is the conscious or unconscious activation of particular associations in memory.
   b. Two-track processing refers to our conscious and unconscious processing of memories.
   c. That Martina is able to retrieve her former classmates' names implies that they already have been encoded.
   d. The serial position effect is the tendency to remember things at the beginning or end of a list better than those in the middle.

29. **b.** is the answer. Being back in the context in which the original experiences occurred triggered memories of these experiences.

a. The memories were triggered by similarity of place, not mood.
c. Implicit memories are procedural memories for automatic skills and classically conditioned associations.
d. Echoic memory refers to momentary memory of auditory stimuli.

Module Review:

30. **c.** is the answer. Although both are explicit memories, semantic memory involves knowledge of facts while episodic memory involves memory of personal events.
   a. & b. Priming is the activation (sometimes unconscious) of associations. Encoding is the processing of information into the memory system.

31. **c.** is the answer. Kandel and Schwartz found that when learning occurred in the sea slug, *Aplysia*, serotonin was released at certain synapses, which then became more efficient at signal transmission.

32. **d.** is the answer. In general, being in a context similar to that in which you experienced something will tend to help you recall the experience.
   a. & b. The learning environment per se—and its familiarity or exoticness—did not affect retention.

33. **c.** is the answer.

34. **c.** is the answer.
   a. & b. The basal ganglia are involved in motor movement, not working or emotional memory.
   d. The basal ganglia are involved in the formation of implicit memories, not explicit memories.

35. **b.** is the answer.
   a. The hippocampus is a temporary processing site for *explicit memories*.
   c. & d. These areas of the brain are not directly involved in the memory system.

36. **a.** is the answer. According to the serial position effect, after a delay, items at the beginning tend to be remembered best.

37. **a.** is the answer.
   b. In the serial position effect, the items in the middle of the list always show the *poorest* retention.
   c. & d. Delayed recall erases the memory facilitation for items at the end of the list.

38. **d.** is the answer. Surprisingly, Lashley found that no matter where he cut, the rats had at least a partial memory of how to solve the maze.
   a. & b. Lashley's studies did not investigate the significance of the interval between learning and cortical lesioning.

39. **d.** is the answer.

Terms and Concepts to Remember:

40. Semantic memory is our explicit conscious memory of facts and general knowledge.

41. Episodic memory is our explicit conscious memory of personally experienced events.

42. The **hippocampus** is a temporal lobe neural center located in the limbic system that is important in the processing of explicit memories for storage.

43. Memory consolidation is the neural storage of a long-term memory.

44. A **flashbulb memory** is an unusually vivid memory of an emotionally important moment or event.

45. Long-term potentiation (LTP) is an increase in a synapse's firing potential following brief, rapid stimulation. LTP is believed to be the neural basis for the learning and memory of associations.

46. Priming is the activation, often unconsciously, of a web of associations in memory in order to retrieve a specific memory.

47. Mood-congruent memory is the tendency to recall experiences that are consistent with our current mood.

48. The **serial position effect** is the tendency for items at the beginning and end of a list to be more easily retained than those in the middle.

MODULE 24 Forgetting, Memory Construction, and Improving Memory

Forgetting

1. forget

2. anterograde amnesia; retrograde amnesia

3. nonverbal tasks; classically conditioned; explicit

4. encoding; enters the memory system

5. encoding; less

6. soon

7. storage decay; memory trace

8. retrieval

9. interference

10. proactive interference; retroactive interference

11. better

12. positive transfer

13. repression

14. rarely

15. retrieval

16. **b.** is the answer.
a., c., & d. Involvement in other activities, even just eating or listening to music, is more disruptive than sleeping.

17. **a.** is the answer. Proactive interference occurs when old information makes it difficult to recall new information.
b. If Carlos were having trouble remembering the old extension, this answer would be correct.
c. & d. Carlos has successfully encoded and stored the extension; he's just having problems retrieving it.

18. **a.** is the answer.
b. Although Lewis' difficulty in recalling these memories could be considered retrieval failure, it is caused by repression, which is therefore the best explanation.
c. Because the torture was traumatic, Lewis would clearly have encoded it.
d. Proactive interference would result in Lewis not being able to recall new information.

19. **b.** is the answer. Retroactive interference is the disruption of something you once learned by new information.
a. Proactive interference occurs when old information makes it difficult to correctly remember new information.
c. & d. Interference produces forgetting even when the forgotten material was effectively encoded and stored. Janice's problem is at the level of retrieval.

Memory Construction Errors

20. reconsolidation

21. misinformation effect; can; imagination inflation; activate similar brain areas

When people viewed a film of a traffic accident and were quizzed a week later, phrasing of questions affected answers; the word "smashed," for instance, made viewers mistakenly think they had seen broken glass.

22. source amnesia; misattribute; déjà vu; temporal lobe; hippocampus; frontal lobe

23. cannot

24. hypnosis

25. **d.** is the answer.
a. This is an example of proactive interference.

b. This is an example of the disruptive effects of depressant drugs, such as alcohol, on the formation of new memories.

c. This is positive transfer.

26. questioned; neutral; nonleading

27. are not

28. 3; infantile amnesia

Improving Memory

29. Survey; Question; Read; Retrieve; Review

Suggestions for improving memory include making the material meaningful rather than mindlessly repeating information. Using mnemonic devices that incorporate vivid imagery is helpful, too. Frequent activation of retrieval cues, such as the context and mood in which the original learning occurred, can also help strengthen memory. Studying should also be arranged to minimize potential sources of interference. And, of course, sleep more, so the brain has a chance to organize and consolidate information. Finally, self-tests in the same format (recall or recognition) that will later be used on the actual test are useful. In testing your knowledge, you are not only rehearsing the information but also finding out what you don't know.

Module Review:

30. b. is the answer. In essence, we construct our memories, bringing them into line with our biases and assumptions, as well as with our subsequent experiences.

a. If this were true, it would mean that memory construction does not occur. Through memory construction, memories may deviate significantly from the original experiences.

c. There is no evidence that such chemical transfers occur.

d. Many long-term memories are apparently unlimited in duration.

31. d. is the answer.

a. Repression involves preventing anxiety-arousing thoughts from entering consciousness.

b. Encoding failure occurs when a person has not processed information sufficiently for it to enter the memory system.

c. With reconsolidation, retrieved memories are potentially changed before being stored again.

32. d. is the answer. It is in both encoding and retrieval that we construct our memories, and as

Loftus' studies showed, leading questions affect people's memory construction.

a. The memory encoding occurred at the time of the event in question, not during questioning by the hypnotist.

b. Déjà vu is the false sense that you have already experienced a current situation.

c. Proactive interference is the interfering effect of prior learning on the recall of new information.

33. c. is the answer. As Ebbinghaus and Bahrick both showed, most of the forgetting that is going to occur happens soon after learning.

34. d. is the answer.

a. & b. This study did not find evidence that memories fade (decay) with time.

c. When one is awake, there are many *more* potential sources of memory interference than when one is asleep.

35. d. is the answer.

36. c. is the answer.

a. This is retrograde amnesia.

b. This is source amnesia.

d. The capacity of working memory *averages* 7 items.

37. c. is the answer. According to Freud, we repress painful memories to preserve our self-concepts.

a. & b. The fact that repressed memories can sometimes be retrieved suggests that they were encoded and have not decayed with time.

38. d. is the answer. When misled by the phrasings of questions, subjects incorrectly recalled details of the film and even "remembered" objects that weren't there.

39. c. is the answer. Speed reading, which entails little active rehearsal, yields poor retention.

40. b. is the answer. Amnesia patients typically have suffered damage to the hippocampus, a brain structure involved in processing explicit memories for facts.

a., c., & d. Amnesia patients do retain implicit memories for how to do things; these are processed in the cerebellum. Motor skills and classically conditioned responses are implicit memories.

41. d. is the answer.

42. c. is the answer. Loftus and Palmer found that eyewitness testimony could easily be altered when questions were phrased to imply misleading information.

a. Although memories *are* constructed during encoding, the misinformation effect is a retrieval,

rather than an encoding, phenomenon.
b. & d. In fact, just the opposite is true.

Terms and Concepts to Remember:

43. **Anterograde amnesia** is an inability to form new memories.

44. **Retrograde amnesia** is an inability to retrieve old memories.

45. **Proactive interference** is the disruptive effect of something you already have learned on your efforts to learn or recall new information.

46. **Retroactive interference** is the disruptive effect of new learning on the recall of old knowledge.

    Memory aid: Retro means "backward." **Retroactive interference** is "backward-acting" interference.

47. **Repression** is an example of motivated forgetting in that anxiety-arousing thoughts, feelings, and memories are prevented from entering consciousness. In psychoanalytic theory, it is the basic defense mechanism.

48. **Reconsolidation** is the process in which retrieved memories are potentially changed before being stored again.

49. The **misinformation effect** is the tendency of eyewitnesses to an event to incorporate misleading information into their memories of the event.

50. At the heart of many false memories, **source amnesia** refers to attributing an event to the wrong source. (Also called *source misattribution*.)

51. **Déjà vu** is the false sense that you have already experienced a current situation.

Essay Question

Experts agree that child abuse is a real problem that can have long-term adverse effects on individuals. They also acknowledge that forgetting of isolated events, both good and bad, is an ordinary part of life.

Although experts all accept the fact that recovered memories are commonplace, they warn that memories "recovered" under hypnosis or with the use of drugs are unreliable, as are memories of events before age 3. Finally, they agree that memories can be traumatic, whether real or false.

Before You Move On

Matching Items

1. m	**6.** e	**11.** j
2. n	**7.** f	**12.** o
3. a	**8.** i	**13.** h
4. l	**9.** b	**14.** d
5. c	**10.** g	**15.** k

True–False Items

1. T	**6.** F
2. T	**7.** T
3. T	**8.** F
4. T	**9.** F
5. F	

Cross-Check

ACROSS
1. repression
4. echoic
6. semantic
7. priming
10. imagery
13. LTP
14. iconic
18. chunking
19. flashbulb
20. amnesia
21. rehearsal

DOWN
1. recognition
2. sensory
3. misinformation
4. effortful
5. hippocampus
8. implicit
9. mnemonics
11. automatic
12. proactive
15. long-term
16. visual
17. déjà vu
22. episodic

Thinking, Language, and Intelligence

Overview

Module 25 deals with thinking, with emphasis on how people logically—or at times illogically—use tools such as algorithms and heuristics when making decisions and solving problems. Also discussed are several common obstacles to problem solving, including fixations that prevent us from taking a fresh perspective on a problem and our bias to search for information that confirms rather than challenges existing hypotheses. The module also discusses the power and perils of intuition and the meaning and development of creativity. It concludes with an exploration of animal cognitive skills.

Module 26 is concerned with language, including its structure, development in children, use by animals, and relationship to thinking. The module introduces Chomsky's theory that humans have a biological predisposition to acquire language, as well as Skinner's view that language develops through association, imitation, and reinforcements. The module also describes the brain's role in language processing and speech.

An ongoing controversy in psychology involves attempts to define and measure intelligence. Module 27 discusses whether intelligence is a single general ability or several specific ones. It also describes the historical origins of intelligence tests and discusses several important issues concerning their use. These include the methods by which intelligence tests are constructed and whether such tests are valid, reliable, and free of bias. The module also explores extremes of intelligenceand how aging affects (or doesn't affect) intelligence. Module 28 examines the extent of genetic and environmental influences on intelligence.

NOTE: Answer guidelines for all Module 25–28 questions begin on page 230.

Outline

Instructions

First, skim each section, noting headings and boldface items. After you have read the section, review each objective by answering the fill-in, essay-type, and multiple-choice questions for that section. In some cases, Study Tips explain how best to learn a difficult concept and Applications and Module Reviews help you to know how well you understand the material. Finally, try to define the important terms and concepts using your own words. As you proceed, evaluate your performance by consulting the answers on page 230. Do not continue until you understand each answer. If you need to, review or reread a troublesome section before continuing.

Before You Move On includes activities that test you on material from the entire unit.

MODULE 25 Thinking

Concepts

Objective 25-1: Define *cognition,* and describe the functions of concepts.

1. Cognition, or _____, can be defined as _____ _____ .

2. People tend to organize similar objects, events, ideas, or people into mental groupings called _____ .

3. Concepts are typically formed through the development of a best example, or _____ , of a category. People more easily detect _____ (male/female) prejudice against _____ (males/females) than vice versa.

APPLICATION:

4. Complete the following analogy: Rose is to flower as
   a. concept is to prototype.
   b. prototype is to concept.
   c. concept is to cognition.
   d. cognition is to concept.

Problem Solving: Strategies and Obstacles

Objective 25-2: Describe the cognitive strategies that assist our problem solving, and identify the obstacles that hinder it.

5. Humans are especially capable of using their reasoning powers for coping with new situations, and thus for _____ _____ .

6. When we try each possible solution to a problem, we are using _____ _____ .

7. Logical, methodical, step-by-step procedures for solving problems are called _____ .

8. Simple thinking strategies that provide us with problem-solving shortcuts are referred to as _____ .

9. When you suddenly realize a problem's solution, _____ has occurred. Research studies show that such moments are preceded by _____ _____ activity involved in focusing attention and accompanied by a burst of activity in the _____ _____ _____ .

10. The tendency of people to look for information that supports their preconceptions is called _____ _____ .

11. It is human nature to seek evidence that _____ our ideas more eagerly than to seek evidence that might _____ them.

12. Not being able to take a new perspective when attempting to solve a problem is referred to as _____ . One example of this obstacle to problem solving is the tendency to repeat solutions that have worked previously; this phenomenon is known as the development of a _____ _____ .

STUDY TIP/APPLICATION: We all use any of four techniques for solving problems: trial and error, algorithms, heuristics, and insight. To test your understanding of these approaches, apply them to a problem you might actually face, such as finding a misplaced set of car keys. Using the chart on the next page, see if you can come up with an example of how you could find your keys using each of the four problem-solving approaches.

13. Problem-Solving Approach	How You Would Find Car Keys Using Each Method
a. Trial and error	
b. Algorithm	
c. Heuristics	
d. Insight	

APPLICATIONS:

14. A dessert recipe that gives you the ingredients, their amounts, and the steps to follow is an example of a(n)

   a. prototype.
   b. algorithm.
   c. heuristic.
   d. mental set.

15. Boris the chess master selects his next move by considering moves that would threaten his opponent's queen. His opponent, a chess-playing computer, selects its next move by considering *all* possible moves. Boris is using a(n) _____ and the computer is using a(n) _____ .

   a. algorithm; heuristic
   b. prototype; mental set
   c. mental set; prototype
   d. heuristic; algorithm

16. Experts in a field prefer heuristics to algorithms because heuristics

   a. guarantee solutions to problems.
   b. prevent mental sets.
   c. often save time.
   d. prevent fixation.

Forming Good and Bad Decisions and Judgments

Objective 25-3: Define *intuition*, and describe how the availability heuristic, overconfidence, belief perseverance, and framing influence our decisions and judgments.

17. Effortless, immediate, and automatic feelings or thoughts characterize our _____ .

18. When we judge the likelihood of something occurring in terms of how readily it comes to mind, we are using the _____ _____ .

Explain how this heuristic may lead us to make judgmental errors.

Objective 25-4: Identify the factors that contribute to our fear of unlikely events.

19. (Thinking Critically) Many people fear flying more than driving. These fears _____ (are/are not) supported by death and injury statistics. This type of faulty thinking occurs because we fear

   a. _____
   b. _____
   c. _____
   d. _____

20. The tendency of people to overestimate the accuracy of their knowledge results in

    _____ .

21. Overconfidence has _____ value because self-confident people tend to live _____ (more/less) happily and seem more _____ .

22. When research participants are given feedback on the accuracy of their judgments, such feedback generally _____ (helps/does not help) them become more realistic about how much they know.

23. Research has shown that once we form a belief or a concept, it may take more convincing evidence for us to change the concept than it did to create it; this is because of _____

    _____ .

24. A cure for this is to _____

    _____ _____ .

25. The way an issue is posed is called _____ . This effect influences political and business decisions, suggesting that our judgments _____ (may/may not) always be well reasoned.

APPLICATIONS:

26. During a televised political debate, the Republican and Democratic candidates each argued that the results of a recent public opinion poll supported their party's platform regarding sexual harassment. Because both candidates saw the information as supporting their belief, it is clear that both were victims of
    a. fixation.
    b. mental set.
    c. belief perseverance.
    d. confirmation bias.

27. In relation to ground beef, consumers respond more positively to an ad describing it as "75 percent lean" than to one referring to its "25 percent fat" content. This is an example of
    a. the framing effect.   c. mental set.
    b. confirmation bias.   d. overconfidence.

28. Most people tend to
    a. accurately estimate the accuracy of their knowledge and judgments.
    b. underestimate the accuracy of their knowledge and judgments.
    c. overestimate the accuracy of their knowledge and judgments.
    d. lack confidence in their decision-making strategies.

29. Dominic is certain that he will be able to finish reading the assigned text chapter over the weekend even though he also has to write a five-page essay on the U.S. political process and will be going to a party on Saturday night. If he's like most people, Dominic
    a. is accurate in knowing how much he can do over the weekend.
    b. underestimates how much he'll get done over the weekend.
    c. overestimates how much he can get done over the weekend.

30. Which of the following illustrates belief perseverance?
    a. Your belief remains intact even in the face of evidence to the contrary.
    b. You refuse to listen to arguments counter to your beliefs.
    c. You tend to become flustered and angered when your beliefs are refuted.
    d. You tend to search for information that supports your beliefs.

31. Marilyn was asked to solve a series of five math problems. The first four problems could only be solved by a particular sequence of operations. The fifth problem could also be solved following this sequence; however, a much simpler solution was possible. Marilyn did not realize this simpler solution and solved the problem in the way she had solved the first four. Her problem-solving strategy was hampered by
    a. fixation.
    b. the overconfidence phenomenon.
    c. mental set.
    d. her lack of a prototype for the solution.

32. The number of airline reservations typically declines after a highly publicized airplane crash because people overestimate the incidence of such disasters. In such instances, their decisions are being influenced by
    a. belief perseverance.
    b. the availability heuristic.
    c. confirmation bias.
    d. fixation.

Objective 25-5: Describe how smart thinkers use intuition.

33. Researchers have shown that in making complex decisions, we benefit from using _____ (rational/intuitive) thinking. Although critics disagree, letting a problem "_____" while we attend to other things can pay dividends.

34. Another advantage of intuition is that it enables us to react quickly, which is _____ .

35. Finally, intuition is _____ knowledge, resulting from experience.

Thinking Creatively

Objective 25-6: Define *creativity*, and explain what fosters it.

36. The ability to produce ideas that are both novel and valuable is called _____ . The relationship between _____ , or what intelligence tests reveal, and creativity holds only up to a certain point. Researchers have found that the brain activity associated with intelligence is _____ (the same as/different from) the activity associated with creativity.

37. Standard intelligence tests, which demand single correct answers to questions, measure _____ thinking. Tests that allow multiple possible answers to problems measure _____ thinking.

Describe five components of creativity.

Describe research findings on how to foster creativity.

APPLICATION:

38. Vanessa is a very creative sculptress. We would expect that Vanessa also
    a. has an exceptionally high aptitude for sculpting.
    b. tries to solve problems in ways that worked before.
    c. has a venturesome personality and is intrinsically motivated.
    d. lacks expertise in most other skills.

Do Other Species Share Our Cognitive Skills?

Objective 25-7: Describe what we know about thinking in other animals.

39. Animals are capable of forming _____ . Wolfgang Köhler demonstrated that chimpanzees also exhibit the "Aha!" reaction that characterizes reasoning by _____ .

40. Forest-dwelling chimpanzees learn to use different sticks as _____ . These behaviors, along with behaviors related to grooming and courtship, _____ (vary/do not vary) from one group of chimpanzees to another, suggesting the transmission of _____ customs.

41. Animals _____ (do/do not) have many other cognitive skills. For example, elephants have demonstrated _____ and chimpanzees have demonstrated _____ , _____ , and group aggression.

MODULE REVIEW:

42. The text defines *cognition* as
    a. silent speech.
    b. all mental activity.
    c. the mental activities associated with thinking, knowing, remembering, and communicating information.
    d. logical reasoning.

43. A mental grouping of similar things, events, or people is called a(n)
    a. prototype.   c. algorithm.
    b. concept.   d. heuristic.

44. When forming a concept, people often develop a best example, or _____ , of a category.
    a. denoter
    b. heuristic
    c. prototype
    d. algorithm

45. Confirmation bias refers to the tendency to
    a. allow preexisting beliefs to distort logical reasoning.
    b. cling to one's initial conceptions after the basis on which they were formed has been discredited.
    c. search randomly through alternative solutions when problem solving.
    d. look for information that is consistent with one's beliefs.

46. Which of the following best describes the relationship between creativity and aptitude?
    a. Creativity appears to depend on the ability to think imaginatively and has little if any relationship to aptitude.
    b. Creativity is best understood as a certain kind of aptitude.
    c. The higher the level of aptitude a person has, the greater his or her creativity.
    d. A certain level of aptitude is necessary but not sufficient for creativity.

47. Mental set is an example of a(n)
    a. algorithm.
    b. heuristic.
    c. fixation.
    d. insight.

48. Thoughts and feelings that are automatic, effortless, immediate, and unreasoned are examples of
    a. mental set.
    b. confirmation bias.
    c. heuristics.
    d. intuition.

49. Which of the following is an example of the use of heuristics?
    a. trying every possible letter ordering when unscrambling a word
    b. considering each possible move when playing chess
    c. using the formula "area = length × width" to find the area of a rectangle
    d. playing chess using a defensive strategy that has often been successful for you

50. The chimpanzee Sultan used a short stick to pull a longer stick that was out of reach into his cage. He then used the longer stick to reach a piece of fruit. Researchers hypothesized that Sultan's discovery of the solution to his problem was the result of:
    a. trial and error.
    b. heuristics.
    c. fixation.
    d. insight.

51. Researchers who are convinced that animals can think point to evidence that
    a. black bears have learned to sort pictures into animal and nonanimal categories.
    b. chimpanzees regularly use sticks as tools in their natural habitats.
    c. chimps invent grooming and courtship customs and pass them on to their peers.
    d. they exhibit all of these skills.

52. A common problem in everyday reasoning is our tendency to
    a. accept as logical those conclusions that agree with our own opinions.
    b. accept as logical those conclusions that disagree with our own opinions.
    c. underestimate the accuracy of our knowledge.
    d. accept as logical conclusions that involve unfamiliar concepts.

53. Availability is an example of
    a. a mental set.
    b. belief bias.
    c. an algorithm.
    d. a heuristic.

54. Assume that Congress is considering revising its approach to welfare and to this end is hearing a range of testimony. A member of Congress who uses the availability heuristic would be most likely to
    a. want to experiment with numerous possible approaches to see which of these seems to work best.
    b. want to cling to approaches to welfare that seem to have had some success in the past.
    c. refuse to be budged from his or her beliefs despite persuasive testimony to the contrary.
    d. base his or her ideas on the most vivid, memorable testimony given, even though many of the statistics presented run counter to this testimony.

55. If you want to be absolutely certain that you will find the solution to a problem you know *is* solvable, you should use
    a. a heuristic.
    b. an algorithm.
    c. insight.
    d. trial and error.

TERMS AND CONCEPTS TO REMEMBER:

56. cognition

57. concept

58. prototype

59. algorithm

60. heuristic

61. insight
62. confirmation bias
63. mental set
64. intuition
65. availability heuristic
66. overconfidence
67. belief perseverance
68. framing
69. creativity
70. convergent thinking
71. divergent thinking

MODULE 26

Language and Thought

Language Structure

Objective 26-1: Describe the structural components of a language.

1. Language is defined as _____ _____ .

2. The smallest distinctive sound units of language are its _____ . English has approximately _____ of these units.

3. Phonemes are grouped into units of meaning called _____ .

4. The system of rules that enables us to use our language to speak to and understand others is called _____ , which consists of the ordering of words, or _____ , and the meaning of words, or _____ .

5. According to linguist _____ , all human languages have the same grammatical building blocks, which suggests that there is a _____ _____ .

6. Behaviorist _____ believed that the diversity of language can be explained by _____ , _____ , and _____ .

7. The fact that preschoolers pick up language so readily and use grammar so well suggests to Chomsky that humans come with a built-in readiness to learn _____ .

APPLICATIONS:

8. The word *predates* contains _____ phonemes and _____ morphemes.
   a. 7; 3   c. 7; 2
   b. 3; 7   d. 3; 2

9. The sentence "Blue jeans wear false smiles" has correct _____ but incorrect _____ .
   a. morphemes; phonemes
   b. phonemes; morphemes
   c. semantics; syntax
   d. syntax; semantics

Language Development

Objective 26-2: Identify the milestones in language development, and describe how we acquire language.

10. By _____ months of age, babies can read lips and discriminate speech sounds. This marks the beginning of their _____ _____ , their ability to comprehend speech. This ability begins to mature before their _____ _____ , or ability to produce words.

11. The first stage of language development, in which children spontaneously utter different sounds, is the _____ stage. This stage typically begins at about _____ months of age. The sounds children make during this stage _____ (do/do not) include only the sounds of the language they hear.

12. Deaf infants _____ (do/do not) babble. Many natural babbling sounds are _____-_____ pairs formed by _____ _____ .

13. By about _____ months of age, infant babbling begins to resemble the household language. At about the same time, the ability to perceive speech sounds outside their native language is _____ (lost/acquired).

14. During the second stage, called the _____-_____ stage, children convey complete thoughts using single words. These words are usually _____

that labels objects or people. This stage begins at about _____ year(s) of age.

15. During the _____-_____ stage, children speak in sentences containing mostly nouns and verbs. This type of speech is called _____ speech. It _____ (does/does not) follow the rules of syntax.

16. Childhood seems to represent a _____ _____ for mastering certain aspects of language. Those who learn a second language as adults usually speak it with the _____ of their first language. Moreover, they typically show _____ (poorer/better) mastery of the _____ of the second language.

17. The window for learning language gradually begins to close after age _____. When a young brain doesn't learn any language, its language-learning capacity _____ (never/may still) fully develop(s).

18. People who learn sign language as teens or adults _____ (eventually do/do not) learn to sign as fluently as those who learned sign as infants.

APPLICATIONS:

19. Complete the following: -ed is to sh- as _____ is to _____.
   a. phoneme; morpheme
   b. morpheme; phoneme
   c. grammar; syntax
   d. syntax; grammar

20. A listener hearing a recording of Japanese, Spanish, and North American children babbling would
   a. not be able to tell them apart.
   b. be able to tell them apart if they were older than 6 months.
   c. be able to tell them apart if they were older than 8 to 10 months.
   d. be able to tell them apart at any age.

21. The child who says "Milk gone" is engaging in _____. This type of utterance demonstrates that children are actively experimenting with the rules of _____.
   a. babbling; syntax
   b. telegraphic speech; syntax
   c. babbling; semantics
   d. telegraphic speech; semantics

The Brain and Language

Objective 26-3: Identify the brain areas involved in language processing and speech.

22. Brain injuries may produce an impairment in language use called _____. Studies of people with such impairments have shown that (a) _____ _____ is involved in producing speech and (b) _____ _____ is involved in understanding speech.

(a) Speaking words (_____ and the motor cortex)

23. Although our conscious experience of language seems indivisible, functional MRI scans show that different _____ _____ are engaged to compute each word's form, sound, and meaning, for example.

(b) Hearing words (auditory cortex and _____)

24. As in other forms of information processing, the brain operates by dividing its mental functions into _____.

APPLICATION:

25. In a soccer game, Laura suffered damage to her left temporal lobe. As a result, she is unable to speak in meaningful sentences. The damage affected
   a. Wernicke's area.
   b. Broca's area.
   c. the hypothalamus.
   d. the hippocampus.

Do Other Species Have Language?

Objective 26-4: Describe what we know about other animals' capacity for language.

26. Animals definitely _____ (do/do not) communicate.

27. The Gardners attempted to communicate with the chimpanzee Washoe by teaching her _____ _____.

28. Most now agree that humans _____ (alone/along with primates) possess language that involves complex grammar.

Summarize some of the arguments of skeptics of the "talking apes" research and some responses of believers.

Thinking and Language

Objective 26-5: Describe the relationship between language and thinking, and discuss the value of thinking in images.

29. According to the _____

_____ hypothesis, language shapes our thinking. The linguist who proposed this hypothesis is _____ .

30. Although this hypothesis is too extreme, many people who are bilingual report feeling a different sense of _____ , depending on which language they are using.

31. In several studies, researchers have found that using the pronoun "he" (instead of "he or she") _____ (does/does not) influence people's thoughts concerning gender.

32. Bilingual people, who learn to inhibit one language while using their other language, are better able to inhibit their _____ to irrelevant information. This has been called the

_____ _____ .

33. One study of Canadian children found that English-speaking children who were _____ in French had increased _____ scores and creativity than control children.

34. It appears that thinking _____ (can/cannot) occur without the use of language. Thinking in terms of mental pictures is called _____ , or _____ .

35. Mental rehearsal can help you achieve an academic goal. In one study of introductory psychology students preparing for a midterm exam, the greatest benefits were achieved by those who visualized themselves _____

(receiving a high grade/studying effectively), which is called _____

_____ .

Summarize the probable relationship between thinking and language.

APPLICATION:

36. Luke is the back-up quarterback for his high school football team. The starting quarterback has been injured, so Luke will play on Saturday. In addition to physical practice, Luke should visualize throwing the ball, a process called

_____ _____ , rather than seeing a touchdown noted on the scoreboard, called _____

_____ .

MODULE REVIEW:

37. The English language has approximately _____ phonemes.
    a. 25   **c.** 40
    b. 30   **d.** 45

38. Which of the following is NOT true of babbling?
    a. It is imitation of adult speech.
    b. It is the same in all cultures.
    c. It typically occurs from about age 4 months to 1 year.
    d. Babbling increasingly comes to resemble a particular language.

39. Which of the following has been argued by critics of ape language research?
    a. Ape language is merely imitation of the trainer's behavior.
    b. Ape vocabularies and sentences are simple, rather like those of a 2-year-old child.
    c. By seeing what they wish to see, trainers attribute greater linguistic ability to apes than actually exists.
    d. All of these are arguments by critics.

40. Whorf's linguistic determinism hypothesis states that
    a. language is primarily a learned ability.
    b. language is partially an innate ability.
    c. the size of a person's vocabulary reflects his or her intelligence.
    d. our language shapes our thinking.

41. Which of the following BEST describes Chomsky's view of language development?
    a. We are born with a built-in specific language.
    b. Language is an innate ability.
    c. Humans have a biological predisposition to acquire language.
    d. There are no cultural influences on the development of language.

42. Damage to _____ will usually cause a person to lose the ability to comprehend language.
    a. any area of the brain
    b. Broca's area
    c. Wernicke's area
    d. frontal lobe association areas

43. Deaf children who are not exposed to sign language until they are teenagers
    a. are unable to master the basic words of sign language.
    b. learn the basic words but not how to order them.
    c. are unable to master either the basic words or syntax of sign language.
    d. never become as fluent as those who learned to sign at a younger age.

44. According to the text, language acquisition is best described as
    a. the result of conditioning and reinforcement.
    b. a biological process of maturation.
    c. an interaction between biology and experience.
    d. a mystery of which researchers have no real understanding.

45. The linguistic determinism hypothesis is challenged by the finding that
    a. chimps can learn to communicate spontaneously by using sign language.
    b. people with no word for a certain color can still perceive that color accurately.
    c. the Eskimo language contains a number of words for snow, whereas English has only one.
    d. infants' babbling contains many phonemes that do not occur in their own language and that they therefore cannot have heard.

46. Phonemes are the basic units of _____ in language.
    a. sound
    b. meaning
    c. grammar
    d. semantics

47. Syntax refers to the
    a. sounds in a word.
    b. rules for ordering words into sentences.
    c. rules by which meaning is derived from sentences.
    d. overall rules of a language.

48. Our ability to learn a new language
    a. diminishes with age.
    b. is limited by a sharply defined critical period.
    c. remains constant throughout our lives.
    d. depends on the language.

49. Many psychologists are skeptical of claims that chimpanzees can acquire language because the chimps have not shown the ability to
    a. use symbols meaningfully.
    b. acquire speech.
    c. acquire even a limited vocabulary.
    d. use syntax in communicating.

50. Which of the following is cited by Chomsky as evidence that humans are born with a predisposition to learn language?
    a. Children master the complicated rules of grammar with ease.
    b. Different languages do not have the same grammatical building blocks.
    c. Children make unpredictable mistakes as they acquire grammar.
    d. Children raised in isolation from language spontaneously begin speaking words.

51. Telegraphic speech is typical of the _____ stage.
    a. babbling
    b. one-word
    c. two-word
    d. three-word

52. Children first demonstrate a rudimentary understanding of syntax during the _____ stage.
    a. babbling
    b. one-word
    c. two-word
    d. three-word

53. The study in which people who immigrated to the United States at various ages were compared in terms of their ability to understand English grammar found that
    a. age of arrival had no effect on mastery of grammar.
    b. those who immigrated as children understood grammar as well as native speakers.

c. those who immigrated as adults understood grammar as well as native speakers.

d. whether English was spoken in the home was the most important factor in mastering the rules of grammar.

54. Researchers taught the chimpanzee Washoe to communicate by using

   a. various sounds.
   b. plastic symbols of various shapes and colors.
   c. sign language.
   d. all of these methods.

55. Regarding the relationship between thinking and language, which of the following most accurately reflects the position taken in the text?

   a. Language determines everything about our thinking.
   b. Language determines the way we think.
   c. Thinking without language is not possible.
   d. Thinking affects our language, which then affects our thought.

56. The bilingual advantage refers to the fact that people who are fluent in two languages are better at

   a. inhibiting their attention to irrelevant information.
   b. acquiring large vocabularies in both languages.
   c. thinking in images.
   d. all of these abilities.

57. Which of the following is true regarding the relationship between thinking and language?

   a. "Real" thinking requires the use of language.
   b. People sometimes think in images rather than in words.
   c. A thought that cannot be expressed in a particular language cannot occur to speakers of that language.
   d. All of these statements are true.

58. One reason an English-speaking adult may have difficulty pronouncing Russian words is that

   a. the vocal tracts of English- and Russian-speaking people develop differently in response to the demands of the two languages.
   b. although English and Russian have very similar morphemes, their phonemic inventories are very different.
   c. although English and Russian have very similar phonemes, their morphemic inventories are very different.

d. after the babbling stage, a child who hears only English stops uttering other phonemes.

TERMS AND CONCEPTS TO REMEMBER:

59. language

60. phoneme

61. morpheme

62. grammar

63. babbling stage

64. one-word stage

65. two-word stage

66. telegraphic speech

67. aphasia

68. Broca's area

69. Wernicke's area

70. linguistic determinism

MODULE 27 Intelligence and Its Assessment

What Is Intelligence?

Objective 27-1: Give psychologists' definition of *intelligence*, and identify the arguments for *g*.

1. Psychologists _____ (do/do not) agree on a definition of intelligence.

2. Intelligence has been defined as whatever _____ _____ measure, but that _____ (does/does not) take into account the different qualities that enable success in different cultures.

3. In any context, intelligence can be defined as _____ _____ _____ .

4. Charles Spearman believed that a factor called *g*, or _____ _____ , runs through the more specific aspects of intelligence.

5. The statistical procedure used to identify clusters of related items is called _____ _____ .

6. Research has found that distinct abilities
_____ (do/do not) tend to cluster together and _____ (do/do not) correlate enough to define a general underlying factor.

Objective 27-2: Compare Gardner's and Sternberg's theories of intelligence, and discuss the criticisms they have faced.

7. People with _____
_____ score at the low end of intelligence tests but possess extraordinary specific skills. Most of these people are _____ (males/females) and many also have _____
_____ _____ .

8. Howard Gardner proposes that there are
_____ _____ , each independent of the others.

9. Gardner has also speculated about a ninth possible intelligence, _____ intelligence, the ability to ponder large questions about life.

10. Sternberg's _____ theory distinguishes three types of intelligence:
_____ intelligence,
_____ intelligence, and
_____ intelligence.

11. Critics of theories of multiple intelligences point out that the world is not so just: General intelligence scores _____ (do/do not) predict performance on various complex tasks and in various jobs. Even so, success requires a combination of talent and _____ . Researchers report a _____-_____ rule for success.

APPLICATIONS:

12. Melvin is limited in mental ability but has an exceptional ability to play complex music on the piano after hearing it only once. He has been diagnosed as having
_____ _____ .

13. Don's intelligence scores were only average, but he has been enormously successful as a corporate manager. Psychologist Sternberg would probably suggest that
   a. Don's verbal intelligence exceeds his performance intelligence.

   b. Don's performance intelligence exceeds his verbal intelligence.
   c. Don's academic intelligence exceeds his practical intelligence.
   d. Don's practical intelligence exceeds his academic intelligence.

Objective 27-3: Describe the four components of emotional intelligence.

14. The know-how involved in comprehending social situations and managing oneself successfully differs from _____ intelligence and is referred to as _____ intelligence.

15. A critical part of social intelligence is
_____ _____ —the ability to _____ ,
_____ , _____ ,
and _____ emotions.

16. More specifically, the four components of emotional intelligence are as follows: the ability to _____ emotions in faces, music, and stories; the ability to _____ them and how they change and blend; the ability to _____ them correctly in varied situations; and the ability to use them to enable _____ or creative thinking.

Briefly describe emotionally intelligent people.

17. Some scholars believe that the concept of
_____ intelligence stretches the idea of multiple intelligences too far.

APPLICATION:

18. Gerardeen has superb social skills, manages conflicts well, and has great empathy for her friends and co-workers. Researchers would probably say that Gerardeen possesses a high degree of
_____ .

Assessing Intelligence

Objective 27-4: Define *intelligence test*, and explain the difference between achievement and aptitude tests.

19. An intelligence test measures people's _____ abilities and _____ them with others.

20. Tests designed to measure what you already have learned are called _____ tests. Tests designed to predict your ability to learn something new are called _____ tests.

APPLICATION:

21. Before becoming attorneys, law students must pass a special licensing exam, which is an _____ test. Before entering college, high school students must take the SAT Reasoning Test, which is an _____ test.

Objective 27-5: Discuss when and why intelligence tests were created, and describe how today's tests differ from early intelligence tests.

22. The French psychologist who devised a test to predict the success of children in school was _____ . Predictions were made by comparing children's chronological ages with their _____ ages, which were determined by the test. This test _____ (was/was not) designed to measure inborn intelligence; Binet and his collaborator, _____ , leaned toward an _____ explanation of intelligence.

23. Lewis Terman's revision of Binet's test is referred to as the _____-_____ . From this test, _____ derived the famous _____ , or _____ .

Give the original formula for computing IQ, and explain any items used in the formula.

24. Today's tests compute _____ (IQ/ an intelligence test score) by comparing the individual's performance to the average performance of people of _____ (the same/different) age(s). These tests are designed so that a score of _____ is considered average.

25. The most widely used intelligence test is the _____ _____ _____ . Consisting of 15 subtests, it provides not only a general intelligence score but also separate scores for _____ , _____ _____ , _____ _____ , and _____ .

APPLICATIONS:

26. Benito was born in 1937. In 1947, he scored 130 on an intelligence test. Using the original IQ formula, Benito's mental age when he took the test was _____ .

27. If asked to guess the intelligence score of a stranger, your best guess would be _____ .

Objective 27-6: Describe a normal curve, and explain what it means to say that a test has been standardized and is reliable and valid.

28. One requirement of a good test is the process of defining meaningful scores relative to a pretested comparison group, which is called _____ .

29. When scores on a test are compiled, they generally result in a bell-shaped pattern, or _____ distribution.

Describe the normal curve, and explain its significance in the standardization process.

30. If a test yields consistent results, it is said to be _____ .

31. To check a test's reliability, researchers test people many times. Two basic methods of checking reliability are

    a. _____

    b. _____

32. The Stanford-Binet, WAIS, and WISC have reliabilities of about _____ .

33. The extent to which a test measures or predicts what it is supposed to is referred to as the test's _____ . The behavior of interest is referred to as the _____ .

34. The extent to which a test measures the behavior it was designed to measure is referred to as the test's _____ _____ .

35. The extent to which a test predicts future performance of a particular behavior is referred to as the test's _____ _____ .

Choose a specific example and use it to illustrate and explain the concept of criterion and its relationship to predictive validity.

36. The predictive validity of these tests _____ (increases/diminishes) as individuals move up the educational ladder.

APPLICATIONS:

37. If you wanted to develop a test of musical aptitude in North American children, which would be the appropriate standardization group?
    a. children all over the world
    b. North American children
    c. children of musical parents
    d. children with known musical ability

38. Jack takes the same test of mechanical reasoning on several different days and gets virtually identical scores. This suggests that the test has
    a. high content validity.
    b. high reliability.
    c. high predictive validity.
    d. been standardized.

39. You would not use a test of hearing ability as an intelligence test because it would lack
    a. content reliability.
    b. predictive reliability.
    c. predictive validity.
    d. content validity.

40. A school psychologist found that 85 percent of those who scored above 115 on an aptitude test were A students and 75 percent of those who scored below 85 on the test were D students. The psychologist concluded that the test had high
    a. content validity because scores on it correlated highly with the criterion behavior.
    b. predictive validity because scores on it correlated highly with the criterion behavior.
    c. reliability because the test yielded inconsistent results.
    d. reliability because the test yielded consistent results.

The Dynamics of Intelligence

Objective 27-7: Discuss how aging affects crystallized and fluid intelligence.

41. The accumulation of knowledge and verbal skills is referred to as _____ intelligence. The ability to reason speedily and abstractly is referred to as _____ intelligence.

42. During adulthood, _____ intelligence declines beginning in the _____ and _____ , slowly until about age _____ , and then more rapidly, especially after about age _____ .

43. When developmental psychologists restudy the same group at different times across their life span, they are using _____ studies. When they compare members of different age groups at the same time, they are using _____-_____ studies.

Objective 27-8: Describe the stability of intelligence scores over the life span.

44. Traditional intelligence tests before age _____ predict future aptitudes only modestly. By age _____ , children's performance on intelligence tests begins to predict their adolescent and adult scores.

45. During childhood, the stability of intelligence scores _____ (increases/ decreases) with age. A long-term study of mental ability in Scottish children revealed that intelligence _____ (does/does not) stabilize through late adulthood.

46. More intelligent children and adults live _____ and _____ . Give four possible reasons for this relationship.

    a. _____

    b. _____

    c. _____

    d. _____

APPLICATIONS:

47. At age 16, Angel's intelligence score was 110. What will her score probably be at age 32?
    a. 125
    b. 110
    c. 115
    d. There is no basis for predicting an individual's future IQ.

48. A psychologist who is looking at a student's intelligence score finds a jump of 30 points between the earliest score at age 2 and the most recent at age 17. The psychologist's knowledge of testing would probably lead her to conclude that such a jump
    a. indicates that different tests were used, creating an apparent change in intelligence level, although it actually remained stable.
    b. signals a significant improvement in the child's environment over this period.
    c. is unsurprising, since intelligence scores do not become stable until adolescence.
    d. is mainly the result of the age at which the first test was taken.

Objective 27-9: Describe the traits of those at the low and high intelligence extremes.

49. Individuals whose intelligence test scores are 70 or below and who have difficulty adapting to life may be labeled _____ _____ . Inability to adapt may be expressed in three areas: _____ skills, _____ skills, and _____ skills.

50. An intellectual disability sometimes has a physical basis, such as _____ _____ , a genetic disorder caused by an extra chromosome.

51. The current view is that people with an intellectual disability might be better able to live independently today because tests have been periodically _____ and those individuals suddenly lost 6 test-score points.

52. At the high extreme, Lewis Terman's "gifted children" turned out to be _____ , well-_____ , and unusually successful _____ .

APPLICATION:

53. Twenty-two-year-old Dan has an intelligence score of 63 and the academic skills of a fourth-grader, and is unable to live independently. Dan probably
    a. has higher fluid intelligence than crystallized intelligence.
    b. has higher crystallized intelligence than fluid intelligence.
    c. is intellectually disabled.
    d. will eventually achieve self-supporting social and vocational skills.

MODULE REVIEW:

54. The existence of _____ reinforces the generally accepted notion that intelligence is a multidimensional quality.
    a. adaptive skills   c. general intelligence
    b. a *g* factor   d. savant syndrome

55. The concept of a *g* factor implies that intelligence
    a. is a single overall ability.
    b. is several specific abilities.
    c. cannot be defined or measured.
    d. is a socially constructed concept.

56. Most experts view intelligence as a person's
    a. ability to perform well on intelligence tests.
    b. innate mental capacity.
    c. potential to learn from experience, solve problems, and adapt to new situations.
    d. diverse skills acquired throughout life.

57. In recent years, researchers are more likely than before to consider intelligence as
    a. a single entity.
    b. primarily determined by heredity.
    c. entirely the product of learning.
    d. made up of several abilities.

58. The psychologist who has proposed that intelligence is composed of analytic, creative, and practical aspects is
    a. Charles Spearman.
    b. Howard Gardner.
    c. Robert Sternberg.
    d. Théodor Simon.

59. A 6-year-old child has a mental age of 9. The child's IQ is
    a. 96.   c. 125.
    b. 100.   d. 150.

60. Standardization refers to the process of
    a. determining the accuracy with which a test measures what it is supposed to.
    b. defining meaningful scores relative to a representative pretested group.
    c. determining the consistency of test scores obtained by retesting people.
    d. measuring the success with which a test predicts the behavior it is designed to predict.

61. Which of the following is NOT a requirement of a good test?
    a. reliability   c. correlation
    b. standardization   d. validity

62. Which of the following statements is true?
    a. The predictive validity of intelligence tests is not as high as their reliability.
    b. The reliability of intelligence tests is not as high as their predictive validity.
    c. Modern intelligence tests have extremely high predictive validity and reliability.
    d. The predictive validity and reliability of most intelligence tests is very low.

63. The bell-shaped distribution of intelligence scores in the general population is called a
    a. reliable distribution.
    b. standardization curve.
    c. bimodal distribution.
    d. normal distribution.

64. The test created by Alfred Binet was designed specifically to
    a. measure inborn intelligence in adults.
    b. measure inborn intelligence in children.
    c. predict school performance in children.
    d. identify intellectually disabled children so that they could be institutionalized.

65. If a test designed to indicate which applicants are likely to perform the best on the job fails to do so, the test has
    a. low reliability.
    b. low content validity.
    c. low predictive validity.
    d. not been standardized.

66. The formula for the intelligence quotient was devised by
    a. Robert Sternberg.   c. Lewis Terman.
    b. Alfred Binet.   d. William Stern.

67. Current intelligence tests compute an individual's intelligence score as
    a. the ratio of mental age to chronological age multiplied by 100.
    b. the ratio of chronological age to mental age multiplied by 100.
    c. the amount by which the test-taker's performance deviates from the average performance of others the same age.
    d. the ratio of the test-taker's verbal intelligence score to his or her nonverbal intelligence score.

68. Originally, IQ was defined as
    a. mental age divided by chronological age and multiplied by 100.
    b. chronological age divided by mental age and multiplied by 100.
    c. mental age subtracted from chronological age and multiplied by 100.
    d. chronological age subtracted from mental age and multiplied by 100.

69. Tests of _____ measure what an individual can do now, whereas tests of _____ predict what an individual will be able to do later.
    a. aptitude; achievement
    b. achievement; aptitude
    c. reliability; validity
    d. validity; reliability

70. Down syndrome is normally caused by
    a. an extra chromosome in the person's genetic makeup.
    b. a missing chromosome in the person's genetic makeup.
    c. malnutrition during the first few months of life.
    d. prenatal exposure to an addictive drug.

71. In his study of children with high intelligence scores, Terman found that
    a. the children were more emotional and less healthy than a control group.
    b. the children were ostracized by classmates.
    c. the children were healthy and well-adjusted, and did well academically.
    d. later, as adults, they nearly all achieved great vocational success.

TERMS AND CONCEPTS TO REMEMBER:

72. intelligence
73. general intelligence (*g*)
74. savant syndrome
75. emotional intelligence
76. intelligence test
77. achievement test
78. aptitude test
79. mental age
80. Stanford-Binet
81. intelligence quotient (IQ)
82. Wechsler Adult Intelligence Scale (WAIS)
83. standardization
84. normal curve
85. reliability
86. validity
87. content validity
88. predictive validity
89. crystallized intelligence
90. fluid intelligence
91. longitudinal studies
92. cross-sectional studies
93. intellectual disability
94. Down syndrome

Essay Question

You have been asked to devise a Psychology Achievement Test (PAT) that will be administered to freshmen who declare psychology as their major. What steps will you take to ensure that the PAT is a good intelligence test? (Use the space below to list the points you want to make, and organize them. Then write the essay on a separate sheet of paper.)

MODULE
28

Genetic and Environmental Influences on Intelligence

Twin and Adoption Studies

Objective 28-1: Discuss the evidence that points to a genetic influence on intelligence, and define *heritability*.

1. The intelligence scores of identical twins raised together are _____ (more/no more) similar than those of fraternal twins. Brain scans also reveal that identical twins have similar volume to their brain's _____ and _____ matter, and those areas associated with _____ and _____ intelligence.

2. The amount of variation in a trait within a group that is attributed to genetic factors is called its _____ . For intelligence, estimates range from _____ to _____ percent.

3. Identical twins exhibit substantial similarity (and _____) in specific talents.

4. Because intelligence is influenced by many genes, it is said to be _____ .

5. Where environments differ widely, as they do among children of _____-_____ parents, environmental differences are _____ (more/less) predictive of intelligence scores.

6. Adoption _____ (does/does not) enhance the intelligence scores of mistreated or neglected children. Similarly, studies of same-age, unrelated siblings adopted as infants and raised together, _____ (show/ do not show) a modest influence of their shared environment.

7. Studies of adopted children and their adoptive and biological families demonstrate that with age, genetic influences on intelligence become _____ (more/less) apparent. Thus, children's intelligence scores are more like those of their _____ (biological/adoptive) parents than their _____ (biological/adoptive) parents.

STUDY TIP: Heritability is a difficult concept to grasp in part because it is often confused with genetic determination, which refers to what causes a characteristic to develop. The number of toes on your feet is genetically determined because your genes cause five toes to develop on each foot. Heritability, on the other hand, is what causes differences in a characteristic. To say that the heritability of intelligence is 50 percent does not mean that half of an individual's intelligence is inherited. Rather, it means that we can attribute to heredity 50 percent of the variation of intelligence among those studied. A good way to keep the two concepts straight is to remember that while the concept of genetic determination makes sense in the case of a single person, heritability does not. Genetic determination is biological; heritability is a statistical measure. Heritability only makes sense relative to differences among groups of people. It doesn't make sense to ask, "What's the heritability of my intelligence?"

APPLICATIONS:

8. Raoul and Fidel are identical twins separated at birth. Because they have similar heredity and different environments, heritability for their intelligence is likely to be _____ (high/low). Ramona was adopted by Francesa's parents when she was 2 months old. The heritability for their intelligence is likely to be _____ (high/low).

9. If you compare the same trait in people of similar heredity who live in very different environments, heritability for that trait will be _____; heritability for the trait is most likely to be _____ among people of very different heredities who live in similar environments.
   a. low; high
   b. high; low
   c. environmental; genetic
   d. genetic; environmental

Environmental Influences

Objective 28-2: Discuss what evidence for environmental influences on intelligence reveals.

10. Studies indicate that neglected children _____ (do/do not) show signs of recovery in intelligence and behavior when placed in more nurturing environments.

11. Although normal brain development can be retarded by _____ , _____ deprivation, and _____ _____ , there is no sure environment that will transform a normal baby into a genius.

12. Research has found that high-quality _____ programs, _____ supplements to pregnant mothers and newborns, and _____ _____ programs result in a rise in intelligence scores.

13. Later _____ also has a positive effect on intelligence and enhances future _____ . One analysis of collegians found that _____ _____ and _____ rivaled aptitude and previous grades as predictors of academic achievement.

Group Differences in Intelligence Test Scores

Objective 28-3: Describe how and why the genders differ in mental ability scores.

14. Girls tend to outscore boys on _____ tests and are more _____ fluent. They also have an edge in _____ objects; in sensitivity to touch, taste, and color; and in _____-detecting ability.

15. Although boys and girls hardly differ in math _____ , boys score higher in _____ _____ and complex _____ _____ . The mental ability scores of males tend to vary _____ (less/more) than those of females.

16. Working from an _____ perspective, some theorists speculate that these gender differences in spatial manipulation helped our ancestors survive.

17. According to many, boys' and girls' interests and abilities are shaped in large part by _____ _____ and opportunities.

Objective 28-4: Describe how and why racial and ethnic groups differ in mental ability scores.

18. Group differences in intelligence scores _____ (do/do not) provide an accurate basis for judging individuals. Individual

differences within a race are _____ (greater than/less than) between-race differences.

Explain why heredity may contribute to individual differences in intelligence but not necessarily contribute to group differences.

19. Under the skin, the races _____ (are/are not) alike. Race _____ (is/is not) a neatly defined biological category.

20. The intelligence test performance of today's population exceeds that of the 1930s population because they are better-_____, better-_____, and more _____-_____.

21. When Blacks and Whites have or receive the same pertinent knowledge, they exhibit similar _____-_____ skill.

22. Although Asian students on the average score _____ (higher/lower) than North American students on math tests, this difference may be due to the fact that _____ _____ _____.

23. Achievement varies with _____ and _____.

APPLICATION:

24. The contribution of environmental factors to racial gaps in intelligence scores is indicated by
   a. evidence that individual differences within a race are much greater than differences between races.
   b. evidence that White and Black infants score equally well on certain measures of infant intelligence.
   c. the fact that Asian students outperform North American students on math achievement and aptitude tests.
   d. all of this evidence.

The Question of Bias

Objective 28-5: Discuss whether intelligence tests are inappropriately biased.

25. In the sense that they detect differences caused by cultural experiences, intelligence tests probably _____ (are/are not) biased.

26. Most psychologists agree that, in terms of predictive validity, the major aptitude tests _____ (are/are not) racially biased.

27. When women and members of ethnic minorities are led to expect that they won't do well on a test, a _____ _____ may result, and their scores may actually be lower.

28. Carol Dweck reports that believing intelligence is changeable fosters a _____ _____, which focuses on learning and growing.

MODULE REVIEW:

29. Studies of adopted children and their biological and adoptive families demonstrate that with age, genetic influences on intelligence
   a. become more apparent.
   b. become less apparent.
   c. become more difficult to disentangle from environmental influences.
   d. become easier to disentangle from environmental influences.

30. Which of the following is NOT true?
   a. In math grades, the average girl typically equals or surpasses the average boy.
   b. The gender gap in math and science scores is increasing.
   c. Women are better than men at detecting emotions.
   d. Males score higher than females on tests of spatial abilities.

31. Most psychologists believe that racial gaps in test scores
   a. have been exaggerated when they are, in fact, insignificant.
   b. indicate that intelligence is in large measure inherited.
   c. are in large measure caused by environmental factors.
   d. are increasing.

TERMS AND CONCEPTS TO REMEMBER:

32. heritability

33. stereotype threat

Before You Move On

Matching Items 1

Match each definition or description with the appropriate term.

Definitions or Descriptions

_____ **1.** the basic distinctive units of sound in a language

_____ **2.** the way an issue or question is posed

_____ **3.** rules for combining words into sentences

_____ **4.** the rules by which meaning is derived from sounds

_____ **5.** presuming that something is likely if it comes readily to mind

_____ **6.** the tendency to overestimate the accuracy of one's judgments

_____ **7.** being unable to see a problem from a different angle

_____ **8.** haphazard problem solving by trying one solution after another

_____ **9.** the sudden realization of the solution to a problem

_____ **10.** the tendency to repeat problem-solving techniques that worked in the past, even though a fresh approach may be more appropriate

_____ **11.** the basic units of meaning in a language

_____ **12.** controls speech production

_____ **13.** responsible for language comprehension

_____ **14.** language disorder

Terms

a. syntax
b. morphemes
c. mental set
d. trial and error
e. availability heuristic
f. phonemes
g. semantics
h. insight
i. framing
j. overconfidence
k. fixation
l. aphasia
m. Broca's area
n. Wernicke's area

Matching Items 2

Match each term with its definition or description.

Terms

_____ 1. intelligence test score
_____ 2. *g*
_____ 3. heritability
_____ 4. savant syndrome
_____ 5. factor analysis
_____ 6. aptitude test
_____ 7. achievement test
_____ 8. Stanford-Binet
_____ 9. criterion
_____ 10. content validity
_____ 11. reliability
_____ 12. fluid intelligence
_____ 13. crystallized intelligence
_____ 14. analytic intelligence
_____ 15. creative intelligence
_____ 16. practical intelligence

Definitions or Descriptions

a. a test designed to predict a person's ability to learn something new
b. a test designed to measure current knowledge
c. the consistency with which a test measures performance
d. the degree to which a test measures what it is designed to measure
e. Terman's revision of Binet's original intelligence test
f. the behavior that a test is designed to predict
g. an underlying, general intelligence factor
h. a person's score on an intelligence test based on performance relative to the average performance of people the same age
i. a very low intelligence score accompanied by one extraordinary skill
j. the proportion of variation among individuals that can be attributed to genes
k. a statistical technique that identifies related items on a test
l. intellectual skills used in everyday problem solving
m. the ability to reason abstractly and quickly
n. accumulated knowledge and verbal skills
o. the capacity for flexible and innovative thinking
p. academic problem solving

True–False Items

Indicate whether each statement is true or false by placing *T* or *F* in the blank next to the item.

_____ 1. The order in which children acquire an understanding of various morphemes is unpredictable.
_____ 2. Most human problem solving involves the use of heuristics rather than reasoning that systematically considers every possible solution.
_____ 3. When asked, most people underestimate the accuracy of their judgments.
_____ 4. Studies have shown that even animals may sometimes have insight reactions.
_____ 5. Although the morphemes differ from language to language, the phonemes for all languages are the same.
_____ 6. Children of all cultures babble using the same phonemes.
_____ 7. Thinking without using language is not possible.
_____ 8. In the current version of the Stanford-Binet intelligence test, one's perfor-

mance is compared only with the performance of others the same age.
_____ 9. Most of the major aptitude tests have higher validity than reliability.
_____ 10. The intelligence scores of adopted children are more similar to those of their adoptive parents than their biological parents.
_____ 11. The consensus among psychologists is that most intelligence tests are extremely biased.
_____ 12. Most psychologists agree that intelligence is mainly determined by heredity.
_____ 13. The variation in intelligence scores within a racial group is much larger than that between racial groups.
_____ 14. Telling students they are unlikely to succeed often erodes their performance on aptitude tests.
_____ 15. By age 60, most people decline in even the most basic cognitive abilities.
_____ 16. Historically, most psychologists have considered intelligence to be composed of several distinct abilities.

Cross-Check

As you learned in Module 2, reviewing and overlearning of material are important to the learning process. After you have written the definitions of the key terms in this unit, you should complete the crossword puzzle to ensure that you can reverse the process—recognize the term, given the definition.

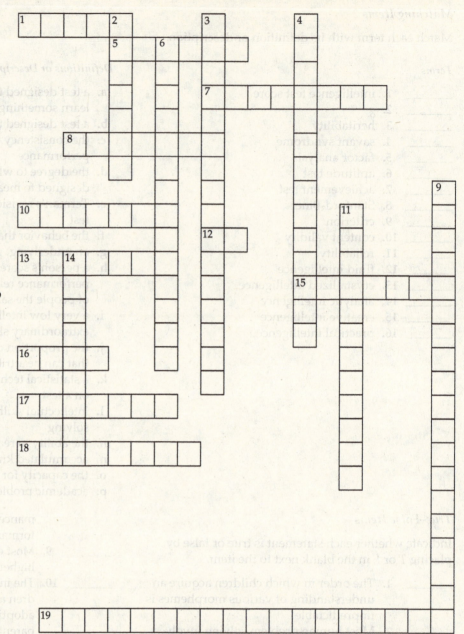

ACROSS

1. French educator who devised a test to predict children's learning potential.
5. The chimpanzee taught by Allen and Beatrice Gardner to use sign language.
7. An inability to approach a problem in a new way.
8. Theorist who argues for the existence of multiple intelligences.
10. Linguist who views language development as a process of maturation.
12. Originally defined as the ratio of mental age to chronological age.
13. The stage of language development between 1 and 2 years of age.
15. Behaviorist who explains language development with familiar learning principles.
16. The most widely used intelligence test (abbreviation).
17. A mental grouping of similar objects.
18. Degree to which a test measures what it is supposed to measure.
19. An obstacle to rational thinking that may be eliminated by considering an opposing viewpoint.

DOWN

2. Stage of language development characterized by the use of telegraphic speech.
3. Tendency of people to search for information that confirms their preconceptions.
4. Statistical procedure that identifies clusters of items that seem to define a common ability.
6. Condition in which a person of limited mental ability has one amazing skill.
9. Charles Spearman's concept of *g*.
11. Heuristic in which we estimate the likelihood of events based on how readily they come to mind.
14. A critical part of social intelligence.

Answers

MODULE
25   **Thinking**

Concepts

1. thinking; the mental activities associated with thinking, knowing, remembering, and communicating
2. concepts
3. prototype; male; females

4. **b.** is the answer. A rose is a prototypical example of the concept *flower*.

c. & d. Cognition is the overall term for thinking. This example is more specific, dealing with a prototype of a concept.

Problem Solving: Strategies and Obstacles

5. problem solving

6. trial and error

7. algorithms

8. heuristics

9. insight; frontal lobe; right temporal lobe

10. confirmation bias

11. verifies; refute

12. fixation; mental set

13. **a.** Trial and error: randomly looking everywhere in the house

   b. Algorithm: methodically checking every possible location in the house as well as all the pockets in your clothes

   c. Heuristics: thinking about the most logical place for you to have left your keys

   d. Insight: suddenly realizing that you left your keys in the car when you took the groceries out

14. **b.** is the answer. Follow the directions precisely and you can't miss!

   a. A prototype is the best example of a concept.

   c. Heuristics are simple thinking strategies that help solve problems but, in contrast to a recipe that is followed precisely, do not guarantee success.

   d. A mental set is a tendency to approach a problem in a way that has been successful in the past.

15. **d.** is the answer.

   b. & c. If Boris always attacks his opponent's queen when playing chess, he is a victim of mental set; prototypes, however, have nothing to do with chess playing.

16. **c.** is the answer.

   a., b., & d. Heuristics do not guarantee solutions or prevent mental sets.

Forming Good and Bad Decisions and Judgments

17. intuition

18. availability heuristic

The availability heuristic leads us to estimate the likelihood of events based on how readily they come to mind. Thus, we may think certain ethnic groups are more likely to be terrorists because of the vividness of the events of September 11, 2001.

19. are not

   a. what our ancestral history has prepared us to fear.

   b. what we cannot control.

   c. what is immediate.

   b. what is most readily available in memory.

20. overconfidence

21. adaptive; more; competent

22. helps

23. belief perseverance

24. consider the opposite

25. framing; may not

26. **d.** is the answer. The confirmation bias is the tendency to search for information that confirms one's preconceptions. In this example, the politicians' preconceptions are biasing their interpretation of the survey results.

   a. Fixation is the inability to see a problem from a fresh perspective

   b. Mental set is the tendency to approach a problem in a particular way. There is no problem per se in this example.

   c. Belief perseverance is the tendency to cling to one's beliefs despite evidence to the contrary.

27. **a.** is the answer. In this example, the way the issue is posed, or framed, has evidently influenced consumers' judgments.

   b. Confirmation bias is the tendency to search for information that confirms one's preconceptions.

   c. Mental set is the tendency to approach a problem in a particular way.

   d. Overconfidence is the tendency to be more confident than correct.

28. **c.** is the answer. This is referred to as overconfidence.

29. **c.** is the answer. Most people are more confident than correct in estimating their knowledge and the amount of time a task will take.

30. **a.** is the answer. Although b. and c. may be true, they do not describe belief perseverance. The d. answer is the confirmation bias.

31. **c.** is the answer. By simply following a strategy that has worked well in the past, Marilyn is hampered by the type of fixation called mental set.

   a. Fixation is a broader term, being unable to conceive of an unusual function for an object.

   b. Overconfidence is exhibited by the person who overestimates the accuracy of his or her judgments.

   d. Prototypes are best examples of categories, not strategies for solving problems.

32. b. is the answer. The publicity surrounding disasters makes such events vivid and seemingly more probable than they actually are.

a. Belief perseverance is the tendency to cling to one's beliefs despite evidence to the contrary.

c. Confirmation bias refers to our tendency to search for information that supports our preconceptions and ignore other information.

d. Fixation operates in situations in which effective problem solving requires using an object in an unfamiliar manner.

33. intuitive; incubate

34. adaptive

35. implicit

Thinking Creatively

36. creativity; aptitude; different from

37. convergent; divergent

Creative people tend to have expertise, or a solid base of knowledge; imaginative thinking skills, which allow them to see things in new ways, to recognize patterns, and to make connections; intrinsic motivation, or the tendency to focus on the pleasure and challenge of their work; and a venturesome personality that tolerates ambiguity and risk and seeks new experiences. Creative people also have generally benefited from living in creative environments.

Research suggests that you can boost your creativity by developing your expertise in an area you care about and enjoy; allow time for a problem to incubate (sleep on it!); set aside time for your mind to roam freely; and experience other cultures and ways of thinking, which will expose you to multiple perspectives and facilitate flexible thinking.

38. c. is the answer.

a. Beyond a certain level of aptitude, creativity and intelligence are not correlated.

b. Just the opposite is true of creative people.

d. This may or may not be true, but most likely it isn't.

Do Other Species Share Our Cognitive Skills?

39. concepts; insight

40. tools; vary; cultural

41. do; self-awareness; altruism; cooperation

Module Review:

42. c. is the answer.

43. b. is the answer.

a. A prototype is the best example of a particular category, or concept.

c. & d. Algorithms and heuristics are problem-solving strategies.

44. c. is the answer.

a. There is no such thing as a "denoter."

b. & d. Heuristics and algorithms are problem-solving strategies.

45. d. is the answer. It is a major obstacle to problem solving.

a. & b. These refer to belief bias and belief perseverance, respectively.

c. This is trial-and-error problem solving.

46. d. is the answer. Creativity is supported by a certain level of aptitude (ability to learn). Yet, there is more to creativity than aptitude, or what intelligence tests reveal. Indeed, creativity engages different brain areas.

a. The ability to think imaginatively and intelligence are *both* components of creativity.

b. Creativity, the capacity to produce ideas that are novel and valuable, is related to and depends in part on aptitude but cannot be considered simply a kind of intelligence.

c. Beyond a certain aptitude there is no correlation between intelligence scores and creativity.

47. c. is the answer. Both involve failing to see a problem from a new perspective.

a. & b. Algorithms and heuristics are problem-solving strategies.

d. Insight is the sudden realization of a problem's solution.

48. d. is the answer.

a. Mental set is the tendency to approach a problem in a particular way that worked previously.

b. Confirmation bias is the tendency to search for information that supports our preconceptions.

c. Heuristics are simple thinking strategies that are based on past successes in similar situations.

49. d. is the answer. Heuristics are simple thinking strategies—such as playing chess defensively—that are based on past successes in similar situations.

a., b., & c. These are all algorithms.

50. d. is the answer. Sultan suddenly arrived at a novel solution to his problem, thus displaying apparent insight.

a. Sultan did not randomly try various strategies of reaching the fruit; he demonstrated the "light bulb" reaction that is the hallmark of insight.

b. Heuristics are simple thinking strategies.

c. Fixation is an impediment to problem solving. Sultan obviously solved his problem.

51. d. is the answer.

52. a. is the answer. Reasoning in daily life is often distorted by our beliefs, which may lead us, for example, to accept conclusions that haven't been arrived at logically.

b., c., & d. These are just the opposite of what we tend to do.

53. **d.** is the answer. This is a simple thinking strategy that allows us to make quick judgments.
a. Mental sets are obstacles to problem solving, in which the person tends to repeat solutions that have worked in the past and is unable to conceive of other possible solutions.
b. Belief perseverance is the tendency to cling to a belief even after the information that led to the formation of the belief is discredited.
c. Algorithms are methodical strategies that guarantee a solution to a particular problem.

54. **d.** is the answer. If we use the availability heuristic, we base judgments on the availability of information in our memories, and more vivid information is often the most readily available.
a. This would exemplify use of the trial-and-error approach to problem solving.
b. This would exemplify a mental set.
c. This would exemplify belief perseverance.

55. **b.** is the answer. Because they involve the systematic examination of all possible solutions to a problem, algorithms guarantee that a solution will be found.
a., c., & d. None of these methods guarantees that a problem's solution will be found.

Terms and Concepts to Remember:

56. **Cognition** refers to all the mental activities associated with thinking, knowing, remembering, and communicating information.

57. A **concept** is a mental grouping of similar objects, events, ideas, or people.

58. A **prototype** is a mental image or best example of a category.

59. An **algorithm** is a methodical, logical rule or procedure that, while sometimes slow, guarantees solving a particular problem.

60. A **heuristic** is a simple thinking strategy that often allows us to make judgments and solve problems efficiently. Although heuristics are more efficient than algorithms, they do not guarantee success and sometimes even impede problem solving.

61. **Insight** is a sudden and often novel realization of the solution to a problem. Insight contrasts with strategy-based solutions.

62. The **confirmation bias** is an obstacle to problem solving in which people tend to search for information that supports their preconceptions and to ignore or distort contradictory evidence.

63. **Mental set** refers to the tendency to continue applying a particular problem-solving strategy even when it is no longer helpful.

64. **Intuition** is an immediate, automatic, and effortless feeling or thought.

65. The **availability heuristic** is based on estimating the likelihood of certain events in terms of how readily they come to mind.

66. Another obstacle to problem solving, **overconfidence** refers to the tendency to overestimate the accuracy of our beliefs and judgments.

67. **Belief perseverance** is the tendency for people to cling to a particular belief even after the information that led to the formation of the belief is discredited.

68. **Framing** refers to the way an issue or question is posed. It can affect people's perception of the issue or answer to the question.

69. Most experts agree that **creativity** refers to an ability to produce novel and valuable ideas.

70. **Convergent thinking** involves narrowing the available solutions to a problem in order to find the best one.

71. **Divergent thinking** is creative thinking that diverges in different directions.

MODULE
26
Language and Thought

Language Structure

1. our spoken, written, or signed words and the ways we combine them to communicate meaning.

2. phonemes; 40

3. morphemes

4. grammar; syntax; semantics

5. Noam Chomsky; universal grammar

6. B. F. Skinner; association; imitation; reinforcement

7. grammatical rules

8. **a.** is the answer. Each sound of the word is a phoneme (note that the second letter "e" does not itself represent a sound); the morphemes are "pre," which means before; "date"; and "s," which indicates the plural.

9. **d.** is the answer. This sentence, although semantically meaningless, nevertheless follows the grammatical rules of English syntax for combining words into sentences.

a. & b. The phonemes (smallest units of sound) and morphemes (smallest units of meaning) of this sentence are equally correct.

Language Development

10. 4; receptive language; productive language
11. babbling; 4; do not
12. do; consonant-vowel; bunching the tongue in the front of the mouth
13. 10; lost
14. one-word; nouns; 1
15. two-word; telegraphic; does
16. critical period; accent; poorer; grammar
17. 7; never
18. do not
19. **b.** is the answer. The morpheme *-ed* changes the *meaning* of a regular verb to form its past tense; the phoneme *sh* is a unique *sound* in the English language.
    c. & d. Syntax, which specifies rules for combining words into grammatical sentences, is one aspect of the grammar of a language.
20. **a.** is the answer.
21. **b.** is the answer. Such utterances, characteristic of a child of about 2 years, are like telegrams, in that they consist mainly of nouns and verbs and show use of syntax.
    a. & c. Babbling consists of phonemes, not words.
    d. Semantics refers to the rules by which meaning is derived from sounds; this speech example indicates nothing in particular about the child's understanding of semantics.

The Brain and Language

22. aphasia; Broca's area; Wernicke's area
23. neural networks
24. subfunctions
25. **a.** is the answer.
    b. Broca's area is involved in speech production.
    c. & d. The hypothalamus and the hippocampus have nothing to do with language.

Do Other Species Have Language?

26. do
27. sign language
28. alone

Chimps have acquired only limited vocabularies and—in contrast to children—have acquired these vocabularies only with great difficulty. Interpreting chimpanzee signs as language may be little more than the trainers' wishful thinking. Believers contend that although animals do not have our facility for language, they have the abilities to communicate. For example, Washoe and Loulis sign spontaneously.

Thinking and Language

29. linguistic determinism; Benjamin Whorf
30. self
31. does
32. attention; bilingual advantage
33. immersed; aptitude
34. can; implicit; nondeclarative (procedural) memory
35. studying effectively; process simulation

The relationship is probably a two-way one: the linguistic determinism hypothesis suggests that language helps shape thought; that words come into the language to express new ideas indicates that thought also shapes language.

36. process simulation; outcome simulation
    Imagining the procedure activates the brain areas involved in actually performing the activity, so process simulation produces better results than outcome simulation.

Module Review:

37. **c.** is the answer.
38. **a.** is the answer. Babbling is not the imitation of adult speech since babbling infants produce phonemes from languages they have not heard and could not be imitating.
39. **d.** is the answer.
40. **d.** is the answer.
    a. The text does not discuss any views that language is primarily learned.
    b. This is Chomsky's position regarding language development.
    c. The linguistic determinism hypothesis is concerned with the content of thought, not intelligence.
41. **c.** is the answer.
    a. Just the opposite is true.
    b. According to Chomsky, although the *ability* to acquire language is innate, the child can only acquire language in association with others.
    d. Cultural influences are an important example of the influence of learning on language development, an influence Chomsky fully accepts.
42. **c.** is the answer.
    b. Broca's area is involved in speech production.
    d. The association areas are involved in higher-order activities such as planning.
43. **d.** is the answer. Compared with deaf children exposed to sign language from birth, those who learn to sign as teens have the same grammatical difficulties as do hearing adults trying to learn a second spoken language.

44. **c.** is the answer. Children are biologically prepared to learn language as they and their caregivers interact.
    a. This would be the view of a behaviorist.
    b. No psychologist, including Chomsky, believes that language is entirely a product of biological maturation.
    d. Although language acquisition is not completely understood, research has shed sufficient light on it to render it less than a complete mystery.

45. **b.** is the answer. The evidence that absence of a term for a color does not affect ability to perceive the color challenges the idea that language always shapes thought.
    a. & d. These findings are not relevant to the linguistic determinism hypothesis, which addresses the relationship between language and thought.
    c. This finding is in keeping with the linguistic determinism hypothesis.

46. **a.** is the answer.
    b. Morphemes are the basic units of meaning.
    c. & d. The text does not refer to basic units of grammar or semantics.

47. **b.** is the answer.
    a. Phonemes are the sounds in a word.
    c. Such rules are known as semantics.
    d. Such rules are the language's grammar, which includes its syntax as well as its semantics.

48. **a.** is the answer.

49. **d.** is the answer. Syntax is one of the fundamental aspects of language, and chimps seem unable, for example, to use word order to convey differences in meaning.
    a. & c. Chimps' use of sign language demonstrates both the use of symbols and the acquisition of fairly sizable vocabularies.
    b. No psychologist would require the use of speech as evidence of language; significantly, all the research and arguments focus on what chimps are and are not able to do in acquiring other facets of language.

50. **a.** is the answer.

51. **c.** is the answer.

52. **c.** is the answer. Although the child's utterances are only two words long, the words are placed in a sensible order. In English, for example, adjectives are placed before nouns.
    a. & b. Syntax specifies rules for *combining* two or more units in speech.
    d. There is no three-word stage.

53. **b.** is the answer.

54. **c.** is the answer.

55. **d.** is the answer.

56. **a.** is the answer.

57. **b.** is the answer.
    a. Researchers do not make a distinction between "real" and other thinking, nor do they consider nonlinguistic thinking less valid than linguistic thinking.
    c. As indicated by several studies cited in the text, this is not true.

58. **d.** is the answer. Following the babbling stage, the child's ability to produce all phonemes becomes in a sense shaped and limited to the ability to produce those phonemes he or she hears.
    a. The vocal tract of *Homo sapiens* does not develop in specialized ways for different languages.
    b. & c. English and Russian differ significantly in both their phonemes and their morphemes. Nor is there any reason why differences in morphemes would in and of themselves cause pronunciation difficulties.

Terms and Concepts to Remember:

59. **Language** refers to spoken, written, or signed words and how we combine them to communicate meaning.

60. **Phonemes** are the smallest distinctive units of sound in a language that are distinctive for speakers of the language.

61. **Morphemes** are the smallest units of language that carry meaning.
    Example: The word "dogs," which contains four phonemes, contains only two **morphemes**— "dog" and "-s." Although most morphemes are combinations of two or more phonemes, the plural "-s" conveys a distinctive meaning of "more than one."

62. **Grammar** is a system of rules that enables us to communicate with and understand others.

63. The **babbling stage** of speech development, which begins around 4 months, is characterized by the spontaneous utterance of speech sounds. During the babbling stage, children the world over sound alike.

64. Between 1 and 2 years of age, children speak mostly in single words; they are therefore in the **one-word stage** of linguistic development.

65. Beginning about age 2, children are in the **two-word stage** and speak mostly in two-word sentences.

66. **Telegraphic speech** is the economical, telegram-like speech of children in the two-word stage. Utterances consist mostly of nouns and verbs; however, words occur in the correct order, show-

ing that the child has learned some of the language's syntactic rules.

67. **Aphasia** is an impairment of language, usually caused by left-hemisphere damage either to Broca's area or to Wernicke's area.

68. **Broca's area,** located in the left frontal lobe, is involved in controlling the motor ability to produce speech.

69. **Wernicke's area,** located in the left temporal lobe, is involved in language comprehension and expression.

70. **Linguistic determinism** is Benjamin Whorf's hypothesis that language determines the way we think.

MODULE
27 Intelligence and Its Assessment

What Is Intelligence?

1. do not

2. intelligence tests; does not

3. the mental potential to learn from experience, solve problems, and use knowledge to adapt to new situations

4. overall (general)

5. factor analysis

6. do; do

7. savant syndrome; males; autism spectrum disorder

8. multiple (8) intelligences

9. existential

10. triarchic; analytical (academic problem-solving); practical; creative

11. do; grit; 10-year

12. savant syndrome

13. **d.** is the answer. Sternberg distinguishes among *academic* intelligence, as measured by intelligence tests; *practical* intelligence, which is involved in everyday life and tasks, such as managerial work; and *creative* intelligence.
a. & b. Verbal and performance intelligence are both measured by standard intelligence tests and would be included in Sternberg's academic intelligence.
c. Academic intelligence refers to skills assessed by intelligence tests; practical intelligence applies to skills required for everyday tasks and, often, for occupational success.

14. academic; social

15. emotional intelligence; perceive; understand; manage; use

16. recognize; predict; express; adaptive

Emotionally intelligent people are both socially aware and self-aware. They can manage their emotions and they can delay gratification. They handle others' emotions skillfully. They also exhibit modestly better job performance.

17. emotional

18. emotional intelligence

Assessing Intelligence

19. mental; compares

20. achievement; aptitude

21. achievement; aptitude

22. Alfred Binet; mental; was not; Théodore Simon; environmental

23. Stanford-Binet; William Stern; intelligence quotient; IQ

In the original formula for IQ, measured mental age is divided by chronological age and multiplied by 100. "Mental age" refers to the chronological age that most typically corresponds to a given level of performance.

24. an intelligence test score; the same; 100

25. Wechsler Adult Intelligence Scale; verbal comprehension; perceptual organization; working memory; processing speed

26. 13. At the time he took the test, Benito's chronological age (CA) was 10. Knowing that IQ = 130 and CA = 10, solving the equation for mental age yields a value of 13.

27. 100. Modern intelligence tests are periodically restandardized so that the average remains near 100.

28. standardization

29. normal

The normal curve describes the distribution of many physical phenomena and psychological attributes (including intelligence test scores), with most scores falling near the average and fewer near the extremes. When a test is standardized on a normal curve, individual scores are assigned according to how much they deviate above or below the distribution's average.

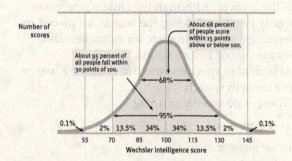

30. reliable
31. **a.** They may retest people using the same test.
    b. They may split the test in half and see whether odd-question scores and even-question scores agree.
32. +.9
33. validity; criterion
34. content validity
35. predictive validity

The criterion is the particular behavior a predictive test, such as an aptitude test, is intended to predict. For example, performance in a relevant job situation would be the criterion for a test measuring managerial aptitude. The criterion determines whether a test has predictive validity. For example, the on-the-job success of those who do well on a job aptitude test would indicate the test has predictive validity.

36. diminishes
37. **b.** is the answer. A standardization group provides a representative comparison for the trait being measured by a test. Because this test will measure musical aptitude in North American children, the standardization group should be limited to North American children but should include children of all degrees of musical aptitude.
38. **b.** is the answer.
39. **d.** is the answer. Because the hearing acuity test would in no way sample behaviors relevant to intelligence, it would not have content validity as a test of intelligence.
    a. & b. There is no such thing as content reliability or predictive reliability.
    c. There is nothing to indicate that, used to test hearing, this test would lack predictive validity.
40. **b.** is the answer.
    a. Content validity is the degree to which a test measures what it claims to measure. The question gives no indication as to the nature of the questions.
    c. & d. Reliability is the degree to which a test yields consistent results. There is no indication in the question as to whether the test's results are consistent or inconsistent.

The Dynamics of Intelligence

41. crystallized; fluid
42. fluid; twenties; thirties; 75; 85
43. longitudinal; cross-sectional
44. 3; 4
45. increases; does

46. longer; healthier
    a. Intelligence facilitates more education, better jobs, and a healthier environment.
    b. Intelligence encourages healthy living: less smoking, better diet, more exercise.
    c. Prenatal events or early childhood illnesses might have influenced both intelligence and health.
    d. A "well-wired body," as evidenced by fast reaction speeds, perhaps fosters both intelligence and longevity.
47. **b.** is the answer. Intelligence scores become quite stable during adolescence.
48. **d.** is the answer. It is not until after age 4 that intelligence-test performance begins to predict adolescent and adult scores.
    a. Such a conclusion is unlikely, given the high validity of the commonly used intelligence tests.
    b. No such conclusion is possible, because intelligence-test performance before age 4 does not predict later aptitude.
    c. Stability in intelligence scores is generally established by late adolescence.
49. intellectually disabled; conceptual; social; practical
50. Down syndrome
51. restandardized
52. healthy; adjusted; academically
53. **c.** is the answer. To be labeled intellectually disabled a person must have a test score below 70 and experience difficulty adapting to the normal demands of living independently.
    a. If Dan is intellectually disabled, it is likely that both his crystallized and fluid intelligence are fairly low.
    d. The text does not suggest that intellectually disabled people eventually become self-supporting.

Module Review:

54. **d.** is the answer. That people with savant syndrome excel in one area but are intellectually disabled in others suggests that there are multiple intelligences.
    a. The ability to adapt defines the capacity we call intelligence.
    b. & c. Spearman hypothesized that we have a general intelligence factor (*g*) rather than multiple intelligences.
55. **a.** is the answer.
56. **c.** is the answer.
    a. Performance ability and intellectual ability are separate traits.

b. This has been argued by some, but certainly not most, experts.

d. Although many experts believe that there are multiple intelligences, this would not be the same thing as diverse acquired skills.

57. **d.** is the answer.
    a. Contemporary researchers emphasize the different aspects of intelligence.
    b. & c. Contemporary researchers see intelligence as the product of both heredity and learning.

58. **c.** is the answer.
    a. Charles Spearman proposed the existence of an underlying general intelligence, which he called *g*.
    b. Howard Gardner proposed that intelligence consists of eight autonomous abilities.
    d. Théodor Simon worked with Alfred Binet to create the first intelligence test.

59. **d.** is the answer. If we divide 9, the measured mental age, by 6, the chronological age, and multiply the result by 100, we obtain 150.

60. **b.** is the answer.
    a. This answer refers to a test's content validity.
    c. This answer refers to test-retest reliability.
    d. This answer refers to predictive validity.

61. **c.** is the answer. Correlation is a measure of the relationship between two variables.

62. **a.** is the answer.
    c. & d. Most modern tests have high reliabilities of about +.9; their validity scores are much lower.

63. **d.** is the answer.
    a. & b. There are no such terms.
    c. A bimodal distribution is one having two (bi-) modes, or averages. The normal distribution has only one mode.

64. **c.** is the answer. French compulsory education laws brought more children into the school system, and the government didn't want to rely on teachers' subjective judgments to determine which children would require special help.
    a. & b. Binet's test was intended for children, and Binet specifically rejected the idea that his test measured inborn intelligence, which is an abstract capacity that cannot be quantified.
    d. This was not a purpose of the test, which dealt with children in the school system.

65. **c.** is the answer. Predictive validity is the extent to which tests predict what they are intended to predict.
    a. Reliability is the consistency with which a test samples the particular behavior of interest.
    b. Content validity is the degree to which a test measures what it is designed to measure.

d. Standardization is the process of defining meaningful test scores based on the performance of a representative group.

66. **d.** is the answer.

67. **c.** is the answer.
    a. This is William Stern's original formula for the intelligence quotient.
    b. & d. Neither of these formulas is used to compute the score on current intelligence tests.

68. **a.** is the answer.

69. **b.** is the answer.
    c. & d. Reliability and validity are characteristics of good tests.

70. **a.** is the answer.
    b. Down syndrome is normally caused by an extra, rather than a missing, chromosome.
    c. & d. Down syndrome is a genetic disorder that is manifest during the earliest stages of prenatal development, well before malnutrition and exposure to drugs would produce their harmful effects on the developing fetus.

71. **c.** is the answer.
    a. & b. There was no evidence of either in the individuals studied by Terman.
    d. Vocational success in adulthood varied.

Terms and Concepts to Remember:

72. Most experts define **intelligence** as the mental potential to learn from experience, solve problems, and use knowledge to adapt to new situations.

73. **General intelligence (*g*)**, according to Spearman and others, is a general intelligence factor that underlies each of the more specific mental abilities identified through factor analysis.

74. A person with **savant syndrome** has a very low intelligence score, yet possesses one exceptional ability, for example, in music or drawing.

75. **Emotional intelligence** is the ability to perceive, manage, understand, and use emotions.

76. **Intelligence tests** measure people's mental aptitudes and compare them with those of others, using numerical scores.

77. **Achievement tests** measure a person's current knowledge.

78. **Aptitude tests** are designed to predict future performance. They measure your capacity to learn new information, rather than measuring what you already know.

79. A concept introduced by Binet, **mental age** is the chronological age that most typically corresponds to a given level of performance.

80. The **Stanford-Binet** is Lewis Terman's widely used revision of Binet's original intelligence test.

81. The **intelligence quotient (IQ)** was defined originally as the ratio of mental age to chronological age multiplied by 100. Contemporary tests of intelligence assign a score of 100 to the average performance for a given age and define other scores as deviations from this average.

82. The **Wechsler Adult Intelligence Scale (WAIS)** is the most widely used intelligence test. It is individually administered, contains 15 subtests, and yields separate scores for verbal comprehension, perceptual organization, working memory, and processing speed, as well as an overall intelligence score.

83. **Standardization** is the process of defining meaningful scores by comparison with a pretested standardization group.

84. The **normal curve** is a bell-shaped curve that represents the distribution (frequency of occurrence) of many physical and psychological attributes. The curve is symmetrical, with most scores near the average and fewer near the extremes.

85. **Reliability** is the extent to which a test produces consistent results.

86. **Validity** is the degree to which a test measures or predicts what it is supposed to.

87. The **content validity** of a test is the extent to which it samples the behavior that is of interest.

88. **Predictive validity** is the extent to which a test predicts the behavior it is designed to predict; also called *criterion-related validity*.

89. **Crystallized intelligence** is the accumulated knowledge and verbal skills that come with education and experience.

90. **Fluid intelligence** is the ability to reason speedily and abstractly.

91. In a **cross-sectional study**, people of different ages are compared with one another.

92. In a **longitudinal study**, the same people are tested and retested over a period of years.

93. The two criteria that designate **intellectual disability** are an intelligence test score of 70 or below and difficulty adapting to the normal demands of independent living; formerly called *mental retardation*.

94. A condition of mild to severe intellectual disability and associated physical disorders, **Down syndrome** is usually the result of an extra copy of chromosome 21.

Essay Question

The first step in constructing the test is to create a valid set of questions that measure psychological knowledge and therefore give the test content validity. If your objective is to predict students' future achievement in psychology courses, the test questions should be selected to measure a criterion, such as information faculty members expect all psychology majors to master before they graduate.

To enable meaningful comparisons, the test must be standardized. That is, the test should be administered to a representative sample of incoming freshmen at the time they declare psychology to be their major. From the scores of your pretested sample you will then be able to assign an average score and evaluate any individual score according to how much it deviates above or below the average.

To check your test's reliability you might retest a sample of people using the same test or another version of it. If the two scores are correlated, your test is reliable. Alternatively, you might split the test in half and determine whether scores on the two halves are correlated.

MODULE
28

Genetic and Environmental Influences on Intelligence

Twin and Adoption Studies

1. more; gray; white; verbal; spatial
2. heritability; 50; 80
3. heritability
4. polygenetic
5. less-educated; more
6. does; show
7. more; biological; adoptive
8. low; high
9. **a.** is the answer. If everyone has nearly the same heredity, then heritability—the variation in a trait attributed to heredity—must be low. If individuals within a group come from very similar environments, environmental differences cannot account for variation in a trait; heritability, therefore, must be high.

Environmental Influences

10. do
11. malnutrition; sensory; social isolation

12. preschool; nutritional; interactive reading
13. schooling; income; study motivation; study skills

Group Differences in Intelligence Test Scores

14. spelling; verbally; locating; emotion
15. computation; spatial ability; math problems; more
16. evolutionary
17. social expectations
18. do not; greater than

Because of the impact of environmental factors such as education and nutrition on intelligence test performance, even if the heritability of intelligence is high within a particular group, differences in intelligence among groups may be environmentally caused. One group may, for example, thrive in an enriched environment while another of the same genetic predisposition may falter in an impoverished one.

19. are; is not
20. fed; educated; test-prepared
21. information-processing
22. higher; Asian students have spent 30 percent more time in school and spend more time studying math
23. time; culture
24. d. is the answer. These reasons, along with other historical and cross-cultural reasons, all argue for the role of environment in creating and perpetuating the gap.

The Question of Bias

25. are
26. are not
27. stereotype threat

Module Review:

28. a. is the answer.
    c. & d. Separating genetic from environmental influences is difficult *at any age*.
29. b. is the answer. As social expectations have changed, the gender gap in math and science scores is narrowing.
30. c. is the answer.
    a. On the contrary, many *group* differences are highly significant, even though they tell us nothing about specific *individuals*.
    b. Although heredity contributes to individual differences in intelligence, it does not necessarily contribute to group differences.
    d. In fact, the difference has diminished somewhat in recent years.
31. growth mind-set

Terms and Concepts to Remember:

32. **Heritability** is the proportion of variation among individuals that can be attributed to genes.
33. **Stereotype threat** is the phenomenon in which a person's concern that he or she will be evaluated based on a negative stereotype (as on an aptitude test, for example) is actually followed by lower performance.

Before You Move On

Matching Items 1

1. f	6. j	11. b
2. i	7. k	12. m
3. a	8. d	13. n
4. g	9. h	14. l
5. e	10. c	

Matching Items 2

1. h	5. k	9. f	13. n
2. g	6. a	10. d	14. p
3. j	7. b	11. c	15. o
4. i	8. e	12. m	16. l

True–False Items

1. F	9. F
2. T	10. F
3. F	11. F
4. T	12. F
5. F	13. T
6. T	14. F
7. F	15. F
8. T	16. F

Cross-Check

ACROSS	DOWN
1. Binet	2. two-word
5. Washoe	3. confirmation bias
7. fixation	4. factor analysis
8. Gardner	6. savant syndrome
10. Chomsky	9. general intelligence
12. IQ	11. availability
13. one-word	14. emotional
15. Skinner	
16. WAIS	
17. concept	
18. validity	
19. belief perseverance	

Motivation and Emotion

Overview

Motivation is the study of forces that energize and direct our behavior. Module 29 discusses various motivational concepts and looks closely at two motives: the need to belong and achievement. Research on the need to belong and social networking reveals that social networking tends to increase self-disclosure and strengthen relationships with people we already know. Research on achievement motivation underscores the importance of self-discipline and persistence in achieving one's goals. Module 30 covers hunger. Research on hunger points to the fact that our biological drive to eat is strongly influenced by psychological and social-cultural factors.

Module 31 discusses the nature of emotion. Emotions are responses of the whole individual, involving physiological arousal, expressive behaviors, and conscious experience. This module discusses several theoretical controversies concerning the relationship and sequence of the components of emotion, primarily regarding whether the body's response to a stimulus causes the emotion and whether thinking is necessary to and must precede the experience of emotion, as well as the physiology of emotion. Module 32 examines how we communicate emotions, as well as the differences in emotional expression and understanding between the genders and among different cultures.

NOTE: Answer guidelines for all Modules 29–32 questions begin on page 258.

Outline

MODULE 29 Basic Motivational Concepts, Affiliation, and Achievement

MODULE 30 Hunger

MODULE 31 Theories and Physiology of Emotion

MODULE 32 Expressing and Experiencing Emotion

Instructions

First, skim each section, noting headings and boldface items. After you have read the section, review each objective by answering the fill-in, essay-type, and multiple-choice questions for that section. In some cases, Study Tips explain how best to learn a difficult concept and Applications and Module Reviews help you to know how well you understand the material. Finally, try to define the important terms and concepts using your own words. As you proceed, evaluate your performance by consulting the answers on page 258. Do not continue until you understand each answer. If you need to, review or reread a troublesome section before continuing.

Before You Move On includes activities that test you on material from the entire unit.

Basic Motivational Concepts, Affiliation, and Achievement

Motivational Concepts

Objective 29-1: Define *motivation* as psychologists use the term, and identify the perspectives from which they view motivated behavior.

1. Motivation is defined as _____ _____ _____ .

2. Four perspectives on motivation are _____ theory (which has been replaced by the _____ perspective), _____ - _____ theory, _____ theory, and the _____ of needs proposed by _____ .

3. As a result of Darwin's influence, many complex behaviors were classified as rigid, unlearned behavior patterns that are characteristic of a species, called _____ . Although early instinct theory _____ (did/did not) explain human motives, the underlying assumption that _____ predispose species-typical behavior remains strong.

4. According to another view of motivation, organisms may experience a physiological _____ , which creates a state of arousal that _____ the organism to reduce the need.

5. The physiological aim of drive reduction is to maintain a steady internal state, called _____ .

6. Behavior is often not so much pushed by our drives as it is pulled by _____ in the environment.

7. Rather than reduce a physiological need, some motivated behaviors actually _____ arousal. This demonstrates that human motives _____ (do/do not) always satisfy some biological need.

8. Human motivation aims not to eliminate _____ but to seek _____ _____ of arousal. The principle that performance increases with arousal only up to a point is the _____ - _____ . Those who enjoy high arousal are called _____ - _____ ; these risk takers may also be motivated by a drive to master their emotions and _____ .

9. Starting from the idea that _____ - _____ needs such as the need for water take precedence over others, Abraham Maslow constructed a hierarchy of needs.

10. According to Maslow, the _____ needs are the most pressing, whereas the highest-order needs relate to _____ and _____ .

11. A criticism of Maslow's theory is that the sequence is _____ and not _____ fixed.

12. Surveys of life satisfaction reveal that _____ satisfaction is strongly predictive of feelings of well-being in poorer nations, whereas _____ matter more in wealthy nations.

APPLICATIONS:

13. Mary loves hang-gliding. It would be most difficult to explain Mary's behavior according to
    a. incentives.
    b. achievement motivation.
    c. drive-reduction theory.
    d. Maslow's hierarchy of needs.

14. For two weeks, Orlando has been on a hunger strike to protest his country's involvement in what he perceives as an immoral war. Orlando's willingness to starve himself to make a political statement conflicts with the theory of motivation advanced by
    a. Darwin.   c. Dodson.
    b. Yerkes.   d. Maslow.

15. Which of the following is NOT an example of homeostasis?
    a. perspiring to restore normal body temperature

b. feeling hungry and eating to restore your energy level

c. feeling hungry at the sight of an appetizing food

d. All of these are examples of homeostasis.

The Need to Belong

Objective 29-2: Describe the evidence that points to our human affiliation need—our need to belong.

16. The Greek philosopher _____ referred to humans as the _____ animal. The deep need to belong—our _____ need—seems to be a basic human motivation.

17. From an evolutionary standpoint, social bonds in humans boosted our ancestors' _____ rates. As adults, those who formed _____ were more likely to _____ and co-nurture their off-spring to maturity.

18. People experience a deep sense of well-being when their need for relatedness is satisfied along with two other basic psychological needs: _____ and _____ .

19. Feeling accepted and loved by others boosts our _____ .

20. Much of our _____ behavior aims to increase our belonging. To gain acceptance, we generally _____ to group standards.

21. We have a need to form and maintain relationships in part because feelings of love activate brain _____ and _____ systems.

22. After years of placing individual refugee and immigrant families in _____ communities, U.S. policies today encourage _____ .

23. _____ (Throughout the world/Only in certain cultures do) people use social exclusion, or _____ , to control social behavior. Researchers have found that social exclusion elicits increased activity in brain areas, such as the _____ _____ _____ ,

that also activate in response to physical _____ .

24. Researchers have found that people who are rejected are more likely to engage in _____ behaviors, to underperform on _____ , and to act in disparaging or _____ ways. Rejection also interfered with their _____ for others.

Objective 29-3: Describe how social networking influences us.

25. Phone talking and e-mailing are being displaced by the greater use of _____ , _____ sites, and other messaging technology.

26. People who are _____ tend to spend greater-than-average time online.

27. The Internet offers opportunities for new _____ , which is also mostly _____ (weakening/strengthening) our connections with the variety of people we already know.

28. Electronic communication can stimulate healthy _____ . When communicating electronically rather than face-to-face, we often are less _____ , and thus less _____ .

29. Generally speaking, social networks _____ (reveal/do not reveal) people's real personalities.

30. People who are overly self-important, self-focused, and self-promoting are said to be _____ . People who score high on this trait tend to be _____ (especially active/less active) on social networking sites.

List some suggestions by experts for maintaining a healthy balance between real-world and online time.

APPLICATIONS:

31. Summarizing her report on the need to belong, Rolanda states that
    a. "Cooperation amongst our ancestors was uncommon."
    b. "Social bonding is not in our nature; it is a learned human trait."
    c. "Because bonding with others increased our ancestors' success at reproduction and survival, it became part of our biological nature."
    d. "Our male ancestors were more likely to bond than were females."

32. Right after dinner, Dennis goes to his room, turns on his computer, and begins chatting with friends on Facebook. Which of the following is true, according to the most recent research?
    a. His connections with friends have been strengthened.
    b. He is more willing to disclose personal thoughts and feelings, which deepens his friendships.
    c. He reveals his true personality to friends and others online.
    d. All of these statements are true.

33. Brad's parents worry that he spends too much time on social networking sites collecting superficial "friends." He also seems excessively self-absorbed and goes to great lengths to promote himself online. A psychologist might say that Brad is showing signs of
    a. ostracism.
    b. narcissism.
    c. autonomy.
    d. competence.

Achievement Motivation

Objective 29-4: Define *achievement motivation*.

34. Psychologists refer to the desire for significant accomplishments, for mastering skills or ideas, for control, and for attaining a high standard as _____ _____ .

35. Research has shown that _____ is a better predictor of school performance than _____ _____ _____ have been. Extremely successful individuals differ from equally talented peers in their _____ , their passionate dedication to a long-term goal.

STUDY TIP: Research studies have shown that people who possess a low need for achievement tend to

prefer situations and tasks that are either very easy or impossibly hard. Conversely, people with a high need for achievement tend to prefer tasks that are moderately difficult. Why do you think this might be? Which types of tasks (for example, college courses) do you prefer?

APPLICATIONS:

36. During a meeting with the parents of a struggling high school student, the guidance counselor notes which of the following as the best predictor of school performance?
    a. attendance
    b. intelligence test scores
    c. talent
    d. self-discipline

37. Shawna's teacher admires the passion and perseverance with which she pursues her long-term goals. A psychologist would say that Shawna has
    a. high intelligence.
    b. needs.
    c. drive.
    d. grit.

MODULE REVIEW:

38. Motivation is best understood as a state that
    a. reduces a drive.
    b. aims at satisfying a biological need.
    c. energizes an organism to act.
    d. energizes and directs behavior.

39. Which of the following is a difference between a drive and a need?
    a. Needs are learned; drives are inherited.
    b. Needs are physiological states; drives are psychological states.
    c. Drives are generally stronger than needs.
    d. Needs are generally stronger than drives.

40. One problem with the idea of motivation as drive reduction is that
    a. because some motivated behaviors do not seem to be based on physiological needs, they cannot be explained in terms of drive reduction.
    b. it fails to explain any human motivation.
    c. it cannot account for homeostasis.
    d. it does not explain the hunger drive.

41. One shortcoming of the instinct theory of motivation is that it
    a. places too much emphasis on environmental factors.

b. focuses on cognitive aspects of motivation.

c. applies only to animal behavior.

d. does not explain human behaviors; it simply names them.

42. Instinct theory and drive-reduction theory both emphasize _____ factors in motivation.

a. environmental   c. psychological

b. cognitive   d. biological

43. Few human behaviors are rigidly patterned enough to qualify as

a. needs.   c. instincts.

b. drives.   d. incentives.

44. According to Maslow's theory

a. the most basic motives are based on physiological needs.

b. needs are satisfied in a specified order.

c. the highest motives relate to self-transcendence.

d. all of these statements are true.

45. Which of the following is INCONSISTENT with the drive-reduction theory of motivation?

a. When body temperature drops below 98.6° Fahrenheit, blood vessels constrict to conserve warmth.

b. A person is driven to seek a drink when his or her cellular water level drops below its optimum point.

c. Monkeys will work puzzles even if not given a food reward.

d. A person becomes hungry when body weight falls below its biological set point.

46. Beginning with the most basic needs, which of the following represents the correct sequence of needs in the hierarchy described by Maslow?

a. safety; physiological; esteem; belongingness and love; self-actualization; self-transcendence

b. safety; physiological; belongingness and love; esteem; self-actualization; self-transcendence

c. physiological; safety; esteem; belongingness and love; self-actualization; self-transcendence

d. physiological; safety; belongingness and love; esteem; self-actualization; self-transcendence

47. Homeostasis refers to

a. the tendency to maintain a steady internal state.

b. the tendency to seek external rewards for behavior.

c. the highest level of needs in Maslow's hierarchy.

d. the optimum level of arousal that most people seek.

48. When asked what makes life meaningful, most people first mention

a. good health.

b. challenging work.

c. satisfying relationships.

d. serving others.

49. Which of the following is NOT an aspect of Murray's definition of achievement motivation?

a. the desire to master skills

b. the desire for control

c. the desire to gain approval

d. the desire to attain a high standard

50. Deliberate social exclusion on another person is called

a. ostracism.

b. narcissism.

c. self-control.

d. autonomy.

51. Affiliation refers to the need to

a. feel competent.

b. build relationships and feel part of a group.

c. have high self-esteem.

d. reproduce.

52. Autonomy refers to our sense of

a. competence.

b. belonging.

c. self-control.

d. well-being.

53. Research studies have shown that being shunned leads to increased activity in which brain area?

a. amygdala

b. hippocampus

c. arcuate nucleus

d. anterior cingulate cortex

TERMS AND CONCEPTS TO REMEMBER:

54. motivation

55. instinct

56. drive-reduction theory

57. homeostasis

58. incentive

59. Yerkes-Dodson law

60. hierarchy of needs

61. affiliation need

62. ostracism

63. narcissism

64. achievement motivation

65. grit

Essay Question

Differentiate the three major theories of motivation and explain why they cannot fully account for human behavior. (Use the space below to list the points you want to make, and organize them. Then write the essay on a separate sheet of paper.)

MODULE 30 Hunger

The Physiology of Hunger

Objective 30-1: Describe the physiological factors that produce hunger.

1. Researchers observed that men became preoccupied with thoughts of food when they underwent _____ .

2. Cannon and Washburn's experiment using a balloon indicated that there is an association between hunger and _____ _____ .

3. When rats had their stomachs removed, hunger _____ (did/did not) continue.

4. A major source of energy in your body is the blood sugar _____ . If the level of this sugar drops, you won't consciously feel the lower blood sugar, but your _____ , _____ , and _____ will signal your brain to motivate eating. Your brain, which is automatically monitoring your _____ _____ and your body's internal state, will then trigger hunger.

5. The brain area that plays a role in hunger and other bodily maintenance functions is the _____ . One area called the _____ _____ has a center that secretes appetite-stimulating hormones. Another neural center secretes appetite-suppressing hormones.

6. The hunger-arousing hormone secreted by an empty stomach is (a) _____ .

7. When a portion of an obese person's stomach is surgically sealed off, the remaining stomach produces _____ (more/less) of this hormone. Other appetite hormones include (b) _____ , which is secreted by the pancreas and controls blood glucose; (c) _____ , which is secreted by fat cells and decreases hunger; (d) _____ , which is secreted by the hypothalamus and triggers hunger; and (e) _____ from the digestive tract, which decreases hunger.

8. The weight level at which an individual's body is programmed to stay is referred to as the body's _____ _____ . A person whose weight goes beyond this level will tend to feel _____ (more/less) hungry than usual and expend _____ (more/less) energy.

9. The rate of energy expenditure in maintaining basic functions when the body is at rest is the _____ _____ rate. When food intake is reduced, the body compensates by _____ (raising/ lowering) this rate.

10. The concept of a precise body set point that drives hunger _____ (is accepted/is not accepted) by all researchers. Some researchers believe that set point can be altered by _____ _____ ,

and that _____ _____ also sometimes drive our feelings of hunger. In support of this idea is evidence that when people are given unlimited access to tasty foods, they tend to _____ and _____ _____ . For these reasons, some researchers prefer to use the term _____ _____ as an alternative to the idea that there is a fixed set point.

APPLICATIONS:

11. Kenny and his brother have nearly identical eating and exercise habits, yet Kenny is obese and his brother is very thin. The MOST LIKELY explanation for the difference in their body weights is that they differ in
    a. their bone structure.
    b. amygdala activity.
    c. their set points and their metabolic rates.
    d. their differing exposure to carbohydrate-laden foods.

12. Lucille has been sticking to a strict diet but can't seem to lose weight. What is the most likely explanation for her difficulty?
    a. Her body has a very low set point.
    b. Her prediet weight was near her body's set point.
    c. Her weight problem is actually caused by an increase in basal metabolic rate.
    d. Lucille is influenced primarily by external factors.

The Psychology of Hunger

Objective 30-2: Discuss cultural and situational factors that influence hunger.

13. Research with patients who had no memory for events occurring more than a minute ago indicates that part of knowing when to eat is our _____ of our last meal.

14. Carbohydrates boost levels of the neurotransmitter _____ , which _____ (calms/arouses) the body.

15. Taste preferences for sweet and salty are _____ (genetic/learned) and _____ . Other influences on taste include _____ and _____ .

16. We have a natural dislike of many foods that are _____ ; this _____ was probably adaptive for our ancestors, and

protected them from toxic substances.

17. Our eating is also controlled by _____ . This phenomenon is called the _____ _____ .

18. Because of _____ facilitation, people tend to eat _____ (less/more) when they are with other people. The phenomenon of _____ _____ is the tendency to mindlessly eat more when portions are larger. Another factor that stimulates eating is food _____ .

APPLICATION:

19. Randy, who has been under a lot of stress lately, has intense cravings for sugary junk foods, which tend to make him feel more relaxed. Which of the following is the most likely explanation for his craving?
    a. Randy feels that he deserves to pamper himself with sweets because of the stress he is under.
    b. The extra sugar gives Randy the energy he needs to cope with the demands of daily life.
    c. Carbohydrates boost levels of serotonin, which has a calming effect.
    d. The extra sugar tends to lower blood insulin level, which promotes relaxation.

Obesity and Weight Control

Objective 30-3: Discuss the factors that predispose some people to become and remain obese.

20. Obesity has been associated with lower psychological _____ , especially among _____ (men/women), and increased _____ . It also increases the likelihood of suffering _____ among 6- to 9-year-olds.

21. An overweight person has a _____ _____ _____ (BMI) of _____ (what number?) or more. A person who is obese has a BMI of _____ or more.

22. In the United States, _____ percent of adults are obese. Significant obesity increases the risk of _____ _____ _____ .

23. Being slightly overweight _____ (poses/does not pose) serious health risks. More important is a person's _____.

24. Obesity has also been linked in women to their risk of late-life _____ decline, including _____ disease, and brain tissue loss.

25. Fat tissue has a _____ (higher/lower) metabolic rate than does muscle. The result is that fat tissue requires _____ (more/less) food energy to be maintained. Also, overweight people tend to move about _____ (more/less) than lean people.

Explain why, metabolically, many obese people find it so difficult to become and stay thin.

26. Studies of adoptees and twins _____ (do/do not) provide evidence of a genetic influence on obesity.

27. Also contributing to the problem of obesity are _____ factors. For example, adults who suffer from _____ _____ are more vulnerable to obesity. Also, people are _____ (less/more) likely to become obese when a friend becomes obese, thus demonstrating _____ influence as a factor in obesity.

28. Two reasons for global increases in the prevalence of obesity are changing _____ and decreased work-related _____ _____.

State several pieces of advice for those who want to lose weight.

APPLICATION:

29. Which of the following would be the WORST piece of advice to offer to someone trying to lose weight?
    a. "To treat yourself to one 'normal' meal each day, eat very little until the evening meal."
    b. "Reduce your consumption of saturated fats."
    c. "Boost your metabolism by exercising regularly."
    d. "Begin only if you feel motivated and self-disciplined."

MODULE REVIEW:

30. Increases in insulin will
    a. lower blood sugar and trigger hunger.
    b. raise blood sugar and trigger hunger.
    c. lower blood sugar and trigger satiety.
    d. raise blood sugar and trigger satiety.

31. The text suggests that a *neophobia* for unfamiliar tastes
    a. is more common in children than in adults.
    b. protected our ancestors from potentially toxic substances.
    c. may be an early warning sign of obesity.
    d. only grows stronger with repeated exposure to those tastes.

32. The brain area known as the arcuate nucleus is notable in the study of motivation because it
    a. secretes hormones that affect appetite.
    b. secretes hormones that cause obesity.
    c. raises blood sugar.
    d. increases the set point.

33. In their study of men on a semistarvation diet, Ancel Keys and his team found that
    a. the metabolic rate of the men increased.
    b. the men eventually lost interest in food.
    c. the men became obsessed with food.
    d. the men's behavior directly contradicted predictions made by Maslow's hierarchy of needs.

34. Research on genetic influences on obesity reveals that
    a. the body weights of adoptees correlate with that of their biological parents.
    b. the body weights of adoptees correlate with that of their adoptive parents.
    c. identical twins usually have very different body weights.
    d. the body weights of identical twin women are more similar than those of identical twin men.

35. Research on obesity indicates that
    a. pound for pound, fat tissue requires more food to maintain than lean tissue.
    b. given an obese parent, boys are more likely than girls to be obese.
    c. overweight people have a higher metabolic rate than lean people.
    d. when weight drops below the set point, hunger increases.

36. Which of the following influences on hunger motivation does NOT belong with the others?
    a. set/settling point
    b. attraction to sweet and salty tastes
    c. reduced production of ghrelin after stomach bypass surgery
    d. memory of time elapsed since your last meal

37. The tendency to overeat when food is plentiful
    a. is a recent phenomenon that is associated with the luxury of having ample food.
    b. emerged in our prehistoric ancestors as an adaptive response to periods when food was scarce.
    c. is greater in developed, than in developing, societies.
    d. is stronger in women than in men.

38. Unit bias refers to the research finding that people tend to
    a. eat more when a portion of food is supersized.
    b. avoid unfamiliar tasting foods.
    c. overeat during celebrations with other people.
    d. do all of these things.

39. Which of the following is NOT necessarily a reason that obese people have trouble losing weight?
    a. Fat tissue has a lower metabolic rate than lean tissue.
    b. Once a person has lost weight, it takes fewer calories to maintain his or her current weight.
    c. The tendency toward obesity may be genetically based.
    d. Obese people tend to lack willpower.

TERMS AND CONCEPTS TO REMEMBER:

40. glucose

41. set point

42. basal metabolic rate

MODULE 31

Theories and Physiology of Emotion

Emotion: Arousal, Behavior, and Cognition

Objective 31-1: Describe how arousal, cognition, and expressive behavior interact in emotion.

1. Emotions have three components: _____ _____ , _____ _____ , and _____ _____ .

2. According to the James-Lange theory, emotional states _____ (precede/follow) bodily responses.

Describe two problems that Walter Cannon identified with the James-Lange theory.

3. Cannon proposed that emotional stimuli in the environment are routed simultaneously to the brain's _____ , which results in awareness of the emotion, and to the _____ nervous system, which causes the body's reaction. Because another scientist concurrently proposed similar ideas, this theory has come to be known as the _____-_____ theory.

4. Cannon's theory _____ (is/is not) contradicted by the fact people with high spinal cord injury _____ (do/do not) report a change in their emotions' intensity.

Objective 31-2: Explain whether we must consciously interpret and label emotions in order to experience them.

5. The two-factor theory of emotion proposes that emotion has two components: _____ arousal and a _____ label. This theory was proposed by _____ and _____ .

6. The *spillover effect* refers to occasions when our _____ response to one event carries over into our response to another event.

7. Schachter and Singer found that physically aroused college men told that an injection would cause arousal _____ (did/did not) become emotional in response to the experimenters' accomplice's aroused behavior. Physically aroused volunteers not expecting arousal _____ (did/did not) become emotional in response to the accomplice's behavior.

8. Arousal _____ emotion; cognition _____ emotion.

9. Robert Zajonc believes that the feeling of emotion _____ (can/cannot) precede our cognitive labeling of that emotion.

Cite two pieces of evidence that support Zajonc's position.

10. According to _____ , a pathway from the _____ via the (a) _____ to the (b) _____ enables us to experience emotion before _____ . For more complex emotions, sensory input is routed through the (c) _____ for interpretation.

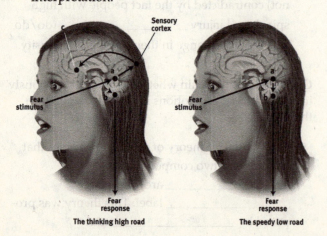

The thinking high road   **The speedy low road**

11. The researcher who disagrees with Zajonc and argues that most emotions require cognitive processing is _____ . According to this view, emotions arise when we _____ an event as beneficial or harmful to our well-being.

12. Complex emotions are affected by our _____ , _____ , and _____ .

Express some general conclusions that can be drawn about cognition and emotion.

_____

STUDY TIP/APPLICATION: The theories of emotion discussed in this module seem so similar that it's often hard to tell them apart. As you think about the theories, remember: The theories differ in the order of importance they assign to the three components of emotions: physical arousal (increased heart rate, for example), the expression of the emotion (feeling angry, for example), and the importance of cognitive appraisal of the situation in which the emotion has occurred. To help ensure your understanding of the theories, see if you can fill in the missing information in the chart below for a common emotional experience: Hearing the screeching of a car's tires. For example, the first response might be a physical reaction such as increased heart beat or an emotional expression of fear, or it might be the opposite.

13. Theory	Stimulus Event	First Response	Second Response	Third Response
James-Lange	Screeching tires			
Cannon-Bard	Screeching tires			
Schachter-Singer	Screeching tires			

APPLICATIONS:

14. You are on your way to school to take a big exam. Suddenly, you notice that your pulse is racing and you are sweating, and so you feel nervous. This fits with the _____-_____ theory of emotion.

15. Two years ago, Maria was in an automobile accident in which her spinal cord was severed, leaving her paralyzed from the neck down. Today, Maria finds that she experiences emotions less intensely than she did before her accident. This tends to support the _____-_____ theory of emotion.

16. After hitting a grand-slam home run, Mike noticed that his heart was pounding. Later that evening, after nearly having a collision while driving on the freeway, Mike again noticed that his heart was pounding. That he interpreted this reaction as fear, rather than as ecstasy, can best be explained by the _____-_____ theory of emotion.

Embodied Emotion

Objective 31-3: Identify some basic emotions.

17. Carroll Izard believes that there are _____ basic emotions, most of which _____ (are/are not) present in infancy.

18. Although others claim that emotions such as pride and love should be added to the list, Izard contends that they are _____ of the basic emotions.

Objective 31-4: Describe the link between emotional arousal and the autonomic nervous system.

19. Describe the major physiological changes that each of the following undergoes during emotional arousal.

   a. heart:_____

   b. liver: _____

   c. respiration: _____

   d. digestion: _____

   e. pupils: _____

   f. blood:_____

   g. skin:_____

20. The responses of arousal are activated by the _____ nervous system. In response to its signal, the _____ glands release the stress hormones _____ and _____ .

21. When the need for arousal has passed, the body is calmed through activation of the _____ nervous system.

22. The body's response to danger is coordinated and adaptive, preparing you to _____ _____ _____ .

Objective 31-5: Discuss whether different emotions activate different physiological and brain-pattern responses.

23. The various emotions are associated with _____ (similar/different) forms of physiological arousal. In particular, the emotions of _____ , _____ , and _____ are difficult to distinguish physiologically.

24. A neural center in the brain called the _____ is activated when we experience negative social emotions such as _____ .

25. The emotions _____ and _____ prompt similar increased _____ _____ , but they stimulate different facial muscles.

26. The brain circuits underlying some of our emotions _____ (are/are not) different. For example, seeing a fearful face elicits greater activity in the _____ than seeing a(n) _____ face. People who have generally negative personalities, and those who are prone to _____, show more _____ _____ lobe activity.

27. When people experience positive moods, brain scans reveal more activity in the _____ _____ _____ .

28. Individuals with more active _____ (right/left) _____ lobes tend to be more cheerful than those in whom this pattern of brain activity is reversed.

Objective 31-6: Discuss the effectiveness of polygraphs in using body states to detect lies.

29. (Thinking Critically) The technical name for the "lie detector" is the _____ . (Thinking Critically) Explain how lie detectors supposedly indicate whether a person is lying.

30. (Thinking Critically) How well the lie detector works depends on whether a person exhibits _____ while lying.

31. (Thinking Critically) Those who criticize lie detectors feel that the tests are particularly likely to err in the case of the _____ (innocent/guilty), because different _____ all register as _____ .

32. (Thinking Critically) By and large, experts _____ (agree/do not agree) that lie detector tests are highly accurate.

33. (Thinking Critically) A test that assesses a suspect's knowledge of details of a crime that only the guilty person should know is the

_____ _____

_____ .

APPLICATIONS:

34. A student participating in an experiment concerned with physical responses that indicate emotions reports that her mouth is dry, her heart is racing, and she feels flushed. Can the emotion she is experiencing be determined?
    a. Yes, it is anger.
    b. Yes, it is fear.
    c. Yes, it is ecstasy.
    d. No, it cannot be determined from the information given.

35. Julio was extremely angry when he came in for a routine EEG of his brain activity. When he later told this to the doctor, she was no longer concerned about the
    a. increased electrical activity in Julio's right frontal lobe.
    b. increased electrical activity in Julio's left frontal lobe.
    c. decreased electrical activity in Julio's amygdala.
    d. increased electrical activity in Julio's amygdala.

36. As part of her job interview, Jan is asked to take a lie-detector test. Jan politely refuses and points out the problems with the test, which are that
    a. _____

    b. _____

37. Nine-month-old Nicole's left frontal lobe is more active than her right frontal lobe. We can expect that, all other things being equal, Nicole
    a. may suffer from mild depression for most of her life.
    b. may have trouble "turning off" upsetting feelings later in her life.
    c. may be more cheerful than those with more active right frontal lobes.
    d. may have trouble expressing feelings later in her life.

MODULE REVIEW:

38. Which division of the nervous system is especially involved in bringing about emotional arousal?
    a. somatic nervous system
    b. peripheral nervous system
    c. sympathetic nervous system
    d. parasympathetic nervous system

39. Concerning emotions and their accompanying bodily responses, which of the following appears to be true?

    a. Each emotion has its own bodily response and underlying brain circuit.
    b. All emotions involve the same bodily response as a result of the same underlying brain circuit.
    c. Many emotions involve similar bodily responses but have different underlying brain circuits.
    d. All emotions have the same underlying brain circuits but different bodily responses.

40. The Cannon-Bard theory of emotion states that

    a. emotions have two ingredients: physical arousal and a cognitive label.
    b. the conscious experience of an emotion occurs at the same time as the body's physical reaction.
    c. emotional experiences are based on an awareness of the body's responses to an emotion-arousing stimulus.
    d. emotional ups and downs tend to balance in the long run.

41. Which of the following was NOT raised as a criticism of the James-Lange theory of emotion?

    a. The body's responses are too similar to trigger the various emotions.
    b. Emotional reactions occur before the body's responses can take place.
    c. The cognitive activity of the cortex plays a role in the emotions we experience.
    d. People with spinal cord injuries at the neck typically experience less emotion.

42. (Thinking Critically) In one study, innocent people taking a polygraph test were declared guilty approximately _____ of the time.

    a. three-fourths   c. one-third
    b. one-half   d. one-fourth

43. In the Schachter-Singer experiment, which college men reported feeling an emotional change in the presence of the experimenter's highly emotional confederate?

    a. those receiving epinephrine and expecting to feel physical arousal
    b. those receiving a placebo and expecting to feel physical arousal
    c. those receiving epinephrine but not expecting to feel physical arousal
    d. those receiving a placebo and not expecting to feel physical arousal

44. Emotions consist of which of the following components?

    a. physiological reactions
    b. behavioral expressions
    c. conscious feelings
    d. all of these components

45. (Thinking Critically) Law enforcement officials sometimes use a lie detector to assess a suspect's responses to details of the crime believed to be known only to the perpetrator. This is known as the

    a. inductive approach.
    b. deductive approach.
    c. guilty knowledge test.
    d. screening examination.

46. In laboratory experiments, fear and joy

    a. result in an increase in heart rate.
    b. stimulate different facial muscles.
    c. increase heart rate and stimulate different facial muscles.
    d. result in a decrease in heart rate.

47. Research with subliminally flashed stimuli supports Robert Zajonc's view that

    a. the heart is always subject to the mind.
    b. emotional reactions involve deliberate rational thinking.
    c. cognition is not necessary for emotion.
    d. responding to a subliminal stimulus is a learned skill.

48. The stress hormones epinephrine and norepinephrine are released by the _____ gland(s) in response to stimulation by the _____ branch of the nervous system.

    a. pituitary; sympathetic
    b. pituitary; parasympathetic
    c. adrenal; sympathetic
    d. adrenal; parasympathetic

49. Which of the following most accurately describes emotional arousal?

    a. Emotions prepare the body to act.
    b. Emotions are voluntary reactions to emotion-arousing stimuli.
    c. Because all emotions have the same physiological basis, emotions are primarily psychological events.
    d. Emotional arousal is always accompanied by cognition.

50. Schachter's and Singer's two-factor theory emphasizes that emotion involves both
    a. the sympathetic and parasympathetic divisions of the nervous system.
    b. verbal and nonverbal expression.
    c. physical arousal and a cognitive label.
    d. universal and culture-specific aspects.

51. Which theory of emotion emphasizes the simultaneous experience of the body's response and emotional feeling?
    a. James-Lange theory
    b. Cannon-Bard theory
    c. two-factor theory
    d. Schachter-Singer theory

52. (Thinking Critically) The polygraph measures
    a. lying.
    b. brain rhythms.
    c. chemical changes in the body.
    d. physiological indexes of arousal.

53. People who are exuberant and persistently cheerful show increased activity in the brain's

    _____ .

    a. right frontal lobe
    b. left frontal lobe
    c. amygdala
    d. thalamus

54. Which theory of emotion implies that every emotion is associated with a unique physiological reaction?
    a. James-Lange theory
    b. Cannon-Bard theory
    c. two-factor theory
    d. Schachter-Singer theory

55. Which of the following was NOT presented in the text as evidence that some emotional reactions involve no deliberate, rational thinking?
    a. Some of the neural pathways involved in emotion are separate from those involved in thinking and memory.
    b. Emotional reactions are sometimes quicker than our interpretations of a situation.
    c. People can develop an emotional preference for visual stimuli to which they have been unknowingly exposed.
    d. Arousal of the sympathetic nervous system will trigger an emotional reaction even when artificially induced by an injection of epinephrine.

56. In an emergency situation, emotional arousal will result in
    a. increased rate of respiration.
    b. increased blood sugar.
    c. a slowing of digestion.
    d. all of these events.

57. Several studies have shown that physical arousal can intensify just about any emotion. For example, when people who have been physically aroused by exercise are insulted, they often misattribute their arousal to the insult. This finding illustrates the importance of
    a. cognitive labels of arousal in the conscious experience of emotions.
    b. a minimum level of arousal in triggering emotional experiences.
    c. the simultaneous occurrence of physical arousal and cognitive labeling in emotional experience.
    d. all of these things.

58. (Thinking Critically) Many psychologists are opposed to the use of lie detectors because
    a. they represent an invasion of a person's privacy and could easily be used for unethical purposes.
    b. there are often serious discrepancies among the various indicators such as perspiration and heart rate.
    c. polygraphs cannot distinguish the various possible causes of arousal.
    d. they are accurate only about 50 percent of the time.

TERMS AND CONCEPTS TO REMEMBER:

59. emotion

60. James-Lange theory

61. Cannon-Bard theory

62. two-factor theory

63. polygraph

Essay Question

Discuss biological influences on emotions. (Use the space below to list the points you want to make, and organize them. Then write the essay on a separate sheet of paper.)

MODULE 32 — Expressing and Experiencing Emotion

Detecting Emotion in Others

Objective 32-1: Describe how we communicate non-verbally.

1. Most people are especially good at reading non-verbal _____ , and we are particularly good at detecting nonverbal _____ . Although we are good at detecting emotions, we find it difficult to detect _____ expressions.

2. Introverts are _____ (better/worse) at reading others' emotions, whereas extraverts are themselves _____ (easier/harder) to read.

3. The absence of nonverbal cues to emotion is one reason that _____ communications are easy to misread.

Gender and Emotion

Objective 32-2: Discuss whether the genders differ in their ability to communicate nonverbally.

4. Women are generally _____ (better/worse) than men at detecting nonverbal signs of emotion. Women possess greater emotional _____ than men, as revealed by the tendency of men to describe their emotions in _____ terms. This gender difference may contribute to women's greater emotional _____ and _____ . Although women are _____ (more/less) likely than men to describe themselves as empathic, physiological measures reveal a much _____ (smaller/larger) gender difference. Women are _____ (more/less) likely than men to express empathy.

APPLICATION:

5. Pat is very accurate at reading others' nonverbal behavior and is more likely to express empathy. Based on body responses, Alex seems to feel almost as much empathy. Pat is _____ (male/female); Alex is _____ (male/female).

Culture and Emotion

Objective 32-3: Explain whether gestures and facial expressions mean the same thing in all cultures.

6. Gestures have _____ (the same/different) meanings in different cultures.

7. Studies of adults indicate that in different cultures facial expressions have _____ (the same/different) meanings. Studies of children indicate that the meaning of their facial expressions _____ (varies/does not vary) across cultures. The emotional facial expressions of blind children _____ (are/are not) the same as those of sighted children.

8. According to _____ , human emotional expressions evolved because they helped our ancestors communicate before language developed. It has also been adaptive for us to _____ faces in particular _____ .

9. Cultures that encourage _____ display mostly visible emotions. In cultures such as that of Japan people _____ emotions from the surrounding context. This points to the importance of realizing that emotions are not only biological and psychological but also _____-_____ .

APPLICATION:

10. Who is the LEAST likely to display personal emotions openly?
    a. Paul, a game warden in Australia
    b. Niles, a stockbroker in Belgium
    c. Deborah, a physicist in Toronto
    d. Yoko, a dentist in Japan

The Effects of Facial Expressions

Objective 32-4: Describe how facial expressions influence our feelings.

11. Darwin believed that when an emotion is accompanied by an outward facial expression, the emotion is _____ (intensified/diminished).

12. In one study, students who were induced to _____ reported feeling a little angry.

13. The _____ effect occurs when expressions amplify our emotions by activating muscles associated with specific states.

14. Studies have found that imitating another person's facial expressions _____ (leads/does not lead) to greater empathy with that person's feelings.

15. Similarly, moving our body as we would when experiencing a particular emotion causes us to feel that emotion. This is the _____ _____ effect.

APPLICATIONS:

16. The candidate stepped before the hostile audience, panic written all over his face. It is likely that the candidate's facial expression caused him to experience
   a. a lessening of his fear.
   b. an intensification of his fear.
   c. a better understanding of the audience.
   d. a desire to run from the scene.

17. Children in New York, Nigeria, and New Zealand smile when they are happy and frown when they are sad. This suggests that
   a. children imitate the facial expressions of their parents.
   b. some emotional expressions are learned at a very early age.
   c. the children have not yet learned their culture's form of expressiveness.
   d. facial expressions of emotion are universal and biologically determined.

MODULE REVIEW:

18. Research on nonverbal communication has revealed that
   a. it is easy to hide your emotions by controlling your facial expressions.
   b. facial expressions tend to be the same the world over, while gestures vary from culture to culture.
   c. most authentic expressions last between 7 and 10 seconds.
   d. most gestures have universal meanings; facial expressions vary from culture to culture.

19. With regard to emotions, Darwin believed that
   a. the expression of emotions helped our ancestors to survive.
   b. all humans express basic emotions using similar facial expressions.
   c. human facial expressions of emotion retain elements of animals' emotional displays.
   d. all of these statements are true.

20. Which of the following is true regarding gestures and facial expressions?
   a. Gestures are universal; facial expressions, culture-specific.
   b. Facial expressions are universal; gestures, culture-specific.
   c. Both gestures and facial expressions are universal.
   d. Both gestures and facial expressions are culture-specific.

TERMS AND CONCEPTS TO REMEMBER:

21. facial feedback effect

22. behavior feedback effect

Essay Question

Discuss cultural influences on emotions. (Use the space below to list the points you want to make, and organize them. Then write the essay on a separate sheet of paper.)

Before You Move On

Matching Items 1

Match each term with its definition or description.

Terms

_____ **1.** set point
_____ **2.** incentive
_____ **3.** homeostasis
_____ **4.** instinct
_____ **5.** hierarchy of needs
_____ **6.** glucose
_____ **7.** ostracism
_____ **8.** narcissism
_____ **9.** grit

Definitions or Descriptions

a. the body's tendency to maintain a balanced internal state
b. excessive self-absorption
c. a complex, species-specific pattern of behavior
d. environmental stimulus that motivates behavior
e. perseverance in the pursuit of long-term goals
f. Maslow's theory of motivation
g. blood sugar
h. deliberately excluding others
i. the body's weight-maintenance setting

Matching Items 2

Match each definition or description with the appropriate term.

Definitions or Descriptions

_____ **1.** emotions consist of physical arousal *and* a cognitive label
_____ **2.** an emotion-arousing stimulus triggers cognitive and body responses simultaneously
_____ **3.** the division of the nervous system that calms the body following arousal
_____ **4.** the division of the nervous system that activates arousal
_____ **5.** a device that measures the physiological correlates of emotion
_____ **6.** we are sad because we cry

Terms

a. two-factor theory
b. sympathetic nervous system
c. James-Lange theory
d. polygraph
e. Cannon-Bard theory
f. parasympathetic nervous system

True–False Items

Indicate whether each statement is true or false by placing *T* or *F* in the blank next to the item.

_____ **1.** In wealthy nations, financial satisfaction more strongly predicts feelings of well-being.
_____ **2.** Intelligence test scores are the best predictors of success.
_____ **3.** When body weight rises above set point, hunger increases.
_____ **4.** All taste preferences are conditioned.
_____ **5.** The hormone insulin controls blood glucose levels.
_____ **6.** Obesity is often a sign of social status and affluence where food is scarce.

_____ **7.** The two-factor theory states that emotions are given a cognitive label before physical arousal occurs.
_____ **8.** All emotions involve conscious thought.
_____ **9.** Men are generally better than women at detecting nonverbal emotional expression.
_____ **10.** The sympathetic nervous system triggers physiological arousal during an emotion.
_____ **11.** When one imitates an emotional facial expression, the body may experience physiological changes characteristic of that emotion.
_____ **12.** Physical arousal can intensify emotion.

Cross-Check

As you learned in Module 2, reviewing and over-learning of material are important to the learning process. After you have written the definitions of the key terms in this unit, you should complete the crossword puzzle to ensure that you can reverse the process—recognize the term, given the definition.

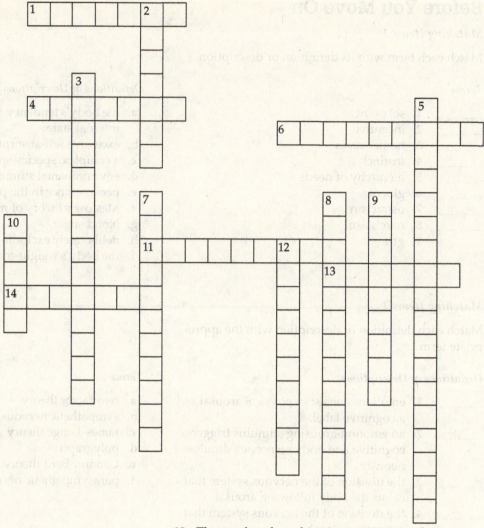

ACROSS

1. A response of the whole organism involving physical arousal, expressive behaviors, and conscious experience.
4. Hormone secreted by an empty stomach.
6. Device that measures several of the physiological responses accompanying emotion.
11. In Maslow's theory, human needs are organized into a _____ .
13. In Maslow's theory, the needs that follow physiological needs in order of priority.
14. Major energy source for the body.

DOWN

2. A BMI of 30 or more.
3. Theory that explains behavior as arising from physiological needs and the states of tension they create.
5. The body's rate of energy expenditure at rest.
7. Type of motivation that reflects the degree to which a person is motivated by a desire for significant accomplishment.
8. In Maslow's theory, the most basic types of needs.
9. Theory that emotions have two ingredients: physical arousal and a cognitive label.
10. Theory that emotional experiences are based on an awareness of the body's responses to emotion-arousing stimuli was proposed by James and

_____ .

12. Theory that the subjective experience of an emotion occurs at the same time as the body's physical reaction.

Answers

MODULE
29

Basic Motivational Concepts, Affiliation, and Achievement

Motivational Concepts

1. a need or desire that energizes and directs behavior
2. instinct; evolutionary; drive-reduction; arousal; hierarchy; Abraham Maslow
3. instincts; did not; genes
4. need; drives
5. homeostasis

6. incentives

7. increase; do not

8. arousal; optimum levels; Yerkes-Dodson law; sensation-seekers; actions

9. lower-level

10. physiological; self-actualization; self-transcendence

11. arbitrary; universally

12. financial; social connections

13. **c.** is the answer. Drive-reduction theory maintains that behavior is motivated when a biological need creates an aroused state, driving the individual to satisfy the need. It is difficult to believe that Mary's hang-gliding is satisfying a biological need.

    a., b., & d. Mary may enjoy hang-gliding because it is a challenge that "is there" (incentive), because it satisfies a need to accomplish something challenging (achievement), or because it increases her self-esteem and sense of fulfillment in life (Maslow's hierarchy of needs).

14. **d.** is the answer. According to Maslow's theory, physiological needs, such as the need to satisfy hunger, must be satisfied before a person pursues loftier needs, such as making political statements.

    a. Darwin proposed evolutionary theory and the idea that genes predispose species-typical behavior.

    b. & c. Yerkes and Dodson were concerned with optimum levels of arousal.

15. **c.** is the answer. This is an example of salivating in response to an incentive rather than to maintain a balanced internal state.

    a. & b. Both examples are behaviors that maintain a balanced internal state (homeostasis).

The Need to Belong

16. Aristotle; social; affiliation

17. survival; attachments; reproduce

18. autonomy; competence

19. self-esteem

20. social; conform

21. reward; safety

22. isolated; chain migration

23. Throughout the world; ostracism; anterior cingulate cortex; pain

24. self-defeating; aptitude tests; aggressive; empathy

25. texting; social media

26. lonely

27. social networks; strengthening

28. self-disclosure; self-conscious; inhibited

29. reveal

30. narcissistic; especially active

To maintain a healthy balance between real-world and online time, experts suggest that you monitor your time and your feelings, "hide from" your more distracting online friends, turn off your mobile devices at certain times, try a social networking fast, and refocus by taking a nature walk.

31. **c.** is the answer.

32. **d.** is the answer.

33. **b.** is the answer.

    a. Ostracism is the deliberate social exclusion of people or groups.

    c. & d. Autonomy and competence are two basic psychological needs, but they have nothing to do with our need to belong.

Achievement Motivation

34. achievement motivation

35. self-discipline; intelligence test scores; grit

36. **d.** is the answer.

37. **d.** is the answer.

Module Review:

38. **d.** is the answer.

    a. & b. Although motivation is often aimed at reducing drives and satisfying biological needs, this is by no means always the case, as achievement motivation illustrates.

    c. Motivated behavior not only is energized but also is directed at a goal.

39. **b.** is the answer. A drive is the psychological consequence of a physiological need.

    a. Needs are unlearned states of deprivation.

    c. & d. Because needs are physical and drives psychological, their strengths cannot be compared directly.

40. **a.** is the answer. The curiosity of a child or a scientist is an example of behavior apparently motivated by something other than a physiological need.

    b. & d. Some behaviors, such as thirst and hunger, are partially explained by drive reduction.

    c. Drive reduction is directly based on the principle of homeostasis.

41. **d.** is the answer.

    a. & b. Instinct theory emphasizes biological factors rather than environmental or cognitive factors.

    c. Instinct theory applies to both humans and other animals.

42. **d.** is the answer.

43. **c.** is the answer.
    a. & b. Needs and drives are biologically based states that stimulate behaviors but are not themselves behaviors.
    d. Incentives are the external stimuli that motivate behavior.

44. **d.** is the answer.

45. **c.** is the answer. Such behavior, presumably motivated by curiosity rather than any biological need, is inconsistent with a drive-reduction theory of motivation.
    a., b., & d. Each of these examples is consistent with a drive-reduction theory of motivation.

46. **d.** is the answer.

47. **a.** is the answer.
    b. This describes incentives.
    c. Maslow's highest level is self-transcendence.
    d. Homeostasis has nothing to do with level of arousal.

48. **c.** is the answer.

49. **c.** is the answer.

50. **a.** is the answer.

51. **b.** is the answer.

52. **c.** is the answer.

53. **d.** is the answer.

Terms and Concepts to Remember:

54. **Motivation** is a need or desire that energizes and directs behavior.

55. An **instinct** is a complex behavior that is rigidly patterned throughout a species and is unlearned.

56. **Drive-reduction theory** attempts to explain behavior as arising from a physiological need that creates an aroused tension state (drive) that motivates an organism to satisfy the need.

57. **Homeostasis** refers to the body's tendency to maintain a balanced or steady internal state.

58. An **incentive** is a positive or negative environmental stimulus that motivates behavior.

59. The **Yerkes-Dodson law** is the principle that performance increases with arousal only up to a certain point, beyond which performance decreases.

60. Maslow's **hierarchy of needs** proposes that human motives may be ranked from the basic, physiological level through higher-level needs for safety, love, esteem, self-actualization, and self-transcendence; until they are satisfied, the more basic needs are more compelling than the higher-level ones.

61. Our **affiliation need** is the need to build relationships and to feel part of a group.

62. **Ostracism** is the deliberate social exclusion of individuals or groups.

63. **Narcissism** is excessive self-absorption and self-love.

64. **Achievement motivation** is a desire for significant accomplishment; for mastery of things, people, or ideas; for control; and for rapidly attaining a high standard.

65. **Grit** refers to an individual's passion and perseverance in the pursuit of long-term goals.

Essay Question

To qualify as an instinct, a complex behavior must have a fixed pattern throughout a species and be unlearned. Such behaviors are common in other species and include imprinting in birds. A few human behaviors, such as infants' innate reflexes to root for a nipple and suck, exhibit unlearned fixed patterns, but many more are directed by both physiological needs and psychological wants. Although instinct theory failed to explain human motives, the underlying assumption that genes predispose many behaviors is as strongly believed as ever.

Instinct theory was replaced by drive-reduction theory and the idea that biological needs create aroused drive states that motivate the individual to satisfy these needs and preserve homeostasis. Drive-reduction theory failed as a complete account of human motivation because many human motives do not satisfy any obvious biological need. Instead, such behaviors are motivated by environmental incentives.

Arousal theory emerged in response to evidence that some motivated behaviors *increase*, rather than decrease, arousal.

MODULE
30   **Hunger**

The Physiology of Hunger

1. semistarvation

2. stomach contractions

3. did

4. glucose; stomach; intestines; liver; blood chemistry

5. hypothalamus; arcuate nucleus

6. ghrelin

7. less; insulin; leptin; orexin; PYY

8. set point; less; more

9. basal metabolic; lowering

10. is not accepted; slow, sustained changes in body weight; psychological factors; overeat; gain weight; settling point

11. **c.** is the answer. Individual differences in metabolism and set point explain why it is possible for two people to have very different weights despite similar patterns of eating and exercise.

12. **b.** is the answer. The body acts to defend its set point, or the weight to which it is predisposed. If Lucille was already near her set point, weight loss would prove difficult.
a. If the weight level to which her body is predisposed is low, weight loss upon dieting should not be difficult.
c. An increase in basal metabolic rate would help her to lose weight.
d. People influenced by external factors might have greater problems losing weight because they tend to respond to food stimuli, but this can't be the explanation in Lucille's case because she has been sticking to her diet.

The Psychology of Hunger

13. memory

14. serotonin; calms

15. genetic; universal; conditioning; culture

16. unfamiliar; neophobia

17. situations; ecology of eating

18. social; more; unit bias; variety

19. **c.** is the answer. Serotonin is a neurotransmitter that is elevated by the consumption of carbohydrates and has a calming effect.
a. & b. These answers do not explain the feelings of relaxation that Randy associates with eating junk food.
d. The consumption of sugar tends to elevate insulin level rather than lower it.

Obesity and Weight Control

20. well-being; women; depression; bullying

21. body mass index; 25; 30

22. 36; diabetes, high blood pressure, heart disease, gallstones, arthritis, and certain types of cancer

23. does not pose; fitness

24. cognitive; Alzheimer's

25. lower; less; less
When an overweight person's body drops below its previous set (or settling) point, the brain triggers increased hunger and decreased metabolism. The body adapts to starvation by burning off fewer calories and seeking to restore lost weight.

26. do

27. environmental; sleep loss; more; social

28. food consumption; activity levels
Begin only if you are motivated and self-disciplined. Exercise and get enough sleep. Minimize exposure to tempting food cues. Limit variety and eat healthy foods. Reduce portion size. Don't starve all day and eat one big meal at night. Beware of binge eating. Before eating with others, decide how much you want to eat. Don't worry about occasional lapses. Connect to a support group.

29. **a.** is the answer. Dieting, including fasting, lowers the body's metabolic rate and reduces the amount of food energy needed to maintain body weight.
b., c., & d. Each of these strategies would be a good piece of advice to a dieter.

Module Review:

30. **a.** is the answer. Increases in insulin increase hunger indirectly by lowering blood sugar, or glucose.

31. **b.** is the answer.
a. Neophobia for taste is typical of all age groups.
c. Neophobia for taste is *not* an indicator of obesity.
d. With repeated exposure, our appreciation for a new taste typically *increases*.

32. **a.** is the answer.

33. **c.** is the answer. The deprived men focused on food almost to the exclusion of anything else.
a. To conserve energy, the men's metabolic rate actually *decreased*.
b. & d. Far from losing interest in food, the men came to care only about food—a finding consistent with Maslow's hierarchy, in which physiological needs are at the base.

34. **a.** is the answer.

35. **d.** is the answer.

36. **d.** is the answer. Memory of the time of the last meal is an example of a psychological influence on hunger motivation.
a., b., & c. Each of these is a biological influence on hunger motivation.

37. **b.** is the answer.
c. If anything, just the opposite is true.
d. Men and women do not differ in the tendency to overeat.

38. **a.** is the answer.
b. This is an example of neophobia.
c. This is an example of social facilitation.

39. **d.** is the answer. Most researchers today discount the idea that people are obese because they lack willpower.

Terms and Concepts to Remember:

40. Glucose, or blood sugar, is the major source of energy for body tissues. Elevating the level of glucose in the body will reduce hunger.

41. Set point is an individual's regulated weight level, which is maintained by adjusting food intake and energy output.

42. Basal metabolic rate is the body's base rate of energy expenditure when resting.

 MODULE **31**

Theories and Physiology of Emotion

Emotion: Arousal, Behavior, and Cognition

1. bodily arousal; expressive behaviors; conscious experience

2. follow

Cannon argued that the body's responses were not sufficiently distinct to trigger the different emotions and, furthermore, that bodily changes occur too slowly to trigger sudden emotion.

3. cortex; sympathetic; Cannon-Bard

4. is; do

5. physical; cognitive; Stanley Schachter; Jerome Singer

6. arousal

7. did not; did

8. fuels; channels

9. can

First, experiments on subliminal perception indicate that although stimuli are not consciously perceived, people later prefer those stimuli to others they have never been exposed to. Second, there is some separation of the neural pathways involved in emotion and cognition.

10. Joseph LeDoux; eye or ear; thalamus; amygdala; cognition; cortex

11. Richard Lazarus; appraise

12. interpretations; expectations; memories

It seems that some emotional responses—especially simple likes, dislikes, and fears—involve no conscious thinking. Other emotions are greatly affected by our interpretations, expectations, and memories.

13. Answers are given in order: first response, second response, third response.
    James-Lange theory: physical arousal, expressed emotion, cognitive appraisal is unimportant

Cannon-Bard theory: physical arousal and cognitive appraisal occur simultaneously, expressed emotion

Schachter-Singer theory: physical arousal, cognitive appraisal, expressed emotion

14. James-Lange. The James-Lange theory proposes that the experienced emotion is an awareness of a prior body response: Your pulse races, and so you feel nervous.

15. James-Lange. According to the James-Lange theory, Maria's emotions should be greatly diminished because her brain is unable to sense physical arousal.

16. two-factor. According to the two-factor theory, it is cognitive interpretation of the same general physiological arousal that distinguishes the two emotions.

Embodied Emotion

17. 10; are

18. combinations

19. a. Heart rate increases.

    b. The liver pours extra sugar into the bloodstream.

    c. Respiration rate increases.

    d. Digestion slows.

    e. Pupils dilate.

    f. If wounded, blood tends to clot more rapidly.

    g. Skin perspires.

20. sympathetic; adrenal; epinephrine (adrenaline); norepinephrine (noradrenaline)

21. parasympathetic

22. fight or flee

23. similar; fear; anger; sexual arousal

24. insula; disgust

25. fear; joy; heart rate

26. are; amygdala; angry; depression; right frontal

27. left frontal lobe

28. left; frontal

29. polygraph

The polygraph measures several of the physiological responses that accompany emotion, such as changes in breathing, cardiovascular activity, and perspiration. The assumption is that lying is stressful, so a person who is lying will become physiologically aroused.

30. anxiety (or guilt)

31. innocent; emotions; arousal

32. do not agree

33. guilty knowledge test

34. d. is the answer.

35. **a.** is the answer. As people experience negative emotions, such as anger, the right frontal lobe becomes more electrically active.
c. & d. The EEG measures electrical activity on the surface of the cortex, not at the level of structures deep within the brain, such as the amygdala.

36. **a.** Our physiological arousal is much the same from one emotion to another.
b. Many innocent people respond with heightened tension to the accusations implied by the critical questions.

37. **c.** is the answer.
a. Individuals with more active right frontal lobes tend to be less cheerful and are more likely to be depressed.
b. In fact, just the opposite is true: people with greater left frontal activity tend to be better able to turn off upsetting feelings.
d. The text does not suggest that greater left or right frontal activity influences a person's ability to express his or her feelings.

Module Review:

38. **c.** is the answer.
a. The somatic division of the peripheral nervous system carries sensory and motor signals to and from the central nervous system.
b. The peripheral nervous system is too general an answer, since it includes the sympathetic and parasympathetic divisions, as well as the somatic division.
d. The parasympathetic nervous system restores the body to its unaroused state.

39. **c.** is the answer. Although many emotions have the same general body arousal, resulting from activation of the sympathetic nervous system, they appear to be associated with different brain circuits.

40. **b.** is the answer.
a. This expresses the two-factor theory.
c. This expresses the James-Lange theory.
d. This theory was not discussed.

41. **d.** is the answer. The finding that people whose brains can't sense the body's responses experience considerably less emotion in fact supports the James-Lange theory, which claims that experienced emotion follows from the body's responses.
a., b., & c. All these statements go counter to the theory's claim that experienced emotion is essentially just an awareness of the body's response.

42. **c.** is the answer.

43. **c.** is the answer. The men who received epinephrine without an explanation felt arousal and experienced this arousal as whatever emotion the experimental confederate in the room with them was displaying.
a. Epinephrine recipients who expected arousal attributed their arousal to the drug and reported no emotional change in reaction to the confederate's behavior.
b. & d. In addition to the two groups discussed in the text, the experiment involved placebo recipients; these subjects were not physically aroused and did not experience an emotional change.

44. **d.** is the answer. These are the three components of emotions identified in the text.

45. **c.** is the answer. If the suspect becomes physically aroused while answering questions about details only the perpetrator of the crime could know, it is presumed that he or she committed the crime.

46. **c.** is the answer. Both fear and joy increase heart rate but stimulate different facial muscles.

47. **c.** is the answer.
a. & b. These answers imply that cognition *always* precedes emotion.
d. These responses are unconscious and automatic and so are not learned.

48. **c.** is the answer.
a., b., & d. The pituitary does not produce stress hormones nor is the parasympathetic division involved in arousal.

49. **a.** is the answer. Emotional arousal activates the sympathetic nervous system, causing the release of sugar into the blood for energy, pupil dilation, and the diverting of blood from the internal organs to the muscles, all of which help prepare the body to meet an emergency.
b. Being autonomic responses, most emotions are *involuntary* reactions.
c. All emotions do *not* have the same physiological basis.
d. Some emotions occur without cognitive awareness.

50. **c.** is the answer. According to Schachter and Singer, the two factors in emotion are (1) physical arousal and (2) conscious interpretation of the arousal.

51. **b.** is the answer.
a. The James-Lange theory states that the experience of an emotion is an awareness of one's physical response to an emotion-arousing stimulus.
c. & d. The two-factor theory, proposed by Schachter and Singer, states that to experience emotion one must be physically aroused and attribute the arousal to an emotional cause.

52. **d.** is the answer. No device can literally measure lying. The polygraph measures breathing, cardiovascular activity, and perspiration for changes indicative of physiological arousal.

53. **b.** is the answer.

54. **a.** is the answer. If, as the theory claims, emotions are triggered by physiological reactions, then each emotion must be associated with a unique physiological reaction.
b. According to the Cannon-Bard theory, the same general body response accompanies many emotions.
c. & d. The two-factor theory, proposed by Schachter and Singer, states that the cognitive interpretation of a general state of physical arousal determines different emotions.

55. **d.** is the answer. As the Schachter-Singer study indicated, physical arousal is not always accompanied by an emotional reaction. Only when arousal was attributed to an emotion was it experienced as such. The results of this experiment, therefore, support the viewpoint that conscious interpretation of arousal must precede emotion.
a., b., & c. Each of these was presented as a supporting argument in the text.

56. **d.** is the answer.

57. **a.** is the answer. That physical arousal can be misattributed demonstrates that it is the cognitive interpretation of arousal, rather than the intensity or specific nature of the body's arousal, that determines the conscious experience of emotions.
b. & c. The findings of these studies do not indicate that a minimum level of arousal is necessary for an emotional experience nor that applying a cognitive label must be simultaneous with the arousal.

58. **c.** is the answer. As heightened arousal may reflect feelings of anxiety or irritation rather than of guilt, the polygraph, which simply measures arousal, may easily err.
a. Misuse and invasion of privacy are valid issues, but researchers primarily object to the use of lie detectors because of their inaccuracy.
b. Although there are discrepancies among the various measures of arousal, this was not what Lykken objected to.
d. The lie detector declares an innocent person guilty about one-third of the time and about one-fourth of the guilty innocent.

Terms and Concepts to Remember:

59. **Emotion** is a response of the whole organism involving three components: (1) bodily arousal, (2) expressive behaviors, and (3) conscious experience.

60. The **James-Lange theory** states that emotional experiences are based on an awareness of the body's responses to emotion-arousing stimuli: A stimulus triggers the body's responses that in turn trigger the experienced emotion.

61. The **Cannon-Bard theory** states that the subjective experience of an emotion occurs at the same time as the body's physical reaction.

62. The **two-factor theory** of emotion proposes that emotions have two ingredients: physical arousal and a cognitive label. Thus, physical arousal is a necessary, but not a sufficient, component of emotional change. For an emotion to be experienced, arousal must be attributed to an emotional cause.

63. The **polygraph**, or lie detector, is a device that measures several of the physiological responses accompanying emotion.

Essay Question

All emotions involve some degree of physiological arousal of the sympathetic nervous system. Although the arousal that occurs with different emotions is in most ways undifferentiated, there may be subtle differences in the brain circuits associated with different emotions.

MODULE
32 **Expressing and Experiencing Emotion**

Detecting Emotion in Others

1. cues; threats; deceiving
2. better; easier
3. electronic
4. better; literacy; simpler; responsiveness; expressiveness; more; smaller; more
5. female; male
6. different
7. the same; does not vary; are
8. Charles Darwin; interpret; contexts
9. individuality; infer; social-cultural
10. **d.** is the answer. In Japan and China, cultures that encourage people to adjust to others, personal emotional displays are less visible.
a., b., & c. In cultures that encourage individuality, as in Western Europe, Australia, and North America, personal emotions are displayed openly.
11. intensified
12. frown

13. facial feedback
14. leads
15. behavior feedback
16. **b.** is the answer. Expressions may amplify the associated emotions.
    a. Laboratory studies have shown that facial expressions *intensify* emotions.
    c. & d. Neither of these reactions are likely.
17. **d.** is the answer.
    a. & c. Both of these contradict the finding that emotional expressions are universal.
    b. Even if it is true that emotional expressions are acquired at an early age, this would not necessarily account for the common facial expressions of children from around the world. If anything, the different cultural experiences of the children might lead them to express their feelings in very *different* ways.

Module Review:

18. **b.** is the answer.
    a. The opposite is true; relevant facial muscles are hard to control voluntarily.
    c. Authentic facial expressions tend to fade within 4 or 5 seconds.
    d. Facial expressions are generally universal; many gestures vary from culture to culture.
19. **d.** is the answer.
20. **b.** is the answer. Whereas the meanings of gestures vary from culture to culture, facial expressions seem to have the same meanings around the world.

Terms and Concepts to Remember:

21. The **facial feedback effect** is the tendency of facial muscles to trigger corresponding feelings.
22. The **behavior feedback effect** is the tendency of our behavior to influence our thoughts, feelings, and actions.

Essay Question

Unlike facial expressions of emotion, the meaning of many gestures is culturally determined. Culture also influences how people express their feelings. In cultures that encourage individuality, for example, personal emotions are displayed openly. In cultures that emphasize human interdependence, the display of personal emotions is discouraged.

Before You Move On

Matching Items 1

1. i	5. f	9. e
2. d	6. g	
3. a	7. h	
4. c	8. b	

Matching Items 2

1. a	4. b
2. e	5. d
3. f	6. c

True–False Items

1. F	7. F
2. F	8. F
3. F	9. F
4. F	10. T
5. T	11. T
6. T	12. T

Cross-Check

ACROSS	**DOWN**
1. emotion	2. obesity
4. ghrelin	3. drive-reduction
6. polygraph	5. basal metabolic rate
11. hierarchy	7. achievement
13. safety	8. physiological
14. glucose	9. two-factor
	10. Lange
	12. Cannon-Bard

Stress, Health, and Human Flourishing

Overview

Behavioral factors play a major role in maintaining health and causing illness. The effort to understand this role more fully has led to the emergence of the interdisciplinary field of behavioral medicine. The subfield of health psychology focuses on questions such as: How do our perceptions of a situation determine the stress we feel? How do our emotions and personality influence our risk of disease? How can psychology contribute to the prevention of illness?

Modules 33 and 34 address key topics in health psychology. Module 33 begins with the important topic of stress—its nature, its effects on the body, psychological factors that determine how it affects us, and how stress contributes to infectious diseases, cancer, and heart disease.

Module 34 looks at physical and psychological factors that promote good health, including aerobic exercise and social support. The last section of this module is a discussion of happiness, the goal of all people everywhere. It begins with an explanation of positive psychology, the study of subjective well-being. The module concludes with an examination of the factors that affect our happiness, as well several suggestions for increasing our happiness..

NOTE: Answer guidelines for all Modules 33 and 34 questions begin on page 281.

Outline

 MODULE 33 Stress and Illness

 MODULE 34 Health and Happiness

Instructions

First, skim each section, noting headings and boldface items. After you have read the section, review each objective by answering the fill-in, essay-type, and multiple-choice questions for that section. In some cases, Study Tips explain how best to learn a difficult concept and Applications and Module Reviews help you to know how well you understand the material. Finally, try to define the important terms and concepts using your own words. As you proceed, evaluate your performance by consulting the answers on page 281. Do not continue until you understand each answer. If you need to, review or reread a troublesome section before continuing.

Before You Move On includes activities that test you on material from the entire unit.

MODULE
33   ## Stress and Illness

Stress: Some Basic Concepts

Objective 33-1: Identify events that provoke stress responses, and describe how we respond and adapt to stress.

1. Stress is not merely a _____ or a _____ . Rather, it is the _____ by which we perceive and respond to environmental threats and challenges. The threat or challenge is the _____ , and our physical and emotional response is the _____ _____ .

2. This definition highlights the fact that stress arises less from the events than from how we _____ them and that stressors can have _____ (only negative/both positive and negative) effects, depending on how they are perceived.

STUDY TIP/APPLICATION: The words *stress* and *stressor* are so similar it's easy to think that they mean the same thing. To understand the difference, remember that *stress* is the process by which we appraise and cope with challenging environmental events (the *stressors*). But they are different concepts describing different aspects of a behavior. It may help you to see the difference between these concepts if you realize that stressors can be external events, such as having your flight cancelled, or internal events, such as worrying about an upcoming term paper assignment, and that stress includes those events plus your response to them. To make sure you understand the differences between stress and stressors, see if you can come up with examples of each as you complete the following chart. The first example has already been filled in.

3. Stressor (Stressful Event)	Appraisal		Response	
	Threat	Challenge	Threat	Challenge
Getting cut off by a driver on the freeway	"I'm going to be in an accident"	"I need to watch more carefully"	Heart races; hit the brakes hard	Heart races; swerve out of the way

4. Catastrophic events, such as floods, hurricanes, and fires, usually result in significant damage to _____ and _____ health.

5. Research studies have found that people who have recently been widowed, fired, or divorced are _____ (more/no more) vulnerable to illness than other people.

6. Another source of stress comes from _____ _____ , such as rush-hour traffic and family frustration. The stresses that accompany poverty and unemployment, for example, often compounded by _____ , drive up _____ _____ levels among African-Americans.

7. In the 1920s, physiologist _____ began studying the effect of stress on the body. He discovered that the hormones _____ and _____ are released by the _____ glands into the bloodstream in response to stress. This and other bodily changes due to stress are mediated by the _____ nervous system, thus preparing the body for _____ _____ _____ .

8. In studying animals' reactions to stressors, Hans Selye referred to the bodily response to stress as the _____ _____ _____ .

9. During the first phase of the GAS—the _____ reaction—the person is in a state of shock due to the sudden arousal of the _____ nervous system.

10. This is followed by the stage of _____, in which the body's resources are mobilized to cope with the stressor.

11. If stress continues, the person enters the stage of _____. During this stage, a person is _____ (more/less) vulnerable to disease.

12. A common response to stress among women has been called _____ _____ _____, which refers to the increased tendency to _____. This tendency in women may in part be due to _____, a stress-moderating hormone.

13. Facing stress, men more often than women tend to _____ socially, turn to _____, or become _____.

APPLICATIONS:

14. Each semester, Bob does not start studying until just before midterms. Then he is forced to work around the clock until after final exams, which makes him sick, probably because he is in the _____ phase of the general adaptation syndrome.
    a. alarm
    b. resistance
    c. exhaustion
    d. depletion

15. Connie complains to the campus psychologist that she has too much stress in her life. The psychologist tells her that the level of stress people experience depends primarily on
    a. how many activities they are trying to do at the same time.
    b. how they appraise the events of life.
    c. their physical hardiness.
    d. how predictable stressful events are.

16. Karen and Kyumi attend different universities, but both have rooms in on-campus dorms. Karen's dorm is large, roomy, with only two students to a suite. Kyumi attends a city school, where the dorms are small, overcrowded, and noisy, with five students to a room, which makes studying very difficult. Which student is probably under more stress?
    a. Karen
    b. Kyumi
    c. There should be no difference in their levels of stress.
    d. It is impossible to predict stress levels in this situation.

Stress and Vulnerability to Disease

Objective 33-2: Describe how stress makes us more vulnerable to disease.

17. The field that integrates behavioral and medical knowledge relevant to health and disease is _____. The subfield of psychology that contributes to behavioral medicine is called _____ psychology.

18. Another subfield, _____, focuses on mind-body interactions. This field investigates how the _____, _____, and _____ systems together affect the immune system and health.

19. The body's system of fighting disease is the _____ system. This system includes two types of white blood cells, called _____: the _____ _____, which mature in the _____ marrow and fight bacterial infections; and the _____ _____, which mature in the _____ and other lymphatic tissue and attack viruses, cancer cells, and foreign substances.

20. Two other immune agents are the _____, which identifies, pursues, and ingests foreign substances, and _____ _____ cells, which pursue diseased cells.

21. Responding too strongly, the immune system may attack the body's tissues and cause an _____ reaction or a _____ disease, such as lupus. _____ (Women/Men) are the immunologically stronger sex, which makes them _____ (more/less) susceptible to the latter.

22. Or the immune system may _____, allowing a dormant herpes virus to erupt or _____ cells to multiply.

23. Stress can suppress the lymphocyte cells, resulting in a(n) _____ (increase/decrease) in disease resistance. Stress diverts energy from the _____ _____ to the _____ and _____, mobilizing the body for action and making us more vulnerable to disease.

24. Worldwide, the sixth leading cause of death is _____, caused by the _____ _____ _____.

25. Stressful life circumstances _____ (have/have not) been shown to accelerate the progression of this chronic disease.

26. Educational initiatives, bereavement support groups, cognitive therapy, and other efforts to control stress _____ (have/have not) been shown to have positive consequences on HIV-positive individuals.

27. Stress _____ (does/does not) create cancer cells. However, some studies find that people are at increased risk for cancer within a year after experiencing _____, _____, or _____.

28. When rodents were inoculated with _____ cells or given _____, tumors developed sooner in those that were also exposed to _____ stress.

APPLICATIONS:

29. A white blood cell that matures in the thymus and that attacks cancer cells is
    a. a macrophage.   c. a T lymphocyte.
    b. a B lymphocyte.   d. any of these cells.

30. When would you expect that your immune responses would be WEAKEST?
    a. during summer vacation
    b. during exam weeks
    c. just after receiving good news
    d. Immune activity would probably remain constant during these times.

Objective 33-3: Explain why some of us are more prone than others to coronary heart disease.

31. The leading cause of death in the United States is _____ _____. List several risk factors for developing this condition: _____ _____ _____ .

32. Friedman, Rosenman, and their colleagues discovered that tax accountants experience an increase in blood _____ level and blood-_____ speed during tax season. This showed there was a link between coronary warning indicators and _____.

Friedman and Rosenman, in a subsequent study, grouped people into Type A and Type B personalities. Characterize these types, and indicate the difference that emerged between them over the course of this nine-year study.

33. The Type A characteristic that is most strongly linked with coronary heart disease is _____ _____, especially _____ _____ .

34. When a _____ (Type A/Type B) person is angered, bloodflow is diverted away from the internal organs, including the liver,

which is responsible for removing
_____ and fat from the blood.
Thus, such people have elevated levels of these
substances in the blood.

35. People with the _____
_____ personality type suppress
their _____ (positive/negative)
emotions to avoid _____
_____ .

36. Another toxic emotion is _____ ;
researchers have found that _____
are more than twice as likely to develop heart
disease as _____ .

37. Depression _____ (increases/
has no effect on) one's risk of having a heart
attack or developing other heart problems.

38. Heart disease and depression may both result
when chronic _____ triggers
persistent _____ .

APPLICATION:

39. Jill is an easygoing, noncompetitive person who
is happy in her job and enjoys her leisure time.
She would PROBABLY be classified as
a. Type A.
b. Type B.
c. Type D.
d. There is too little information to tell.

Objective 33-4: Discuss how strategies for handling
anger compare in their effectiveness.

40. The belief that expressing pent-up emotion is
adaptive is most commonly found in cultures that
emphasize _____ . This is called
_____ . In cultures that emphasize _____ , such as those of
_____ or _____ ,
expressions of anger are less common.

41. Expressing anger can be temporarily calming if it
does not leave us _____ or
_____ .

Identify some potential problems with expressing
anger.

42. List three suggestions offered by experts for
handling anger.
a. _____
b. _____
c. _____

43. If used wisely, anger can communicate
_____ and _____ ,
and it can motivate people to take action and
achieve _____ .

44. Researchers have found that students who
_____ someone who had hurt
them had increased _____ to
brain regions that help people understand their
own emotions and make socially appropriate
decisons.

APPLICATIONS:

45. Who will probably be angrier after getting a
parking ticket?
a. Bob, who has just awakened from a nap
b. Veronica, who has just finished eating a big
lunch
c. Dan, who has just completed a tennis match
d. Alicia, who has been reading a romantic novel

46. Marysol was so mad at her brother that she
exploded at him when he entered her room. That
she felt less angry afterward is best explained by
a. persistent inflammation.
b. physiological arousal.
c. bloodflow to the amygdala.
d. catharsis.

47. Expressing anger can be adaptive when you
a. retaliate immediately.
b. have mentally rehearsed all the reasons for
your anger.
c. count to 10, then blow off steam.
d. first wait until the anger subsides, then deal
with the situation in a civil manner.

MODULE REVIEW:

48. Researchers Friedman and Rosenman refer
to individuals who are very time-conscious,
supermotivated, verbally aggressive, and easily
angered as
a. ulcer-prone personalities.
b. cancer-prone personalities.
c. Type A.
d. Type B.

49. During which stage of the general adaptation syndrome is a person especially vulnerable to disease?
    a. alarm reaction   c. stage of exhaustion
    b. stage of resistance d. stage of adaptation

50. The leading cause of death in the United States is
    a. lung cancer.
    b. AIDS.
    c. coronary heart disease.
    d. alcohol-related accidents.

51. Stress has been demonstrated to place a person at increased risk of
    a. cancer.
    b. progressing from HIV infection to AIDS.
    c. bacterial infections.
    d. all of these conditions.

52. *Stress* is defined as
    a. unpleasant or aversive events that cannot be controlled.
    b. situations that threaten health.
    c. the process by which we perceive and respond to challenging or threatening events.
    d. anything that decreases immune responses.

53. Behavioral and medical knowledge about factors influencing health form the basis of the field of
    a. health psychology.
    b. holistic medicine.
    c. behavioral medicine.
    d. osteopathic medicine.

54. In order, the sequence of stages in the general adaptation syndrome is
    a. alarm reaction, stage of resistance, stage of exhaustion.
    b. stage of resistance, alarm reaction, stage of exhaustion.
    c. stage of exhaustion, stage of resistance, alarm reaction.
    d. alarm reaction, stage of exhaustion, stage of resistance.

55. AIDS is a disorder that causes a breakdown in the body's
    a. endocrine system.
    b. circulatory system.
    c. immune system.
    d. respiratory system.

56. *Tend and befriend* refers to
    a. the final stage of the general adaptation syndrome.
    b. the health-promoting impact of having a strong system of social support.
    c. an alternative to the fight-or-flight response that may be more common in women.
    d. the fact that spiritual people typically are not socially isolated.

57. Which of the following statements concerning Type A and Type B persons is true?
    a. Even when relaxed, Type A persons have higher blood pressure than Type B persons.
    b. When stressed, Type A persons redistribute bloodflow to the muscles and away from internal organs.
    c. Type B persons tend to suppress anger more than Type A persons.
    d. Type A persons tend to be more outgoing than Type B persons.

58. The disease- and infection-fighting cells of the immune system are
    a. B lymphocytes.
    b. T lymphocytes.
    c. macrophages.
    d. all of these types of cells.

59. Which of the following is true of Type D personalities?
    a. They have reactive personalities and anger easily.
    b. They suppress negative emotions to avoid social disapproval.
    c. They are relaxed and easygoing.
    d. They are competitive and hard-driving.

60. One effect of stress on the body is to
    a. suppress the immune system.
    b. facilitate the immune system response.
    c. increase disease resistance.
    d. increase the growth of B and T lymphocytes.

61. Compared with men, women
    a. have stronger immune systems.
    b. are less susceptible to infections.
    c. are more susceptible to self-attacking diseases such as multiple sclerosis.
    d. have all these characteristics.

62. Allergic reactions and self-attacking diseases are caused by
   a. an overreactive immune system.
   b. an underreactive immune system.
   c. the presence of B lymphocytes.
   d. the presence of T lymphocytes.

63. Research on cancer patients reveals that
   a. stress affects the growth of cancer cells by weakening the body's natural resources.
   b. patients' attitudes can influence their rate of recovery.
   c. cancer occurs slightly more often than usual among those widowed, divorced, or separated.
   d. all of these statements are true.

64. The component of Type A behavior that is the most predictive of coronary disease is
   a. time urgency.   c. high motivation.
   b. competitiveness.   d. anger.

65. The field of psychoneuroimmunology is concerned with
   a. thoughts and feelings.
   b. the brain.
   c. the endocrine system.
   d. all of these things.

66. Concerning catharsis, which of the following is true?
   a. Expressing anger can be temporarily calming if it does not leave one feeling guilty or anxious.
   b. The arousal that accompanies unexpressed anger never dissipates.
   c. Expressing one's anger always calms one down.
   d. Psychologists agree that under no circumstances is catharsis beneficial.

TERMS AND CONCEPTS TO REMEMBER:

67. stress
68. general adaptation syndrome (GAS)
69. tend and befriend
70. health psychology
71. psychoneuroimmunology
72. coronary heart disease

73. Type A
74. Type B
75. catharsis

MODULE
34 **Health and Happiness**

Coping With Stress

Objective 34-1: Identify two ways that people try to alleviate stress.

1. People learn to _____ with stress by finding _____ , _____ , or _____ ways to alleviate it.

2. When we cope directly with a stressor, we are using _____-_____ coping.

3. When we attempt to alleviate stress by avoiding it and attending to emotional needs, we are using _____-_____ coping.

4. People tend to use _____-_____ coping when they feel a sense of _____ over a situation. They turn to _____-_____ coping when they cannot or believe they cannot _____ a situation.

STUDY TIP/APPLICATION: Two basic strategies for coping with stressors are problem-focused coping and emotion-focused coping. *Problem-focused coping* is an action-oriented strategy in which we attempt to reduce stress by changing the stressor or the way we interact with that stressor. In contrast, with *emotion-focused coping* we focus on our feelings and try to change how we think about stressors. Think about how you typically cope with stress. Do you more often rely on problem-focused coping or emotion-focused coping? Now complete the chart on the next page. For each stressor, write down one example of a problem-focused strategy and one example of an emotion-focused strategy.

5. Stressor	Emotion-Focused Strategy	Problem-Focused Strategy
You are worried about the amount of reading needed to prepare for an exam.	To take your mind off things, you go to a movie.	You divide the reading into manageable, daily sessions, and get started!
a. You get into an argument with your roommate.		
b. Your car muffler falls off.		
c. You develop a cold sore on your lip the day of an important dance.		

APPLICATIONS:

6. Velma has been unable to resolve a stressful relationship with a family member. To cope, she turns to a close friend for social support. Velma's coping strategy is an example of
   a. problem-focused coping.
   b. emotion-focused coping.
   c. managing rather than coping.
   d. self-control.

7. To help him deal with a stressful schedule of classes, work, and studying, Randy turns to a regular program of exercise and relaxation training. Randy's strategy is an example of
   a. problem-focused coping.
   b. emotion-focused coping.
   c. managing rather than coping.
   d. self-control.

Objective 34-2: Explain how a perceived lack of control can affect health.

8. Negative situations are especially stressful when they are appraised as _____.

9. Seligman found that exposure to inescapable punishment produced a passive resignation in behavior, which he called _____ _____. Perceiving a loss of _____, humans become more vulnerable to ill health.

10. With higher economic status comes lower risks of infant _____, low _____, smoking, and _____.

11. In animals and humans, sudden lack of control is followed by a drop in immune responses, a(n) _____ (increase/decrease) in blood pressure, and a rise in the levels of _____ _____.

12. Individuals who have an _____ _____ _____ perceive that chance or outside forces control their fate. People who perceive an _____ _____ _____ _____ believe they control their own destiny.

13. Research studies demonstrate that people who perceive an _____ (internal/external) locus of control achieve more in school and work, feel less _____, and enjoy better _____.

14. Compared with their parents' generation, more young Americans express an _____ (external/internal) locus of control, which may help explain an associated increase in rates of _____ .

Objective 34-3: Describe how our self-control can be depleted, and explain why it is important to build this strength.

15. Self-control is the ability to control _____ and delay _____-_____ for longer-term rewards.

16. Research studies demonstrate that self-control is associated with _____ _____ .

17. Our self-control is _____ (stable/constantly changing).

18. Exercising willpower _____ (increases/decreases) neural activation in brain regions associated with mental control. Sugar has the _____ (same/opposite) effect.

19. Developing self-discipline in one area of life may _____ _____ into other areas as well.

Objective 34-4: Describe how an optimistic outlook affects health and longevity.

20. People who have an optimistic outlook on life expect to have more _____ , to _____ better with stressful events, and to enjoy better _____ .

21. Optimists respond to stress with smaller increases in _____ _____ , and recover more _____ (quickly/slowly) from heart bypass surgery.

22. Optimistic students tend to get better _____ .

23. Studies of identical twins reveal that optimism _____ (runs/does not run) in families.

24. One genetic marker of optimism is a gene that enhances the hormone _____ .

25. People _____ (can/cannot) learn to become more optimistic.

Objective 34-5: Describe how social support promotes good health.

26. Another buffer against the effects of stress is _____ support.

27. People in _____ (collectivist/individualist) cultures tend to keep their struggles to themselves; people in _____ (collectivist/individualist) cultures feel more comfortable turning to friends and family.

28. Longitudinal research reveals that a _____ _____ at age 50 predicts healthy aging better than _____ _____ at the same age.

State some possible reasons for the link between health and social support.

29. Some research studies suggest that the presence of _____ increases the odds of survival after a heart attack.

30. James Pennebaker has found that emotional _____ can adversely affect our physical health.

31. Health can be improved by _____ about personal traumas in a diary. Another way to reduce stress is to talk about it. In another study, Holocaust survivors who were the most _____ had the most improved health.

APPLICATIONS:

32. You have just transferred to a new campus and find yourself in a potentially stressful environment. According to the text, which of the following would help you cope with the stress?

a. believing that you have some control over your environment

b. having a friend to confide in

c. feeling optimistic that you will eventually adjust to your new surroundings

d. All of these behaviors would help.

33. Which of the following would be the best piece of advice to offer a person who is trying to minimize the adverse effects of stress on his or her health?

a. "Avoid challenging situations that may prove stressful."

b. "Learn to play as hard as you work."

c. "Maintain a sense of control and a positive approach to life."

d. "Keep your emotional responses in check by keeping your feelings to yourself."

Reducing Stress

Objective 34-6: Discuss the effectiveness of aerobic exercise as a way to manage stress and improve well-being.

34. Sustained exercise that increases heart and lung fitness is known as _____ exercise.

35. Exercise helps fight heart disease by increasing _____ and lowering _____ _____ .

36. Aerobic exercise can also reduce _____ , _____ , and _____ .

37. Exercise increases the body's production of mood-boosting neurotransmitters such as _____ , _____ , and the _____ . It also may foster _____ .

Objective 34-7: Describe the ways in which relaxation and meditation might influence stress and health.

38. A system for recording a physiological response and providing information concerning it is called _____ . The instruments used in this system _____ (pro-

vide/do not provide) the individual with a means of monitoring physiological responses. Current research indicates that this method works best on _____ _____ .

39. Simple relaxation procedures have been shown to help alleviate _____ , _____ , _____ , and _____ .

40. Many stress management programs today are built around _____ _____ , in which a person learns to relax and silently attend to his or her inner state, without _____ it.

State some of the benefits of mindfulness meditation.

41. Mindfulness strengthens connections in regions of the brain associated with _____ _____ .

42. When labeling emotions, "mindful people" show less activation in the _____ , and more activation in the _____ .

43. Emotionally unpleasant images also trigger _____ (weaker/stronger) electrical brain responses in mindful people than in their less mindful counterparts.

Objective 34-8: Describe the faith factor, and offer some possible explanations for the link between faith and health.

44. Several recent studies demonstrate that religious involvement _____ (predicts/does not predict) health and longevity.

State two possible intervening variables that might account for the *faith factor* in health.

APPLICATION:

45. Concluding her presentation on spirituality and health, Maja notes that
    a. religion promotes self-control.
    b. religious involvement predicts health and longevity.
    c. people who attend religious services weekly have healthier lifestyles.
    d. all of these statements are true.

Happiness

Objective 34-9: Define the *feel-good, do-good phenomenon*, and describe the focus of positive psychology research.

46. Happy people tend to perceive the world as _____ and feel more _____ .They are _____ and live more energized and satisfied lives.

47. Happy people are also _____ (more/less) willing to help others. This is called the _____-_____, _____-_____ phenomenon.

48. Researchers working in the area of _____ _____ use scientific methods to study human flourishing. In particular, they are studying positive _____, _____ , and _____ _____ .

49. An individual's self-perceived happiness or satisfaction with life is called his or her _____ _____ .

Objective 34-10: Describe how time, wealth, adaptation, and comparison affect our happiness levels.

50. Tracking positive and negative emotion words in billions of Facebook entries, a social psychologist found that the most positive moods days of the week are _____ and _____ .

51. Positive emotions _____ (rise/fall) in the early to middle part of most days. The gloom of stressful events usually _____ (is gone by/continues into) the next day.

52. After experiencing tragedy or dramatically positive events, people generally _____ (regain/do not regain) near-normal levels of happiness.

53. Most people tend to _____ (underestimate/overestimate) the duration of emotions and _____ (underestimate/overestimate) their resiliency and capacity to adapt.

54. Researchers have found that, after people achieve a certain level of income, money _____ (does/does not) increase their feelings of happiness.

55. During the last half-century, buying power in the United States has almost tripled; personal happiness has _____ (increased/ decreased/remained almost unchanged).

56. Increasing real incomes in Europe, Australia, and Japan _____ (has/has not) produced increasing happiness.

57. The idea that happiness is relative to one's recent experience is stated by the _____-_____ phenomenon.

Explain how this principle accounts for the fact that, for some people, material desires can never be satisfied.

58. The principle that one feels worse off than others is known as _____ _____ . This helps to explain why the middle- and upper-income people who compare themselves with the relatively poor are _____ (more/less/equally) satisfied with life.

59. Over the last half-century, inequality in Western countries has _____ (increased/decreased). Places with great inequality have higher _____ rates,

_____ , _____ ,

and _____ _____ ,

and lower _____ .

Objective 34-11: Identify some predictors of happiness, and show how we can be happier.

60. List six factors that have been shown to be positively correlated with feelings of happiness.

_____

_____

_____

_____

_____

_____

61. List three factors that are evidently unrelated to happiness.

_____

_____

_____

62. Research studies of identical and fraternal twins have led to the estimate that _____ percent of the variation in people's happiness ratings is heritable. But personal history and _____ also matter.

State several evidence-based suggestions for increasing your happiness.

APPLICATIONS:

63. As elderly Mr. Hooper crosses the busy intersection, he stumbles and drops the packages he is carrying. Which passerby is most likely to help Mr. Hooper?
   a. Drew, who has been laid off from work for three months
   b. Leon, who is on his way to work
   c. Bonnie, who earned her doctoral degree the day before
   d. Nancy, whose father recently passed away

64. Cindy was happy with her promotion until she found out that Janice, who has the same amount of experience, receives a higher salary. Cindy's feelings are best explained according to
   a. the adaptation-level phenomenon.
   b. subjective well-being.
   c. the concept of catharsis.
   d. the principle of relative deprivation.

65. When Professor Simon acquired a spacious new office, he was overjoyed. Six months later, however, he was taking the office for granted. His behavior illustrates the
   a. relative deprivation principle.
   b. adaptation-level phenomenon.
   c. catharsis theory.
   d. concept of subjective well-being.

MODULE REVIEW:

66. Which of the following is true regarding happiness?
   a. People with less education tend to be happier.
   b. Beautiful people tend to be happier than plain people.
   c. Women tend to be happier than men.
   d. People who are socially outgoing or who exercise regularly tend to be happier.

67. Research indicates that a person is most likely to be helpful to others if he or she
   a. is feeling guilty about something.
   b. is happy.
   c. recently received help from another person.
   d. recently offered help to another person.

68. A graph depicting the course of positive emotions over the hours of the day since waking would
   a. start low and rise steadily until bedtime.
   b. start high and decrease steadily until bedtime.
   c. remain at a stable, moderate level throughout the day.
   d. rise over the early hours and fall during the day's last several hours.

69. When students studied others who were worse off than themselves, they felt greater satisfaction with their own lives. This is an example of the principle of
   a. relative deprivation.
   b. adaptation level.
   c. behavioral contrast.
   d. opponent processes.

70. Which of these factors have researchers NOT found to correlate with happiness?
   a. age
   b. high self-esteem
   c. religious faith
   d. optimism

MODULE REVIEW:

71. Attempting to alleviate stress directly by changing a stressor or how we interact with it is an example of
   a. problem-focused coping.
   b. emotion-focused coping.
   c. managing rather than coping with stress.
   d. self-control.

72. A study in which Holocaust survivors spent time recalling their experiences found that
   a. most did not truthfully report feelings and events.
   b. all survivors experienced a sustained increase in blood pressure until they finished talking about their experiences.
   c. those who were most self-disclosing later had the most improved health.
   d. all the survivors denied undergoing concentration camp horrors.

73. Which of the following was NOT mentioned in the text as a potential health benefit of exercise?
   a. Exercise can increase ability to cope with stress.
   b. Exercise can lower blood pressure.
   c. Exercise can reduce stress, depression, and anxiety.
   d. Exercise improves functioning of the immune system.

74. Social support _____ our ability to cope with stressful events.
   a. has no effect on
   b. usually increases
   c. usually decreases
   d. has an unpredictable effect on

75. Research has demonstrated that as a predictor of health and longevity, religious involvement
   a. has a small, insignificant effect.
   b. is more accurate for women than men.
   c. is more accurate for men than women.
   d. equals nonsmoking and exercise.

76. Which of the following was NOT suggested as a possible explanation of the faith factor in health?
   a. Having a coherent worldview is a buffer against stress.
   b. Religious people tend to have healthier lifestyles.
   c. Those who are religious have stronger networks of social support.
   d. Because they are more affluent, religiously active people receive better health care.

TERMS AND CONCEPTS TO REMEMBER:

77. coping

78. problem-focused coping

79. emotion-focused coping

80. learned helplessness

81. external locus of control

82. internal locus of control

83. self-control

84. aerobic exercise

85. mindfulness meditation

86. feel-good, do-good phenomenon

87. positive psychology

88. subjective well-being

89. adaptation-level phenomenon

90. relative deprivation

Essay Question

Discuss several factors that enhance a person's ability to cope with stress. (Use the space below to list the points you want to make, and organize them. Then write the essay on a separate sheet of paper.)

Before You Move On

Matching Items

Match each definition or description with the appropriate term.

Definitions or Descriptions

_____ 1. the tendency to react to changes on the basis of recent experience

_____ 2. an individual's self-perceived happiness

_____ 3. emotional release

_____ 4. the tendency to evaluate our situation negatively against that of other people

_____ 5. the scientific study of optimal human functioning

_____ 6. the process by which we perceive and respond to threatening events

_____ 7. the coronary-prone behavior pattern

_____ 8. the coronary-resistant behavior pattern

_____ 9. attempting to alleviate stress by avoiding a stressor

_____ 10. the tendency of people to be helpful when they are in a good mood

_____ 11. attempting to alleviate stress by managing how we interact with the stressor

Terms

a. adaptation-level phenomenon
b. positive psychology
c. catharsis
d. Type A
e. Type B
f. problem-focused
g. emotion-focused
h. stress
i. relative deprivation principle
j. feel-good, do-good phenomenon
k. subjective well-being

True–False Items

Indicate whether each statement is true or false by placing *T* or *F* in the blank next to the item.

_____ 1. Stressors tend to increase activity in the immune system and in this way make people more vulnerable to illness.

_____ 2. Our satisfaction with life generally is not influenced by factors under our control.

_____ 3. Optimism tends to run in families.

_____ 4. Events are most stressful when perceived as both negative and controllable.

_____ 5. People who experience tragedy generally recover near-normal levels of happiness.

_____ 6. Optimists cope more successfully with stressful events than do pessimists.

_____ 7. Wealthy people tend to be much happier than middle-income people.

_____ 8. Religiously active people tend to live longer than those who are not religiously active.

_____ 9. Aerobic exercise can reduce stress, depression, and anxiety.

_____ 10. Type A persons are more physiologically reactive to stress than are Type B persons.

_____ 11. People with few social and community ties are more likely to die prematurely than are those with many social ties.

Cross-Check

As you learned in Module 2, reviewing and overlearning of material are important to the learning process. After you have written the definitions of the key terms in this unit, you should complete the crossword puzzle to ensure that you can reverse the process—recognize the term, given the definition.

ACROSS

4. Emotional release.
5. Coronary-prone behavior pattern.
7. Phenomenon in which people tend to be helpful when they are in a good mood.
8. During the _____ stage of the stress reaction, the body's sympathetic nervous system is suddenly activated.
9. The process by which people appraise and react to events they perceive as threatening.
11. White blood cells of the immune system that fight bacterial infections and viruses, cancer cells, and foreign substances in the body.

DOWN

1. Principle that we are worse off relative to those with whom we compare ourselves.
2. The "big eater" of the immune system.
3. Friedman and Rosenman's term for easygoing, relaxed people.
6. Type of exercise that may help alleviate anxiety.
8. Phenomenon referring to our tendency to judge things relative to our prior experience.
10. Psychologist who first described the general adaptation syndrome.

Answers

MODULE
33 **Stress and Illness**

Stress: Some Basic Concepts

1. stimulus; response; process; stressor; stress reaction
2. appraise; both positive and negative

3. Many answers will complete the table. Just think about stressful events in your life—an upcoming exam, a first date, a job interview. For each one, consider how you would appraise it (as a subject beyond your ability or as a task to be completed with extra work), then ask yourself how you would respond (if beyond your ability, you might go out with friends the night before the exam; as a challenge, you would stay home and study hard).

4. emotional; physical

5. more

6. daily hassles; racism; blood pressure

7. Walter Cannon; epinephrine; norepinephrine; adrenal; sympathetic; fight or flight

8. general adaptation syndrome

9. alarm; sympathetic

10. resistance

11. exhaustion; more

12. tend and befriend; seek and give support; oxytocin

13. withdraw; alcohol; aggressive

14. c. is the answer. According to Selye's general adaptation syndrome, diseases are most likely to occur in this final stage.
    a. & b. Resistance to disease is greater during the alarm and resistance phases because the body's mobilized resources are not yet depleted.
    d. There is no such thing as the "depletion phase."

15. b. is the answer.
    a., c., & d. Each of these is a factor in coping with stress, but it is how an event is perceived that determines whether it is stressful.

16. b. is the answer. Living under crowded conditions contributes to feeling a lack of control, which is the situation in Kyumi's case.

Stress and Vulnerability to Disease

17. behavioral medicine; health

18. psychoneuroimmunology; psychological, neurological; endocrine

19. immune; lymphocytes; B lymphocytes; bone; T lymphocytes; thymus

20. macrophage; natural killer (NK)

21. allergic; self-attacking; Women; more

22. underreact; cancer

23. decrease; immune system; brain; muscles

24. AIDS; human immunodeficiency virus (HIV)

25. have

26. have

27. does not; depression; helplessness; bereavement

28. tumor; carcinogens; uncontrollable

29. c. is the answer.
    a. Macrophages are immune agents that search for and ingest harmful invaders.
    b. B lymphocytes mature in the bone marrow and release antibodies that fight bacterial infections.

30. b. is the answer. Stressful situations, such as exam weeks, decrease immune responses.

31. coronary heart disease; high blood pressure, a family history of the disease, smoking, obesity, high-fat diet, physical inactivity, elevated cholesterol level, stress responses, personality traits

32. cholesterol; clotting; stress

Type A people are reactive, competitive, hard-driving, supermotivated, impatient, time-conscious, verbally aggressive, and easily angered. Type B people are more relaxed and easygoing. In the Friedman and Rosenman study, heart attack victims came overwhelmingly from the Type A group.

33. negative emotions; the anger associated with an aggressively reactive temperament

34. Type A; cholesterol

35. Type D; negative; social disapproval

36. pessimism; pessimists; optimists

37. increases

38. stress; inflammation

39. b. is the answer.
    a. Type A persons are hard-driving and competitive.
    c. Type D people have the negative emotions of Type A people, but they suppress them. This makes them equally susceptible to heart disease.

40. individualism; catharsis; interdependence; Tahiti; Japan

41. guilty; anxious

One problem with expressing anger is that it breeds more anger, in part because it may trigger retaliation. Expressing anger can also magnify anger and reinforce its occurrence.

42. a. Wait to calm down.
    b. Find a healthy distraction or support.
    c. Distance yourself.

43. strength; competence; goals

44. forgave; bloodflow

45. c. is the answer. Because physical arousal tends to intensify emotions, Dan (who is likely to be physically aroused after playing tennis) will probably be angrier than Alicia, Bob, or Veronica, who are in more relaxed states.

46. d. is the answer. In keeping with the idea of catharsis, Jane feels less angry after releasing her aggression.

47. d. is the answer.

a. Venting anger immediately may lead you to say things you later regret and/or may lead to retaliation by the other person.

b. Going over the reasons for your anger merely prolongs the emotion.

c. Counting to 10 may give you a chance to calm down, but "blowing off steam" may rekindle your anger.

Module Review:

48. c. is the answer.

a. & b. Researchers have not identified such personality types.

d. Individuals who are more easygoing are labeled Type B.

49. c. is the answer.

a. & b. During these stages, the body's defensive mechanisms are at peak function.

d. This is not a stage of the GAS.

50. c. is the answer. Coronary heart disease is followed by cancer, stroke, and chronic lung disease. AIDS is the world's fourth leading cause of death.

51. d. is the answer. Because stress depresses the immune system, stressed individuals are prone to all of these conditions.

52. c. is the answer.

a., b., & d. Whether an event is stressful depends on how it is appraised.

53. c. is the answer.

a. Health psychology is a subfield of behavioral medicine.

b. Holistic medicine is an older term that refers to medical practitioners who take more of an interdisciplinary approach to treating disorders.

d. Osteopathy is a medical therapy that emphasizes manipulative techniques for correcting physical problems.

54. a. is the answer.

55. c. is the answer.

56. c. is the answer.

a. The final stage of the general adaptation syndrome is exhaustion.

b. & d. Although both of these are true, neither has anything to do with "tend and befriend."

57. b. is the answer. The result is that their blood may contain excess cholesterol and fat.

a. Under relaxed situations, there is no difference in blood pressure.

c. Anger, both expressed and suppressed, is more characteristic of Type A people.

d. The text doesn't indicate that Type A persons are more outgoing than Type B persons.

58. d. is the answer. B lymphocytes fight bacterial infections; T lymphocytes attack cancer cells, viruses, and foreign substances; and macrophages ingest harmful invaders.

59. b. is the answer.

a & d. These refer to Type A personalities.

c. This refers to a Type B personality.

60. a. is the answer. A variety of studies have shown that stress depresses the immune system, increasing the risk and potential severity of many diseases.

61. d. is the answer.

62. a. is the answer.

b. An *under*reactive immune system would make an individual more susceptible to infectious diseases or the proliferation of cancer cells.

c. & d. Lymphocytes are disease- and infection-fighting white blood cells in the immune system.

63. d. is the answer.

64. d. is the answer. The crucial characteristic of Type A behavior seems to be a tendency to react with negative emotions, especially anger; other aspects of Type A behavior appear not to predict heart disease, and some appear to be helpful to the individual.

65. d. is the answer.

66. a. is the answer.

b. The opposite is true. Any emotional arousal will simmer down if you wait long enough.

c. Catharsis often magnifies anger, escalates arguments, and leads to retaliation.

d. When counterattack is justified and can be directed at the offender, catharsis may be helpful.

Terms and Concepts to Remember:

67. Stress refers to the process by which we perceive and respond to events, called *stressors*, that we perceive as threatening or challenging.

68. The **general adaptation syndrome (GAS)** is the three-stage sequence of bodily reaction to stress outlined by Hans Selye.

69. Tend and befriend refers to the tendency of some people (especially women) to provide support (tend) and seek support from others (befriend) when under stress.

70. **Health psychology** is a subfield of psychology that provides psychology's contribution to behavioral medicine.

71. **Psychoneuroimmunology** is the study of how psychological, neural, and endocrine processes affect the immune system and resulting health.

72. The leading cause of death in the United States today, **coronary heart disease** results from the clogging of the vessels that nourish the heart muscle.

73. **Type A** is Friedman and Rosenman's term for the coronary-prone behavior pattern of competitive, hard-driving, impatient, verbally aggressive, and anger-prone people.

74. **Type B** is Friedman and Rosenman's term for the coronary-resistant behavior pattern of easygoing, relaxed people.

75. **Catharsis** is emotional release; in psychology, the idea that "releasing" aggressive energy (through action or fantasy) relieves aggressive urges.

MODULE 34 **Health and Happiness**

Coping With Stress

1. cope; emotional; cognitive; behavioral
2. problem-focused
3. emotion-focused
4. problem-focused; control; emotion-focused; change
5. **a.** Emotion-focused: You go next door to be comforted by another close friend.
    Problem-focused: You talk with your roommate about resolving your disagreement.
    b. Emotion-focused: You call a friend but keep driving, leaving the muffler where it is and listening to the loud noises of the car.
    Problem-focused: You immediately drive to the nearest muffler shop to have a new muffler put on.
    c. Emotion-focused: You start crying, saying you can't possibly go to the dance.
    Problem-focused: You go to the local drug store to find out what kind of cream you can buy to get rid of the cold sore.
6. **b.** is the answer. Velma is attempting to address her emotional needs, since she has been unable to alleviate stress directly.
7. **c.** is the answer.
8. uncontrollable
9. learned helplessness; control
10. mortality; birth weight; violence

11. increase; stress hormones
12. external locus of control; internal locus of control
13. internal; depressed; health
14. external; depression
15. impulses; short-term gratification
16. good health, higher income, better grades
17. constantly changing
18. decreases; opposite
19. spill over
20. control; cope; health
21. blood pressure; quickly
22. grades
23. runs
24. oxytocin
25. can
26. social
27. collectivist; individualist
28. good marriage; low cholesterol

Close relationships provide the opportunity to confide painful feelings, which may mitigate physical reactions to stressful events. Social support calms us and reduces blood pressure and stress hormones. Social support fosters stronger immune functioning.

29. pets
30. suppression
31. writing; self-disclosing
32. **d.** is the answer.
33. **c.** is the answer.
    a. This is not realistic.
    b. & d. These might actually increase the health consequences of potential stressors.

Reducing Stress

34. aerobic
35. bloodflow; blood pressure
36. stress; depression; anxiety
37. norepinephrine; serotonin; endorphins; neurogenesis
38. biofeedback; provide; tension headaches
39. headaches; hypertension; anxiety; insomnia
40. mindfulness meditation; judging

The benefits of mindfulness meditation may include improved immune system functioning; and reductions in sleep problems, cigarette use, binge eating, and alcohol and other substance use disorders.

41. focusing our attention, processing what we see and hear, and being reflective and aware
42. amygdala; prefrontal cortex
43. weaker

44. predicts

Religiously active people have healthier lifestyles. They also tend to have stronger networks of social support and are more likely to be married.

45. **d.** is the answer.

Happiness

46. safer; confident; healthier

47. more; feel-good, do-good

48. positive psychology; well-being; character; groups, communities, and cultures

49. subjective well-being

50. Friday; Saturday

51. rise; is gone by

52. regain

53. overestimate; underestimate

54. does not

55. remained almost unchanged

56. has not

57. adaptation-level

If we acquire new possessions, we feel an initial surge of pleasure. But we then adapt to having these new possessions, come to see them as normal, and require other things to give us another surge of happiness.

58. relative deprivation; more

59. increased; crime; obesity, anxiety; drug use; life expectancy

60. high self-esteem; satisfying marriage or close friendships; active religious faith; optimistic, outgoing, and agreeable personality; sleeping well and exercising; having work and leisure that engage our skills

61. age; gender; physical attractiveness

62. 50; culture

Realize that happiness doesn't come from financial success. Take control of your time. Act happy. Seek work and leisure that engage your skills. Buy shared experiences rather than things. Engage in regular aerobic exercise. Get plenty of sleep. Give priority to close relationships. Focus beyond self. Be grateful. Nurture your spiritual self.

63. **c.** is the answer. People who are in a good mood are more likely to help others. Bonnie, who is probably pleased with herself for earning a Ph.D., is likely to be in a better mood than Drew, Leon, or Nancy.

64. **d.** is the answer. Cindy is unhappy with her promotion because she feels deprived relative to Janice.

a. The adaptation-level phenomenon would predict that Cindy's raise would cause an increase in her happiness, since her most recent experience was to earn a lower salary.
b. Subjective well-being refers simply our self-perceived happiness. It does not involve a comparison with others.
c. The catharsis hypothesis maintains that venting one's anger may relieve aggressive urges.

65. **b.** is the answer. Professor Simon's judgment of his office is affected by his recent experience: When that experience was of a smaller office, his new office seemed terrific; now, however, it is commonplace.
a. Relative deprivation is the sense that one is worse off than those with whom one compares oneself.
c. Catharsis refers to the release of emotion.
d. Subjective well-being refers to our self-perceived happiness or satisfaction with life. It does not deal with comparisons.

Module Review:

66. **d.** is the answer. Education level, gender, and physical attractiveness seem unrelated to happiness.

67. **b.** is the answer.
a., c., & d. Research studies have not found these factors to be related to altruistic behavior.

68. **d.** is the answer.

69. **a.** is the answer. The principle of relative deprivation states that happiness is relative to others' attainments. This helps explain why those who are relatively well off tend to be slightly more satisfied than the relatively poor, with whom the better-off can compare themselves.
b. Adaptation level is the tendency for our judgments to be relative to our prior experience.
c. This phenomenon has nothing to do with the interpretation of emotion.
d. Opponent processes are not discussed in the text in relation to emotion.

70. **a.** is the answer.

71. **a.** is the answer.
b. In emotion-focused coping, we attempt to alleviate stress by avoiding or ignoring it.
c. This is an example of coping rather than managing stress because it involves an attempt to actually alleviate a stressor.
d. Self-control may be involved but it is not the overall method of alleviating stress in this case.

72. **c. is the answer.** The finding that talking about grief leads to better health makes a lot of sense in light of this physiological finding.
a., b., & d. The study by Pennebaker did not find these to be true.

73. **d. is the answer.** Regular aerobic exercise has been shown to increase ability to cope with stress, lower blood pressure, and reduce depression and anxiety. The text does not cite evidence that exercise enhances immune function.

74. **b. is the answer.**

75. **d. is the answer.**
b. & c. The text does not indicate that a gender difference exists in the "faith factor" in health.

76. **d. is the answer.** As a group, religiously active people are no more affluent than other people.

Terms and Concepts to Remember:

77. **Coping** refers to any effort to alleviate stress using emotional, cognitive, or behavioral methods.

78. **Problem-focused coping** involves attempting to alleviate stress directly by changing a stressor or how we interact with it.

79. **Emotion-focused coping** involves attempting to alleviate stress by avoiding or ignoring a stressor and attending to the emotional reactions it triggers.

80. **Learned helplessness** is a state of hopelessness and passive resignation acquired when an animal or human is unable to avoid repeated aversive events.

81. An **external locus of control** is the perception that chance or outside forces beyond our control determine our destiny.

82. An **internal locus of control** is the perception that you control your own destiny.

83. **Self-control** is the ability to control impulses and delay short-term gratification in order to obtain greater long-term rewards.

84. **Aerobic exercise** is any sustained activity such as running, swimming, or cycling that promotes heart and lung fitness and may help alleviate depression and anxiety.

85. **Mindfulness meditation** is a reflective practice in which people focus on their current experiences in a nonjudgmental manner.

86. The **feel-good, do-good phenomenon** is the tendency of people to be helpful when they are in a good mood.

87. **Positive psychology** is the scientific study of human functioning, focusing on the strengths and virtues that help individuals and communities thrive.

88. **Subjective well-being** refers to a person's sense of satisfaction with his or her life.

89. The **adaptation-level phenomenon** refers to our tendency to judge things relative to a neutral level defined by our prior experience.

90. The principle of **relative deprivation** is the perception that we are worse off relative to those with whom we compare ourselves.

Essay Question

If stressors cannot be eliminated, aerobic exercise, biofeedback, relaxation, meditation, and spirituality can help the person cope. Aerobic exercise can reduce stress, depression, and anxiety, perhaps by increasing production of mood-boosting neurotransmitters. Research demonstrates that people who regularly practice relaxation techniques enjoy a greater sense of tranquility and have lower blood pressure and stronger immune responses. Numerous studies have confirmed the psychological benefits of meditation. Today, it has found a new home in stress management programs, such as mindfulness meditation. People with strong social ties eat better, exercise more, and smoke and drink less. Social support may also help people evaluate and overcome stressful events. In addition, confiding painful feelings to others has been demonstrated to reduce the physiological responses linked to stress. Finally, religiously active people tend to live longer than those who are not religiously active.

Before You Move On

Matching Items

1. a	5. b	9. g
2. k	6. h	10. j
3. c	7. d	11. f
4. i	8. e	

True–False Items

1. F	5. T	9. T
2. F	6. T	10. T
3. T	7. F	11. T
4. F	8. T	

Cross-Check

ACROSS	DOWN
4. catharsis	1. relative deprivation
5. Type A	2. macrophage
7. feel-good, do-good	3. Type B
8. alarm	6. aerobic
9. stress	8. adaptation level
11. lymphocyte	10. Selye

Social Psychology

Overview

Module 35 demonstrates the powerful influences of social situations on the behavior of individuals. Central to this topic are research studies on attitudes and actions, conformity, obedience, and group and cultural influences. The social principles that emerge help us to understand how individuals are influenced by advertising, political candidates, and the various groups to which they belong. Although social influences are powerful, it is important to remember the significant role of individuals in choosing and creating the social situations that influence them.

Modules 36 and 37 discuss how people relate to one another, from the negative—developing prejudice and behaving aggressively—to the positive—being attracted to people who are nearby and/or similar and behaving altruistically.

Module 37 concludes with a discussion of situations that provoke conflict and techniques that have been shown to promote conflict resolution.

Although there is some terminology for you to learn in these modules, your primary task is to absorb the findings of the many research studies discussed. The module headings, which organize the findings, should prove especially useful to you here. In addition, you might, for each main topic (conformity, group influence, aggression, etc.), ask yourself the question, "What situational factors promote this phenomenon?" The research findings can then form the basis for your answers.

NOTE: Answer guidelines for all Modules 35–37 questions begin on page 306.

Outline

Instructions

First, skim each section, noting headings and boldface items. After you have read the section, review each objective by answering the fill-in, essay-type, and multiple-choice questions for that section. In some cases, Study Tips explain how best to learn a difficult concept and Applications and Module Reviews help you to know how well you understand the material. Finally, try to define the important terms and concepts using your own words. As you proceed, evaluate your performance by consulting the answers on page 306. Do not continue until you understand each answer. If you need to, review or reread a troublesome section before continuing.

Before You Move On includes activities that test you on material from the entire unit.

MODULE 35 Social Thinking and Social Influence

Objective 35-1: Identify what social psychologists study, and discuss how we tend to explain others' behavior and our own.

1. Psychologists who study how we think about, influence, and relate to one another are called _____ _____ .

Social Thinking

2. Fritz Heider's theory of how we explain others' behavior is the _____ theory. According to this theory, we attribute behavior either to an internal cause, which is called a _____ _____ , or to an external cause, which is called a _____ _____ .

3. Most people tend to _____ (overestimate/underestimate) the extent to which people's actions are influenced by social situations because their _____ is focused on the person. This tendency is called the _____ _____ . When explaining our own behavior, or that of someone we know well, this tendency is _____ (stronger/weaker). When observers view the world from others' perspectives, attributions are _____ (the same/reversed).

4. People in _____ (Western/East Asian) cultures more often attribute behavior to people's personal traits, while people in _____ (Western/East Asian) cultures are somewhat more sensitive to the power of the situation.

Give an example of the practical consequences of attributions.

STUDY TIP: To drive home the concept of the fundamental attribution error, think about a recent embarrassing moment. Perhaps you made an unkind remark that you later regretted. In explaining your behavior, you likely would say, "I was caught up in the moment," or "It was the people I was with." These are *external* (situational) attributions. Now think about how you would explain the same type of behavior in another person, especially someone you have just met. If you committed the fundamental attribution error, you would be less likely to "forgive" the person by making an external attribution. Instead, you would attribute it to personality and expect the person to behave similarly in the future.

APPLICATION:

5. Professor Washington's students did very poorly on the last exam. The tendency to make the fundamental attribution error might lead her to conclude that the class did poorly because
   a. the test was unfair.
   b. not enough time was given for students to complete the test.
   c. students were distracted by some social function on campus.
   d. students were unmotivated.

Objective 35-2: Discuss how attitudes and actions interact.

6. Feelings, often influenced by our beliefs, that predispose our responses are called _____ . When people focus on an issue and respond favorably to an argument, _____ _____ has occurred. Persuasion may also occur through the _____ (slower/faster) _____ as people respond to incidental cues such as a speaker's appearance.

7. Attitudes are especially likely to affect behavior when external influences are _____ , when the attitude is _____ , specific to the behavior, and easily _____ .

8. Many research studies demonstrate that our attitudes are strongly influenced by our _____ . One example of this is the tendency for people who agree to a small request to comply later with a larger one. This is the _____ - _____ - _____ - _____ phenomenon.

9. When you follow the social prescriptions for how you should act as, say, a college student, you are adopting a _____ .

10. Taking on a set of behaviors, or acting in a certain way, generally _____ (changes/does not change) people's attitudes.

11. According to _____ _____ theory, thoughts and feelings change because people are motivated to justify actions that would otherwise seem hypocritical. This theory was proposed by _____ .

12. Dissonance theory predicts that people induced (without coercion) to behave contrary to their true attitudes will be motivated to reduce the resulting _____ by changing their _____ .

STUDY TIP/APPLICATION: Cognitive dissonance theory and the foot-in-the-door phenomenon are two powerful examples of our attitudes following our actions. Think about these examples as you complete the following exercises.

13. a. Using the foot-in-the-door technique, how might you persuade a friend to take on an important, time-consuming task such as becoming treasurer of a ski club?

b. Suppose your roommate thinks climate change is nothing more than a hoax foisted by politicians on a gullible public. Using cognitive dissonance theory, how might you go about changing your roommate's attitude?

APPLICATIONS:

14. Which of the following is an example of the foot-in-the-door phenomenon?
a. To persuade a customer to buy a product, a store owner offers a small gift.
b. After agreeing to wear a small "Enforce Recycling" lapel pin, a woman agrees to collect signatures on a petition to make recycling required by law.
c. After offering to sell a car at a ridiculously low price, a car salesperson is forced to tell the customer the car will cost $1000 more.
d. All of these are examples.

15. Which of the following situations should produce the GREATEST cognitive dissonance?
a. A soldier is forced to carry out orders he finds disagreeable.
b. A student who loves animals has to dissect a cat in order to pass biology.
c. As part of an experiment, a participant is directed to deliver electric shocks to another person.
d. A student volunteers to debate an issue, taking the side he personally disagrees with.

16. Before she gave a class presentation favoring gun control legislation, Wanda opposed it. Her present attitude favoring such legislation can best be explained by
a. attribution theory.
b. cognitive dissonance theory.
c. role playing.
d. the fundamental attribution error.

Social Influence

Objective 35-3: Describe how culture affects our behavior.

17. The enduring behaviors, ideas, attitudes, values, and traditions of a group of people and transmitted from one generation to the next defines the group's _____ .

18. One landmark of human culture is the preservation of _____ , which is derived from our mastery of _____ , so that we can pass it on to future generations. Culture also enables an efficient division of _____ .

19. All cultural groups evolve their own rules for expected behavior, called _____ .

20. The speed at which culture changes is much _____ (faster/slower) than the pace of evolutionary changes in the human _____ _____ .

Objective 35-4: Describe automatic mimicry, and explain how conformity experiments reveal the power of social influence.

21. People take on the _____ tones of others around them. This natural tendency to automatically _____ others' expressions, postures, and voice tones is called the _____ _____ _____. This helps us to feel what they are feeling, referred to as _____ . It also helps explain why studies of British workers have revealed _____ _____ — sharing up and down moods.

22. The term that refers to the tendency to adjust one's behavior to coincide with some group standard is _____ .

23. The psychologist who first studied the effects of group pressure on conformity is _____ .

24. In this study, when the opinion of other group members was contradicted by objective evidence, research participants _____ (were/were not) willing to conform to the group opinion.

1	2	3

List the conditions under which we are more likely to conform.

25. One reason that people comply with social pressure is to gain approval or avoid rejection; this is called _____ _____ .

26. Another reason people comply is that they have genuinely been influenced by what they have learned from others; this type of influence is called _____ _____ _____ .

27. Compared with cultures that prize collectivism, cultures that prize _____ (individualism/collectivism) have _____ (higher/lower) conformity rates.

APPLICATION:

28. Maria recently heard a speech calling for a ban on aerosol sprays that endanger the earth's ozone layer. Maria's subsequent decision to stop using aerosol sprays is an example of

a. informational social influence.
b. normative social influence.
c. the fundamental attribution error.
d. the foot-in-the-door phenomenon.

Objective 35-5: Describe what Milgram's obedience experiments taught us about the power of social influence.

29. The classic social psychology studies of obedience were conducted by _____ . When ordered by the experimenter to electrically shock the "learner," the majority of participants (the "teachers") in these studies _____ (complied/refused). More recent studies have found that women's compliance rates in similar situations were _____ (higher than/lower than/similar to) men's.

List the conditions under which obedience was highest in Milgram's studies.

30. In getting people to administer increasingly larger shocks, Milgram was in effect applying the _____-_____ -_____-_____ technique.

31. The Milgram studies demonstrate that strong
_____ influences can
make _____ people
_____ to falsehoods and
commit cruel acts.

32. José is the one student member on his school's
board of trustees. At the board's first meeting,
José wants to disagree with the others on several
issues but in each case decides to say nothing.
Studies on conformity suggest all except one of
the following are factors in José's not speaking
up. Which one is NOT a factor?
   a. The board is a large group.
   b. The board is prestigious and most of its members are well known.
   c. The board members are already aware that
José and the student body disagree with them
on these issues.
   d. Because this is the first meeting José has
attended, he feels insecure and not fully competent.

33. Twenty-year-old Marge belonged to a sorority. During pledge week, she was ordered to
force potential members to strip in front of their
friends. Although Marge disapproved of asking
fellow students to embarrass themselves, she
did it anyway. She respected the sorority officers, and all her fellow sisters were also hazing
the pledges. How would Milgram explain Marge's
behavior?

Objective 35-6: Describe how our behavior is affected
by the presence of others.

34. The tendency to perform a task better when other
people are present is called _____
_____ . In general, people
become aroused in the presence of others, and
arousal enhances the correct response on a(n)
_____ (easy/difficult) task. Later
research revealed that arousal strengthens the
response that is most _____
in a given situation.

35. Researchers have found that the reactions of people in crowded situations are often
_____ (lessened/amplified).

36. Researchers found that people worked
_____ (harder/less hard) in a
team tug-of-war than they had in an individual
contest. This phenomenon has been called
_____ _____ . It
is especially common among men in
_____ cultures.

Give the reasons that this diminished effort may
occur in group tasks.

37. The feeling of anonymity and loss of self-restraint
that an individual may develop when in a group
is called _____ .

STUDY TIP: To help solidify the idea of social facilitation in your mind, think about sports you play—or
don't play (because you do not do well). Think about
your friends in similar situations, your children if you
are a parent. Then think about professional athletes.
Does the same hold true for the performing arts (acting, playing a musical instrument, dancing)? What
about your everyday activities?

38. Which of the following would most likely be subject to social facilitation?
   a. proofreading a page for spelling errors
   b. typing a letter with accuracy
   c. playing a difficult piece on a musical
instrument
   d. running quickly around a track

39. Concluding her presentation on deindividuation,
Renée notes that deindividuation is less likely in
situations that promote
   a. anonymity.
   b. decreased self-awareness.
   c. increased self-awareness.
   d. increased arousal.

Objective 35-7: Explain group polarization and groupthink, and describe how much power we have as individuals.

40. Over time, the initial differences between groups usually _____ (increase/decrease).

41. The enhancement of each group's prevailing tendency over time is called _____ _____ . Electronic discussions in _____ groups provide a medium for this tendency.

42. When the desire for group harmony overrides realistic thinking in individuals, the phenomenon known as _____ has occurred. This phenomenon is made possible by overconfidence, _____ , self-justification, and _____ _____ .

43. In considering the power of social influence, we cannot overlook the interaction of _____ _____ (the power of the situation) and _____ _____ (the power of the individual).

44. The power of one or two individuals to sway the opinion of the majority is called _____ _____ .

45. A minority opinion will have the most success in swaying the majority if it takes a stance that is _____ (unswerving/flexible).

APPLICATION:

46. Jane and Sandy were best friends in their first year of university. Jane joined a sorority; Sandy didn't. By the end of their last year, they found that they had less in common with each other than with the other members of their respective circles of friends. Which of the following phenomena most likely explains their feelings?
    a. group polarization   c. deindividuation
    b. groupthink   d. social facilitation

MODULE REVIEW:

47. According to cognitive dissonance theory, dissonance is most likely to occur when
    a. a person's behavior is not based on strongly held attitudes.
    b. two people have conflicting attitudes and find themselves in disagreement.
    c. an individual does something that is personally disagreeable.

    d. an individual is coerced into doing something that he or she does not want to do.

48. Which of the following phenomena is best explained by cognitive dissonance theory?
    a. group polarization
    b. the foot-in-the-door phenomenon
    c. normative social influence
    d. informational social influence

49. Which of the following is true?
    a. Attitudes and actions rarely correspond.
    b. Attitudes predict behavior about half the time.
    c. Attitudes are excellent predictors of behavior.
    d. Attitudes predict behavior under certain conditions.

50. Which of the following describes how we explain others' behavior as being due to internal dispositions or external situations?
    a. cognitive dissonance theory
    b. peripheral route persuasion
    c. central route persuasion
    d. attribution theory

51. *Culture* is best defined as
    a. the enduring behaviors, ideas, attitudes, values, and traditions of a group of people.
    b. a social system that is unique to people with a specific ethnic background.
    c. the set of enacted and enforced laws in a society.
    d. rules for expected behavior for a specific group of people at a certain moment in history.

52. In his study of obedience, Stanley Milgram found that the majority of participants
    a. refused to shock the learner even once.
    b. complied with the experiment until the "learner" first indicated pain.
    c. complied with the experiment until the "learner" began screaming in agony.
    d. complied with all the demands of the experiment.

53. Which of the following statements is true?
    a. Groups are almost never swayed by minority opinions.
    b. Group polarization is most likely to occur when group members frequently disagree with one another.
    c. Groupthink provides the consensus needed for effective decision making.
    d. A group that is like-minded will probably not change its opinions through discussion.

54. Conformity increased under which of the following conditions in Asch's studies of conformity?
    a. The group had three or more people.
    b. The group had high status.
    c. Individuals were made to feel insecure.
    d. All of these conditions increased conformity.

55. The phenomenon in which individuals lose their identity and relinquish normal restraints when they are part of a group is called
    a. groupthink.   c. empathy.
    b. social loafing.   d. deindividuation.

56. Subjects in Asch's line-judgment experiment conformed to the group standard when their judgments were observed by others but not when they were made in private. This tendency to conform in public demonstrates
    a. social facilitation.
    b. overjustification.
    c. informational social influence.
    d. normative social influence.

57. Based on findings from Milgram's obedience studies, participants would be LESS likely to follow the experimenter's orders when
    a. they hear the "learner" cry out in pain.
    b. they merely administer the test while someone else delivers the shocks.
    c. the "learner" is an older person or mentions having some physical problem.
    d. they see another person disobey instructions.

58. Which of the following most accurately states the effects of crowding on behavior?
    a. Crowding makes people irritable.
    b. Crowding sometimes intensifies people's reactions.
    c. Crowding promotes unselfish behavior.
    d. Crowding usually weakens the intensity of people's reactions.

59. Research has found that for a minority to succeed in swaying a majority, the minority must
    a. make up a sizable portion of the group.
    b. express its position as consistently as possible.
    c. express its position in the most extreme terms possible.
    d. be able to convince a key majority leader.

60. Which of the following conclusions did Milgram derive from his studies of obedience?
    a. Even ordinary people, without any particular hostility, can become agents in a destructive process.
    b. Under the proper circumstances, most people can suppress their natural aggressiveness.

    c. The need to be accepted by others is a powerful motivating force.
    d. He reached all of these conclusions.

61. Which of the following best summarizes the relative importance of personal control and social control of our behavior?
    a. Situational influences on behavior generally are much greater than personal influences.
    b. Situational influences on behavior generally are slightly greater than personal influences.
    c. Personal influences on behavior generally are much greater than situational influences.
    d. Situational and personal influences interact in determining our behavior.

62. Which of the following is important in promoting conformity in individuals?
    a. whether an individual's behavior will be observed by others in the group
    b. whether the individual is male or female
    c. the size of the group's meeting room
    d. whether the individual is of a higher status than other group members

63. Which of the following is most likely to promote groupthink?
    a. The group's leader fails to take a firm stance on an issue.
    b. A minority faction holds to its position.
    c. The group consults with various experts.
    d. Group polarization is evident.

TERMS AND CONCEPTS TO REMEMBER:
64. social psychology
65. attribution theory
66. fundamental attribution error
67. attitude
68. peripheral route persuasion
69. central route persuasion
70. foot-in-the-door phenomenon
71. role
72. cognitive dissonance theory
73. culture
74. norm
75. conformity
76. normative social influence
77. informational social influence
78. social facilitation
79. social loafing
80. deindividuation
81. group polarization
81. groupthink

Essay Question

The Panhellenic Council on your campus has asked you to make a presentation on the topic "Social Psychology" to all freshmen who have signed up to "rush" a fraternity or sorority. In a fit of cynicism following your rejection last year by a prestigious fraternity or sorority, you decide to speak on the negative influences of groups on the behavior of individuals. What will you discuss? (Use the space below to list the points you want to make, and organize them. Then write the essay on a separate sheet of paper.)

MODULE 36 Antisocial Relations

Prejudice

Objective 36-1: Define *prejudice*, and identify its social and emotional roots.

1. Prejudice is an _____ and usually _____ attitude toward a group that involves overgeneralized beliefs known as _____ .

2. Like all attitudes, prejudice is a mixture of _____ , _____ , and predispositions to _____ .

3. Prejudice is a negative _____ , and _____ is a negative _____ .

4. Americans today express _____ (less/the same/more) racial prejudice than they did some 50 years ago. Yet, as _____ prejudice wanes, _____ prejudice lingers, which may take the form of "_____ ," such as race-related traffic stops.

5. Blatant forms of prejudice _____ (have/have not) diminished. However, even people who deny holding prejudiced attitudes may carry negative _____ about race.

6. Studies of prejudice indicate that it is often an unconscious, or _____ , action. For example, people who more quickly associate good things with White names or faces also are the quickest to perceive _____ and apparent _____ in Black faces.

7. Our perceptions are also influenced by our _____ . Research has shown that _____ people with a flashed Black rather than White face makes them _____ (more/ less) likely to perceive a flashed tool as a gun.

8. Overt gender prejudice has also _____ (increased/decreased). However, worldwide, _____ (women/men) are more likely to live in poverty, and are more likely to be _____ . People also tend to perceive their fathers as being more _____ than their mothers.

9. Prejudice against _____ and _____ people still exists throughout most of the world. Without protection from hate crimes and discrimination, these people experience substantially higher rates for _____ and related disorders.

10. For those with money, power, and prestige, prejudice often serves as a means of _____ social inequalities.

11. The belief that people get what they deserve— that the good are rewarded and the bad punished—is expressed in the _____-_____ phenomenon.

12. Discrimination increases prejudice through the tendency of people to _____ victims for their plight.

13. Through our _____ , we associate ourselves with certain groups and contrast ourselves with others.

14. Prejudice is also fostered by the _____ _____ , a tendency to favor groups to which one belongs— called the _____ —while excluding others, or the _____ .

15. That prejudice derives from attempts to blame others for one's frustration is proposed by the _____ theory.

16. People who feel loved and supported become more _____ to and _____ of those who differ from them.

17. Prejudice is also nourished by _____ emotions.

Objective 36-2: Identify the cognitive roots of prejudice.

18. Research suggests that prejudice may also derive from _____ , the process by which we attempt to simplify our world by classifying people into groups. One by-product of this process is that people tend to _____ and _____ the similarity of those within a group; they perceive _____ _____ .

19. Our greater recognition of faces of our own race is the _____-_____ _____ , which emerges in infancy, between _____ of age.

20. Another factor that fosters the formation of group stereotypes and prejudice is the tendency to _____ from vivid or memorable cases.

21. The belief that people get what they deserve is based in part on _____ _____ , the tendency to believe that one would have foreseen how something turned out.

APPLICATIONS:

22. Students at State University are convinced that their school is better than any other; this most directly illustrates
    a. an ingroup bias.
    b. prejudice and discrimination.
    c. the scapegoat effect.
    d. the just-world phenomenon.

23. Alexis believes that all male athletes are self-centered and sexist. Her beliefs are an example of
    a. in-group bias.
    b. hindsight bias.
    c. stereotypes.
    d. own-age bias.

24. Ever since their cabin lost the camp softball competition, the campers have become increasingly hostile toward one camper in their cabin, blaming her for every problem in the cabin. This behavior is best explained in terms of
    a. the ingroup bias.
    b. prejudice.
    c. the scapegoat theory.
    d. catharsis.

25. Given the tendency of people to categorize information according to preformed schemas, which of the following stereotypes would Juan, a 65-year-old political liberal and fitness enthusiast, be most likely to have?
    a. "People who exercise regularly are very extraverted."
    b. "All political liberals are advocates of a reduced defense budget."
    c. "Young people today have no sense of responsibility."
    d. "Older people are lazy."

Aggression

Objective 36-3: Explain how psychology's definition of *aggression* differs from everyday usage, and identify the biological factors that make us more prone to hurt one another.

26. Aggressive behavior is defined by psychologists as _____ _____ . Thus, psychologists _____ (do/do not) consider assertive salespeople to be aggressive.

27. Like other behaviors, aggression emerges from the interaction of _____ and _____ .

28. Today, most psychologists _____ (do/do not) consider human aggression to be instinctive.

29. In humans, aggressiveness _____ (varies/does not vary) greatly from culture to culture, era to era, and person to person.

30. That there are genetic influences on aggression can be shown by the fact that many species of animals have been _____ for aggressiveness.

31. Twin studies suggest that genes _____ (do/do not) influence human aggression. One genetic marker of those who commit the most violence is the _____ chromosome. Another marker is the _____ _____ _____ gene, which helps break down neurotransmitters such as _____ and serotonin.

32. There _____ (is/is not) one spot in the brain that controls aggression. Aggression is a complex behavior that _____ (does/does not) occur in particular contexts. However, animal and human brains have _____ _____ that, given provocation, will either inhibit or facilitate aggression.

33. Studies of violent criminals reveal diminished activity in the brain's _____ _____, which play an important role in controlling _____.

34. The aggressive behavior of animals can be manipulated by altering the levels of the hormone _____. When this level is _____ (increased/decreased), aggressive tendencies are reduced.

35. Humans are _____ (more/less) sensitive to hormonal changes.

36. One drug that unleashes aggressive responses to provocation is _____.

Objective 36-4: Outline psychological and social-cultural factors that may trigger aggressive behavior.

37. According to the _____-_____ principle, inability to achieve a goal leads to anger, which may generate aggression.

38. Other aversive stimuli can provoke hostility, including _____ _____.

39. Aggressive behavior can be learned through _____, as shown by the fact that people use aggression where they've found it pays, and through _____ of others.

40. Parent-training programs often advise parents to avoid _____ violence by screaming and hitting. Instead, parents should _____ desirable behaviors and frame statements _____.

41. Crime rates are higher in countries in which there is a large disparity between those who are _____ and those who are _____. High violence rates also are typical of cultures and families in which there is minimal _____ _____.

42. Repeatedly viewing on-screen violence may create _____ _____ to which people respond when they are in new situations or are uncertain how to act.

Comment on the effects of viewing sexual violence on attitudes and behavior.

Summarize the findings of the study in which undergraduates viewed either sexually explicit films or nonerotic films.

43. Video games can _____ aggressive thoughts, decrease _____, and increase _____.

44. Kids who play a lot of violent video games see the world as more _____, get into more _____ and _____, and earn poorer _____.

45. Many factors contribute to aggression, including _____ factors, such as an increase in testosterone; _____ factors, such as frustration; and _____ factors, such as deindividuation.

APPLICATIONS:

46. Summarizing his report on the biology of aggression, Sam notes that
    a. biology does not significantly influence aggression.
    b. when one identical twin has a violent temperament, the other member of the twin pair rarely does.
    c. hormones and alcohol influence the neural systems that control aggression.
    d. testosterone reduces dominance behaviors in animals.

47. After waiting in line for an hour to buy concert tickets, Teresa is told that the concert is sold out. In her anger she pounds her fist on the ticket counter, frightening the clerk. Teresa's behavior is best explained by
    a. evolutionary psychology.
    b. deindividuation.
    c. genetics.
    d. the frustration-aggression principle.

MODULE REVIEW:

48. Violent criminals often have diminished activity in the _____ of the brain, which play(s) an important role in _____.
    a. occipital lobes; aggression
    b. hypothalamus; hostility
    c. frontal lobes; controlling impulses
    d. temporal lobes; patience

49. *Aggression* is defined as behavior that
    a. hurts another person.
    b. is intended to hurt another person.
    c. is hostile, passionate, and produces physical injury.
    d. has all of these characteristics.

50. Which of the following is true about aggression?
    a. It varies too much to be instinctive in humans.
    b. It is just one instinct among many.
    c. It is instinctive but shaped by learning.
    d. It is the most important human instinct.

51. Research studies have found a positive correlation between aggressive tendencies in animals and levels of the hormone
    a. estrogen.   c. noradrenaline.
    b. adrenaline.   d. testosterone.

52. Research studies have indicated that the tendency of viewers to see sexual violence as less serious is
    a. increased by exposure to pornography.
    b. not changed after exposure to pornography.
    c. decreased in men by exposure to pornography.
    d. decreased in both men and women by exposure to pornography.

53. Which of the following was NOT mentioned in the text discussion of the roots of prejudice?
    a. people's tendency to overestimate the similarity of people within groups
    b. people's tendency to assume that exceptional, or especially memorable, individuals are unlike the majority of members of a group
    c. people's tendency to assume that the world is just and that people get what they deserve
    d. people's tendency to discriminate against those they view as "outsiders"

54. The belief that those who suffer deserve their fate is expressed in the
    a. just-world phenomenon.
    b. phenomenon of ingroup bias.
    c. frustration-aggression principle.
    d. cross-race effect.

55. Which of the following is an example of implicit prejudice?
    a. Jake, who is White, gives higher evaluations to essays he believes to be written by Blacks than to White-authored essays.
    b. Carol believes that White people are arrogant.
    c. Brad earns more than Jane, despite having the same skills, performance level, and seniority.
    d. In certain countries, women are not allowed to drive.

56. We tend to perceive the members of an ingroup as _____ and the members of an outgroup as _____.

    a. similar to one another; different from one another

    b. different from one another; similar to one another

    c. above average in ability; below average in ability

    d. below average in ability; above average in ability

57. Regarding the influence of alcohol and testosterone on aggressive behavior, which of the following is true?

    a. Consumption of alcohol increases aggressive behavior; injections of testosterone reduce aggressive behavior.

    b. Consumption of alcohol reduces aggressive behavior; injections of testosterone increase aggressive behavior.

    c. Consumption of alcohol and injections of testosterone both promote aggressive behavior.

    d. Consumption of alcohol and injections of testosterone both reduce aggressive behavior.

58. Research studies have shown that frequent exposure to sexually explicit films

    a. leads to less aggressive behavior toward women.

    b. diminishes the attitude that sexual violence is serious.

    c. may lead individuals to see their partners as more attractive.

    d. may produce all of these effects.

59. Most researchers agree that

    a. media violence is a factor in aggression.

    b. there is a negative correlation between media violence and aggressiveness.

    c. paradoxically, watching excessive pornography ultimately diminishes an individual's aggressive tendencies.

    d. media violence is too unreal to promote aggression in viewers.

60. People with power and status may become prejudiced because

    a. they tend to justify the social inequalities between themselves and others.

    b. those with less status and power tend to resent them.

    c. those with less status and power appear less capable.

    d. they feel proud and are boastful of their achievements.

TERMS AND CONCEPTS TO REMEMBER:

61. prejudice

62. stereotype

63. discrimination

64. just-world phenomenon

65. ingroup

66. outgroup

67. ingroup bias

68. scapegoat theory

69. other-race effect

70. aggression

71. frustration-aggression principle

72. social script

MODULE 37 Prosocial Relations

Attraction

Objective 37-1: Explain why we befriend or fall in love with some people but not with others.

1. A prerequisite for, and perhaps the most powerful predictor of, attraction is _____ .

2. When people are repeatedly exposed to unfamiliar stimuli, their liking of the stimuli _____ (increases/decreases). This phenomenon is the _____ _____ effect.

3. Compared with relationships formed in person, Internet-formed relationships are _____ (more/less) likely to last and be satisfying. Studies of people who engage in _____ dating reveal that observers can read a _____ (woman's/man's) level of romantic interest more accurately than a _____ (woman's/man's).

4. Our first impression of another person is most influenced by the person's _____ .

5. In a sentence, list several of the characteristics that physically attractive people are judged to possess: _____ _____ .

6. A person's attractiveness _____ (is/is not) strongly related to his or her self-esteem or happiness.

7. Cross-cultural research reveals that men judge women as more attractive if they have a

_____ , _____ appearance, whereas women judge men who appear _____ , _____ , _____ , and as more attractive. When people rate opposite-sex faces and bodies separately, the _____ tends to be the better predictor of overall physical attractiveness. A person is also judged more physically attractive if he or she has appealing

_____ .

8. Compared with strangers, friends and couples are more likely to be similar in terms of

_____

_____ .

Explain what a reward theory of attraction is and how it can account for the three predictors of liking—proximity, attractiveness, and similarity.

9. Ahmed and Monique are on a blind date. Which of the following will probably be MOST influential in determining whether they like each other?
   a. their personalities
   b. their beliefs
   c. their social skills
   d. their physical attractiveness

10. Having read this section, which of the following is best borne out by research on attraction?
   a. Birds of a feather flock together.
   b. Opposites attract.
   c. Familiarity breeds contempt.
   d. Absence makes the heart grow fonder.

Objective 37-2: Describe how romantic love typically changes as time passes.

11. Two types of love are _____ love and _____ love.

12. According to the two-factor theory, emotions have two components: physical _____ and a _____ label. When college men were placed in an aroused state, their feelings toward an attractive woman _____ (were/were not) more positive than those of men who had not been aroused.

13. As love matures, the flood of passion-facilitating hormones (testosterone, _____ , adrenaline) subsides and another hormone, _____ , supports feelings of trust, calmness, and bonding with the mate.

14. Companionate love is promoted by _____ —mutual sharing and giving by both partners. Another key ingredient of loving relationships is the revealing of intimate aspects of ourselves through _____ . A third key to enduring love is _____

_____ .

APPLICATION:

15. Opening her mail, Joan discovers a romantic greeting card from her boyfriend. According to the two-factor theory, she is likely to feel the most intense romantic feelings if, prior to reading the card, she has just
   a. completed her daily run.
   b. finished reading a long section in her psychology textbook.
   c. awakened from a nap.
   d. finished eating lunch.

Altruism

Objective 37-3: Identify the times when people are most—and least—likely to help.

16. An unselfish regard for the welfare of others is called _____ .

Give an example of altruism.

17. According to Darley and Latané, people will help only if a three-stage decision-making process is completed: Bystanders must first _____ the incident, then _____ it as an emergency, and finally _____ _____ for helping.

18. When people who overheard a seizure victim calling for help thought others were hearing the same plea, they were _____ (more/less) likely to go to his aid than when they thought no one else was aware of the emergency.

19. In a series of staged accidents, Latané and Darley found that a bystander was _____ (more/less) likely to help when more people shared responsibility for helping, that is, when there was a _____ _____ .

This phenomenon has been called the _____ _____ .

Identify the circumstances in which a person is most likely to offer help during an emergency.

STUDY TIP: As with other concepts, altruism is best understood by relating it to your own experiences. Can you think of instances of altruism in your home town? At school? Have you personally stopped to help a person who seemed to be in need—for example, an older woman struggling to carry groceries to her car? What are some other examples of truly altruistic behavior?

Objective 37-4: Discuss how social exchange theory and social norms explain helping behavior.

20. The idea that social behavior aims to maximize rewards and minimize costs is proposed by the _____ _____ theory.

21. One rule of social behavior tells us to return help to those who have helped us; this is the _____ norm.

22. Another rule tells us to help those who need our help; this is the _____-_____ norm.

Peacemaking

Objective 37-5: Explain how social traps and mirror-image perceptions fuel social conflict.

23. A perceived incompatibility of actions, goals, or ideas is called a _____ . This perception can take place between _____ at war, _____ groups feuding within a society, or _____ sparring in a relationship.

24. Situations in which conflicting parties become caught in mutually destructive behavior by pursuing their own self-interests are called _____ _____ .

25. The distorted images people in conflict form of each other are called _____-_____ perceptions. These perceptions can often feed a vicious cycle of hostility. As a result, perceptions can become _____ _____ .

Objective 37-6: Discuss how we can transform feelings of prejudice, aggression, and conflict into attitudes that promote peace.

26. Establishing contact between two conflicting groups _____ (is/is not) always sufficient to resolve conflict.

27. In Muzafer Sherif's study, two conflicting groups of campers were able to resolve their conflicts by working together on projects in which they shared _____ goals. Shared _____ breed solidarity, as demonstrated by a surge in the use of the word _____ in the weeks after 9/11.

28. When conflicts arise, a third-party _____ may facilitate communication and promote understanding.

29. Charles Osgood has advanced a strategy of conciliation called GRIT, which stands for _____ and _____ in _____-_____ . The key to this method is each side's offering of a small _____ gesture in order to increase mutual trust and cooperation.

APPLICATIONS:

30. Mr. and Mrs. Samuels are constantly fighting, and each perceives the other as hard-headed and insensitive. Their conflict is being fueled by
    a. self-disclosure.
    b. inequity.
    c. a social trap.
    d. mirror-image perceptions.

31. Which of the following strategies would be MOST likely to foster positive feelings between two conflicting groups?
    a. Take steps to reduce the likelihood of mirror-image perceptions.
    b. Separate the groups so that tensions diminish.
    c. Increase the amount of contact between the two conflicting groups.
    d. Have the groups work on a superordinate goal.

MODULE REVIEW:

32. Increasing the number of people that are present during an emergency tends to
    a. increase the likelihood that people will cooperate in rendering assistance.
    b. decrease the empathy that people feel for the victim.
    c. increase the role that social norms governing helping will play.
    d. decrease the likelihood that anyone will help.

33. The mere exposure effect demonstrates that
    a. familiarity breeds contempt.
    b. opposites attract.
    c. birds of a feather flock together.
    d. familiarity breeds fondness.

34. In one experiment, college men were physically aroused and then introduced to an attractive woman. Compared with men who had not been aroused, these men
    a. reported more positive feelings toward the woman.
    b. reported more negative feelings toward the woman.
    c. were ambiguous about their feelings toward the woman.
    d. were more likely to feel that the woman was "out of their league" in terms of attractiveness.

35. The deep affection that is felt in long-lasting relationships is called _____ love; this feeling is fostered in relationships in which _____ .
    a. passionate; there is equity between the partners
    b. passionate; traditional roles are maintained
    c. companionate; there is equity between the partners
    d. companionate; traditional roles are maintained

36. Which of the following is associated with an increased tendency on the part of a bystander to offer help in an emergency situation?
    a. being in a good mood
    b. having recently needed help and not received it
    c. observing someone as he or she refuses to offer help
    d. being a female

37. Most people prefer mirror-image photographs of their faces. This is best explained by
    a. the principle of equity.
    b. the principle of self-disclosure.
    c. the mere exposure effect.
    d. mirror-image perceptions.

38. Research studies indicate that in an emergency situation, the presence of others often
    a. prevents people from even noticing the situation.
    b. prevents people from interpreting an unusual event as an emergency.
    c. prevents people from assuming responsibility for assisting.
    d. leads to all of these behaviors.

39. Which of the following factors is the MOST powerful predictor of friendship?
    a. similarity in age
    b. common racial and religious background
    c. similarity in physical attractiveness
    d. physical proximity

40. When male students in an experiment were told that a woman to whom they would be speaking had been instructed to act in a friendly or unfriendly way, most of them subsequently attributed her behavior to
    a. the situation.
    b. the situation *and* her personal disposition.
    c. her personal disposition.
    d. their own skill or lack of skill in a social situation.

41. Which of the following BEST describes how GRIT works?
    a. The fact that two sides in a conflict have great respect for the other's strengths prevents further escalation of the problem.
    b. The two sides engage in a series of reciprocated conciliatory acts.
    c. The two sides agree to have their differences settled by a neutral, third-party mediator.
    d. The two sides engage in cooperation in those areas in which shared goals are possible.

TERMS AND CONCEPTS TO REMEMBER:

42. mere exposure effect
43. passionate love
44. companionate love
45. equity
46. self-disclosure
47. altruism
48. bystander effect
49. social exchange theory
50. reciprocity norm
51. social-responsibility norm
52. conflict
53. social trap
54. mirror-image perceptions
55. self-fulfilling prophecy
56. superordinate goals
57. GRIT

Before You Move On

Matching Items

Match each term with the appropriate definition or description.

Terms

_____ 1. social facilitation
_____ 2. social loafing
_____ 3. bystander effect
_____ 4. conformity
_____ 5. ingroup bias
_____ 6. normative social influence
_____ 7. informational social influence
_____ 8. group polarization
_____ 9. stereotype
_____ 10. attribution
_____ 11. altruism
_____ 12. mere exposure effect
_____ 13. central route persuasion
_____ 14. social script

Definitions or Descriptions

a. a causal explanation for someone's behavior
b. a generalized belief about a group of people
c. people work less hard in a group
d. performance is improved by an audience
e. the tendency to favor one's own group
f. the effect of social approval or disapproval
g. adjusting one's behavior to coincide with a group standard
h. group discussion enhances prevailing tendencies
i. the effect of accepting others' opinions about something
j. unselfish regard for others
k. the tendency that a person is less likely to help someone in need when others are present
l. the increased liking of a stimulus that results from repeated exposure to it
m. responding favorably to arguments as a result of systematic thinking about an issue
n. a culturally specific model of how to act in a given situation

True–False Items

Indicate whether each statement is true or false by placing T or F in the blank next to the item.

_____ 1. When explaining another's behavior, we tend to underestimate situational influences.

_____ 2. When explaining our own behavior, we tend to underestimate situational influences.

_____ 3. An individual is more likely to conform when the rest of the group is unanimous.

_____ 4. The tendency of people to conform is influenced by their culture.

_____ 5. A bystander is more likely to offer help in an emergency if other bystanders are present.

_____ 6. Counterattitudinal behavior (acting contrary to our beliefs) often leads to attitude change.

_____ 7. Human aggression is instinctual.

_____ 8. Group polarization tends to prevent groupthink from occurring.

_____ 9. Crowded conditions usually subdue people's reactions.

_____ 10. When individuals lose their sense of identity in a group, they often become more uninhibited.

_____ 11. Peripheral route persuasion allows for fast responding to an issue.

_____ 12. In our relations with others of similar status, we tend to give more than we receive.

Cross-Check

As you learned in Module 2, reviewing and overlearning of material are important to the learning process. After you have written the definitions of the key terms in this unit, you should complete the crossword puzzle to ensure that you can reverse the process—recognize the term, given the definition.

ACROSS

4. A generalized belief about a group of people.

5. A strategy of conflict resolution in which both groups make conciliatory gestures. (abbrev.)

6. Theory that proposes that prejudice provides an outlet for anger by finding someone to blame.

8. The tendency to change one's attitudes to coincide with those held by a group.

9. An unselfish regard for the welfare of others.

12. Mutual giving and receiving in a relationship.

13. Type of love that refers to an aroused state of intense positive absorption in another person.

14. Perceived incompatibility between individuals or groups.

15. Personal beliefs and feelings that influence our behavior.

DOWN

1. A person's tendency not to offer help to someone if others are present.

2. Type of social influence that results when one goes along with a group when one is unsure of what to do.

3. Psychological discomfort we experience when two of our thoughts conflict.

7. Phenomenon whereby people who agree to a small request are more likely to comply later with a larger request.

8. Type of love in which there is a deep, enduring attachment.

10. Our tendency to underestimate situational influences and overestimate dispositional influences upon the behavior of others is the _____ attribution error.

11. A causal explanation of a given behavior.

Answers

Social Thinking and Social Influence

1. social psychologists

Social Thinking

2. attribution; dispositional attribution; situational attribution

3. underestimate; attention; fundamental attribution error; weaker; reversed

4. Western; East Asian

Our attributions—to individuals' dispositions or to situations—have important practical consequences. A hurtful remark from an acquaintance, for example, is more likely to be forgiven if it is attributed to a temporary situation than to a mean disposition.

5. **d.** is the answer. The fundamental attribution error refers to the tendency to underestimate situational influences in favor of this type of dispositional attribution when explaining the behavior of other people.
   a., b., & c. These are situational attributions.

6. attitudes; central route persuasion; faster; peripheral route

7. minimal; stable; recalled

8. actions (or behavior); foot-in-the-door

9. role

10. changes

11. cognitive dissonance; Leon Festinger

12. dissonance; attitudes

13. No single answer is correct. A possible answer for a. is to ask the friend to check some figures from the monthly expenses. For b., you might get your roommate to debate the issue and have him or her argue that climate change is a major concern.

14. **b.** is the answer. In the foot-in-the-door phenomenon, compliance with a small initial request, such as wearing a lapel pin, later is followed by compliance with a much larger request, such as collecting petition signatures.

15. **d.** is the answer. In this situation, the counterattitudinal behavior is performed voluntarily and cannot be attributed to the demands of the situation.
    a., b., & c. In all of these situations, the counterattitudinal behaviors should not arouse much dissonance because they can be attributed to the demands of the situation.

16. **b.** is the answer. Dissonance theory focuses on what happens when our actions contradict our attitudes.
    a. Attribution theory holds that we give causal explanations for others' behavior, often by crediting either the situation or people's dispositions.
    c. Role playing would mean she is simply pretending to favor gun control legislation. Nothing in the question indicates she's pretending.
    d. The fundamental attribution error refers to the tendency to underestimate the influence of the situation.

Social Influence

17. culture

18. innovation; language; labor

19. norms

20. faster; gene pool

21. emotional; mimic; chameleon effect; empathy; mood linkage

22. conformity

23. Solomon Asch

24. were

We are more likely to conform when we are made to feel incompetent or insecure, when the group has at least three people, when everyone else in the group agrees, when we admire the group's status and attractiveness, when we have not made a prior commitment to any response, when others will observe our behavior, and when our culture encourages respect for social standards.

25. normative social influence

26. informational social influence

27. individualism; lower

28. **a.** is the answer. As illustrated by Maria's decision to stop buying aerosol products, informational social influence occurs when people have genuinely been influenced by what they have learned from others.
    b. Had Maria's behavior been motivated by the desire to avoid rejection or to gain social approval (which we have no reason to suspect is the case), it would have been an example of normative social influence.
    c. The fundamental attribution error is the tendency to underestimate the influence of the situation.
    d. The foot-in-the-door phenomenon is the tendency for people who agree to a small request to comply later with a larger request.

29. Stanley Milgram; complied; similar to

Obedience was highest when the person giving the orders was close at hand and perceived to be a legitimate authority figure, the authority figure was supported by a prestigious institution, the victim was depersonalized or at a distance, and when there were no role models for defiance.

30. foot-in-the-door

31. social; ordinary; conform

32. **c.** is the answer. Prior commitment to an opposing view generally tends to work against conformity. In contrast, large group size, prestigiousness of a group, and an individual's feelings of incompetence and insecurity all strengthen the tendency to conform.

33. Milgram would say that Marge's behavior was a product of the situation, not her personal traits. She respected the officers of the sorority and everyone else was participating in the hazing.

34. social facilitation; easy; likely

35. amplified

36. less hard; social loafing; individualist

Social loafing is caused because as part of a group, people feel less accountable, and they view their individual contributions as dispensable. Also, because group members share benefits equally no matter what their contribution, some people may free ride on others' efforts.

37. deindividuation

38. **d.** is the answer. Social facilitation, or better performance in the presence of others, occurs for easy tasks but not for more difficult ones. For tasks such as proofreading, typing, playing an instrument, or giving a speech, the arousal resulting from the presence of others can lead to mistakes.

39. **c.** is the answer. Deindividuation involves the loss of self-awareness and self-restraint in group situations that involve arousal and anonymity, so (a.), (c.), and (d.) cannot be right.

40. increase

41. group polarization; Internet

42. groupthink; conformity; group polarization

43. social control; personal control

44. minority influence

45. unswerving

46. **a.** is the answer. Group polarization means that the tendencies within a group—and therefore the differences among groups—grow stronger over time. Thus, because the differences between the sorority and nonsorority students have increased, Jane and Sandy are likely to have little in common.

b. Groupthink is the tendency for realistic decision making to disintegrate when the desire for group harmony is strong.
c. Deindividuation is the loss of self-restraint and self-awareness that sometimes occurs when one is part of a group.
d. Social facilitation refers to improved performance of a task in the presence of others.

Module Review:

47. **c.** is the answer. Cognitive dissonance is the tension we feel when we are aware of a discrepancy between our thoughts and actions, as would occur when we do something we find distasteful.
a. Dissonance requires strongly held attitudes, which must be perceived as not fitting behavior.
b. Dissonance is a personal cognitive process.
d. In such a situation the person is less likely to experience dissonance, since the action can be attributed to "having no choice."

48. **b.** is the answer.
a. Group polarization involves group opinions.
c. & d. Normative and informational social influence have to do with reasons for influence.

49. **d.** is the answer. Our attitudes are more likely to guide our actions when other influences are minimal, especially when the attitude is stable, specific to the behavior, and easily recalled. The presence of other people would more likely be an outside factor that would lessen the likelihood of actions being guided by attitude.

50. **d.** is the answer.

51. **a.** is the answer

52. **d.** is the answer. In Milgram's initial experiments, more than 60 percent of the participants complied fully with the experiment.

53. **d.** is the answer. In such groups, discussion usually strengthens prevailing opinion; this phenomenon is known as group polarization.
a. Minority opinions, especially if consistently and firmly stated, can sway the majority in a group.
b. Group polarization, or the strengthening of a group's prevailing tendencies, is most likely in groups where members agree.
c. When groupthink occurs, there is so much consensus that decision making becomes less effective.

54. **d.** is the answer.

55. **d.** is the answer.
a. Groupthink refers to the mode of thinking that occurs when the desire for group harmony overrides realistic and critical thinking.

b. Social loafing refers to the tendency for people in a group to exert less effort when pooling their efforts

c. Empathy is feeling what another person feels.

56. **d.** is the answer. Normative social influence refers to influence on behavior that comes from a desire to look good to others. Participants who were observed conformed because they didn't want to look like oddballs.

a. Social facilitation involves performing tasks better or faster in the presence of others.

b. Overjustification occurs when a person is rewarded for doing something that is already enjoyable.

c. Informational social influence is the tendency of individuals to accept the opinions of others, especially in situations where they themselves are unsure.

57. **d.** is the answer. Role models for defiance reduce levels of obedience.

a. & c. These did not result in diminished obedience.

b. This "depersonalization" of the victim resulted in increased obedience.

58. **b.** is the answer.

a. & c. Crowding may amplify irritability or unselfish tendencies that are already present. Crowding does not, however, produce these reactions as a general effect.

d. In fact, just the opposite is true. Crowding often intensifies people's reactions.

59. **b.** is the answer.

a. Even if they made up a sizable portion of the group, although still a minority, their numbers would not be as important as their consistency.

c. & d. These aspects of minority influence were not discussed in the text; however, they are not likely to help a minority sway a majority.

60. **a.** is the answer.

61. **d.** is the answer. The text emphasizes the ways in which personal and social controls interact in influencing behavior. It does not suggest that one factor is more influential than the other.

62. **a.** is the answer. As Solomon Asch's experiments demonstrated, individuals are more likely to conform when they are being observed by others in the group. The other factors were not discussed in the text and probably would not promote conformity.

63. **d.** is the answer. Group polarization, or the enhancement of a group's prevailing attitudes, promotes groupthink, which leads to the disintegration of critical thinking.

a. Groupthink is more likely when a leader highly favors an idea, which may make members reluctant to disagree.

b. A strong minority faction would probably have the opposite effect: It would diminish group harmony while promoting critical thinking.

c. Consulting experts would discourage groupthink by exposing the group to other opinions.

Terms and Concepts to Remember:

64. **Social psychology** is the scientific study of how we think about, influence, and relate to one another.

65. **Attribution theory** deals with our causal explanations of behavior. We attribute behavior to the individual's disposition or to the situation.

66. The **fundamental attribution error** is our tendency to underestimate the impact of situations and to overestimate the impact of personal dispositions upon the behavior of others.

67. **Attitudes** are feelings, often influenced by our beliefs, that may predispose us to respond in particular ways to objects, people, and events.

68. **Peripheral route persuasion** occurs when people are influenced by incidental cues, such as a speaker's appearance.

69. **Central route persuasion** occurs when interested people focus on the arguments and respond with favorable thoughts

70. The **foot-in-the-door phenomenon** is the tendency for people who agree to a small request to comply later with a larger request.

71. A **role** is a set of explanations (norms) about how people in a specific social position ought to behave.

72. **Cognitive dissonance theory** refers to the theory that we act to reduce the psychological discomfort (dissonance) we experience when our behavior conflicts with what we think and feel, or more generally, when two of our thoughts are inconsistent. This is frequently accomplished by changing our attitude rather than our behavior.

Memory aid: Dissonance means "lack of harmony." **Cognitive dissonance** occurs when two thoughts, or cognitions, are at variance with one another.

73. A **culture** is the enduring behaviors, ideas, attitudes, values, and traditions shared by a group of people and transmitted from one generation to the next.

74. A **norm** is an understood rule for accepted and expected behavior.

75. **Conformity** is the tendency to change one's thinking or behavior to coincide with a group standard.

76. **Normative social influence** refers to the pressure on individuals to conform to avoid rejection or gain social approval.

    Memory aid: *Normative* means "based on a norm, or pattern, regarded as typical for a specific group." **Normative social influence** is the pressure groups exert on the individual to behave in ways acceptable to the group standard.

77. **Informational social influence** results when one is willing to accept others' opinions about reality.

78. **Social facilitation** is stronger performance of simple or well-learned tasks that occurs when other people are present.

79. **Social loafing** is the tendency for individual effort to be diminished when one is part of a group working toward a common goal.

80. **Deindividuation** refers to the loss of self-restraint and self-awareness that sometimes occurs in group situations that foster arousal and anonymity.

    Memory aid: As a prefix, *de-* indicates reversal or undoing. To **deindividuate** is to undo one's individuality.

81. **Group polarization** refers to the enhancement of a group's prevailing tendencies through discussion, which often has the effect of accentuating the group's differences from other groups.

    Memory aid: To *polarize* is to "cause thinking to concentrate about two poles, or contrasting positions."

82. **Groupthink** refers to the unrealistic thought processes and decision making that occur within groups when the desire for group harmony overrides a realistic appraisal of alternatives.

    Example: The psychological tendencies of overconfidence, self-justification, conformity, and group polarization foster the development of the "team spirit" mentality known as **groupthink**.

Essay Question

Your discussion might focus on some of the following topics: normative social influence; conformity, which includes suggestibility; obedience; group polarization; and groupthink.

As a member of any group with established social norms, individuals will often act in ways that enable them to avoid rejection or gain social approval. Thus, a fraternity or sorority pledge would probably be very suggestible and likely to eventually conform to the attitudes and norms projected by the group—or be rejected socially. In extreme cases of pledge hazing, acute social pressures may lead to atypical and antisocial individual behaviors—for example, on the part of pledges complying with the demands of senior members of the fraternity or sorority. Over time, meetings and discussions will probably enhance the group's prevailing attitudes (group polarization). This may lead to the unrealistic and irrational decision making that is groupthink. The potentially negative consequences of groupthink depend on the issues being discussed, but may include a variety of socially destructive behaviors.

MODULE 36 Antisocial Relations

Prejudice

1. unjustifiable; negative; stereotypes
2. beliefs; emotions; action
3. attitude; discrimination; behavior
4. less; overt; subtle; "microaggressions"
5. have; associations
6. implicit; anger; threat
7. expectations; priming; more
8. decreased; women; illiterate; intelligent
9. gay; lesbian; depression
10. justifying
11. just-world
12. blame
13. social identities
14. ingroup bias; ingroup; outgroup
15. scapegoat
16. open; accepting
17. negative
18. categorization; stereotype; overestimate; outgroup homogeneity
19. other-race effect (cross-race effect or own-race bias); 3 and 9 months
20. overgeneralize
21. hindsight bias
22. **a.** is the answer.
    b. Prejudices are unjustifiable and usually negative attitudes toward other groups. They may result from an ingroup bias, but they are probably not why students favor their own university.
    c. Scapegoats are individuals or groups toward which prejudice is directed as an outlet for the anger of frustrated individuals or groups.

d. The just-world phenomenon is the tendency for people to believe that others "get what they deserve."

23. **c.** is the answer.
    a. The ingroup bias is the tendency to favor one's own group.
    b. Hindsight bias contributes to the belief that people get what they deserve.
    d. The own-age bias refers to better recognition memory for faces of one's own age group.

24. **c.** is the answer. According to the scapegoat theory, when things go wrong, people look for someone on whom to take out their anger and frustration.
    a. These campers are venting their frustration on a member of their *own* cabin group (although this is not always the case with scapegoats).
    b. Prejudice refers to an unjustifiable and usually negative attitude toward another group.
    d. Catharsis is the idea that releasing aggressive energy relieves aggressive urges.

25. **c.** is the answer. People tend to overestimate the similarity of people within groups other than their own. Thus, Juan is not likely to form stereotypes of fitness enthusiasts (a.), political liberals (b.), or older adults (d.), because these are groups to which he belongs.

Aggression

26. any physical or verbal behavior intended to hurt or destroy; do not

27. biology; experience

28. do not

29. varies

30. bred

31. do; Y; monoamine oxidase A (MAOA); dopamine

32. is not; does; neural systems

33. frontal lobes; impulses

34. testosterone; decreased

35. less

36. alcohol

37. frustration-aggression

38. physical pain, personal insults, foul odors, hot temperatures, cigarette smoke, crowding

39. rewards; observation (or imitation)

40. modeling; reinforce; positively

41. rich; poor; father care

42. social scripts

Pornography that portrays sexual aggression as pleasurable for the victim increases the acceptance of coercion in sexual relationships. Repeatedly watching X-rated films and Internet pornography also makes sexual aggression seem less serious.

The study found that after viewing sexually explicit films for several weeks, undergraduates were more likely to recommend a lighter prison sentence for a convicted rapist than were those who viewed nonerotic films.

43. prime; empathy; aggression

44. hostile; arguments; fights; grades

45. biological; psychological; social-cultural

46. **c.** is the answer.
    a. & b. Biology is an important factor in aggressive behavior. This includes genetics, which means identical twins would have similar temperaments.
    d. Just the opposite is true.

47. **d.** is the answer. According to the frustration-aggression principle, the blocking of an attempt to achieve some goal—in Teresa's case, buying concert tickets—creates anger and can generate aggression.
    a. Evolutionary psychology maintains that aggressive behavior is a genetically based drive. Teresa's behavior clearly was a reaction to a specific situation.
    b. Deindividuation refers to loss of self-restraint in group situations that foster arousal. Teresa's action has only to do with her frustration.
    c. Nothing in the question suggests that Teresa inherited a tendency to be aggressive or to lose her temper easily.

Module Review:

48. **c.** is the answer.

49. **b.** is the answer. Aggression is any behavior, physical or verbal, that is intended to hurt or destroy.
    a. A person may accidentally be hurt in a nonaggressive incident; aggression does not necessarily prove hurtful.
    c. Verbal behavior, which does not result in physical injury, may also be aggressive. Moreover, acts of aggression may be cool and calculated, rather than hostile and passionate.

50. **a.** is the answer. The very wide variations in aggressiveness from culture to culture indicate that aggression cannot be considered an unlearned instinct.

51. **d.** is the answer.

52. **a.** is the answer.

53. **b.** is the answer. In fact, people tend to overgeneralize from vivid cases, rather than assume that they are unusual.

a., c., & d. Each of these is an example of a cognitive (a. & c.) or a social (d.) root of prejudice.

54. **a.** is the answer.

b. Ingroup bias is the tendency of people to favor their own group.

c. The frustration-aggression principle is the idea that frustration creates anger, which can spark aggression.

d. The cross-race effect (other-race effect) refers to the tendency to recall the faces of our own race more accurately than those of other races.

55. **a.** is the answer.

b. This is an example of overt prejudice.

c. & d. These are examples of discrimination.

56. **b.** is the answer.

a. We are keenly sensitive to differences within our group, less so to differences within other groups.

c. & d. Although we tend to look more favorably on members of the ingroup, the text does not suggest that ingroup bias extends to evaluations of abilities.

57. **c.** is the answer.

58. **b.** is the answer.

59. **a.** is the answer.

60. **a.** is the answer. Such justifications arise as a way to preserve inequalities. The just-world phenomenon presumes that people get what they deserve. According to this view, someone who has less must deserve less.

Terms and Concepts to Remember:

61. **Prejudice** is an unjustifiable (and usually negative) attitude toward a group and its members.

62. A **stereotype** is a generalized (sometimes accurate but often overgeneralized) belief about a group of people.

63. **Discrimination** is unjustifiable negative behavior toward a group and its members.

64. The **just-world phenomenon** is a manifestation of the commonly held belief that good is rewarded and evil is punished. People get what they deserve and deserve what they get.

65. The **ingroup** refers to the people and groups with whom we share a common identity.

66. The **outgroup** refers to the people and groups that are excluded from our ingroup.

67. The **ingroup bias** is the tendency to favor our own group.

68. The **scapegoat theory** proposes that prejudice provides an outlet for anger by finding someone to blame.

69. The **other-race effect** is our tendency to recall the faces of our own race more accurately than those of other races. Also called the *cross-race effect* or *own-race bias.*

70. **Aggression** is any physical or verbal behavior intended to harm someone physically or emotionally.

71. The **frustration-aggression principle** states that aggression is triggered when people become angry because their efforts to achieve a goal have been blocked.

72. A **social script** is a culturally specific model of how to behave in various situations.

MODULE
37   Prosocial Relations

Attraction

1. proximity
2. increases; mere exposure
3. more; speed; man's; woman's
4. appearance
5. Attractive people are perceived as healthier, happier, more sensitive, more successful, and more socially skilled.
6. is not
7. youthful; fertile; mature; dominant; masculine; affluent; face; traits
8. attitudes, beliefs, interests, religion, race, education, intelligence, smoking behavior, economic status, and age

A reward theory of attraction says that we are attracted to, and continue relationships with, those people whose behavior provides us with more benefits than costs. Proximity makes it easy to enjoy the benefits of friendship at little cost, attractiveness is pleasing, and similarity is reinforcing to us.

9. **d.** is the answer. Hundreds of experiments indicate that first impressions are most influenced by physical appearance.

10. **a.** is the answer. Friends and couples are much more likely than randomly paired people to be similar in views, interests, and a range of other factors.

b. The opposite is true.

c. The mere exposure effect demonstrates that familiarity tends to breed fondness.

d. This is unlikely, given the positive effects of proximity and intimacy.

11. passionate; companionate

12. arousal; cognitive; were

13. dopamine; oxytocin

14. equity; self-disclosure; positive support

15. **a.** is the answer. According to the two-factor theory, physical arousal can intensify whatever emotion is currently felt. Only in the situation described in (a.) is Joan likely to be physically aroused.

Altruism

16. altruism

An example of altruism is giving food and shelter to people displaced by a hurricane or other major disaster without expectation of reward.

17. notice; interpret; assume responsibility

18. less

19. less; diffusion of responsibility; bystander effect

People are most likely to help someone when they have just observed someone else being helpful; when they are not in a hurry; when the victim appears to need and deserve help; when they are in some way similar to the victim; when the person is a woman; when in a small town or rural area; when feeling guilty; when not preoccupied; and when in a good mood.

20. social exchange

21. reciprocity

22. social-responsibility

Peacemaking

23. conflict; nations; cultural; partners

24. social traps

25. mirror-image; self-fulfilling prophecies

26. is not

27. superordinate; predicaments; "we"

28. mediator

29. Graduated; Reciprocated Initiatives; Tension-Reduction; conciliatory

30. **d.** is the answer. The couple's similar, and presumably distorted, feelings toward each other fuel their conflict.
    a. Self-disclosure, or the sharing of intimate feelings, fosters love.
    b. Their relationship may not be equitable, but that's not a factor in this question.
    c. With a social trap, both parties pursue their self-interest, which also may be the case here but not what is described in the question.

31. **d.** is the answer. Sherif found that hostility between two groups could be dispelled by giving the groups superordinate, or shared, goals.
    a. Although reducing the likelihood of mirror-image perceptions might reduce mutually destructive behavior, it would not lead to positive feelings between the groups.
    b. Such segregation would likely increase ingroup bias and group polarization, resulting in further group conflict.
    c. Contact by itself is not likely to reduce conflict.

Module Review:

32. **d.** is the answer. This phenomenon is known as the bystander effect.
    a. This answer is incorrect because individuals are less likely to render assistance at all if others are present.
    b. Although people are less likely to assume responsibility for helping, this does not mean that they are less empathic.
    c. This answer is incorrect because norms such as the social responsibility norm encourage helping others, yet people are less likely to help with others around.

33. **d.** is the answer. Being repeatedly exposed to novel stimuli increases our liking for them.
    a. For the most part, the opposite is true.
    b. & c. The mere exposure effect concerns our tendency to develop likings on the basis, not of similarities or differences, but simply of familiarity, or repeated exposure.

34. **a.** is the answer. This result supports the two-factor theory of emotion and passionate attraction, according to which arousal from any source can facilitate an emotion, depending on how we label the arousal.

35. **c.** is the answer. Deep affection is typical of companionate love, rather than passionate love, and is promoted by equity, whereas traditional roles may be characterized by the dominance of one sex.

36. **a.** is the answer.
    b. & c. These factors would most likely decrease a person's altruistic tendencies.
    d. There is no evidence that one sex is more altruistic than the other.

37. **c.** is the answer. The mere exposure effect refers to our tendency to like what we're used to, and we're used to seeing mirror images of ourselves.
    a. Equity refers to equality in giving and taking between the partners in a relationship.

b. Self-disclosure is the sharing of intimate feelings with a partner in a loving relationship.

d. Although people prefer mirror images of their faces, mirror-image perceptions are often held by parties in conflict. Each party views itself favorably and the other negatively.

38. **d.** is the answer.

39. **d.** is the answer. Because it provides people with an opportunity to meet, proximity is the most powerful predictor of friendship, even though, once a friendship is established, the other factors mentioned become more important.

40. **c.** is the answer. In this example of the fundamental attribution error, even when given the situational explanation for the woman's behavior, students ignored it and attributed her behavior to her personal disposition.

41. **b.** is the answer.
    a. GRIT is a technique for reducing conflict through a series of conciliatory gestures, not for maintaining the status quo.
    c. & d. These measures may help reduce conflict but they are not aspects of GRIT.

Terms and Concepts to Remember:

42. The **mere exposure effect** refers to the fact that repeated exposure to an unfamiliar stimulus increases our liking of it.

43. **Passionate love** refers to an aroused state of intense positive absorption in another person, especially at the beginning of a relationship.

44. **Companionate love** refers to a deep, enduring, affectionate attachment to those with whom we share our lives.

45. **Equity** refers to the condition in which there is mutual giving and receiving between the partners in a relationship.

46. **Self-disclosure** refers to a person's revealing intimate aspects of oneself to others.

47. **Altruism** is unselfish regard for the welfare of others.

48. The **bystander effect** is the tendency of a person to be less likely to offer help to someone if there are other people present.

49. **Social exchange theory** states that our social behavior revolves around exchanges, in which we try to minimize our costs and maximize our benefits.

50. The **reciprocity norm** is the expectation that people will help, not hurt, those who have helped them.

51. The **social-responsibility norm** is the expectation that people will help those who depend on them.

52. **Conflict** is a perceived incompatibility of actions, goals, or ideas between individuals or groups.

53. A **social trap** is a situation in which conflicting parties become caught in mutually destructive behaviors because each persists in pursuing its own self-interest rather than the good of the group.

54. **Mirror-image perceptions** are the negative, mutual views that conflicting people often hold about one another.

55. A **self-fulfilling prophecy** is a belief that leads to its own fulfillment.

56. **Superordinate goals** are mutual goals that require the cooperation of individuals or groups otherwise in conflict.

57. **GRIT** (Graduated and Reciprocated Initiatives in Tension-Reduction) is a strategy of conflict resolution based on the defusing effect that conciliatory gestures can have on parties in conflict.

Before You Move On

Matching Items

1. d	**6.** f	**11.** j
2. c	**7.** i	**12.** l
3. k	**8.** h	**13.** m
4. g	**9.** b	**14.** n
5. e	**10.** a	

True–False Items

1. T	**6.** T	**11.** T
2. F	**7.** F	**12.** F
3. T	**8.** F	
4. T	**9.** F	
5. F	**10.** T	

Cross-Check

ACROSS	DOWN
4. stereotype	1. bystander effect
5. GRIT	2. informational
6. scapegoat	3. cognitive dissonance
8. conformity	7. foot-in-the-door
9. altruism	8. companionate
12. equity	10. fundamental
13. passionate	11. attribution
14. conflict	
15. attitudes	

Personality

Overview

Personality refers to each individual's characteristic pattern of thinking, feeling, and acting. Modules 38 and 39 examine four perspectives on personality. Psychodynamic theories emphasize the unconscious and irrational aspects of personality. Humanistic theory draws attention to the concept of self and to the human potential for healthy growth. Trait theory led to advances in techniques for evaluating and describing personality. The social-cognitive perspective emphasizes the effects of our interactions with the environment. Module 38 describes and then evaluates the contributions, shortcomings, and historical significance of the psychodynamic and humanistic perspectives. Module 39 turns to contemporary research on personality, focusing on how the trait and social-cognitive perspectives explore and assess traits and the focus of many of today's researchers on the concept of self.

NOTE: Answer guidelines for all Modules 38 and 39 questions begin on page 331.

Outline

Instructions

First, skim each section, noting headings and boldface items. After you have read the section, review each objective by answering the fill-in, essay-type, and multiple-choice questions for that section. In some cases, Study Tips explain how best to learn a difficult concept and Applications and Module Reviews help you to know how well you understand the material. Finally, try to define the important terms and concepts using your own words. As you proceed, evaluate your performance by consulting the answers on page 331. Do not continue until you understand each answer. If you need to, review or reread a troublesome section before continuing.

Before You Move On includes activities that test you on material from the entire unit.

Classic Perspectives on Personality

What Is Personality?

Objective 38-1: Identify the theories that inform our understanding of personality.

1. Personality is defined as an individual's characteristic pattern of _____ , _____ , and _____ .

2. The psychoanalytic perspective on personality was proposed by _____ . A second, historically significant perspective was the _____ approach, which focused on people's capacities for _____ and _____ .

3. Later theorists built upon these two broad perspectives. Characteristic patterns of behavior are the focus of _____ theories, while _____-_____ theories explore the interaction between people's traits (including their thinking) and their social context.

The Psychodynamic Theories

Objective 38-2: Discuss how Sigmund Freud's treatment of psychological disorders led to his view of the unconscious mind.

4. Theories that view human behavior as an interaction between the _____ and _____ minds are referred to as _____ theories. These theories are descended from Freud's theory and associated techniques, called _____ .

5. Sigmund Freud was a medical doctor who specialized in _____ disorders.

6. Freud developed his theory in response to his observation that many patients had disorders that did not make _____ sense.

7. At first, Freud thought _____ would unlock the door to the unconscious.

8. The technique later used by Freud, in which the patient relaxes and says whatever comes to mind, is called _____ _____ .

9. According to this theory, many of a person's thoughts, wishes, and feelings are hidden in a large _____ region. Some of the thoughts in this region can be retrieved at will into consciousness; these thoughts are said to be _____ . Many of the memories of this region, however, are blocked, or _____ , from consciousness.

10. Freud believed that a person's _____ wishes are often reflected in his or her beliefs, habits, and troubling _____ .

Objective 38-3: Describe Freud's view of personality.

11. Freud believed that all facets of personality arise from conflict between our _____ internalized urges and the _____ controls over them.

12. According to Freud, personality consists of three interacting structures: the (a) _____ , the (b) _____ , and the (c) _____ .

13. The id is a reservoir of psychic energy that is primarily _____ (conscious/unconscious) and operates according to the _____ principle in order to satisfy basic _____ and _____ drives.

14. The ego develops _____ (before/after) the id and consists of thoughts, judgments, and memories that are mostly _____ (conscious/unconscious). The ego operates according to the _____ principle.

Explain why the ego is considered the "executive" of personality.

15. The personality structure that reflects moral values is the _____ , which Freud

believed began emerging at about age

_____ .

16. A person with a _____ (strong/weak) superego may be self-indulgent; one with an unusually _____ (strong/weak) superego may be virtuous but guilt-ridden.

17.

Conflict	The Id's Response	The Ego's Response	The Superego's Response
a. The driver ahead of you is driving 10 miles/hour below the speed limit.			
b. You have pledged a charitable donation but now need money to buy a new sweater.			
c. You've procrastinated about completing a term paper and a friend suggests buying one online.			

APPLICATION:

18. A psychoanalyst would characterize a person who is impulsive and self-indulgent as possessing a strong _____ and a weak _____ .

   a. id and ego; superego   **c.** ego; superego
   b. id; ego and superego   **d.** id; superego

Objective 38-4: Identify the developmental stages proposed by Freud.

19. According to Freud, personality is formed as the child passes through a series of _____ stages, each of which is focused on a distinct body area called an _____ .

20. The first stage is the _____ stage, which takes place during the first 18 months of life. During this stage, the id's energies are focused on behaviors such as _____ .

21. The second stage is the _____ stage, which lasts from about age _____ months to _____ months.

22. The third stage is the _____ stage, which lasts roughly from ages _____ to _____ years. During this stage, the id's energies are focused on the _____ . Freud also believed that during this stage children develop sexual desires for the _____ (same/opposite)-sex parent. Freud referred to these feelings as the _____ _____ in boys. Some psychoanalysts in Freud's era believed that girls experience a parallel _____ _____ .

23. Freud believed that _____ with the same-sex parent provided the basis for what psychologists now call _____ _____ .

Explain how this complex of feelings is resolved through the process of identification.

24. During the next stage, sexual feelings are repressed: this phase is called the _____ stage and lasts until puberty.

25. The final stage of development is called the _____ stage.

26. According to Freud, it is possible for a person's development to become blocked in any of the stages; in such an instance, the person is said to be _____ .

APPLICATIONS:

27. Jill has a biting, sarcastic manner. According to Freud, she is
   a. projecting her anxiety onto others.
   b. fixated in the oral stage of development.
   c. fixated in the anal stage of development.
   d. identifying with her mother.

28. Song Yi works in a smoke-free office. So, she frequently has to leave work and go outside to smoke a cigarette. Freud would probably say that Song Yi is _____ at the _____ stage of development.

Objective 38-5: Describe how Freud thought people defended themselves against anxiety.

29. The ego attempts to protect itself against anxiety through the use of _____ _____ . The process underlying each of these mechanisms is _____ .

30. All defense mechanisms function _____ and _____ .

31. Freud also viewed jokes and dreams as expressions of repressed sexual and aggressive tendencies. He called the remembered content of dreams the _____ _____ , which he believed to be a censored version of the dream's true _____ _____ .

32. Dealing with anxiety by returning to an earlier stage of development is called _____ .

33. When a person reacts in a manner opposite that of his or her true feelings, _____ _____ is said to have occurred.

34. When a person attributes his or her own feelings to another person, _____ has occurred.

35. When a person offers a false, self-justifying explanation for his or her actions, _____ has occurred.

36. When impulses are directed toward an object other than the one that caused arousal, _____ has occurred.

37. When a person refuses to believe or even perceive a painful reality, he or she is experiencing _____ .

APPLICATIONS:

38. According to the psychoanalytic perspective, a child who frequently "slips" and calls her teacher "Mom" PROBABLY
   a. has some unresolved conflicts concerning her mother.
   b. is fixated in the oral stage of development.
   c. is ruled by the pleasure principle.
   d. has a superego that overrides her id.

39. Match each defense mechanism in the following list with the proper example of how it could show itself.

Defense Mechanisms

_____ 1. displacement
_____ 2. projection
_____ 3. reaction formation
_____ 4. rationalization
_____ 5. regression
_____ 6. denial

Example

a. nail biting or thumb sucking in an anxiety-producing situation
b. overzealous crusaders against "immoral behaviors" who don't want to admit to their own sexual desires
c. saying you drink "just to be sociable" when in reality you have a drinking problem
d. a parent will not admit that her child could cheat on a test
e. thinking someone hates you when in reality you hate that person
f. a child who is angry at his parents and vents this anger on the family pet, a less threatening target

40. Suzy bought a used, high-mileage automobile because it was all she could afford. Attempting to justify her purchase, she raves to her friends about the car's attractiveness, good acceleration, and stereo. According to Freud, Suzy is using the defense mechanism of

a. displacement.   c. rationalization.
b. reaction formation.   d. projection.

Objective 38-6: Identify which of Freud's ideas were accepted or rejected by his followers.

41. The theorists who established their own, modified versions of psychoanalytic theory are called

_____-_____ .

These theorists typically place _____ (more/less) emphasis on the conscious mind than Freud did and _____ (more/less) emphasis on sex and aggression.

Briefly summarize how each of the following theorists departed from Freud.

a. Adler _____

_____

b. Horney _____

_____

c. Jung _____

_____

42. Today's psychologists _____ (accept/reject) the idea of inherited experiences, which _____ (which theorist?)

called a _____

_____ , a reservoir of images, or
_____ .

43. More recently, some of Freud's ideas have been incorporated into _____ theory. Unlike Freud, the theorists advocating this perspective do not believe that _____ is the basis of personality. They do agree, however, that much of mental life is _____ , that _____ shapes personality, and that we often struggle with _____ _____ .

Objective 38-7: Describe projective tests and how they are used, and discuss some criticisms of them.

44. Tests that provide test-takers with ambiguous stimuli for interpretation are called _____ tests. One such test, in which people view ambiguous pictures and then make up stories about them, is called the _____ _____ _____ , was developed by _____ .

45. The most widely used projective test is the _____ , in which people are shown a series of _____ . Critics contend that these tests have _____ (little/significant) validity and reliability.

APPLICATION:

46. Teresa is taking a personality test that asks her to describe random patterns of dots. This is a _____ test.

Objective 38-8: Discuss how contemporary psychologists view Freud's psychoanalysis.

47. Contrary to Freud's theory, research indicates that human development is _____ (fixed in childhood/lifelong), children gain their gender identity at a(n) _____ (earlier/later) age, and the presence of a same-sex parent _____ (is/is not) necessary for the child to become strongly masculine or feminine.

48. Research also disputes Freud's belief that dreams disguise and fulfill _____ and that defense mechanisms disguise _____ and _____ impulses. Another Freudian idea that is no longer widely accepted is that psychological disorders are caused by _____ _____.

49. Criticism of psychoanalysis as a scientific theory centers on the fact that it provides _____-_____ _____ explanations and does not offer _____ _____ .

50. Psychoanalytic theory rests on the assumption that the human mind often _____ painful experiences. Many of today's researchers think that this process is much _____ (more common/rarer) than Freud believed. They also believe that when it does occur, it is a reaction to terrible _____ .

Objective 38-9: Discuss how modern research has developed our understanding of the unconscious.

51. Today's psychologists agree with Freud that we have limited access to all that goes on in our minds. However, they believe that the unconscious involves the _____ that control our perceptions and interpretations, the _____ of stimuli not con-

sciously attended, the _____ that activate instantly, and our _____ memories, for example.

52. There is also research support for two of Freud's defense mechanisms. For example, one study demonstrated _____ _____ (trading unacceptable impulses for their opposite).

53. The defense mechanism that Freud called _____ is what researchers today call the _____ _____ effect. This refers to our tendency to _____ the extent to which others share our beliefs and behaviors.

54. Another Freudian idea that has received support is that people defend themselves against _____ . However, defense mechanisms seem motivated less by the sexual and aggressive undercurrents that Freud imagined than by our need to protect our _____ .

State several of Freud's ideas that have endured.

Humanistic Theories

Objective 38-10: Describe how humanistic psychologists viewed personality, and explain their goal in studying personality.

55. Two influential theories of humanistic psychology were proposed by _____ and _____ . These theorists offered a _____-_____ perspective that emphasized human _____ .

56. According to Maslow, humans are motivated by needs that are organized into a _____ . Maslow refers to the process of fulfilling one's potential as _____ and the process of finding meaning, purpose, and communion beyond the self as _____ . Many people who fulfill their potential have been moved by _____ that surpass ordinary consciousness.

List some of the characteristics Maslow associated with those who fulfilled their potential.

57. According to Rogers, a person nurtures growth in a relationship by being _____ , _____ , and _____ .

58. People who are accepting of others offer them _____ _____ . By so doing, they enable others to be _____ without fearing the loss of their esteem.

59. For both Maslow and Rogers, an important feature of personality is how an individual perceives himself or herself; this is the person's _____ .

Objective 38-11: Explain how humanistic psychologists assessed a person's sense of self.

60. Humanistic psychologists sometimes use _____ to assess personality, that is, to evaluate the _____ .

61. One questionnaire, inspired by Carl Rogers, asked people to describe themselves both as they would _____ like to be and as they _____ are. When these two selves are alike, the self-concept is _____ .

62. Some humanistic psychologists feel that questionnaires are _____ and prefer to use _____ to assess personality.

Objective 38-12: Describe how humanistic theories have influenced psychology, and discuss the criticisms they have faced.

63. Humanistic psychologists have influenced such diverse areas as _____ , _____ , _____ _____ , and _____ . They have also had a major impact on today's _____ psychology. And they laid the groundwork for today's _____ _____ scientific subfield.

64. Critics contend that the concepts of humanistic theory are _____ and _____ .

65. Another criticism of humanistic theory is that it encourages _____ , which can lead to _____ .

66. A third criticism of humanistic theory is that it is _____ , and fails to appreciate the human capacity for _____ .

APPLICATIONS:

67. Professor Minton believes that people are basically good and are endowed with self-actualizing tendencies. Evidently, Professor Minton is a proponent of
a. behaviorism.
b. psychodynamic theory.
c. the humanistic perspective.
d. self-concept theory.

68. Andrew's grandfather, who has lived a rich and productive life, is a spontaneous, loving, and self-accepting person. Maslow might say that he
a. is at the middle rung of the hierarchy of needs.
b. has passed the need for self-transcendence.
c. still has to satisfy his basic, physiological needs.
d. is a self-actualizing person.

69. The school psychologist believes that having a positive self-concept is necessary before students can achieve their potential. Evidently, the school psychologist is working within the _____ perspective.
a. trait
b. psychodynamic
c. humanistic
d. behaviorist

70. Wanda wishes to instill in her children an accepting attitude toward other people. Maslow and Rogers would probably recommend that she
    a. teach her children first to accept themselves.
    b. use discipline sparingly.
    c. be affectionate with her children only when they behave as she wishes.
    d. exhibit all of these behaviors.

MODULE REVIEW:

71. The text defines *personality* as
    a. the set of personal attitudes that characterizes a person.
    b. an individual's characteristic pattern of thinking, feeling, and acting.
    c. a predictable set of responses to environmental stimuli.
    d. an unpredictable set of responses to environmental stimuli.

72. Which of the following places the greatest emphasis on the unconscious mind?
    a. the humanistic perspective
    b. the social-cognitive perspective
    c. the trait perspective
    d. the psychoanalytic perspective

73. Which of the following is the correct order of psychosexual stages proposed by Freud?
    a. oral; anal; phallic; latency; genital
    b. anal; oral; phallic; latency; genital
    c. oral; anal; genital; latency; phallic
    d. anal; oral; genital; latency; phallic

74. According to Freud, defense mechanisms are methods of reducing
    a. anger.   c. anxiety.
    b. fear.   d. lust.

75. Neo-Freudians such as Adler and Horney believed that
    a. Freud placed too great an emphasis on the conscious mind.
    b. Freud placed too great an emphasis on sexual and aggressive instincts.
    c. the years of childhood were more important in the formation of personality than Freud had indicated.
    d. Freud's ideas about the id, ego, and superego as personality structures were incorrect.

76. Which of Freud's ideas would NOT be accepted by most contemporary psychologists?
    a. Development is essentially fixed in childhood.
    b. Sexuality is a potent drive in humans.
    c. The mind is an iceberg with consciousness being only the tip.
    d. Repression can be the cause of forgetting.

77. Projective tests such as the Rorschach inkblot test have been criticized because
    a. their scoring system is too rigid and leads to unfair labeling.
    b. they were standardized with unrepresentative samples.
    c. they have low reliability and low validity.
    d. it is easy for people to fake answers in order to appear healthy.

78. Id is to ego as _____ is to _____ .
    a. reality principle; pleasure principle
    b. pleasure principle; reality principle
    c. conscious forces; unconscious forces
    d. conscience; "personality executive"

79. Contemporary research has provided more support for defense mechanisms such as _____ than for defense mechanisms such as _____ .
    a. projection; displacement
    b. displacement; projection
    c. displacement; regression
    d. regression; displacement

80. According to Freud's theory, personality arises in response to conflicts between
    a. our unacceptable urges and our tendency to become self-actualized.
    b. the process of identification and the ego's defense mechanisms.
    c. the collective unconscious and our individual desires.
    d. our biological impulses and the social restraints against them.

81. The Oedipus and Electra complexes have their roots in the
    a. anal stage.   c. latency stage.
    b. oral stage.   d. phallic stage.

82. Which of the following was NOT mentioned in the text as a criticism of Freud's theory?
    a. The theory is sexist.
    b. It offers few testable hypotheses.
    c. There is no evidence of anything like an "unconscious."
    d. The theory ignores the fact that human development is lifelong.

83. According to Freud, _____ is the process by which children incorporate their parents' values into their _____ .
   a. reaction formation; superegos
   b. reaction formation; egos
   c. identification; superegos
   d. identification; egos

84. Which of the following refers to the tendency to overestimate the extent to which others share our beliefs?
   a. displacement
   b. projection
   c. rationalization
   d. the false consensus effect

85. Humanistic theories of personality
   a. emphasize the difference between conscious and unconscious thoughts.
   b. emphasize the growth potential of "healthy" individuals.
   c. focus on the past rather than the present or future.
   d. emphasize scientific objectivity.

86. According to Rogers, three conditions are necessary to promote growth in personality. These are
   a. honesty, sincerity, and empathy.
   b. high self-esteem, honesty, and empathy.
   c. high self-esteem, genuineness, and acceptance.
   d. genuineness, acceptance, and empathy.

87. For humanistic psychologists, many of our behaviors and perceptions are ultimately shaped by whether our _____ is _____ or _____ .
   a. genuineness; real; feigned
   b. empathy; internal; external
   c. personality structure; introverted; extraverted
   d. self-concept; positive; negative

88. Which of the following is a common criticism of the humanistic perspective?
   a. Its concepts are vague and subjective.
   b. The emphasis on the self encourages selfishness in individuals.
   c. Humanism fails to appreciate the reality of evil in human behavior.
   d. All of these are common criticisms.

89. In promoting personality growth, the person-centered perspective emphasizes all but
   a. empathy.
   b. acceptance.
   c. genuineness.
   d. altruism.

TERMS AND CONCEPTS TO REMEMBER:
90. personality
91. psychodynamic theories
92. psychoanalysis
93. unconscious
94. free association
95. id
96. ego
97. superego
98. psychosexual stages
99. Oedipus complex
100. identification
101. fixation
102. defense mechanisms
103. repression
104. collective unconscious
105. projective tests
106. Thematic Apperception Test (TAT)
107. Rorschach inkblot test
108. humanistic theories
109. self-actualization
110. unconditional positive regard
111. self-concept

Contemporary Perspectives on Personality

Trait Theories

Objective 39-1: Explain how psychologists use traits to describe personality.

1. Gordon Allport developed trait theory, which defines personality in terms of people's stable and enduring _____ and _____ . Unlike Freud, he was generally less interested in _____ individual traits than in _____ them.

2. To reduce the number of traits to a few basic ones, psychologists use the statistical procedure of _____ _____ .

The Eysencks think that two or three personality dimensions are sufficient; these include (a) _____–_____ and (b) emotional _____–_____ .

Moody
Anxious
Rigid
Sober
Pessimistic
Reserved
Unsociable
Quiet
(a)
Passive
Careful
Thoughtful
Peaceful
Controlled
Reliable
Even-tempered
Calm
(b)

Touchy
Restless
Aggressive
Excitable
Changeable
Impulsive
Optimistic
Active
(a)
Sociable
Outgoing
Talkative
Responsive
Easygoing
Lively
Carefree
Leadership

(b)

3. Some researchers believe that extraverts seek stimulation because their level of _____ _____ is relatively low. PET scans reveal that an area of the brain's _____ lobe involved in behavior inhibition is less active in _____ (extraverts/introverts) than in _____ (extraverts/ introverts). Dopamine and dopamine-related neural activity tend to be higher in _____ (extraverts/introverts).

4. Biology influences our personality in others ways as well. Twin and adoption studies indicate that our _____ play an important role in defining our _____ and _____ style.

5. Children's shyness and inhibition may differ as an aspect of _____ _____ _____ reactivity.

6. Personality differences among dogs, birds, and other animals _____ (are/are not) evident and consistently judged.

APPLICATIONS:

7. Isaiah is sober and reserved; Rashid is fun-loving and affectionate. The Eysencks would say that Isaiah _____ and Rashid _____ .

   a. is emotionally unstable; is emotionally stable
   b. is emotionally stable; is emotionally unstable
   c. is an extravert; is an introvert
   d. is an introvert; is an extravert

8. Because you have a relatively low level of brain arousal, a trait theorist would suggest that you are an _____ who would naturally seek _____ .

   a. introvert; stimulation
   b. introvert; isolation
   c. extravert; stimulation
   d. extravert; isolation

9. Nadine has a relatively high level of brain arousal. Trait theorists would probably predict that she is an _____ .

Objective 39-2: Identify some common misunderstandings about introversion, and discuss whether extraversion leads to greater success than introversion.

10. (Thinking Critically) Western cultures prize _____ (introversion/extraversion), which tends to be equated with _____ , over _____ (introversion/extraversion), which is often equated with _____ .

11. (Thinking Critically) Introversion is often equated with _____ , although they are not the same thing.

12. (Thinking Critically) Introverts seek _____ (high/low) levels of stimulation from the environment because they are _____ . Shy people remain quiet because they fear others will _____ .

Objective 39-3: Describe personality inventories, and discuss their strengths and weaknesses as trait-assessment tools.

13. Questionnaires that categorize personality traits are called _____ _____ .

14. The most widely used of all such personality tests is the _____ _____ _____ _____ ; its questions are grouped into _____ (how many?) clinical scales. This test also has a _____ _____ , which assesses faking.

15. This test was developed by testing a large pool of items and selecting those that differentiated particular individuals; in other words, the test was _____ derived.

APPLICATION:

16. A psychologist at the campus mental health center administered an empirically derived personality test to diagnose an emotionally troubled student. Which test did the psychologist most likely administer?
   a. the MMPI
   b. the Neuroticism Index
   c. the Big Five Questionnaire
   d. the Eysenck Personality Questionnaire

Objective 39-4: Identify the traits that seem to provide the most useful information about personality variation.

17. Researchers have arrived at a cluster of five factors that seem to describe the major features of personality. List and briefly describe the Big Five.
   a. _____
   b. _____
   c. _____
   d. _____
   e. _____

18. Personality continues to develop and change through late childhood and adolescence. By adulthood, the Big Five traits are quite _____ (stable/variable). Up to age 40, we show signs of a _____ _____: We become more conscientious and agreeable and less neurotic (emotionally unstable).

19. Heritability of the Big Five is estimated at _____ percent or more for each dimension. Moreover, these traits _____ (do/do not) predict other attributes.

APPLICATION:

20. For his class presentation, Bruce plans to discuss the Big Five personality factors used by people throughout the world to describe others or themselves. Which of the following is NOT a factor that Bruce will discuss?
   a. extraversion   c. independence
   b. openness   d. conscientiousness

Objective 39-5: Discuss whether research supports the consistency of personality traits over time and across situations.

21. Human behavior is influenced both by our inner _____ and by the external _____ . The issue of which of these is the more important influence on personality is called the _____-_____ controversy.

22. To be considered a personality trait, a characteristic must persist over _____ and across _____ . Research studies reveal that personality trait scores _____ (correlate/do not correlate) with scores obtained seven years later. The consistency of specific behaviors from one situation to the next is _____ (predictably consistent/not predictably consistent).

23. An individual's score on a personality test _____ (is/is not) very predictive of his or her behavior in any given situation.

Explain the apparent contradiction between behavior in specific situations and average behavior patterns.

24. People's expressive styles, which include their _____ , manner of _____ , and _____ , are quite _____ (consistent/inconsistent), which _____ (does/does not) reveal distinct personality traits.

Social-Cognitive Theories

Objective 39-6: Describe how social-cognitive theorists view personality development, and explain how they explore behavior.

25. Social-cognitive theory, which focuses on how the individual and the _____ interact, was proposed by _____ .

26. Social-cognitive theorists propose that personality is shaped by the mutual influence of our internal _____, our _____, and _____ factors, as reflected in the _____ approach to personality. This is the principle of _____ _____ .

Describe three different ways in which the environment and personality interact.

27. In addition to the interaction of internal personal factors, the environment, and our behaviors, we also experience _____- _____ interaction.

28. It follows from the social-cognitive perspective that the best means of predicting people's future behavior is their _____ _____ .

29. Modern studies indicate that assessment center exercises are more revealing of visible dimensions, such as _____ _____, than others, such as _____ _____ drive.

Objective 39-7: Discuss the criticisms social-cognitive theorists have faced.

30. Social-cognitive theories build from research on _____ and _____ .

31. The major criticism of the social-cognitive perspective is that it fails to appreciate a person's _____ _____ .

32. Ramona identifies with her politically conservative parents. At college, most of her friends also held conservative views. After four years in this environment, Ramona's politics have become even more conservative. According to the social-cognitive perspective, in this case Ramona's parents (_____ factor) helped shape her political beliefs (_____ factor), which influenced her choice of college (also a _____ factor) and created an _____ that fostered her already formed political attitudes.

33. In high school, Chella and Nari were best friends. They thought they were a lot alike, as did everyone else who knew them. After high school, they went on to very different colleges, careers, and life courses. Now, at their twenty-fifth reunion, they are shocked at how little they have in common. Bandura would suggest that their differences reflect the interactive effects of environment, personality, and behavior, which he refers to as _____ _____ .

Exploring the Self

Objective 39-8: Explain why psychology has generated so much research on the self, and discuss the importance of self-esteem to our well-being.

34. One of Western psychology's most vigorously researched topics today is the _____ .

35. One example of thinking about self is the concept of _____ _____, which emphasizes how our aspirations motivate us through specific goals.

36. Our tendency to overestimate the extent to which others are noticing and evaluating us is called the _____ _____ .

37. According to self theorists, personality development hinges on our feelings of self-worth, or _____ . Our sense of competence on a task, or our _____, is also important. People who feel good about themselves are relatively _____ (dependent on/independent of) outside pressures.

38. In a series of experiments, researchers found that people who were made to feel insecure were _____ (more/less) critical of other persons or tended to express heightened _____ _____ .

39. The behavior of many people has been described in terms of a *spotlight effect*. This means that they
   a. tend to see themselves as being above average in ability.
   b. perceive that their fate is determined by forces not under their personal control.
   c. overestimate the extent to which other people are noticing them.
   d. do all of these things.

Objective 39-9: Describe the evidence that reveals self-serving bias, and differentiate between defensive and secure self-esteem.

40. People tend to be most overconfident of their abilities in areas where they are, in fact, most _____ (competent/incompetent).

41. The tendency of people to judge themselves favorably is called the _____ bias. The phenomenon, which reflects overestimating the self as well as the desire to maintain a positive self-view, is less striking in _____ , where people value _____ .

42. Responsibility for success is generally accepted _____ (more/less) readily than responsibility for failure.

43. Most people perceive their own behavior and traits as being _____ (above/ below) average.

44. Bushman and Baumeister found that students with unrealistically _____ (low/high) self-esteem were most likely to become exceptionally aggressive after criticism. Some psychologists believe that today's new generation expresses more _____ than earlier generations.

Identify some of the attitudes and behaviors that seem to be on the rise in *Generation Me*.

45. Some researchers distinguish _____ self-esteem, which is fragile and sensitive to _____ , from _____ self-esteem, which is less focused on _____ evaluations.

46. James attributes his failing grade in chemistry to an unfair final exam. His attitude exemplifies
   a. self-efficacy.
   b. narcissism.
   c. self-serving bias.
   d. reciprocal determinism.

Objective 39-10: Discuss how individualist and collectivist cultures differ in their values and goals.

47. Cultures based on _____ give relatively greater priority to personal _____ and define their identity mostly in terms of personal _____ . Examples of such cultures occur in _____ , _____ , and _____ .

48. In contrast, cultures based on _____ give priority to the goals of one's _____ and define their _____ accordingly. Examples of such cultures occur in _____ and _____ .

49. (Table 39.3) In contrasting individualist and collectivist cultures, we say that in defining the self, individualists value _____ , while collectivists value _____ .

50. Whereas people in _____ cultures value freedom, they suffer more _____ , divorce, _____ , and _____ -related disease.

51. The new field of _____ is studying how neurobiology and cultural traits influence each other.

MODULE REVIEW:

52. Which two dimensions of personality have the Eysencks emphasized?
    a. extraversion–introversion and emotional stability–instability
    b. narcissism and self-serving bias
    c. self-esteem and emotional stability–instability
    d. conscientiousness and neuroticism

53. With regard to personality, it appears that
    a. there is little consistency of behavior from one situation to the next and little consistency of traits over the life span.
    b. there is little consistency of behavior from one situation to the next but significant consistency of traits over the life span.
    c. there is significant consistency of behavior from one situation to the next but little consistency of traits over the life span.
    d. there is significant consistency of behavior from one situation to the next and significant consistency of traits over the life span.

54. A major criticism of trait theory is that it
    a. places too great an emphasis on early childhood experiences.
    b. overestimates the consistency of behavior in different situations.
    c. underestimates the importance of heredity in personality development.
    d. places too great an emphasis on positive traits.

55. In studying personality, a trait theorist would most likely
    a. interview the person.
    b. observe a person in a variety of situations.
    c. use a personality inventory.
    d. test the effect of lowering a person's self-esteem.

56. The Minnesota Multiphasic Personality Inventory (MMPI) is a(n)
    a. projective personality test.
    b. empirically derived and objective personality test.
    c. personality test developed mainly to assess job applicants.
    d. personality test used primarily to assess self-serving bias.

57. Trait theory attempts to
    a. show how development of personality is a lifelong process.
    b. describe and classify people in terms of their predispositions to behave in certain ways.

    c. determine which traits are most conducive to individual self-actualization.
    d. explain how behavior is shaped by the interaction between traits, behavior, and the environment.

58. The Big Five personality factors are
    a. emotional stability, openness, introversion, sociability, locus of control.
    b. neuroticism, extraversion, openness, emotional stability, sensitivity.
    c. neuroticism, gregariousness, extraversion, impulsiveness, conscientiousness.
    d. emotional stability, extraversion, openness, agreeableness, conscientiousness.

59. Research on the Big Five personality factors provides evidence that
    a. some tendencies decrease during adulthood, while others increase.
    b. these traits only describe personality in Western, individualist cultures.
    c. the heritability of individual differences in these traits generally runs about 25 percent or less.
    d. all of these statements are true.

60. Regarding high self-esteem, psychologists who study the self have found that self-affirming thinking
    a. is generally maladaptive to the individual because it distorts reality by overinflating self-esteem.
    b. is generally adaptive to the individual because it reduces shyness, anxiety, and loneliness.
    c. tends to prevent the individual from viewing others with compassion and understanding.
    d. tends *not* to characterize people who exhibit narcissism.

61. Which of the following is the major criticism of the social-cognitive perspective?
    a. It focuses too much on early childhood experiences.
    b. It focuses too little on the inner traits of a person.
    c. It provides descriptions but not explanations.
    d. It lacks appropriate assessment techniques.

62. Which personality theory emphasizes the interaction between the individual and the environment in shaping personality?
    a. psychodynamic   c. humanistic
    b. trait   d. social-cognitive

63. Research has shown that individuals who are made to feel insecure are subsequently
    a. more critical of others.
    b. less critical of others.
    c. more likely to display self-serving bias.
    d. less likely to display self-serving bias.

64. An example of self-serving bias described in the text is the tendency of people to
    a. see themselves as average on nearly any desirable dimension.
    b. accept more responsibility for successes than failures.
    c. be overly critical of other people.
    d. exhibit heightened racial prejudice.

65. Which of the following statements about self-esteem is NOT correct?
    a. People with low self-esteem tend to be negative about others.
    b. People with high self-esteem are more persistent at difficult tasks.
    c. People with low self-esteem tend to be nonconformists.
    d. People with high self-esteem have fewer sleepless nights.

66. In studying personality, a social-cognitive theorist would most likely make use of
    a. personality inventories.
    b. projective tests.
    c. observing behavior in different situations.
    d. factor analyses.

TERMS AND CONCEPTS TO REMEMBER:

67. trait
68. personality inventory
69. Minnesota Multiphasic Personality Inventory (MMPI)
70. empirically derived test
71. social-cognitive perspective
72. reciprocal determinism
73. self
74. spotlight effect
75. self-esteem
76. self-efficacy
77. self-serving bias
78. narcissism
79. individualism
80. collectivism

Before You Move On

Matching Items 1

Match each definition or description with the appropriate term.

Definitions or Descriptions

_____ 1. redirecting impulses to a less threatening object
_____ 2. test consisting of a series of inkblots
_____ 3. the conscious executive of personality
_____ 4. personality inventory
_____ 5. disguising an impulse by imputing it to another person
_____ 6. switching an unacceptable impulse into its opposite
_____ 7. the unconscious repository of instinctual drives
_____ 8. a statistical technique that identifies clusters of personality traits
_____ 9. personality structure that corresponds to a person's conscience
_____ 10. providing self-justifying explanations for an action

Terms

a. id
b. ego
c. superego
d. reaction formation
e. rationalization
f. displacement
g. factor analysis
h. projection
i. Rorschach
j. MMPI

Matching Items 2

Match each term with the appropriate definition or description.

Terms

_____ 1. projective test
_____ 2. identification
_____ 3. collective unconscious
_____ 4. reality principle
_____ 5. psychosexual stages
_____ 6. pleasure principle
_____ 7. empirically derived test
_____ 8. reciprocal determinism
_____ 9. personality inventory
_____ 10. Oedipus complex
_____ 11. preconscious

Definitions or Descriptions

a. the id's demand for immediate gratification
b. a boy's sexual desires toward his mother
c. information that is retrievable but currently not in conscious awareness
d. stages of development proposed by Freud
e. questionnaire used to assess personality traits
f. the two-way interactions of behavior with personal and environmental factors
g. personality test that provides ambiguous stimuli
h. the repository of universal memories proposed by Jung
i. the process by which children incorporate their parents' values into their developing superegos
j. the process by which the ego seeks to gratify impulses of the id in nondestructive ways
k. developed by testing a pool of items and then selecting those that discriminate the group of interest

Essay Question

You are an honest, open, and responsible person. Discuss how these characteristics would be explained according to the major perspectives on personality. (Use the space below to list points you want to make, and organize them. Then write the essay on a separate piece of paper.)

Cross-Check

As you learned in Module 2, reviewing and overlearning of material are important to the learning process. After you have written the definitions of the key terms in this unit, you should complete the crossword puzzle to ensure that you can reverse the process—recognize the term, given the definition.

ACROSS

3. In Freud's theory, the area of the unconscious containing material that is retrievable into conscious awareness.
6. Type of questionnaire used by trait theorists to assess personality.
8. A person's characteristic pattern of behavior.
9. In Freud's theory, the conscious division of personality.
10. The ego's methods of unconsciously protecting itself against anxiety.
13. According to Freud, _____ occurs when development becomes arrested in an immature psychosexual stage.

DOWN

1. Defense mechanism in which an impulse is shifted to an object other than the one that originally aroused the impulse.
2. The interacting influences of behavior, internal cognition, and environment.
3. An individual's characteristic pattern of thinking, feeling, and acting.
4. In Freud's theory, the complex developed by boys in which they are sexually attracted to their mother and resent their father.
5. In Freud's theory, the process by which the child's superego develops and incorporates the parents' values.
7. A widely used test in which people are asked to interpret 10 inkblots.
11. The most widely used personality inventory.
12. In Freud's theory, the personality system consisting of basic sexual and aggressive drives.

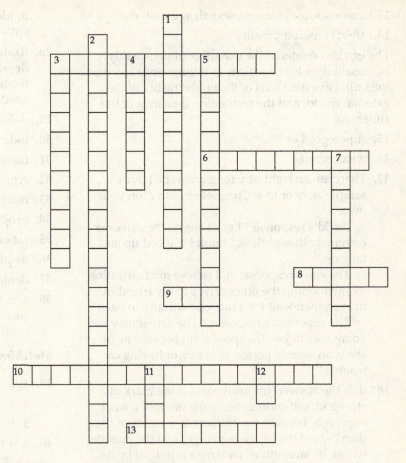

Answers

MODULE
38
Classic Perspectives on Personality

What Is Personality?

1. thinking; feeling; acting
2. Sigmund Freud; humanistic; growth; self-fulfillment
3. trait; social-cognitive

The Psychodynamic Theories

4. conscious; unconscious; psychodynamic; psycho-analysis
5. nervous
6. neurological
7. hypnosis
8. free association
9. unconscious; preconscious; repressed
10. unconscious; symptoms
11. biological; social
12. id; ego; superego

13. unconscious; pleasure; sexual; aggressive

14. after; conscious; reality

The ego is considered the executive of personality because it directs our actions as it intervenes among the impulsive demands of the id, the reality of the external world, and the restraining demands of the superego.

15. superego; 4 or 5

16. weak; strong

17. There are no right or wrong answers. Here's a sample answer to a. Complete b. and c. on your own.

a. The id's response: "I'm so angry; the driver is extremely thoughtless. I think I'll speed up and tailgate."

The ego's response: "I'll relieve my frustration by mentioning the other driver to my friend in the car, then wait for a safe opportunity to pass."

The superego's response: "The driver may be going way below the speed limit because he or she is an elderly person or is sick or having car trouble."

18. d. is the answer. Impulsiveness is the mark of a strong id; self-indulgence is the mark of a weak superego. Because the ego serves to mediate the demands of the id, the superego, and the outside world, its strength or weakness is judged by its decision-making ability, not by the character of the decision—so the ego is not relevant to the question asked.

19. psychosexual; erogenous zone

20. oral; sucking (also biting, chewing)

21. anal; 18; 36

22. phallic; 3; 6; genitals; opposite; Oedipus complex; Electra complex

23. identification; gender identity

Children eventually cope with their feelings for the opposite-sex parent by repressing them and by identifying with the rival (same-sex) parent. Through this process children incorporate many of their parents' values, thereby strengthening the superego.

24. latency

25. genital

26. fixated

27. b. is the answer. Sarcasm is said to be an attempt to deny the passive dependence characteristic of the oral stage.

a. A person who is projecting attributes his or her own feelings to others.

c. Such a person might be either messy and disorganized or highly controlled and compulsively neat.

d. Identification involves incorporating the parent's values into one's superego.

28. fixated; oral. Song Yi was probably orally deprived (weaned too early) as an infant, so she is fixated at the oral stage. Smoking satisfies her id's needs.

29. defense mechanisms; repression

30. indirectly; unconsciously

31. manifest content; latent content

32. regression

33. reaction formation

34. projection

35. rationalization

36. displacement

37. denial

38. a. is the answer. Freud believed that dreams and such slips of the tongue reveal unconscious conflicts.

Matching Items

39. 1. f   4. c
    2. e   5. a
    3. b   6. d

40. c. is the answer. Suzy is trying to justify her purchase by generating (inaccurate) explanations for her behavior.

a. Displacement is the redirecting of impulses toward an object other than the one responsible for them.

b. Reaction formation is the transformation of unacceptable impulses into their opposites.

d. Projection is the attribution of one's own unacceptable thoughts and feelings to others.

41. neo-Freudians; more; less

a. Adler emphasized the social, rather than the sexual, tensions of childhood and said that much of behavior is driven by the need to overcome feelings of inferiority.

b. Horney questioned the male bias in Freud's theory, such as the assumptions that women have weak egos and suffer "penis envy." Like Adler, she emphasized social tensions.

c. Jung emphasized an inherited collective unconscious.

42. reject; Jung; collective unconscious; archetypes

43. psychodynamic; sex; unconscious; childhood; inner conflicts

44. projective; Thematic Apperception Test (TAT); Henry Murray

45. Rorschach; inkblots; little

46. projective
47. lifelong; earlier; is not
48. wishes; sexual; aggressive; sexual suppression
49. after-the-fact; testable predictions
50. represses; rarer; trauma
51. schemas; priming; emotions; implicit
52. reaction formation
53. projection; false consensus; overestimate
54. anxiety; self-image

Freud drew attention to the unconscious and the irrational, to human defenses against anxiety, to the importance of human sexuality, and to the tension between our biological impulses and our social well-being.

Humanistic Theories

55. Abraham Maslow; Carl Rogers; third-force; potential
56. hierarchy; self-actualization; self-transcendence; peak experiences

For Maslow, such people were self-aware, self-accepting and open, spontaneous, loving and caring, not paralyzed by others' opinions, secure, and problem-centered rather than self-centered.

57. genuine; accepting; empathic
58. unconditional positive regard; spontaneous
59. self-concept
60. questionnaires; self-concept
61. ideally; actually; positive
62. depersonalizing; interviews
63. counseling; education; child raising; management; popular; positive psychology
64. vague; subjective
65. individualism; self-indulgence, selfishness, and an erosion of moral restraints
66. naive; evil
67. c. is the answer.
   b. & c. Neither of these theories offers any particular explanation of this tendency.
   d. Self-concept is an aspect of humanistic theory.
68. d. is the answer.
69. c. is the answer.
   a., b., & d. The self-concept is not relevant to any of these theories.
70. a. is the answer.
   b. The text does not discuss the impact of discipline on personality.
   c. This would constitute conditional, rather than unconditional, positive regard and would likely

cause the children to be less accepting of themselves and others.

Module Review:

71. b. is the answer. Personality is defined as patterns of response—of thinking, feeling, and acting—that are relatively consistent across a variety of situations.
72. d. is the answer.
   a. & b. Conscious processes are the focus of these perspectives.
   c. The trait perspective focuses on the description of behaviors.
73. a. is the answer.
74. c. is the answer. According to Freud, defense mechanisms reduce anxiety unconsciously, by disguising one's threatening impulses.
   a., b., & d. Unlike these specific emotions, anxiety need not be focused. Defense mechanisms help us cope when we are unsettled but are not sure why.
75. b. is the answer.
   a. According to most neo-Freudians, Freud placed too great an emphasis on the *unconscious* mind.
   c. Freud placed great emphasis on early childhood, and the neo-Freudians basically agreed with him.
   d. The neo-Freudians accepted Freud's ideas about the basic personality structures.
76. a. is the answer. Developmental research indicates that development is lifelong.
   b., c., & d. To varying degrees, research has partially supported these Freudian ideas.
77. c. is the answer. As scoring is largely subjective and the tests have not been very successful in predicting behavior, their reliability and validity have been called into question.
   a. This is untrue.
   b. Unlike empirically derived personality tests, projective tests are not standardized.
   d. Although this may be true, it was not mentioned as a criticism of projective tests.
78. b. is the answer. In Freud's theory, the id operates according to the pleasure principle; the ego operates according to the reality principle.
   c. The id is presumed to be unconscious.
   d. The superego is, according to Freud, the equivalent of a conscience; the ego is the "personality executive."
79. b. is the answer.
80. d. is the answer.

a. Self-actualization is a concept of the humanistic perspective.

b. Through identification, children *reduce* conflicting feelings as they incorporate their parents' values.

c. Jung, rather than Freud, proposed the concept of the collective unconscious.

81. **d.** is the answer.

82. **c.** is the answer. Although many researchers think of the unconscious as information processing without awareness rather than as a reservoir of repressed information, they agree with Freud that we do indeed have limited access to all that goes on in our minds.

83. **c.** is the answer.

a. & b. Reaction formation is the defense mechanism by which people transform unacceptable impulses into their opposites.

d. It is the superego, rather than the ego, that represents parental values.

84. **d.** is the answer.

85. **b.** is the answer.

a. & c. These are true of psychodynamic theories.

d. This is true of behaviorism.

86. **d.** is the answer.

87. **d.** is the answer.

88. **d.** is the answer.

89. **d.** is the answer.

Terms and Concepts to Remember:

90. **Personality** is an individual's characteristic pattern of thinking, feeling, and acting.

91. **Psychodynamic theories** view human behavior as a dynamic interaction between the conscious and unconscious minds. They stress the importance of childhood experiences.

92. **Psychoanalysis** is Freud's theory of personality that attributes thoughts and actions to unconscious motives and conflicts; also, the techniques used in treating psychological disorders by seeking to expose and interpret the tensions within a patient's unconscious.

93. In Freud's theory, the **unconscious** is the reservoir of mostly unacceptable thoughts, wishes, feelings, and memories. According to contemporary psychologists, it is a level of information processing of which we are unaware.

94. **Free association** is the Freudian technique in which the person is encouraged to say whatever comes to mind as a means of exploring the unconscious.

95. In Freud's theory, the **id** is the unconscious system of personality, consisting of basic sexual and aggressive drives, that supplies psychic energy to personality. It operates on the *pleasure principle*.

96. In psychoanalytic theory, the **ego** is the largely conscious, "executive" division of personality that attempts to mediate among the demands of the id, the superego, and reality. It operates on the *reality principle*.

97. In Freud's theory, the **superego** is the division of personality that represents internalized ideals and provides standards for judgment (the conscience) and for future aspirations.

98. Freud's **psychosexual stages** are developmental periods children pass through during which the id's pleasure-seeking energies are focused on different erogenous zones.

99. According to Freud, boys in the phallic stage develop a collection of feelings, known as the **Oedipus complex**, that center on sexual attraction to the mother and resentment of the father. Some psychologists of that time believed that girls have a parallel *Electra complex*.

100. In Freud's theory, **identification** is the process by which the child's superego develops and incorporates the parents' values. Freud saw identification as crucial, not only to resolution of the Oedipus complex, but also to the development of what psychologists now call *gender identity*.

101. In Freud's theory, **fixation** occurs when development becomes arrested, due to unresolved conflicts, in an earlier psychosexual stage.

102. In psychoanalytic theory, **defense mechanisms** are the ego's methods of unconsciously protecting itself against anxiety by distorting reality.

103. In psychoanalytic theory, **repression** is the unconscious exclusion of anxiety-arousing thoughts, feelings, and memories from consciousness; the basis of all defense mechanisms.

104. The **collective unconscious** is Jung's concept of an inherited unconscious shared by all people and deriving from our species' history.

105. **Projective tests**, such as the Rorschach, present ambiguous stimuli onto which people supposedly *project* their own inner feelings.

106. The **Thematic Apperception Test (TAT)** is a projective test in which people express their inner feelings and interests through the stories they make up about ambiguous scenes.

107. The **Rorschach inkblot test**, the most widely used projective test, consists of 10 inkblots that people are asked to interpret; it seeks to identify people's inner feelings by analyzing their interpretations of the blots.

108. **Humanistic theories** of personality focus on our potential for healthy personal growth.

109. In Maslow's theory, **self-actualization** describes the process of fulfilling one's potential and becoming spontaneous, loving, creative, and self-accepting. Self-actualization becomes active only after the more basic physical and psychological needs have been met.

110. According to Rogers, **unconditional positive regard** is an attitude of total acceptance toward another person.

111. **Self-concept** refers to one's personal awareness of "who I am." In the humanistic perspective, the self-concept is a central feature of personality; life happiness is significantly affected by whether the self-concept is positive or negative.

MODULE
39 Contemporary Perspectives on Personality

Trait Theory

1. behaviors; motives; explaining; describing

2. factor analysis; extraversion–introversion; stability–instability

3. brain arousal; frontal; extraverts; introverts; extraverts

4. genes; temperament; behavioral

5. autonomic nervous system

6. are

7. **d.** is the answer.
   a. & b. These traits are unrelated to whether a person is reserved or fun-loving.

8. **c.** is the answer.
   a. & b. According to this theory, introverts have relatively high levels of arousal, causing them to crave solitude.
   d. Isolation might lower arousal level even further.

9. introvert

10. extraversion; success; introversion; weakness

11. shyness

12. low; sensitive; evaluate them negatively

13. personality inventories

14. Minnesota Multiphasic Personality Inventory; 10; lie scale

15. empirically

16. **a.** is the answer.
   b. & c. There are no such tests.
   d. A personality test that measures personality traits would not be helpful in identifying troubled behaviors.

17. **a.** Conscientiousness: from disciplined to impulsive
   b. Agreeableness: from soft-hearted to ruthless
   c. Neuroticism (emotional stability): on a continuum from calm to anxious; secure to insecure
   d. Openness: from preference for variety to routine
   e. Extraversion: from sociable to retiring

18. stable; maturity principle

19. 40; do

20. **c.** is the answer.

21. traits (or dispositions); situation (or environment); person-situation

22. time; situations; correlate; not predictably consistent

23. is not
At any given moment a person's behavior is powerfully influenced by the immediate situation, so that it may appear that the person does not have a consistent personality. But averaged over many situations a person's outgoingness, happiness, and carelessness, for instance, are more predictable.

24. animation; speaking; gestures; consistent; does

Social-Cognitive Theories

25. environment; Albert Bandura

26. cognition; behaviors; environmental; biopsychosocial; reciprocal determinism
Different people choose different environments partly on the basis of their dispositions. Our personality shapes how we interpret and react to events. It also helps create the situations to which we react.

27. gene-environment

28. past behavior in similar situations

29. communication ability; inner achievement

30. learning; cognition

31. inner traits

32. situational; internal; situational; environment. This shows the interaction of internal and situational factors, using the social-cognitive view of how personality develops.

33. reciprocal determinism. This shows how the interaction of behavior, internal personal factors, and environment can change behavior.

Exploring the Self

34. self

35. possible selves

36. spotlight effect

37. self-esteem; self-efficacy; independent of

38. more; racial prejudice

39. **c.** is the answer.
    a. This describes self-serving bias.
    b. The spotlight effect has nothing to do with control.

40. incompetent

41. self-serving; Asia; modesty

42. more

43. above

44. high; narcissism

Narcissism correlates with materialism, the desire to be famous, inflated expectations, more hookups with fewer committed relationships, more gambling, and more cheating, all of which have been on the rise.

45. defensive; criticism; secure; external

46. **c.** is the answer.

47. individualism; goals; traits; North America; Western Europe; Australia; New Zealand

48. collectivism; group; identity; Japan; China

49. independence; interdependence

50. individualist; loneliness; homicide; stress

51. cultural neuroscience

Module Review:

52. **a.** is the answer.

53. **b.** is the answer. Studies have shown that people do not act with predictable consistency from one situation to the next. But, over a number of situations, consistent patterns emerge, and this basic consistency of traits persists over the life span.

54. **b.** is the answer. In doing so, it underestimates the influence of the environment.
    a. The trait perspective does not emphasize early childhood experiences.
    c. This criticism is unlikely since trait theory does not seek to explain personality development.
    d. Trait theory does not look on traits as being "positive" or "negative."

55. **c.** is the answer. Personality inventories are the major assessment method used by trait theorists.

56. **b.** is the answer. The MMPI was developed by selecting from many items those that differentiated between the groups of interest; hence, it was empirically derived. That it is an objective test is shown by the fact that it can be scored by computer.
    a. Projective tests present ambiguous stimuli for people to interpret; the MMPI is a questionnaire.
    c. Although sometimes used to assess job applicants, the MMPI was developed to assess emotionally troubled people.
    d. The MMPI does not focus on control but, rather, measures various aspects of personality.

57. **b.** is the answer. Trait theory attempts to describe behavior and not to develop explanations or applications. The emphasis is more on consistency than on change.

58. **d.** is the answer.

59. **a.** is the answer. Neuroticism, extraversion, and openness tend to decrease, while agreeableness and conscientiousness tend to increase.
    b. The Big Five dimensions describe personality in various cultures reasonably well.
    c. Heritability generally runs 40 percent for each dimension.

60. **b.** is the answer. Psychologists who study the self emphasize that for the individual, self-affirming thinking is generally adaptive. People with high self-esteem have fewer sleepless nights, succumb less easily to pressures to conform, and are just plain happier.

61. **b.** is the answer. The social-cognitive theory has been accused of putting so much emphasis on the situation that inner traits are neglected.
    a. Such a criticism has been made of the psychodynamic perspective but is not relevant to the social-cognitive perspective.
    c. Such a criticism might be more relevant to the trait perspective; the social-cognitive perspective offers an explanation in the form of reciprocal determinism.
    d. There are assessment techniques appropriate to the theory, namely, questionnaires and observations of behavior in situations.

62. **d.** is the answer.
    a. This perspective emphasizes unconscious dynamics in personality.
    b. This perspective is more concerned with *describing* than *explaining* personality.
    c. This perspective emphasizes the healthy, self-actualizing tendencies of personality.

63. **a.** is the answer. Feelings of insecurity reduce self-esteem, and those who feel negative about themselves tend to feel negative about others.

64. **b.** is the answer.

65. **c.** is the answer. In actuality, people with *high* self-esteem are generally more independent of pressures to conform.

66. **c.** is the answer. In keeping with their emphasis on interactions between people and situations, social-cognitive theorists would most likely make use of observations of behavior in relevant situations.
    a. & d. Personality inventories and factor analyses would more likely be used by a trait theorist.
    b. Projective tests would more likely be used by a psychologist working within the psychodynamic perspective.

Terms and Concepts to Remember:

67. A **trait** is a characteristic pattern of behavior or a disposition to feel and act.

68. **Personality inventories,** associated with the trait perspective, are questionnaires used to assess personality traits.

69. Consisting of 10 clinical scales, the **Minnesota Multiphasic Personality Inventory (MMPI)** is the most widely researched and clinically used personality inventory.

70. An **empirically derived test** is one developed by testing many items to see which best distinguish between groups of interest.

71. According to the **social-cognitive perspective,** behavior is the result of interactions between people's traits (including their thinking) and their social context.

72. According to the social-cognitive perspective, personality is shaped through **reciprocal determinism,** or the interacting influences of behavior, internal cognition, and environment.

73. In contemporary psychology, the **self** is the organizer of our thoughts, feelings, and actions.

74. The **spotlight effect** is the tendency of people to overestimate the extent to which other people are noticing and evaluating their appearance, performance, and blunders.

75. **Self-esteem** refers to an individual's feeling of self-worth.

76. **Self-efficacy** is one's sense of competence and effectiveness.

77. **Self-serving bias** is the tendency to perceive oneself favorably.

78. **Narcissism** is excessive self-love and self-absorption.

79. **Individualism** is giving priority to personal goals over group goals and defining one's identity in terms of personal traits rather than group identification.

80. **Collectivism** is giving priority to the goals of one's group and defining one's identity accordingly.

Before You Move On

Matching Items 1

1. f	**5.** h	**9.** c
2. i	**6.** d	**10.** e
3. b	**7.** a	
4. j	**8.** g	

Matching Items 2

1. g	**5.** d	**9.** e
2. i	**6.** a	**10.** b
3. h	**7.** k	**11.** c
4. j	**8.** f	

Essay Question

Since you are apparently in good psychological health, according to the psychodynamic perspective you must have experienced a healthy childhood and successfully passed Freud's stages of psychosexual development. Freud would also say that your ego is functioning well in balancing the demands of your id with the restraining demands of your superego and reality. Freud might also say that your honest nature reflects a well-developed superego, while Jung might say it derives from a universal value found in our collective unconscious.

According to the humanistic perspective, your open and honest nature indicates that your basic needs have been met and you are in the process of self-actualization or even self-transcendence (Maslow). Furthermore, your openness indicates that you have a healthy self-concept and were likely nurtured by genuine, accepting, and empathic caregivers (Rogers). More recently, researchers who emphasize the self would also focus on the importance of a positive self-concept.

Trait theorists would be less concerned with explaining these specific characteristics than with describing them, determining their consistency, and classifying your personality type. Some trait theorists, such as Allport, Eysenck, and Kagan, attribute certain trait differences to biological factors such as autonomic reactivity and heredity.

According to the social-cognitive perspective, your personal factors, behavior, and environmental influences interacted in shaping your personality and behaviors. The fact that you are a responsible person indicates that you perceive yourself as controlling, rather than as controlled by, your environment.

Cross-Check

ACROSS	DOWN
3. preconscious	1. displacement
6. inventory	2. reciprocal determinism
8. trait	3. personality
9. ego	4. Oedipus
10. defense mechanisms	5. identification
13. fixation	7. Rorschach
	11. MMPI
	12. id

Psychological Disorders

Overview

Although there is no clear-cut line between normal and abnormal behavior, we can characterize as abnormal those behaviors that represent a clinically significant disturbance in a person's cognition, emotion regulation, or behavior. Modules 40–43 discuss anxiety disorders, obsessive-compulsive disorder, posttraumatic stress disorder, major depressive disorder, bipolar disorder, schizophrenia, dissociative disorders, personality disorders, and eating disorders, as classified by the *Diagnostic and Statistical Manual of Mental Disorders* (DSM-5). Although this classification system follows a medical model, in which disorders are viewed as illnesses, the modules discuss psychological as well as physiological factors, as advocated by the current biopsychosocial approach. Thus, psychoanalytic theory, learning theory, social-cognitive theory, and other psychological perspectives are drawn on when relevant.

Your major task in this unit is to learn about psychological disorders, their various characteristics, and their possible causes. Since the material to be learned is extensive, it may be helpful to rehearse it by mentally completing the questions for each module several times.

NOTE: Answer guidelines for all Module 40–43 questions begin on page 357.

Outline

Instructions

First, skim each section, noting headings and boldface items. After you have read the section, review each objective by answering the fill-in, essay-type, and multiple-choice questions for that section. In some cases, Study Tips explain how best to learn a difficult concept and Applications and Module Reviews help you to know how well you understand the material. Finally, try to define the important terms and concepts using your own words. As you proceed, evaluate your performance by consulting the answers on page 357. Do not continue until you understand each answer. If you need to, review or reread a troublesome section before continuing.

Before You Move On includes activities that test you on material from the entire unit.

Basic Concepts of Psychological Disorders

Understanding Psychological Disorders

Objective 40-1: Discuss how we draw the line between normality and disorder.

1. A psychological disorder is defined as a

   _____

   _____ .

2. Such behaviors are dysfunctional, or

   _____ , and they are often

   accompanied by _____ . They

   _____ (have/have not) varied

   over time.

STUDY TIP: To be said to have a psychological disorder, a person must exhibit a clinically significant disturbance in cognition, emotion regulation, or behavior. Most people sometimes behave in ways that seem disturbed yet fall short of being clinically significant; the behaviors don't interfere with the person's daily life. For example, a fear of horses may be abnormal, but if you have no contact with horses, your fear doesn't affect your life and so is not disordered. Think about your own behavior patterns and see if you can think of examples that fit the criteria that characterize psychological disorders.

APPLICATION:

3. Kitty has agreed to appear on the TV show *Survivor*. Her test involves eating roaches, a practice that disgusts most North Americans, including Kitty. Although Kitty feels disgust for her task, her disgust at eating roaches does not interfere with her _____ and so she is not considered to have a disorder.

Objective 40-2: Discuss how the *medical model* and the biopsychosocial approach influence our understanding of *psychological disorders*.

4. The view that psychological disorders are sicknesses is the basis of the _____ model. According to this view, psychological disorders are viewed as mental _____ , or _____ , diagnosed on the basis of _____ and cured through _____ .

5. One of the first reformers to advocate this position and call for providing more humane living

conditions for the mentally ill was

_____ .

6. Today's psychologists recognize that all behavior arises from the interaction of _____ and _____ . To presume that a person is "mentally ill" attributes the condition solely to a "_____" that must be identified and cured.

7. Major psychological disorders such as _____ and _____ are universal; others, such as _____ _____ and _____ _____ , are culture-bound. These culture-bound disorders may share an underlying dynamic, such as _____ , yet differ in their _____ .

8. Today, psychologists take a _____ approach, whereby they assume that disorders result from the interaction of _____ , _____ , and _____ influences.

Influences:
- evolution
- individual genes
- brain structure and chemistry

Influences:
- stress
- trauma
- learned helplessness
- mood-related perceptions and memories

Psychological disorder

Influences:
- roles
- expectations
- definitions of *normality* and *disorder*

9. Epigenetics is the study of _____ influences on _____ expression that occur without a change in _____ .

STUDY TIP: Think about the implications of the medical model and the biopsychosocial approach to psychological disorders. If a behavior pattern that represents a clinically significant disturbance in a person's cognition is caused by a brain abnormality, for example, how would you answer the following questions?

1. How should this behavior be diagnosed?
2. How should this behavior be treated in efforts to cure it?

3. How will people view people who are diagnosed with this disorder? For example, are they to blame for their plight?

Now think about a disordered behavior that is caused by a person's environment, thinking patterns, and habits. Would your answers to these questions change for this type of behavior? Why or why not?

APPLICATION:

10. Haya, who suffers from *taijin-kyofusho*, is afraid of direct eye contact with another person. A therapist who believes in the medical model would say that her problem has a _____ basis. A biopsychosocial therapist would want to look into the interaction of her _____ , _____ , and _____-environment.

Classifying Disorders—and Labeling People

Objective 40-3: Describe how and why clinicians classify psychological disorders, and explain why some psychologists criticize the use of diagnostic labels.

11. The most widely used system for classifying psychological disorders is the American Psychiatric Association manual, commonly known by its abbreviation, _____ . This manual aims to _____ a disorder and to _____ its future course, which suggests appropriate _____ and stimulates research into its _____ .

12. Real-world tests (_____ _____) have assessed the reliability of the new categories. Some, such as adult _____ _____ _____ , have fared well; others, such as _____ _____ _____ have not. Critics fear that the new DSM will extend the _____ of everyday life.

13. The more fundamental complaint of critics of the DSM is that these labels are at best _____ and at worst _____ _____ .

14. Studies have shown that labeling has _____ (little/a significant) effect on our interpretation of individuals and their behavior.

Outline the pros and cons of labeling psychological disorders.

Objective 40-4: Explain why there is controversy over the diagnosis of attention-deficit/hyperactivity disorder.

15. (Thinking Critically) ADHD, or _____-_____/ _____ _____ , plagues children who display its three key symptoms: extreme _____ , _____ , and _____ .

16. (Thinking Critically) ADHD is diagnosed more often in _____ (boys/girls). In the decade after 1987, the proportion of American children being treated for this disorder _____ (increased/decreased) dramatically. Experts _____ (agree/ do not agree) that ADHD is a real disorder.

17. (Thinking Critically) ADHD _____ (is/is not) thought by some to be heritable, and it _____ (is/is not) caused by eating too much sugar or poor schools. ADHD is often accompanied by a _____ disorder or with behavior that is _____ or temper-prone.

APPLICATION:

18. (Thinking Critically) Thirteen-year-old Ronald constantly fidgets in his seat at school, frequently blurts out answers without being called, and is extremely distractible. A psychiatrist might diagnose Ronald with _____-_____/ _____ .

Objective 40-5: Discuss whether psychological disorders predict violent behavior.

19. (Thinking Critically) Most people with psychological disorders _____ (are/are not) violent. Better predictors of violence are a history of violence, use of _____ or _____ , and access to a _____ .

Rates of Psychological Disorders

Objective 40-6: State how many people have, or have had, a psychological disorder, and discuss whether poverty is a risk factor.

20. Research reveals that just over _____ (how many?) adult Americans suffer a clinically significant mental disorder in a given year.

21. The incidence of serious psychological disorders is _____ (higher/lower) among those below the poverty line.

22. In terms of age of onset, most psychological disorders appear by _____ (early/middle/late) adulthood. Some, such as the _____ _____ and _____ , appear during childhood.

MODULE REVIEW:

23. The criteria for classifying behavior as psychologically disordered
    a. vary from culture to culture.
    b. vary from time to time.
    c. vary by culture and with time.
    d. have remained largely unchanged over the course of history.

24. Today, psychologists take the view that disordered behaviors
    a. are usually genetically triggered.
    b. are organic diseases.
    c. arise from the interaction of nature and nurture.
    d. are the product of learning.

25. The view that all behavior arises from the interaction of heredity and environment is referred to as the _____ approach.
    a. biopsychosocial   c. medical
    b. psychodynamic   d. conditioning

26. In a given year, which of the following is (are) the most commonly reported of the psychological disorders?
    a. depressive disorders
    b. schizophrenia
    c. OCD
    d. generalized anxiety disorder

27. Evidence of environmental effects on psychological disorders is seen in the fact that certain disorders, such as _____ , are universal, whereas others, such as _____ , are culture-bound.
    a. schizophrenia; depression
    b. depression; schizophrenia
    c. antisocial personality; neurosis
    d. depression; anorexia nervosa

28. Mental health workers use the DSM-5 to
    a. guide medical diagnoses and treatment.
    b. identify the cause of a disorder.
    c. determine the relative contributions of nature and nurture on disordered behavior.
    d. do all of these things.

29. Which of the following is true concerning a "clinically significant disturbance"?
    a. It has had the same meaning since behavior was first studied.
    b. It interferes with normal day-to-day life.
    c. It involves an intense emotion but does not affect normal activities.
    d. It does not involve feelings of distress.

30. The fact that disorders such as schizophrenia are universal, whereas other disorders such as anorexia nervosa are culture-bound provides evidence for the _____ model of psychological disorders.
    a. medical   c. social-cultural
    b. biopsychosocial   d. psychodynamic

31. Our early ancestors commonly attributed disordered behavior to
    a. "bad blood."   c. brain injury.
    b. evil spirits.   d. laziness.

32. Which of the following statements concerning the labeling of disordered behaviors is NOT true?
    a. Labels interfere with effective treatment of psychological disorders.
    b. Labels promote research studies of psychological disorders.
    c. Labels may create preconceptions that bias people's perceptions.
    d. Labels may influence behavior by creating self-fulfilling prophecies.

33. Which of the following is true of the medical model?
   a. In recent years, it has been in large part discredited.
   b. It views psychological disorders as sicknesses that are diagnosable and treatable.
   c. It emphasizes the role of psychological factors in disorders over that of physiological factors.
   d. It focuses on cognitive factors.

34. Behavior is classified as disordered when it represents a significant dysfunction in
   a. an individual's cognitions.
   b. an individual's emotions.
   c. an individual's behaviors.
   d. all of these aspects.

TERMS AND CONCEPTS TO REMEMBER:

35. psychological disorder

36. medical model

37. epigenetics

38. DSM-5

39. attention-deficit/hyperactivity disorder (ADHD)

Essay Question

Clinical psychologists label people disordered if their behavior represents a "clinically significant disturbance in their cognition, emotion regulation, or behavior." Demonstrate your understanding of the classification process by giving examples of behaviors that might be considered disordered but, because they do not interfere with daily life, would not necessarily be labeled disordered. (Use the space below to list the points you want to make, and organize them. Then write the essay on a separate piece of paper.)

MODULE
41

Anxiety Disorders, OCD, and PTSD

Anxiety Disorders

Objective 41-1: Distinguish among *generalized anxiety disorders, panic disorder*, and phobias.

1. Anxiety disorders are psychological disorders characterized by _____ _____ .

2. Three anxiety disorders discussed in the text are _____ _____ _____, _____ _____, and _____ .

3. When a person is continually tense, apprehensive, and physiologically aroused for no apparent reason, he or she is diagnosed as suffering from a _____ disorder. In Freud's term, the anxiety is _____-_____ .

4. Generalized anxiety disorder can lead to physical problems, such as _____ _____ _____ .

   In some instances, anxiety may intensify dramatically and unpredictably and be accompanied by heart palpitations or choking, for example; people with these symptoms are said to have _____ _____ . This anxiety may escalate into a minutes-long episode of intense fear, or a _____ . _____ .

5. Fear or avoidance of situations in which escape might be difficult when panic strikes is called _____ .

6. People who _____ have at least a doubled risk of a _____ _____ because _____ is a stimulant.

7. When a person has an irrational fear of a specific object, activity, or situation, the diagnosis is a _____ . Although in many situations, the person can live with the problem, some _____ _____ , such as a fear of thunderstorms, are incapacitating.

8. When a person has an intense fear of other people's negative judgments, the diagnosis is a _____ _____ _____ .

Obsessive-Compulsive Disorder

Objective 41-2: Describe *OCD*.

9. When a person cannot control repetitive thoughts and actions, an _____-_____ disorder is diagnosed. Older people are _____ (more/less) likely than teens and young adults to suffer from this disorder.

10. An analysis of 14 twin studies indicates that OCD _____ (does/does not) have a genetic basis.

Posttraumatic Stress Disorder

Objective 41-3: Describe *PTSD*.

11. Traumatic stress, such as that associated with witnessing atrocities or combat, can produce _____ _____ _____ disorder. The symptoms of this disorder include _____ _____ , _____ , _____ , _____ , _____ , and trouble _____ .

12. People who have a sensitive _____ _____ are more vulnerable to this disorder. The odds of getting the disorder are higher in _____ (men/women) than in _____ (men/women).

13. Researchers who believe this disorder may be overdiagnosed point to the _____ _____ of most people who suffer trauma.

14. Irene occasionally experiences unpredictable episodes of intense dread accompanied by heart palpitations and a sensation of smothering. Since her symptoms have no apparent cause, they would probably be classified as indicative of
    a. a phobia.
    b. generalized anxiety disorder.
    c. agoraphobia.
    d. panic attack.

15. Han has an intense, irrational fear of snakes. He is suffering from
    a. generalized anxiety disorder.
    b. obsessive-compulsive disorder.
    c. a phobia.
    d. a panic attack.

16. Isabella is continually tense, jittery, and apprehensive for no specific reason. She would probably be diagnosed as suffering from
    a. a phobia.
    b. posttraumatic stress disorder.
    c. obsessive-compulsive disorder.
    d. generalized anxiety disorder.

17. Jason is so preoccupied with staying clean that he showers as many as 10 times each day. Jason would be diagnosed as suffering from
    a. panic attacks.
    b. generalized anxiety disorder.
    c. agoraphobia.
    d. obsessive-compulsive disorder.

18. Although she escaped from war-torn Bosnia two years ago, Zheina still has haunting memories and nightmares. Because she is also severely depressed, her therapist diagnoses her condition as
    a. panic disorder.
    b. obsessive-compulsive disorder.
    c. generalized anxiety disorder.
    d. posttraumatic stress disorder.

Understanding Anxiety Disorders, OCD, and PTSD

Objective 41-4: Describe how conditioning, cognition, and biology contribute to the feelings and thoughts that mark anxiety disorders, OCD, and PTSD.

19. Freud assumed that anxiety disorders are symptoms of submerged mental energy that derives from intolerable impulses that were _____ during childhood.

20. Drawing on research in which rats are given unpredictable electric shocks, theorists link general anxiety with _____ conditioning of _____ .

21. Some fears arise from _____ _____ , such as when a person who fears heights after a fall also comes to fear airplanes.

22. Phobias and compulsive behaviors reduce feelings of anxiety and thereby are _____ . Through _____ learning, someone might also learn fear by seeing others display their own fears.

23. The anxiety response probably _____ (is/is not) genetically influenced. There may be anxiety _____ that affect brain levels of the neurotransmitter _____ , which influences mood, as well as the neurotransmitter _____ , which regulates the brain's alarm centers.

24. Among PTSD patients, a history of _____ _____ leaves long-term _____ marks that increase the likelihood that a genetic vulnerability to the disorder will be expressed.

25. Brain scans of persons with obsessive-compulsive disorder reveal excessive activity in a brain region called the _____ _____ cortex. Some _____ drugs dampen this fear-circuit activity, thus reducing this behavior.

26. Humans probably _____ (are/are not) biologically prepared to develop certain fears. Compulsive acts typically are exaggerations of behaviors that contributed to our species' _____ .

STUDY TIP: Phobias are persistent fears of certain objects, activities, or situations. They are irrational because they are much stronger than the actual danger. Also, many *specific phobias* may be unrelated to a direct, negative experience with the feared object. Are there any specific objects, activities, or situations that you find particularly frightening? How do you think you acquired these fears? Can you remember a bad experience? Did you see someone else have a problem? Does your fear ever interfere with your daily life?

APPLICATIONS:

27. Julia's psychologist believes that Julia's fear of heights can be traced to a conditioned fear she developed after falling from a ladder. This explanation suggests that her fear resulted from
    a. reinforcement.
    b. observational learning.
    c. repression.
    d. stimulus generalization.

28. Before he can study, Rashid must arrange his books, pencils, paper, and other items on his desk so that they are "just so." The campus counselor suggests that Rashid's compulsive behavior may help alleviate his feelings of anxiety about failing in school. The counselor is suggesting that Rashid's compulsive behavior continues because of
    a. reinforcement.
    b. stimulus generalization.
    c. observational learning.
    d. natural selection.

29. When Olivia and her mother were working in the garden, her mother was stung by a bee, which was very painful. Olivia now will not work in the garden any more for fear of being stung by a bee. Olivia's fear is based on _____ .

30. To which of the following is a person MOST likely to acquire a phobia?

   a. heights

   b. being in public

   c. being dirty

   d. All of these are equally likely.

MODULE REVIEW:

31. Because of some troubling thoughts, Carl recently had a PET scan of his brain that revealed excessive activity in the anterior cingulate area. Carl's psychiatrist believes that Carl suffers from

   a. social anxiety disorder.

   b. posttraumatic stress disorder.

   c. a phobia.

   d. obsessive-compulsive disorder.

32. Which of the following was presented in the text as evidence of biological influences on anxiety disorders, OCD, and PTSD?

   a. Identical twins often develop similar phobias.

   b. Brain scans of persons with obsessive-compulsive disorder reveal unusually high activity in the anterior cingulate cortex.

   c. Drugs that dampen the brain's fear-circuit activity also alleviate OCD.

   d. All of these findings were presented.

33. Freud's psychoanalytic theory would most likely view phobias as

   a. conditioned fears.

   b. displaced responses to incompletely repressed impulses.

   c. biological predispositions.

   d. manifestations of self-defeating thoughts.

34 . Which of the following provides evidence that human fears have been subjected to the evolutionary process?

   a. Compulsive acts typically exaggerate behaviors that contributed to our species' survival.

   b. Most phobias focus on objects that our ancestors also feared.

   c. It is easier to condition some fears than others.

   d. All of these provide evidence.

35. The most common explanation of OCD and PTSD is that the symptoms of these disorders represent the person's attempt to deal with

   a. unconscious conflicts.

   b. anxiety.

   c. unfulfilled wishes.

   d. unpleasant responsibilities.

TERMS AND CONCEPTS TO REMEMBER:

36. anxiety disorders

37. generalized anxiety disorder

38. panic disorder

39. phobia

40. obsessive-compulsive disorder (OCD)

41. posttraumatic stress disorder (PTSD)

MODULE 42 Major Depressive Disorder and Bipolar Disorder

Major Depressive Disorder and Bipolar Disorder

Objective 42-1: Distinguish between *major depressive disorder* and *bipolar disorder*.

1. A persistent state of hopelessness and lethargy with no discernible cause is called _____ _____ disorder. When a person's mood alternates between depression and the hyperactive state of _____, _____ disorder is diagnosed. For some people, symptoms may have a _____ pattern, with depression returning each fall or winter, and mania possibly arriving with spring.

2. The possible symptoms of depression include _____ _____ .

3. Major depressive disorder occurs when at least five signs of depression last _____ or more with no apparent cause.

4. Although _____ are more common, _____ is the number one reason that people seek mental health services. It is also the leading cause of disability worldwide.

5. Symptoms of mania include _____ _____ .

6. Bipolar disorder is less common among creative professionals who rely on _____ and _____ than among those who rely on _____ expression and vivid _____ . With DSM-5, bipolar diagnoses among children and adolescents may decrease because of the new classification of _____ _____ _____ _____ in those with emotional volatility.

7. For the past six months, 25-year-old Haeji has complained of feeling isolated from others, dissatisfied with life, uninterested in most activities, and discouraged about the future. Haeji could be diagnosed as suffering from
   a. bipolar disorder.
   b. major depressive disorder.
   c. disruptive mood dysregulation disorder.
   d. mania.

8. On Monday, Delon felt optimistic, energetic, and on top of the world. On Tuesday, he felt hopeless and lethargic, and thought that the future looked very grim. Delon would MOST likely be diagnosed as having
   a. bipolar disorder.
   b. major depressive disorder.
   c. a seasonal pattern of depression.
   d. mania.

Understanding Major Depressive Disorder and Bipolar Disorder

Objective 42-2 Describe how the biological and social-cognitive perspectives help us understand major depressive disorder and bipolar disorder.

9. Depression is accompanied by many _____ and _____ changes.

10. The commonality of depression suggests that its _____ must also be common.

11. Compared with men, women are _____ (more/less) vulnerable to depression. In general, women are most vulnerable to disorders involving _____ states, such as _____ _____ .

12. Men's disorders tend to be more _____ and include _____ _____ .

13. Most people suffering major depression _____ (do/do not) eventually return to normal _____ (with/

without) professional help. It usually _____ (is/is not) the case that a depressive episode has been triggered by a stressful event. An individual's vulnerability to depression also increases following, for example, _____ .

14. With each new generation, the rate of depression is _____ (increasing/decreasing) and the disorder is striking _____ (earlier/later). In North America, today's young adults are _____ (how many?) times more likely than their grandparents to suffer depression.

15. Major depressive disorder and bipolar disorder _____ (do/do not) to run in families. Studies of _____ also reveal that genetic influences on major depressive disorder and bipolar disorder are _____ (weak/strong).

16. To determine which genes are involved in depression, researchers use _____ _____ , in which they examine the _____ of both affected and unaffected family members.

17. The brains of depressed people tend to be _____ (more/less) active, especially in an area of the _____ _____ lobe and an adjacent brain _____ _____ .

18. Depression may also be caused by _____ (high/low) levels of two neurotransmitters, _____ and _____ .

19. Drugs that decrease mania reduce _____ ; drugs that relieve depression increase _____ or _____ supplies by blocking either their _____ or their chemical _____ . The risk of depression, which (like heart disease) is associated with _____ , is reduced by a heart-healthy "Mediterranean diet."

20. Not only our biology but also our actions contribute to depression. Diet, drugs, stress, and other life experiences lay down _____ marks, which are often organic molecules.

21. According to the social-cognitive perspective, depression may be linked with _____ beliefs and a _____ style. Such beliefs may arise from _____ _____ , the feeling that can arise when the individual repeatedly experiences uncontrollable, painful events.

22. Gender differences in responding to _____ help explain why women have been twice as vulnerable to depression. According to Susan Nolen-Hoeksema, when trouble strikes, men tend to _____ and women tend to _____ .

Describe how depressed people differ from others in their explanations of failure and how such explanations tend to feed depression.

23. According to Martin Seligman, depression is more common in Western cultures that emphasize _____ and that have shown a decline in commitment to _____ and family.

24. Depression-prone people respond to bad events in an especially _____ way.

25. Being withdrawn, self-focused, and complaining tends to elicit social _____ (empathy/rejection).

Outline the vicious cycle of depression.

26. Ken's therapist suggested that his depression is a result of his self-defeating thoughts and negative assumptions about himself, his situation, and his future. Evidently, Ken's therapist is working within the _____ perspective.

   a. learning   c. biological
   b. social-cognitive   d. psychoanalytic

27. Alicia's doctor, who thinks that Alicia's depression has a biochemical cause, prescribes a drug that

   a. reduces norepinephrine.
   b. increases norepinephrine.
   c. reduces serotonin.
   d. increases acetylcholine.

28. Complete the following flow chart comparing how a depressed person and a person who is not depressed would deal with this situation.

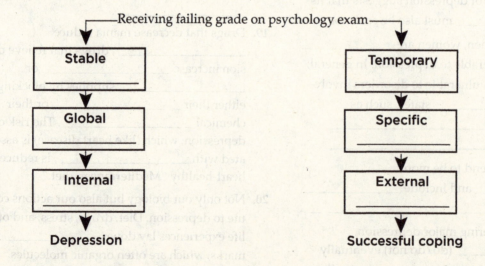

Objective 42-3: Identify the factors that increase the risk of suicide, and describe what we know about nonsuicidal self-injury.

Identify several group differences in suicide rates.

29. Factors that affect suicide are _____ use disorder and social _____ . For the elderly, it may be an alternative to current or future _____ . People who engage in nonsuicidal self-injury do so to gain relief from intense _____ , to ask for help and gain _____ , to relieve _____ , to get others to change their negative behavior, or to fit in with a peer group.

30. Important warning signs to watch for in suicide prevention efforts include _____ _____ , giving _____ _____ , or _____ and _____ _____ .

MODULE REVIEW:

31. Gender differences in the prevalence of depression may partly result from the fact that when stressful experiences occur
    a. women tend to act, while men tend to think.
    b. women tend to think, while men tend to act.
    c. women tend to distract themselves by drinking, while men tend to delve into their work.
    d. women tend to delve into their work, while men tend to distract themselves by drinking.

32. Which of the following is NOT true concerning depression?
    a. Depression is more common in women than in men.
    b. Most depressive episodes appear not to be preceded by any particular factor or event.
    c. With each new generation, depression is striking earlier.
    d. Most people recover from depression without professional therapy.

33. In treating depression, a psychiatrist would probably prescribe a drug that would
    a. increase levels of acetylcholine.
    b. decrease levels of dopamine.
    c. increase levels of norepinephrine.
    d. decrease levels of serotonin.

34. In general, women are more vulnerable than men to
    a. external disorders such as anxiety.
    b. internal disorders such as depression.
    c. external disorders such as antisocial conduct.
    d. internal disorders such as alcohol use disorder.

35. Which neurotransmitter is present in overabundant amounts during the manic phase of bipolar disorder?
    a. dopamine   c. epinephrine
    b. serotonin   d. norepinephrine

36. The DSM-5's new diagnosis of disruptive mood dysregulation disorder
    a. will clearly help parents who struggle with unstable children.
    b. will turn temper tantrums into a mental disorder.
    c. will lead to overmedication.
    d. will reduce the number of child and adolescent bipolar diagnoses.

37. Social-cognitive theorists contend that depression is linked with
    a. negative moods.
    b. maladaptive explanations of failure.
    c. self-defeating beliefs.
    d. all of these characteristics.

38. Which of the following is NOT true of major depressive disorder and bipolar disorder, according to the biological perspective?
    a. Activity in the left frontal lobe is increased during a depressed state.
    b. Norepinephrine is scarce during depression.
    c. Brain reward centers are less active during a depressed state.
    d. Serotonin is scarce or inactive during depression.

TERMS AND CONCEPTS TO REMEMBER:

39. major depressive disorder
40. bipolar disorder
41. mania
42. rumination

MODULE 43 Schizophrenia and Other Disorders

Schizophrenia

Objective 43-1: Describe the patterns of perceiving, thinking, and feeling that characterize schizophrenia.

1. Schizophrenia, or "split mind," refers not to a split personality but rather to a split from _____ . This disorder is an example of a _____ _____ , a broad term for _____ .

2. People with schizophrenia who display inappropriate behavior are said to have _____ _____ .

3. Those with toneless voices, expressionless faces, or mute and rigid bodies are said to have _____ _____ .

4. The disturbed perceptions of people suffering from schizophrenia may take the form of _____ , which usually are _____ (sights/sounds).

5. The distorted, false beliefs of schizophrenia patients are called _____ . Jumbled ideas may make no sense even within sentences, forming what is known as _____ _____ .

6. Many psychologists attribute the disorganized thinking of schizophrenia to a breakdown in the capacity for _____ _____ .

7. The difficulty most people with schizophrenia have perceiving facial emotions is a sign of an impaired _____ _____ _____ .

8. Some victims of schizophrenia lapse into an emotionless _____ _____ state of no apparent feeling; others, who exhibit _____ , may remain motionless for hours or perform compulsive actions, such as continually rocking, or rubbing an arm, or being severely and dangerously agitated.

Objective 43-2: Distinguish between *chronic* and *acute* schizophrenia.

9. When schizophrenia develops slowly (called _____ schizophrenia), recovery is _____ (more/less) likely than when it develops rapidly in reaction to particular life stresses (called _____ schizophrenia).

APPLICATION:

10. Claiming that she heard a voice commanding her to warn other people that eating is harmful, Sandy attempts to convince others in a restaurant not to eat. The psychiatrist to whom she is referred finds that Sandy's thinking and speech are often fragmented and incoherent. In addition, Sandy has an unreasonable fear that someone is "out to get her" and consequently trusts no one. Her condition is most indicative of _____ symptoms of schizophrenia.

Objective 43-3: Identify the brain abnormalities associated with schizophrenia.

11. The brain tissue of schizophrenia patients has been found to have an excess of receptors for the neurotransmitter _____ . Drugs that block these receptors have been found to _____ (increase/decrease) schizophrenia symptoms.

12. Brain scans have shown that some people suffering from schizophrenia have abnormally _____ (high/low) brain activity in the _____ lobes.

13. Enlarged, _____-filled areas and a corresponding _____ of cerebral tissue is also characteristic of schizophrenia. Two smaller-than-normal areas are the _____ and the _____ _____ connecting the brain's two hemispheres. Schizophrenia patients also have a smaller-than-normal _____ ,

which may account for their difficulty in filtering _____ and focusing _____ .

Objective 43-4: Identify the prenatal events associated with increased risk of developing schizophrenia.

14. Some scientists contend that the brain abnormalities of schizophrenia may be caused by a prenatal problem, such as _____ _____ _____ , maternal _____ , older _____ age, and _____ during delivery. Another possible culprit is a mid-pregnancy _____ _____ .

List several pieces of evidence for the fetal-virus idea.

Objective 43-5: Describe how genes influence schizophrenia.

15. Twin studies _____ (support/do not support) the contention that heredity plays a role in schizophrenia.

16. The role of the prenatal environment in schizophrenia is demonstrated by the fact that identical twins who share the same _____ , and are therefore more likely to experience the same prenatal _____ , are more likely to share the disorder.

17. Adoption studies _____ (confirm/do not confirm) a genetic link in the development of schizophrenia.

18. It appears that for schizophrenia to develop there must be both a _____ predisposi-

tion and other _____ factors such as those listed earlier that "_____ _____ " the _____ that predispose this disease.

19. Wayne has been diagnosed with schizophrenia. His doctor attempts to help Wayne by prescribing a drug that blocks receptors for _____ .

20. Janet, whose class presentation is titled "Current Views on the Causes of Schizophrenia," concludes her talk with the statement
    a. "Schizophrenia is caused by intolerable stress."
    b. "Schizophrenia is inherited."
    c. "Genes may predispose some people to react to particular experiences by developing schizophrenia."
    d. "As of this date, schizophrenia is completely unpredictable and its causes are unknown."

Other Disorders

Objective 43-6: Describe *dissociative disorders*, and discuss why they are controversial.

21. In _____ disorders, a person's conscious awareness _____ from painful memories, thoughts, and feelings. A sudden loss of memory or change in identity, is called a _____ .

22. Dissociation itself _____ (is/is not so) rare.

23. A person who develops two or more distinct personalities is suffering from _____ _____ disorder.

24. Skeptics express three concerns about the existence of DID. First, they find it suspicious that it has such a short and _____ history. Second, they note that DID _____ (varies/does not vary) by culture. Third, as shown by Nicholas Spanos, such people may merely be playing different _____ .

25. Those who accept this as a genuine disorder point to evidence that differing personalities may be associated with distinct _____ and _____ states. Some clinicians include dissociative disorders under the umbrella of _____ _____ disorder, a natural, protective response to traumatic experiences during childhood.

Identify two pieces of evidence brought forth by those who do not accept dissociative identity disorder as a genuine disorder.

26. The psychodynamic and learning perspectives view dissociative disorders as ways of dealing with _____ . Others view them as a desperate effort to _____ from a horrific existence. Skeptics claim these disorders are sometimes contrived by _____-_____ people and sometimes constructed out of the _____-_____ interaction.

APPLICATIONS:

27. Multiple personalities have long been a popular subject of films and novels. For example, Dr. Jekyll, whose second personality was Mr. Hyde, had _____ _____ disorder.

28. As a child, Monica was criticized severely by her mother for not living up to her expectations. This criticism was always followed by a beating with a whip. As an adult, Monica is generally introverted and extremely shy. Sometimes, however, she acts more like a young child, throwing tantrums if she doesn't get her way. At other times, she is a flirting, happy-go-lucky young lady. Most likely, Monica is

    a. experiencing a fugue state.
    b. suffering from posttraumatic stress disorder.
    c. suffering from dissociative identity disorder.
    d. a fantasy-prone person playing a role.

Objective 43-7: Identify the three clusters of *personality disorders*, and describe the behaviors and brain activity that characterize the *antisocial personality*.

29. Personality disorders exist when an individual has character traits that are enduring and impair _____ _____ .

30. A fearful sensitivity to rejection may predispose the _____ personality disorder. Eccentric behaviors, such as emotionless disengagement, are characteristic of the _____ personality disorder. The third cluster exhibits dramatic or _____ behaviors, such as the _____ or _____ personality disorders.

31. An individual who seems to have no conscience, lies, steals, is generally irresponsible, and may be criminal is said to have an _____ personality. He or she may show lower _____ _____ . Previously, this person was labeled a _ _____ .

32. Studies of biological relatives of those with antisocial and unemotional tendencies suggest that there _____ (may/may not) be a biological predisposition to such traits.

33. Antisocial adolescents tend to have been _____ , _____ , unconcerned with _____ , _____ , and low in _____ .

34. In people with antisocial criminal tendencies, the emotion-controlling _____ is smaller. PET scans of murderers' brains reveal reduced activity in the _____ _____ , an area of the cortex that helps control _____ .

35. As in other disorders, in antisocial personality, genetics _____ (is/is not) the whole story. Rather, genes, in combination with negative _____ influences such as _____ _____ , help wire the brain.

APPLICATION:

36. Ming has never been able to keep a job. He's been in and out of jail for charges such as theft, sexual assault, and spousal abuse. Ming would most likely be diagnosed as having
a. a dissociative identity disorder.
b. schizotypal personality disorder.
c. a fugue state.
d. an antisocial personality.

Objective 43-8: Identify the three main eating disorders, and explain how biological, psychological, and social-cultural influences make people more vulnerable to them.

37. The disorder in which a person becomes significantly underweight and yet feels fat is known as _____ _____ .

38. A more common disorder is
_____ _____ ,
which is characterized by repeated
_____ -
episodes and by feelings of depression or anxiety. When bouts of excessive eating followed by remorse are not accompanied by purging or fasting, the _____ -
_____ disorder may be diagnosed.

39. The families of anorexia patients tend to be
_____ , _____ ,
_____ , and _____ .

40. Genetic factors _____
(may/do not) influence susceptibility to eating disorders.

41. Those most vulnerable to eating disorders are also those (usually women or gay men) who most idealize _____ and have the greatest body _____ .

42. In impoverished areas of the world, where thinness can signal poverty, _____ is better. In _____ cultures, however, the rise in eating disorders has coincided with an increasing number of women having a poor _____
_____ .

43. When young women were shown pictures of unnaturally thin models, they felt more
_____ , _____ , and
_____ with their own bodies.

APPLICATION:

44. Of the following individuals, who might be most prone to developing an eating disorder?
a. Jason, an adolescent boy who is somewhat overweight and is unpopular with his peers
b. Jennifer, a teenage girl who has a poor self-image and a fear of not being able to live up to her parents' high standards
c. Susan, a 35-year-old woman who is a "workaholic" and devotes most of her energies to her high-pressured career
d. Bill, a 40-year-old man who has had problems with alcohol use and is seriously depressed after losing his job of 20 years

MODULE REVIEW:

45. Which of the following is NOT true regarding schizophrenia?
a. It occurs more frequently in people born in winter and spring months.
b. It occurs more frequently when mothers are sick with influenza during pregnancy.
c. It occurs more frequently in lightly populated areas.
d. It usually appears during adolescence or early adulthood.

46. The effect of drugs that block receptors for dopamine is to
a. lessen the hallucinations of schizophrenia.
b. alleviate catatonia.
c. increase the hallucinations of schizophrenia.
d. make catatonia more likely.

47. Most of the hallucinations of schizophrenia patients involve the sense of
a. smell.   c. hearing.
b. vision.   d. touch.

48. Hearing voices would be _____ ; believing that you are Napoleon would be _____ .
a. word salad; catatonia
b. catatonia; word salad
c. a delusion; a hallucination
d. a hallucination; a delusion

49. When schizophrenia is slow to develop, called _____ schizophrenia, recovery is _____ .
a. acute; unlikely   c. chronic; unlikely
b. chronic; likely   d. acute; likely

50. Many psychologists believe the disorganized thoughts of people with schizophrenia result from a breakdown in
   a. selective attention.
   b. memory storage.
   c. motivation.
   d. memory retrieval.

51. Research evidence links the brain abnormalities of schizophrenia to _____ during prenatal development.
   a. maternal stress
   b. a viral infection contracted
   c. abnormal levels of certain hormones
   d. the weight of the unborn child

52. Among the following, which is generally accepted as a possible cause of schizophrenia?
   a. an excess of endorphins in the brain
   b. being a twin
   c. extensive learned helplessness
   d. a genetic predisposition

53. When expecting to be electrically shocked, people with an antisocial personality disorder, as compared with normal people, show
   a. less fear and greater arousal of the autonomic nervous system.
   b. less fear and less autonomic arousal.
   c. greater fear and greater autonomic arousal.
   d. greater fear and less autonomic arousal.

54. Which of the following is true concerning eating disorders?
   a. Genetic factors may influence susceptibility.
   b. Cultural pressures for thinness strongly influence teenage girls.
   c. Family background is a significant factor.
   d. All of these statements are true.

55. Nicholas Spanos considers dissociative identity disorder to be
   a. a genuine disorder.
   b. merely role playing.
   c. a disorder that cannot be explained according to the learning perspective.
   d. a biological phenomenon.

56. Although the cause of eating disorders is still unknown, proposed explanations focus on all the following, EXCEPT
   a. metabolic factors.
   b. genetic factors.
   c. family background factors.
   d. cultural factors.

TERMS AND CONCEPTS TO REMEMBER:

57. schizophrenia

58. psychosis

59. delusions

60. chronic schizophrenia

61. acute schizophrenia

62. dissociative disorders

63. dissociative identity disorder (DID)

64. personality disorders

65. antisocial personality disorder

66. anorexia nervosa

67. bulimia nervosa

68. binge-eating disorder

Before You Move On

SUMMARY STUDY TIP: This unit discusses categories of psychological disorders. To help organize your study of this material, complete the following table. For each category, list the specific disorders discussed. Then, for each disorder, give a description and a brief explanation of possible causes of the disorders. To get you started, portions of the first category of disorders, plus some random information, has been provided.

Category	Specific Disorders	Description of the Disorder	Possible Explanations of Causes
Anxiety disorders	Generalized anxiety disorder Panic disorder Phobias	Distressing, persistent anxiety or maladaptive behaviors that reduce anxiety	Conditioning and reinforcement of fears. For example, stimulus generalization. Also, observational learning. Pairing of a traumatic event with a genetic predisposition.
Obsessive-compulsive disorder			
Posttraumatic stress disorder			
Major depressive disorder			
Bipolar disorder			
Schizophrenia			
Dissociative disorders			
Personality disorders			
Eating disorders			

Matching Items 1

Match each term with the appropriate definition or description.

Terms

_____ 1. dissociative disorder
_____ 2. medical model
_____ 3. major depressive disorder
_____ 4. social anxiety disorder
_____ 5. biopsychosocial approach
_____ 6. mania
_____ 7. obsessive-compulsive disorder
_____ 8. schizophrenia
_____ 9. hallucination
_____ 10. panic attack
_____ 11. survivor resiliency

Definitions or Descriptions

a. psychological disorder in which lethargy and feelings of hopelessness impair daily living
b. an extremely elevated mood
c. a false sensory experience
d. approach that considers behavior disorders as illnesses that can be diagnosed, treated, and, in most cases, cured
e. a sudden escalation of anxiety often accompanied by a sensation of choking or other physical symptoms
f. a disorder in which conscious awareness becomes separated from previous memories, feelings, and thoughts
g. approach that considers behavior disorders to be the result of biological, psychological, and social-cultural influences
h. intense fear of being scrutinized by others
i. a group of disorders marked by disorganized thinking, disturbed perceptions, and inappropriate emotions and actions
j. a disorder characterized by repetitive thoughts and actions
k. the ability to recover after severe stress

Matching Items 2

Match each term with the appropriate definition or description.

Terms

_____ 1. dissociative identity disorder
_____ 2. phobia
_____ 3. dopamine
_____ 4. panic disorder
_____ 5. antisocial personality
_____ 6. norepinephrine
_____ 7. serotonin
_____ 8. bipolar disorder
_____ 9. delusions
_____ 10. agoraphobia
_____ 11. psychosis
_____ 12. anorexia nervosa

Definitions or Descriptions

a. a neurotransmitter for which there are excess receptors in some schizophrenia patients
b. a neurotransmitter that is overabundant during mania and scarce during depression
c. an individual who seems to have no conscience
d. false beliefs that may accompany psychological disorders
e. an anxiety disorder marked by a persistent, irrational fear of a specific object, activity, or situation
f. a disorder formerly called multiple personality disorder
g. a neurotransmitter possibly linked to anxiety disorders
h. a type of mood disorder
i. an anxiety disorder marked by episodes of intense dread
j. a fear of situations in which help might not be available during a panic attack
k. marked by irrationality and loss of contact with reality
l. a type of eating disorder

Cross-Check

As you learned in Module 2, reviewing and overlearning of material are important to the learning process. After you have written the definitions of the key terms in this unit, you should complete the crossword puzzle to ensure that you can reverse the process—recognize the term, given the definition.

ACROSS

3. A persistent state of lethargy is a symptom of _____ _____ disorder.
16. A euphoric, hyperactive state.
17. Generalized anxiety disorder is often accompanied by depressed _____ .
18. Mood disorder in which a person alternates between depression and mania.
19. Category of disorders that includes phobias.

DOWN

1. When schizophrenia is a slow-developing process, it is said to be _____ .
2. A widely used system of classifying psychological disorders.
4. A psychological disorder characterized by extreme inattention, for example.
5. Disorders that involve a separation of conscious awareness from one's previous memories, thoughts, and feelings.
6. A persistent, irrational fear of a specific object or situation.
7. Biomedical research technique used to determine which genes are involved in a specific psychological disorder.
8. Approach that assumes that genes, psychological factors, and social and cultural circumstances combine and interact to produce psychological disorders.
9. False sensory experiences.
10. The viewpoint that psychological disorders are illnesses.
11. False beliefs that often are symptoms of schizophrenia.

12. A possible cause of schizophrenia is a _____ mishap, such as oxygen deprivation.
13. Neurotransmitter for which there are excess receptors in the brains of schizophrenia patients.
14. Category of schizophrenia symptoms that includes having a toneless voice, expressionless face, and a mute or rigid body.
15. Neurotransmitter that influences sleep and mood and that therefore may be a factor in anxiety disorders.

Answers

 ## Basic Concepts of Psychological Disorders

Understanding Psychological Disorders

1. syndrome marked by a clinically significant disturbance in a person's cognition, emotion regulation, or behavior.

2. maladaptive; distress; have

3. day-to-day life

4. medical; illness; psychopathology; symptoms; therapy

5. Philippe Pinel

6. nature; nurture; sickness

7. depression; schizophrenia; anorexia nervosa; bulimia nervosa; anxiety; symptoms

8. biopsychosocial; biological; psychological; social-cultural

9. environmental; gene; DNA

10. biological; biology; psychology; social-cultural. Haya's behavior is directed by a specific situation. Because it does not interfere with her everyday life, it is not considered disordered.

Classifying Disorders—and Labeling People

11. DSM-5; describe; predict; treatment; causes

12. field trials; posttraumatic stress disorder; antisocial personality disorder; pathologizing

13. subjective; value judgments

14. a significant

Psychological labels may be arbitrary. They can create preconceptions that bias our perceptions and interpretations and they can affect people's self-images. Moreover, labels can change reality, by serving as self-fulfilling prophecies. Despite these drawbacks, labels are useful in describing, treating, and researching the causes of psychological disorders.

15. attention-deficit/hyperactivity disorder; inattention; hyperactivity; impulsivity

16. boys; increased; do not agree

17. is; is not; learning; defiant

18. attention-deficit/hyperactivity disorder

19. are not; alcohol; drugs; gun

Rates of Psychological Disorders

20. 1 in 4

21. higher

22. early; antisocial personality; phobias

Module Review:

23. c. is the answer.

24. c. is the answer. Most clinicians agree that psychological disorders may be caused by both psychological (d.) and physical (a. and b.) factors.

25. a. is the answer.

26. a. is the answer.

27. d. is the answer. Although depression is universal, anorexia nervosa and bulimia are rare outside of Western culture.

a. & b. Schizophrenia and depression are both universal.
c. The text mentions only schizophrenia and depression as universal disorders. Furthermore, neurosis is no longer a category of diagnosis.

28. a. is the answer.
b. & c. The DSM-5 describes disordered behaviors but does not attempt to identify the causes.

29. b. is the answer.
a. The meaning of a clinically significant disturbance has varied over time.
c. & d. By definition, a clinically significant disturbance interferes with daily life and involves distress in the person suffering from a psychological disorder.

30. b. is the answer. The fact that some disorders are universal implicates biological factors in their origin. The fact that other disorders appear only in certain parts of the world implicates sociocultural and psychological factors in their origin.

31. b. is the answer.

32. a. is the answer. In fact, just the opposite is true. Labels are useful in promoting effective treatment of psychological disorders.

33. b. is the answer.
a. This isn't the case; in fact, the medical model has gained credibility from recent discoveries of genetic and biochemical links to some disorders.
c. & d. The medical perspective tends to place more emphasis on physiological factors.

34. d. is the answer.

Terms and Concepts to Remember:

35. A **psychological disorder** is a syndrome marked by a "clinically significant disturbance in an individual's cognition, emotion regulation, or behavior."

36. The **medical model** holds that psychological disorders are illnesses that can be diagnosed, treated, and, in most cases, cured, often through treatment in a psychiatric hospital.

37. **Epigenetics** is the study of environmental influences on gene expression that occur without a change in DNA.

38. **DSM-5** is a short name for the American Psychiatric Association's *Diagnostic and Statistical Manual of Mental Disorders* (*Fifth Edition*), which provides a system of classifying psychological disorders.

39. **Attention-deficit/hyperactivity disorder (ADHD)** is a psychological disorder characterized by the appearance by age 7 of one or more

of three symptoms: extreme inattention, hyperactivity, and impulsivity.

Essay Question

There is more to a psychological disorder than a temporary state of sadness or a fear of bugs, for example. Behaviors are more likely to be considered disordered when judged as distressful and dysfunctional to the individual. Prolonged feelings of depression or the use of drugs to avoid dealing with problems are examples of behaviors that may signal a psychological disorder if the person is unable to function, to perform routine behaviors (becomes dysfunctional).

 # Anxiety Disorders, OCD, and PTSD

Anxiety Disorders

1. distressing, persistent anxiety and often dysfunctional behaviors that reduce anxiety

2. generalized anxiety disorder; panic disorder; phobias

3. generalized anxiety; free-floating

4. high blood pressure; panic disorder; panic attack

5. agoraphobia

6. smoke; panic attack; nicotine

7. phobia; specific phobias

8. social anxiety disorder

Obsessive-Compulsive Disorder

9. obsessive-compulsive; less

10. does

Posttraumatic Stress Disorder

11. posttraumatic stress; haunting memories; nightmares; social withdrawal; jumpy anxiety; numbness of feeling; sleeping

12. limbic system; women; men

13. survivor resiliency

14. **d.** is the answer.
   a. & c. There is no indication that she has an irrational fear of a specific object.
   b. Generalized anxiety disorder is characterized by a continually tense, apprehensive state.

15. **c.** is the answer. An intense fear of a specific object is a phobia.
   a. His fear is focused on a specific object, not generalized.
   b. In this disorder a person is troubled by repetitive thoughts and actions.

d. A panic attack does not involve a specific object, such as a snake.

16. **d.** is the answer.
   a. In phobias, anxiety is focused on a specific object.
   b. Posttraumatic stress disorder is tied to a specific traumatic experience.
   c. The obsessive-compulsive disorder is characterized by repetitive and unwanted thoughts and/or actions.

17. **d.** is the answer. Jason is obsessed with cleanliness; as a result, he has developed a compulsion to shower.
   a. Panic attacks are minutes-long episodes of intense fear.
   b. Generalized anxiety disorder does not have a specific focus.
   c. Agoraphobia is fear or avoidance of situations in which escape might not be possible.

18. **d.** is the answer.
   a. There is no evidence that Zheina is having panic attacks.
   b. Zheina shows no signs of being obsessed with certain thoughts or behaviors.
   c. Zheina's problem is tied to a very specific traumatic event.

19. repressed

20. classical; fears

21. stimulus generalization

22. reinforced; observational

23. is; genes; serotonin; glutamate

24. child abuse; epigenetic

25. anterior cingulate; antidepressant

26. are; survival

27. **d.** is the answer. A phobia, such as Julia's, is seen as a conditioned fear that results from stimulus generalization.

28. **a.** is the answer. Compulsive behaviors are reinforced because they reduce the anxiety created by obsessive thoughts. Rashid's obsession concerns failing, and his desk-arranging compulsive behaviors apparently help him control these thoughts.

29. observational learning. Olivia observed her mother's painful experience and is now afraid of being stung by a bee.

30. **a.** is the answer. Humans seem biologically prepared to develop a fear of heights and other dangers that our ancestors faced.

Module Review:

31. d. is the answer. This area shows increased activity during compulsive behaviors.

32. d. is the answer.

33. b. is the answer.
a. This answer reflects the learning perspective.
c. Although certain phobias are biologically predisposed, this could not fully explain phobias, nor is it the explanation offered by psychodynamic theory.
d. Social-cognitive theorists propose self-defeating thoughts as a cause of depression.

34. d. is the answer.

35. b. is the answer. The psychodynamic explanation is that these disorders are a manifestation of incompletely repressed impulses over which the person is anxious. According to the learning perspective, the troubled behaviors that result from these disorders have been reinforced by anxiety reduction.
a. & c. These are true of the psychodynamic, but not the learning, perspective.

Terms and Concepts to Remember:

36. Anxiety disorders involve distressing, persistent anxiety and often dysfunctional behaviors that reduce anxiety.

37. In the **generalized anxiety disorder**, the person is continually tense, apprehensive, and in a state of autonomic nervous system arousal for no apparent reason.

38. A **panic disorder** is an anxiety disorder marked by unpredictable, minutes-long episodes of intense dread accompanied by chest pain, dizziness, or choking. It is essentially an escalation of the anxiety associated with generalized anxiety disorder.

39. A **phobia** is an anxiety disorder in which a person has a persistent, irrational fear and avoidance of a specific object, activity, or situation.

40. Obsessive-compulsive disorder (OCD) is a disorder in which the person experiences uncontrollable and repetitive thoughts (obsessions) and actions (compulsions).

41. Posttraumatic stress disorder (PTSD) is a disorder characterized by haunting memories, nightmares, social withdrawal, jumpy anxiety, numbness of feeling, and/or insomnia lasting four weeks or more following a traumatic experience.

Major Depressive Disorder and Bipolar Disorder

Major Depressive Disorder and *Bipolar Disorder*

1. major depressive; mania; bipolar; seasonal

2. lethargy, feelings of worthlessness, and reduced interest or enjoyment in most activities most of the time

3. two weeks

4. phobias; depression

5. hyperactivity and a wildly optimistic state

6. precision; logic; emotional; imagery; disruptive mood dysregulation disorder

7. **b.** is the answer. The fact that this woman has had these symptoms for more than two weeks indicates that she is suffering from major depressive disorder. Disruptive mood dysregulation disorder occurs in children and adolescents.

8. **a.** is the answer. Delon's alternating states of the hopelessness and lethargy of depression and the energetic, optimistic state of mania are characteristic of bipolar disorder.
b. Although he was depressed on Tuesday, Delon's manic state on Monday indicates that he is not suffering from major depressive disorder.
c. Delon changed from mania to depression within a day, not by season.
d. Delon is also depressed, not just manic.

Understanding Major Depressive Disorder and Bipolar Disorder

9. behavioral; cognitive

10. causes

11. more; internal; depression, anxiety, and inhibited sexual desire

12. external; alcohol use disorder, antisocial conduct, and lack of impulse control

13. do; without; is; a family member's death, loss of a job, a ruptured marriage, or a physical assault

14. increasing; earlier; three

15. do; twins; strong

16. linkage analysis; DNA

17. less; left frontal; reward center

18. low; norepinephrine; serotonin

19. norepinephrine; norepinephrine; serotonin; reuptake; breakdown; inflammation

20. epigenetic

21. self-defeating; negative explanatory; learned help-lessness

22. stress; act; overthink (ruminate)

Depressed people are more likely than others to explain failures or bad events in terms that are stable (it's going to last forever), global (it will affect every-thing), and internal (it's my fault). Such explanations lead to feelings of hopelessness, which in turn feed depression.

23. individualism; religion

24. self-blaming

25. rejection

Depression is often brought on by negative, stressful experiences. Depressed people brood over such expe-riences with maladaptive explanations that produce self-blame and amplify their depression, which in turn triggers other symptoms of depression. In addi-tion, being withdrawn and complaining tends to elicit social rejection and other negative experiences.

26. **b.** is the answer.

27. **b.** is the answer. Norepinephrine, which increas-es arousal and boosts mood, is scarce during depression. Drugs that relieve depression tend to increase norepinephrine.

c. Increasing serotonin, which is sometimes scarce during depression, might relieve depression.

d. This neurotransmitter is involved in motor responses but has not been linked to psychologi-cal disorders.

28. There are no right or wrong answers to this. Possible responses of a depressed person might be "I'll never be able to pass this course (stable),""I'm never going to do well in any college courses (global)," and "It's my fault; I didn't study hard enough (internal)."

Suicide rates are higher among White and Native Americans, the rich, older people, the nonreligious, and those who are single, widowed, or divorced. Although women more often attempt suicide, men are more likely to succeed. Suicide rates also vary widely around the world.

29. alcohol; suggestion; suffering; negative thoughts; attention; guilt

30. verbal hints; possessions away, withdrawal; pre-occupation with death

Module Review:

31. **b.** is the answer.

c. & d. Men are more likely than women to cope with stress in these ways.

32. **b.** is the answer. Depression is often preceded by a stressful event related to work, marriage, or a close relationship.

33. **c.** is the answer. Drugs that relieve depression tend to increase levels of norepinephrine.

a. Acetylcholine is a neurotransmitter involved in muscle contractions.

b. It is in certain types of schizophrenia that decreasing dopamine levels is helpful.

d. On the contrary, it appears that a particular type of depression may be related to *low* levels of serotonin.

34. **b.** is the answer.

a. Anxiety is an internal disorder.

d. Alcohol use disorder is an external disorder.

35. **d.** is the answer. In bipolar disorder, norepineph-rine appears to be overabundant during mania and in short supply during depression.

a. There is an overabundance of dopamine recep-tors in some schizophrenia patients.

b. Serotonin sometimes appears to be scarce dur-ing depression.

c. Epinephrine has not been implicated in psycho-logical disorders.

36. **d.** is the answer.

37. **d.** is the answer.

38. **a.** is the answer. Just the opposite is true.

Terms and Concepts to Remember:

39. **Major depressive disorder** occurs when a person experiences five or more symptoms, at least one of which must be either (1) depressed mood or (2) reduced interest or enjoyment in most activi-ties, for two or more weeks and for no discernible reason.

40. **Bipolar disorder** is the mood disorder in which a person alternates between depression and the euphoria of a manic state.

Memory aid: *Bipolar* means having two poles, that is, two opposite qualities. In **bipolar disorder,** the opposing states are mania and depression.

41. **Mania** is the wildly optimistic, hyperactive state that alternates with depression in the bipolar dis-order.

42. **Rumination** is overthinking about our problems and their causes.

⟶ Schizophrenia and Other Disorders

Schizophrenia

1. reality; psychotic disorder; a group of psychologi-cal disorders marked by irrational ideas, distorted perceptions, and a loss of contact with reality

2. positive symptoms

3. negative symptoms

4. hallucinations; sounds

5. delusions; word salad

6. selective attention

7. theory of mind

8. flat affect; catatonia

9. chronic; less; acute

10. positive

11. dopamine; decrease

12. low; frontal

13. fluid; shrinkage; cortex; corpus callosum; thalamus; sensory input; attention

14. low birth weight; diabetes; paternal; oxygen deprivation; viral infection

Risk of schizophrenia increases for those who undergo fetal development during a flu epidemic, or simply during the flu season. People born in densely populated areas and those born during winter and spring months are at increased risk. The months of excess schizophrenia births are reversed in the Southern Hemisphere, where the seasons are the reverse of the Northern Hemisphere's. Mothers who were sick with influenza during their pregnancy may be more likely to have children who develop schizophrenia. Blood drawn from pregnant women whose children develop schizophrenia have higher-than-normal levels of viral infection antibodies.

15. support

16. placenta; viruses

17. confirm

18. genetic; epigenetic; turn on; genes

19. dopamine

20. c. is the answer.

Other Disorders

21. dissociative; separates (dissociates); fugue state

22. is not so

23. dissociative identity

24. localized; varies; roles

25. brain; body; posttraumatic stress

Skeptics point out that the recent increase in the number of reported cases of dissociative identity disorder indicates that it has become a fad. The fact that the disorder is much less prevalent outside North America also causes skeptics to doubt the disorder's genuineness.

26. anxiety; detach; fantasy-prone; therapist-patient

27. dissociative identity

28. c. is the answer.
    a. A fugue state involves a loss of memory or change in identity.
    b. DID may be considered under the umbrella of PTSD but it is still a separate disorder.
    d. That is the view of skeptics of DID, but there's no clue that that is the case here.

29. social functioning

30. avoidant; schizotypal; impulsive; borderline; narcissistic

31. antisocial; emotional intelligence; psychopath (or sociopath)

32. may

33. impulsive; uninhibited; social rewards; anxiety

34. amygdala; frontal lobes; impulses

35. is not; environmental; childhood abuse

36. d. is the answer. Repeated wrongdoing and aggressive behavior are part of the pattern associated with antisocial personality disorder, which may also include marital problems and an inability to keep a job.
    a. & c. Although a fugue state and dissociative identity disorder may involve an aggressive personality, there is nothing in the example to indicate a dissociation.
    b. Nothing in the question indicates that Ming shows eccentric or odd behavior.

37. anorexia nervosa

38. bulimia nervosa; binge-purge; binge-eating

39. competitive; high achieving; protective

40. may

41. thinness; dissatisfaction

42. bigger; Western; body image

43. ashamed; depressed; dissatisfied

44. b. is the answer. Adolescent females with low self-esteem and high-achieving families seem especially prone to eating disorders such as anorexia nervosa.
    a. & d. Eating disorders occur much more frequently in women than in men.
    c. Eating disorders usually develop during adolescence, rather than during adulthood.

Module Review:

45. c. is the answer.

46. a. is the answer.
    b. & d. Catatonia is a zombie-like state and is unrelated to the presence or absence of dopamine.

47. c. is the answer.

48. **d.** is the answer. Hallucinations are false sensory experiences; delusions are false beliefs.
    a. & b. Word salad is jumbled speech and catatonia is a zombie-like state.

49. **c.** is the answer.

50. **a.** is the answer. Schizophrenia sufferers are easily distracted by irrelevant stimuli, evidently because of a breakdown in the capacity for selective attention.

51. **b.** is the answer.

52. **d.** is the answer. Risk for schizophrenia increases for individuals who are related to a schizophrenia victim, and the greater the genetic relatedness, the greater the risk.
    a. Schizophrenia victims have an overabundance of the neurotransmitter dopamine, not endorphins.
    b. Being a twin is, in itself, irrelevant to developing schizophrenia.
    c. Although learned helplessness has been suggested by social-cognitive theorists as a cause of self-defeating depressive behaviors, it has not been suggested as a cause of schizophrenia.

53. **b.** is the answer. Those with an antisocial personality disorder show less autonomic arousal in such situations, and emotions, such as fear, are tied to arousal.

54. **d.** is the answer.

55. **b.** is the answer.
    c. Playing a role is most definitely a learned skill.
    d. Role playing, being completely learned, is not biologically based.

56. **a.** is the answer. The text does not indicate whether their metabolism is higher or lower than most.
    b., c., & d. Genes, family background, and cultural influence have all been proposed as factors in eating disorders.

Terms and Concepts to Remember:

57. **Schizophrenia** is a psychological disorder characterized by delusions, hallucinations, disorganized speech, and/or diminished, inappropriate emotional expression.

58. **Psychotic disorders,** such as schizophrenia, are psychological disorders in which a person loses contact with reality and experiences irrational ideas and distorted perceptions.

59. **Delusions** are false beliefs that often are symptoms of psychotic disorders.

60. **Chronic schizophrenia** (also called *process schizophrenia*) is a form of schizophrenia that usually appears by late adolescence or early adulthood.

61. **Acute schizophrenia** (also called *reactive schizophrenia*) can begin at any age, and frequently occurs in response to an emotionally traumatic event.

62. **Dissociative disorders** involve a separation of conscious awareness from previous memories, thoughts, and feelings.
    Memory aid: To *dissociate* is to separate or pull apart. In the **dissociative disorders** a person becomes dissociated from his or her memories and identity.

63. The **dissociative identity disorder (DID)** is a dissociative disorder in which a person exhibits two or more distinct and alternating personalities; formerly called *multiple personality disorder.*

64. **Personality disorders** are characterized by inflexible and enduring maladaptive character traits that impair social functioning.

65. The **antisocial personality disorder** is a personality disorder in which the person (usually a man) may be aggressive and ruthless or a clever con artist, and shows no sign of a conscience that would inhibit wrongdoing.

66. **Anorexia nervosa** is an eating disorder, most common in adolescent females, in which a person restricts food intake to become significantly underweight and yet still feels fat.

67. **Bulimia nervosa** is an eating disorder characterized by episodes of overeating followed by purging (by vomiting or laxative use) or fasting.

68. **Binge-eating** disorder is characterized by episodes of overeating, followed by distress, but without the purging or fasting that marks bulimia nervosa.

Before You Move On

Summary Study Tip: Using the text discussion and tables to complete this chart will enhance your understanding of the material in this unit.

Matching Items 1

1. f	**5.** g	**9.** c
2. d	**6.** b	**10.** e
3. a	**7.** j	**11.** k
4. h	**8.** i	

Matching Items 2

1. f	**5.** c	**9.** d
2. e	**6.** b	**10.** j
3. a	**7.** g	**11.** k
4. i	**8.** h	**12.** l

Cross-Check

ACROSS
3. major depressive
16. mania
17. mood
18. bipolar
19. anxiety

DOWN
1. chronic
2. DSM-5
3. ADHD
4. dissociative
5. phobia
6. linkage analysis
7. biopsychosocial
8. hallucinations
9. medical model
10. delusions
11. prenatal
12. dopamine
13. negative
14. serotonin

Therapy

Overview

Modules 44 and 45 discuss the major psychotherapies and biomedical therapies for maladaptive behaviors. The various psychotherapies all derive from the personality theories discussed earlier, namely, the psychodynamic, humanistic, behavioral, and cognitive theories. Module 44 groups the therapies by perspective but also emphasizes the common threads that run through them. In evaluating the therapies, the module points out that, although people who are untreated often improve, those receiving psychotherapy tend to improve somewhat more, regardless of the type of therapy they receive. This module includes a discussion of two popular alternative therapies.

In Module 45, the biomedical therapies discussed are drug therapies, electroconvulsive therapy and other forms of brain stimulation, and psychosurgery, which is seldom used. By far the most important of these, drug therapies are being used in the treatment of psychotic, anxiety, and depressive disorders.

Because the origins of problems often lie beyond the individual, Module 45 concludes with approaches that aim at preventing psychological disorders by focusing on the family or on the larger social environment as possible contributors to psychological disorders.

NOTE: Answer guidelines for all Modules 44 and 45 questions begin on page 381.

Outline

Instructions

First, skim each section, noting headings and boldface items. After you have read the section, review each objective by answering the fill-in, essay-type, and multiple-choice questions for that section. In some cases, Study Tips explain how best to learn a difficult concept and Applications and Module Reviews help you to know how well you understand the material. Finally, try to define the important terms and concepts using your own words. As you proceed, evaluate your performance by consulting the answers on page 381. Do not continue until you understand each answer. If you need to, review or reread a troublesome section before continuing.

Before You Move On includes activities that test you on material from the entire unit.

MODULE
44

Introduction to Therapy and the Psychological Therapies

Treating Psychological Disorders

Objective 44-1: Discuss how *psychotherapy* and the *biomedical therapies* differ.

1. The treatment of people with psychological disorders has often been harsh. Reformers _____ and _____ pushed for gentler, more humane treatments and for constructing mental hospitals.

2. Modern Western therapies are classified as either _____ therapies or _____ therapies. Some therapists combine techniques in an integrative, _____ approach.

Psychoanalysis and Psychodynamic Therapies

Objective 44-2: Describe the goals and techniques of psychoanalysis, and discuss how they have been adapted in psychodynamic therapy.

3. The goal of Freud's psychoanalysis is to help the patient gain _____ .

4. Freud assumed that many psychological problems originate in childhood impulses and conflicts that have been _____ .

5. Psychoanalysts attempt to bring _____ feelings into _____ awareness where they can be dealt with.

6. Freud's technique in which a patient says whatever comes to mind is called _____ _____ .

7. When, in the course of therapy, a person omits shameful or embarrassing material, _____ is occurring. Insight is facilitated by the analyst's _____ of the meaning of such omissions, of dreams, and of other information revealed during therapy sessions.

8. When strong feelings, similar to those experienced in other important relationships, are developed toward the therapist, _____ has occurred.

9. Today, psychoanalysis _____ (is/is not) commonly practiced in the United States. Critics point out that psychoanalysts' interpretations are hard to _____ or _____ and that therapy takes a long time and is very _____ .

10. Therapists who are influenced by Freud's psychoanalysis but who talk to the patient face-to-face are _____ therapists. These therapists work with patients only _____ (how often?) and for only a few weeks or months. These therapists try to help people understand their current symptoms by focusing on _____ across important relationships.

11. Without embracing all aspects of Freud's theory, psychodynamic therapists aim to help people gain beneficial insight into their _____ experiences and _____ dynamics.

APPLICATIONS:

12. During a session with his psychoanalyst, Jamal hesitates while describing a highly embarrassing thought. In the psychoanalytic framework, this is an example of

    a. transference.   **c.** mental repression.
    b. insight.   **d.** resistance.

13. During psychoanalysis, Jane has developed strong feelings of hatred for her therapist. The analyst interprets Jane's behavior in terms of a _____ of her feelings toward her father.

14. Ernesto is seeing a psychodynamic therapist. Unlike a psychoanalyst, his therapist does not talk about _____ , _____ , and _____ , but rather about themes across important _____ .

15. Isadora's psychoanalyst would be most likely to interpret her fear of intimate relationships in terms of _____ _____ .

Humanistic Therapies

Objective 44-3: Identify the basic themes of humanistic therapy, and describe the specific goals and techniques of Rogers' client-centered approach.

16. Humanistic therapies attempt to help people meet their potential for _____ . Like psychodynamic therapies, humanistic therapies attempt to reduce inner conflicts by providing clients with new _____ .

List several ways that humanistic therapy differs from psychodynamic therapy.

17. The humanistic therapy based on Rogers' theory is called _____-_____ therapy, which is described as _____ therapy because the therapist _____ (interprets/does not interpret) the person's problems.

18. To promote growth in clients, Rogerian therapists exhibit _____, _____, and _____ .

19. Rogers' technique of echoing, restating, and seeking clarification of what a person is saying is called _____ .

20. Given a nonjudgmental environment that provides _____ _____, patients are better able to accept themselves as they are and to feel valued and whole.

21. Three tips for listening more actively in your own relationships are to _____, _____ _____, and _____ _____ .

Behavior Therapies

Objective 44-4: Explain how the basic assumption of behavior therapy differs from the assumptions of psychodynamic and humanistic therapies, and describe the techniques used in exposure therapies and aversive conditioning.

22. Behavior therapy applies principles of _____ to eliminate troubling behaviors.

Contrast the basic assumption of the behavior therapies with the assumptions of psychodynamic and humanistic therapies.

23. One cluster of behavior therapies is based on the principles of _____ _____, as developed in Pavlov's experiments. This technique, in which a new, incompatible response is substituted for a maladaptive one, is called _____ . Two examples of this technique are _____ _____ and _____ _____ .

24. The most widely used types of behavior therapies are the _____ . The first attempt at this type of therapy was made by _____ ; her technique was later refined by _____ into the _____ therapies used today. Systematic desensitization assumes that one cannot simultaneously be _____ and relaxed.

25. The first step in systematic desensitization is the construction of a list of _____-arousing stimuli. The second step involves training in _____ _____ . In the third step, the person is trained to associate the _____ state with the _____-arousing stimuli. Finally,

you will move to _____
_____ and practice what you
had only imagined before, beginning with relatively easy tasks.

26. For those who are unable to visually imagine
an anxiety-arousing situation, or too afraid or
embarrassed to do so, _____
_____ _____
therapy offers a promising alternative.

27. In aversive conditioning, the therapist attempts
to substitute a _____ (positive/
negative) response for one that is currently
_____ (positive/negative) to a
harmful stimulus. In this technique, a person's
unwanted behaviors become associated with
_____ feelings. In the long run,
aversive conditioning _____
(does/does not) work.

APPLICATIONS:

28. To help Sam quit smoking, his therapist blew a
blast of smoke into Sam's face each time Sam
inhaled. Which technique is the therapist using?
   a. exposure therapy
   b. behavior modification
   c. systematic desensitization
   d. aversive conditioning

29. To help him overcome his fear of flying, Duane's
therapist has him construct a list of anxiety-
triggering stimuli and then learn to associate
each with a state of deep relaxation. Duane's
therapist is using the technique called
   a. systematic desensitization.
   b. aversive conditioning.
   c. transference.
   d. free association.

Objective 44-5: State the main premise of therapy
based on operant conditioning principles, and
describe the views of its proponents and critics.

30. Reinforcing desired behaviors and withholding
reinforcement for or punishing undesired behaviors are key aspects of _____
_____ .

31. Therapies that influence behavior by controlling
its consequences are based on principles of
_____ conditioning. One appli-
cation of this form of therapy to institutional
settings is the _____
_____ , in which desired
behaviors are rewarded.

State two criticisms of behavior modification.

State some responses of proponents of behavior
modification.

STUDY TIP/APPLICATION: Each type of behavior therapy
discussed is derived from principles of either classical conditioning or operant conditioning. Classical
conditioning is based on the formation of a learned
association between two stimulus situations or
events. Operant conditioning is based on the use of
reinforcement and punishment to modify the future
likelihood of behaviors. Several problem behaviors
are described in the chart on the next page. Test
your understanding of behavior therapy by completing the chart and explaining how you would treat the
problem behavior using one of the behavior therapies. Be sure to identify any reinforcers, conditioned
stimuli, and unconditioned stimuli that you would
use. The first example is completed for you.

32. Situation	Type of Conditioning	Procedure
A friend is trying to quit smoking	Aversive conditioning, a type of counterconditioning (classical conditioning)	Each time your friend puffs the cigarette, the taste of the cigarette (conditioned stimulus) is paired with a blast of hot air delivered to his/her face (unconditioned stimulus).
a. A relative has a fear of flying (Hint: use imagined situations)		
b. The parents of a sloppy teenager want to get him to clean up his room		
c. A child is terrified of dogs (Hint: use real situations)		

Cognitive Therapies

Objective 44-6: Discuss the goals and techniques of cognitive therapy and of cognitive-behavioral therapy.

33. The vicious cycle of depression is maintained by _____ and _____ explanations of bad events. Therapists who teach people new, more constructive ways of thinking are using _____ therapy.

34. One variety of cognitive therapy attempts to reverse the _____ beliefs often associated with _____ by helping clients see their irrationalities. This therapy was developed by _____ .

35. To change negative self-talk, therapists teach people to _____ their thinking in _____ situations. Depression-prone children, teens, and college students trained to talk back to their _____ thoughts are _____ (more/less) likely to experience future depression.

36. An integrative therapy that combines an attack on negative thinking with efforts to modify behavior is known as _____-_____ therapy. This type of therapy is an effective treatment program for anxiety, depressive disorders, and bipolar disorder, because they share a common problem: _____ _____ . It is also useful for _____-_____ _____ ; people are taught to relabel their problem behaviors.

37. A newer form of CBT that helps change harmful and even suicidal behavior patterns is called _____ _____ therapy. This type of therapy combines cognitive tactics for tolerating distress and regulating emotions with _____ _____ _____ and _____ _____ .

APPLICATIONS (REVIEW OF ALL PSYCHOTHERAPIES):

38. Given that Don Carlo's therapist attempts to help him by offering genuineness, acceptance, and empathy, she is probably practicing _____ therapy.

39. To help Sam lose weight by eating fewer sweets, his therapist laced a batch of cookies with a nausea-producing drug. Which technique is the therapist using? _____ _____

40. B.J.'s therapist interprets her psychological problems in terms of repressed impulses. Which type(s) of therapy is she using? _____

41. Leota is startled when her therapist says that she needs to focus on eliminating her problem behavior rather than gaining insight into its underlying cause. Most likely, Leota has consulted a _____ therapist.
    a. behavior   c. cognitive
    b. humanistic   d. psychoanalytic

42. Ben is a cognitive-behavioral therapist. Compared with Rachel, who is a behavior therapist, Ben is more likely to
    a. base his therapy on principles of operant conditioning.
    b. base his therapy on principles of classical conditioning.
    c. address clients' attitudes as well as behaviors.
    d. focus on clients' unconscious urges.

43. A patient in a hospital receives poker chips for making her bed, being punctual at meal times, and maintaining her physical appearance. The poker chips can be exchanged for privileges, such as television viewing, snacks, and magazines. This is an example of the
    a. psychodynamic therapy technique called systematic desensitization.
    b. behavior therapy technique called a token economy.
    c. cognitive therapy technique called a token economy.
    d. humanistic therapy technique called systematic desensitization.

44. After Darnel dropped a pass in an important football game, he became depressed and vowed to quit the team because of his athletic incompetence. The campus psychologist used gentle questioning to reveal to Darnel that his thinking was irrational: his "incompetence" had earned him an athletic scholarship. The psychologist's response was most typical of a _____ therapist.
    a. behavior   c. client-centered
    b. psychodynamic   d. cognitive

Group and Family Therapies

Objective 44-7: Discuss the aims and benefits of group and family therapies.

List several advantages of group therapy.

45. Although _____ therapy does not provide the same degree of therapist involvement with each client, it does save time and money and permits therapeutic benefits from _____ interaction.

46. The type of group interaction that focuses on the fact that we live and grow in relation to others is _____ _____ .

47. In this type of group, therapists focus on improving _____ within the family.

48. Many people also participate in _____ - _____ and _____ groups. One such group is _____ _____ .

STUDY TIP/APPLICATION: To organize your thinking about the modern psychological therapies discussed in this module, complete the chart below and on the next page. For each category of therapy, state the assumed underlying cause of psychological disorders, the overall goal of therapy, and the role of the therapist. To help you get started, the first example is already filled in.

49. Type of Psychotherapy	Assumed Cause of Psychological Disorder	Goal of Therapy	Role of Therapist
Psychodynamic Therapies	Unconscious conflicts from childhood	Self-insight	Interpreting patients' memories and feelings
Humanistic Therapies			
Behavior Therapies			

49. Continued

Type of Psychotherapy	Assumed Cause of Psychological Disorder	Goal of Therapy	Role of Therapist
Cognitive Therapies			
Cognitive-Behavioral Therapy			
Group and Family Therapies			

Evaluating Psychotherapies

Objective 44-8: Discuss whether psychotherapy works, and explain how we can know.

50. A majority of psychotherapy clients express _____ (satisfaction/dissatisfaction) with their therapy.

Give three reasons that client testimonials are not persuasive evidence for psychotherapy's effectiveness.

51. Clinicians tend to _____ (overestimate/underestimate) the effectiveness of psychotherapy.

52. One reason clinicians' perceptions of the effectiveness of psychotherapy are inaccurate is that clients justify entering therapy by emphasizing their _____ and justify leaving therapy by emphasizing their _____ .

53. In hopes of better assessing psychotherapy's effectiveness, psychologists have turned to _____ research studies.

54. The debate over the effectiveness of psychotherapy began with a study by _____ ; it showed that the rate of improvement for those who received therapy _____ (was/was not) higher than the rate for those who did not.

55. In the best studies of the effectiveness of therapy, researchers randomly assign people on a waiting list to therapy or no therapy and later evaluate everyone. These are _____ _____ trials.

56. Overall, the results of meta-analyses of research outcome studies indicate that psychotherapy is _____ (somewhat effective/ineffective).

Objective 44-9: Discuss whether some psychotherapies are more effective than others for specific disorders.

57. Comparisons of the effectiveness of different forms of therapy reveal _____ (clear/no clear) differences, that the type of therapy provider _____ (matters greatly/does not matter), and that whether therapy is provided by an individual therapist or within a group _____ (makes a difference/does not make a difference).

58. Some therapies _____ (are/are not) better at treating particular problems. With phobias, compulsions, and other specific behavior problems, _____ _____ therapies have been the most effective. With mild to moderate depression, _____ counseling often helps Other studies have demonstrated that anxiety, posttraumatic stress disorder, and depression may be effectively treated with _____ or _____-_____ therapy.

59. As a rule, psychotherapy is most effective with problems that are _____ (specific/nonspecific).

60. Therapies with no scientific support, such as _____ therapies, recovered-_____ therapies, and _____ therapies that involve reenacting the trauma of birth, should be avoided.

61. Clinical decision making that integrates research with clinical expertise and patient preferences and characteristics is called _____-_____.

APPLICATION:

62. Your best friend Armand wants to know which type of therapy works best. You should tell him that
   a. psychotherapy does not work.
   b. behavior therapy is the most effective.
   c. cognitive therapy is the most effective.
   d. no one type of therapy is consistently the most successful.

Objective 44-10: Discuss how alternative therapies fare under scientific scrutiny.

63. Today, many forms of _____ _____ are touted as effective treatments for a variety of complaints.

64. Aside from testimonials, there is very little evidence based on _____ research for such therapies.

65. In one popular alternative therapy, a therapist triggers eye movements in patients while they imagine _____. This therapy, called _____ _____ _____ _____, has proven _____ (completely ineffective/somewhat effective) as a treatment for nonmilitary _____ _____. However, skeptics point to evidence that _____ _____ is just as effective as triggered eye movements in producing beneficial results. The key seems to be

in the person's _____ traumatic memories and in a _____ effect.

66. For people with a _____ _____ of depression symptoms, timed _____ _____ therapy may be beneficial.

APPLICATION:

67. A close friend who for years has suffered from wintertime depression is seeking your advice regarding the effectiveness of light exposure therapy. What should you tell your friend?
   a. "Don't waste your time and money. It doesn't work."
   b. "A more effective treatment for a seasonal pattern of depression symptoms is eye movement desensitization and reprocessing."
   c. "You'd be better off with a prescription for lithium."
   d. "It might be worth a try. There is some evidence that morning light exposure produces relief."

Objective 44-11: Describe the three elements shared by all forms of psychotherapy.

68. All forms of psychotherapy offer three benefits: _____ for demoralized people; a new _____ on oneself; and a relationship that is _____, _____, and _____.

69. The emotional bond between therapist and client—the _____ _____—is a key aspect of effective therapy. In one study of depression treatment, the most effective therapists were those who were perceived as most _____ and _____.

Objective 44-12: Discuss how culture and values influence the therapist-client relationship.

70. Psychotherapists _____ (do/do not) differ from one another and _____ (may/may not) differ from their clients. This is particularly significant when the therapist and client are from different _____. Another area of potential value conflict is _____.

71. In North America, Europe, and Australia, most therapists reflect their culture's _____ . Clients with a _____ perspective, as with many from Asian cultures, may assume people will be more mindful of others' expectations.

72. Differences in values may help explain the reluctance of some _____ populations to use mental health services.

Objective 44-13: Identify what a person should look for when selecting a therapist.

73. The American Psychological Association suggests that a person should seek help when he or she has feelings of _____ , a deep and lasting _____ , _____ behavior, disruptive _____ , sudden _____ shifts, and _____ rituals, for example.

APPLICATION:

74. Seth enters therapy to talk about some issues that have been upsetting him. The therapist prescribes some medication to help him. The therapist is most likely a
   a. clinical psychologist.
   b. psychiatrist.
   c. psychiatric social worker.
   d. clinical social worker.

MODULE REVIEW:

75. The technique in which a person is asked to report everything that comes to his or her mind is called _____ ; it is favored by_____ therapists.
   a. active listening; cognitive
   b. unconditional positive regard; humanistic
   c. free association; psychoanalytic
   d. systematic desensitization; behavior

76. Of the following categories of psychotherapy, which is known for its nondirective nature?
   a. psychoanalysis   c. behavior therapy
   b. humanistic therapy   d. cognitive therapy

77. Which of the following is NOT a common criticism of psychoanalysis?
   a. It emphasizes the existence of repressed memories.
   b. It provides interpretations that are hard to disprove.

c. It is generally a very expensive process.
   d. It gives therapists too much control over patients.

78. Which of the following is NOT necessarily an advantage of group therapies over individual therapies?
   a. They tend to take less time for the therapist.
   b. They tend to cost less money for the client.
   c. They are more effective.
   d. They allow the client to test new behaviors in a social context.

79. Cognitive-behavioral therapy (CBT) aims to
   a. alter the way people act.
   b. make people more aware of their irrational negative thinking.
   c. alter the way people think and act.
   d. countercondition anxiety-provoking stimuli.

80. An eclectic psychotherapist is one who
   a. takes a nondirective approach in helping clients solve their problems.
   b. views psychological disorders as usually stemming from one cause, such as a biological abnormality.
   c. uses one particular technique, such as psychoanalysis or counterconditioning, in treating disorders.
   d. uses a variety of techniques, depending on the client and the problem.

81. The technique in which a therapist echoes and restates what a person says in a nondirective manner is called
   a. active listening.
   b. free association.
   c. systematic desensitization.
   d. transference.

82. The technique of systematic desensitization is based on the premise that maladaptive symptoms are
   a. a reflection of irrational thinking.
   b. conditioned responses.
   c. expressions of unfulfilled wishes.
   d. all of these things.

83. The operant conditioning technique in which desired behaviors are rewarded with points or poker chips that can later be exchanged for various rewards is called
   a. counterconditioning.
   b. systematic desensitization.
   c. a token economy.
   d. exposure therapy.

84. One variety of _____ therapy is based on the finding that depressed people often attribute their failures to _____ .
    a. humanistic; themselves
    b. behavior; external circumstances
    c. cognitive; external circumstances
    d. cognitive; themselves

85. Carl Rogers was a _____ therapist who was the creator of _____ .
    a. behavior; systematic desensitization
    b. psychoanalytic; insight therapy
    c. humanistic; client-centered therapy
    d. cognitive; cognitive therapy for depression

86. Using techniques of classical conditioning to develop an association between unwanted behavior and an unpleasant experience is known as
    a. aversive conditioning.
    b. systematic desensitization.
    c. transference.
    d. exposure therapy.

87. Which type of psychotherapy emphasizes the individual's inherent potential for self-fulfillment?
    a. behavior therapy
    b. psychodynamic therapy
    c. humanistic therapy
    d. biomedical therapy

88. Which type of psychotherapy focuses on changing unwanted behaviors rather than on discovering their underlying causes?
    a. behavior therapy
    b. cognitive therapy
    c. humanistic therapy
    d. psychodynamic therapy

89. The techniques of counterconditioning are based on principles of
    a. observational learning.
    b. classical conditioning.
    c. operant conditioning.
    d. behavior modification.

90. In which of the following does the client learn to associate a relaxed state with a list of anxiety-arousing situations?
    a. cognitive therapy
    b. aversive conditioning
    c. counterconditioning
    d. systematic desensitization

91. Principles of operant conditioning underlie which of the following techniques?
    a. counterconditioning
    b. systematic desensitization
    c. aversive conditioning
    d. the token economy

92. Which of the following is NOT a common criticism of behavior therapy?
    a. Clients may rely too much on extrinsic rewards for their new behaviors.
    b. Behavior control is unethical.
    c. Outside the therapeutic setting, the new behavior may disappear.
    d. All of these are criticisms of behavior therapy.

93. Which type of therapy focuses on eliminating irrational thinking?
    a. psychodynamic therapy
    b. client-centered therapy
    c. cognitive therapy
    d. behavior therapy

94. Family therapy differs from other forms of psychotherapy because it focuses on
    a. using a variety of treatment techniques.
    b. conscious rather than unconscious processes.
    c. the present instead of the past.
    d. how family tensions may cause individual problems.

95. One reason that aversive conditioning may only be temporarily effective is that
    a. for ethical reasons, therapists cannot use sufficiently intense unconditioned stimuli to sustain classical conditioning.
    b. patients are often unable to become sufficiently relaxed for conditioning to take place.
    c. patients know that outside the therapist's office they can engage in the undesirable behavior without fear of aversive consequences.
    d. most conditioned responses are elicited by many nonspecific stimuli and it is impossible to countercondition them all.

96. The effectiveness of psychotherapy has been assessed both through clients' perspectives and through controlled research studies. What have such assessments found?
    a. Clients' perceptions and controlled studies alike strongly affirm the effectiveness of psychotherapy.
    b. Whereas clients' perceptions strongly affirm the effectiveness of psychotherapy, studies point to more modest results.

c. Whereas studies strongly affirm the effectiveness of psychotherapy, many clients feel dissatisfied with their progress.

d. Clients' perceptions and controlled studies alike paint a very mixed picture of the effectiveness of psychotherapy.

97. The results of outcome research on the effectiveness of different psychotherapies reveal that

a. no single type of therapy is consistently superior.

b. behavior therapies are most effective in treating specific problems, such as phobias.

c. cognitive therapies are most effective in treating depressed emotions.

d. all of these statements are true.

98. A person can derive benefits from psychotherapy simply by believing in it. This illustrates the importance of

a. client-centered therapy.

b. the placebo effect.

c. evidence-based practice.

d. clinicians' perceptions.

99. Before 1950, the main mental health providers were

a. psychologists.   c. psychiatrists.

b. paraprofessionals.   d. the clergy.

100. Light exposure therapy has proven useful as a form of treatment for people suffering from

a. bulimia nervosa.

b. a seasonal pattern in depression symptoms.

c. obsessive-compulsive disorder.

d. anxiety.

101. Which form of therapy is MOST likely to be successful in treating depression?

a. behavior modification

b. psychoanalysis

c. cognitive therapy

d. humanistic therapy

102. The common ingredients of the psychotherapies include

a. the offer of a therapeutic relationship.

b. the expectation among clients that the therapy will prove helpful.

c. the chance to develop a fresh perspective on oneself and the world.

d. all of these elements.

TERMS AND CONCEPTS TO REMEMBER:

103. psychotherapy

104. biomedical therapy

105. eclectic approach

106. psychoanalysis

107. resistance

108. interpretation

109. transference

110. psychodynamic therapy

111. insight therapies

112. client-centered therapy

113. active listening

114. unconditional positive regard

115. behavior therapy

116. counterconditioning

117. exposure therapies

118. systematic desensitization

119. virtual reality exposure therapy

120. aversive conditioning

121. token economy

122. cognitive therapy

123. cognitive-behavioral therapy

124. group therapy

125. family therapy

126. evidence-based practice

127. therapeutic alliance

MODULE 45
The Biomedical Therapies and Preventing Psychological Disorders

Drug Therapies

Objective 45-1: Identify and describe the drug therapies, and explain how double-blind studies help researchers evaluate a drug's effectiveness.

1. Therapy involving changing the brain's functioning is referred to as _____ therapy. The most widely used biomedical treatments are the _____ therapies. Thanks to these therapies and support from community

mental health programs, the number of residents in mental hospitals has _____ (increased/ decreased) sharply.

2. The field that studies the effects of drugs on mind and behavior is _____ .

3. To guard against the _____ effect and normal _____ , neither the patients nor the staff involved in a study may be aware of which condition a given individual is in; this is called a _____-_____ procedure.

4. The revolution in drug therapy began with the discovery that some drugs, used for other medical purposes, calmed people with _____ . One effect of _____ drugs such as _____ is to help those experiencing _____ (positive/negative) symptoms of schizophrenia by decreasing their responsiveness to irrelevant stimuli.

5. The antipsychotic drugs work by occupying the _____ receptor sites and blocking the activity of the neurotransmitter _____ .

6. Long-term use of antipsychotic drugs can produce _____ _____ , which involves involuntary movements of the muscles of the _____ , _____ , and _____ . Many of the newer antipsychotics such as risperidone have _____ (more/fewer) of these effects.

7. Xanax and Ativan are classified as _____ drugs.

8. These drugs depress activity in the _____ _____ .

9. When used in combination with _____ _____ , these drugs can help people cope with frightening situations.

10. Antianxiety drugs have been criticized for merely reducing _____ , rather than resolving underlying _____ . These drugs can also be _____ .

11. Drugs that are prescribed to alleviate depression are called _____ drugs. Because

the most commonly prescribed drugs in this group are increasingly being used to treat strokes and other disorders, including _____ disorders, _____-_____ disorder, and _____ they are more commonly called _____-_____ inhibitors.

12. One example of this type of drug is _____ , which works by blocking the normal reuptake of _____

from synapses. Increased serotonin promotes _____ , the development of new brain cells, which reverses stress-induced neuron loss. Drugs that work by blocking the reabsorption or breakdown of norepinephrine and serotonin are called _____-_____ drugs. These drugs have _____ (more/fewer) side effects.

13. Also effective in calming anxious people and energizing depressed people is _____ _____ , which has positive side effects. Even better is to use antidepressant drugs, which work _____ (bottom-up/top-down) on the limbic system, in conjunction with _____-_____ therapy, which works _____ (bottom-up/top-down), starting with the frontal lobes.

14. Although people with depression often improve after one month on antidepressants, studies demonstrate that a large percentage of the effectiveness is due to _____ or a _____ .

15. To treat the emotional highs and lows of _____ disorder, a

_____-_____
drug such as the simple salt _____
is often prescribed.

16. Another effective drug in the control of mania was originally used to treat epilepsy; it is _____ .

APPLICATIONS:

17. In an experiment testing the effects of a new antipsychotic drug, neither Dr. Cunningham nor her patients know whether the patients are in the experimental or the control group. This is an example of
   a. a placebo effect.
   b. within-subjects research.
   c. the double-blind procedure.
   d. the single-blind procedure.

18. Linda's doctor prescribes medication that blocks the activity of dopamine in her nervous system. Evidently, Linda is being treated with an _____ drug.
   a. antipsychotic   c. antidepressant
   b. antianxiety   d. anticonvulsive

19. Abraham's doctor prescribes medication that increases the availability of norepinephrine or serotonin in his nervous system. Evidently, Abraham is being treated with a(n) _____ drug.
   a. antipsychotic
   b. mood-stabilizing
   c. antidepressant
   d. anticonvulsive

20. A psychiatrist has diagnosed a patient as having bipolar disorder. It is likely that she will prescribe
   a. an antipsychotic drug.
   b. lithium.
   c. an antianxiety drug.
   d. a drug that blocks receptor sites for serotonin.

Brain Stimulation

Objective 45-2: Describe the use of brain stimulation techniques and psychosurgery in treating specific disorders.

21. The therapeutic technique in which the patient receives an electric shock to the brain is referred to as _____ therapy, abbreviated as _____ .

22. ECT is most often used with patients suffering from severe _____ . Research evidence _____ (confirms/does not

confirm) ECT's effectiveness with patients who have not responded to drug therapy.

23. The mechanism by which ECT works is _____ .

24. A gentler procedure called _____ _____ aims to treat depression by presenting pulses through a magnetic coil held close to a person's skull. Unlike ECT, this procedure produces no _____ , _____ loss, or other side effects. Although how it works is unclear, one explanation is that it energizes the brain's left _____ , which is relatively inactive in depressed patients. Repeated stimulation may cause nerve cells to form new functioning circuits through _____ _____ .

25. Another treatment being investigated for treatment of patients with depression is _____-_____ stimulation of a neural hub that bridges the frontal lobes to the limbic system.

Psychosurgery

26. The biomedical therapy in which a portion of brain tissue is removed or destroyed is called _____ .

27. In the 1930s, Moniz developed an operation called the _____ . In this procedure, the _____ lobe of the brain is disconnected from the rest of the brain.

28. Today, most psychosurgery has been replaced by the use of _____ or some other form of treatment.

APPLICATION:

29. In concluding her talk titled "Psychosurgery Today," Ashley states that
   a. "Psychosurgery is still widely used throughout the world."
   b. "Electroconvulsive therapy is the only remaining psychosurgical technique that is widely practiced."
   c. "With advances in psychopharmacology, psychosurgery has largely been abandoned."
   d. "Although lobotomies remain popular, other psychosurgical techniques have been abandoned."

Therapeutic Lifestyle Change

Objective 45-3: Describe how, by taking care of themselves with a healthy lifestyle, people might find some relief from depression, and explain how this reinforces the idea that we are biopsychosocial systems.

30. One approach to therapy promotes _____ change, which includes regular aerobic exercise, adequate sleep, light exposure, social connection, anti-rumination, and nutritional supplementation.

31. The relative success of this _____ approach seems to confirm that everything psychological is also biological and that we are all social creatures.

Preventing Psychological Disorders and Building Resilience

Objective 45-4: Explain the rationale of preventive mental health programs, and discuss why it is important to develop resilience.

32. Psychotherapies and biomedical therapies locate the cause of psychological disorders within the _____ . An alternative viewpoint is that many psychological disorders are responses to _____ _____ .

33. According to this viewpoint, it is not just the _____ who needs treatment but also the person's _____ _____ .

34. One advocate of _____ mental health, George Albee, believes that many social stresses undermine people's sense of _____ , _____ _____ , and _____ . These stresses include _____ , work that is _____ , constant _____ , _____ , _____ , and _____ .

35. _____ psychologists aim to enhance people's competence, health, and well-being.

36. Lifestyle changes may also help prevent some disorders by building an individual's _____ . In some cases, struggling with challenging crises can lead to _____ _____ .

37. A psychotherapist who believes that the best way to treat psychological disorders is to prevent them from developing would be MOST likely to view disordered behavior as
    a. maladaptive thoughts and actions.
    b. expressions of unconscious conflicts.
    c. conditioned responses.
    d. an understandable response to stressful social conditions.

38. Electroconvulsive therapy is most useful in the treatment of
    a. schizophrenia. c. personality disorders.
    b. depression. d. anxiety disorders.

39. Which biomedical therapy is MOST likely to be practiced today?
    a. psychosurgery
    b. electroconvulsive therapy
    c. drug therapy
    d. lobotomy

40. The antipsychotic drugs appear to produce their effects by blocking the receptor sites for
    a. dopamine. c. norepinephrine.
    b. epinephrine. d. serotonin.

41. Psychologists who advocate a _____ approach to mental health contend that many psychological disorders could be prevented by changing the disturbed individual's _____ .
    a. biomedical; diet
    b. family; behavior
    c. humanistic; feelings
    d. preventive; environment

42. Antidepressant drugs are believed to work by affecting serotonin or
    a. dopamine. c. norepinephrine.
    b. lithium. d. acetylcholine.

43. After many years of taking antipsychotic drugs, Greg's facial muscles sometimes twitch involuntarily. This behavior is called
    a. tardive dyskinesia. c. rTMS.
    b. the placebo effect. d. EMDR.

44. Which of the following is the mood-stabilizing drug most commonly used to treat bipolar disorder?
    a. Ativan c. Xanax
    b. chlorpromazine d. lithium

45. The type of drugs criticized for reducing symptoms without resolving underlying problems are the _____ drugs.

- **a.** antianxiety
- **b.** antipsychotic
- **c.** antidepressant
- **d.** amphetamine

46. The lobotomy procedure is not widely used today because

- **a.** it produces a lethargic, immature personality.
- **b.** it is irreversible.
- **c.** calming drugs became available in the 1950s.
- **d.** of all of these reasons.

Before You Move On

Matching Items 1

Match each term with the appropriate definition or description.

Terms

_____ **1.** cognitive therapy
_____ **2.** behavior therapy
_____ **3.** systematic desensitization
_____ **4.** cognitive-behavioral therapy
_____ **5.** client-centered therapy
_____ **6.** exposure therapy
_____ **7.** aversive conditioning
_____ **8.** psychoanalysis
_____ **9.** preventive mental health
_____ **10.** biomedical therapy
_____ **11.** counterconditioning
_____ **12.** insight therapy

Definitions or Descriptions

a. associates unwanted behavior with unpleasant experiences

b. associates a relaxed state with anxiety-arousing stimuli

c. emphasizes the social context of psychological disorders

d. integrative therapy that focuses on changing self-defeating thinking and unwanted behavior

e. category of therapies that teach people more adaptive ways of thinking and acting

f. the most widely used method of behavior therapy

g. therapy developed by Carl Rogers

h. therapy based on Freud's theory of personality

i. treatment with psychosurgery, electroconvulsive therapy, or drugs

j. classical conditioning procedure in which new responses are conditioned to stimuli that trigger unwanted behaviors

k. category of therapies based on learning principles derived from classical and operant conditioning

l. therapies that aim to increase the client's awareness of underlying motives and defenses

Matching Items 2

Match each term with the appropriate definition or description.

Terms

_____ 1. active listening
_____ 2. token economy
_____ 3. placebo effect
_____ 4. lobotomy
_____ 5. lithium
_____ 6. psychopharmacology
_____ 7. double-blind technique
_____ 8. Xanax
_____ 9. free association
_____ 10. evidence-based practice

Definitions or Descriptions

a. type of psychosurgery
b. mood-stabilizing drug
c. clinical decision making that integrates research, clinical expertise, and patient characteristics
d. empathic technique used in person-centered therapy
e. the beneficial effect of a person's expecting that treatment will be effective
f. antianxiety drug
g. technique of psychoanalytic therapy
h. an operant conditioning procedure
i. the study of the effects of drugs on the mind and behavior
j. experimental procedure in which both the patient and staff are unaware of a patient's treatment condition

Essay Question

Willie has been diagnosed as suffering from major depressive disorder. Describe the treatment he might receive from a psychodynamic therapist, a cognitive therapist, and a biomedical therapist. (Use the space below to list points you want to make, and organize them. Then write the essay on a separate sheet of paper.)

Cross-Check

As you learned in Module 2, reviewing and overlearning of material are important to the learning process. After you have written the definitions of the key terms in this unit, you should complete the crossword puzzle to ensure that you can reverse the process—recognize the term, given the definition.

ACROSS

1. Therapy that teaches people new and more adaptive ways of thinking.
5. Approach that draws on a variety of forms of therapy to best suit clients' needs.
9. Blocking anxiety-provoking memories from consciousness.
13. Therapy that attempts to change behavior by removing or destroying brain tissue.
14. Therapy that uses prescribed medications or medical procedures to treat psychological disorders.
15. Conditioning in which an unpleasant state is associated with an unwanted behavior.

DOWN

2. Nondirective technique in which the listener echoes and restates, but does not interpret, clients' remarks.
3. Integrative therapy that focuses on changing self-defeating thinking and unwanted behaviors.
4. Humanistic therapy developed by Carl Rogers.
6. Behavior therapy in which new responses are classically conditioned to stimuli that trigger unwanted behaviors.
7. Psychoanalytic term for the analyst's helping a client to gain deeper insights into unwanted thoughts and behaviors.
8. Therapy that views problem behaviors as partially engendered by the client's environment.
10. Biomedical therapy often used to treat severe depression.
11. Therapy developed by Sigmund Freud.
12. Therapy that applies principles of operant or classical conditioning to eliminate problem behaviors.

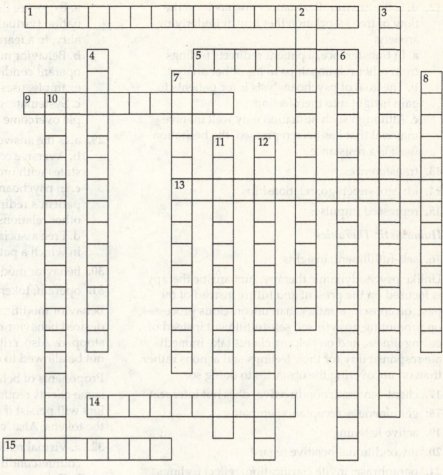

Answers

 MODULE 44

Introduction to Therapy and the Psychological Therapies

Treating Psychological Disorders

1. Philippe Pinel; Dorothea Dix
2. psychological; biomedical; eclectic

Psychoanalysis and Psychodynamic Therapies

3. insight
4. repressed
5. repressed; conscious
6. free association
7. resistance; interpretation
8. transference
9. is not; prove or disprove; expensive
10. psychodynamic; once or twice a week; themes
11. childhood; unconscious

12. d. is the answer. Resistances are blocks in the flow of free association that hint at underlying anxiety.
a. In transference, a patient redirects feelings from other relationships to his or her analyst.
b. The goal of psychoanalysis is for patients to gain insight into their feelings.
c. Although such hesitation may well involve material that has been repressed, the hesitation itself is a resistance.

13. transference

14. id; ego; superego; relationships

15. repressed impulses

Humanistic Therapies

16. self-fulfillment; insights

Unlike psychodynamic therapy, humanistic therapy is focused on the present and future instead of the past, on conscious rather than unconscious processes, on promoting growth and self-fulfillment instead of curing illness, and on helping clients take immediate responsibility for their feelings and actions rather than on uncovering the obstacles to doing so.

17. client-centered; nondirective; does not interpret

18. genuineness; acceptance; empathy

19. active listening

20. unconditional positive regard

21. paraphrase; invite clarification; reflect feelings

Behavior Therapies

22. learning

Whereas the psychodynamic and humanistic therapies assume that problems diminish as self-awareness grows, behavior therapists doubt that self-awareness is the key. Instead of looking for the inner cause of unwanted behavior, behavior therapy applies learning principles to directly attack the unwanted behavior itself.

23. classical conditioning; counterconditioning; exposure therapies; aversive conditioning

24. exposure therapies; Mary Cover Jones; Joseph Wolpe; exposure; anxious

25. anxiety; progressive relaxation; relaxed; anxiety; actual situations

26. virtual reality exposure

27. negative; positive; unpleasant; does not

28. d. is the answer. Aversive conditioning is the classical conditioning technique in which a positive response is replaced by a negative response. (In this example, the US is the blast of smoke, the CS is the taste of the cigarette as it is inhaled, and the intended CR is aversion to cigarettes.)

a. Exposure therapy exposes someone, in imagination (virtual reality exposure therapy) or actuality, to a feared situation.
b. Behavior modification applies the principles of operant conditioning and thus, in contrast to the example, uses reinforcement.
c. Systematic desensitization is used to help people overcome specific anxieties.

29. a. is the answer.
b. Aversive conditioning associates unpleasant states with unwanted behaviors.
c. In psychoanalytic therapy, transference is the patient's redirecting to the analyst emotions from other relationships.
d. Free association is a psychoanalytic technique in which a patient says whatever comes to mind.

30. behavior modification

31. operant; token economy

Behavior modification is criticized because the desired behavior may stop when the rewards are stopped. Also, critics contend that one person should not be allowed to control another.

Proponents of behavior modification contend that some clients request this therapy and that the behaviors will persist if patients are properly weaned from the tokens. Also, control already exists.

32. a. Virtual reality exposure therapy, a type of counterconditioning (classical conditioning).
b. Token economy, based on operant conditioning principles.
c. Systematic desensitization, an exposure therapy, which is a form of counterconditioning. Specific procedures may vary. Refer to the text for general descriptions.

Cognitive Therapies

33. self-blaming; overgeneralized; cognitive

34. catastrophizing; depression; Aaron Beck

35. restructure; stressful; negative; less

36. cognitive-behavioral; emotion regulation; obsessive-compulsive disorder

37. dialectical behavior; social skills training; mindfulness meditation

38. humanistic

39. aversive conditioning

40. psychoanalysis

41. a. is the answer.
b. & c. These types of therapists are more concerned with promoting self-fulfillment (humanistic) and healthy patterns of thinking (cognitive) than with correcting specific problem behaviors.

d. Psychoanalysts see the behavior merely as a symptom and focus their treatment on its presumed underlying cause.

42. **c.** is the answer.
a. & b. Behavior therapists make extensive use of techniques based on both operant and classical conditioning.
d. Neither behavior therapists nor cognitive behavioral therapists focus on clients' unconscious urges.

43. **b.** is the answer.

44. **d.** is the answer. Because the psychologist is focusing on Darnel's irrational thinking, this response is most typical of Beck's cognitive therapy for depression.
a. Behavior therapists treat behaviors rather than thoughts.
b. Psychoanalysts focus on helping patients gain insight into previously repressed feelings.
c. Client-centered therapists attempt to facilitate clients' growth by offering a genuine, accepting, empathic environment.

Group and Family Therapies

Group therapy saves therapists time and clients money. It offers a social laboratory for exploring social behaviors and developing social skills. It enables people to see that others share their problem. It provides feedback as clients try out new ways of behaving.

45. group; social

46. family therapy

47. communication

48. self-help; support; Alcoholics Anonymous

49. Humanistic therapies focus on the present and future, conscious thoughts, and having the person take responsibility for his or her feelings and actions. The goal is self-fulfillment. The therapist is genuine, accepting, and empathic and uses active listening in this nondirective therapy.

Behavior therapies focus on the problem behavior. The goal is to change undesirable behaviors to desirable behaviors. They use techniques based on classical and operant conditioning principles—for example, exposure therapies, aversive conditioning, and token economies.

Cognitive therapies focus on the person's way of thinking about himself or herself. Self-blaming and overgeneralized explanations of bad events cause the problem. The goal is to change the person's negative thinking. They use gentle questioning to reveal the patient's irrational thinking and persuade a depressed person, for example, to adopt a more positive attitude.

Cognitive-behavioral therapy (CBT) is an integrative therapy that focuses training people to change their self-harmful thoughts and behaviors. Its goal is to make people aware of their irrational negative thinking, to replace it with new ways of thinking, and to apply that to their everyday behavior.

Group and family therapies assume that problems arise from social interactions. They help people to see that others have similar problems and that communication can resolve most problems. During sessions, for example, they try to guide family members toward positive relationships and improved communication.

Evaluating Psychotherapies

50. satisfaction

People often enter therapy in crisis. When the crisis passes, they may attribute their improvement to the therapy. Clients, who may need to believe the therapy was worth the time, effort, and money, may overestimate its effectiveness. Clients generally find positive things to say about their therapists, even if their problems remain.

51. overestimate

52. unhappiness; well-being

53. controlled

54. Hans Eysenck; was not

55. randomized clinical

56. somewhat effective

57. no clear; does not matter; does not make a difference

58. are; behavioral conditioning; nondirective; cognitive; cognitive-behavioral

59. specific

60. energy; memory; rebirthing

61. evidence-based practice

62. **d.** is the answer.
a. Psychotherapy has proven "somewhat effective" and more cost-effective than physician care for psychological disorders.
b. & c. Behavior and cognitive therapies are both effective in treating depression, and behavior therapy is effective in treating specific problems such as phobias.

63. alternative therapy

64. controlled

65. traumatic events; eye movement desensitization

and reprocessing (EMDR); somewhat effective; posttraumatic stress disorder; finger tapping; reliving; placebo

66. seasonal pattern; light exposure

67. **d.** is the answer.
a. In fact, there is evidence that light exposure therapy can be effective in treating a seasonal pattern of depression.
b. There is no evidence that EMDR is effective as a treatment for a seasonal pattern of depression.
c. Lithium is a mood-stabilizing drug that is often used to treat bipolar disorder.

68. hope; perspective; caring; trusting; empathic

69. therapeutic alliance; empathic; caring

70. do; may; cultures; religion

71. individualism; collectivist

72. minority

73. hopelessness; depression; self-destructive; fears; mood; compulsive

74. **b.** is the answer. Psychiatrists are physicians who specialize in treating psychological disorders. As doctors they can prescribe medications.
a., c., & d. These professionals cannot prescribe drugs.

Module Review:

75. **c.** is the answer.
a. & b. Active listening and unconditional positive regard are Rogerian techniques.
d. Systematic desensitization is a process in which a person is conditioned to associate a relaxed state with anxiety-triggering stimuli.

76. **b.** is the answer.

77. **d.** is the answer. This is not among the criticisms commonly made of psychoanalysis. (It would more likely be made of behavior therapies.)

78. **c.** is the answer. There is no indication that they are more effective than individual therapies.

79. **c.** is the answer.

80. **d.** is the answer.
a. An eclectic therapist may use a nondirective approach with certain behaviors; however, a more directive approach might be chosen for other clients and problems.
b. In fact, just the opposite is true. Eclectic therapists generally view disorders as stemming from many influences.
c. Eclectic therapists, in contrast to this example, use a combination of treatments.

81. **a.** is the answer.

82. **b.** is the answer.
a. This reflects a cognitive perspective.

c. This reflects a psychodynamic perspective.

83. **c.** is the answer.
a. & b. Counterconditioning is the replacement of an undesired response with a desired one by means of aversive conditioning or systematic desensitization.
d. Exposure therapy exposes a person (in imagination or in actuality) to a feared situation.

84. **d.** is the answer.

85. **c.** is the answer.
a. This answer would be a correct description of Joseph Wolpe.
b. There is no such thing as insight therapy.
d. This answer would be a correct description of Aaron Beck.

86. **a.** is the answer.
b. & d. In systematic desensitization, a type of exposure therapy, a hierarchy of anxiety-provoking stimuli is gradually associated with a relaxed state.
c. Transference refers to a patient's transferring of feelings from other relationships onto his or her psychoanalyst.

87. **c.** is the answer.
a. Behavior therapy focuses on behavior, not self-awareness.
b. Psychodynamic therapy focuses on bringing unconscious feelings into awareness.
d. Biomedical therapy focuses on physical treatment through drugs, ECT, or deep-brain stimulation.

88. **a.** is the answer. For behavior therapy, the problem behaviors *are* the problems.
b. Cognitive therapy teaches people to think and act in more adaptive ways.
c. Humanistic therapy promotes growth and self-fulfillment by providing an empathic, genuine, and accepting environment.
d. Psychodynamic therapy focuses on uncovering and interpreting unconscious feelings.

89. **b.** is the answer. Counterconditioning techniques involve taking an established stimulus, which triggers an undesirable response, and pairing it with a new stimulus in order to condition a new, and more adaptive, response.
a. As indicated by the name, counterconditioning techniques are a form of conditioning; they do not involve learning by observation.
c. & d. The principles of operant conditioning are the basis of behavior modification, which, in contrast to counterconditioning techniques, involves use of reinforcement.

90. **d.** is the answer.

a. This is a confrontational therapy, which is aimed at teaching people to think and act in more adaptive ways.

b. Aversive conditioning is a form of counterconditioning in which unwanted behavior is associated with unpleasant feelings.

c. Counterconditioning is a general term, including not only systematic desensitization, in which a hierarchy of fears is desensitized, but also other techniques, such as aversive conditioning.

91. d. is the answer.

a., b., & c. These techniques are based on classical conditioning.

92. d. is the answer.

93. c. is the answer.

a. Psychodynamic therapy focuses on unconscious forces and childhood conflict and has the goal of self-insight.

b. In this humanistic therapy, the therapist facilitates the client's growth by offering a genuine, accepting, and empathic environment.

d. Behavior therapy concentrates on modifying the actual symptoms of psychological problems.

94. d. is the answer.

a. This is true of most forms of psychotherapy.

b. & c. This is true of humanistic, cognitive, and behavior therapies.

95. c. is the answer. Although aversive conditioning may work in the short run, the person's ability to discriminate between the situation in which the aversive conditioning occurs and other situations can limit the treatment's effectiveness.

a., b., & d. These are not limitations of the effectiveness of aversive conditioning.

96. b. is the answer. Clients' testimonials regarding psychotherapy are generally very positive. The research, in contrast, seems to show that therapy is only *somewhat* effective.

97. d. is the answer.

98. b. is the answer.

a. Client-centered therapy is Rogers' method of psychotherapy.

c. Evidence-based practice integrates the best available research with clinical expertise and patient characteristics and preferences.

d. The question has nothing to do with clinicians' perceptions.

99. c. is the answer.

100. b. is the answer.

101. c. is the answer.

a. Behavior modification is most likely to be successful in treating specific behavior problems, such as bed-wetting.

b. & d. The text does not single out particular disorders for which these therapies tend to be most effective.

102. d. is the answer.

Terms and Concepts to Remember:

103. Psychotherapy is an interaction between a trained therapist and someone seeking to overcome psychological difficulties or achieve personal growth.

104. Biomedical therapy is the use of prescribed medications or medical procedures that act on a person's physiology to treat psychological disorders.

105. With an **eclectic approach**, therapists are not locked into one form of psychotherapy, but draw on whatever combination seems best suited to a client's problems.

106. Psychoanalysis, the therapy developed by Sigmund Freud, attempts to give clients self-insight by bringing into awareness and interpreting previously repressed feelings.

Example: The tools of the **psychoanalyst** include free association, the analysis of dreams and transferences, and the interpretation of repressed impulses.

107. Resistance is the psychoanalytic term for the blocking from consciousness of anxiety-laden memories. Hesitation during free association may reflect resistance.

108. Interpretation is the psychoanalytic term for the analyst's helping the patient to understand resistances and other aspects of behavior, so that the patient may gain deeper insights.

109. Transference is the psychoanalytic term for a patient's redirecting to the analyst emotions from other relationships.

110. Derived from the psychoanalytic tradition, **psychodynamic therapy** seeks to enhance patients' self-insight into their symptoms by focusing on childhood experiences and important relationships in addition to unconscious forces.

111. Insight therapies such as psychodynamic and humanistic therapies aim to improve psychological functioning by increasing the person's awareness of underlying motives and defenses.

112. Client-centered therapy is a humanistic nondirective therapy developed by Carl Rogers, in which growth and self-awareness are facilitated in an environment that offers genuineness, acceptance, and empathy. Also called *person-centered therapy*.

113. **Active listening** is a nondirective technique of Rogers' client-centered therapy, in which the listener echoes, restates, and seeks clarification of, but does not interpret, clients' remarks.

114. **Unconditional positive regard** refers to the accepting, nonjudgmental attitude that is the basis of Rogers' client-centered therapy.

115. **Behavior therapy** is therapy that applies learning principles to the elimination of unwanted behaviors.

116. **Counterconditioning** is a category of behavior therapy in which new responses are classically conditioned to stimuli that trigger unwanted behaviors; include exposure therapies and aversive conditioning.

117. **Exposure therapies** treat anxiety by exposing people (in imagination or actual situations) to things they normally fear and avoid. Among these therapies are systematic desensitization and virtual reality exposure therapy.

118. **Systematic desensitization** is a type of exposure therapy in which a state of relaxation is classically conditioned to a hierarchy of gradually increasing anxiety-provoking stimuli.

    Memory aid: This is a form of **counterconditioning** in which sensitive, anxiety-triggering stimuli are *desensitized* in a progressive, or **systematic**, fashion.

119. **Virtual reality exposure therapy** progressively exposes people to electronic simulations of feared situations to treat their anxiety.

120. **Aversive conditioning** is a form of counterconditioning in which an unpleasant state is associated with an unwanted behavior.

121. A **token economy** is an operant conditioning procedure in which desirable behaviors are promoted in people by rewarding them with tokens, or positive reinforcers, which can be exchanged for privileges or treats. For the most part, token economies are used in hospitals, schools, and other institutional settings.

122. **Cognitive therapy** focuses on teaching people new and more adaptive ways of thinking. The therapy is based on the idea that thoughts intervene between events and our emotional reactions.

123. **Cognitive-behavioral therapy (CBT)** is a popular integrative therapy that focuses on changing self-defeating thinking (cognitive therapy) and unwanted behaviors (behavior therapy).

124. **Group therapy** is therapy conducted with groups rather than individuals.

125. **Family therapy** treats the family as a system and so views problem behavior as influenced by, or directed at, other members of the individual's family.

126. **Evidence-based practice** is clinical decision making that integrates the best available research with clinical expertise and patient characteristics and preferences.

127. A **therapeutic alliance** is the bond of trust that develops between a therapist and client working together to overcome the client's problem.

MODULE 45

The Biomedical Therapies and Preventing Psychological Disorders

Drug Therapies

1. biomedical; drug; decreased
2. psychopharmacology
3. placebo; recovery; double-blind
4. psychoses; antipsychotic; chlorpromazine (Thorazine); positive
5. dopamine
6. tardive dyskinesia; face; tongue; limbs; fewer
7. antianxiety
8. central nervous system
9. psychological therapy
10. symptoms; problems; addictive
11. antidepressant; anxiety; obsessive-compulsive; posttraumatic stress disorder; selective-serotonin-reuptake
12. fluoxetine (Prozac); serotonin; neurogenesis; dual-action; more
13. aerobic exercise; bottom-up; cognitive-behavioral; top-down
14. natural recovery; placebo effect
15. bipolar; mood-stabilizing; lithium
16. Depakote
17. c. is the answer.
    a. The placebo effect refers to the result of an experiment, arising from the patient's positive expectations; it is not the experiment itself.
    b. In this design, which is not mentioned in the text, there is only a single research group.

d. This answer would be correct if the experimenter, but not the research participants, knew which condition was in effect.

18. **a.** is the answer.

19. **c.** is the answer.

20. **b.** is the answer.

Brain Stimulation

21. electroconvulsive; ECT

22. depression; confirms

23. unknown

24. repetitive transcranial magnetic stimulation (rTMS); seizures; memory; frontal lobe; long-term potentiation

25. deep-brain

Psychosurgery

26. psychosurgery

27. lobotomy; frontal

28. drugs

29. **c.** is the answer.
    b. Although still practiced, electroconvulsive therapy is not a form of psychosurgery.

Therapeutic Lifestyle Change

30. therapeutic lifestyle

31. biopsychosocial

Preventing Psychological Disorders and Building Resilience

32. person; a disturbing and stressful society

33. person; social context

34. preventive; competence; personal control; self-esteem; poverty; meaningless; criticism; unemployment; racism; sexism

35. Community

36. resilience; posttraumatic growth

37. **d.** is the answer.
    a. This would be the perspective of a cognitive-behavioral therapist.
    b. This would be the perspective of a psychoanalyst.
    c. This would be the perspective of a behavior therapist.

Module Review:

38. **b.** is the answer. Although no one is sure how ECT works, one possible explanation is that it increases release of norepinephrine, the neurotransmitter that elevates mood.

39. **c.** is the answer.
    a. The fact that its effects are irreversible makes psychosurgery a drastic procedure, and with advances in psychopharmacology, psychosurgery was largely abandoned.
    b. ECT is still widely used as a treatment of severe depression, but in general it is not used as frequently as drug therapy.
    d. A lobotomy is a psychosurgical procedure once used to calm uncontrollably emotional or violent patients.

40. **a.** is the answer. By occupying receptor sites for dopamine, these drugs block its activity and reduce its production.

41. **d.** is the answer.

42. **c.** is the answer.

43. **a.** is the answer.

44. **d.** is the answer. Lithium works as a mood stabilizer.
    a. & c. Ativan and Xanax are antianxiety drugs.
    b. Chlorpromazine is an antipsychotic drug.

45. **a.** is the answer.

46. **d.** is the answer.

Terms and Concepts to Remember:

47. **Psychopharmacology** is the study of the effects of drugs on mind and behavior.
    Memory aid: Pharmacology is the science of the uses and effects of drugs. **Psycho**pharmacology is the science that studies the psychological effects of drugs.

48. **Antipsychotic drugs** are used to treat schizophrenia and other severe thought disorders.

49. **Antianxiety drugs** help control anxiety and agitation by depressing activity in the central nervous system.

50. **Antidepressant drugs** treat depression, anxiety disorders, obsessive-compulsive disorder, and posttraumatic stress disorder. (Several widely used antidepressant drugs are selective-serotonin-reuptake-inhibitors—SSRIs.)

51. In **electroconvulsive therapy (ECT)**, a biomedical therapy often used to treat severe depression, a brief electric shock is passed through the brain of an anesthetized patient.

52. **Repetitive transcranial magnetic stimulation (rTMS)** is the delivery of repeated pulses of magnetic energy to stimulate or suppress brain activity.

53. **Psychosurgery** is a biomedical therapy that attempts to change behavior by removing or destroying brain tissue. Since drug therapy

became widely available in the 1950s, psychosurgery has been infrequently used.

54. Once used to control violent patients, the **lobotomy** is a form of psychosurgery in which the nerves linking the emotion centers of the brain to the frontal lobes are severed.

55. **Resilience** is a person's ability to cope with stress and recover from adversity and even trauma.

56. **Posttraumatic growth** is positive psychological changes as a result of struggling with extremely challenging circumstances and life crises.

Before You Move On

Matching Items 1

1. e	5. g	9. c
2. k	6. f	10. i
3. b	7. a	11. j
4. d	8. h	12. l

Matching Items 2

1. d	5. b	9. g
2. h	6. i	10. c
3. e	7. j	
4. a	8. f	

Essay Question

Psychodynamic therapists assume that psychological problems such as depression are caused by unconscious conflicts from childhood experiences. A psychodynamic therapist would probably attempt to bring these feelings into Willie's conscious awareness and interpret those memories and feelings in order to help him gain insight into his depression.

Cognitive therapists assume that a person's emotional reactions are influenced by the person's thoughts in response to the event in question. A cognitive therapist would probably try to teach Willie new and more constructive ways of thinking in order to reverse his catastrophizing beliefs about himself, his situation, and his future.

Biomedical therapists attempt to treat disorders by altering the functioning of the patient's brain. A biomedical therapist would probably prescribe an antidepressant drug such as fluoxetine to increase the availability of norepinephrine and serotonin in Willie's nervous system. If Willie's depression is especially severe, a *psychiatrist* might treat it with several sessions of electroconvulsive therapy.

Cross-Check

ACROSS
1. cognitive therapy
5. eclectic
9. resistance
13. psychosurgery
14. biomedical
15. aversive

DOWN
2. active listening
3. cognitive-behavioral
4. client-centered
6. counterconditioning
7. interpretation
8. family therapy
10. electroconvulsive
11. psychoanalysis
12. behavior therapy

Statistical Reasoning
in Everyday Life

Appendix A Overview

A basic understanding of statistical reasoning has become a necessity in everyday life. Statistics are tools that help the psychologist and layperson to interpret the vast quantities of information they are confronted with on a daily basis. Appendix A discusses how statistics are used to describe data and to generalize from instances.

In studying this appendix, you must concentrate on learning a number of procedures and understanding some underlying principles in the science of statistics. The graphic and computational procedures in the section called "Describing Data" include how data are distributed in a sample; measures of central tendency such as the mean, median, and mode; variation measures such as the range and standard deviation; and correlation, or the degree to which two variables are related. Most of the conceptual material is then covered in the section titled "Significant Differences." You should be able to discuss three important principles concerning populations and samples, as well as the concept of significance in testing differences. The ultimate goal is to make yourself a better consumer of statistical research by improving your critical thinking skills.

NOTE: Answer guidelines for all questions in Appendix A begin on page 396.

Outline

 Describing Data

 Significant Differences

Instructions

First, skim each section, noting headings and boldface items. After you have read the section, review each objective by answering the fill-in, essay-type, and multiple-choice questions for that section. In some cases, Study Tips explain how best to learn a difficult concept and Applications and Section Reviews help you to know how well you understand the material. Finally, try to define the important terms and concepts using your own words. As you proceed, evaluate your performance by consulting the answers on page 396. Do not continue with the next section until you understand each answer. If you need to, review or reread the section in the textbook before continuing.

Appendix A Review includes activities that test you on material from the entire appendix.

Describing Data

Measures of Central Tendency and Measures of Variation

Objective A-1: Explain how we describe data using three measures of central tendency, and discuss the relative usefulness of the two measures of variation.

1. Researchers use _____ to help them see and interpret their observations.

2. Once researchers have gathered their _____ , they may use _____ _____ to _____ that data meaningfully. One simple way of visually representing data is to use a _____ _____ . It is important to read the _____ _____ and note the _____ to avoid being misled by misrepresented data.

3. The three measures of central tendency are the _____ , the _____ , and the _____ .

4. The most frequently occurring score in a distribution is called the _____ .

5. The mean is computed as the _____ _____ of all the scores divided by the _____ of scores.

6. The median is the score at the _____ percentile.

7. When a distribution is lopsided, or _____ , the _____ (mean/median/mode) can be biased by a few extreme scores.

8. Averages derived from scores with _____ (high/low) variability are more reliable than those with _____ (high/low) variability.

9. The measures of variation include the _____ and the _____ _____ .

10. The range is computed as the _____ _____ .

11. The range provides a(n) _____ (crude/accurate) estimate of variation because it _____ (is/is not) influenced by extreme scores.

12. The standard deviation is a _____ (more accurate/less accurate) measure of variation than the range. Unlike the range, the standard deviation _____ (does/does not) use information from each score in the distribution.

13. The symmetrical, bell-shaped distribution in which most scores fall near the _____ with fewer and fewer near the extremes is called the _____ _____ .

14. In this distribution, approximately _____ percent of the individual scores fall within 1 standard deviation on either side of the mean. Within 2 standard deviations on either side of the mean fall _____ percent of the individual scores.

Explain what it means to score 116 on the normally distributed Wechsler IQ test. (Recall that the mean is 100; the standard deviation is ±15 points. Hint: You might find it helpful to draw the normal curve first.)

APPLICATIONS:

15. The football team's punter wants to determine how consistent his punting distances have been during the past season. He should compute the
    a. mean.
    b. median.
    c. mode.
    d. standard deviation.

16. Esteban refuses to be persuaded by an advertiser's claim that people using their brand of gasoline average 50 miles per gallon. His decision probably is based on
    a. the possibility that the average is the mean, which could be artificially inflated by a few extreme scores.
    b. the absence of information about the size of the sample studied.
    c. the absence of information about the variation in sample scores.
    d. all of these statements.

17. Bob scored 43 out of 70 points on his psychology exam. He was worried until he discovered that most of the class earned the same score. Bob's score was equal to the

  a. mean.   **c.** mode.

  b. median.   **d.** range.

18. The four families on your block all have annual household incomes of $25,000. If a new family with an annual income of $75,000 moved in, which measure of central tendency would be most affected?

  a. mean   **c.** mode

  b. median   **d.** standard deviation

Correlation: A Measure of Relationships

Objective A-2: Explain what it means when we say two things are correlated, and describe positive and negative correlations.

19. A measure of the direction and extent of relationship between two sets of scores is called the

_____ _____ .

Numerically, this measure can range from

_____ to _____ .

20. To depict a correlation, researchers create a graph called a _____ , which uses dots to represent the values of the two variables.

21. When there is no relationship at all between two sets of scores, the correlation coefficient is

_____ . If two factors increase or

decrease together, they are _____

_____ . If, however, one decreases

as the other increases, they are

_____ _____ .

Another way to state the latter is that the two

variables relate _____ .

Using the space below, draw scatterplots showing patterns of correlation.

Perfect positive correlation (+1.00)

No relationship (0.00)

Perfect negative correlation (–1.00)

Cite an example of a positive correlation and a negative correlation. You can use previous examples in the text or you can base your examples on observations from daily life.

An example of a positive correlation is

An example of a negative correlation is

22. The correlation coefficient _____ (gives/does not give) information about cause-effect relationships. It does, however, tell how well one factor _____ the other related factor.

APPLICATIONS:

23. Meagan has found a positive correlation between the height and body weight of students at her school. Which of the following is true?

  a. There is a cause-effect relationship between height and weight.

  b. As height increases, weight decreases.

  c. Knowing a person's height, one can predict his or her weight.

  d. All of these statements are true.

24. Given the positive correlation found by Meagan, how should she depict the relationship on a scatterplot?
    a. All the points should fall on a straight line.
    b. The points should be spread randomly about the plot.
    c. All the points should fall on a curved line.
    d. It is impossible to determine from the information given.

Regression Toward the Mean

Objective A-3: Define *regression toward the mean*.

25. A correlation that is perceived but doesn't really exist is called an _____ _____ .

26. When we believe that a relationship exists between two things, we are most likely to recall instances that _____ (confirm/disconfirm) our belief.

27. This type of correlation feeds the illusion of _____—that we can control events that actually are due to _____ .
    It is also fed by a statistical phenomenon called _____ _____ _____ _____ , the idea that average results are more typical than extreme results.

APPLICATIONS:

28. Which of the following exemplifies regression toward the mean?
    a. In his second season of varsity basketball, Edward averaged 5 points more per game than in his first season.
    b. A gambler rolls 5 consecutive "sevens" using her favorite dice.
    c. After earning an unusually low score on the first exam in a class, a "B student" scores much higher on the second exam.
    d. A student who usually gets Bs earns grades of A, C, C, and A on four exams, thus maintaining a B average overall for the class.

29. Joe believes that his basketball game is always best when he wears his old gray athletic socks. Joe is a victim of the phenomenon called
    a. regression toward the mean.
    b. the availability heuristic.
    c. illusory correlation.
    d. skewed scoring.

30. The first step in constructing a bar graph is to
    a. measure the standard deviation.
    b. organize the data.
    c. calculate a correlation coefficient.
    d. determine the range.

31. What is the mean of the following distribution of scores: 2, 3, 7, 6, 1, 4, 9, 5, 8, 2?
    a. 5   c. 4.7
    b. 4   d. 3.7

32. What is the median of the following distribution of scores: 1, 3, 7, 7, 2, 8, 4?
    a. 1   c. 3
    b. 2   d. 4

33. What is the mode of the following distribution: 8, 2, 1, 1, 3, 7, 6, 2, 0, 2?
    a. 1   c. 3
    b. 2   d. 7

34. The most frequently occurring score in a distribution is the
    a. mean.   c. mode.
    b. median.   d. range.

35. In the following distribution, the mean is _____ the mode and _____ the median: 4, 6, 1, 4, 5.
    a. less than; less than
    b. less than; greater than
    c. equal to; equal to
    d. greater than; equal to

36. Why is the median at times a better measure of central tendency than the mean?
    a. It is more sensitive to extreme scores.
    b. It is less sensitive to extreme scores.
    c. It is based on more of the scores in the distribution than the mean.
    d. Both a. and c. explain why.

37. A lopsided set of scores that includes a number of extreme or unusual values is said to be
    a. symmetrical.   c. skewed.
    b. normal.   d. dispersed.

38. Which of the following is the measure of central tendency that would be most affected by a few extreme scores?
    a. mean   c. median
    b. range   d. mode

39. Which of the following is NOT a measure of central tendency?
   a. mean
   b. range
   c. median
   d. mode

40. The symmetrical, bell-shaped distribution in which most scores are near the mean and fewer near the extremes forms a
   a. skewed curve.
   b. bimodal curve.
   c. normal curve.
   d. bar graph.

41. A homogeneous sample with little variation in scores will have a(n) _____ standard deviation.
   a. small
   b. moderate
   c. large
   d. unknown (It is impossible to determine.)

42. The following scatterplot depicts a correlation coefficient that would be close to

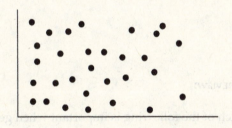

   a. +1.0.
   b. −1.0.
   c. 0.00.
   d. 0.50.

43. Which of the following correlation coefficients indicates the strongest relationship between two variables?
   a. −.73
   b. +.66
   c. 0.00
   d. −.50

44. A correlation coefficient
   a. indicates the direction of relationship between two variables.
   b. indicates the strength of relationship between two variables.
   c. does *not* indicate whether there is a cause-effect relationship between two variables.
   d. does all of these things.

45. Which of the following statistics must fall on or between −1.00 and +1.00?
   a. the mean
   b. the standard deviation
   c. the correlation coefficient
   d. none of these statistics

46. The *value* of the correlation coefficient indicates the _____ of relationship between two variables, and the *sign* (positive or negative) indicates the _____ of the relationship.
   a. direction; strength
   b. strength; direction
   c. direction; reliability
   d. reliability; strength

47. If two sets of scores are negatively correlated, it means that
   a. as one set of scores increases, the other decreases.
   b. as one set of scores increases, the other increases.
   c. there is only a weak relationship between the sets of scores.
   d. there is no relationship at all between the sets of scores.

48. Illusory correlation refers to
   a. the perception that two negatively correlated variables are positively correlated.
   b. the perception of a relationship between two unrelated variables.
   c. an insignificant correlation coefficient.
   d. a correlation coefficient that equals −1.00.

49. Gamblers who blow on their dice "for luck" are victims of
   a. regression toward the mean.
   b. the illusion of control.
   c. a skewed distribution.
   d. a standard deviation.

50. Regression toward the mean is the
   a. tendency for unusual scores to fall back toward a distribution's average.
   b. basis for all tests of statistical significance.
   c. reason the range is a more accurate measure of variation than the standard deviation.
   d. reason the standard deviation is a more accurate measure of variation than the range.

51. In a normal distribution, what percentage of scores fall between +2 and −2 standard deviations of the mean?
   a. 50 percent
   b. 68 percent
   c. 95 percent
   d. 99.7 percent

TERMS AND CONCEPTS TO REMEMBER:

52. mode

53. mean

54. median

55. range

56. standard deviation
57. normal curve
58. correlation coefficient
59. scatterplot
60. regression toward the mean

Significant Differences

Objective A-4: Explain how we know whether an observed difference can be generalized to other populations.

61. The best basis for generalizing is not from _____ cases but from a _____ sample of cases.

62. Observations are more reliable when they are based on scores with _____ (high/low) variability.

63. Averages based on a large number of cases are _____ (more/less) reliable than those based on a few cases.

64. Tests of statistical _____ are used to estimate whether observed differences are real, that is, to make sure they are not simply the result of _____ variation. The differences are probably real if the sample averages are _____ and the difference between them is _____ .

APPLICATIONS:

65. Dr. Salazar recently completed an experiment in which she compared reasoning ability in a sample of women and a sample of men. The means of the female and male samples equaled 21 and 19, respectively, on a 25-point scale. A statistical test revealed that her results were not statistically significant. What can Dr. Salazar conclude?

  a. Women have superior reasoning ability.
  b. The difference in the means of the two samples is probably due to chance variation.
  c. The difference in the means of the two samples is reliable.
  d. She cannot reach any of these conclusions.

Objective A-5: Define *cross-sectional studies* and *longitudinal studies*, and discuss why it is important to know which method was used.

66. (Thinking Critically) Researchers use _____-_____ studies to investigate a randomly sampled group of

people of _____ (the same/different) age(s). This type of study generally extends over a very _____ (long/short) period of time.

67. (Thinking Critically) Researchers use _____ studies to study, test, and re-test _____ (the same/different) group(s) over a _____ (long/short) period of time.

68. (Thinking Critically) The first kind of study found evidence of intellectual _____ (stability/decline) during adulthood; the second found evidence of intellectual _____ (stability/decline).

(Thinking Critically) Explain why the conflicting results of these two types of studies point to the importance of knowing how researchers reached their conclusions.

SECTION REVIEW:

69. Which of the following is important when generalizing from a sample to the population?
  a. The sample is representative of the population.
  b. The sample is large.
  c. The scores in the sample have low variability.
  d. All of these conditions exist.

70. When a difference between two groups is statistically significant, this means that
  a. the difference is statistically real but of little practical significance.
  b. the difference is probably the result of sampling variation.
  c. the difference is not likely to be due to chance variation.
  d. all of these statements are true.

71. In generalizing from a sample to the population, it is important that
  a. the sample be representative.
  b. the sample be nonrandom.
  c. the sample not be too large.
  d. all of these conditions exist.

72. The set of scores that would likely be most representative of the population from which it was drawn would be a sample with a relatively
   a. large standard deviation.
   b. small standard deviation.
   c. large range.
   d. small range.

73. If a difference between two samples is NOT statistically significant, which of the following can be concluded?
   a. The difference is probably not a true one.
   b. The difference is probably not reliable.
   c. The difference could be due to sampling variation.
   d. All of these conclusions can be reached.

74. Which of the following is true of the longitudinal method?
   a. It compares people of different ages.
   b. It studies the same people at different times.
   c. It usually involves a larger sample than do cross-sectional tests.
   d. It usually involves a smaller sample than do cross-sectional tests.

75. In which type of study are the same people tested and retested over a period of years?
   a. cross-sectional
   b. correlational
   c. longitudinal
   d. scatterplot

76. Which of the following is true of the cross-sectional method?
   a. It compares people of different ages with one another.
   b. It studies the same group of people at different times.
   c. It tends to paint too favorable a picture of the effects of aging on intelligence.
   d. It is more appropriate than the longitudinal method for studying intellectual change over the life span.

TERMS AND CONCEPTS TO REMEMBER:

77. cross-sectional study
78. longitudinal study
79. statistical significance

Appendix A Review

Matching Items

Match each term with the appropriate definition or description.

Terms

_____ 1. bar graph
_____ 2. median
_____ 3. normal curve
_____ 4. regression toward the mean
_____ 5. mode
_____ 6. range
_____ 7. standard deviation
_____ 8. skewed
_____ 9. mean
_____ 10. measures of central tendency
_____ 11. measures of variation

Definitions or Descriptions

a. the mean, median, and mode
b. the difference between the highest and lowest scores
c. the arithmetic average of a distribution
d. the range and standard deviation
e. a symmetrical, bell-shaped distribution
f. the most frequently occurring score
g. the tendency for extremes of unusual scores to fall back toward the average
h. a graph depicting a table of data
i. the middle score in a distribution
j. an asymmetrical distribution
k. the square root of the average squared deviation of scores from the mean

True–False Items

Indicate whether each statement is true or false by placing a *T* or *F* in the blank next to the item.

_____ 1. The first step in describing raw data is to organize it.

_____ 2. In almost all distributions, the mean, the median, and the mode will be the same.

_____ 3. When a distribution has a few extreme scores, the range is more misleading than the standard deviation.

_____ 4. If increases in the value of variable *x* are accompanied by decreases in the value of variable *y*, the two variables are negatively correlated.

_____ 5. Over time, extreme results tend to fall back toward the average.

_____ 6. If a sample has low variability, it cannot be representative of the population from which it was drawn.

_____ 7. The mean is always the most precise measure of central tendency.

_____ 8. Averages that have been derived from scores with low variability are more reliable than those derived from scores that are more variable.

_____ 9. A relationship between two variables is depicted on a scatterplot.

_____ 10. Small samples are less reliable than large samples for generalizing to the population.

Essay Question

Discuss several ways in which statistical reasoning can improve your own everyday thinking. (Use the space below to list the points you want to make, and organize them. Then write the essay on a separate sheet of paper.)

Answers

 Describing Data

Measures of Central Tendency and *Measures of Variation*

1. statistics

2. data; descriptive statistics; organize; bar graph; scale labels; range

3. mode; median; mean

4. mode

5. total sum; number

6. 50th

7. skewed; mean

8. low; high

9. range; standard deviation

10. difference between the lowest and highest scores

11. crude; is

12. more accurate; does

13. mean; normal curve (normal distribution)

14. 68; 95

Because the mean equals 100 and the standard deviation is 15 points, a score of 116 is just over one standard deviation unit above the mean. Because 68 percent of the population's scores fall within one standard deviation on either side of the mean, 34 percent fall between 0 and +1 standard deviation unit. By definition, 50 percent of the scores fall below the mean. Therefore, a score at or above 115 is higher than that obtained by 84 percent of the population (50 percent + 34 percent = 84 percent).

15. **d.** is the answer. A small or large standard deviation indicates whether a distribution is homogeneous or variable.
a., b., & c. These statistics would not give any information regarding the consistency of performance.

16. **d.** is the answer.

17. **c.** is the answer.
a. The mean is computed as the sum of the scores divided by the number of scores.
b. The median is the midmost score in a distribution.
d. The range is the difference between the highest and lowest scores in a distribution.

18. **a.** is the answer. The mean is strongly influenced by extreme scores. In this example, the mean would change from $25,000 to (75,000 + 25,000 + 25,000 + 25,000 + 25,000)/5 = $35,000.

b. & c. Both the median and the mode would remain $25,000, even with the addition of the fifth family's income.

d. The standard deviation is a measure of variation, not central tendency.

19. correlation coefficient; +1.00; –1.00

20. scatterplot

21. 0.00; positively correlated; negatively correlated; inversely

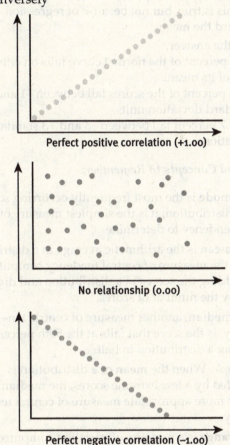

Perfect positive correlation (+1.00)

No relationship (0.00)

Perfect negative correlation (–1.00)

An example of a positive correlation is the relationship between air temperature and ice cream sales: As one increases so does the other.

An example of a negative correlation is the relationship between good health and the amount of stress a person is under: As stress increases, the odds of good health decrease.

22. does not give; predicts

23. **c.** is the answer. If height and weight are positively correlated, increased height is associated with increased weight. Thus, one can predict a person's weight from his or her height.
a. Correlation does not imply causality.
b. This situation depicts a negative correlation between height and weight.

24. **a.** is the answer. Because the two variables—height and weight—correlate perfectly, they would vary together perfectly and form a straight line.

25. illusory correlation

26. confirm

27. control; chance; regression toward the mean

28. **c.** is the answer. Regression toward the mean is the phenomenon that average results are more typical than extreme results. Thus, after an unusual event (the low exam score in this example) things tend to return toward their average level (in this case, the higher score on the second exam).
a. Edward's improved average indicates only that, perhaps as a result of an additional season's experience, he is a better player.
b. Because the probability of rolling 5 consecutive "sevens" is very low, the gambler's "luck" will probably prove on subsequent rolls to be atypical and things will return toward their average level. This answer is incorrect, however, because it states only that 5 consecutive "sevens" were rolled.
d. In this example, although the average of the student's exam grades is her usual grade of B, they are all extreme grades and do not regress toward the mean.

29. **c.** is the answer. A correlation that is perceived but doesn't actually exist, as in the example, is known as an illusory correlation.
a. Regression toward the mean is the tendency for extreme scores to fall back toward the average.
b. The availability heuristic is the tendency of people to estimate the likelihood of something in terms of how readily it comes to mind (see Chapter 9).
d. There is no such thing as skewed scoring.

Section Review:

30. **b.** is the answer. A bar graph is based on a data distribution.

31. **c.** is the answer. The mean is the sum of scores divided by the number of scores. [(2 + 3 + 7 + 6 + 1 + 4 + 9 + 5 + 8 + 2)/10 = 4.7.]

32. **d.** is the answer. When the scores are put in order (1, 2, 3, 4, 7, 7, 8), 4 is at the 50th percentile, splitting the distribution in half.

33. **b.** is the answer. The mode is the most frequently occurring score. Because there are more 2s than any other number in the distribution, 2 is the mode.

34. **c.** is the answer.

a. The mean is the arithmetic average.

b. The median is the score that splits the distribution in half.

d. The range is the difference between the highest and lowest scores.

35. c. is the answer. The mean, median, and mode are equal to 4.

36. b. is the answer.

a. In fact, just the opposite is true.

c. Both the mean and the median are based on all the scores in a distribution. The median is based on the number of scores, while the mean is based on the average of their sum.

d. The mean is the arithmetic average.

37. c. is the answer.

38. a. is the answer. As an average, calculated by adding all scores and dividing by the number of scores, the mean could easily be affected by the inclusion of a few extreme scores.

b. The range is not a measure of central tendency.

c. & d. The median and mode give equal weight to all scores; each counts only once and its numerical value is unimportant.

39. b. is the answer.

40. c. is the answer.

a. A skewed curve is formed from an asymmetrical distribution.

b. A bimodal curve has two modes; a normal curve has only one.

d. A bar graph depicts a distribution of scores.

41. a. is the answer. The standard deviation is the average deviation in a distribution; therefore, if variation (deviation) is small, the standard deviation will also be small.

42. c. is the answer.

a. & b. These are "perfect" correlations of equal strength.

d. This indicates a much stronger relationship between two sets of scores than does a coefficient of 0.00.

43. a. is the answer. . The closer the correlation coefficient is to either +1 or –1, the stronger the relationship between the variables.

44. d. is the answer.

45. c. is the answer.

46. b. is the answer.

47. a. is the answer.

b. This situation indicates that the two sets of scores are positively correlated.

c. Whether a correlation is positive or negative does not indicate the strength of the relationship, only its direction.

d. In negative correlations, there *is* a relationship; the correlation is negative because the relationship is an inverse one.

48. b. is the answer.

49. b. is the answer.

50. a. is the answer.

b. Regression toward the mean has nothing to do with tests of statistical significance.

c. In fact, just the opposite is true.

d. This is true, but not because of regression toward the mean.

51. c. is the answer.

a. 50 percent of the normal curve falls on either side of its mean.

b. 68 percent of the scores fall between –1 and +1 standard deviation units.

d. 99.7 percent fall between –3 and +3 standard deviations.

Terms and Concepts to Remember:

52. The **mode** is the most frequently occurring score in a distribution; it is the simplest measure of central tendency to determine.

53. The **mean** is the arithmetic average in a distribution; the measure of central tendency computed by adding the scores in a distribution and dividing by the number of scores.

54. The **median**, another measure of central tendency, is the score that falls at the 50th percentile, cutting a distribution in half.

Example: When the **mean** of a distribution is affected by a few extreme scores, the **median** is the more appropriate measure of central tendency.

55. The **range** is a measure of variation computed as the difference between the highest and lowest scores in a distribution.

56. The **standard deviation** is a computed measure of how much scores in a distribution deviate around the mean. Because it is based on every score in the distribution, it is a more precise measure of variation than the range.

57. The **normal curve** (*normal distribution*) is the symmetrical, bell-shaped distribution describing many types of psychological data, in which most scores fall near the mean, with fewer and fewer at the extremes.

58. The **correlation coefficient** is a statistical measure of the relationship between two things. It can be positive or negative (from –1 to +1).

Example: If there is a positive correlation between air temperature and ice cream sales, the warmer (higher) it is, the more ice cream is sold. If there is a negative correlation between air temperature and sales of cocoa, the cooler (lower) it is, the more cocoa is sold.

59. A **scatterplot** is a depiction of the relationship between two variables by means of a graphed cluster of dots.

60. **Regression toward the mean** is the tendency for extreme or unusual scores or events to fall back (regress) toward the average.

Significant Differences

61. exceptional (memorable); representative
62. low
63. more
64. significance; chance; reliable; large
65. **b.** is the answer.
   a. If the difference between the sample means is not significant, then the groups probably do not differ in the measured ability.
   c. When a result is not significant it means that the observed difference is unreliable.
66. cross-sectional; different; short
67. longitudinal; the same; long
68. decline; stability

Because cross-sectional studies compare people not only of different ages but also of different eras, education levels, family size, and affluence, it is not surprising that such studies reveal cognitive decline with age. In contrast, longitudinal studies test one group over a span of years. However, because those who survive to the end of longitudinal studies may be the brightest and healthiest, these studies may underestimate the average decline in intelligence. It is therefore important to know what type of methodology was used and whether the sample was truly representative of the population being studied.

69. **d.** is the answer.
70. **c.** is the answer.
   a. A statistically significant difference may or may not be of practical importance.
   b. This is often the case when a difference is *not* statistically significant.
71. **d.** is the answer.
72. **b.** is the answer.
73. **d.** is the answer.
74. **b.** is the answer.
75. **c.** is the answer.
76. **a.** is the answer.

Terms and Concepts to Remember:

77. In a **cross-sectional study,** people of different ages are compared with one another.
78. In a **longitudinal study,** the same people are tested and retested over a period of years.
79. **Statistical significance** means that an obtained result, such as the difference between the averages for two samples, very likely reflects a real difference rather than sampling variation or chance factors. Tests of statistical significance help researchers decide when they can justifiably generalize from an observed instance.

Appendix A Review

Matching Items

1. h	**5.** f	**9.** c
2. i	**6.** b	**10.** a
3. e	**7.** k	**11.** d
4. g	**8.** j	

True–False Items

1. T	**6.** F
2. F	**7.** F
3. T	**8.** T
4. T	**9.** T
5. T	**10.** T

Essay Question

The use of tables and bar graphs is helpful in accurately organizing, describing, and interpreting events, especially when there is too much information to remember and one wishes to avoid conclusions based on general impressions. Computing an appropriate measure of central tendency provides an index of the overall average of a set of scores. Knowing that the mean is the most common measure of central tendency, but that it is very sensitive to unusually high or low scores, can help one avoid being misled by claims based on misleading averages. Being able to compute the range or standard deviation of a set of scores allows one to determine how homogeneous the scores in a distribution are and provides a basis for realistically generalizing from samples to populations. Understanding the correlation coefficient can help us to see the world more clearly by revealing the extent to which two things relate. Being aware that unusual results tend to return to more typical results (regression toward the mean) helps us to avoid the practical pitfalls associated with illusory correlation. Finally, understanding the basis for tests of statistical significance can make us more discerning consumers of research reported in the media.

Psychology at Work

Appendix B Overview

Appendix B discusses work motivation. People who view their work as a meaningful calling, those working in jobs that optimize their skills, and those who become absorbed in activities that result in flow find work satisfying and enriching. Effective leaders recognize this and develop management styles that focus on workers' strengths and adapt their leadership style to the situation. Research on achievement motivation underscores the importance of self-discipline and persistence in achieving one's goals. Human factors psychologists focus on developing ways of making machines and work settings user-friendly.

NOTE: Answer guidelines for all Appendix B questions begin on page 406.

Outline

 Personnel Psychology

 Organizational Psychology

 The Human Factor

Instructions

First, skim each section, noting headings and boldface items. After you have read the section, review each objective by answering the fill-in, essay-type, and multiple-choice questions for that section. In some cases, Study Tips explain how best to learn a difficult concept and Applications and Section Reviews help you to know how well you understand the material. Finally, try to define the important terms and concepts using your own words. As you proceed, evaluate your performance by consulting the answers on page 406. Do not continue with the next section until you understand each answer. If you need to, review or reread the section in the textbook before continuing.

Appendix B Review includes activities that test you on material from the entire appendix.

Introduction

Objective B-1: Define *flow*, and identify key subfields related to industrial-organizational psychology.

1. People who view their work as an unfulfilling but necessary way to make money see it as a _____ . Those who see it as an opportunity to advance from one position to a better one view work as a _____ . People who view their work as a _____ report the greatest satisfaction.

2. Psychologist Mihaly Csikszentmihalyi formulated the concept of _____ , which is defined as a focused state of _____ and diminished awareness of _____ and time. People who experience this state also experience increased feelings of _____ , _____ , and _____ .

3. In many nations, the nature of work has changed, from _____ to _____ to _____ .

4. The sense of mutual obligations between workers and employers is called the _____ _____ .

5. The field of _____-_____ psychology applies psychology's principles to the workplace. The subfield of _____ psychology focuses on employee recruitment, training, appraisal, and development. Another subfield, _____ psychology, examines how work environments and _____ styles influence worker motivation, satisfaction, and productivity. A related but independent field, _____ _____ psychology, focuses on the design of appliances, machines, and work environments.

APPLICATION:

6. Which of the following individuals would be characterized as experiencing flow?

    a. Sheila, who, despite viewing her work as merely a job, performs her work conscientiously

    b. Larry, who sees his work as an artist as a calling

    c. Arnie, who views his present job as merely a stepping stone in his career

    d. Montel, who often becomes so immersed in his writing that he loses all sense of self and time

⟶ Personnel Psychology

Objective B-2: Describe how personnel psychologists help with job seeking, employee selection, work placement, and performance appraisal.

7. Researchers note that the first step to a stronger organization is to institute a _____-_____ selection system, which matches strengths to work.

8. A career counseling science aims, first, to assess our differing values, _____ , and, especially, _____ , which _____ (are/are not) stable. Second, it aims to alert us to well-matched vocations—vocations with a good _____-_____ fit.

9. Satisfied and successful people devote less time to _____ than to _____ .

10. Interviewers tend to _____ (feel confident/lack confidence) in their ability to predict job performance from unstructured interviews. These impressions tend to be highly _____ (accurate/error-prone).

11. The best predictor of long-term job performance for most jobs is _____ _____ _____ . Interviewers tend to _____ (over/under)estimate their interviewing skills and intuition—a phenomenon labeled the _____ _____ .

State five effects that fuel this phenomenon.

12. A more disciplined method of collecting information from job applicants is the
_____ _____ ,
which asks the same questions of all applicants. This method enhances the
_____ accuracy of the interview process; it also reduces _____ .

13. Performance appraisal has several purposes, including helping organizations decide
_____ ,
how to appropriately _____
_____ ,
and how to better harness employees'
_____ . Performance appraisal methods include _____ ,
_____ _____ scales,
and _____ _____ scales.

14. Some organizations practice _____-
_____ feedback, in which employees not only rate themselves but also their supervisors and other colleagues, and vice versa.

15. Performance appraisal is subject to bias. When the overall evaluation of an employee biases ratings of work-related behaviors, a
_____ _____
has occurred. The tendency to be too easy or too harsh results in _____ and
_____ errors, respectively. When raters focus on easily remembered recent behavior, they are committing the
_____ error.

⟶ Organizational Psychology

B-3: Describe the role of organizational psychologists.

16. Positive moods at work contribute to worker
_____ , _____ , and
_____ .

17. Researchers have also found a positive correlation between measures of organizational success and employee _____ , or the extent of workers' involvement, satisfaction, and enthusiasm.

APPLICATION:

18. Darren, a sales clerk at a tire store, enjoys his job, not so much for the money as for its challenge and the opportunity to interact with a variety of people. The store manager asks you to recommend a strategy for increasing Darren's motivation. Which of the following is most likely to be effective?
   a. Create a competition among the salespeople so that whoever has the highest sales each week receives a bonus.
   b. Put Darren on a week-by-week employment contract, promising him continued employment only if his sales increase each week.
   c. Leave Darren alone unless his sales drop and then threaten to fire him if his performance doesn't improve.
   d. Involve Darren as much as possible in company decision making and use rewards to inform him of his successful performance.

Objective B-4: Describe some effective leadership techniques.

19. The best managers help people to
_____ , match tasks to _____ , care how their people feel about their work, and
_____ positive behaviors.

20. Higher worker achievement is motivated by a leader who sets _____ ,
_____ goals. When people state goals together with _____ and
_____ _____ , they become more focused in their work.

21. Managers who are directive, set clear standards, organize work, and focus attention on specific goals are said to employ _____
_____ . More democratic managers who aim to build teamwork and mediate conflicts in the work force employ
_____ _____ .

22. Effective leaders tend to exude a self-confident _____ that is a mix of a
_____ of some goal, an ability to _____ the goal clearly, and enough optimism to _____ others to follow. Leadership that inspires others to transcend their own self-interests for the sake of the group is called _____ leadership.

23. The most effective style of leadership _____ (varies/does not vary) with the situation and/or the person.

24. Effective managers _____ (rarely/often) exhibit a high degree of both task and social leadership. The _____ effect occurs when people respond more positively to managerial decisions on which they have voiced an opinion.

STUDY TIP: Think about several leaders you know. These might be group leaders, employers, teachers, and relatives. Of these people, whose leadership skills do you admire the most? Why? What type of leadership style (e.g., social leadership, task leadership) best characterizes this person? What specific aspects of this leadership style does the person exhibit?

 The Human Factor

Objective B-5: Describe how human factors psychologists work to create user-friendly machines and work settings.

25. Human factors psychologists help to design machines and work settings that fit our natural _____ and _____. They also work to devise ways to reduce the _____, _____, and _____ that contribute to traffic accidents.

26. One example of good design is the use of _____ _____ that broadcast sound directly through a person's own hearing aid. This is an example of an effective _____ _____ technology.

27. Safe, easy, and effective machine designs have not been more common because developers sometimes assume that others share their expertise, called the _____ _____ _____.

Appendix B Review

Multiple-Choice Questions

1. People who view work as a calling see it as
   a. an unfulfilling but necessary way to make money.
   b. an opportunity to advance to a better position.
   c. a fulfilling and socially useful activity.
   d. all of these things.

2. Workers who report the highest satisfaction with their work and their lives tend to view their work as
   a. a calling.   c. a job.
   b. a career.   d. a hobby.

3. Who first described the concept of flow?
   a. Maslow   c. Owen
   b. Csikszentmihalyi d. Norman

4. *Flow* is best described as
   a. a completely involved, focused state of consciousness on a task.
   b. goal-oriented leadership.
   c. group-oriented leadership.
   d. a state of heightened awareness of self and time.

5. In many nations, work has shifted from
   a. knowledge work to farming.
   b. knowledge work to manufacturing.
   c. manufacturing to knowledge work.
   d. knowledge work to skill work.

6. Who is most likely to focus on selecting employees and performance appraisal?
   a. personnel psychologist
   b. organizational psychologist
   c. human factors psychologist
   d. engineering psychologist

7. Who is most likely to focus on maximizing worker satisfaction and productivity?
   a. personnel psychologist
   b. organizational psychologist
   c. human factors psychologist
   d. engineering psychologist

8. Who is most likely to focus on the design of optimal work environments?
   a. personnel psychologist
   b. organizational psychologist
   c. human factors psychologist
   d. engineering psychologist

9. The sense of mutual obligations between workers and employers is known as
   a. flow.
   b. task leadership.
   c. social leadership.
   d. the psychological contract.

10. The first step in establishing workplace effectiveness is
   a. identifying people's strengths and matching those to work.
   b. hiring a boss who focuses on task leadership.
   c. establishing a fair system of worker compensation.
   d. hiring a boss who focuses on group leadership.

11. The best predictor of on-the-job performance for all but less-skilled jobs is
   a. age.
   b. general mental ability.
   c. motivation.
   d. stated intentions.

12. To increase employee productivity, industrial-organizational psychologists advise managers to
   a. adopt a directive leadership style.
   b. adopt a democratic leadership style.
   c. instill competitiveness in each employee.
   d. deal with employees according to their individual motives.

13. For as long as she has been the plant manager, Juanita has welcomed input from employees and has delegated authority. Bill, in managing his department, takes a more authoritarian, iron-fisted approach. Juanita's style is one of _____ leadership, whereas Bill's is one of _____ leadership.
   a. task; social
   b. social; task
   c. directive; democratic
   d. democratic; participative

14. Dr. Iverson conducts research focusing on how management styles influence worker motivation. Dr. Iverson would most accurately be described as a(n)
   a. motivation psychologist.
   b. personnel psychologist.
   c. organizational psychologist.
   d. human factors psychologist.

15. Which of the following was NOT identified as a contributing factor in the interviewer illusion?
   a. The fact that interviews reveal applicants' intentions but not necessarily their habitual behaviors.
   b. The tendency of interviewers to think that interview behavior only reflects applicants' enduring traits.
   c. The tendency of interviewers to more often follow the successful careers of applicants they hired rather than those who were not hired.
   d. The tendency of most interviewers to rely on unstructured rather than structured interviews.

16. Munson is conducting his annual appraisal of employees' performance. Which of the following is NOT a type of appraisal method?
   a. graphic rating
   b. behavior rating
   c. checklist
   d. unstructured interview

17. Because Brent believes that his employees are intrinsically motivated to work for reasons beyond money, Brent would be described as a(n) _____ manager.
   a. directive
   b. social-oriented
   c. task-oriented
   d. charismatic

18. Jack works for a company that requires employees to periodically rate their own performance and to be rated by their managers, other colleagues, and customers. This type of assessment is called
   a. 360-degree feedback.
   b. multifactorial evaluation.
   c. analytical performance review.
   d. human resource management.

19. Thanks to _____ , TiVo and DVR have solved the TV recording problem caused by the complexity of VCRs.
   a. parapsychologists
   b. human factors psychologists
   c. psychokineticists
   d. Gestalt psychologists

Matching Items

Match each term with its definition or description.

Terms

_____ 1. human factors psychology
_____ 2. personnel psychology
_____ 3. organizational psychology
_____ 4. flow
_____ 5. task leadership
_____ 6. social leadership
_____ 7. structured interview
_____ 8. industrial-organizational psychology

Definitions or Descriptions

a. state of focused consciousness
b. applies psychological concepts and methods to optimizing human behavior in workplaces.
c. seeks to optimize person-machine interactions
d. applies psychological methods and principles to the selection and evaluation of workers
e. goal-oriented leadership that sets standards, organizes work, and focuses attention on goals
f. seeks to maximize worker satisfaction and productivity
g. group-oriented leadership that builds teamwork, mediates conflict, and offers support
h. technique in which all job applicants are asked the same questions

Essay Question

Your aunt, who is the Chief Executive Officer of a large company that manufactures electronic circuits, wonders whether an industrial-organizational psychologist could benefit her employees and business. What should you tell her?

Terms and Concepts to Remember

1. flow
2. industrial-organizational (I/O) psychology
3. personnel psychology
4. organizational psychology
5. human factors psychology
6. structured interviews
7. task leadership
8. social leadership

Answers

Introduction

1. job; career; calling
2. flow; consciousness; self; self-esteem, competence, well-being
3. farming; manufacturing; knowledge work
4. psychological contract
5. industrial-organizational; personnel; organizational; management; human factors
6. d. is the answer.

⟫ Personnel Psychology

7. strengths-based
8. personalities; interests; are; person-environment
9. correcting deficiencies; accentuating strengths
10. feel confident; error-prone
11. general mental ability; over; interviewer illusion

Five effects that fuel the interviewer illusion are

   a. Interviews disclose the interviewee's good intentions, which are less revealing than their typical behaviors.
   b. Interviewers tend to follow the successful careers of people they hired and lose track of those they did not hire.
   c. Interviewers mistakenly presume that *how* interviewees present themselves reflects only their enduring traits.

d. Interviewers' preconceptions and moods influence their perceptions of job applicants.

e. Interviewers judge people relative to those interviewed just before and after them.

12. structured interview; predictive; bias

13. who to retain; reward and pay workers; strengths; checklists; graphic rating; behavior rating

14. 360-degree

15. halo error; leniency; severity; recency

Organizational Psychology

16. creativity; persistence; helpfulness

17. engagement

18. d. is the answer. Because Darren appears to resonate with the principle that people are intrinsically motivated to work for reasons beyond money, giving him feedback about his work and involving him in decision making are probably all he needs to be very satisfied with his situation.

a., b., & c. Creating competitions and using controlling, rather than informing, rewards may have the opposite effect and actually undermine Darren's motivation.

19. identify and measure their strengths; strengths; reinforce

20. specific; challenging; subgoals; implementation intentions

21. task leadership; social leadership

22. charisma; vision; communicate; inspire; transformational

23. varies

24. often; voice

The Human Factor

25. perceptions; inclinations; distractions; fatigue; inattention

26. loop systems; assistive listening

27. curse of knowledge

Appendix B Review

Multiple-Choice Questions

1. c. is the answer.
   a. This is characteristic of those who view work as merely a job.
   b. This is true of those who view work as a career.

2. a. is the answer.

3. b. is the answer.

4. a. is the answer.
   b. & c. Goal- and task-orientations are two styles of leadership.
   d. Flow is a stated of *reduced* awareness of self and time.

5. c. is the answer.

6. a. is the answer.
   b. Organizational psychologists focus on maximizing worker satisfaction and productivity.
   c. & d. Human factors psychologists (also called engineering psychologists) focus on the design of optimal work environments.

7. b. is the answer.
   a. Personnel psychologists focus on selecting employees and performance appraisal.
   c. & d. Human factors psychologists (also called engineering psychologists) focus on the design of optimal work environments.

8. d. is the answer.
   a. Personnel psychologists focus on selecting employees and performance appraisal.
   b. Organizational psychologists focus on maximizing worker satisfaction and productivity.
   c. This answer is too general. I/O psychologists include personnel psychologists, organizational psychologists, and human factors psychologists.

9. d. is the answer.
   a. Flow is a completely involved, focused state of consciousness on a task.
   b. Task leadership is goal-oriented leadership that sets standards, organizes work, and focuses attention on goals.
   c. Social leadership is group-oriented leadership that builds teamwork, mediates conflict, and offers support.

10. a. is the answer.

11. b. is the answer.

12. d. is the answer. As different people are motivated by different things, to increase motivation and thus productivity, managers are advised to learn what motivates individual employees and to challenge and reward them accordingly.
    a. & b. The most effective management style will depend on the situation.
    c. This might be an effective strategy with some, but not all, employees.

13. b. is the answer.
    a. Bill's style is one of task leadership, whereas Juanita's is one of social leadership.
    c. Juanita's style is democratic, whereas Bill's is directive.

d. Participative is another term used to refer to the social or group-oriented style of leadership.

14. c. is the answer.

15. d. is the answer. Although unstructured interviews *are* more prone to bias than structured interviews, the text does not suggest that they are used more often.

16. d. is the answer.
a., b., & c. These are all performance appraisal methods used by supervisors.

17. b. is the answer.
a. & c. Directive, or task-oriented, managers are likely to assume that worker motivation is low.
d. The most effective leaders are generally charismatic, which has nothing to do with whether they are directive or democratic leaders.

18. a. is the answer.

19. b. is the answer.

a. Parapsychologists study claims of ESP.

c. Psychokineticists are people who claim ESP has the power of "mind over matter."

d. Gestalt psychologists emphasize the organization of sensations into meaningful perceptions.

Matching Items

1. c   5. e
2. d   6. g
3. f   7. h
4. a   8. b

Essay Question

You should tell your aunt that industrial-organizational psychologists work in varied areas as research scientists, consultants, and management professionals. A personnel psychologist could assist her in selecting, placing, and training employees, as well as in developing criteria to measure their performance and that of the overall organization. An organizational psychologist could assist in facilitating organizational changes to maximize the satisfaction and productivity of her employees. Finally, a human factors psychologist could assist in designing an optimum work environment for employees.

Terms and Concepts to Remember

1. **Flow** is a completely involved, focused state of consciousness on a task that optimally engages a person's skills, accompanied by a diminished awareness of self and time.

2. **Industrial-organizational (I/O) psychology** is a profession that applies psychological concepts and methods to optimizing human behavior in workplaces.

3. **Personnel psychology** is a subfield of I/O psychology that applies psychological methods and principles to the selection and evaluation of workers.

4. **Organizational psychology** is a subfield of I/O psychology that explores how work environments and management styles affect worker motivation, satisfaction, and productivity.

5. **Human factors psychology** is a branch of psychology that explores how people and machines interact and how physical environments can be made safer and easier to use.

6. A **structured interview** is one in which an interviewer asks the same job-relevant questions of all interviewees, who are then rated on established evaluation scales.

7. **Task leadership** is goal-oriented leadership that sets standards, organizes work, and focuses attention on goals.

8. **Social leadership** is group-oriented leadership that builds teamwork, mediates conflict, and offers support.